SKILL BUILDERS — APPROPRIATENESS

SKILL	USE	PROCEDURE	EXAMPLE
Using language that adapts to a specific person or persons and the context of the conversation.	To increase interaction effectiveness.	1. Adapt formality of language to the person and situation. 2. Be wary of jargon and slang. 3. Avoid crude language. 4. Demonstrate sensitivity. 5. Avoid racist labels.	Kevin (who is angry about a grade) approaches his professor: "Dr. Allensmith, I was interested in why you evaluated my essay as you did. I'm not sure that other professors would have viewed my topic as being trivial, so I'd like to hear more about your philosophy."

SKILL BUILDERS — DATING INFORMATION

SKILL	USE	PROCEDURE	EXAMPLE
Including a specific time referent that indicates when a fact was true.	To avoid the pitfalls of language that allow you to speak of a dynamic world in static terms.	1. Before you make a statement, consider or find out when the information was true. 2. If not based on present information, verbally acknowledge when it was true.	When Jake says, "How good a hitter is Steve?" Mark replies by dating his evaluation: "When I worked with him two years ago, he couldn't hit the curve."

SKILL BUILDERS — OWNING FEELINGS OR OPINIONS

SKILL	USE	PROCEDURE	EXAMPLE
Making an "I" statement to identify yourself as the source of an idea or feeling.	To help others understand that the feeling or opinion is yours.	When an idea, opinion, or feeling is yours, say so.	Instead of saying, "Maury's is the best restaurant in town," say, "I believe Maury's is the best restaurant in town."

SKILL BUILDERS — INDEXING GENERALIZATIONS

SKILL	USE	PROCEDURE	EXAMPLE
Mentally or verbally accounting for individual differences.	To avoid "allness" in speaking.	1. Before you make a statement, consider whether it pertains to a specific object, person, or place. 2. If you use a generalization, inform the listener that it is not necessarily accurate.	"He's a politician and I don't trust him, although he may be different from most politicians I know."

SKILL BUILDERS — OTHER-CENTERED MESSAGES

SKILL	USE	PROCEDURE	EXAMPLE
Expressing compassion and understanding and encouraging partners to talk about what has happened and to explore their feelings about the situation.	To help partners in their efforts to cognitively reappraise an emotionally disturbing event.	1. Ask questions that prompt the person to tell and elaborate on what happened. 2. Emphasize your willingness to listen to an extended story. 3. Use vocalized encouragement and nonverbal behavior to communicate your continued interest without interrupting your partner as the account unfolds. 4. Affirm, legitimize, and encourage exploration of the feelings expressed by your partner. 5. Demonstrate that you understand and connect with what has happened but avoid changing the focus to you.	Angie begins to express what has happened to her. Allison says: "Really, what happened then?" As Angie utters one more sentence and then stops, Allison says: "You've simply got to tell me *all* about it, and don't worry about how long it takes. I want to hear the whole thing from start to finish." During Angie's discussion, Allison shows her encouragement: "Go on. . .," "Wow. . .," "Uh huh. . .," and she nods her head, leans forward, etc. To affirm, Allison says: "Yes, I can see that you're disappointed. Most people would be disappointed in this situation. Is this as difficult as when. . .?" Allison then continues: "I know that I felt angry when my sister did that to me. So what happened then?"

SKILL BUILDERS — POSITIVE FACEWORK

SKILL	USE	PROCEDURE	EXAMPLE
Messages affirming a person or a person's actions in the face of a difficult situation.	To protect the other's positive face needs (to be respected, liked, and valued) in situations where other messages are perceived to be FTAs.	1. Describe and convey positive feelings about what the other has said or done in the situation. 2. Express your admiration for the person's courage or effort in the situation. 3. Acknowledge how difficult the situation is. 4. Express your belief that the other has the qualities and skills to endure or succeed.	Jan has learned that Ken has suffered his brother's anger when Ken intervened in order to help him. Jan says: "I really respect you for the way you have acted during this. It takes a lot of guts to hang in there like you've been doing, especially when you've been attacked for doing so. I know that you've got the skills to help you get through this."

SKILL BUILDERS — SPEAKING MORE CLEARLY

SKILL	USE	PROCEDURE	EXAMPLE
Clarify meaning by selecting a less ambiguous word, by narrowing from a general category to a particular group within that category, by selecting a word that is a more precise choice, or by using concrete details or examples.	To help the listener picture thoughts analogous to the speaker's.	1. Assess whether the word is less specific or precise than it should be. 2. Pause to mentally brainstorm alternatives. 3. Select a more specific, precise word and/or add details or an example.	Instead of saying, "Bring the stuff for the audit," say, "Bring the records and receipts from the last year for the audit." Or, instead of saying, "Paul is very loyal," say "Paul is very loyal. He will back you up when you're under fire."

Message Formation (continued)

SKILL BUILDERS   **CREDITING THE SOURCE**

SKILL	USE	PROCEDURE	EXAMPLE
Verbally identifying the source of ideas you are using.	To give credit to sources of information we present in order to clarify the origin of the ideas and to avoid possible hard feelings.	Include the specific source of ideas, whether written or oral.	At a meeting of a group's fund-raising committee, Tina says, "What about buying a television at discount and selling raffle tickets? George was the first one to think of the idea and I think it's a great one. We could probably make a couple of hundred dollars."

Listening for Understanding

SKILL BUILDERS   **TURNTAKING**

SKILL	USE	PROCEDURE	EXAMPLE
Engaging in appropriate conversational sequencing.	Determining when a speaker is at a place where another person may talk if he or she wants to.	1. Take your share of turns. 2. Gear turn length to the behavior of partners. 3. Give and watch for turn-taking and turn-exchanging cues. Avoid giving inadvertent turn-taking cues. 4. Observe and use conversation-directing behavior. 5. Limit interruptions.	When John lowers his voice as he says "I really thought they were going to go ahead during those last few seconds," Melissa, noticing he appears to be finished, says, "I did, too. But did you notice. . ."

SKILL BUILDERS   **PARAPHRASING**

SKILL	USE	PROCEDURE	EXAMPLE
A response that conveys your understanding of another person's message.	To increase listening efficiency; to avoid message confusion; to discover the speaker's motivation.	1. Listen carefully to the message. 2. Notice what images and feelings you have experienced from the message. 3. Determine what the message means to you. 4. Create a message that conveys these images and/or feelings.	Grace says, "At two minutes to five, the boss gave me three letters that had to be in the mail that evening!" Bonita replies, "If I understand, you were really resentful that your boss dumped important work on you right before quitting time, when she knows that you have to pick up the baby at daycare."

SKILL BUILDERS · CLARIFYING SUPPORTIVE INTENTIONS

SKILL

Openly stating that your goal in the conversation is to support and help your partner.

USE

To enable your partner to easily interpret messages without searching for a hidden agenda. To communicate that someone is "on their side" and to provide a context for understanding supportive comments.

PROCEDURE

1. Directly state your intentions, emphasizing your desire to help.
2. Remind your partner about your ongoing relationship.
3. Indicate that helping is your only motive.
4. Phrase your clarification in a way that reflects helpfulness.

EXAMPLE

After listening to Sonja complain about flunking her geology midterm, her friend Deepak replies:
"Sonja, you're a dear friend, and I'd like to help if you want me to. I did well enough on the midterm that I think I could be of help; maybe we could meet once a week to go over the readings and class notes together."

SKILL BUILDERS · NEGATIVE FACEWORK

SKILL

Using verbally indirect methods when offering information, opinions, or advice.

USE

To protect the other's negative face needs (for independence and autonomy) when presenting opinions or advice.

PROCEDURE

1. Ask for permission before making suggestions or giving advice.
2. After stating the advice verbally defer to the opinions and preferences of the other person.
3. Use tentative language to hedge and qualify opinions and advice.
4. Offer suggestions indirectly by telling stories or describing hypothetical options.

EXAMPLE

Judy has learned that Gloria has really been hurt by the rejection from a best friend. Judy says: "Would you like any advice on this?" Gloria says yes, Judy then offers suggestion.
"These are just a few suggestions, but I think you should go with what you think is best. Now, I'm not sure that these are the only way to go, but I think . . ."
After stating her opinions, Judy says "Depending on what you want to accomplish, I can see a couple ways that you might proceed . . .

 **SKILL BUILDERS**  **PERCEPTION CHECKING**

SKILL	**USE**	**PROCEDURE**	**EXAMPLE**
A statement that expresses the meaning you get from the non-verbal behavior of another.	To clarify the meaning of nonverbal behavior.	1. Watch the behavior of another. 2. Ask yourself: What does that behavior mean to me? 3. Describe the behavior (to yourself or aloud) and put your interpretation of the nonverbal behavior into words to verify your perception.	As Dale frowns while reading Paul's first draft of a memo, Paul says, "From the way you're frowning, I take it that you're not too pleased with the way I phrased the memo."

SKILL BUILDERS **QUESTIONING**

SKILL	**USE**	**PROCEDURE**	**EXAMPLE**
Phrasing a response designed to get further information, to clarify information already received, or to encourage another to continue speaking.	To help get a more complete picture before making other comments; to help a shy person open up; to clarify meaning.	1. Note the kind of information you need to increase your understanding of the message. 2. Phrase questions as specific, complete sentences. 3. Deliver questions in a sincere tone of voice. 4. Put the burden of ignorance on your own shoulders.	When Connie says, "Well, it would be better if she weren't so sedentary," Jeff replies, "I'm not sure I understand what you mean by 'sedentary'—would you explain?"

Disclosure

 **SKILL BUILDERS** **ASKING FOR CRITICISM**

SKILL	**USE**	**PROCEDURE**	**EXAMPLE**
Asking others for their reaction to you or to your behavior.	To get information that will help you understand yourself and your effect on others.	1. Outline the kind of criticism you are seeking. 2. Avoid verbal or nonverbal negative reactions to the criticism. 3. Paraphrase what you hear. 4. Give positive reinforcement to those who take your requests seriously.	Lucy asks, "Tim, when I talk with the boss, do I sound defensive?" Tim replies, "I think so—your voice gets sharp and you lose eye contact, which makes you look nervous." "So you think that the tone of my voice and my eye contact lead the boss to perceive me as defensive." "Yes." "Thanks Tim. I've really got to work on this."

Responding Supportively

SKILL BUILDERS — EMPATHIZING

SKILL
The cognitive process of identifying with or the vicarious experiencing of the feelings, thoughts, or attitudes of another.

USE
To prepare yourself for making an appropriate comforting response.

PROCEDURE
1. Show respect for the person by actively attending to what the person says.
2. Concentrate on observing and understanding both the verbal and nonverbal messages, using paraphrases and perception checking to aid you.
3. Experience an emotional response parallel to another person's actual or anticipated display of emotion, imagine yourself in the place of the person, feel concern, compassion, or sorrow for the person because of his or her situation or plight.

EXAMPLE
When Jerry says, "I was really hurt when Sarah returned the ring I had given her," Mary experiences an emotional response parallel to Jerry's, imagines herself in Jerry's situation, or feels concern, compassion, or sorrow for Jerry.

SKILL BUILDERS — FRAMING

SKILL
Offering information, observations, and opinions with the goal of helping the receiver to understand or reinterpret an event or circumstance.

USE
To support others when you believe that people have made interpretations based on incomplete information or have not considered other viable explanations that would be less threatening to their self-esteem.

PROCEDURE
1. Listen to how your partner is interpreting events.
2. Notice information that your partner may be overlooking or over-emphasizing in the interpretation.
3. Clearly present relevant, truthful information, observations, and opinions that enable your partner to develop a less ego-threatening explanation of what has happened.

EXAMPLE
Pam: "Katie must be really angry with me. Yesterday she walked right by me at the market and didn't even say 'Hi'."
Paula: "Are you sure she's angry? She hasn't said anything to me. And you know, when she's mad I usually hear about it. Maybe she just didn't see you."

SKILL BUILDERS — GIVING ADVICE

SKILL
Presenting suggestions and proposals a partner could use to satisfactorily resolve an emotionally difficult situation.

USE
To comfort our partners when we have established a supportive climate and they are unable to find their own solutions.

PROCEDURE
1. Ask for permission to give advice.
2. Word the message as *one* suggestion in a way that the recipient can understand.
3. Present any potential risks or costs associated with the following the advice.
4. Indicate that you will not be offended should your partner choose to ignore your recommendation or look for another choice.

EXAMPLE
After a friend has explained a difficult situation she faces, Felicia might say: "I have a suggestion if you'd like to hear it. As I see it, one way you could handle this is to . . .
"This is just one idea—you may come up with a different solution that's just as good. So think this one over, and do what you believe is best for you."

Disclosure (continued)

SKILL BUILDERS  ASSERTIVENESS

SKILL
Standing up for yourself and doing so in interpersonally effective ways that describe your feelings honestly and exercise your personal rights while respecting the rights of others.

USE
To show clearly what you think or feel.

PROCEDURE
1. Identify what you are thinking or feeling.
2. Analyze the cause of these feelings.
3. Choose the appropriate skills necessary to communicate these feelings, as well as any outcome you desire.
4. Communicate these feelings to the appropriate person. Remember to own your feelings.

EXAMPLE
When Gavin believes that he is being unjustly charged, he says, "I have never been charged for a refill on iced tea before—has there been a change in policy?"

SKILL BUILDERS  DESCRIBING BEHAVIOR, CONSEQUENCES, AND FEELINGS SEQUENCE

SKILL
Describing the basis of a conflict in terms of behavior, consequences, and feelings (b-c-f).

USE
To help the other person understand the problem completely.

PROCEDURE
1. Own the message.
2. Describe the behavior that you see or hear.
3. Describe the consequences that result.
4. Describe your feelings.

EXAMPLE
Jason says, "I have a problem that I need your help with. When I tell you what I'm thinking and you don't respond (b), I start to think you don't care about me or what I think (c), and this causes me to get very angry with you (f)."

SKILL BUILDERS GIVING CONSTRUCTIVE CRITICISM

SKILL
Describing the specific negative behaviors or actions of another and the effects that the behavior has on others.

USE
To help people see themselves as others see them.

PROCEDURE
1. Describe the person's behavior accurately.
2. Preface negative statements with positive ones if possible.
3. Be specific.
4. When appropriate, suggest how the person can change the behavior.

EXAMPLE
Carol says, "Bob, I've noticed something about your behavior with Jenny. Would you like to hear it?" After Bob assures her that he would, Carol continues, "Although you seem really supportive of Jenny, there are times when Jenny starts to relate an experience and you interrupt her and finish telling the story."

Disclosure (continued)

SKILL
Putting emotional state into words.

USE
For self-disclosure; to teach people how to treat you.

PROCEDURE
1. Indicate what has triggered the feeling.
2. Mentally identify what you are feeling–think specifically. Am I feeling hate? Anger? Joy?
3. Verbally own the feeling. For example, "I'm (name the emotion)."

EXAMPLE
"As a result of not getting the job, I feel depressed and discouraged" or "Because of the way you stood up for me when I was being put down by Leah, I'm feeling very warm and loving toward you."

SKILL
Describing the specific positive behaviors or accomplishments of another and the effects that the behaviors have on others.

USE
To help people see themselves positively.

PROCEDURE
1. Make note of the specific behavior or accomplishment that you want to reinforce.
2. Describe the specific behavior and/or accomplishment.
3. Describe the positive feelings or outcomes that you or others experience as a result of the behavior or accomplishment.
4. Phrase the response so that the level of praise appropriately reflects the significance of the behavior or accomplishment.

EXAMPLE
"Marge, that was an excellent writing job on the Miller story. Your descriptions were particularly vivid."

SKILL
Accurately recounting the specific actions of another without commenting on their appropriateness.

USE
Holding ourselves accountable for our observations and any resulting conclusions we have drawn.

PROCEDURE
1. Identify the generalized perception you are experiencing.
2. Recall the specific behaviors that have led you to this perception.
3. Form a message in which you report only what you have seen or heard without judging its appropriateness.

EXAMPLE
Instead of saying "She is such a snob," say "She has walked by us three times now without speaking."

Inter-Act TENTH EDITION

Interpersonal Communication Concepts, Skills, and Contexts

Kathleen S. Verderber
NORTHERN KENTUCKY UNIVERSITY

Rudolph F. Verderber
UNIVERSITY OF CINCINNATI

New York   Oxford
Oxford University Press
2004

Oxford University Press

Oxford New York
Auckland Bangkok Buenos Aires Cape Town Chennai
Dar es Salaam Delhi Hong Kong Istanbul Karachi Kolkata
Kuala Lumpur Madrid Melbourne Mexico City Mumbai
Nairobi São Paulo Shanghai Taipei Tokyo Toronto

Published by Oxford University Press, Inc.
198 Madison Avenue, New York, New York 10016
http://www.oup-usa.org

Library of Congress Cataloging-in-Publication Data

Verderber, Kathleen S., 1949-
   Inter-act : interpersonal communication concepts, skills, and contexts / Kathleen S.
   Verderber, Rudolph F. Verderber.—10th ed.
      p. cm.
   Includes bibliographical references and index.
   ISBN 0-19-516847-X
   1. Interpersonal communication. 2. Interpersonal relations. I. Verderber, Rudolph F. II.
Title.

BF637.C45V47 2004
158.2—dc21   2003042967

Printing number: 9 8 7 6 5 4 3 2

Printed in the United States of America on acid-free paper

Brief Contents

PREFACE   xiv

PART I
Understanding Interpersonal Communication

CHAPTER 1   An Orientation to Interpersonal Communication   1

CHAPTER 2   Forming and Using Social Perceptions   30

CHAPTER 3   Communication in Relationships: Basic Concepts   60

CHAPTER 4   Verbal Communication   90

CHAPTER 5   Communicating Through Nonverbal Behaviors   120

PART II
Developing Interpersonal Communication Skills

CHAPTER 6   Holding Effective Conversations   148

CHAPTER 7   Listening Effectively   178

CHAPTER 8   Responding with Understanding and Comforting Others   208

CHAPTER 9   Sharing Personal Information: Self-Disclosure and Feedback   242

CHAPTER 10   Using Interpersonal Influence Ethically   272

CHAPTER 11   Managing Conflict   302

PART III
Using Communication Skills to Improve Relationships

CHAPTER 12   Communicating in Intimate Relationships: Friends, Spouses, and Family   336

CHAPTER 13   Communicating in the Workplace   364

CHAPTER 14   Electronically Mediated Interpersonal Communication   398

REFERENCES   422

GLOSSARY   430

INDEX   436

PHOTO CREDITS   444

Contents

Preface   xiv

PART I   Understanding Interpersonal Communication

CHAPTER 1   An Orientation to Interpersonal Communication   1

Interpersonal Communication Defined   3
The Functions of Interpersonal Communication   4
The Interpersonal Communication Process   5
   Participant Characteristics and Roles   6
   Context   7
   Message Formation   8
   Channels   9
   Noise   9
   Feedback Messages   9
   The Process in Action   10
Interpersonal Communication Principles   11
   Interpersonal Communication Has Purpose   11
   Interpersonal Communication Is Continuous   12
   Interpersonal Communication Messages Vary in Conscious Encoding   12
   Interpersonal Communication Is Relational   12
   Interpersonal Communication Is Learned   14
The Ethics of Interpersonal Communication   14
Interpersonal Communication and Diversity   16
   Diverse Voices: *Arturo Madrid, Social Perception*   19
Increasing Interpersonal Communication Competence   20
   Understanding the Concepts and Developing Skills that Lead
     to Competence   21
   Spotlight on Scholars: *Brian Spitzberg on Interpersonal Communication
     Competence*   23
   Writing Communication Improvement Goal Statements   24
Summary   26
Chapter Resources   28
  Key Words   28
  Inter-Act with Media   28

CHAPTER 2 Forming and Using Social Perceptions 30

The Perception Process 32
  Attention and Selection 33
  Organization of Stimuli 33
  Interpretation of Stimuli 34
Perceptions of Self: Self-Concept and Self-Esteem 35
  Forming and Maintaining a Self-Concept 35
  Developing and Maintaining Self-Esteem 38
  Accuracy of Self-Concept and Self-Esteem 38
  Spotlight on Scholars: *Michael Hecht on Interethnic Communication
    and Ethnic Identity* 41
  Presenting Ourselves 42
  Self-Concept, Self-Esteem, and Communication 44
  Diverse Voices: *Dolores V. Tanno, I Am. . .* 45
  Cultural and Gender Differences 47
Perception of Others 48
  Physical Characteristics and Social Behaviors 49
  Stereotyping 50
  Emotional States 52
  Cultural and Gender Differences 53
Improving Social Perception 54
Summary 56
What Would You Do? A Question of Ethics 57
Chapter Resources 58
  Communication Improvement Plan: Perception 58
  Key Words 58
  Inter-Act with Media 58

CHAPTER 3 Communicating in Relationships:
Basic Concepts 60

Types of Relationships 63
  Acquaintances 63
  Friends 63
  Close Friends or Intimates 64
  Disclosure and Feedback Ratios 65
Communication Patterns During Stages of Relationships 68
  Beginning and Developing Relationships 68
  Spotlight on Scholars: *Steven Duck on Personal Relationships* 69
  Diverse Voices: *Brenda J. Allen, Friendships that Bridge Differences* 73
  Communication in Stabilizing Relationships 75
  Relationship Disintegration 79
Theoretical Perspectives on Relationships 81
  Interpersonal Needs Theory 81
  Exchange Theory 83

What Would You Do? A Question of Ethics 85
Summary 86
Chapter Resources 88
    Communication Improvement Plan: Relationships 88
    Key Words 88
    Inter-Act with Media 88

CHAPTER 4 Verbal Communication 90

The Nature and Use of Language 93
    Language and Meaning 94
    Language and Culture 96
Increasing Language Clarity 100
    Diverse Voices: *Castelan Cargile, Accents and Language* 101
    Develop Your Vocabulary 102
    Choose Specific Language 103
    Date Information 106
    Index Generalizations 108
Speaking Appropriately 110
    Adapt Formality to the Situation 110
    Be Wary of Jargon and Slang 111
    Avoid Crude Language 111
    Demonstrate Sensitivity 111
    Spotlight on Scholars: *Molefi Kete Asante on The Language of Prejudice and Racism* 115
Summary 116
What Would You Do? A Question of Ethics 117
Chapter Resources 118
    Communication Improvement Plan: Verbal Communication 118
    Key Words 118
    Inter-Act with Media 118

CHAPTER 5 Communicating Through Nonverbal Behaviors 120

The Nature of Nonverbal Communication Behavior 123
Body Motions 123
    Types of Body Motions 123
    How Body Motions Are Used 125
    Cultural Variations 127
    Gender Variations 128
Paralanguage 129
    Vocal Characteristics 129
    Vocal Interferences 129

Self-Presentation 131
  Clothing and Personal Grooming 131
  Poise 132
  Touch 132
  Time 133
  Cultural Variations in Self-Presentation 134
Communication Through Management of Your Environment 135
  Space 135
  Spotlight on Scholars: *Judee K. Burgoon on Nonverbal Expectancy Violation Theory* 137
  Temperature, Lighting, and Color 140
  Diverse Voices: *Elizabeth Lozano,* Latin American and Anglo Use of Personal Space in Public Places 141
  Cultural Variations in Management of the Environment 142
  Increasing Accuracy of Nonverbal Communication 143
What Would You Do? A Question of Ethics 144
Summary 145
Chapter Resources 146
  Communication Improvement Plan: Nonverbal Communication 146
  Key Words 146
  Inter-Act with Media 146

PART II Developing Interpersonal Communication Skills

CHAPTER 6 Holding Effective Conversations 148
Characteristics of Conversation 150
Types and Structures of Conversation 151
  Parts of a Conversation 151
  Two Common Types of Conversation 152
  The Structure of Casual Social Conversation 153
  The Structure of Problem-Consideration Conversations 154
Rules of Conversations 155
  Characteristics of Rules 156
  The Cooperative Principle 157
  Diverse Voices: *Gwendolyn Gong, Ph.D., When Mississippi Chinese Talk* 159
Guidelines for Effective Conversationalists 161
  Prepare to Contribute Interesting Information 161
  Ask Questions that Motivate Others to Respond 162
  Provide Free Information 163
  Credit the Sources of Your Ideas 163
  Practice Appropriate Turn-Taking 164
  Maintain Conversational Coherence 166

Practice Politeness   167

Engage in Ethical Dialogue   170

Cultural Variations in Effective Conversation   171

What Would You Do? A Question of Ethics   171

Summary   172

Inter-Action Dialogue: Conversations   174

Chapter Resources   176

Communication Improvement Plan: Conversation   176

Key Words   176

Inter-Act with Media   176

CHAPTER 7   Listening Effectively   178

Attending: Focusing Attention   182

Diverse Voices: *Dawn O. Braithwaite and Charles A. Braithwaite,*
Communication Between Able-Bodied Persons and Persons
with Disabilities   185

Understanding: Listening Actively   187

Identifying the Organization   187

Attend to Nonverbal Cues   188

Ask Questions   188

Paraphrasing   191

Remembering: Retaining Information   194

Repeat Information   194

Construct Mnemonics   194

Spotlight on Scholars: *Robert Bostrom on Listening*   195

Take Notes   196

Evaluating: Listening Critically   198

Separate Factual Statements from Inferences   198

Evaluating Inferences   200

What Would You Do? A Question of Ethics   203

Summary   203

Inter-Action Dialogue: Listening Effectively   204

Chapter Resources   206

Communication Improvement Plan: Listening   206

Key Words   206

Inter-Act with Media   206

CHAPTER 8   Responding with Understanding and
Comforting Others   208

Empathy   211

Approaches to Empathy   211

Improving Our Ability to Empathize   212

Diverse Voices: *Linda Howard, Black and White*   213

Cultural Considerations   216

Understanding Emotional Support 217
   Supporting 218
   Spotlight on Scholars: *Brant Burleson on Comforting* 219
Characteristics of Effective and Ineffective Emotional Support Messages 221
   Supportive Interaction Phases 222
Supportive Message Skills 224
   Clarifying Supportive Intentions 225
   Buffering Face Threats 226
   Other-Centered Messages 228
   Framing 230
   Giving Advice 233
Gender and Cultural Similarity and Differences in Comforting 235
What Would You Do? A Question of Ethics 236
Summary 237
Inter-Action Dialogue: Responding and Comforting 238
Chapter Resources 240
   Communication Improvement Plan: Responding 240
   Key Words 240
   Inter-Act with Media 240

CHAPTER 9 Sharing Personal Information:
Self-Disclosure and Feedback

    242

Self-Disclosure 245
   Guidelines for Appropriate Self-Disclosure 245
   Cultural and Gender Differences 247
Disclosing Feelings 247
   Masking Feelings 247
   Displaying Feelings 249
   Describing Feelings 250
   Owning Feelings and Opinions 256
Giving Personal Feedback 257
   Describing Behavior 257
   Praise 259
   Giving Constructive Criticism 261
Asking for Criticism 264
What Would You Do? A Question of Ethics 266
Summary 267
Inter-Action Dialogue: Self-Disclosure 268
Chapter Resources 270
   **Communication Improvement Plan: Developing Relationships Through
   Self-Disclosure and Feedback** 270
   Key Words 270
   Inter-Act with Media 270

CHAPTER 10 Using Interpersonal Influence Ethically   272

Interpersonal Power in Relationships   274
Perception of Coercive Power   275
Reward Power   275
Legitimate Power   276
Expert Power   276
Referent Power   277

Types of Persuasive Messages   277
Giving Good Reasons   277
Personal Credibility   279
Spotlight on Scholars: *Richard Petty on Attitude Change*   281
Emotion Appeals   284

Compliance-Gaining Strategies   285
Supporting-Evidence Strategies   285
Exchange Strategies   286
Direct-Request Strategies   286
Empathy-Based Strategies   286
Face-Maintenance Strategies   286
Other-Benefit Strategies   287
Distributive Strategies   287
Choosing a Strategy   287
Overcoming Resistance   288

Assertiveness   288
Contrasting Methods of Expressing Our Needs and Rights   289
Distinguishing Among Passive, Aggressive, and Assertive Responses   290
Characteristics of Assertive Messages   292
Assertiveness in Cross-Cultural Relationships   293

What Would You Do? A Question of Ethics   295
Summary   296
Inter-Action Dialogue: Influence   298
Chapter Resources   300
Communication Improvement Plan: Influencing Ethically   300
Key Words   300
Inter-Act with Media   300

CHAPTER 11 Managing Conflict   302

Types of Interpersonal Conflict   305
Pseudoconflict   305
Fact Conflict   306
Value Conflict   306
Policy Conflict   307
Ego Conflict   308

Styles of Managing Conflict   310
   Withdrawal   310
   Diverse Voices: *Bruce A. Jacobs, Conversing about Racism*   311
   Accommodating   313
   Forcing   314
   Compromising   315
   Collaborating   315
Communication Skills that Promote Successful Conflict Management   318
   Communication Skills for Initiating Conflict   318
   Spotlight on Scholars: *Daniel J. Canary on Conflict Management*   321
   Communication Skills for Responding to Conflict   323
   Communication Skills for Mediating Conflict   325
   Recovering from Conflict-Management Failures   327
What Would You Do? A Question of Ethics   328
Summary   329
Inter-Action Dialogue: Conflict   330
Chapter Resources   334
   Communication Improvement Plan: Conflict Management   334
   Key Words   334
   Inter-Act with Media   334

PART III Using Communication Skills to Improve Relationships

CHAPTER 12 Communicating in Intimate Relationships: Friends, Spouses, and Family

                                                    336
Characteristics of Intimate Relationships   339
   Warmth and Affection   339
   Trust   339
   Self-Disclosure   340
   Commitment   340
Types of Intimate Relationships and Relational Styles   341
   Male Relationships   341
   Female Relationships   343
   Gender Differences in Intimacy   343
   Male–Female Relationships   344
   Marriage Relationships   345
   Spotlight on Scholars: *Mary Anne Fitzpatrick on Couple Types*
      and Communication   347
   Family Relationships   349
   Diverse Voices: *Elisa Martinez, Having a Choice of Who to Be*   351
   Improving Family Communication   353

Problem Areas in Intimate Relationships   357
   Jealousy   357
   Sex-Role Stereotyping   358
What Would You Do? A Question of Ethics   360
Summary   361
Chapter Resources   362
   Communication Improvement Plan: Intimate Relationships   362
   Key Words   362
   Inter-Act with Media   362

CHAPTER 13 Communicating in the Workplace   364

Presenting Yourself During the Hiring Process   367
   Presenting Yourself in Writing   367
   Presenting Yourself During an Interview   372
Interviewing Others   374
   Beginning the Interview   374
   Questions Used in the Body of the Interview   374
   Concluding an Interview   376
Managing Relationships at Work   377
   Communicating in Managerial Relationships   377
   Communicating in Co-Worker Relationships   379
   Diverse Voices: *Sheryl Lindsley, Understanding Our Mexican Co-Workers*   381
Leadership in Work Relations   384
   Leadership Traits   385
   Leadership Styles   385
   Preparing for Leadership   386
   Coaching Others at Work   386
   Spotlight on Scholars: *Gail T. Fairhurst on Leadership in Work
      Organizations*   387
   Counseling Others at Work   389
   Leading Group Discussion and Decision Making   390
What Would You Do? A Question of Ethics   394
Summary   394
Chapter Resources   396
   Communication Improvement Plan: Workplace Communication   396
   Key Words   396
   Inter-Act with Media   396

CHAPTER 14 Electronically Mediated (EM) Interpersonal
Communication   398

Cellular and Digital Telephones   401
The Internet   403
   Internet Terminology   403
Communicating Online   405
   E-Mail   405
   Newsgroups   408
   Internet Chat   409
Role of Electronic Communication in Building Relationships   410
   Development of Electronically Mediated Relationships   411
   From Online to In-Person Relationships   413
The Dark Side of Electronically Mediated Communication   413
Interpersonal Communication Skills in Cyber Relationships   415
   Sender Skills   415
   Receiver Skills   416
What Would You Do? A Question of Ethics   418
Summary   419
Chapter Resources   420
   Communication Improvement Plan: Communicating Electronically   420
   Key Words   420
   Inter-Act with Media   420

References   422
Glossary   430
Index   436
Photo Credits   444

Preface

We are excited to present to you the tenth edition of *Inter-Act*, now published by Oxford University Press. When we began writing the first edition of this text, the field of interpersonal communication was relatively new, with few theories and scant research to guide us. Interpersonal communication as a field of study has matured since then, and the concepts and skills we present are grounded in well-developed communication theories that continue to be refined through scholarly research. Today the best communication scholarship not only helps us understand how our relationships work, but it also provides us with insights into how we can improve our own communication practices. Although most of us realize that we need to improve our interpersonal communication skills in order to help maintain and improve our relationships with those who are dear to us, we must also develop and improve our relationships with those who differ from us, whether those differences are in personal philosophy, political perspective, gender, age, race, religion, or culture. In this new edition, we present the theories, concepts, and skills that can help us be more effective in all our relationships.

Philosophy of the Text

We believe that the field of interpersonal communication, like the field of medicine, is a practical study. One studies interpersonal communication in order to understand and become skillful in relating with others. Thus, this text presents not only the theories of interpersonal communication, but it also identifies specific communication skills that make interactions more effective and satisfying. The text encourages students to practice and adopt new ways of interacting. The course to which *Inter-Act* is ideally suited is one whose goals include helping students practice and become more skilled. Since there is cultural variation in what behaviors are deemed to be effective, the text strives to sensitize students to these differences and teach them about the flexibility needed to be effective in various contexts.

Specific Goals

The overall vision of *Inter-Act* continues to be supported with seven specific goals: (1) to present important communication propositions, theories, and assumptions that have been consistently supported by careful research so that the conceptual foundations of interpersonal relationship competence can be more clearly understood; (2) to teach communication skills that facilitate effective relationships; (3) to challenge students to think critically and creatively about the concepts and skills that they are learning; (4) to present ethical frameworks that guide competent communication early in the text and weave discussions of ethical issues throughout the book; (5) to consider how communication needs, rules, and processes differ among diverse people; (6) to provide additional pedagogical features that significantly enhance students' enjoyment of the challenge of learning; and (7) to freshen and update the text's content and style so that it remains appealing, relevant, and reflective of the digital age.

Chapters and Key Features

For the convenience of those who are familiar with the previous edition of *Inter-Act*, the chapter order, main headings, and many of the key features remain the same. As a result, the overall feel of this edition is similar to the last edition and will be comfortable to users of previous editions. Nevertheless, this edition incorporates new insights provided by theory and research and new examples that freshen and bring a contemporary relevance to the concepts and skills.

New Feature: Inter-Action Dialogues and Analyses

In this new feature, six dialogues demonstrate how specific skills presented in the text can be used to create more effective conversations. Transcriptions of the conversations are printed in the text, and video footage of conversations appear on the CD-ROM included with each new text. Each dialogue is accompanied by an analysis. Two of the analyses are provided in the text. The others are available on the Inter-Action! CD-ROM that is packaged with this text. Conversations can be used for class discussion or as analytical assignments.

Chapters and Features Strengthened in this Edition

- **Chapter 8, Responding with Understanding and Comforting Others,** has been retitled to reflect its thorough revision. The new chapter presents the current scholarship on supportive communication and teaches five skills for comforting others.
- **Chapter 4, Verbal Communication,** has been revised so that emphasis is placed on the central role that speech communities play in determining language, meaning, and the complex relationships between them. This discussion of cultural influences on language and meaning lays the foundation for understanding the skills that can help increase the clarity and appropriateness of messages.
- **Chapter 14, Electronically Mediated Interpersonal Communication,** incorporates new research related to the use of cellular phones and e-mail and how online relationships are developed and maintained.
- **Chapter 7, Listening Effectively,** presents the five-step active listening process and now includes the skills of questioning and paraphrasing.

- **Chapter 10, Using Interpersonal Influence Ethically,** has been reorganized so that a discussion of power at the beginning of the chapter provides the base for understanding influence theory and the skills that follow.
- **Focus on Skills.** Previous users of *Inter-Act* will find that most of the skills presented in previous editions remain unchanged. However, in this edition we have refined our skill list so that all skills require overt behaviors, not just cognitive processing. While we present these cognitive processes, we do not label them as skills. We have also added new skills that are based on recent scholarship. The skills are described and exemplified in the text and in Skill Builders boxes, which highlight each skill with the definition of the skill, a brief description of its use, the steps for enacting the skill, and an example that illustrates the skill in use.
- **Student Activities** presented in the text have been streamlined. The Observe & Analyze activities have been edited so that they provide clearer directions for students. All can be used as journal or short paper assignments.
- **Spotlight on Scholars** features continue to explore the work of eleven eminent communication scholars. Based on interviews with the scholars, these features have been updated to reflect the recent work of each scholar. This feature is designed to help undergraduates understand the research and theory building process and what motivates the people who do this work.
- **Diverse Voices,** excerpts of previously published selections, appear in most chapters of the text to give voice to the experiences of people from a wide range of backgrounds and cultural experiences. A third of these excerpts are new to this edition. This popular feature highlights the personal thoughts and experiences of individuals on topics related to the content of the chapter, helping students to understand how other cultural perspectives view a particular concept.
- **Text Yourself Exercises** are short self-tests that challenge students to practice the material they have read. We have increased the number of tests in this edition.
- **Communication Improvement Plans** are provided at the end of each chapter. In accord with the findings of noteworthy research, students are encouraged to set specific goals for development by writing a skill improvement plan.
- **What Would You Do? A Question of Ethics** is a feature that outlines ethical challenges and requires students to think critically in sorting through a variety of ethical dilemmas faced by communicators. Material in Chapter 1 lays the groundwork for the criteria on which students may make their assessments. In each case, the dilemma posed focuses on issues raised in the specific chapter.
- **Skills Chart.** A convenient tear-out chart at the beginning of the book provides a summary of all Skill Builders. The skills in the chart have been grouped into categories for easy reference.

Supplementary Materials

As a user of this text you also have access to supplementary materials developed at Oxford University Press. Materials prepared by Oxford are divided into those that are relevant for students and those for faculty.

Student Materials

- **CD-Rom.** New to this edition is an exciting student CD-ROM, which is packaged in each new copy of *Inter-Act*, tenth edition. The CD-ROM expands text content in a variety of ways. First, it contains video footage of four of the Inter-Action Dialogues which appear in the textbook. Students can watch these videos and then use the CD-ROM to analyze the skills that are demonstrated in each conversation. A click of a button allows students to compare their analyses to those written by the authors. The CD-ROM also links students to the *Inter-Act* companion Web site at Oxford University Press.

- **Student Workbook.** Available with this edition is a revised student workbook, written by Mary Hoeft and Sharon Rubin, both at the University of Wisconsin-Barron County. This workbook offers a wealth of exercises that reinforce text content. For each chapter, students will find an interactive chapter outline, a key terms list, a variety of exercises, helpful URLs, and a chapter quiz. This is an invaluable student resource.

- **Companion Web Site: For Students.** The companion Web site for *Inter-Act*, tenth edition can be found at http://www.oup.com/us/highered/interact. It contains additional helpful resources for students wishing to reinforce their study of interpersonal communications. On the companion Web site, students will find: an online glossary, links to all Web sites mentioned in the text, and a variety of exercises designed to help students think further about material they encounter in the textbook. Also provided is a link to an Oxford site called "Now Playing," which discusses interpersonal communication issues as seen in recent popular films.

Faculty Materials

- **Instructor's Resource Manual.** For the tenth edition of *Inter-Act*, the Instructor's Resource Manual has been revised by Lori E. Zakel and Lynn M. Disbrow, both of Sinclair Community College. The Instructor's Resource Manual features new teaching resources, including class-tested exercises, surveys, role-playing exercises, experiential learning exercises, suggested journal topics, discussion questions, written assignments, possible course schedule, and an extensive test bank.

- **Computerized Test Bank.** The test bank from the Instructor's Resource Manual is also available on CD-ROM. The electronic format allows users to customize tests to suit any style of exam.

- **Companion Web Site: For Instructors.** The companion web site for *Inter-Act*, tenth edition can be found at: http://www.oup.com/us/highered/interact. It contains additional helpful resources for instructors teaching classes in interpersonal communication. On the web site, instructors will find:

  - **Media Guide for Interpersonal Communication, by Charles G. Apple, University of Michigan, Flint.** This Media Guide is a wonderful resource, expanding on the Inter-Act with Media listings that accompany each chapter in the text. The Media Guide provides compelling examples of interpersonal communication in an engaging format that generates student interest and motivates learning through the use of films, books, plays, Web sites, and journal articles.

- **Power Point Presentations.** A Power Point presentation for each chapter of the book is provided. Slides highlight important concepts from each chapter in a dynamic, visual way. Instructors can use these slides to enhance their lecture periods.

For additional information regarding these supplementary materials, please call your Oxford sales representative at 1-800-280-0280, or visit the Oxford Higher Education Web site at http://www.oup-usa.org/highered.

Acknowledgments

We would like to begin by expressing our gratitude to the team at our new publisher, Oxford University Press. Our editor, Peter Labella, has worked hard to make this a smooth transition. We especially want to thank Linda Harris and her staff, whose professional advice has made our book stronger. We thank Terry Deal Michelet, our production editor, and all the others at Oxford who were involved in this revision. We are pleased to again have Charles Apple working with us on the Inter-Act with Media feature. We owe special gratitude to Brant Burleson, Professor of Communication at Purdue University, who provided us with guidance in the extensive revision of Chapter 8. We are responsible for what appears in this book, yet the content reflects the thoughts of a great many people. We would like to thank the following colleagues who reviewed the last edition and provided guidance for the changes we have made in this tenth edition: Joseph S. Coppolino, Nassau Community College; Kathryn Dindia, University of Wisconsin, Milwaukee; Aloysia F. Hard, Olympic College; Cheri Frey-Hartel, Cardinal Stritch University; Vickie Harvey, California State University, Stanislau; David E. Majewski, Richard Bland College; Randall R. Mueller, Gateway Technical College; George Nagel, Ferris State University; Mary T. Newman, Wharton County Jr. College.

Kathleen S. Verderber
Rudolph F. Verderber

Inter-Act

**Interpersonal Communication
Concepts, Skills, and Contexts**

CHAPTER 1

An Orientation to Interpersonal

Communication

After you have read this chapter, you should be able to answer these questions:

- What is interpersonal communication?
- Why is interpersonal communication important?
- How does the interpersonal communication process work?
- What principles provide the foundation for interpersonal communication?
- What is communication competence?
- What are major ethical issues facing communicators?
- Why should a communicator be concerned about diversity?
- How can you improve your interpersonal communication?

"Hello?"

"Hi—you sound a little spaced—like you just got up."

"No . . ."

"Well, it's something about your voice—but I didn't call to talk about that. Listen . . ."

"Is this Brad?"

"Brad! You've got to be kidding. Brad hasn't got here by nine o'clock in the morning for a month."

"Listen, I'm embarrassed, but I don't recognize your voice."

"I hear you. Kara was telling me she talked to her sister for about ten minutes the other morning before she caught on to who she was."

"Who's Kara?"

"Come off it, Maria—you know darn well who Kara is. Now you're just trying to jive me."

"Maria! I'm not Maria!"

"You're not? Then where's Maria?"

"How should I know? Who is this?"

"This is Thomas."

"Thomas? Well, I don't know any Thomas and I'm not Maria and no Maria lives here."

"Uh—then this isn't 532-7649?"

"No, it is not!"

"Well . . . uh . . . it's been good talking to you—you wouldn't want to meet me for coffee sometime, would you?"

Click.

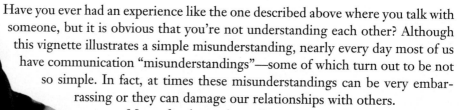

Have you ever had an experience like the one described above where you talk with someone, but it is obvious that you're not understanding each other? Although this vignette illustrates a simple misunderstanding, nearly every day most of us have communication "misunderstandings"—some of which turn out to be not so simple. In fact, at times these misunderstandings can be very embarrassing or they can damage our relationships with others.

Most of us learned to talk and listen before we can remember. You probably learned many basic and vital human interaction skills by observing and imitating the communication behaviors of those around you. Through these observations you formed your own "theories of communication." You draw on these "implicit theories" to help you when you need to communicate with others. When your personal theories are correct, you are effective in your interactions with others, but when your theories are incorrect or incomplete, you may create misunderstanding and harm your relationships.

During this term you will begin a formal study of the theories of interpersonal communication that are based on the research of communication scholars—theories that are more valid, reliable, and complete than many of your personal theories. By understanding the concepts, relationships, and predictions of these theories, you will become better equipped to behave in ways that result in improved relationships. Moreover, you will learn and practice a variety of communication skills in a "safe" classroom setting before you try them out in your other relationships.

In this first chapter, we present introductory information for this study. We (1) define interpersonal communication, (2) discuss the functions that it serves, (3) present a basic description of how the process of interpersonal communication works, (4) identify the basic principles that are fundamental to understanding interpersonal communication, (5) discuss the ethical principles that underlie interpersonal communication, (6) explain how human diversity complicates the interpersonal communication process, and (7) describe what it means to be competent in interpersonal communication.

Interpersonal Communication Defined

We define **interpersonal communication** as the process through which people create and manage their relationships, exercising mutual responsibility in creating meaning. Let's explore this definition to see its importance.

First, interpersonal communication is a process. A process is a systematic series of behaviors with a purpose that occurs over time. During a twenty-minute phone call with your mother to catch up on family news or during a five-minute impromptu meeting with a co-worker to solve a customer problem, a series of behaviors is occurring. These behaviors are purposeful. You ask your mom for your brother's new pager number so you can get in touch with him about sharing the cost of an anniversary present for your grandparents. You tell your co-worker the background of the customer complaint so that she can help you arrive at a solution that is fair to the customer and in keeping with company policy.

Second, interpersonal communication occurs between and among the people involved. For instance, when Crestin (who is trying to get to work on time) shows his impatience with his six-year-old daughter (who is slow to finish her breakfast) by saying "Alisha, quit dawdling!" Alisha might burst into tears, or she might say, "Yes, Daddy," and quickly finish her breakfast. So, what has taken place between the father and his daughter does not depend on what one of them says or does, but rather depends on the meaning that is created between them. What this short exchange means to their relationship is the result of what both of them say and do.

Interpersonal communication—the process through which people create and manage their relationships, exercising mutual responsibility in creating meaning.

OBSERVE & ANALYZE

Journal Activity

Communication Processes Define Relationships

Think about one relationship you have that is "easy" and very satisfying. Then think about one relationship you have that is "difficult" and not satisfying. Briefly describe the last conversation you had with each person. How do these conversations compare to each other? Describe how they are similar; then describe how they differ. How does your communication pattern change? ■

Third, as we communicate, we create and manage our relationships. Without communication your relationships could not exist. A relationship begins when you meet someone. Over time, through your interactions with that person you continue to define the nature of the relationship and what it will become. Is the relationship more personal or impersonal, closer or more distant, romantic or platonic, healthy or unhealthy, dependent or interdependent? The answer to these questions depends on how the people in the relationship talk and behave toward each other. Some communication patterns move relationships to deeper, more satisfying levels while others lead to unhealthy relationships. (For example, some communication processes move relationships to more personal levels while others are designed to maintain relationships at impersonal levels.) Most of us recognize flirting as a communication process that signals the desire to explore a romantic relationship with another. But because the meaning of any communication behavior depends on the response, whether the relationship becomes romantic depends on whether or not the flirting is recognized and reciprocated.

The Functions of Interpersonal Communication

You may have registered for this course because you were curious, because a friend or a teacher recommended it, because it fit your schedule, or because it is a requirement for your major. Whatever may have brought you to this class, we believe that before the term is over you'll be thankful that you have studied interpersonal communication. Why? Because interpersonal communication serves at least 5 functions that are important to your social and psychological health.

1. Through interpersonal communication we attempt to meet our social/psychological needs. Because we are by nature social animals, we need to interact with other people just as we need food, water, and shelter. Often what we talk about is unimportant. We may just "hang out" conversing happily for hours about relatively inconsequential matters, exchanging little real information or we may have "heart to hearts" where we probe deep feelings that are central to our well-being. Regardless of how serious or important the conversation may be, we may carry away from the it a pleasant, satisfied feeling that comes from having met the need to talk with someone.

2. Through interpersonal communication we develop a sense of self. Through our communication and relationships, we learn who we are, what we are good at, and how people react to how we behave. We explore this important function of interpersonal communication in detail in Chapter 2, "Forming and Using Social Perceptions."

3. Through interpersonal communication we fulfill social obligations. We use such statements as "How are you doing?" with a person we sat next to in class last quarter

How are our social needs met in large gatherings?

and "What's happening?" or simply "Hi" when we pass people we know in order to meet social obligations. By saying "Hi, Josh, how's it going?" we acknowledge a person we recognize. By not speaking we risk being perceived as arrogant or insensitive.

4. Through interpersonal communication we acquire information. Accurate and timely information is a key to effective decision making. While we get some information through direct observation, some through reading, and some through the media, we receive a great deal of the information upon which we base our decisions during our conversations with others. For example, Jeff runs out to get a bagel and coffee. When he returns, Tom asks, "What's it like out there this morning?" Jeff replies, "Wow, it's cold—it couldn't be more than twenty degrees." Tom reacts to this news by sighing and says, "I was just going to wear a sweatshirt, but I guess I'd better break out the old winter coat." From decisions as mundane as this one to others that are more important, we acquire a great deal of information on which we act from conversing with others.

5. Through interpersonal communication we influence and are influenced by others. When what a person wants or needs depends on the agreement or cooperation of other people, interpersonal communication is used to influence the ideas and behaviors of others. In a typical day you engage in countless exchanges where the purpose is to influence. From convincing your roommate to loan you a sweater, to listening to a political candidate who is campaigning door-to-door, to persuading your children to do their homework, to (an old favorite) trying to convince an instructor to change your course grade, you use interpersonal communication to entice others into thinking or acting as you wish them to. And others use the same process to try to influence you. Some communication theorists argue that the primary purpose of all communication efforts is to influence the ideas and behavior of others.

The Interpersonal Communication Process

Because you've been communicating for as long as you can remember, you really don't consciously think about the process—the methodical series of thoughts and behaviors that you use when you communicate with someone. These thoughts and behaviors have become automatic. In reality, however, any interpersonal communication episode is the result of a complex series of both cognitions (thinking) and behaviors (doing). Let's begin by describing the elements that make up the communication process (see Figure 1.1) and then we will explain how the process works.

Participant Characteristics and Roles

Participants–the people who communicate by assuming the roles of senders and receivers during the communication.

The **participants** are the people who communicate, assuming the roles of senders and receivers during the communication. As senders, participants form messages and attempt to communicate them to others through verbal symbols and nonverbal behavior. As receivers, they process the messages and behaviors that they receive and react to them. Participating in interpersonal communication can be thought of as playing two roles, sender and receiver. In most interpersonal situations participants enact the two roles simultaneously. Nevertheless, it is useful to describe the primary activities of each role.

In general, it is easier for participants to share meaning when they are similar and have a common base for understanding. According to E. Aronson (1999), we more easily identify with those with whom we share similar physical characteristics (p. 380). The more we perceive ourselves as being different from one another, the more difficult our communication tends to be. Similarities and differences that are likely to have the greatest effect on participants are physical (race, sex, age), psychological (personality, attitudes, values, levels of self-confidence), social (levels of experience in dealing with others and with complex situations), intellectual (knowledge and skills), and gender or cultural characteristics.

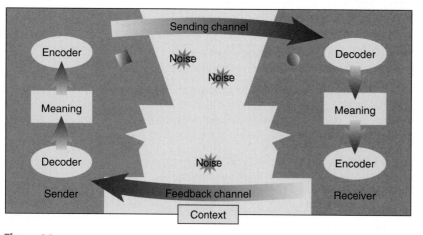

Figure 1.1

A model of communication between two individuals

Context

Context is the setting in which a communication encounter occurs, including what precedes and follows what is said. The context affects the expectations of the participants, the meaning these participants receive, and their subsequent behavior. Context includes the (1) physical, (2) social, (3) historical, (4) psychological, and (5) cultural circumstances that surround a communication episode.

Context—the setting in which communication occurs, including what precedes and follows what is said.

Physical Context The **physical context** includes its location, the environmental conditions (temperature, lighting, noise level), the distance between communicators, seating arrangements, and time of day. Each of these factors can affect the communication. For instance, the meaning shared in a conversation may be affected by whether it is held in a crowded company cafeteria, an elegant candlelit restaurant, over the telephone, or on the Internet.

Physical context—where communication takes place, the environmental conditions (temperature, lighting, noise level), the distance between communicators, seating arrangements, and time of day.

Social Context The **social context** is the type of relationship that may already exist between the participants. Whether communication takes place among family members, friends, acquaintances, work associates, or strangers influences what and how messages are formed, shared, and understood. For instance, most people change how they interact when talking with their parents or siblings as compared to how they interact when talking with their friends.

Social context—the nature of the relationship that exists between the participants.

Historical Context The **historical context** is the background provided by previous communication episodes between the participants. It influences understandings in the current encounter. For instance, suppose one morning Chad tells Shelby that he will get the draft of the report that they had left for their boss to read. As Shelby enters the office that afternoon, she sees Chad and says, "Did you get it?" Another person listening to the conversation would have no idea what the "it" is to which Shelby is referring. Yet Chad may well reply, "It's on my desk." Shelby and Chad understood one another because of the contents of the earlier exchange.

Historical context—the background provided by the previous communication episodes between the participants that influences understandings in the current encounter.

Psychological Context The **psychological context** includes the moods and feelings each person brings to the interpersonal encounter. For instance, suppose Corinne is under a great deal of stress. The person she hired to type the report into her computer couldn't get it done. So the time Corinne has to spend typing the report cuts into the time she was expecting to have to finish the outline for a speech she is to give to the crime task force the next day. Suppose as she is typing, her roommate bounds into their apartment and jokingly suggests that she take a speed-typing course. Corinne, who is normally good-natured, may explode with an angry tirade. Why? Because her stress level provides the psychological context within which she hears this message and it taints what she understands.

Psychological context—the moods and feelings each person brings to an interpersonal encounter.

Cultural Context The **cultural context** includes the beliefs, values, attitudes, meanings, social hierarchies, religion, notions of time, and roles of the group of people (Samovar & Porter, 2000, p. 7). In the United States, the dominant ethnic cultural context has been a European American one. Many "white" Americans seldom think of themselves as "ethnic," but as Sonia Nieto (2000) points out, "we are all ethnic, whether we choose to identify ourselves in this way or not" (p. 27). In

Cultural context—the set of beliefs, values, attitudes, meanings, social hierarchies, religion, notions of time, and roles of the group of people.

the United States, the dominant ethnic cultural context is European American, so the assumption when interacting with others is that they share the beliefs, values, and norms common to this American experience. But in reality the United States is a nation of immigrants and culturally we are quite diverse. As a result, many cultural contexts exist and influence what happens in communication encounters.

Message Formation

Messages—a person's verbal utterances and nonverbal behaviors to which meaning is attributed during communication.

Interpersonal communication takes place through sending and receiving **messages,** which are a person's verbal utterances and nonverbal behaviors to which meaning is attributed. To appreciate the complex way in which messages work, you need to understand meaning, symbols, encoding and decoding, and message form or organization.

Meaning—the substance of messages that you send—the ideas and feelings in your mind.

Meaning Meanings are the ideas and feelings that exist in your mind. You may have ideas about how to study for your next exam, what your career goal is, and whether taxes should be raised or lowered; you also may have feelings such as jealousy, anger, and love. The meanings you have within you, however, cannot be transferred magically into another person's mind.

Symbols—words, sounds, and actions that are generally understood to represent meaning.

Symbols To share meanings, you form messages comprising verbal symbols and nonverbal behaviors. **Symbols** are words, sounds, and actions that are widely understood to represent specific ideas and feelings. As you speak, you choose word symbols to convey your meaning. At the same time facial expressions, eye contact, gestures, and tone of voice—all symbolic nonverbal cues—accompany your words and affect the meaning your listener receives. As a listener, the meaning you attribute to the message is affected by both verbal symbols and nonverbal cues.

Encoding—the cognitive thinking process the sender uses to transform ideas and feelings into symbols and to organize them into a message.

Decoding—the process the receiver uses to transform the messages that are received into the receiver's own ideas and feelings.

Encoding and Decoding Encoding is the cognitive thinking process the sender uses to transform ideas and feelings into symbols and to organize them into a message. **Decoding** is the process the receiver uses to transform the messages that are received into the receiver's own ideas and feelings. Ordinarily you do not consciously think about either the encoding or the decoding process. Only when there is a difficulty (such as speaking in a second language or not being understood) do you become aware of encoding or decoding. Normally, when your eyelids grow heavy and you say "I'm beat," you aren't consciously thinking, "I wonder what symbols I can use to best express the sensation I am now experiencing." Conversely, if you are a native English speaker, when you hear the words "I'm beat" and see the red, heavy-lidded eyes of another person, you are not likely to think, "Beat means to hit, but it is also slang for tired, which means growing weary or feeling a need for sleep; therefore, the person's verbal utterance expresses a need for sleep and the nonverbal behavior of the eyes confirms the accuracy of the statement." (Whew! That was a mouthful.)

The encoding process is made more difficult when verbal and nonverbal cues conflict. For instance, if a co-worker says, "Yes, I'm very interested in the way you arrived at that decision," the meaning you decode will be very different if the person leans forward and looks interested or yawns and looks away.

Form or Organization When messages are long and meanings complex, how well they are organized will affect how accurately they are understood. For instance, when Olga tells Connie about the apartment she looked at yesterday, Connie is more likely to understand the apartment layout if Olga describes the apartment spatially from room to room.

Channels

Channels are both the route traveled by the message and the means of transportation. Messages are transmitted through sensory channels. Face-to-face communication has two basic channels: sound (verbal symbols) and light (nonverbal cues). Although interpersonal communication usually uses these two basic channels—sound and light—people can and do communicate through any of the five sensory channels. A fragrant scent and a firm handshake may be as important as what is seen or heard.

Channels—both the route traveled by the message and the means of transportation.

Noise

Noise is any stimulus that interferes with the sharing of meaning. Noise can be external, internal, or semantic.

Noise—any stimulus that gets in the way of sharing meaning.

External noises are sights, sounds, and other stimuli in the environment that draw people's attention away from what is being said or done. For instance, while a person is giving directions on how to work the new MP3 player, your attention may be drawn away by the external noise of a radio playing an old favorite song of yours. External noise does not have to be a sound, however. Perhaps, while the person gives the directions, your attention is drawn momentarily to an attractive man or woman. Such visual distractions are also external noise.

External noises—the sights, sounds, and other stimuli that draw people's attention away from intended meaning.

Internal noises are thoughts and feelings that compete for attention and interfere with the communication process. If you have tuned out the words of the person with whom you are communicating and tuned into a daydream or a past conversation, then you have experienced internal noise.

Internal noises—the thoughts and feelings that interfere with meaning.

Semantic noises are unintended meanings aroused by certain symbols that inhibit the accuracy of decoding. If a friend describes a forty-year-old secretary as "the girl in the office," and you think "girl" is an odd and condescending term for a forty-year-old woman, you might not even hear the rest of what your friend has to say. Use of ethnic slurs, profanity, and vulgar speech can have the same effect.

Semantic noises—unintended meanings aroused by a speaker's symbols.

Feedback Messages

Feedback is the response to messages that indicates to the sender whether and how that message was heard, seen, and understood. If the verbal or nonverbal response indicates to the sender that the intended meaning was not shared, the originator may try to find a different way of encoding the message in order to align the meaning that was understood with the initiator's original personal meaning. This reencoded message is also feedback because it is a response to the original receiver's response.

Feedback—responses to messages.

OBSERVE & ANALYZE

Journal Activity

The Communication Process

Describe two recent communication episodes that you participated in. One should be an episode that you thought went really well. The other should be one that you thought went poorly. Compare and contrast the episodes. Describe the context factors in the episode, the participant similarities and differences, the messages that were used to create the meaning, the channels used, any noise that interfered with the messages and meaning, and the feedback that was shared. ■

The Process in Action

So far we have explained each of the elements in the interpersonal communication process. Now we will describe how the process works. A person becomes a sender when there is a thought or a feeling that he or she wants to share. To turn the meaning into a message, the sender draws on the vocabulary, grammar, and communication rules of the appropriate language and culture and encodes the thoughts and feelings into a verbal message and behavior. The message is transmitted by way of the channels of sound (speech) and light (nonverbal behavior).

The message is interpreted and assigned meaning by the receiver through the decoding process. Upon decoding the message, the original receiver encodes verbal and nonverbal reactions to the original message. This feedback message is transmitted back to the sender through the selected channels. The sender who receives the feedback decodes it in order to interpret the response he or she is getting from the receiver. The process repeats.

This communication takes place in a context that includes the physical, social, historical, psychological, and cultural environments. The context influences how the message is formed and how it is understood. During the entire transaction, external, internal, and semantic noise may be occurring at various points. This noise affects the ability of the sender and receiver to share meanings.

Let's walk through an example of this process. At the breakfast table (physical context), Joel winks, smiles, and says to his wife (social context), Deborah, "Hey, Babe (potential semantic noise), what do you say we go out to dinner tonight?"

TEST YOURSELF

Identifying Communication Elements

For the following episode identify the contextual factors, participant differences, channels, messages, noise, and feedback.

Jessica and her daughter Rita are shopping. As they walk through an elegant boutique, Rita, who is feeling particularly happy, sees a blouse she wants. With a look of great anticipation and excitement Rita says, "Look at this, Mom—it's beautiful. Can I try it on?" Jessica, who is worried about the cost, frowns, shrugs her shoulders, and says hesitantly, "Well—yes—I guess so." Rita, noticing her mother's hesitation, continues, "And it's marked down to twenty-seven dollars!" Jessica relaxes, smiles, and says, "Yes, it is attractive—try it on. If it fits let's buy it."

(message) Deborah frowns and says, "I don't know that going out for a pizza does much for me" (feedback message based on historical context). Joel sees that Deborah has not understood his meaning and seeks to remedy this. Putting a lilt in his voice he says, "I meant let's go to the Chateau!" Deborah's eyes widen and she bursts out, "The Chateau—are you kidding? Deal." Because the participants are now satisfied with the meaning that has been shared, they may end their interaction or change topics.

Interpersonal Communication Principles

Now that we have described the interpersonal communication process, we will explain the six basic principles (or essential qualities) that describe interpersonal communication: (1) Interpersonal communication is purposeful. (2) Interpersonal communication is continuous. (3) Interpersonal communication messages vary in conscious encoding. (4) Interpersonal communication is relational. (5) Interpersonal communication is learned.

Communication Has Purpose

When people communicate with one another, they have a purpose for doing so. Or, as Kathy Kellermann (1992), a leading researcher on interpersonal contexts, puts it—all communication is goal-directed whether or not the purpose is conscious (p. 288). The purpose of a given transaction may be serious or trivial, but one way to evaluate the success of the communication is to ask whether it achieved its purpose. When Beth calls Leah to ask whether she'd like to join her for lunch to discuss a project they are working on, her purpose may be to resolve a misunderstanding, to encourage Leah to work more closely with her, or simply to establish a cordial atmosphere. When Kareem shares statistics he has found with other members of student government to show the extent of drug abuse on campuses, his purpose may be to contribute information to a group discussion or to plead a case for confronting the problem of drug abuse. Depending on the speaker's purpose, even an apparently successful transaction may fail to achieve its goal. And, of course, different purposes call for different communication strategies.

People may not always be aware of their purpose. For instance, when Jamal passes Tony on the street and says lightly, "Tony, what's happening?" Jamal probably doesn't consciously think, "Tony's an acquaintance and I want him to understand that I see him and consider him worth recognizing." In this case the social obligation to recognize Tony is met spontaneously with the first acceptable expression that comes to Jamal's mind. Regardless of whether Jamal consciously thinks about the purpose, it still motivates his behavior. In this case Jamal will have achieved his goal if Tony responds with an equally casual greeting.

Interpersonal Communication Is Continuous

Because interpersonal communication can be nonverbal as well as verbal, we are always sending "messages" from which others may draw inferences or meaning. Whenever two people are in each other's presence and awareness, communication is occurring. Even if you are silent, another person may infer meaning from your silence. Why? Because your silence is a message that represents a reaction to your environment and to the people around you. If you are cold, you may shiver; if you are hot or nervous, you may perspire; if you are bored, happy, or confused, your face may show it. Whether you like or dislike what you are hearing, your body will reflect it. As skilled communicators, we need to be aware of the messages, whether explicit or implicit, we are constantly sending to others.

Interpersonal Communication Messages Vary in Conscious Encoding

As we discussed earlier in the chapter, sharing meaning with another person involves encoding personal meaning into verbal messages and nonverbal symbols. This encoding process may occur spontaneously, may be based on a "script" that you have learned or rehearsed, or may be "constructed" based on your understanding of the situation in which you find yourself (Reardon, 1987, p. 11).

For each of us there are times when our interpersonal communication reflects a **spontaneous expression** of emotion. When this happens, our messages are encoded without conscious thought. For example, when you burn your finger, you may blurt out "Ouch." When something goes right, you may break out in a broad smile.

At other times, however, our communication is **scripted;** that is, we use conversational phrases that we have learned from past encounters and judge to be appropriate to the present situation. To use scripted reactions effectively, we learn or practice them until they become automatic. Many of these scripts are learned in childhood. As a result, they reflect the cultural background of our family. For example, when you want the sugar bowl but cannot reach it, you may say "Please pass the sugar," followed by "Thank you" when someone complies. This conversational sequence comes from a "table manners script" which you may have had drilled into you at home. Scripts enable us to use messages that are appropriate to the situation and are likely to increase the effectiveness of our communication. One goal of this text is to acquaint you with general scripts (or skills) that can be adapted for use in your communication encounters across a variety of relationships, situations, and cultures.

Finally, messages may be carefully constructed to meet a particular situation. **Constructed messages** are those that we can consciously encode to respond to an immediate situation for which our known scripts are inadequate. These messages help us communication both effectively and appropriately.

Interpersonal Communication Is Relational

In many interpersonal communication settings people not only share content meaning, but also negotiate their relationship. For instance, when Laura says to

Spontaneous expression— messages that are encoded without much conscious thought.

Scripts— conversational phrases we have learned from our past encounters.

Constructed messages— those we encode at the moment to respond to a situation for which our known scripts are inadequate.

Jenny "I've remembered to bring the map," she is not only reporting information, but through the way she says it she may also be communicating "You can always depend on me" or "I am superior to you—if it weren't for me we'd be missing an important document for our trip."

Two aspects of relationships can be negotiated during an interaction. One aspect is the affect (love to hate) present in the relationships. For instance, when Jose says "Hal, good to see you," the nonverbal behavior that accompanies the words may show Hal whether Jose is genuinely happy to see him (positive affect) or not. For instance, if Jose smiles, has a sincere sound to his voice, looks Hal in the eye, and perhaps pats him on the back or shakes hands firmly, then Hal will recognize the signs of affection. If, however, Jose speaks quickly with no vocal inflection and a deadpan facial expression, Hal will perceive the comment as solely meeting some social expectation.

Another aspect of the relational nature of interpersonal communication seeks to define who is in control (Watzlawick, Beavin, & Jackson, 1967, p. 51). Thus, when Tom says to Sue, "I know you're concerned about the budget, but I'll see to it that we have money to cover everything," he can, through his words and the sound of his voice, be saying that he is "in charge" of finances, that he is in control. It is how Sue responds to Tom, however, that determines the true nature of the relationship. The control aspect of the relationship can be viewed as complementary or symmetrical.

In a **complementary relationship** one person lets the other define who is to have greater power. Thus, the communication messages of one person may assert dominance while the communication messages of the other person accept the

Complementary relationships—relationships in which one person lets the other define who is to have greater power.

What messages about affect and control do wedding couples send as they feed each other cake?

assertion. In some cases the relationship is clarified in part by the nature of the context. For instance, in traditional American business most boss–employee relationships are complementary, with the boss in the control position.

In a **symmetrical relationship** people do not agree about who is in control. When one person asserts control, the other challenges that assertion. Or, as one person abdicates dominance, the other refuses to assume it. For example, Tom may say "I think we need to cut back on credit card expenses for a couple of months," to which Sue may respond "No way! I need a new suit for work, the car needs new tires, and you promised we could replace the couch." Here, both people are asserting control.

Control is not negotiated in a single exchange. Relational control is determined through many message exchanges over time. When relationships are complementary, conflict is less likely to be openly expressed than in symmetrical relationships. But in symmetrical relationships power is more likely to be evenly shared than in complementary relationships, where one person is more likely to dominate the other.

Symmetrical relationships— relationships in which people do not agree about who is in control.

Interpersonal Communication Is Learned

Your interpersonal effectiveness is a direct result of the language skills and conversational scripts you have learned. If your family spoke German, you learned to communicate in German. If your family believed it rude to look a person directly in the eyes while speaking, you learned to lower your eyes when talking. If your family yelled and screamed, then quickly made up, you learned to do this as well. When you went to school, if your teacher insisted you refer to older people by their title and surname, you learned to call adults Mr. and Ms. As you grew, you developed peer group friends who may have taught you a whole new vocabulary and encouraged you to adopt language patterns that were very different from those you had learned at home. Up until now your learning about interpersonal communication has probably been informal and limited. Through your formal study and practice in this course you can assess your interpersonal skills and begin to improve those you see as weak.

The Ethics of Interpersonal Communication

In any encounter we choose whether or not we will communicate ethically. **Ethics** is a set of moral principles that may be held by a society, a group, or an individual. Although in this book we are focusing on the word *ethics*, as Terkel and Duval (1999) point out in their *Encyclopedia of Ethics*, the words *ethics* and *morals* are often used interchangeably. They go on to say that even though some philosophers show shades of difference in the words by holding that ethics refers to "cultivation of character and practical decision making" and morals refers to "the set of practices that society holds to be right or just," a considerable overlap is clearly recognized (Terkel & Duval, 1999, p. 80).

Ethics—a set of moral principles that may be held by a society, a group, or an individual.

In this text then, we are particularly interested in ethical issues, which, according to Richard Johannesen, a noted communication scholar in the field, "denotes general and systematic study of what ought to be the grounds and principles for right and wrong human behavior" (p. 2). Although what is considered ethical is to some extent a personal matter, we still expect society to uphold certain standards that can help us with our personal value judgments. A concern of many is an apparent erosion in moral and ethical standards (Edmunds, 1998, pp. 14–15). Families, schools, and religion all share the responsibility of helping individuals develop ethical standards that can be applied to specific situations. As Carl Wellman (1988), a noted philosopher, has pointed out, a person cannot choose and act rationally without some explicit or implicit ethical system (p. 305). Although an ethical theory does not tell us what to do in any given situation, it does tell us what to consider in making our decisions. It directs our attention to the reasons that determine the rightness or wrongness of any act.

Although ethical theory tells us what is acceptable or unacceptable in general, each of us develops a personal ethic—one that guides our specific behavior. Your personal ethic is based on your belief and acceptance of what the communities or groups with which you most closely identify consider moral and ethical. When you behave ethically, you voluntarily act in a manner that complies with expected behavior. Why do people internalize morals and develop a personal ethic? Because most of us regard ourselves as accountable for our conduct, and even to some extent for our attitudes and character, and blame ourselves when we fall short of these ideal principles (Pritchard, 1991, p. 39).

When we communicate, we make choices with ethical implications. So we should understand the general ethical principles that form a basis for ethical interpersonal communication.

1. Ethical communicators are truthful and honest. Truthfulness and **honesty** are standards that compel us to refrain from lying, cheating, stealing, or deception. "An honest person is widely regarded as a moral person, and honesty is a central concept to ethics as the foundation for a moral life" (Terkel & Duval, 1999, p. 122).

Truthfulness and **honesty**— refraining from lying, cheating, stealing, or deception.

Although most people accept truthfulness and honesty as a standard, they still confess to lying on occasion. But even when we face what appears to be a **moral dilemma,** a choice involving an unsatisfactory alternative, we should look for a response that doesn't require us to lie.

Moral dilemma—a choice involving unsatisfactory alternatives.

An operating moral rule is to tell the truth if you possibly can. The fundamental requirement of this rule is that we should not intentionally deceive, or try to deceive, others or even ourselves. Only when we are confronted with a true moral dilemma involving making a choice that most people would deem justified by the circumstances (such as lying to avoid warning an enemy about a planned attack in order to save lives) or selecting the lesser of two evils (lying to protect confidentiality) should we even consider lying. Usually we can avoid direct lies by simply refusing to discuss the issue.

2. Ethical communicators act with integrity. Integrity means maintaining a consistency of belief and action (keeping promises). Terkel and Duval (1999) say, "A person

Integrity—having a consistency of belief and action (keeping promises).

who has integrity is someone who has strong moral principles and will successfully resist the temptation to compromise those principles" (p.135). Integrity then is the opposite of hypocrisy. A person who had promised to take a friend to the doctor would live up to this promise even if he or she had an opportunity to go out with another friend.

Fairness—achieving the right balance of interests without regard to one's own feelings and without showing favor to any side in a conflict.

3. Ethical communicators behave fairly. Fairness means achieving the right balance of interests without regard to one's own feelings and without showing favor to any side in a conflict. Fairness implies impartiality or lack of bias. To be fair to someone is to gather all the relevant facts, consider only circumstances relevant to the decision at hand, and not be swayed by prejudice or irrelevancies. For example, if two of her children are fighting, a mom is exercising fairness if she allows both children to explain "their side" before she decides who is at fault.

Respect—showing regard or consideration for a person and for that person's rights.

Responsibility—accountable for one's actions.

4. Ethical communicators demonstrate respect for the ideas, opinion, and feelings of others. Respect means showing regard or consideration for a person and for that person's rights. Often we talk of respecting another as a fellow human being. For instance someone's affluence, job status, or ethnic background should not influence how we communicate with the person. We demonstrate respect through listening and understanding others' points of view, even when they are vastly different from our own.

5. Ethical communicators are responsible. Responsibility means being accountable for one's actions. A responsibility is something that one is bound to do either through promise or obligation or because of one's role in a group or community. A responsibility may indicate a duty to the moral law or a duty to another human being. Some would argue that we have a responsibility not to harm or interfere with others. Others would argue that not only do we have a responsibility to not harm others, but that we also have a responsibility to help others.

At various places in this text we will confront situations where these issues come into play. We face ethical dilemmas where we must sort out what is more or less right or wrong. In making these choices, we usually reveal what values we hold most dear. So in this book, at the end of each chapter, you will be asked to think about and discuss various ethical dilemmas that relate to the chapter content.

INTER-ACT WITH

Technology

Interested in better understanding ethical dilemmas? You may be interested in a Web site sponsored by the Markkula Center for Applied Ethics at Santa Clara University. This site, called Ethics Connection, is open to anyone, but it was designed with students in mind. It focuses on such issues as how to recognize ethical dilemmas and how to think through to resolutions. Issues covered range from those in health care, social policy, business and technology, human rights, and everyday decision making. The Ethics Connection: http://www.scu.edu/ethics/ ■

Interpersonal Communication and Diversity

Diversity—variations between and among people.

Diversity, variations between and among people, affects nearly every aspect of the communication process we have just discussed. We'd like to think that just because we all speak the English language, then using the right words guarantees that

How does diversity affect aspects of the communication process?

everyone will understand what we say. But whether we understand each other depends as much on who we are as it does on the words we use. We in the United States are part of a multicultural nation—in fact, we may be the most diverse nation on earth. Although many people try to emphasize racial, gender, and cultural disharmony, there is no other nation in the world with such large populations of diverse people who make their way into all walks of life.

Throughout the history of the United States, we've experienced huge migrations of people from different parts of the world. According to the *New York Times Almanac* (2002), the latest figures for the 2000 census show that, today, the largest number of new immigrants are from Latin America and Asia. At the end of the twentieth century people of Latin and Asian descent constituted 12.5 percent and 3.6 percent, respectively of the total U.S. population. Combined with the approximately 13 percent of our population that is of African descent, these three groups accounted for nearly 30 percent of the total population (Wright, 271). Within the next twenty years this figure is predicted to rise to more than 40 percent.

Of course in your own corner of the world the ratios may be tremendously different. Various regions in the United States have far different percentages of populations of African, European, Latin American, and Asian descent. For instance, in 1996 in Los Angeles, a city of approximately 3.5 million people, more than one million (29 percent) were Hispanic American; in San Francisco, a city of 750,000 people, more than 250,000 (39 percent) were Asian American; and in several midwestern cities, such as Cincinnati and St. Louis, 40 percent or more of the population were African American (Carpenter, 1996). In contrast, many rural areas and even several states are 90 percent or more European American (Horner, 1998).

Culture—systems of knowledge shared by a relatively large group of people.

Certainly the most widely discussed aspect of diversity is cultural. You'll recall from our discussion of the cultural context of communication that **culture** may be defined as systems of knowledge shared by a relatively large group of people. It includes a system of shared beliefs, values, symbols, and behaviors. Peter Andersen, a well-respected intercultural communication scholar, goes so far as to say that "culture is a critical concept to communication scholars because every communicator is a product of his or her culture" (Andersen, 2000, p. 260). Thus, as we become more balanced in our diversity, the study of intercultural communication is more important than ever.

We need to take a careful look at ourselves and our communication behavior because, as we interact with others with cultural backgrounds that differ from our own, we are vulnerable to unintentionally communicating in ways that are culturally inappropriate or insensitive and in so doing to undermining our relationships.

Although the most widely discussed aspect of diversity is cultural, we must also be sensitive to how differences among people based on gender, age, physical characteristics, and sexual preference affect communication. Failure to take those differences into account when we interact can also lead us to behave inappropriately.

Within each chapter of this book we will discuss the diverse ways people act in communication situations. In addition, the feature "Diverse Voices" provides opportunities for us to empathize with the communication experiences of a variety of individuals whose voices are being heard. In this chapter we present the voice of Arturo Madrid. Although writing as a Latino, Madrid expresses sentiments that capture the feelings and experiences of a vast number of Americans. We who live in the United States of America hold to the ideal that this is the "land of opportunity" and a place where "all men are created equal," while simultaneously knowing that it is also a land of hypocrisy, where people are afforded unequal treatment and opportunity based on their race, sex, religion, class, ability, country of origin, or sexual orientation. Indeed, it is because we as a country hold such high ideals that you, the people who will shape our country's future, must be willing to "step out of your box," your comfort zone, and expose yourselves to viewpoints and realities that are different from your own.

Over the years as authors we have been increasingly aware of how the cultural diversity of our country makes simplistic prescriptions about interpersonal communication a problem and how our own cultural perspectives limit our viewpoints on these issues. We are increasingly sensitive to the cultural blinders of our white, well-educated, upper-middle-class, middle-aged, mid-western, married-with-children, heterosexual, Christian, European American perspective. When we write, no matter how much we read and how sensitive we try to be, our writings will continue to be informed by these perspectives. We hope that when you encounter these, you will consider alternative perspectives critically and offer your thoughts to your classmates.

Social Perception *By Arturo Madrid*

Arturo Madrid is the Norine R. and T. Frank Murchison Distinguished Professor of Humanities at Trinity University. From 1984 to 1993 he served as the founding President of Tomas Rivera Center, the nation's first institute for policy studies on Latino Issues. In 1996 he was awarded the Charles Frankel Prize in Humanities by the National Endowment for the Humanities. In this classic selection, Madrid describes the conflicting experiences of those who see themselves as different from what has stereotypically been described as "American." Experiencing one-self and being perceived as "other" and "invisible" are powerful determinants of one's self-concept and form a very special filter through which one communicates with others.

My name is Arturo Madrid. I am a citizen of the United States, as are my parents and as were my grandparents, and my great-grandparents. My ancestors' presence in what is now the United States antedates Plymouth Rock, even without taking into account any American Indian heritage I might have.

I do not, however, fit those mental sets that define America and Americans. My physical appearance, my speech patterns, my name, my profession (a professor of Spanish) create a text that confuses the reader.

I am very clearly the *other,* if only your everyday, garden-variety, domestic *other.* I've always known that I was the *other,* even before I knew the vocabulary or understood the significance of otherness.

Despite the operating myth of the day, school did not erase my *otherness.* The true test was not our speech, but rather our names and our appearance, for we would always have an accent, however perfect our pro-nunciation, however excellent our enunciation, however divine our diction. That accent would be heard in our pigmentation, our physiognomy, our names. We were, in short, the *other.*

Being the *other* involves a contradictory phenomenon. On the one hand, being the *other* frequently means being invisible. On the other hand, being the *other* sometimes involves stick-ing out like a sore thumb. What is she/he doing here?

If one is the *other,* one will inevitably be seen stereotypi-cally; will be defined and limited by mental sets that may not bear much relation to existing reali-ties.

There is sometimes a darker side to otherness as well. The *other* disturbs, disquiets, discom-forts. It provokes distrust and suspicion. The *other* frightens, scares.

For some of us being the *other* is only annoying; for others it is debilitating; for still others it is damning. For the majority oth-erness is permanently sealed by physical appearance. For the rest otherness is betrayed by ways of being, speaking, or of doing.

The first half of my life I spent downplaying the significance and consequences of otherness. The second half has seen me wrestling to understand its com-plex and deeply ingrained reali-ties; striving to fathom why oth-erness denies us a voice or visibility or validity in American society and its institutions; strug-gling to make otherness familiar, reasonable, even normal to my fellow Americans.

One of the principal strengths of our society is its ability to address on a continuing and substantive basis the real eco-nomic, political, and social prob-lems that have faced and con-tinue to face us. What makes the United States so attractive to immigrants are the protections and opportunities it offers; what keeps our society together is tol-erance for cultural, religious, social, political, and even linguis-tic difference; what makes us a unique, dynamic, and extraordi-nary nation are the power and creativity of our diversity.

The true history of the U.S. is the one of struggle against intol-erance, against oppression, against xenophobia, against those forces that have prohibited persons from participating in the larger life of the society on the basis of their race, their gender, their religion, their national origin, their linguistic and cultural background. These phenomena are not only consigned to the past. They remain with us and frequently take on virulent dimensions.

If you believe, as I do, that the well-being of a society is directly related to the degree and extent to which all of its citizens participate in its institutions, then you will have to agree that we have a challenge before us. In view of the extraordinary changes that are taking place in our society we need to take up the struggle again, unpleasant as it is. As educated and educator members of this society we have a special

responsibility for assuring that all American institutions, not just our elementary and secondary schools, our juvenile halls, or jails, reflect the diversity of our society. Not to do so is to risk greater alienation on the part of a growing segment of our society; is to risk increased social tension in an already conflictive world; and, ultimately, is to risk the survival of a range of institutions that, for all their defects and deficiencies, provide us the opportunity and the freedom to improve our individual and collective lot.

Let me urge you, as you return to your professional responsibilities and to your personal spaces, to reflect on these two words—*quality* and *diversity*—and on the mental sets and behaviors that

flow out of them. And let me urge you further to struggle against the notion that quality is finite in quantity, limited in its manifestations, or is restricted by considerations of class, gender, race, or national origin; or that quality manifests itself only in leaders and not in followers, in managers and not in workers; or that it has to be associated with verbal agility or elegance of personal style; or that it cannot be seeded, or nurtured, or developed. ■

Excerpted from Madrid, A. (1994). Diversity and its discontents. In *Intercultural Communication: A Reader* (7th ed., pp. 127–131). L. A. Samovar & R. E. Porter (Eds.), Belmont, Calif.: Wadsworth. Reprinted by permission of Black Issues in Higher Education.

Increasing Interpersonal Communication Competence

Communication competence—the impression that communicative behavior is both appropriate and effective in a given relationship.

Communication competence is the impression that communicative behavior is both appropriate and effective in a given relationship (Spitzberg, 2000, p. 375). Communication is *effective* when it achieves its goals; it is *appropriate* when it conforms to what is expected in a relationship. Specifically, when communication is appropriate, each person believes that the other person has abided by the social rules of behavior that apply to the type of relationship they have and the conversational situation they are in.

The definition of competent communication acknowledges that competence is an impression or judgment that one person makes about another. We create the perception that we are competent communicators by the verbal messages we send and the nonverbal behaviors that accompany them.

Since communication is at the heart of how we relate to one another, one of your goals in this course will be to learn those things that will increase the likelihood that others will view you as competent. In the Spotlight on Scholars on pages 23 and 24, we feature Brian Spitzberg on Interpersonal Communication

Competence. Spitzberg believes that perceptions of competence depend in part on personal motivation, knowledge, and skills (see also Spitzberg, 2000, p. 377).

First, as communicator motivation increases, communicator competence increases. That is, perceived competence depends in part on how much a person wants to make a good impression and communicate effectively. People are likely to be more motivated if they are confident and if they see potential rewards. Suppose Annette would like to talk with her boss about increasing her responsibilities. If she has confidence in her ability to persuade her boss and/or if she thinks it's likely that the conversation will result in more challenging job responsibilities, then her motivation to behave in ways that could be seen as competent will be high.

Second, as communicator knowledge increases, communicator competence increases. In addition to being motivated, people also need knowledge about communication to be effective. The more people understand how to behave in a given situation, the more likely they are to be perceived as competent. We gain knowledge about how to interact by observing what others do, by asking others how we should behave, by engaging in formal study, and by learning through trial and error. For instance, Annette may be highly motivated to be competent in talking with her boss about increasing her responsibilities, but she must also know about the various ways of couching her request that her boss would find acceptable and persuasive. As our knowledge and understanding of how and when to ask questions, disclose information, or describe feelings increases, the likelihood that others will see us as competent is likely to increase as well.

Third, as communicator skill increases, communicator competence increases. People who are motivated to be effective and who have knowledge about communication must still act in ways that are consistent with their communication knowledge. **Skills** are goal-oriented actions or action sequences that we can master and repeat in appropriate situations. The more skills you have, the more likely you are to be able to structure your messages to be effective and appropriate. For instance, Annette must not only know how to express her concerns, she must also be able to do so during the actual conversation. The more practice she has had in using specific skills, the more likely it is that she will be able to draw on these skills in real situations.

The combination of our motivation, knowledge, and skills leads us to perform confidently in our encounters with others. The rest of this book is aimed at helping you increase the likelihood that you will be perceived as competent. In the pages that follow you will learn about theories of interpersonal communication that can increase your knowledge and your motivation. You will also find how to perform specific skills, and you will be provided with opportunities to practice them. Through this practice you can increase the likelihood that you can actually perform these skills during conversations.

Skills—goal-oriented actions or action sequences we can master and repeat in appropriate situations.

Understanding the Concepts and Developing Skills that Lead to Competence

Throughout this book we will describe skills or master scripts that you can draw upon to help you become more competent as a communicator. These skills are based on interpersonal communication theories and research. Understanding this knowledge base is critical if you are to become more competent in interpersonal settings. So we will be introducing you to important concepts and theories that will lay a foundation for skill development. By understanding the concepts and theories, you will be better prepared to know when, where, and how to apply specific skills to the communication situations you encounter. Further, by understanding why certain behaviors and skills are effective, you will be better equipped to improvise and creatively use the skill concepts or "scripts" in unfamiliar and ambiguous situations. We will also point out some of the more recent research findings that relate to the theories, concepts, and skills that we discuss. Communication scholars are continually studying interpersonal behavior, and we continue to learn more about how people interact and what specific behaviors, messages, and strategies help to develop and maintain relationships.

Although each skill can be used in a variety of settings and all skills contribute to perceptions of competence, we have grouped the skills into diagnostic categories so that you may review the skills more easily when you are searching for help with improving a particular aspect of your communication repertoire. These five categories are as follows:

1. **Message-formation skills** increase the accuracy and clarity of the messages you send.

2. **Conversational-climate skills** increase the likelihood that you and your partner will develop a supportive relationship in which you trust each other.

3. **Listening-for-understanding skills** increase the likelihood that you are able to understand the meaning of another person.

4. **Empathic-response skills** increase the likelihood that you are able to understand and respond to the emotional experiences of another person.

5. **Disclosure skills** increase the likelihood that you will share your ideas and feelings in an honest and sensitive manner.

Some of the specific skills in each of these categories you already know and use, although you may not be aware of why you use them or why they work. Other skills may not currently be part of your repertoire. You will enhance your competence as you work hard and learn these new interpersonal skills during this course.

Some of the skills presented in this book are universal. Others are grounded in the dominant cultural system of the United States and they may seem odd to you if you are from a different cultural background. Throughout the text you will notice that we try to point out how cultural differences may affect skill usage. We invite you to be active in this process and to think about and discuss in class any observations, insights, and concerns that you have about the appropriateness and effectiveness of these skills for communicating in other cultures with which you are familiar.

Learning to use new skills is difficult. You must not only understand the skills but also become comfortable using them in real-life situations. It's one thing to enjoy rap music, but quite another to be able to perform it. Because some of the communication skills may not be in your repertoire now, as you work on them you

Brian Spitzberg, Professor of Communication at San Diego State University, on

Interpersonal Communication Competence

Although Brian Spitzberg has made many contributions to our understanding of interpersonal communication, he is best known for his work in interpersonal communication competence. This interest in competence began at the University of Southern California. For an interpersonal communication seminar assignment he read the research that had been done on interpersonal competence and found that the research conclusions went in different directions. Spitzberg believed the time was ripe for someone to synthesize these perspectives into a comprehensive theory of competence. His final paper for the seminar was his first effort into trying to construct a competence theory.

Today, the model of interpersonal communication competence that Spitzberg has formulated guides most of our thinking and research in this area. He views competence neither as a trait nor a set of behaviors. Rather Spitzberg says that interpersonal communication competence is a perception that people have about themselves or another person. Since competence is a perception, then it follows that your perception of

your interpersonal communication competence or that of your relationship partner would affect to how you feel about that relationship. So people are more likely to be satisfied in a relationship when they perceive themselves and the other person as competent. According to Spitzberg, we make these competence judgments based on how each of us acts when we talk together. But what determines how we act in a particular conversation?

As Spitzberg was trying to organize his thinking about competence, he was taking another course in which he became acquainted with theories of dramatic acting. These theories held that an actor's performance depended on the actor's motivation, knowledge of the script, and acting skills. Spitzberg found that these same variables could be applied to communication competence and he incorporated them into his theory. How we behave in a conversation depends first, on how personally motivated we are to have the conversation; second, on how personally knowledgeable we are about what behavior is appropriate in situations like this; and third, on how person-

ally skilled we are at actually using the appropriate behaviors during the conversation. In addition, Spitzberg's theory suggests that context variables such as the ones discussed in this chapter also affect how we choose to act in a conversation and the perceptions of competence that they create.

While Spitzberg formed most of these ideas while he was still in graduate school, he and others have spent the last eighteen years refining the theory, conducting programs of research based on his theory, and measuring the effectiveness of the theory. The research has fleshed out parts of the theory and provided some evidence of the theory's accuracy. Over the years Spitzberg has developed about a dozen specific instruments to measure parts of the theory. One of these measures, the Conversational Skills Rating Scale, has been adopted as the standard measure of interpersonal communication skills by the National Communication Association (a leading national organization of communication scholars, teachers, and practitioners). His most recent work involves translating the model and measures of competence into the computer-mediated context. To what extent are the skills we use in face-to-face communication similar to those we use in computer-based interaction? Several research projects are currently investigating this question.

Spitzberg's continuing interest in communication competency has led him to study abusive or dysfunctional relationships from a competence perspective. Recently he has studied obsessive relational intrusion (ORI) and stalking. In ORI and stalking situations, the intruder's motivation is at odds with the motivation of the victim. Specifically the

intruder is wishing to begin, escalate, or to continue a relationship with the victim, who does not agree with the relationship definition that the intruder is operating under. Their interactions, then, are really "arguments" over the very definition of the relationship. The intruders may perceive themselves to be "competent" within what they consider the relationship to be, while victims may respond in ways they believe to be "competent" within their definition. Spitzberg's research with his colleagues has begun to identify the profile of ORI, which may signal the development of stalk-

ing. Such a profile could assist relationship partners to see the stalking coming and remove themselves from the relationship before it becomes dangerous. Recently, Spitzberg has expanded his ORI work to examine the new phenomenon of "cyber-stalking."

Whether the situation is a first date or a job interview, a conflict with a roommate or an intimate discussion of your feelings, Spitzberg believes it is important that others perceive you to be competent. For a list of a few of Spitzberg's publications on competence, see the references list at the end of this book. ■

are likely to feel awkward and to see the skills as creating unrealistic or "phony" sounding messages. Just as rap artists practice the verbal sequences of their songs in order to perform with rhythmic precision, so too communication skills or scripts must be practiced if you are to use them skillfully. As you learn them and become comfortable with their patterns, like the rap artists you can move to "interpreting" these basic patterns in ways that fit with your personality and your manner of expression. We hope that you will find that the material in this book is presented in a way that helps you practice and claim the skills as your own.

Writing Communication Improvement Goal Statements

You are unlikely to master all of these skills during a single course. Becoming competent in our communication is a lifelong journey. This course will be one opportunity to focus your energy on learning about communication and working to improve your skillfulness. If you want to get the most from this course, we suggest that you set personal goals to improve specific skills in your own interpersonal communication repertoire. One way we recommend you do this is to commit to specific goals by writing formal communication improvement plans.

Why written improvement plans? A familiar saying goes, "The road to hell is paved with good intentions." Regardless of how serious you are about changing some aspect of your communication, bringing about changes in behavior takes time and effort. Writing specific plans makes it more likely that your good intentions to improve don't get lost in the busyness of your life.

Psychologists who study motivation have found that when people set specific, challenging goals they achieve at a higher level than when they simply commit to "do their best" (Locke, Latham, & Enez, 1988). Research also shows that by writing down a description of the change you wish to make, formulating a plan for completing it, and having another person witness your pledge, you are more likely to honor the commitment you have made than you would be if you simply made a mental resolution.

Before you can set goals or write communication improvement goal statements, you must first analyze your current communication skills repertoire and determine where you can make improvement. We recommend that after you have studied and practiced using the skills in each chapter of the book, you choose the one or two that you think would help you the most. Once you have identified these, you should write a communication improvement goal statement.

1. **State the problem.** Start by stating a communication problem that you have. For example: "Problem: Even though my boss consistently gives all the interesting tasks to co-workers, I haven't spoken up because I'm not very good at describing my feelings."

2. **State the specific goal.** A goal is *specific* if it is measurable and you know when you have achieved it. For example, to deal with the problem stated above, you might write, "Goal: To describe my feelings about task assignments to my boss."

3. **Outline a specific procedure for reaching the goal.** To develop a plan for reaching your goal, first consult the chapter that covers the skill you wish to hone. Then translate the general steps recommended in the chapter to your specific situation. This step is critical because successful behavioral change requires that you state your objective in terms of specific behaviors you can adopt or modify. For example: "Procedure: I will practice the steps of describing feelings. (1) I will identify the specific feeling I am experiencing. (2) I will encode the emotion I am feeling accurately. (3) I will include what has triggered the feeling. (4) I will own the feeling as mine. (5) I will then put that procedure into operation when I am talking with my boss."

4. **Devise a method of determining when the goal has been reached.** A good goal is measurable, and the fourth part of your goal-setting effort is to determine your minimum requirements for knowing when you have achieved a given goal. For example: "Test of Achieving Goal: This goal will be considered achieved when I have described my feelings to my boss on the next occasion when he bypasses me for an interesting assignment."

At the end of each chapter you will be challenged to develop a goal statement related to the material presented. Figure 1.2 provides another example of a communication improvement plan, this one relating to a public-speaking problem.

Once you have written a communication improvement goal statement, you may want to present it to another person who will witness your commitment and

Figure 1.2 Communication Improvement Plan

GOAL STATEMENT

Problem: I have developed the bad habit of ending sentences with "you know." This has become noticeable and results in others perceiving me as less self-assured. I tend to use this language when the person with whom I am speaking is not providing enough nonverbal feedback. I need to become aware of when I am using this phrase and consciously choose to avoid saying it.

Goal: To improve my message formation skills by avoiding the overuse of "you know" by specifically requesting feedback.

Procedure: I will monitor my messages for excessive use of "you know." When I detect a problem I will use the skill of questioning to get direct feedback from the receiver.

Test of Achieving Goal: This goal will be considered achieved when I am aware of excessive "you knows" and able to reduce my usage by directly requesting feedback.

serve as a consultant, coach, and support person. This gives you someone to talk with about your progress. You might choose to form a partnership with a classmate from this course, with each of you serving as witness and consultant for the other. When one of your goals relates to a particular relationship you have with another person, you should also consider telling that person about your goal. If that person knows what you are trying to do, he or she may be willing to help. If you have a consultant, you might meet with this person periodically to assess your progress, troubleshoot problems, and develop additional procedures for reaching your goal.

Summary

We have defined interpersonal communication as the process through which people create and manage their relationships, exercising mutual responsibility in creating meaning.

Interpersonal communication is important because it helps us meet our social/psychological needs, maintain our sense of self, fulfill social obligations, acquire information, and influence others.

In the communication process participants create meaning by encoding and decoding messages which are conveyed through sensory channels that become distorted by noise. The meaning and messages are influenced by the contexts in which the conversation occurs.

Six principles underlie our interpersonal communication. (1) Interpersonal communication is purposeful. (2) Interpersonal communication is continuous. (3) Interpersonal communication messages vary in degree of conscious encoding. Messages may be spontaneous, scripted, or contrived. (4) Interpersonal communication is relational, defining the power and affection between people. Relational definitions can be complementary or symmetrical. (5) Interpersonal communication is learned.

Ethics is a set of moral principles that may be held by a society, a group, or an individual. When we communicate, we make choices with ethical implications involving truthfulness and honesty, integrity, fairness, respect, and responsibility. These and other issues are dramatized in Ethical Interaction boxes at the end of each chapter.

Diversity, variations between and among people, affects nearly every aspect of the communication process we have just discussed. Certainly the most widely discussed aspect of diversity is culture, but diversity also encompasses differences among people based on gender, age, physical characteristics, and sexual preference. The Diverse Voices feature in various chapters provides a different sort of learning about diversity and interpersonal communication processes.

A primary goal of this course is to become a more competent interpersonal communicator. Competence is the impression that our communication behavior is both appropriate and effective in a given relationship. It involves increasing motivation, knowledge, and skills. The five categories are message-formation, conversational-climate, listening-for-understanding, empathic-response, and disclosure skills.

These skills can be learned, developed, and improved. You can enhance your learning this term by writing goal statements to systematically improve your skills repertoire.

Chapter Resources

Key Words

Interpersonal communication, *p. 3*
Participants, *p. 6*
Context, *p. 7*
Physical context, *p. 7*
Social context, *p. 7*
Historical context, *p. 7*
Psychological context, *p. 7*
Cultural context, *p. 7*
Messages, *p. 8*
Meaning, *p. 8*
Symbols, *p. 8*
Encoding, *p. 8*
Decoding, *p. 8*
Channels, *p. 9*
Noise, *p. 9*
External noise, *p. 9*
Internal noise, *p. 9*
Semantic noise, *p. 9*

Feedback, *p. 9*
Spontaneous expression, *p. 12*
Scripts, *p. 12*
Constructed messages, *p. 12*
Complementary relationships, *p. 13*
Symmetrical relationships, *p. 14*
Ethics, *p. 14*
Truthfulness and honesty, *p. 15*
Moral dilemma, *p. 15*
Integrity, *p. 15*
Fairness, *p. 16*
Respect, *p. 16*
Responsibility, *p. 16*
Diversity, *p. 16*
Culture, *p. 18*
Communication competence, *p. 20*
Skills, *p. 21*

Inter-Act with Media

CINEMA

Mark Stevenson Johnson (Director). (1998). *Simon Birch* Ian Michael Smith, Joseph Mazzello, Ashley Judd, Oliver Platt, David Straithairn, Dana Ivey, Beatrice Winde, Jan Hooks, Jim Carrey.

Brief Summary: The movie is based on the John Irving bestseller, *A Prayer for Owen Meany.* While the movie reduces the book down to some of the most basic plot elements, it does an excellent job of displaying the various relationships in the story. The story is about a very small young boy, Simon, and his best friend, Joe. Simon believes that he was created so small in order to fulfill a special purpose in life. He believes that he will be ultimately redeemed by completing a special task..

IPC Concepts: The movie illustrates the importance of such interpersonal concepts as truth and respect. The local minister has to deal with his secret past. Joe must learn how to relate to Simon after his part in a tragic accident. Simon must deal with his own self-talk and guilt after the accident. The two boys relate to each other, in part, through small micro rituals that they have developed.

THEATER

William Shakespeare. *A Midsummer Night's Dream.*

Brief Summary: This is the story of a night when the world of humans overlaps with the world of the Faeries following a wedding feast for Hyppolyta and Theseus. After a series of misunderstandings, several characters wander into the forest, only to walk into the middle of a disagreement between Oberon and Titania, the King and Queen of the Faeries. The resulting comic interactions serve to illustrate a wide range of communication principles, including misunderstandings, perceptions, and failures to listen effectively. The story is also filled with symbols of love and marriage.

IPC Concepts: Relationships, listening, perception, shields, personal bias, point of view.

LITERATURE

John Irving. (1989). *A Prayer for Owen Meany.* New York: Morrow.

Brief Summary: While this book served as the basis for the film *Simon Birch,* the book is far more complex in its treatment of both story and character development. This book is a fascinating treatment of the relationship between Owen Meany (Simon Birch) and his best friend—the narrator in both treatments.

IPC Concepts: Illustrates the importance of such interpersonal concepts as truth and respect. The local minister has to deal with his secret past. Joe must learn how to relate to Simon after his part in a tragic accident. Simon must deal with his own self-talk and guilt after the accident. The two boys relate to each other, in part, through small micro rituals that they have developed.

Harper Lee. (1960). *To Kill a Mockingbird.* New York: HarperCollins.

Brief Summary: This book is a classic of American literature and frequently appears on lists of the best in American novels. It takes us through even more of the culture of the south during the 1930s. We learn and experience more about the people in the town, and about the children and their adventures. The book closes with a masterful statement on empathy when Scout stands on the front porch of the Radley home and realizes how the world has looked in the eyes of Boo (Arthur) Radley.

IPC Concepts: Illustrates virtually every aspect of the communication process in interpersonal relationships. It deals with trust, perception, empathy, conflict, stereotyping, listening, cultural diversity, and the development of the self.

ACADEMIC WORK

Ronald C. Arnett & Pat Arneson. (1999). *Dialogic Civility in a Cynical Age: Community, Hope, and Interpersonal Relationships.* New York: SUNY Press.

Brief Summary: This book is a necessary shot of optimism and substance for believers in dialogue. It offers an optimistic, philosophical, and practical approach to making dialogue a reality in interpersonal relationships. The richness of the book comes from the review of a wide range of dialogical voices that include: Martin Buber, Carl Rogers, Carol Gilligan, Paulo Freire, Victor Frank, Nel Noddings, Sissela Bok, Abraham Maslow, and Robert Bellah.

IPC Concepts: Communication process and dialogue.

Kenneth N. Cissna and Rob Anderson. (1990). The contributions of Carl R. Rogers to a philosophical praxis of dialogue. *Western Journal of Speech Communication, 54*(2), 125–147.

Brief Summary: Cissna argues that Carl Rogers should be appreciated for being far more than a therapist—he should also be regarded as having made a substantial contribution to the nature and practice of dialogue. The article describes the contribution of Rogers as that of practical philosophy, which helps to extend the work of martin Buber in I and Thou. The article delineates the qualities inherent in Rogers's work that are applicable to interpersonal communication. These include: contact, congruence, positive regard, and empathy.

IPC Concepts: Dialogue, qualities for effective, growth-oriented interpersonal communication, and relational development.

WHAT'S ON THE WEB

COMFLE.

http://commfaculty.fullerton.edu/jreinard/internet.htm#INTERPER

Brief Summary: A set of hyperlinks to a wide variety of topics in communication theory. This Web address links to the other topics listed in interpersonal communication.

IPC Concepts: In addition to a wide range of other communication research interests, this Web site contains links on the following interpersonal topics: empathy, temperament, gender, nonverbal, and conflict. There are also good links on language and intercultural communication.

Interpersonal Communication articles Web site.

http://www.pertinent.com/articles/communication/index.asp

Brief Summary: This is an interesting Web site that offers a variety of articles regarding communication. It provides a good overview on the communication process.

IPC Concepts: Self, relationships, culture, conflict, and interpersonal communication at work.

CHAPTER 2

Forming and Using

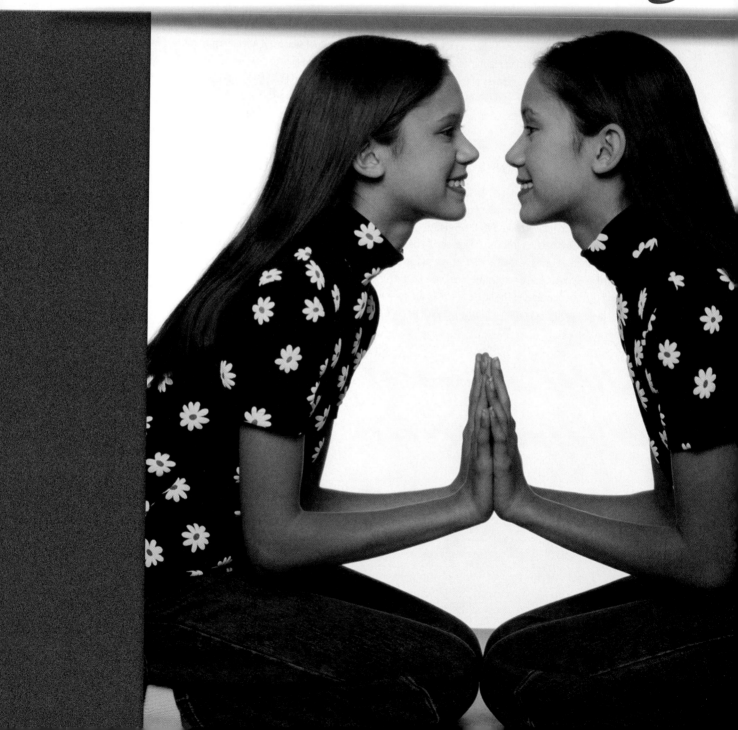

Social Perceptions

After you have read this chapter, you should be able to answer these questions:

- What is perception?
- How does the mind select, organize, and interpret information?
- What is the self-concept, and how is it formed?
- What is self-esteem, and how is it developed?
- How do our self-concept and self-esteem affect our communication with others?
- What affects how accurately we perceive others?
- What methods can we use to improve the accuracy of social perception?

"As Dwayne and Miguel are leaving Spanish Literature class on the first day of the semester, Dwayne comments: "Man, I can't believe it! This course is going to be impossible—I don't know if I can do it."

"Really?" replies Miguel, "I thought the course sounded really interesting. The Prof. seems interesting to listen to and I really liked the idea that we could choose our own term paper topic."

"But Miguel, did you see what we're reading? We've got five books to read—with a test after each book, and then we're supposed to write a term paper!"

"But Dwayne, they're fiction. I mean we start with Don Quixote and then read four other books written over a two-hundred–year period—we'll really get an interesting look at Spanish society and culture. And since the Prof. has obviously visited and studied in Spain, he'll really be able to give us an insider's look."

"Right—as if I need an insider's look. I'm taking four other courses that look pretty heavy. Sure, I wouldn't have signed up for the course if I didn't like Spanish, but five books and a term paper!"

"The way I see it, the term paper is going to be a blast. I'm sure we're going to see some real contrasts in views of life over that time period—writing the paper is going to be fun."

"Fun? Shooting baskets, playing video games, going out on dates—that's fun. Writing a term paper? That's work."

Have you and a friend had this kind of disagreement after a first day of class? Why are their views so different? And how do we come to have different takes on the same event? If we analyze this conversation we can see that Dwayne focuses on the time requirements and workload in the class while Miguel focuses on the class's potential for learning, and his interest in the subject. They attended the same class, but carried away different perceptions. Because much of the meaning we share with others is based on our perceptions, a careful study of interpersonal communications begins with understanding the perceptual process and social perceptions.

In this chapter we describe the basic process of perception. Then we examine how the perceptions we have about ourselves are formed and changed. Next we explain how we perceive others. Finally, we discuss how you can increase the accuracy of both your self-perception and your perceptions of others. As you will see, perception is a foundation piece in both our own communication and our evaluation of the communication of others.

The Perception Process

Perception—the process of selectively attending to information and assigning meaning to it.

Perception is the process of selectively attending to information and assigning meaning to it. At times our perceptions of the world, other people, and ourselves agree with the perceptions of others. At other times our perceptions are significantly different from the perceptions of other people. We base our communication and behavioral responses on what we perceive. So when our perceptions are different from those with whom we interact, sharing meaning becomes more challenging.

Your brain selects the information it receives from your sense organs, organizes the information selected, interprets it, and then evaluates it.

Attention and Selection

Although we are subject to a constant barrage of sensory stimuli, we focus attention on relatively little of it. How we choose depends in part on our needs, interests, and expectations.

Needs We are likely to pay attention to information that meets our biological and psychological needs. When you go to class, how well in tune you are to what is being discussed is likely to depend on whether you believe the information is important to you—that is, does it meet a personal need?

Interests We are likely to pay attention to information that pertains to our interests. For instance, you may not even recognize that music is playing in the background until you find yourself suddenly listening to some "old favorite." Similarly, when we are really interested in a person, we are more likely to pay attention to what that person is saying.

Expectations Finally, we are likely to see what we expect to see and to ignore information that violates our expectations. Take a quick look at the phrases in the triangles in Figure 2.1 (p. 34).

If you have never seen these triangles, you probably read "Paris in the springtime," "Once in a lifetime," and "Bird in the hand." But if you reexamine the words, you will see that what you perceived was not exactly what is written. Do you now see the repeated words? It is easy to miss the repeated word because we don't *expect* to see the word repeated.

Organization of Stimuli

Even though our attention and selection process limits the stimuli our brain must process, the absolute number of discrete stimuli we attend to at any one moment is still substantial. Our brains use certain principles to arrange these stimuli to make sense out of them. Two of the most common principles we use are simplicity and pattern.

Simplicity If the stimuli we attend to are very complex, the brain simplifies the stimuli into some commonly recognized form. Based on a quick perusal of what someone is wearing, how she is standing, and the expression on her face, we may perceive her as "a successful

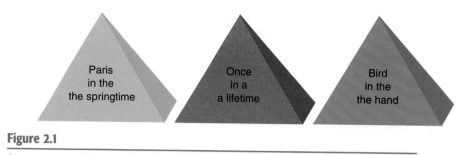

Figure 2.1

A sensory test of expectation

businesswoman," "a flight attendant," or "a soccer mom." Similarly, we simplify the verbal messages we receive. So, for example, Tony might walk out of his hour-long performance review meeting with his boss in which the boss described four of Tony's strengths and three areas for improvement and say to Jerry, his co-worker, "Well, I better shape up or I'm going to get fired!"

Pattern A second principle the brain uses when organizing information is to find **patterns,** sets of characteristics that differentiate some things from others used to group those items having the same characteristics. A pattern makes it easy to interpret stimuli. For example, when you see a crowd of people, instead of perceiving each individual human being, you may focus on the characteristic of sex and "see" men and women, or you may focus on age and "see" children, teens, adults, and seniors.

In our interactions with others we try to find patterns that will enable us to interpret and respond to their behavior. For example, each time Jason and Bill encounter Sara, she hurries over to them and begins an animated conversation. Yet when Jason is alone and runs into Sara, she barely says "Hi." After a while Jason may detect a pattern to Sara's behavior. She is warm and friendly when Bill is around and not so friendly when Bill is absent.

> **Patterns**—sets of characteristics that differentiate some things from others used to group those items having the same characteristics.

Interpretation of Stimuli

As the brain selects and organizes the information it receives from the senses, it also interprets the information by assigning meaning to it. Look at these three sets of numbers. What do you make of them?

A. 631 7348

B. 285 37 5632

C. 4632 7364 2596 2174

In each of these sets, your mind looked for clues to give meaning to the numbers. Because you use similar patterns of numbers every day, you probably interpret A as an in-area telephone number. How about B? A likely interpretation is a Social Security number. And C? People who use credit cards may interpret this set as a credit card number.

Because two people are unlikely to select the same stimuli, or organize stimuli in the same way, they are also not likely to arrive at the same interpretation of events or other people. Yet the unique portrait we derive from a situation directly affects our communication and our behavior. For instance, suppose Sal and Daniel pass Tito on the way to eat lunch. Even though they both greet him, Tito walks past without saying a word. Sal notices that Tito looks troubled, is walking quickly, and is carrying a load of books. Daniel notices that Tito glanced at them quickly, grimaced, and then averted their eyes. "Boy," says Sal, "I guess Tito must really be worried about the paper that is due in history." "You think so?" Daniel replies. "I'd say that he's still angry at me for hitting on Carmen."

While general perception processes are used to make sense of both physical and social phenomena, the study of **social perception,** or **social cognition,** has focused on the specific processes by which people perceive themselves and others. In the study of social perception particular emphasis is placed on how people interpret their own and others' behavior, how people categorize themselves and others, and how people form impressions of themselves and others. Since social perceptions form the basis of our interpersonal communication, understanding them is critical to interpersonal competence.

In the remainder of this chapter we will apply this basic information about perception to the study of perceptions of self and others in our communication.

Social perception—a set of processes by which people perceive themselves and others (also known as social cognition).

Perceptions of Self: Self-Concept and Self-Esteem

Self-concept and self-esteem are the two self-perceptions that have the greatest impact on how we communicate. **Self-concept** is one's self-identity (Baron & Byrne, 2000, p. 160). It is the idea or mental image that you have about your skills, your abilities, your knowledge, your competencies, and your personality. **Self-esteem** is your overall evaluation of your competence and personal worthiness (based on Mruk, 1999, p. 26). In this section we explain how we form our self concepts and how we develop our self-esteem to understand who we are and how we determine whether what we are is good. Then we describe what determines how well our self-perceptions match others' perceptions of us and the role these self-perceptions play when we communicate with others.

Self-concept—self-identity-the idea or mental image that we have about our skills, our abilities, our knowledge, our competencies, and our personality.

Self-esteem—our overall evaluation of our competence and personal worthiness.

Forming and Maintaining a Self-Concept

How do we learn what our skills, abilities, knowledge, competencies, and personality are? Our self-concept comes from the unique interpretations about ourselves that we make based on our experience and from others' reactions and responses to us.

Self-Perception We form impressions about ourselves based on our own perceptions. Through our experiences, we develop our own sense of our skills, our abilities, our knowledge, our competencies, and our personality. For example, if you perceive that it is easy for you to strike up conversations with strangers and that you enjoy chatting with them, you may conclude that you are outgoing or friendly (Kenny, 1994, p. 220).

If we form impressions about ourselves based on our own perceptions gained through our experiences, how does practice affect our perceptions about how well we will perform?

We place great emphasis on the first experience we have with a particular phenomenon (Centi, 1981). For instance, someone who is rejected in his first try at dating may perceive himself to be unattractive to the opposite sex. If additional experiences produce results similar to the first experience, the initial perception will be strengthened. But even when the first experience is not repeated, it is likely to take more than one contradictory additional experience to change the original perception.

When we have positive experiences, we are likely to believe we possess the personal characteristics that we associate with that experience, and these characteristics become part of our picture of who we are. So if Sonya quickly debugs a computer program that Jackie has struggled with, she is more likely to incorporate "competent problem solver" into her self-concept. Her positive experience confirms that she has that skill, so it is reinforced as part of her self-concept. Likewise, if our experiences have been negative, we are not as likely to describe ourselves as having these characteristics. For example, when David began school, he found that he disliked arithmetic and could not understand math concepts as quickly as other children. As time went on, he continued to struggle in mathematics. If asked to describe his strengths, David would be unlikely to say that he is good at math.

Reactions and Responses of Others In addition to our self-perceptions, our self-concept is formed and maintained by how significant others react and respond to us (Rayner, 2001, p. 43). For example, if during a brainstorming session at work, one of your co-workers tells you "You're really a creative thinker," you may decide that this comment fits your image of who you are. And as Rayner suggests, such comments are especially powerful in affecting your self-perception if you respect the person making the comment. Moreover, the power of such comments is increased when the praise is immediate rather than delayed (Hattie, 1992, p. 251). We use other people's comments as a check on our own self-descriptions. They serve to validate, reinforce, or alter our perception of who and what we are.

Some people have very rich or strong self-concepts; they can describe numerous skills, abilities, knowledge, competencies, and personality characteristics that they possess. Others have weak self-concepts; they cannot describe the skills, abilities, knowledge, competencies, or the personality characteristics that they have. The stronger our self-concept, the better we know and understand who we are and the better we are able to cope with the challenges we will face as we interact with others.

Our self-concept begins to form early in life, and information we receive from our families shapes our self-concept (Demo, 1987). One of the major responsibilities that family members have is to talk and act in ways that will help develop accurate and strong self-concepts in other family members. For example, the mother who says "Roberto, your room looks very neat; you are very organized" or

the brother who comments "Kisha, lending Tomika five dollars really helped her out; you are very generous" is helping Roberto or Kisha to recognize important parts of their personalities.

Unfortunately, in some families members do not fulfill these responsibilities. We have a friend who is a terrific artist, but she didn't discover she had this talent until she was forty-five. Why? Because as a child her mother had told her, "I have no artistic talent, and neither do you." So she never took an art class, and her natural talent went undeveloped for years.

Sometimes family members actually do real damage to each other's self-image, especially to the developing self-images of children. Communicating blame, calling names, and repeatedly pointing out another's shortcomings are particularly damaging. When Dad shouts, "Terry, you are so stupid! If you had only stopped to think, this wouldn't have happened," he is damaging Terry's belief in his own intelligence. When big sister teases, "Hey, Dumbo, how many times do I have to tell you, you're too clumsy to be a ballet dancer," she is undermining her younger sister's perception of her gracefulness. As we mentioned, statements like these are more damaging if they are the first ones heard, so these kinds of statements are particularly destructive to young children who are in the beginning stages of learning about themselves. If someone has called you "stupid" since the day you were born, it is unlikely that one or two good grades in school will overcome your self-image of "stupid." Negative and evaluative comments are also damaging to teenagers, whose self-concepts are in flux as they try to separate who they were as children from who they are to become as adults.

But even adults in a family can have their self-concept undermined by repeated attacks. In abusive relationships one person may "browbeat" or verbally humiliate another to such an extent that victims become unsure of what skills, abilities, knowledge, competencies, or personality is theirs. In any family there will be occasional negative statements. The rare put-down will probably not have any lasting effect on a person's self-image, but if the communication messages a person receives are humiliating, blaming, psychologically abusive, then family members will likely have damaged self-concepts that do not accurately reflect their skills, etc. While we should understand our shortcomings—who and what we are not—we have greater need to understand who and what we are.

Journal Activity

Who Am I?

Write a short essay on the subject "Who am I?" To begin this task, list all of the skills, abilities, knowledges, competencies, and personality characteristics that you believe describe you. To generate this list, think of list the skills, abilities, knowledge, competencies, and personality characteristics that describe how you see yourself. To begin, try completing the sentences: "I am skilled at. . .," "I have the ability to. . .," "I know things about. . .," I am competent at doing. . . ," and "One part of my personality is that I am. . . ." Do this over and over again. List as many characteristics in each category as you can think of.

Then develop a second list, only this time, complete the following statements: "Other people believe that I am skilled at. . .," "Other people believe that I have the ability to. . .," "Other people believe that I know things about. . . .," "Other people believe that I am competent at doing. . . ," and "One part of my personality is that other people believe that I am. . . ." Again, complete these statements over and over, as many times as you can.

Compare your two lists of self-perceptions and others' perceptions. How are they similar? Where are they different? Do you understand why they differ? Are your lists long or short? Why do you suppose that is? Reflect on how your own interpretations of your experiences and what others have told you about you have influenced your self-concept. Now organize the lists you have created, perhaps finding a way to group characteristics. Use this information to write an essay titled "Who I Am, and How I Know This." ■

Developing and Maintaining Self-Esteem

You'll recall that our *self-esteem* is our overall evaluation of our competence and personal worthiness—it is our positive or negative evaluation of our self-concept. Our evaluation of our personal worthiness is rooted in our values and develops over time as a result of our experiences. As Mruk (1999, p. 27) points out, self-esteem is not just how well or poorly we do things (self-concept), but the importance or value we place on what we do well or poorly. For instance, as part of Chad's self-concept, he believes he is physically strong. But if he doesn't believe that physical strength or other characteristics he possesses are worthwhile or valuable characteristic to have, then he will not have high self-esteem. Mruk explains that it takes both the perception of having a characteristic and a personal belief that the characteristic is of positive value to produce high self-esteem.

When we successfully use our skills, abilities, or knowledge in worthwhile endeavors, we raise our self-esteem. When we are unsuccessful in using our skills, abilities, and/or when we use them in unworthy endeavors, we lower our self-esteem.

It is important to notice that self-esteem depends on what each individual views as worthwhile. Yet we know that what we believe to be valuable is based both on our personal ideas and on the ideas, morals, and values of the society or group with which we identify. In the dominant culture of the United States, as elsewhere, some skills, abilities, knowledge, competencies, and personality characteristics are valued more than others. People who perceive that they have these characteristics are likely to have higher self-esteem than those who have other characteristics that are less valued. For example, since education is valued, people who finish high school and graduate from college raise their self-esteem. Likewise, people who accept the dominant culture's valuing of education and who drop out of school will lower their self-esteem. In fact according to Rayner (2001) research consistently finds high correlation between academic achievement and self-concept (p. 42).

Accuracy of Self-Concept and Self-Esteem

The accuracy of our self-concept and self-esteem depends on the accuracy of our own perceptions and how we process others' perceptions of us. All of us experience success and failure and all of us hear praise and criticism. If we are overly attentive to successful experiences and positive responses, our self-concept may become overdeveloped and our self-esteem inflated. If, however, we perceive and dwell on failures and give little value to our successes, or if we only remember the criticism we receive, our self-image may be underformed and our self-esteem low. In neither case does our self-concept or self-esteem accurately reflect who we are.

Incongruence, the gap between our inaccurate self-perceptions and reality, is a problem because our perceptions of self are more likely to affect our behavior than our true abilities (Weiten, 1998, p. 491). For example, Sean may actually possess all the skills, abilities, knowledge, competencies, and personality characteristics for effective leadership, but if he doesn't perceive that he has these characteristics, he won't step forward when leadership is needed. Unfortunately, individuals tend to reinforce their self-perceptions by adjusting their behavior to conform with perceived self-conceptions. That is, people with high self-esteem tend to behave in ways that lead to more affirmation, whereas people with low self-esteem tend to act in ways that confirm the low esteem in which they hold themselves. The inaccuracy of a distorted picture of oneself is magnified through self-fulfilling prophecies and by filtering messages.

> **Incongruence**—the gap between our inaccurate self-perceptions and reality.

Self-Fulfilling Prophecies **Self-fulfilling prophecies** are events that happen as the result of being foretold, expected, or talked about. They may be self-created or other-imposed.

Self-created prophecies are those predictions you make about yourself. We often "talk ourselves into" success or failure. For example, Stefan sees himself as quite social and able to get to know people easily; he says, "I'm going to have fun at the party tonight." As a result of his positive self-concept, Stefan looks forward to encountering strangers and, just as he predicted, makes several new acquaintances and enjoys himself. In contrast, Aaron sees himself as unskilled in establishing new relationships; he says, "I doubt I'll know hardly anyone—I'm going to have a miserable time." Because Aaron fears encountering strangers, he feels awkward about introducing himself and, just as he predicted, spends much of his time standing around alone thinking about when he can leave.

> **Self-fulfilling prophecies**— events that happen as the result of being foretold, expected, or talked about.

Self-esteem has an important effect on the prophecies people make. For instance, people with positive self-esteem view success positively and confidently prophesy that they can repeat successes; people with low self-esteem attribute their successes to luck and so prophesy that they will not repeat them (Hattie, 1992, p. 253).

The prophecies others make about you also affect your performance. For example, if the debate coach tells Javier, "I can see that you have a terrific ability to remember details. I know that you will be an outstanding member of the debate team," Javier is likely to believe this and will come to act in ways that are consistent with the prophecy.

Other-created prophecies have a powerful way of changing our self-concepts. For instance, doctors report that when they tell their patients they will recover, a much higher percentage improve than when doctors are noncommittal or show doubt about recovery. In other words, the doctor's statement about the person's health seems to invoke the self-perception "healthy," which leads to real health. Similarly, there have been countless cases of teachers imposing prophecies on students that the students then lived up—or down—to. When teachers believe that their students are able, students "buy into" the expectation and succeed. A lesson to be learned from this is that we should take care what we say to others lest we place unnecessary limitations on them. For instance, in the family, a parent should avoid predicting failure for a child.

Filtering Messages A second way that our self-perceptions can become distorted is through the way we filter what others say to us. We are prone to pay attention to messages that reinforce our current self-image while messages that contradict this image may not "register" or may be downplayed. For example, suppose you prepare an agenda for your study group. Someone comments that you're a good organizer. You may not really hear it, ignore it, or reply, "Anyone could have done that—it was nothing special." If, however, you think you are a good organizer, you will pay attention to the compliment and may even reinforce it by responding, "Thanks, I've worked hard to learn how to do this, but it was worth it. It comes in handy."

Changing Self-Concepts and Self-Esteem Self-concept and self-esteem are enduring characteristics, but they can be changed. At times, comments that contradict self-prophecies will get past the filter and can begin to change the self-image. Then, the newly changed self-perceptions begin to filter other comments and are used as the basis of new self-created, self-fulfilling prophecies. So over the course of your life, your self-concept and self-esteem may change.

Certain situations seem to lend themselves to expediting this process. When people experience profound changes in their social environments, they are likely to drop their filters and absorb information that in other circumstances they would filter out. Life transitions can be times when we become more susceptible to dropping our filters. So, when children begin school, when teens begin the independence process, when young adults leave home, when people start new jobs or begin college, fall in love, marry, divorce, become parents, retire, and grieve the death of someone they love, they are more likely to attend to messages that are at odds with their current self-conceptions. As a result of these new experiences, people change their picture of who they are and begin to predict new things for themselves.

The phenomenal growth of the self-help movement in the United States bears eloquent testimony to the ability of people to work actively to develop self-perceptions that are congruent with their actual personal characteristics. For example, Alcoholics Anonymous and other twelve-step groups help members overcome inaccurate perceptions of self-worth by replacing self-conceptions such as "weak-willed" with more accurate self-descriptors. In his analysis of numerous other research studies, Christopher Mruk (1999) found that self-esteem is increased through "hard work and practice, practice, practice—there is simply no

Michael L. Hecht, Professor of Speech Communication, Head of the Department of Speech Communication, College of Arts and Sciences, Pennsylvania State University, on

Interethnic Communication and Ethnic Identity

Michael L. Hecht's passion is people. His native curiosity has led him to devote his life to scholarly endeavors that help us understand how people from different ethnic backgrounds interact in ways that they perceive are satisfying and effective. When he was in graduate school many scholars were interested in studying ineffective communication. But Hecht, an optimist, was more interested in understanding what led people to feel satisfied with a conversation. For his Ph.D. dissertation at the University of Illinois, Hecht developed a theory to help us understand and to measure communication satisfaction. His theory and measures are widely used today. But Hecht's contribution to our understanding of communication satisfaction and effectiveness did not end when he received his degree, instead, it provided the foundation from which he continues to explore what leads people to be effective and satisfied with their conversations.

As a Jewish American, Hecht has always been interested in intergroup communication. His earliest work in this area examined perceptions of conversa-tional satisfaction in conversations between African Americans and European Americans. After graduate school, Hecht teamed up with a grad school contemporary and friend, Sidney Ribeau (who is now President of Bowling Green State University), to study communication satisfaction between African Americans and European Americans. At that time, communication satisfaction had been studied only from a European American perspective.

Hecht and Ribeau discovered that African Americans and European Americans abide by different communication rules. Thus when African Americans and European Americans interact, one party is likely to violate the communication rules expected by the other. These rule violations make conversations between people from these two groups less likely to be perceived as satisfying.

Hecht is also fascinated with how people form and communicate their personal identities. Recently, he formulated the Communication Theory of Identity. The basic premise of this theory is that identity is a communicative process. Hecht and his co-authors believe that there are four different "frames" or perspectives from which we can understand identity.

First, we can view identity through a personal frame. This would suggest that identity is based on your self-concept or self-image derived from your own feelings, self-knowledge, or spiritual sense of self. A second way to view identity is to see that identity is enactment; that is, you act out who you are as you talk. During interaction with others, we consciously and unconsciously communicate our identity to others. Third, you can view identity from a relational perspective. In this light, you negotiate your identity within a particular relationship. You may interact differently in a relationship where you are a parent than in a relationship where you are a child. In addition, while talking with a parent, a child works out what it means to her to be a "child." The relational perspective also allows us to notice how relationships take on identities themselves. When people get married they often find that others see them as a couple or that they perceive themselves to be a couple. As a couple, their identity is different from what it was when they were not "being a couple." Finally, according to this theory, we can think of identities from a communal frame. Groups of people have identities that bond them to one another. These communities develop certain behaviors which they teach to new members and expect members to enact. Hecht and his colleagues suggest that if we want to understand identities, we must look at all four levels in combination. I work out who I am (personal identity) by trying out certain behaviors as I interact (enacted) with others in my relationships (relational). In part, how I act is based on the behavior that is expected of members of those groups to which I see myself belonging (communal).

Recently Hecht's research has combined his interest in understanding identity theory with a desire to use his research to help others. So Hecht has worked with an interdisciplinary team to identify strategies

(refuse, explain, avoid, and leave) that teens use to resist invitations to use drugs. An educational program using these strategies was developed for groups of ethnically diverse junior high students. Early results suggest that this approach is slowing the rate at which students begin using drugs. In addition, the study has provided evidence that Latino American and African American teens who are proud of their ethnic identity are less prone to drug use. This finding is in keeping with the Communication Theory of Identity.

Although it is common for faculty to invite graduate students to work with them on projects, Hecht finds doing research with undergraduate students to be especially rewarding. Hecht has created undergraduate research apprenticeship programs. In the program, undergraduates receive classroom credit for becoming part of research teams. Some students

make substantial contributions to projects and are invited to co-author scholarly articles.

Michael Hecht is currently serving as the Head of the Department of Speech Communication. Since his drug resistance studies are financed by large grants from outside agencies to whom he must account and report, Hecht finds himself doing more administrative work these days. Nonetheless, Professor Hecht still finds time for his first love, teaching courses in interpersonal and nonverbal communication at the undergraduate level and courses in identity and intergroup communication at the graduate level.

Hecht and his colleagues created a multicultural prevention program for the seventh grade in Phoenix and reduced alcohol, marijuana and tobacco use. This program is one of the few that are effective and targeted to Mexican American youth. ■

escaping this basic existential fact" (p. 112). So why is this important? Because our self-esteem affects with whom we choose to form relationships. Researchers have found that "people with high self-esteem are more committed to partners who perceive them very favorably, while people with low self-esteem are more committed to partners who perceive them less favorably (Leary, 2002, p. 130).

Role—a pattern of learned behaviors that people use to meet the perceived demands of a particular context.

Presenting Ourselves

We present our self-image and self-esteem to others through the roles we enact. A **role** is a pattern of learned behaviors that people use to meet the perceived demands of a particular context. For instance, during the day you may enact the roles of "student," "brother/sister," and "salesclerk."

Roles that we enact may result from our own needs, relationships that we form, cultural expectations, the groups we choose to be part of, and our own conscious decisions. From our experiences each of us has developed a prototype, or model, of what behaviors are expected of occupants of specific roles. We understand what the proper behaviors for a physician are, how a waitress should act, and what dads are supposed to do. Not only does our own experience inform us about what the proper behavior is when enacting a certain role, but the expectations of a specific group may also influence what we perceive to be role-appropriate behavior. Our family, our religious community, our athletic team, our theater club—every group has expectations about what behavior is appropriate for people in certain roles.

Everyone enacts numerous roles each day and we draw on different skills and attributes as we enact these roles. For instance, Sam, who is perceived as a warm, quiet, sensitive person in her family group, may choose to enact the role of a boisterous "party animal" in a friendship group. With each new situation, we may test a role we know how to enact or we may decide to try to enact a new role.

Michael Hecht and his colleagues believe that our identity is developed and manifested through our communication. This Communication Theory of Identity suggests that there are four different aspects of identity which we work out in our transactions relationships with others. In the Spotlight on Scholars that appears on pages 41 and 42, you can read about Michael Hecht and the Communication Theory of Identity.

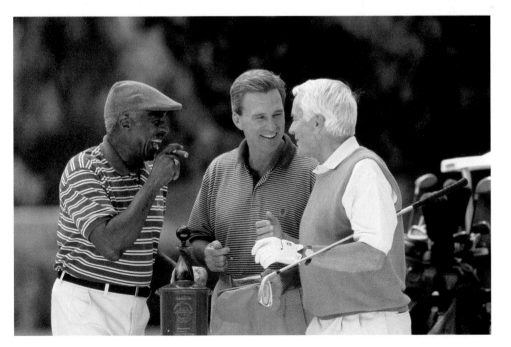

We present our self-image and self-esteem to others through the roles we enact.

In the Diverse Voices selection in this chapter (see pages 45 and 46), Dolores V. Tanno explains the origin and meaning of the various communal frames that she uses in presenting herself to others.

Self-Concept, Self-Esteem and Communication

Just as our self-concept and self-esteem affect how accurately we perceive ourselves, so too do they influence our communication by moderating competing internal messages in our self-talk and influencing our personal communication style.

Self-talk—the internal conversations we have with ourselves.

Self-Perceptions Moderate Self-Talk Self-talk is the internal conversations we have with ourselves. When we face a decision, we may be especially conscious of the different and often competing "voices" in our head. Listen to the self-talk Corey had upon returning from a job interview.

"I think I made a pretty good impression on the personnel director—I mean, she talked with me for a long time."

"Well, she talked with me, but maybe she was just trying to be nice. After all, it was her job."

"No, she didn't have to spend that much time with me. And she really lit up when I talked about the internship I had at Federated."

"So, she said she was interested in my internship. Talking about that is not exactly telling me that it would make a difference in her view of me as a prospective employee."

Notice that several of the messages in this internal conversation are competing. What determines which voice Corey listens to is likely to depend on his self-perceptions. If Corey has high self-esteem, he will probably conclude that the interviewer was sincere, and he'll feel good about the interview. If, on the other hand, he has low self-esteem, and his self-concept doesn't include competence in the skills and abilities that are relevant to the job, he is more likely to "listen" to the negative voices in his head and conclude that he doesn't have a chance for the job.

Self-Perception Influences How We Talk about Ourselves with Others If we feel good about ourselves, we are likely to communicate positively. For instance, people with a strong self-concept and higher self-esteem usually take credit for their successes. Likewise, people with healthy self-perceptions are inclined to defend their views even in the face of opposing arguments. If we feel bad about ourselves, we are likely to communicate negatively by downplaying our accomplishments.

Why do some people put themselves down regardless of what they have done? People who have low self-esteem are likely to be unsure of the value of their contributions and expect others to view them negatively. As a result, perhaps, people with a poor self-concept or low self-esteem find it less painful to put themselves down than to hear the criticism of others. Thus, to preempt the likelihood that others will comment on their unworthiness, they do it first.

I Am . . . *By Dolores V. Tanno*

How do you behave when you are asked to talk about yourself, especially when you are perceived as "different," whether that difference is by sex, religion, or ethnicity? Delores V. Tanno, University of Nevada Las Vegas, describes how each ethnic self-reference communicates a story, and multiple stories provide significance to determining who "I am."

Over the course of my life one question has been consistently asked of me: *"What are you?"* I used to reply that I was American, but it quickly became clear this was unacceptable because what came next was, "No, really what are you?" In my more perverse moments I responded, "I am human." I stopped when I realized that people's feelings were hurt. Ironic? Yes, but the motive behind the question often justified hurt feelings. I became aware of this only after asking a question of my own: "Why do you ask?"

Confronting the motives of people has forced me to examine who I am. In the process I have had to critically examine my own choices, in different times and contexts, of the names by which I am placed in society. The names are "Spanish," "Mexican American," "Latina," and "Chicana."

"I am Spanish." Behind this label is the story of my childhood in northern New Mexico. New Mexico was the first permanent Spanish settlement in the Southwest, and New Mexicans have characterized themselves as Spanish for centuries. My parents, grandparents, and great-grandparents consider them-

selves Spanish; wrongly or rightly they attribute their customs, habits, and language to their Spanish heritage, and I followed suit. In my young mind, the story of being Spanish did not include concepts of racial purity or assimilation; what it did do was allow me to begin my life with a clearly defined identity and a place in the world. For me, the story of being Spanish incorporates into its plot the innocence of youth, before the reality of discrimination became an inherent part of the knowledge of who I am.

"I am Mexican American." When I left New Mexico, my sense of belonging did not follow me across the state border. When I responded to the question, "What are you?" by saying, "I am Spanish," people corrected me: "You mean Mexican, don't you?" My initial reaction was anger; how could they know better than I who I was? But soon my reaction was one of puzzlement, and I wondered just why there was such insistence that I be Mexican. Reading and studying led me to understand that the difference between Spanish and Mexican could be found in the legacy of colonization. Thus behind the name "Mexican American" is the story of classic colonization that

allows for prior existence and that also communicates duality. As Richard A. Garica argues: "Mexican in culture and social activity, American in philosophy and politics." As native born Mexican Americans we also have dual visions: the achievement of the American Dream and the preservation of cultural identity.

"I am Latina." If the story behind the name Mexican American is grounded in duality, the story behind the name "Latina" is grounded in cultural connectedness. The Spaniards proclaimed vast territories of North and South American as their own. They intermarried in all the regions in which they settled. These marriages yielded offspring who named themselves variously as Cubans, Puerto Ricans, Colombians, Mexicans, and so forth, but they connect culturally with one another when they name each other Latinas. To use the name *Latina* is to communicate acceptance and belonging in a broad cultural community.

"I am Chicana." This name suggests a smaller community, a special kind of Mexican American awareness that does not involve others (Cubans, Puerto Ricans, etc.). The name was the primary political as well

Diverse Voices... I Am . . . *continued*

as rhetorical strategy of the Chicano movement of the 1960s. Mirande and Enriquez argue that the dominant characteristic of the name "Chicana" is that it admits a "sense of marginality." There is a political tone and character to "Chicana" that signifies a story of self-determination and empowerment. As such, the name denotes a kind of political becoming. As the same time, however, the name communicates the idea of being American, not in a "melting pot" sense that presupposes assimilation, but rather in a pluralistic sense that acknowledges the inalienable right of existence for different peoples.

What, then, am I? The truth is I am all of these. Each name reveals a different facet of identity that allows symbolic, historical, cultural, and political connectedness. These names are no

different than other multiple labels we take on. For example, to be mother, wife, sister, and daughter, is to admit to the complexity of being female. Each name implies a narrative of experiences gained in responding to circumstances, time, and place and motivated by a need to belong.

In my case, I resort to being Spanish and all it implies whenever I return to my birthplace, in much the same way that we often resort to being children again in the presence of our parents. But I am also Mexican American when I balance the two important cultures that define me; Latina when I wish to emphasize cultural and historical connectedness with others; and Chicana whenever opportunities arise to promote political empowerment and assert political pride.

It is sometimes difficult for people to understand the "both/and" mentality that results from this simultaneity of existence. We are indeed enriched by belonging to two cultures. We are made richer still by having at our disposal several names by which to identify ourselves. Singly the names Spanish, Mexican American, Latina, and Chicana communicate a part of a life story. Together they weave a rhetorically powerful narrative of ethnic identity that combines biographical, historical, cultural, and political experiences.

Excerpted from Tanno, D. V. (2001). Names, narratives, and the evolution of ethnic identity. In A. Gonzalez, M. Houston, & V. Chen (Eds.), *Our Voices-Essays in Cultural Ethnicity and Communication* (3rd ed., pp. 25–28). Los Angeles, Calif.: Roxbury Publishing Company.

Self-Perceptions Affect Our Perceptions of Others Self-image and self-esteem are important not only because of the way they moderate our self-talk, but also because they affect how we perceive others. First, the more accurate our self-image, the more accurately we are likely to perceive others. Both self-perception and perception of others start with our ability to process data accurately. Second, the higher our self-esteem, the more likely we are to see others favorably. Studies have shown that those people who accept themselves as they are tend to be more accepting of others; similarly, those with low self-esteem are more likely to find fault in others. Third, our own personal characteristics influence the type of characteristics we are likely to perceive in others. For example, people who are secure tend to see others positively rather than negatively. If you recall that we respond to the world as we perceive it to be (and not necessarily as it is), you can readily see how low self-esteem can account for misunderstandings and communication breakdowns.

Self-Perceptions Influence Communication Style Research demonstrates that we communicate our self-concept and our self-esteem when we interact with others (Campbell, 1990, p. 538). For instance, Jan, who has low self-esteem, may comment to her friend David, "What I did probably wasn't that important to the company, so I don't deserve a raise and won't get one." Or Troy, who is unclear about his abilities, may say, "Please go ahead and take that book. I probably wouldn't be able to understand it anyway." In contrast, people with richer self-concepts and higher self-esteem usually present themselves positively and make statements that show an expectation of acceptance. They are likely to take credit for their successes: "My suggestions helped the Kappa Xi Phi recruit new members, so I think I'm likely to be asked to run for president next year." Likewise, people with healthy self-perceptions are likely to defend their views even in the face of opposing arguments. For instance, when criticized Amber might say, "You may not like my position, but I've thought this through carefully and believe that I have good reasons to support my position."

Cultural and Gender Differences

Your cultural background influences your perception and affects your views of self. Many Americans share what is called the "Western view of self," which says that the individual is an autonomous entity with distinct abilities, traits, motives, and values, and that these attributes cause behavior. Moreover, people with this Western view see the individual as the most basic social unit. So, the notion of self-concept and self-esteem are built on the notions of independence from others and discovering and expressing individual uniqueness.

People who share an "Eastern view of self" believe the family, not the individual, is the smallest social unit. In these cultures the skills, abilities, knowledge, and personality characteristics that are valued are profoundly different. Children raised in Western cultures will come to value those personal characteristics that are associated with independence, and will develop high self-esteem from them. In Eastern cultures, however, the child is acculturated toward greater interdependency (Jordan, 1991, p. 137). So, these children will develop higher self-esteem when they perceive themselves to be cooperative, helpful, and self-effacing.

Similarly, men and women are socialized to view themselves differently and to value who they are based on whether their behavior corresponds to the behavior expected of their sex in their culture. If women are expected to be nurturing caregivers who attend to home and family life, then those women who perceive that they have the skills, abilities, knowledge, competencies, and personality characteristics needed for these jobs will have enriched self-concepts and high self-esteem. But women who do not have these attributes are likely to be less confident of who they are and are likely to have lower self-esteem.

Perception of Others

As you encounter others, you are faced with a number of questions: Do you have anything in common? Will they accept you? Will you be able to get along? Because this uncertainty is uncomfortable you will try to alleviate it by finding answers to questions. Charles Berger and James Bradac (1982) suggested that **uncertainty reduction theory** explains the ways individuals monitor their social environments in order to know more about themselves and others (Littlejohn, 2002, p. 243).

We seek information about others because if we are uncertain about what they are like, we will have a difficult time predicting their behavior, and this uncertainty will make us uncomfortable.

Uncertainty reduction theory—explains the ways individuals monitor their social environments and come to know more about themselves and others.

What are the individuals in this group communicating through their physical appearance, dress, and behavior?

When two people meet, they form initial impressions to guide their behavior. As people continue to interact, these perceptions will be reinforced, intensified, or changed. Just as with our self-perceptions, our social perceptions are not always accurate. The factors that are likely to influence our perceptions of others include physical characteristics and social behaviors, stereotyping, and emotional states.

Physical Characteristics and Social Behaviors

Social perceptions, especially the important first impressions, are often made on the basis of physical characteristics and social behaviors. We use our first impressions to help us make sense of others. On the basis of a person's physical attractiveness (facial characteristics, height, weight, grooming, dress, sound of voice), we are likely to categorize people as friendly, courageous, intelligent, cool, or their opposites (Aronson, 1999, p. 380). We use physical characteristics in this order: race, gender, age, appearance, facial expressions, eye contact, movement, personal space, and touch. In one study, professional women dressed in jackets were assessed as more powerful than professional women dressed in other clothing (Temple & Loewen, 1993, p. 345). Show a friend a picture of your child, uncle, or grandmother, and your friend may well form impressions of your relative's personality on the basis of that photo alone!

Early impressions are also made on the basis of a person's social behaviors. Sometimes our impressions are formed by observing a single behavior. For instance, after a company party Caleb asked Sara what she thought of Gavin, the customer service rep. Sara, who had noticed Gavin interrupt Yolanda once, replied, "Gavin? Oh, he's really rude."

Some judgments of other people are based on what are called "implicit personality theories," which are assumptions people have developed about which physical characteristics and personality traits or behaviors are associated with another (Michener & DeLamater, 1999, p. 106).

Because your own implicit personality theory says that certain traits go together, you are likely to perceive that a person has a whole set of characteristics when you have actually observed only one characteristic, trait, or behavior. When you do this, your perception is exhibiting what is known as the **halo effect.** For instance, Heather sees Martina personally greeting and welcoming every person who arrives at the meeting. Heather's implicit personality theory views this behavior as a sign of the characteristic of warmth. She further associates warmth with goodness and goodness with honesty. As a result, she perceives that Martina is good and honest as well as warm.

In reality, Martina may be a con artist who uses her warmth to lure people into a false sense of trust. This example demonstrates a "positive halo" (Heather assigned Martina positive characteristics), but we also use implicit personality theory to inaccurately impute bad characteristics. In fact, Hollman (1972) found that negative information more strongly influences our impressions of others than does positive information. So we are more likely to negatively halo others than to positively halo them.

Halo effect—perceiving that a person has a whole set of characteristics when you have actually observed only one characteristic, trait, or behavior.

Halo effects seem to occur most frequently under one or more of three conditions: (1) when the perceiver is judging traits with which he or she has limited experience, (2) when the traits have strong moral overtones, and (3) when the perception is of a person that the perceiver knows well.

In both cases, women and men differ in attributes they perceive in others. Scholar Leslie Zebrowitz (1990) says that men and boys are more likely to describe others in terms of their abilities ("She writes well"), whereas women and girls are more likely to describe others in terms of their self-concepts ("She thinks she's a good writer"). In addition, Zebrowitz has found that males' descriptions include more nonsocial activities ("She likes to fly model airplanes"), whereas females include more interpersonal interactions ("He likes to get together with his friends") (p. 24).

Given limited amounts of information, then, we fill in details. This tendency to fill in details leads to a second factor that influences social perception: stereotyping.

Stereotyping

Perhaps the most commonly known factor that influences our perception of others is stereotyping. **Stereotypes** are a "set of beliefs or expectations that we have about people based solely on their group membership," (Jones, 2002, p. 4). So, when we find out that someone is Hispanic or Muslim, a skateboarder, chess player, an elementary school teacher or a nurse—in short any "identifiable group"—we use this information to attribute to the person a host of characteristics. These perceived group characteristics, taken as a whole, may be positive or negative and they may be accurate or inaccurate (Jussim, McCauley, & Lee, 1995, p. 6).

We are likely to develop generalized perceptions about any group we come in contact with. Subsequently, any number of perceptual cues—skin color, style of dress, a religious medal, gray hair, sex, and so on—can lead us to stereotype our generalizations onto a specific individual.

Stereotyping contributes to perceptual inaccuracies because it ignores individual differences. For instance, if part of Dave's stereotype of personal injury lawyers is that they are unethical, then he will use this stereotype when he meets Denise, a highly principled woman who happens to be a successful personal injury lawyer. You may be able to think of instances when you have been the victim of a stereotype based on your gender, age, ethnic heritage, social class, physical characteristics, or other group identity. If so, you know how hurtful the use of stereotypes can be.

When we use stereotypes as the basis of our social interaction, we risk creating miscommunication and hard feelings. A friend of ours who was raised in a middle-class African American home tells the following story about his first day at college. He was at the registration center, where he had just completed selecting his classes. As he was about to walk over to the cashier's line to write a check for his tuition, the dean of the college greeted him warmly, welcomed him to campus, and directed him to the financial aid line. He was stung. It seems that part of the dean's stereotype was the belief that only white students pay their own tuition bills.

Stereotypes—set of beliefs or expectations that we have about people based solely on their group membership.

As this example suggests, stereotyping can lead to prejudice and discrimination. According to Jones (2002), **prejudice** is a positive or negative attitude or judgment directed toward people simply because they happen to be members of a specific group (p. 4). Notice the distinction between a stereotype and a prejudice. Whereas a stereotype is a set of beliefs or expectations, a prejudice is positive or negative attitude—both relate to group membership. Stereotypes and prejudice are cognitive—things we think. **Discrimination,** on the other hand, is a negative action toward a social group or its members on account of group membership (Jones, 2002, p. 8). The contrast is that whereas prejudice and stereotype deal with attitudes, discrimination involves negative action. For instance, when Laura discovers that Wasif, a man she has just met, is a Muslim, she may stereotype him as a chauvinist. If she is a feminist, she may use this stereotype to prejudge him and assume that he will expect women to be subservient. Thus she holds a prejudice about him. If she acts on her prejudice, she may discriminate against him by refusing to partner with him on a class project. So, without really having gotten to know Wasif, Laura prejudges him and discriminates. In this case, Wasif may never get the chance to be known for who he really is, and Laura may have lost an opportunity to get to work with the best student in class.

Stereotypes, prejudice, and discrimination, like self-concept and self-esteem, can be difficult to change. People are likely to maintain their stereotypes and prejudices and continue to discriminate against others even in the face of evidence that disproves their stereotypes.

Let's consider another example. Richard may stereotype people with tattoos as being rowdy. From that stereotype he develops a prejudice against people with tattoos. He thinks of them as being untrustworthy. Then when a person with a tattoo applies for a job, Richard accepts the application and later throws it in the wastebasket, muttering to himself, "I can't believe a guy like that thinks I'm going to hire him to manage money."

Racism, ethnocentrism, sexism, ageism, able-ism, and other "-isms" occur when a powerful group believes its members are superior to those of another group and that this superiority gives the powerful group the right to dominate or discriminate against the "inferior" group. Because "-isms" can be deeply ingrained and subtle, it is easy to overlook behaviors we engage in that are racist, sexist, or ableist.

All people can be prejudiced and can discriminate. Nevertheless, "prejudices of groups with power are farther reaching in their consequences than others" (Sampson, 1999, p. 131). Because such attitudes can be deeply ingrained and are often subtle, it is easy to overlook behaviors we engage in that in some way meet this definition. The behavior may seem insignificant, such as directing an African American student to the financial aid line. It may appear innocuous, such as leaving more space between you and a blind person on a bus than you would if the other person were sighted. Telling jokes, laughing at jokes, or encouraging repetition of jokes that demean women is sexist behavior. So is assuming that the women in the office should plan the holiday party because, well, you know, they're just better at that. Ignoring the presence or the comments of another person

Prejudice—a positive or negative attitude or judgment directed toward people simply because they happen to be members of a specific group.

Discrimination—a negative action toward a social group or its members on account of group membership.

Racism, ethnocentrism, sexism, ageism, able-ism—beliefs that the behaviors or characteristics of one group are inherently superior to those of another group and that this gives the "superior" group the right to dominate or discriminate against the "inferior" group.

because that person is of another race or the opposite sex is racist/sexist behavior. We may say, "But I didn't mean anything by what I did." Nonetheless, our behavior will be perceived as racist/sexist, and it will seriously harm our attempts to communicate.

Most definitions of both racism and sexism acknowledge that the "superior" group member must have the power to impose discriminatory behavior. From this perspective, some people are in a better position than others to be racist or sexist, ageist or able-ist. At the present time in the United States, in both government and industry, European American males are disproportionately represented in positions of power. Therefore, European American males are in a better position to use their stereotypes and prejudices to discriminate against other groups. Hence we generally speak of whites as being "racist" and males as being "sexist." This, of course, does not mean that any particular European American or any individual male is a racist or sexist. But because of our tendencies to stereotype, many innocent people are so labeled.

Although it is important for us to understand these different concepts from an interpersonal communication standpoint, whether we have societal power or not, when we act on stereotypes and prejudices we undermine our ability to develop and maintain a relationship. Because racial and gender stereotypes are so deeply ingrained in our culture, very few people manage to completely avoid behaving or thinking in a prejudiced manner. By becoming aware of our own attitudes and behaviors, we can guard against inhibiting communication by automatically assuming that other people feel and act the same way we do. We can also guard against saying or doing things that offend other people and perpetuate outdated racial and sex-role stereotypes. If people are confronted with enough information over a long enough period, their attitudes may change.

How is this person's emotional state likely to affect the conversation she will have when the partner arrives.

Emotional States

A final factor that affects how accurately we perceive others is our emotional state at the time of the interaction. Based on his studies, Joseph Forgas (1991) has concluded that "there is a broad and pervasive tendency for people to perceive and interpret others in terms of their [own] feelings at the time" (p. 288). If, for example, you get the internship that you had applied for, your good mood—brought on by your good fortune—is likely to spill over so that you perceive other things and other people more positively than you might have under different circumstances. If, however, you received a low grade on a paper you thought was well written, your perceptions of people around you are likely to be colored by your disappointment or anger due to this grade.

Our emotions also cause us to engage in selective perceptions, ignoring inconsistent information. For instance, if Donna sees Nick as a man with whom she would like to develop a strong relationship, she will tend to see the positive side of Nick's personality and overlook or ignore the negative side that is apparent to others.

Our emotions may also affect our attributions (Forgas, 2000, p. 397). **Attributions** are reasons we give for others' behavior. In addition to making judgments about people, we attempt to construct reasons why people behave as they do. According to attribution theory, what we determine—rightly or wrongly—to be the causes of others' behavior has a direct impact on our perceptions of them. For instance, suppose a co-worker with whom you had a noon luncheon has not arrived by 12:20. If you like and respect your co-worker, you are likely to attribute his lateness to something external: an important phone call at the last minute, the need to finish a job before lunch, or some accident that may have occurred. If you are not particularly fond of your co-worker, you are likely to attribute his lateness to something internal: forgetfulness, inconsiderateness, or malicious intent. In either case, your causal attribution further affects your perception of the person.

Attributions—reasons we give for others' behavior.

Like prejudices, causal attributions may be so strong that they resist contrary evidence. If you do not particularly care for the person, when he does arrive and explains that he had an emergency long-distance phone call, you are likely to disbelieve the reason or discount the urgency of the call. Being aware of the human tendency toward such cognitive biases can help you correct your perceptions and thus improve your communication.

In the final part of this chapter we focus on procedures that will enable us to improve our social perceptions of people regardless of their culture or gender.

Cultural and Gender Differences

Members of the opposite sex or people from different cultures talking with each other are likely to experience difficulty sharing meaning because they approach the world with different perspectives. You may think that you don't have to be concerned with cultural differences because most of your communication will be with people similar to yourself. But you don't have to cross national borders to encounter different cultures. As we mentioned earlier, the United States contains within it a diversity of cultures. This can be shown by the fact that there are now some 176 living languages spoken in the United states (http://www.ethnologue.com, 2002). Cultural differences can also be experienced across generations, regions, social classes, and even neighborhoods.

When we are confronted with strangers who are of the opposite sex, or people from different cultures, or differently able people, we tend to see these differences as barriers to communication because differences increase uncertainty. The more one person differs from another, the less either person is able to predict the behavior of the other. When people are uncertain about how another person will behave, they become anxious. Some people express their fear by withdrawing or becoming compliant; others mask their fear with aggressive behavior. Clearly, none

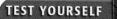

TEST YOURSELF

Factors Leading to Misperceptions of Others

For the following situation, list each of the factors discussed in this section that contributed to the inaccuracy of the initial perception of the other person. Be able to defend your answers in class.

Amanda was depressed. Her daughter was having problems in school, she had just been informed that her work hours were being cut back, and her mother was facing possible surgery. On her way home from campus, she stopped at the dry cleaner to pick up her laundry. There was a new man working the counter. From looking at him, Amanda could tell he was quite old. She thought to herself that he could be a problem. When she requested her laundry, he asked to see her claim check. Because no one had ever asked her for this before, Amanda had started throwing these away so she responded that she had thrown the receipt away. "Well," the man firmly replied, "I'm not able to give you clothes without a claim check. It's store policy." After demanding to see the manager and being informed that she had left for the day, Amanda stormed out of the store. "I'll fix him," she fumed to herself. "It's just like an old man to be so rigid!"

of these behaviors improves communication. All of these cultural and gender differences argue for a greater need to confront our ignorance about what people are thinking, feeling, and valuing. In the final part of this chapter we focus on procedures that will enable us to improve our social perceptions of people regardless of their culture or gender.

Improving Social Perception

Because inaccuracies in perception are common and because they influence how we communicate, improving perceptual accuracy is an important first step in becoming a competent communicator. The following guidelines can aid you in constructing a more realistic impression of others as well as in assessing the validity of your own perceptions.

1. Question the accuracy of your perceptions. Questioning accuracy begins by saying, "I know what I think I saw, heard, tasted, smelled, or felt, but I could be wrong. What other information should I be aware of?" By accepting the possibility that you have overlooked something, you will become interested in increasing your accuracy. In situations where the accuracy of perception is important, take a few seconds to double-check. It will be worth the effort.

2. Seek more information to verify perceptions. If your perception has been based on only one or two pieces of information, try to collect further information so that your perceptions are better grounded. Note that your perception is tentative—that is, subject to change.

The best way to get additional information about people is to talk with them. Unfortunately, we tend to avoid people who are different from us and so we don't know much them. As a result we base our perceptions (and then our behavior) on stereotypes. It's OK to be unsure about how to treat someone from another group. But rather than letting your uncertainty cause you to make mistakes, talk with the person and ask for the information you need to become more comfortable.

3. Realize that your perceptions of a person will change over time. People often base their behavior on perceptions that are old or based on incomplete information. Just as you have changed, so too have other people. So when you encounter someone you haven't seen for a while, you will want to become reacquainted and let their current behavior rather than their past actions or reputation inform your perceptions.

Just because a former classmate was "wild" in high school does not mean that the person has not changed and become a mature responsible adult.

4. Use the skill of perception checking to verify your impressions. A **perception check** is a message that reflects your understanding of the meaning of another person's *nonverbal* behavior. Perception checking calls for you to (1) watch the behavior of the other person, (2) ask yourself "What does that behavior mean to me?" and (3) describe the behavior and put your interpretation of the nonverbal behavior you observed into words to verify your perception.

The following examples illustrate the use of perception checking. In each of the examples the final sentence is a perception check. Notice that body language sometimes provides the perceptual information that needs to be checked out, whereas at other times the tone of voice does. Also notice that the perception-checking statements do not express approval or disapproval of what is being received—they are purely descriptive statements of the perceptions.

> Valerie walks into the room with a completely blank expression. She neither speaks to Ann nor does she acknowledge that Ann is even in the room. Valerie sits down on the edge of the bed and stares into space. Ann says, "Valerie, did something happen? You look like you're in a state of shock. Am I right? Is there something I can do?"
>
> Tad, the company messenger, delivers a memo to Erin. As Erin reads the note, her eyes brighten and she breaks into a smile. Tad says, "Hey, Erin, you look really pleased. Am I right?"
>
> Cesar, speaking in short, precise sentences with a sharp tone of voice, gives Bill his day's assignment. Bill says, "From the sound of your voice, Cesar, I get the impression that you're upset with me. Are you?"

So when we use the skill of perception checking we encode the meaning that we have perceived from someone's nonverbal behavior and feed it back so that it can be verified or corrected. For instance, when Bill says, "I can't help but get the impression that you're upset with me. Are you?" Cesar may say (1) "No, whatever gave you that impression?" in which case Bill can further describe the cues that he received; (2) "Yes, I am," in which case Bill can get Cesar to specify what has caused the feelings; or (3) "No, it's not you; it's just that three of my team members didn't show up for this shift." If Cesar is not upset with him, Bill can

Perception check—a message that reflects your understanding of the meaning of another person's *nonverbal* behavior.

TEST YOURSELF

Perception Checking

Write well-phrased perception checks for each of the following situations:

Franco comes home from the doctor's office with pale face and slumped shoulders. Glancing at you with a forlorn look, he shrugs his shoulders.

You say:

As you return the tennis racket you borrowed from Liam, you smile and say, "Here's your racket." Liam stiffens, grabs the racket, and starts to walk away.

You say:

Natalie dances into the room with a huge grin on her face.

You say:

In the past, your advisor has told you that almost any time would be all right for working out your next term's schedule. When you tell her you'll be in Wednesday at 4 p.m., she pauses, frowns, sighs, and says "Uh-huh" and nods.

You say:

Compare your written responses to the guidelines for effective perception checking discussed earlier. Edit your responses where necessary in order to improve them. Now say them aloud. Do they sound "natural"? If not, revise them until they do.

SKILL	USE	PROCEDURE	EXAMPLE
A statement that expresses the meaning you get from the nonverbal behavior of another.	To clarify the meaning of nonverbal behavior.	1. Watch the behavior of another. 2. Ask yourself: What does that behavior mean to me? 3. Describe the behavior (to yourself or aloud) and put your interpretation of the nonverbal behavior into words to verify your perception.	As Dale frowns while reading Paul's first draft of a memo, Paul says, "From the way you're frowning, I take it that you're not too pleased with the way I phrased the memo."

examine what caused him to misinterpret Cesar's feelings; if Cesar is upset with him, Bill has the opportunity to change the behavior that caused Cesar to be upset.

To see what might happen when we respond without checking the accuracy of our perceptions, suppose that in place of the descriptive perception check Bill were to say, "Why are you so upset with me?" Bill would not be describing his perception; he would be making a judgment based on his perception. Replying as if his perception is "obviously" accurate amounts to mindreading.

Perhaps you are thinking, "Well, I know how to read other people's signals. I can tell perfectly well when another person is upset (happy, angry) with me." And perhaps you are correct—most of the time. But if you do not check out your perception, you are still guessing what the other person is feeling and whether the person's anger or happiness is centered on you. If you reply judgmentally, the other person may well become defensive about the feelings you appear to be challenging. The response is then likely to be something like "Who said I'm upset?" or, more harshly, "What the hell are you talking about?" Such responses are likely to trigger an escalating round of emotional outbursts and complete misunderstanding.

You will want to check your perceptions whenever the accuracy of your understanding is important (1) to your current communication, (2) to the relationship you have with the other person, or (3) to the conclusions you draw about that person. Perception checking is especially important in new relationships or when you haven't talked with someone for a long time.

Summary

Perception is the process of selectively attending to information and assigning meaning to it. Our perceptions are a result of our selection, organization, and interpretation of sensory information. Inaccurate perceptions cause us to see the world not as it is but as we would like it to be.

Self-concept, our self-identity, is the idea or mental image that we have about our skills, our abilities, our knowledge, our competencies, and our personality. Self-esteem is our overall evaluation of our competence and personal worthiness. Self-concepts come from interpretations of self based on our experience and reactions and responses of others. The inaccuracy of a distorted picture of oneself becomes magnified through self-fulfilling prophecies and filtering messages. Our self-concept and self-esteem moderate competing internal messages in our self-talk, influence our perception of others, and influence our personal communication style.

Perception also plays an important role in forming impressions of others. Factors that are likely to influence our social perceptions are physical characteristics and social behaviors, stereotyping, and emotional states. Because research shows that the accuracy of people's perceptions and judgments varies considerably, your communication will be most successful if you do not rely entirely on your impressions to determine how another person feels or what that person is really like. You will improve (or at least better understand) your perceptions of others if you take into account physical characteristics and social behaviors, stereotyping, and emotional states.

You can learn to improve perception if you actively question the accuracy of your perceptions, seek more information to verify perceptions, talk with the people about whom you are forming perceptions, realize that perceptions of people need to change over time, and check perceptions verbally before you react.

WHAT WOULD YOU DO?

A Question of Ethics

Rustown was a small midwest factory town. Over the years the white, middle-class citizens had grown together to form a close-knit community that prided itself on its unity. Corpex, a large out-of-town corporation, which had just bought out the town's major factory, decided to move its headquarters there and to expand the current plant, creating hundreds of new jobs. This expansion meant that the new people coming into the town to manage and work in the factory would spend money and build homes, but also it meant that the composition of the small community would change.

Rustown inhabitants had mixed reactions to this takeover. The owners of land and shops were excited by the increased business that was expected, but many in the community recognized that since most people in town had been born and raised there, the inhabitants of Rustown were pretty much

alike—and they liked it that way. They knew that many of the new factory managers as well as some of the new employees were African and Latin Americans. Rustown had never had a black or Latino family in its community and some of the town's people openly worried about the effects these newcomers would have on their community.

Otis Carr was one of the Corpex managers who had agreed to move to Rustown because of the opportunities that appeared to await him and his family, even though he recognized that as a black man he might experience resentment. At work on the first day, Otis noticed that the workers seemed very leery of him, but by the end of the first week the plant was running smoothly and Otis was feeling the first signs of acceptance. On Monday morning of the next week, Otis accidentally overheard a group of workers talking on their break, trading stereotypes

about African Americans and Latinos and using vulgarities and racist slurs in discussing specific new co-workers.

A bit shaken, Otis returned to his office. He had faced racism before, but this time it was different. This time he had power and the responsibility to make a difference. He wanted to reach his workers for the sake of the company, the town, and other minority group members who would be coming to Rustown. Although he knew he had to do something, he realized that just using his power would get him nowhere. In a sick way he understood their prejudices, but not how to change them. How could he reach his workers?

Devise a plan for Otis. How could he use his own social perceptions of Rustown to address this problem in a way that is within ethical interpersonal communication guidelines? ■

Chapter Resources

Communication Improvement Plan: Perception

Would you like to improve your use of the following aspects of forming and using social perception discussed in this chapter?

> Forming self-concepts
> Developing and maintaining self-esteem
> Presenting self
> Perception checking

Pick one of the above and write a communication improvement plan

Skill: _____

Problem: _____

_____

_____

_____

Goal: _____

_____

_____

_____

Procedure:

1. _____

2. _____

3. _____

Test of Achieving Goal: _____

_____

Key Words

Perception, *p. 32*
Patterns, *p. 34*
Social perception, *p. 35*
Self-esteem, *p. 35*
Self-concept, *p. 35*
Incongruence, *p. 39*
Self-fulfilling prophecies, *p. 39*
Role, *p. 42*
Self-talk, *p. 44*
Uncertainty reduction theory, *p. 48*
Halo effect, *p. 49*
Stereotypes, *p. 50*
Prejudice, *p. 51*
Discrimination, *p. 51*
Racism, ethnocentrism, sexism, ageism, able-ism, *p. 51*

Attributions, *p. 53*
Perception check, *p. 53*

Inter-Act with Media

CINEMA

Ron Howard (Director). (2001). *A Beautiful Mind.* Russell Crowe, Jennifer Connelly, Ed Harris, Christopher Plummer.

Brief Summary: Based on the true story of Nobel Prize winning mathematician, John F. Nash, the film portrays the pain and complexity of Nash's struggle with schizophrenia and his remarkably successful use of his own self-talk and perception-checking approach to overcome the illness and manage his life. The film also examines the effect of the illness on Nash's personal and professional relationships.

Both *Nixon* and *Music of the Heart* also examine similar issues of perception in forming social relationships.

IPC Concepts: Perception, self-talk.

Bob Clark (Director). (1983). *A Christmas Story.* Peter Billingsley, Darren McGavin.

Brief Summary: This film is based on the memoirs of jean Shepherd about growing up in the 1940s and centers on a young boy's quest for the Christmas gift of his dreams, a Red Ryder BB gun. The boy, Ralph, his little brother, and their friends have a series of adventures at school and on the way to and from school. We also see the relationship and parenting approaches of both parents. Of real interest for perception is the scene where mom and dad take Ralph and his brother to the department store to see Santa Claus. Each child travels up a long ramp to Santa's throne, filled with anticipation until face-to-face with Santa, at which time terror at the reality of this huge and strange grownup takes hold. When Ralph reaches Santa, the camera shows the entire experience from Ralph's eyes—a wonderful opportunity to practice empathy and to apply perception theory.

IPC Concepts: perception and empathy.

Blake Edwards (Director). (1982). *Victor/Victoria.* Julie Andrews, James Garner, Robert Preston, Leslie Ann Warren, Alex Karras, and John Rhys-Davies.

Brief Summary: The story is about a gay man (Robert Preston) and a straight woman, (Julie Andrews) who are struggling entertainers in Paris. The man suggests that the woman perform her normal nightclub act as a man pretending to be a woman. The con works so well that she becomes a major celebrity, and the pair attract the attention of an American gangster played by James Garner, his mistress (Leslie Ann Warren), and his attendant (Alex Karras). The resolution is amusing and charming. The film is a brilliant depiction of the role of perception in meeting and evaluating others and how social stereotypes affect our interactions with others and with ourselves. The inner turmoil of James Garner and Alex Karras is effectively portrayed as they respond to their perceptions of Julie Andrews and Robert Preston.

IPC Concepts: Perception, stereotyping, and the impact on relationship development.

THEATER

Alain Boublil, and Claude-Michel Schonberg, lyrics by Herbert Kretzmer. (1985). *Les Miserables.*

Brief Summary: Set during the revolution in France in 1832, this play dramatizes the development of several relationships, and gives us insight into the moral choices that these characters must make. It gives us a glimpse into their inner struggle and the corresponding self-talk. Of special interest is the self-talk of Jean Valjean in the song, "Who Am I?" and Javert's self-talk when he decides to commit suicide.

IPC Concepts: Perception, self-talk, and self-concept by Javert, and the self-talk of Jean Valjean confronted by the wrong of being arrested for his "crime."

LITERATURE

James Baldwin. (1953). *Go Tell It on the Mountain.*

Brief Summary: This is the powerful story of John Grimes and his family on the occasion of his fourteenth birthday. It tells of his conversion and dedication to God, and focuses on the prayers of his mother, Elizabeth, his stepfather, Gabriel, and his aunt, Florence. The novel does a really good job of depicting John's low self-esteem, self-perception as unattractive, and his near obsession with needing to serve the Lord in order to redeem his otherwise worthless life.

IPC Concepts: Perception of self, self-esteem, prayer as a form of self-talk.

ACADEMIC WORK

Joan Borysenko. (1987). *Minding the Body, Mending the Mind.* Boston: Addison-Wesley.

Note: Actually, any book by Joan Borysenko is a good experience.

Brief Summary: Joan Borysenko is one of those rare people who combine the world of medicine, psychology, communication, philosophy, and theology in a clear, practical, and reasonable manner. This book combines her work at Harvard and her personal experiences with some of the best theory on all of the above topics. She offers both clear discussions of the theory, real-life examples of its power, and simple exercises for enacting these ideas. This can be a life-changing book.

IPC Concepts: Self-talk, meditation, breathing, visualization, inner choice making.

Charles V. Roberts & Kittie W. Watson (Eds.). (1989). *Intrapersonal Communication Processes: Original Essays.* New Orleans: Spectra Incorporated, Publishers.

Brief Summary: This compilation of twenty-four essays deals with the nature, characteristics, and approaches to intrapersonal communication. The essays discuss cognitive and psychological approaches, affective and nonconscious processes, and the role of listening in self-talk.

IPC Concepts: Self-talk.

Annie Murphy Paul. (1998, May/June). Where bias begins: The truth about stereotypes. *Psychology Today, 31*(3)52–55, 82.

Brief Summary: A discussion of the psychology of bias and its development that focuses on how stereotypes can develop unconsciously. This is a good discussion of the process of perception and the process of stereotyping.

IPC Concepts: Stereotypes, perception.

WHAT'S ON THE WEB

Perception Web site

http://www.perceptionweb.com/percsup.html

Brief Summary: This online journal deals with perception from a psychological and physiological point of view. It contains journal article abstracts and abstracts of papers presented at various conferences.

IPC Concepts: Perception.

Constructive Love: The Lesson by Thom Rutledge

http://www2.seescape.com/support/lesson.htm

Brief Summary: A really good reinforcer for a discussion on who is in charge of our beliefs, feelings, and actions, this Web site reinforces Ellis' theory of the ABC process in self-talk and emotion.

IPC Concepts: Perception, choice, relationships.

CHAPTER 3

Communicating in

Relationships:

Basic Concepts

After you have read this chapter, you should be able to answer these questions:

- What are the major types of relationships?
- What is a "Johari window"?
- What are effective ways of starting a relationship?
- What are the roles of descriptiveness, openness, tentativeness, and equality in maintaining relationships?
- What are interpersonally effective methods of ending a relationship?
- What is interpersonal needs theory?
- What is exchange theory?

> "Yvonne, wasn't that Pauli that I saw you with again? I thought Lonnie was your man."
>
> "He is. Pauli and I are just friends—we've got a really solid relationship."
>
> "Just friends! Come on, girl, I see you with him a lot. Are you sure he doesn't see it differently?"
>
> "Yeah, I see him a lot because I am really able to talk with him. We're just comfortable with each other. But before you get too worried about his feelings, he and Leona have been an item for months."
>
> "And she doesn't mind you spending time with her man? Are you sure you're not just fooling yourself?"
>
> "Hey, I don't know whether she minds, but Pauli and I just aren't romantically involved—there's no chemistry. Actually, he's more like a brother to me. I tell him my fears and anxieties as well as what's going right with me. And he talks with me about his problems, too. If something happened between us, I'd really miss him."

Relationship—a set of expectations two people have for their behavior based on the pattern of interaction between them.

Interpersonal relationship—a series of interactions between two individuals known to each other.

Good relationship—one in which the interactions are satisfying to and healthy for those involved.

Yvonne is lucky because she has someone she can really talk with—she has a good relationship. The interpersonal skills we will study can help you start, build, and maintain healthy relationships with others. "A **relationship** is a set of expectations two people have for their behavior based on the pattern of interaction between them" (Littlejohn, 2002, p. 234). An **interpersonal relationship** may be defined as "a series of interactions between two individuals known to each other" (Duck & Gilmour, 1981, p. 2). A **good relationship** is one in which the interactions are satisfying to and healthy for those involved.

Good relationships do not just happen, nor do they grow and maintain themselves automatically. In fact, as Canary and Dainton (2002, p. xiii) state, "Most sane people know that relationships require work. That is, partners need to spend time and effort to maintain functional, satisfying relationships. Without such efforts, relationships tend to deteriorate." In this chapter we will explain the nature of relationships, consider two theories of why relationships develop, and then discuss the stages that typically comprise the life cycle of a relationship. Along the way we will present the skills that help create a positive climate for maintaining a relationship.

Types of Relationships

Our relationships vary in their intensity from impersonal to personal (LaFollette, 1996, p. 4). An **impersonal relationship** is one in which a person relates to the other merely because the other fills a role or satisfies an immediate need. In these circumstances, neither party is likely to care who occupies the role or fulfills the need, so long as it is done well. At a restaurant, for instance, Elaine may prefer a particular server, but she will be satisfied if whoever waits on her does it competently. A **personal relationship** is one in which people disclose information to each other and work to meet each other's interpersonal needs. So if Elaine and Juanita enjoy talking with each other and helping each other out, they have a personal relationship.

> **Impersonal relationship**—one in which a person relates to the other merely because the other fills a role or satisfies an immediate need.

> **Personal relationship**—one in which people share large amounts of information with each other and meet each other's interpersonal needs.

We also classify the people with whom we have relationships as acquaintances, friends, and close friends or intimates.

Acquaintances

Acquaintances are people we know by name and talk with when the opportunity arises, but with whom our interactions are limited. Many acquaintance relationships grow out of a particular context. We become acquainted with those who live in our apartment building or dorm or in the house next door, who sit next to us in class, who go to our church or belong to our club. Thus Melinda and Paige, who meet in biology class, may talk with each other about class-related issues, but they make no effort to share personal ideas or to see each other outside of class.

> **Acquaintances**—people we know by name and talk with when the opportunity arises, but with whom our interactions are limited.

Friends

Over time some acquaintances become our friends. **Friends** are people with whom we have negotiated more personal relationships voluntarily (Patterson, Bettini, and Nussbaum, 1993, p. 145). As friendships develop, people move toward interactions that are less role bound. For example, Melinda and Paige, who are acquaintances in biology class and have only talked about class-related subjects, may decide to get together after school one afternoon just to talk. If they find that they enjoy each other's company, they may continue to meet ouside of class and eventually become friends.

> **Friends**—people with whom we have negotiated more personal relationships voluntarily.

Some of our friendships are context bound. Thus, people often refer to their tennis friends, office friends, or neighborhood friends. These context friendships may fade if the context changes. For instance, your friendship with a person at the office may fade if you or your friend take a job with a different company.

What We Look for in Our Friends We tend to choose people as friends who possess qualities or attributes that we believe are desirable. These are likely to include attractiveness, social skills, responsiveness, and similarity (Fehr, 1996, pp. 52–58).

- **Attractiveness.** Physical appearance is important in the development of same- and other-sex friendships. Although the importance of attractiveness wanes as relationships develop, it is especially important in getting people to talk with each other initially.

INTER-ACT WITH

Technology

Record a portion of a movie or TV program where friends are having a conversation. Analyze it on the basis of expectations of friendship, including enjoyment of talking with each other, trust, sharing of personal feelings, high level of commitment, and enduring nature of friendship. Which of these seem evident in the conversation? What other elements were shown in the conversation? Did these seem to contribute to or detract from the relationship? Explain. ■

- **Social skills.** We are likely to form friendships with people whose social skills are well developed. Perception of the presence of social skills seems particularly important in the early stages of relationship development.

- **Responsiveness.** We are drawn to people who respond to us; that is, when someone shows interest in what we do and is concerned for our feelings, we are more likely to want that person as a friend.

- **Similarity.** We are drawn to people whom we perceive as having similar values, attitudes, personalities, cultural backgrounds, social interests, and work interests. The more similarity people have, the more they are attracted to each other.

  Although we are most likely to form friendships with those who are similar, relationships may also develop when there are dissimilarities in personality. The saying "opposites attract" is as accurate as "birds of a feather flock together." Stated theoretically, relationships depend on mutual need fulfillment, so people can be attracted to those who are different from them in order to fulfill their needs. Thus, opposites attract when the differences between the people are seen as complementary (Winstead, Derlega, and Rose, 1997, p. 26). For instance, a very outgoing person and a very shy person, though opposite in personality, may be attracted to each other because they "fit" together—each provides something the other needs.

What We Expect from Our Friends Although people may be drawn to each other for many reasons, a variety of research shows that maintaining a real friendship is marked by a high degree of positiveness, assurance, openness, networking, and task sharing (Dindia, 2000, p. 291; Guerrero and Andersen, 2000, p. 178; Stafford and Canary, 1991).

- **Positiveness.** Friends spend time with each other because they reap positive benefits in doing so. They enjoy each other's company, they enjoy talking with each other, and they enjoy sharing experiences.

- **Assurance.** Friends **trust** each other. They risk putting their well-being in the hands of another because they trust the other not to intentionally harm their interests.

- **Openness.** Friends share personal feelings with each other.

- **Networking.** Friends show a high level of commitment not only to each other but to each other's friends and family. They are likely to sacrifice their time and energy to engage in activities with family and friends of friends.

- **Task sharing.** Friends help each other with work.

Trust—to risk putting your well-being in the hands of another.

Close Friends or Intimates

Close friends or **intimates**—those with whom we share our deepest feelings.

Close friends or **intimates** are those with whom we share our deepest feelings. People may have countless acquaintances and many friends, but they are likely to have only a few truly intimate friends.

Close friends or intimates differ from "regular" friends mostly in degree of commitment, trust, disclosure, and enjoyment in their relationships. For instance, although friends engage in some self-disclosure, they are not likely to share the secrets of their lives; intimate friends, on the other hand, often gain knowledge of the innermost being of their partner. As a result of this increasing amount of disclosure, close friends or intimates increase their investment in the relationship and develop a sense of "we-ness."

Likewise, the degree of intimacy between friends is often characterized by the extent to which one person gives up other relationships in order to devote more time and energy to the primary relationship. Especially when two people are testing the suitability of an enduring relationship as best friends or romantic partners, they spend long periods of time together.

A person's first intimate friendships are likely to be with family members. For instance, small children first rely on their parents, then perhaps on a brother or sister, and ultimately on intimate friendships with people outside the family. But friendships don't develop automatically—they are often a result of exploratory behavior. When people see the possibility of building a friendship with another, they explore to determine the kinds of satisfaction they get from being together.

Intimate relationships may or may not be sexual. In fact research has found that where sexual attraction is strong, premature sexual relations may actually disrupt the development of relational intimacy. While sexual attraction can lead to a healthy intimate relationship, most intimate relationships are platonic. Because intimate relationships are central to our lives, in Chapter 12, we'll describe the theories and research related to intimate relationships.

OBSERVE & ANALYZE
Journal Activity

Types of Relationships

Make a list of the people you have spoken with in the last day or two other than members of your family. First indicate how many of these people were acquaintances, friends, or intimates. Then, for each friend or intimate briefly recount how each of these relationships began. Finally, answer the following two questions: (1) What are the major differences in the relationships between those people you categorized as acquaintances and those you categorized as friends or intimates? (2) What are the qualities that you find most important in your friend and intimate relationships that makes them endure? ■

Disclosure and Feedback Ratios

As people interact in a relationship they choose to disclose or not to disclose personal information and they also choose to give or not to give feedback to each other. If acquaintances begin to disclose and provide feedback to one another their relationship will likely evolve into friendship; if their disclosures and feedback move to even deeper levels, they are likely to become intimates.

A healthy interpersonal relationship is marked by an appropriate balance of **self-disclosure** (sharing biographical data, personal ideas, and feelings that are unknown to the other person) and **feedback** (the verbal and physical responses to people and/or their messages) within the relationship. The **Johari window,** named after its two originators, Jo Luft and Harry Ingham, is a tool for examining the extent of and relationship between disclosure and feedback in the relationship (Luft, 1970). The window represents all of the information about you that can be known. You and your partner each know some (but not all) of this information.

Self-disclosure—sharing biographical data, personal ideas, and feelings that are unknown to the other person.

Feedback—verbal and physical responses to people and/or their messages.

Johari window—a tool for examining the relationship between disclosure and feedback.

	Known to self	Not known to self
Known to others	Open	Blind
Not known to others	Secret	Unknown

Figure 3.1

The Johari Window

The window has four "panes" or quadrants, as shown in Figure 3.1. The first quadrant is called the "open" pane of the window because it represents the information about you that both you and your partner know. It includes information that you have disclosed and the observations about you that your partner has shared with you. It might include mundane information that you share with most people, such as your college major, but it also may include information that you disclose to relatively few people. Similarly it could include simple observations that your partner has made, such as how cute you look when you wrinkle your nose, or more serious feedback you have received from your partner about your interpersonal style. In preparing a Johari window to represent your side of your relationship with a specific person, you would include in the open pane all the items of information about yourself that you would feel free to share with that other person.

The second quadrant is called the "secret" pane. It contains all those things that you know about yourself but that your partner does not yet know about you. This information may run the gamut from where you keep your pencils to your religious practice to deep secrets whose revelation threatens you. To prepare a Johari window to represent your side of your relationship with a specific person, you would include in the secret pane all the items of information that you know about yourself but have not shared with that other person. Secret information is made known through the process of self-disclosure. When you choose to share the information with your partner, the information moves into the open pane of the window. For example, suppose that you had been engaged to be married but on the day of the wedding your fiancé had backed out. You may not want to share this part of your history with casual acquaintances, so it will be in the secret pane of your window in many of your relationships. But when you disclose this fact to a friend, it moves into the open part of your Johari window with this person. As you disclose information, the secret pane of the window becomes smaller and the open pane is enlarged.

The third quadrant is called the "blind" pane. This is the place for information that the other person knows about you, but about which you are unaware. Most people have blind spots—parts of their behavior or the effects of their behavior of which they are unaware. For example, Charley may not know that he snores when he sleeps or that he frowns when he is concentrating. But both of these behaviors are known by someone who has slept in the same room with him or been with him when he attends class lectures. Information moves from the blind area of the window to the open area through feedback from others. If no one has ever told Charley about these behaviors, or if he has refused to believe it when he has been told about them, this information will remain in the blind part of his Johari window. When someone tells him about the behaviors and he accepts the feedback, then the information will move into the open pane of Charley's Johari window with this person. Thus, like disclosure, feedback enlarges the open pane of the Johari window, but in this case it is the blind pane that becomes smaller.

The fourth quadrant is called the "unknown" pane. It contains information about you that you don't know and neither does your partner. Obviously, you cannot develop a list of this information. So how do we know that it exists? Well, because periodically we "discover" it. If, for instance, you have never tried hang gliding, then neither you nor anyone else can really know how you will react at the point of takeoff. You might chicken out or follow through, do it well or crash, love every minute of it or be paralyzed with fear. But until you try it, all of this information is unknown. Once you try it, you gain information about yourself that becomes part of the secret pane, which you can move to the open pane through disclosure. Also once you have tried it, others who observe your flight will have information about your performance that you may not know unless they give you feedback.

As you disclose and receive feedback, the sizes of the various window panes change. These changes reflect the relationships. As the relationship moves from acquaintances to friends to intimates, the open pane of both partners' windows becomes larger, while the secret and hidden parts become smaller.

In Figure 3.2A we see an example of a relationship where there is little disclosure or feedback occurring. This person has not shared much information with the other, and has received little feedback from this partner as well. We would expect to see this pattern in a new relationship or one between casual acquaintances.

Figure 3.2B shows a relationship in which a person is disclosing to a partner, but the partner is providing little feedback. As you can see, the secret pane is smaller, but the hidden pane is unchanged. A window like this indicates that the individual is able to disclose information but the partner is unable or unwilling to give feedback (or, perhaps, that the individual refuses to accept the feedback that is being given). Since part of the way that we learn about who we are comes from the feedback we receive from others, relationships in which one partner does not provide feedback can become very unsatisfying to the other individual.

Figure 3.2C shows a relationship where a partner is good at providing feedback, but where the individual is not disclosing. Since most of us disclose only when we trust our partners, this pattern may be an indication that the individual does not have confidence in the relational partner.

OBSERVE & ANALYZE

Journal Activity

Johari Windows

Working with a friend, each of you should draw a window that represents your perception of your relationship with the other. Then each of you should draw a window that represents what you perceive to be the other's relationship with you. Share the windows. How do they compare? If there are differences in the representations, talk with your friend about them. ■

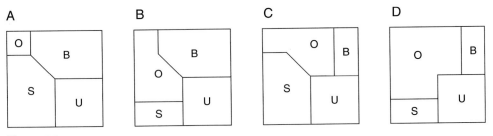

Figure 3.2

Sample Johari windows: (A) low disclosure, low feedback; (B) high disclosure, low feedback; (C) low disclosure, high feedback; (D) high disclosure, high feedback

Figure 3.2D shows a relationship in which the individual has disclosed information and received feedback. So the open pane of the window has enlarged as a result of both processes. Windows that look like this indicate that there is sufficient trust and interest in the relationship that both partners are willing to risk by disclosing and giving feedback.

Obviously, to get a complete "picture" of a relationship each partner's Johari window would need to be examined. A healthy interpersonal relationship is marked by a balance of disclosure and feedback, so that both people are participating.

Communication Patterns During Stages of Relationships

Even though no two relationships develop in exactly the same manner, they tend to move through identifiable stages that follow a "life cycle" that includes beginning and developing, stabilizing, and deteriorating stages (Baxter; 1982, Duck, 1987; Knapp and Vangelisti, 2000; Taylor & Altman, 1987). How quickly a relationship moves through these stages depends on the interpersonal communication between relational partners. "Talking is fundamental to relationships—whether they are starting, getting better, getting worse, or just carrying on" (Duck, 1998, p. 7). In fact, as our Spotlight on Scholars: Steven Duck on Personal Relationships shows, how we talk with one another may be the most important variable in starting and building relationships.

Beginning and Developing Relationships

The communication during the first stage, beginning and building relationships, is focused on getting information about the other person, initiating conversations, keeping conversations flowing, and gradually moving to more intimate conversational topics.

Getting Information about the Other Person Fundamental to beginning and developing a relationship is the need to reduce uncertainty (Berger & Bradac, 1982; Littlejohn, 2002, pp. 243–244). All prospective relationships begin with uncertainty. If we don't know anything about another person, we don't know how to treat that person because we don't know how to predict his or her behavior. As we gather information, we can make decisions about how to react with the other person.

Three strategies can be used to gain information and reduce uncertainty. You use a **passive strategy** when you get information about another by observing the person as he or she interacts with others. By observing others you can often find out how they communicate. You use an **active strategy** when you get information about another by asking people who know the person you are interested in. The most direct way of acquiring information about a person is with an **interactive strategy**—getting information about another by conversing with the person in question.

Passive strategy—getting information about another by observing the person as he or she interacts with others.

Active strategy—getting information about another by asking people who know the person you are interested in.

Interactive strategy—getting information about another by conversing with the person in question.

Steven Duck, Daniel and Amy Starch Research Chair at the Communication Studies Department at the University of Iowa, on

Personal Relationships

What began as a personal curiosity about the friendships he developed as a college student has turned out to be the focus of Steve Duck's lifelong work. He was curious about why some people become close friends, while others remain acquaintances, so he selected this topic for a research term paper assigned in one of his classes. At that time, Duck's hypothesis was that people who have similar attitudes are likely to become attracted to each other and to become friends. Over the years his understanding of how relationships are formed, developed, and maintained has changed considerably. In fact, in Duck's work you can see how scholars develop and test theories only to replace them with more meaningful theories.

Many of Duck's breakthroughs in relationship theory came from his interdisciplinary study in psychology, sociology, family studies, and communication. Duck saw the need to integrate research findings across disciplines as so important that he founded the International Network on Personal Relationships and two international conferences on the subject to promote interdisciplinary scholarship.

While many disciplines have contributed to how he views relationships, Duck believes that his move to the University of Iowa, where he encountered colleagues whose backgrounds were in rhetoric, caused a fundamental shift in his thinking. Based on discussions with these colleagues, who assume that people are connected to one another through language, Duck began to see that conversations and talk were more than the instrument through which relationships were developed.

Duck's early theories were based on the premise that what makes a relationship work is the degree of similarity between the personalities, backgrounds, etc. of the participants. He saw "talk" as simply the channel through which these similarities are uncovered. This model can be seen in the operation of most dating services. Clients with similar profiles are "matched" and come together to talk to each other in order to learn about their similarities. Then presto, the relationship develops. Although people with many similarities often don't develop lasting relationships, this premise dominated the thinking on personal relationships for many years.

In his 1994 article in the *Handbook of Interpersonal Communication,* Duck first proposed a revision to his original premise. He argued that we "do" our relationships in the everyday talk that happens as we interact. "I just don't enjoy talking with him," "I really feel like she listens to me and understands," "We seem to have a lot in common, but we just can't seem to connect," and "We've gotten good at talking things out so that we work through our differences and both feel good about it" are not simple statements about the communication in the relationship—they are statements about relationship itself.

Thus, according to Duck's new model, when two people begin to date, the way their relationship develops most directly depends on how they talk to each other, not simply whether they have similar personalities. If this is so, then from a practical standpoint, it is important to pay attention to how we say things and to how we respond to what others say. So while a dating service may be a convenient way to meet new people with similar interests, whether and what kind of a relationship develops depends on how the two people manage the relationship as they talk.

Duck thinks that it is time for scholars to focus more of their analysis on people's everyday talk in their ordinary conversations, rather than on what he calls the "peaks and valleys," since it is at the heart of understanding how relationships grow, stabilize, and change. For example, while we have studied how people deal with significant conflict, we have paid scant attention to studying how people manage minor conversational annoyances, such as unwanted swearing behavior. In addition, Professor Duck admires recent work on "the dark side of relationships," and has recently published an article on understanding "enemyship."

Duck, who received his Ph.D. from the University of Sheffield, U.K., in 1971, has taught in the United States for seventeen years. He has authored or edited over thirty-five books and hundreds of articles and papers on personal relationships. A prolific scholar, Duck still recognizes the need to refresh his own ideas by engaging in intense study of the work of other scholars. Periodically, professors take a break from the rigors of the classroom, administrative responsibilities, and discovery research and go back into a "learning model" on what is called a sabbatical. In the spring of 2000, Professor Duck spent his sabbatical in the library, reading and thinking about the recent work of other scholars of personal relationships. Refreshed by this intense study period, Duck returned to his classes and his scholarship prepared to continue making contributions to our knowledge of personal relationships. For a list of some of Duck's major publications, see the reference list for this chapter at the end of the book.

Duck's work highlights the importance of integrating insights from a variety of disciplines as we seek to understand and manage our relationships. ∎

While reducing uncertainty is important to people of all cultures, people in some cultures are more likely to rely on passive methods for getting information, while people from other cultures may rely on more active or interactive strategies (Gudykunst & Kim, 1997, p. 309).

Keep in mind that the purpose of acquiring information is to be able to predict the behavior of the potential partner in a relationship. We are interested in whether continued communication is likely to produce positive or negative outcomes for us. So, it isn't just how much a person knows about another person, but how much that person wants to know that is significant (Kellermann & Reynolds, 1990).

Initiating Conversations Regardless of your thoughts, no relationship can begin until you talk with that other person. One of the most stressful times for many people is during an initial interaction with a complete stranger. Many people are so uncomfortable that even if they are seated next to a person whom they find attractive, they are unwilling or afraid to say a word.

In most encounters, what happens in the first few minutes of an initial interaction will have a profound effect on the nature of the relationship that develops. As the old saying goes, you seldom get a second chance to create a first impression. How do you go about talking with a stranger in a way that will make a positive first

No matter how attractive you find another person no relationship can begin until you take the opportunity to talk with the other person. How might the woman in this photo begin a conversation with the man?

impression? Although finding and using "getting to know you" lines is easy for some, many people become tongue-tied when they want to meet someone and, as a result, make a bad first impression. For those of us who find talking with strangers difficult, the following four strategies may be useful. Notice that each of these strategies results in question asking. A cheerful answer to your question followed by a question to you suggests the person is interested in continuing a conversation. A refusal to answer or a curt reply may mean that the person isn't really interested in talking at this time.

1. **Begin by introducing yourself.** "Hi, my name is Gordon. What's yours?"
2. **Refer to the physical context.** "This is awful weather for a game, isn't it?" "I wonder how they are able to keep such a beautiful garden in this climate" or "Darlene and Verne have sure done a lovely job of remodeling this home. Did you ever see it before the renovation?"
3. **Refer to your thoughts or feelings.** "I really like parties, don't you?" "I live on this floor, too—do these steps bother you as much as they do me?" or "Doesn't it seem stuffy in here?"
4. **Refer to another person.** "Marge seems to be an excellent hostess—have you known her long?" or "I don't believe I've had the pleasure of seeing you before—do you work with Evan?"

Small talk—conversation that meets social needs with relatively low amounts of risk.

Idea exchange messages—messages that focus on conveying facts, opinions, and beliefs.

Gossip—talking about people who are not present.

Keeping Conversations Flowing Once two people have begun a conversation, they are likely to engage in **small talk** (conversation that meets social needs with relatively low amounts of risk) characterized by idea exchange and gossip.

Idea exchange messages focus on conveying facts, opinions, and beliefs. Idea exchange is a common type of communication between both new acquaintances and friends. At the office Dan may ask Walt about last night's sports scores, Maria may talk with Louise about new cars, and Pete may discuss an upcoming event with Teresa. Or, on a more serious level, Jan may talk with Gloria about the U.S. role in the Middle East or Dave may seek Bill's views on abortion. Although the discussion of foreign policy and abortion is "deeper" than the discussion about sports or cars, both discussions represent idea exchanges. During early stages of a relationship, this type of communication is important because through it you learn what the other person values and how he or she thinks. Based on this information you can assess how much effort you want to put into developing and sustaining this relationship.

Gossip, talking about other people who are not present, is one of the most common forms of interpersonal communication. On one hand, it's an easy way to talk with people without sharing much information about yourself. Statements such as "Do you know Bill? I hear he has a really great job," "Would you believe that Mary Simmons and Tom Johnson are going together? They never seemed to hit it off too well in the past," and "My sister Eileen is really working hard at losing weight. I saw her the other day, and all she talked about was the diet she's on" are all examples of gossip. Gossip is benign when what is discussed is common knowledge. People do break up, lose their jobs, get in accidents, win prizes, etc. In these circumstances, there's nothing secret—and if the person were there he or she would likely talk about what happened.

This kind of small talk occurs during all phases of a relationship but is used in new relationships because it is safe. You can gossip for a long time with another person without really saying anything about yourself or learning anything about the other person. Also, gossip may be a pleasant way to pass time with people you know but with whom you have no desire or need for a deeper relationship. It also provides a safe way to explore the potential for the relationship to grow since it allows each person to see whether the other reacts similarly to the views expressed about the object of the gossip. This is why conversations at parties are composed largely of gossip.

On the other hand, gossip can be unethical and malicious. If the gossip discloses information that is private or if it is inaccurate, the gossip may damage both the relationship in which it was exchanged and other relationships as well. Perhaps the most malicious kind of gossip is that which is engaged in for purposes of hurting or embarrassing the person who is not present. For instance, saying "Lonnie had an automobile accident—he ran into another car," is a form of gossip, but if it is factual, it is harmless. If a person goes on to say, "And you know it's probably because of what he had to drink—I hear that Lonnie's really been hitting the sauce, lately" the gossip goes far beyond reporting what happened. Gossip quickly turns into rumor, and rumors can destroy a person's life.

Friendships that Bridge Differences By Brenda J. Allen

How do we come to develop relationships with people of different backgrounds? Brenda J. Allen, University of Colorado, describes her interracial friendship with a lesbian woman and how the two overcame sanctions against such a relationship. As you read try to identify the different stages of their relationship to determine how their windows of self-disclosure and feedback changed as the relationship developed.

I expected to like Anna even before I met her. . . . Since that time over six years ago, Anna and I have evolved from colleagues to best friends. From the beginning, Anna seemed to exchange cordial greetings as we passed in the halls. Students liked and respected her and I heard many comments about her excellence in teaching. Because I enjoyed a similar reputation as a teacher, I felt a sort of kinship with Anna. In addition, she dressed with a certain flair that I appreciated because in the public housing development (a.k.a "the projects") where I grew up, we black people took a special pride in how we looked. I admired how Anna, a white woman, knew how to coordinate her clothes and jewelry.

As luck would have it, Anna and I were assigned adjacent desks. As a result of such proximity, I couldn't help but hear how she interacted with her students. I often teased her about her den-mother approach to their problems. She began to do the same with me and we would laugh at ourselves but feel good about our mutual concerns for the students' welfare. Anna and I also found that we had similar ideas about issues, activities, and improvements on our own critical thinking skills in the classroom.

We soon discovered that we had much more in common than our teaching philosophies. We were both baby boomers from the Midwest, only months apart in age. We also came from lower-class families, and religion played a strong role in our childhoods. We were both spiritually grounded and sometimes prayed together. We were both raised to be caring and nurturing. Early in our relationship I began to appreciate the strong sense of reciprocity that I felt with Anna because she often gave to me which I would usually give to others yet rarely receive anything in return.

About a year into our friendship, a major turning point occurred in our relationship. Anna invited me to lunch off campus, and when I met her at the restaurant, she seemed somber. "I have something that I must tell you because our friendship is important to me." She took at deep breath and told me that she was a lesbian. After my initial surprise I thanked her for sharing something so personal and assured her that it would never negatively affect our friendship.

To the contrary, we have grown closer. As a heterosexual I had never before given much thought to sexual orientation of gays, "coming out of the closet." Thanks to Anna, I have become far more sensitive and enlightened. When she first invited me to her home, she showed me the room that had become her bedroom when family members visited because only a few people know that she and her "roommate" were partners. I was amazed by the extent of the masquerade that she felt compelled to perform to maintain a façade of being straight. Anna has since related many stories about the effort that she and gays make to maintain a heterosexual image.

I tend to be a private person with a clear demarcation between my work and my personal life. Nonetheless, after Anna opened up to me about her personal life I began to reciprocate. We now discuss every aspect of our relationships with family, friends, significant others, colleagues, and students. Whenever I find a prospective mate, Anna is usually the first and often only person I will tell. Once the relationship fizzles, she is always there to help me to get back out there in my quest for a significant other. I have often been pleasantly surprised by the similarities of issues that confront us both as we try to develop and maintain positive, intimate relationships.

I have grown comfortable enough with Anna to let her in on the "black" ways of communicating. I find myself calling her "Girl," an affectionate appellation that I normally reserve for African American sisters.

When I moved from a predominately white neighborhood to a racially mixed neighborhood, Anna understood why I felt more at home in my new surroundings. She had felt the same way in settings with a majority of gays and lesbians. We both seem to enjoy a similar sense of validation and contentment that differs from how we

feel at work, where I am the only African American and she is the only lesbian on the faculty.

Anna and I laugh a great deal, often at each other, as well as cry together about personal trials and tribulations and the plight of our world.

Despite our similarities in personal style and background, Anna and I would probably not have become such good friends if she were straight. Because of her sexual orientation she can be empathetic with me in ways that my other white straight friends cannot. Thus, I believe that our marginalized positions in society and academia have been a major factor in forming the center of our friendship.

In regard to the title of this essay, Sapphire was a black

female character in the old radio and television series *Amos 'n' Andy.* She was sassy, verbose, and intensely expressive. Sappho was a Greek poet (circa 600 B.C.) from the isle of Lesbos who wrote about romantic love between women. Each of these characters personifies one aspect of the multifaceted identifies that Anna and I rarely allow others to see. Because we trust and respect one another, we are comfortable being our authentic selves—in all their complexities—with one another. ■

Excerpted from Allen, B. J. (2001). Sapphire and Sappho: Allies in authenticity. In A. Gonzalez, M. Houston, & V. Chen (Eds.), *Our Voices-Essays in Cultural Ethnicity and Communication,* (3rd ed., pp. 179–183). Los Angeles: Roxbury Publishing Company.

Moving to More Intimate Levels   In addition to engaging in small talk, people who are exploring moving to more intimate levels will also begin to talk about more serious ideas, to share their feelings about important matters, and to use affectionate communication. Through the sharing of feelings and the process of self-disclosure you come to know and to understand another person. When people find that they get satisfaction out of being together and are able to share ideas and feelings, their friendship grows.

Particularly important to the development of intimate relationships is using affectionate communication (Floyd & Morman, 1998, p. 157). Affectionate communication includes such nonverbal behaviors as holding hands, putting an arm around a shoulder, sitting close to each other, or looking into each other's eyes. In relationships that have romantic overtones, it might include hugging each other or kissing. Affectionate communication also includes saying "I enjoy being with you," "This relationship is really important to me," "I like you very much," and "You're a real friend."

People who are increasing the intimacy of their relationship begin to share feelings and disclose more personal information. At this stage they are likely to seek each other out for help with a problem and talk for hours, sharing both the joys and the sorrows of their lives. In Chapter 9, Sharing Personal Information, we will discuss in some detail self-disclosure, describing feelings, and giving personal feedback.

Although the "getting to know you stage" may go quite smoothly with people who are similar to you, the process becomes more difficult when you try to move a relationship with someone different from you to a deeper level. In the Diverse Voices selection that appears on pages 73 and 74, Brenda Allen describes the process that resulted in her developing a deep intimate friendship with a person who differed from her in many ways. Perhaps as a result of reading this selection you will feel more comfortable in making the effort to get to know people from whom you differ.

Communication in Stabilizing Relationships

People can have satisfactory relationships as acquaintances, as friends, or as intimates. When relational partners are both satisfied with the level of their relationship, they begin to stabilize the relationship at that level. **Stabilization** occurs when each person in a relationship is satisfied with what he or she is receiving from the relationship. Stability is maintained if both parties help create a **positive communication climate** that encourages the mutually satisfying discussion of ideas. **Defensiveness** is a negative feeling or behavior that results when a person feels threatened. Positive climates are characterized by messages that are descriptive rather than evaluative, open rather than closed (hiding feelings), tentative rather than dogmatic (leaving no room for discussion), and equal rather than superior.

Speaking Descriptively Speaking **descriptively** is stating what you see or hear in objective language devoid of evaluation and judgment. What's wrong with evaluations and judgment? They are likely to make other people believe that you are attacking them. So they become defensive. When people are defensive they feel threatened and are motivated to strike back.

Let's consider an example. After a team meeting to consider how to change the workflow, Juan asks Maria "Why didn't they pay any attention to my idea?"

Maria: *"Juan, your idea was similar to the one we talked about a few weeks ago."*

Maria: *"Juan, that was a stupid idea when we talked about it last week, and everyone knew it."*

The first reply is descriptive. It presents information without a judgment. Juan might disagree, but not without the presence of strong counterinformation. The second reply contains the highly charged word "stupid." Although Maria doesn't call Juan stupid directly, he is likely to feel defensive.

Most of us find speaking descriptively difficult. Oftentimes we base our remarks on our first impression, which involves judgment. Consider each of the following ways a coach might respond to a situation:

The coach pulls Arnold from the basketball game and says to him,

"Keep up show-off play like that and you'll be on the bench permanently."

Or alternatively, the coach says, *"Arnold, you're not following the plans. The last two times you had the ball, you had a chance to pass to an open man—in both cases,*

Stabilization—when each person in a relationship is satisfied with what he or she is receiving from the relationship.

Positive communication climate—one that encourages the mutually satisfying discussion of ideas.

Defensiveness—a negative feeling or behavior that results when a person feels threatened.

Speaking descriptively—stating what you see or hear in objective language devoid of evaluation and judgment.

you took off-balance shots where you had little chance for success. If you continue to play as if you were alone, I'll put you on the bench for the rest of the game."

In the first case, while Arnold may recognize that he made some offensive or defensive mistakes, the phrase "show-off play" is perjorative and may make Arnold defensive. The second statement, however, identifies Arnold's specific behavior and gives the consequences for repeating the behavior. Arnold knows that it is his behavior that is troubling the coach, and that there are negative consequences for continuing the behavior.

Speaking descriptively encompasses two skills: (1) describing behavior ("Did you know your eyes sparkle when you're happy?" or "Are you aware how much you increase the volume of your voice when you show me the mistakes that I made?") and (2) describing feelings ("When you look at me like that, I feel warm inside" or "When you use that tone of voice, I get very defensive"). More detailed discussion of describing feelings and describing behavior will be presented in Chapter 9.

Speaking Openly Speaking **openly** is honestly sharing thoughts and feelings. Stable relationships exist in a climate where both people are candid. Suppose Shelby's friend had helped her with her writing. If there is a positive communication climate, Shelby would feel comfortable saying, "Thank you for helping me with the report—your editing really made the report clearer."

We are uncomfortable openly expressing thoughts and feelings when we fear they will be intrusive or may be misinterpreted or rejected. For instance, suppose that Shelby has been wanting to find out whether Brent, a known procrastinator, has followed through and scheduled a band for the company's holiday party. She may be reluctant to ask him directly, so she might take an indirect approach, saying, "Brent, I appreciate your willingness to take the time to schedule a band for the company's holiday party" and hope that in his response he will volunteer what he has done. But Brent, not understanding Shelby's hidden agenda, might simply reply, "Thanks Shelby." If Shelby continues using indirect probes Brent may begin to wonder about her real motive. And he may become offended when he discovers what she really wanted. If she wants to maintain a positive communication climate, Shelby should be direct. She might ask, "Brent, have you been able to schedule a band for the company's holiday party yet?"

Communication between people who are trying to build a good relationship works best when the people involved understand what is going on in their conversations. When people aren't open about their reasons for talking, they risk erecting communication barriers.

Speaking Tentatively Speaking **tentatively** means phrasing ideas and opinions in a way that acknowledges that what you are saying could be inaccurate or there may be other ways to see things. Consider the wording and the "sound" of each of the following pairs:

"If I remember correctly, Dalton was the sales leader last month."
"I'm sure that Dalton had the most sales last month."

Speaking openly—honestly sharing thoughts and feelings.

Speaking tentatively—phrasing ideas and opinions in a way that acknowledges that what you are saying could be inaccurate or there may be other ways to see things.

"I think you might consider talking with Glenna before doing anything on this project."

"You must talk with Glenna before doing anything on this project."

What differences did you notice? The first sentence of each pair is stated tentatively; the second asserts an opinion. Why are the first sentences more likely to result in better interpersonal communication? First, the tentative phrasings are less likely to antagonize. Second, they acknowledge that the speaker's ideas may be inaccurate or incorrect. "I'm sure that" leaves no room for possible error; "If I remember correctly" not only leaves room for error but also shows that it is the speaker's recollection and not a statement of universal certainty.

Speaking tentatively may seem wishy-washy, and if carried to extremes, it can be. But there is a world of difference between stating what you think to be true and

Who is the boss? Or are these two people co-workers? What led you to this conclusion?

phrasing your views in a way that is likely to arouse hostility. Speaking tentatively nurtures a positive communication climate by acknowledging the possibility for differences in perspectives.

Speaking to Others as Equals Relationships thrive in climates where the people perceive themselves to be peers rather than in climates characterized by feelings of inferiority and superiority. **Speaking equally** means phrasing messages that are plain, natural, and down to earth and convey respect for the other person. When messages are condescending and patronizing they create feelings of inferiority that can lead to anger, resentment, and defensiveness. Effective communicators can speak equally even in relationships where they have greater knowledge, power, or authority.

For instance, in a work setting a boss has authority over a secretary. But a boss who wants to maintain a positive communication climate will frame messages that acknowledge that the secretary is also a competent adult. So, instead of saying, "Bethany, get on this letter right away—I want it on my desk in twenty minutes," the boss could say, "Bethany, I got behind on framing this letter, and it really should be in the 3:00 mail. Do you think you could get it typed by 2:30 for me?" Even though the person is "the boss," the second phrasing respects the secretary by requesting rather than demanding.

You may know more about a subject than your partner, but you can form messages that convey your knowledge without seeming arrogant. In addition to choos-

Speaking equally–phrasing messages that are plain, natural, and down to earth and convey respect for the other person.

TEST YOURSELF

Descriptive, Open, Tentative, Equal

Label the following statements as E (evaluative), C (closed), D (dogmatic), or S (superior). In each case, rephrase the statement so that it is descriptive, tentative, or equal. The first one is completed for you. When you are done, share your revisions with other members of the class. ■

_D_ 1. "Shana—turn that off! No one can study with the radio on!"
Suggested rephrasing: "Shana—I'd suggest turning the radio down or off. You may find that you can study better without the distraction."

____2. "Did you ever hear of such a tacky idea as having a formal wedding and using paper plates?"

____3. "That advertising program will never sell."

____4. "Oh Jack—you're so funny wearing plaids with stripes. Well, I guess that's a man for you!"

____5. "Paul—we've seen that Charlie has difficulty making sound decisions."

____6. Hoping Gloria might volunteer, Ed says, "Gloria, I wonder if you know someone who could take charge."

Answers 2. E 3. D 4. S 5. D 6. C

ing language that conveys equality, we must also be conscious of the effects that our tone of voice and facial expressions have on the message. As we will see in Chapter 5, our nonverbal communication can totally negate the meaning of the words we use.

Relationship Disintegration

Over time a relationship may become less satisfying to one or both relational partners. When this happens the partner or partners will change the relationship so that it is less intimate or may terminate the relationship altogether. If the partners agree to reduce the level of disclosure and feedback, intimate relationships may devolve to friendships, and friendships to acquaintances. The relationship may stabilize at the new level, or may continue to deteriorate until the partners end it. The communication in deteriorating relationships is marked by three stages: the recognition of dissatisfaction, the process of disengaging, and ending.

Recognition of Dissatisfaction The first signs that a relationship is becoming unstable are subtle indications of dissatisfaction. When one person begins to lose interest in the opinions and feelings of the other, the orientation of that person changes from *we* to *I.* Subjects that once yielded free and open discussion become off limits or sources of conflict. As the relationship begins to be characterized by an increase in "touchy" subjects and more unresolved conflicts, partners become more defensive and less willing to foster a positive communication climate.

Why does this happen? For a variety of reasons. Sometimes it happens because people rushed into a more advanced relationship than they could really sustain. In romantic relationships it's common for people who are desiring long-term intimacy to rush the process. For instance, Germaine and Leroy meet and find that they both enjoy rap music and dancing. As they develop the relationship, they believe they have discovered other similarities that make them "just right" for each other. Within a short time they're going together, and they're sure that they'll be spending their lifetime together.

Before long, however, each notices things about the other that are annoying. For instance, Germaine really likes to be around lots of people and constantly arranges for them to attend parties. Leroy, on the other hand, really likes to be alone with Germaine. Even when they go where others congregate, he likes to sit with Germaine alone. Over time they discover that they aren't really socially compatible. As more of these differences are discovered, they reevaluate their compatibility. If they are unable or unwilling to confront these differences and reach a mutually satisfying solution, they will begin to drift apart.

OBSERVE & ANALYZE

Journal Activity

Positive and Negative Climates

Think of two recent interactions you have had. Choose one that was characterized by a positive communication climate and one that was characterized by a negative climate. Recall as best you can some of the specific conversation dialogue from each interaction. Write this down like a script. Now, analyze each script. Count specific instances of being descriptive and evaluative. Recall whether hidden agendas were evidenced. Count instances of provisional wordings and of dogmatic wordings. Look for instances where equality of interactants was present and instances where one person spoke in a way that conveyed an attitude of superiority. Discuss your results. How much did using or failing to use the four skills presented in this section contribute to the climate you experienced? ■

"If you really cared about me, you would dump me."

Often dissatisfaction occurs over time as people change. For instance, Leroy says, "Germaine, you always used to enjoy going to games with me. Early on most of our social life was spent attending football and basketball games." Germaine replies, "That's right. I used to really enjoy that, but I don't anymore. I wasn't fooling you—I've changed." Or Germaine says, "Leroy, you always used to enjoy going on vacations with my family." Leroy replies, "That's right. I used to really enjoy that, but I don't anymore."

Disengaging As deterioration progresses, people begin to drift apart. Their communication changes from deep sharing of ideas and feelings to small talk and other "safe" communication to no significant communication at all. It may seem strange that people who had so much to share can find themselves with nothing to talk about. But in this stage people don't see the need for an effort to build or maintain the relationship. Not only are they no longer interested in exchanging significant ideas, they may begin to avoid each other altogether, seeking out other people with whom to share interests and activities. Hostility need not be present; rather, this stage is likely to be marked by *indifference*.

There are long-time married couples whose relationship has deteriorated over the years. Why would anyone want to be a part of such a relationship? Some people maintain such a relationship "for the children." Others maintain such a relationship because it is economically advantageous, and still others because of deeply held religious convictions. In other words, the relationship continues to serve the needs of the individuals even though it does not appear to meet their interpersonal needs for intimacy. Exchange theory, which is discussed later in this chapter, helps us to understand how people begin, maintain, or end relationships.

Ending When a relationship can't be stabilized at a different level, it will end. A relationship has ended when the people no longer interact with each other. As Cupach and Metts (1986) show, people give many reasons for terminating relationships, including poor communication, lack of fulfillment, differing lifestyles, interests, rejection, outside interference, absence of rewards, and boredom.

Unfortunately, when people decide to end a relationship, they sometimes look for reasons to blame each other rather than to finding equitable ways of bringing the relationship to an acceptable conclusion. When this happens, other relationships are usually affected. According to Leslie Baxter (1982), in the termination stage people are likely to use strategies of manipulation, withdrawal/avoidance, and only occasionally to do so with positive tone.

Manipulation strategies of termination (put the blame on Mame) involve intentionally presenting evidence of a serious breach of faith, then leaving it to the other party to take direct action about the situation. These strategies are manipulative because those who employ them are afraid to take responsibility for their actions. Instead, they feel a need to make themselves the "hurt" party. For instance,

Manipulation strategies of termination—intentionally presenting evidence of a serious breach of faith, then leaving it to the other party to take direct action about the situation.

suppose Paul wants to terminate his marriage but does not want to take responsibility for suggesting the break. Over a period of months he sees to it that his wife will hear of his affair with another woman; he purposely sees to it that his shirts show lipstick stains and smell of perfume scents that are not his wife's. At some point his wife may then "kick him out of the house." This is an interpersonally ineffective strategy because it is dishonest.

Withdrawal/avoidance strategies of termination (what you don't know can't hurt you) use indirect tactics to achieve the goal of termination. For instance, suppose Judy has difficulty with her parents, especially her mother, who continues to try to direct Judy's life even though Judy is twenty-five years old and a successful professional. In order to end this troublesome relationship (you can't very well divorce your parents), Judy takes a job in a different state where she avoids seeing her parents (mother) except once a year. Although withdrawal/avoidance provides a solution to interpersonal problems, it doesn't really deal with the issues that caused the interpersonal difficulty.

Positive tone strategies of termination (I/we've benefited, but it's time to move on) use direct positive communication methods that respect the other. Notice how the person in the following example terminates a relationship in an open and honest way that is likely to preserve respect for both parties: "Geoff, we've been going out together for a long time. And I think we've both enjoyed our relationship. But as much as I treasure our friendship, I've come to realize that I no longer have romantic feelings for you. Although this is hard, I respect you, and I wanted to be up front about my feelings. I hope that we'll be able to continue our friendship."

Journal Activity

Life Cycle of Relationships

1. Identify five people you consider to be your friends. In what kind of context did you first meet? What attracted you to them? What aspects of attraction proved to be the most important as the relationships developed?

2. Identify five people you consider to be acquaintances. List the ways in which communication with your acquaintances differs from communication with your friends.

3. Consider a recent relationship that has deteriorated. When did you notice that deterioration was taking place? What kinds of communication behavior marked the stages of deterioration? ▪

Withdrawal/avoidance strategies of termination—use of indirect methods to achieve the goal of termination.

Positive tone strategies of termination—use of direct positive communication methods that respect others.

Theoretical Perspectives on Relationships

What determines whether or not we will try to build a lasting relationship with another person? Why do some relationships never move beyond a certain level or begin to deteriorate? Two theories, interpersonal needs theory and exchange theory, offer insights that help us to answer these questions.

Interpersonal Needs Theory

Relationships, like communication itself, exist in part because they satisfy basic human needs. **Interpersonal needs theory** proposes that whether or not a relationship is started, built, or maintained depends on how well each person meets the interpersonal needs of the other. Psychologist William Schutz (1966, pp. 18–20) has identified three basic interpersonal needs that all of us have: affection, inclusion, and control.

Interpersonal needs theory—whether or not a relationship is started, built, or maintained depends on how well each person meets the interpersonal needs of the other.

Affection need—a desire to express and to receive love.

Inclusion need—a desire to be in the company of other people.

Control need—a desire to influence the events and people around us.

The need for **affection** reflects a desire to express and to receive love. The people you know probably run the gamut of showing and expressing affection both verbally and nonverbally. At one end of the spectrum are the "underpersonal" individuals—those who avoid close ties, seldom show strong feelings toward others, and shy away from people who show or want to show affection. At the other end of the spectrum are the "overpersonal" individuals—those who thrive on establishing "close" relationships with everyone. They think of all others as intimates, immediately confide in persons they have met, and want everyone to consider them close friends. Somewhere in between these two extremes are "personal" people—those who can express and receive affection easily and who derive pleasure from many kinds of relationships with others.

The need for **inclusion** reflects a desire to be in the company of other people. According to Schutz, everyone has a need to be social. Yet people differ in the amount of interaction with others that will satisfy this need. At one extreme are "undersocial" persons—those who usually want to be left alone. Occasionally, they seek company or enjoy being included with others if specifically invited, but they do not require a great deal of social interaction to feel satisfied. At the other extreme are "oversocial" persons—those who need constant companionship and feel tense when they must be alone. If a party is happening, they must be there; if there is no party, they start one. Their doors are always open—everyone is welcome, and they expect others to welcome them. Of course, most of us do not belong to either of these extreme types. Rather, we are sometimes comfortable being alone and at other times need and enjoy interacting with others.

The need for **control** reflects a desire to influence the events and people around us. As with the other two interpersonal needs, people vary in how much control they require. At one extreme are persons who need no control, who seem to shun responsibility and do not want to be in charge of anything. The "abdicrats," as Schutz calls them, are extremely submissive and are unlikely to make decisions or accept responsibility. At the other extreme are persons who like to be—indeed, who feel they must be—in charge. Such "autocrats" need to dominate others at all times and become anxious if they cannot. They usurp responsibility from those who may have the authority to control a situation, and they try to determine every decision. Again, most people fall somewhere between these two extremes. These "democrats" need to lead at certain times, but at other times they are content to follow the lead of others. Democrats can stand behind their ideas, but they also can be comfortable submitting to others, at least some of the time.

How can this analysis help us understand communication in relationships? Relationships develop and are sustained in part because the partners choose to meet each other's interpersonal needs. This can be difficult in relationships where individuals have incompatible needs. Through verbal and nonverbal communication behavior, we display cues that reveal the level of our immediate interpersonal needs. As you interact with others, you can detect whether their needs for affection, inclusion, and control seem compatible with yours. Suppose that Emily and Dan have been seeing each other regularly and both see their relationship as close. If in response to Dan's attempt to put his arm around Emily while they are watching television, Emily slightly stiffens, it might suggest that Emily doesn't have quite the same need for affection as Dan. It should be emphasized that people's needs do differ; moreover, people's needs change over time. When other people's needs at any given time differ significantly from ours and we fail to understand that, we can misunderstand what's going wrong in our relationships.

Schutz's theory of interpersonal needs is useful because it helps explain a great deal of interpersonal behavior (Trenholm, 1991, p. 191). In addition, research on this model has been generally supportive of its major themes (Shaw, 1981, pp. 228–231). Interpersonal needs theory does not, however, explain how people adjust to one another in their ongoing relationships. The next theory we discuss will help us develop this understanding.

Exchange Theory

Another way of analyzing our relationships is on the basis of exchange ratios. **Exchange theory,** originated by John W. Thibaut and Harold H. Kelley, explains that relationships can be understood in terms of the exchange of rewards and costs that takes place during the individuals' interaction (Thibaut & Kelley, 1986, pp. 9–30). **Rewards** are outcomes that are valued by a person. Some common rewards are good feelings, prestige, economic gain, and fulfillment of emotional needs. **Costs** are outcomes that a person does not wish to incur and include time, energy, and anxiety. For instance, Sharon may be eager to spend time talking with Jan if she anticipates feeling good as a result; she may be reluctant to spend that time if she expects to be depressed at the end of the conversation.

According to Thibaut and Kelley, people seek interaction situations in which their behaviors will yield an outcome of high reward and low cost. For example, if Jill runs into Sarah on campus, Jill has several communication options: She can ignore Sarah, she can smile, she can say "hi" in passing, or she can try to start a conversation. What Jill does will depend in part on her cost/reward analysis of the outcome of the interaction. For instance, if Jill had been thinking about calling Sarah to arrange a game of tennis, she will probably take the time now to seek that outcome; she will be willing to pay the cost, in time and energy, in hopes of receiving a suitable reward, a tennis date. If Jill and Sarah do talk, the interchange will continue until one or both realize that the cost/reward ratio is falling below the satisfactory level. For Jill, this point might be reached once a tennis game is set. For Sarah, it might be reached when she perceives Jill's current lack of interest in other topics of conversation.

This analysis can be extended from single interactions to relationships. If, over an extended period, a person's net rewards (reward minus cost) in a relationship fall below a certain level, that person will come to view the relationship itself as unsatisfactory or unpleasant. But if the net rewards are higher than the level viewed as satisfactory, the person will regard the relationship or interaction as pleasant and satisfying.

Thibaut and Kelley suggest that the most desirable ratio between cost and reward varies from person to person and within one person from time to time.

Exchange theory—says that relationships can be understood in terms of the exchange of rewards and costs that takes place during the individuals' interaction.

Rewards—outcomes that are valued by a person.

Costs—outcomes that a person does not wish to incur.

One reason people differ in their assessments of costs and rewards is that they have different definitions of what is satisfying. If people have a number of relationships they perceive as giving them a good cost/reward ratio, they will set a high satisfaction level and will probably not be satisfied with low-outcome relationships. By contrast, people who have few positive interactions will be satisfied with relationships and interactions that people who enjoy high-outcome relationships would find unattractive. For instance, Calvin may continue to go out with Erica even if she treats him very poorly because based on experiences he has in his other relationships, the rewards he gets from the relationship are on par.

The ratio of costs and rewards determines how attractive or unattractive a relationship or an interaction is to the individuals involved, but it does not indicate how long the relationship or interaction will last. Although it seems logical that people will terminate a relationship or an interaction in which costs exceed rewards, circumstances sometimes dictate that people stay in a relationship that is plainly unsatisfactory.

Thibaut and Kelley's explanation for such a situation involves what they call the **comparison-level of alternatives,** other choices a person perceives as being available that affect the decision of whether to continue in a relationship. A person who feels dissatisfied will tend to leave a relationship or interaction if there is a realistic alternative that seems to promise a higher level of satisfaction. But if there are no such alternatives, the person may choose to stay in the situation because, unsatisfactory though it is, it is the best the person believes can be attained at that time. Thus, if Joan has four or five men she gets along well with, she is less likely

Comparison-level of alternatives—other choices a person perceives as being available that affect the decision of whether to continue in a relationship.

What costs or rewards may be accruing to each person in this photo?

to put up with Charley, who irritates her. If, however, Joan believes that Charley is the only man who can provide the companionship she is seeking, she will be more inclined to tolerate his irritating habits.

Like Schutz's interpersonal needs theory, Thibaut and Kelley's exchange theory helps illuminate important aspects of relationship development. Yet critics of this theory point out an important limitation. Exchange theory suggests that people consciously and deliberately weigh the costs and rewards associated with any relationship or interaction. That is, people rationally choose to continue or terminate relationships. Thus, the theory assumes that people behave rationally from an economic standpoint: They seek out relationships that benefit them and avoid those that are costly (Trenholm, 1991, p. 72). In fact, although people may behave rationally in most situations, rational models such as Thibaut and Kelley's cannot

WHAT WOULD YOU DO?

A Question *of* Ethics

Sally and Ed had been seeing each other for over three years when Ed moved 150 miles away to attend college. When he left, they promised to continue to see each other and agreed that should either of them want to start seeing someone else, they would tell the other person before doing so. During the first five months that he was away, the two talked on the phone twice a week and Ed came home every other weekend.

During this time, Sally became friendly with Jamie, a co-worker at the child care center on the campus of the local junior college where she was also a part-time student. On several occasions they had dinner together before their night class, usually at Jamie's request, and on a couple of the weekends that Ed hadn't come home they had gone to a movie together. As time went on, it became apparent to Sally that Jamie's interest in her was going beyond the point of just being friends. Since she didn't want to risk losing his companionship, Sally had never mentioned Ed. One night during dinner, Jamie brought up the subject of past rela-

tionships, suggesting that he had not been committed to anyone since the middle of high school. When he asked about her Sally seemed momentarily distracted and then abruptly changed the subject. Confused, Jamie let the matter drop.

On Friday of that week, just as Sally and Jamie were about to leave work and head for a movie, the door swung open and in walked Ed. Sally hadn't been expecting him, but she took one look at him, broke into a big smile and ran over and gave him a warm embrace and welcoming kiss. Jamie was shocked and disappointed. Too absorbed with her own excitement, Sally didn't even notice Jamie's discomfort. She quickly introduced Ed to him and then casually said to Jamie, "See you Monday!" and left with Ed.

Over the weekend, Ed confessed that he wanted to end their relationship. He had gone out with a woman who lived down the hall from him in his dorm a couple times and saw the relationship blossoming. Sally was outraged. She accused him of acting dishonestly by violating their agreement about

seeing other people and told him that he had used her until he was secure at college. Their conversation continued to go downhill and eventually Ed left.

On Monday, Sally was looking forward to seeing Jamie because she really needed a friend she could talk with. When she saw Jamie he was very aloof and curt. She asked him if he wanted to get a bite to eat before class and was genuinely surprised when he answered with an abrupt "no." As Sally ate alone she pondered her behavior and wondered if and how she could ever rectify her relationship with Jamie.

1. Sort out the ethical issues in this case. Identify where Sally's, Ed's, and Jamie's behaviors would be considered (1) ethical and (2) unethical.

2. Using guidelines from this chapter, role-play different key moments in the above scenario, changing them in order to improve the communication ethics and outcome of the situation. ■

always explain complex human behavior. Nevertheless, it can be useful to examine your relationships from a cost/reward perspective. Especially if the relationship is stagnating, you may recognize areas where costs are greater than rewards, either for you or for the other person. If so, you may be able to change some aspects of the relationship before it deteriorates completely.

You may discover that it is fruitful to use both of these theories. What you (or your partner) count as "costs" and "rewards" may depend significantly on what your particular needs are. If your needs differ, you may misunderstand the other person's perceptions of rewards and costs. Looking at relationships in this way might help resolve misunderstandings and make you less defensive. That is, if you understand the other person's needs and can take his or her perceived costs and rewards into account, you may understand the situation better and in a way that is less destructive to your own self-esteem.

Summary

One of the main purposes of interpersonal communication is developing and maintaining relationships. A good relationship is one in which the interactions are satisfying to and healthy for those involved.

People have three types of relationships. Acquaintances are people we know by name and talk with, but with whom our interactions are limited in quality and quantity. Friends are people we spend time with voluntarily. We choose friends on the basis of attractiveness, social skills, responsiveness, and similarity; we expect positiveness, assurance, openness, networking, and task sharing from our friends. Close or intimate friendships are those in which we share our deepest feelings, spend great amounts of time together, and mark the relationship in some special way. People can examine the balance in their relationships by drawing a Johari window to see whether both parties are sharing information in ways that help the relationship to grow.

Relationships go through a life cycle that includes building and developing, stabilizing, and ending. In the starting or building stage people are attracted to each other, strike up a conversation, keep conversations going, and move to more intimate levels. People nurture good relationships by using messages that show descriptiveness, openness, tentativeness, and equality. Many of our relationships end. We may terminate them in interpersonally sound ways or in ways that destroy our chances for ever continuing the relationship on any meaningful level.

Two theories are especially useful for explaining the dynamics of relationships. Schutz sees relationships in terms of their ability to meet the interpersonal needs of affection, inclusion, and control. Thibaut and Kelley see relationships as exchanges: People evaluate relationships through a cost/reward analysis, weighing the energy, time, and money invested against the satisfaction gained.

Chapter Resources

Communication Improvement Plan: Relationships

Do you have a relationship that you would like to change? Do you want to build, stabilize, or end the relationship? Using information in this chapter write a communication plan to accomplish your goal.

Skill: _____

Problem: _____

_____

_____

_____

Goal: _____

_____

_____

_____

Procedure:

1. _____

2. _____

3. _____

Test of Achieving Goal: _____

Key Words

Relationship, *p. 62*
Interpersonal relationship, *p. 62*
Good relationship, *p. 62*
Impersonal relationship, *p. 63*
Personal relationship, *p. 63*
Acquaintances, *p. 63*
Friends, *p. 63*
Trust, *p. 64*
Close friends or intimates, *p. 64*
Self-disclosure, *p. 65*
Feedback, *p. 65*
Johari window, *p. 65*
Passive strategy, *p. 68*
Active strategy, *p. 68*
Interactive strategy, *p. 68*
Small talk, *p. 72*
Idea exchange messages, *p. 72*
Gossip, *p. 72*
Stabilization, *p. 75*
Positive communication climate, *p. 75*

Defensiveness, *p. 75*
Speaking descriptively, *p. 75*
Speaking openly, *p. 76*
Speaking tentatively, *p. 76*
Speaking equally, *p. 78*
Manipulation strategies of termination, *p. 80*
Withdrawal/avoidance strategies of termination, *p. 80*
Positive tone strategies of termination, *p. 81*
Interpersonal needs theory, *p. 81*
Affection need, *p. 81*
Inclusion need, *p. 82*
Control need, *p. 82*
Exchange theory, *p. 83*
Rewards, *p. 83*
Costs, *p. 83*
Comparison-level of alternatives, *p. 84*

Inter-Act with Media

CINEMA

Gus Van Sant (Director). (2000). *Finding Forrester.* Sean Connery, Rob Brown, F. Murray Abraham, Anna Paquin, Busta Rhymes.

Brief Summary: This story about an aging, reclusive writer and a brilliant, inner city, high school student covers the gamut of basic relational elements. These two people must build their own relationship, while having their overall relational patterns affected at the same time. They slowly increase self-disclosure. They develop conflict management skills. Ultimately, the story reaches a climax dealing with communication ethics.

IPC Concepts: Relationships, self-disclosure, conflict management, ethics.

Jon Avnet (Director). (1991). *Fried Green Tomatoes.* Kathy Bates, Jessica Tandy, Mary Stuart Masterson, Mary-Louise Parker, Cicely Tyson, Chris O'Donnell, Stan Shaw.

Brief Summary: An excellent adaptation of Fannie Flagg's novel, the film does a brilliant job of introducing the viewer to diversity issues as it takes us through a story-within-a-story. We follow a young woman in Alabama, Evelyn (Kathy Bates), and her troubles relating to herself and to her husband. In a nursing home, Evelyn meets an elderly lady, Mrs. Threadgoode, who serves as her mentor through her telling the story of her life and the history of the Whistle Stop Café in her home-town during the 1920s. The film rotates between 1986 and the 1930s, as it relates the past and present. In so doing, it covers issues in the relationships of the major characters, how Idgie, in particular, becomes a caring, nurturing rebel; how Southern racism touches the lives of everyone in Whistle Stop; and how the people of this community work together in order to help each other make it through the Great Depression.

IPC Concepts: Relationships, turning points, trust, disclosure, diversity.

Stuart Gordon (Director). (1998). *The Wonderful Ice Cream Suit.* Joe Montegna, Esai Morales, Edward James Olmos, Clifton Collins, Jr., Liz Torres, Gregory Sierra, Sid Caesar, Howard Morris.

Brief Summary: *The Wonderful Ice Cream Suit* tells the story of five young men: Gomez (Montegna), the fast-talking schemer; Vamenos (Olmos), the tramp; Martinez (Collins, Jr.), the innocent;

Villanazul (Sierra), the intellectual; and Dominguez (Morales), the romantic. Gomez gathers the four other men, all about the same size, and they all chip in $20 to purchase and share a beautiful white suit. It does not take long for the five men to discover that the wearer of the suit has his wishes come true. The adventures they share change their lives in hilarious and meaningful ways, and through the gift of sharing the five men become great friends.

IPC Concepts: Relationships, culture, identification, self, face.

THEATER

Bernard Slade. (1978). *Same Time Next Year.*

Brief Summary: This play illustrates a rather unique type of relationship. A couple meets and begins an extramarital affair. Their assignations occur only once a year when they travel tot he same meeting place. The total affair lasts for twenty six years. We see them go through personal changes, changes in clothing styles, priorities, obsessions, personal phases, and fads. The two people reflect extraordinary trust and closeness, while they also realize that they have no real wish to marry. This play raises questions about the limits and functions of various types of relationships.

IPC Concepts: Types of relationships, needs and exchange theory, cycles, trust, support, disclosure, ethics.

Tennessee Williams. (1947). *A Streetcar Named Desire.*

Brief Summary: This play is set in the apartment of Stanley and Stella Kowalski in the French Quarter of New Orleans. Two streetcars, one named Desire and the other named Cemetery, once rattled through this neighborhood. When Stella's sister, Blanche, comes to visit unexpectedly, Stanley cannot cope with what he perceives to be an intruder and a liar in the middle of his marriage. His violent and manipulative handling of Blanche dramatizes the impact of such behavior on the lives of all involved.

IPC Concepts: Types of relationships, needs and exchange theory, cycles, trust, support, disclosure, ethics.

LITERATURE

Ernest Hemingway. (1929). *A Farewell to Arms.*

Brief Summary: This is Hemingway's story about a tragic love affair set on the Italian front during World War I. The story is about an American, Lieutenant Frederic Henry, who volunteers as an ambulance driver and is wounded and falls in love with his nurse, Catherine Barkley ("Cat"). The couple enjoys a wonderfully romantic year until Cat's tragic death.

IPC Concepts: Relationship and attraction, needs, disclosure, support.

Carson McCullers. (1940). *The Heart Is a Lonely Hunter.* New York: Houghton Mifflin.

Brief Summary: The heroine is a young girl named Mick Kelly. The story is set in a small, Southern town. The characters are all lonely, broken people, some of whom fight their loneliness with violence and depravity, and some with sex or alcohol. Mick searches for beauty. When John Singer shoots himself, the characters of the novel are left with intense loneliness and with a feeling of having been cheated out of someone special.

IPC Concepts: Types of relationships, needs theory, handling of emotion, self-esteem.

ACADEMIC WORK

Harvey A. Hornstein. (1991). *A Knight in Shining Armor: Understanding Men's Romantic Illusions.* New York: William Morrow and Company, Inc.

Brief Summary: This book is an interesting discussion of the emotional needs that many have when they initiate a relationship. Several paradigms are offered that describe patterns of male relational behavior. The author suggests that because of illusions regarding the nature of a relationship, it is difficult to really know the male partner because of the masks they feel compelled to wear.

IPC Concepts: Relationship types, needs and exchange theory, patterns of communicative behavior in relationships, gender.

Donald Horton & R. Richard Wohl. (1956). *Mass Communication and Parasocial Interaction: Observation on Intimacy at a Distance. Psychiatry, 19,* 215–229.

Brief Summary: This is a landmark article about the impact of television, and by present extension, of any form of media on the development of pseudo relationships between the viewer and the celebrity on the television/in the media. Horton and Wohl made some fascinating discoveries of how people feel about celebrities on television. Viewers are not only refer to celebrities by their first name (Dan, Walter, Johnny, Jay, Dave, etc.), but they also feel as though they know the person and feel a sense of loss or abandonment when the celebrity does not appear when expected.

IPC Concepts: Relationship types, needs theory.

WHAT'S ON THE WEB

Guidelines on Effective Communication, healthy Relationships, and Successful Living by Dr. Larry Alan Nadig
http://www.drnadig.com

Brief Summary: Dr. Nadig is a relationship counselor. His site includes guidelines on effective communication, healthy relationships, listening, and relational conflict.

IPC Concepts: Relationships.

Love Test
http://www.lovetest.com

Brief Summary: A fun and somewhat silly exercise that can put students in the mood or mindset to discuss various attraction variables in relationships.

IPC Concepts: Relationships, attraction variables.

CHAPTER 4

Verbal

Communication

After you have read this chapter, you should be able to answer these questions:

- What is the relationship between language and meaning?

- How does language change?

- What is the difference between denotative and connotative meaning?

- What is a speech community?

- Why do dialects emerge?

- How do cultural differences affect language use?

- How do gendered language differences affect social perceptions?

- How can you increase the clarity of your messages?

- How can you improve your language usage so that it is more specific?

- How can you use the skills of dating and indexing generalizations to increase the accuracy of your messages?

- How can you phrase messages so that they are perceived as appropriate for the situation?

> "Madge, Ed and I are having a really tough time."
>
> "I'm sorry to hear that Donna. What's happening?"
>
> "Well, you know, it's just the way he acts."
>
> "Is he being abusive?"
>
> "Uh, no—it's not that. I just can't seem to figure him out."
>
> "Well is it the way he says things?"
>
> "No, it's more what he doesn't say."
>
> "What do you mean 'what he doesn't say'?"
>
> "You know, he comes home and I ask him where he's been."
>
> "And. . ."
>
> "He says he was working overtime."
>
> "And you don't believe him?"
>
> "No, I believe him, it's just that he's working so much I'm just lonely."
>
> "Have you talked with him about this?"
>
> "No, I don't think he'd understand me."

Given what Donna has said and the way she has said it, would you understand? Sometimes, for a variety of reasons, the way we form our messages makes it difficult for others to understand. Sometimes the problem is what we say—other times it's how we say it. In this chapter we will explain how the language we use to form our messages affects how accurately and easily we are understood.

As Thomas Holtgraves (2002) reminds us, "Language is one of those things that we often take for granted. It's almost like breathing—necessary for life but not something we pay much attention to unless problems develop. But unlike breathing, language has profound implications for our social existence. It plays a role in virtually every aspect of our dealings with others. . . . Understanding what we are doing when we use language can aid our understanding of what it means to be a social being" (p. 8).

We begin this chapter by defining and describing the nature of language and its use, including how people from different subcultures and people of different genders vary in their verbal message construction. Then we examine the relationship between language and meaning, with emphasis on the differences between the denotative and connotative meanings of the words we use. Finally, we consider specific communication skills that can help form verbal messages that are clear and appropriate to the context.

The Nature and Use of Language

Language is both the body of words and the systems for their use in messages that are common to the people of the same speech community.

A **speech community** is a group of people who speak the same language. There are between three thousand and four thousand speech communities in the world, with the number of native speakers ranging from over a hundred million to communities with only a few remaining native speakers. Around 60 percent of the world's speech communities have less than ten thousand speakers. The five largest speech communities in order are Mandarin Chinese, English, Spanish, Arabic, and Hindi (Encyclopedia.com, 2002).

Words are arbitrary symbols used by a speech community to represent objects, ideas, and feelings. While what word is used to represent the object or idea is arbitrary, for a word to be a symbol it must be recognized by members of the speech community as standing for a particular object, idea, or feeling. So different speech communities use different word symbols for the same phenomenon. The season for planting is called "spring" in English-speaking communities, but "pretemps" in French-speaking communities.

Speech communities not only vary in the words that they use but they also vary in how words are put together to form messages. The structure a message takes depends on the rules of grammar and syntax that have evolved in a particular speech community.

1. We use language to name, describe, classify, and limit. This is the first and most obvious purpose of language—it answers who? And what? For instance, in response to the question, "Who's that person I saw talking with you at the meeting?" Tom might respond by saying "Oh, that's my friend Jim. He's a chemist at Procter and Gamble." First, since Tom was asked who, he names Jim. He then classifies him as a friend and a chemist, which limits the description to these two categories. Had Tom said, "He's

OBSERVE & ANALYZE

Journal Activity

Different Languages

Interview a person whose first language is different from your own. Ask the person to speak to you in that language and to translate what they have said into English but in the exact word order that they used in their native language. Then ask them to tell you how the grammar and syntax in that language differs from the grammar and syntax of English. Ask the person to discuss what aspect of the English language was particularly difficult for them to learn and ask them to explain what made this particularly challenging. As you listen to the person speak English, observe whether the person uses nonstandard English grammar or syntax and whether this reflects the grammar and syntax rules in the person's native language. If the person speaks additional languages, ask them to comment on the similarities and differences between the languages they speak. Come to class prepared to share a two-minute oral report about the most interesting thing you learned about language during this interview. ■

Language—the body of words and the systems for their use in messages that are common to the people of the same speech community.

Speech community—a group of people who speak the same language.

Words—arbitrary symbols used by a speech community to represent objects, ideas, and feelings.

a scratch golfer," instead of "chemist," he would have classified and limited under-standing of who Jim is in a different way. The point is, whatever words I choose, my listener will perceive only a partial view of the person being described.

2. We use language to evaluate. Language scholars emphasize that language is inher-ently value laden: We give the things we talk about a positive or negative slant sim-ply by the words we use to refer to them (Richards, 1965, p. 3). Sometimes the slant depends on the shared mindset of speaker and listener. Consider this statement: "The chairs in the den are pea green." Even this description may be perceived as a judg-ment on the taste of the owner of the chairs, depending on the aesthetic associations that the speaker and listener share concerning the color "pea green." Other word choices convey evaluations that are more immediately apparent. For instance, if you see Hallie taking more time than others to make a decision, you could describe Hallie as either "thoughtful" or "dawdling." Likewise, someone may choose to refer to the object on the grill as either "prime filet mignon" or "dead animal flesh." Because there is an evaluative component to much of our language choice, we need to select our words carefully to avoid unintentionally misleading and/or offending others.

3. We use language to discuss things outside our immediate experience. Language enables us to speak hypothetically, to talk about past and future events, and to communi-cate about people and things that are not present. Through language, we can dis-cuss where we hope to be in five years, analyze a conversation two acquaintances had last week, or learn about the history that shapes the world we live in. Language enables us to learn from others' experiences, to share a common heritage, and to develop a shared vision for the future.

4. We can use language to talk about language. As a result of this self-reflexive aspect of language, we can discuss how well we are communicating. For example, when Rodney describes Professor Greer's lectures as "boring," John may question his word choice by saying, "Wouldn't 'confusing' be the more precise word for describing his lectures?"

While the purpose of language is to help members of speech communities understand and relate to each other, the very nature of language and meaning cre-ates the likelihood of misunderstanding. To clarify this we consider how language conveys meaning.

Language and Meaning

On the surface, the relationship between language and meaning seems perfectly clear: We select the correct words, structure them using the rules of syntax and grammar agreed upon by our speech community, and people will interpret our mean-ings correctly. In fact, the relationship between language and meaning is not nearly so simple for several reasons: language is learned, word meanings change over time, the use of language is a creative act, and people interpret words differently.

The first reason the relationship between language and meaning is compli-cated is that since we are not born knowing a language each generation within a speech community learns the language anew. We learn much of our language early in life from our families; much more we learn in school. But we do not all learn to use the same words in the same way.

A second reason the relationship between language and meaning is complicated is that younger generations will invent new words or assign different meanings to the words they learn. For instance, *Merriam-Webster's Collegiate Dictionary: Deluxe Edition* (1998) contains ten thousand new words and usages. Words such as *mediagenic* (attractive and appealing to viewers and readers of the news media) and *hip-hop* (street subculture language including rap) have come into common usage to express ideas that were unthinkable to your grandparents. In addition, members of the speech community will invent new meanings for old words in order to differentiate themselves from other subgroups of the language community. For instance, in some parts of the country to teenagers *stupid* means *cool*, as in "That's a really stupid shirt" and *played* means *tiresome* or *boring*, as in "This party is played, let's split." Likewise, to some college students *apes* means *fraternity brothers* and a *cheesebox* is a *computer* (Dickson, 1998).

Of course, new meanings and new words don't become a part of our "dictionary" until enough people in a language community accept the meaning. So, although in each of the past ten years some hundred thousand new words and changes in meanings have been observed, the compilers of the *Merriam-Webster Dictionary* believed that only ten thousand of them had gained broad enough usage in the general American English language community to recognize them as part of the language.

A third reason the relationship between language and meaning is complicated is that even though languages have systems of syntax and grammar, each utterance is a creative act. When we speak, we use language to create new sentences that represent our meaning. Although on occasion we repeat other people's sentence constructions to represent what we are thinking or feeling, most of our talk is unique.

Language creativity is especially noticeable in children. When children don't know the common designation for a thought, they create one out of the context. For instance, a child may refer to a restaurant as a "meal store" or describe sirens as "scary whistles." While creativity is obvious in children's speech, all of us use our creativity when sharing our ideas and experiences.

A fourth reason language and meaning is so complicated is that as a result of different kinds of meaning, people interpret words differently. Thus, when Melissa tells Trish that her dog died, what Trish understands Melissa to mean depends on both word denotation and connotation.

Denotation The direct, explicit meaning a speech community formally gives a word is its **denotation,** the meaning found in a dictionary. So denotatively, when Melissa said her dog died, she meant that her domesticated canine no longer demonstrates physical life. In some situations the denotative meaning of a word may not be clear. Why? First, dictionary definitions reflect current and past practice in the speech community; and second, the dictionaries use words to define words. The end result is that in addition to words being defined differently in various dictionaries, they may also have multiple meanings that change over time.

In addition, meaning may vary depending on the syntactic context (the position of a word in a sentence and the other words around it) in which the word is used. For instance, in the same sentence a person might say, "I love vacationing in mountain areas. Mornings are really cool. Moreover, by getting out early you can

Denotation—the direct, explicit meaning a speech community formally gives a word.

see some really cool animals." Most listeners would understand that "mornings are really cool" refers to temperature and "see some really cool animals" refers to animals that are uncommon or special.

Connotation The feelings or evaluations we personally associate with a word represent the **connotation** and may be even more important to our understanding of meaning.

C. K. Ogden and I. A. Richards (1923) were among the first scholars to consider the misunderstandings resulting from the failure of communicators to realize that people's subjective reactions to words will be a product of their life experiences. For instance, when Tina says, "We bought an SUV, I think it's the biggest one Chevy makes," Kim might think "Why in the world would anyone want one of those gas guzzlers that take up so much space to park?" and Lexia might say "Oh, I envy you. I'd love to afford a vehicle that has so much power and sits so high on the road."

Word denotation and connotation are important because the only message that counts is the message that is understood, regardless of whether it is the one you intended.

Connotation—the feelings or evaluations we personally associate with a word.

Dialects—variations on a core language that allow a subgroup in a speech community to share meanings unique to their experience.

How do we determine meaning when words can have different connotative or denotative meanings?

Language and Culture

Meaning varies across different speech communities and among subgroups in a single speech community. A large speech community may include subgroups with unique cultures and language systems. Because the United States is a large country of immigrants, it has many dialects, some of which are ethnically based and others that are geographical. As Hecht, Collier, and Ribeau (1993) point out, "Cultural groups define themselves in part through language, and members establish identity through language use" (p. 84).

Subgroups then develop variations on the core language called dialects. **Dialects** are variations on a core language that allow a subgroup in a speech community to share meanings unique to their experience. The official dialect of a speech community is the form of that language that is privileged and taught in school. It is the dialect of the speech community that becomes the standard from which other dialects are judged (Encyclopedia.com, 2002). For example, in the U.S. job market, using standard English marks a person as well educated while use of dialects whose grammar and syntax are markedly different yields the opposite conclusion.

In addition to subgroups based on race, religion, or national origin, we are also experiencing an unprecedented growth in subgroup cultures and language communities associated with generation, social class, and political interest groups. The need for awareness and sensitivity in applying our communication skills doesn't depend on someone's being an immigrant or from a different ethnic

background. Rather, the need for being aware of potential language differences is important in every interpersonal communication. Developing our language skills so that the messages we send are clear and sensitive will increase our interpersonal effectiveness in every situation.

Understanding Cultural Effects on Language Because language and culture are inseparable, we need to understand how cultures differ and how these differences are reflected in language. Thus, in this section, we look at four dimensions of culture that answer why differences in connotations of language occur.

Culture provides people with a theory about how to behave in various situations and how to interpret others' behavior in these same situations. People learn the theories of their cultures through the socialization process. And, as we would imagine, people from different cultures learn different theories that they use to guide their behavior. Of course, not every individual within a cultural group shares precisely the same theories.

One way that cultures vary is in whether the individual or group goals and needs are viewed as most important (Gudykunst & Matsumoto, 1996, p. 21). In **individualistic cultures** individual goals are emphasized more than group goals, because these cultures value uniqueness. As a result, their people are more likely to look after themselves and their immediate family. In contrast, in **collectivistic cultures** group goals are emphasized more than individual goals, because these cultures value harmony and solidarity. As a result, their people are more likely to belong to in-groups or collectives that are supposed to look after them in exchange for their loyalty to the group (Hofstede, 1991, p. 67).

Hofstede (1991, p. 53) cites Australia, Belgium, Canada, Denmark, France, Germany, Great Britain, Ireland, Israel, Italy, the Netherlands, New Zealand, Norway, Sweden, Switzerland, and the United States as individualistic cultures; among the collectivistic cultures are Brazil, China, Colombia, Egypt, Greece, India, Japan, Kenya, Korea, Mexico, Nigeria, Pakistan, Panama, Peru, Saudi Arabia, Thailand, Venezuela, and Vietnam. A close look at this list suggests that individualistic cultures are mostly Western European, North American, and Australian, while collectivistic cultures are mostly Asian, African, and South American.

Individualistic cultures (German, Swiss, American) give rise to speech communities that use low-context communication. **Low-context communication** is communication where information is (1) present in the messages transmitted and (2) presented directly. Collectivistic cultures (Native American, Latin American, Oriental), however, have speech communities with high-context communication. In **high-context communication** people (1) expect others to know how they're thinking and feeling and (2) present messages indirectly. Thus, speech communities with low-context cultures operate on the principle of saying what you mean and getting to the point; in contrast, high-context cultural speech communities communicate in ways that are often ambiguous and indirect (Gudykunst & Matsumoto, 1996, pp. 29–30). So, in a low-context culture "Yes" means "Affirmative, I agree with what you have said." In a high-context culture "Yes" may mean "Affirmative, I agree with what you have said," or it may mean "In this setting it would embarrass you if I said 'No,' so I will say 'Yes' to be polite, but I

Individualistic cultures—cultures in which individuals' goals are emphasized more than group goals, because these cultures value uniqueness.

Collectivistic cultures—cultures in which group goals are emphasized more than individual goals, because these cultures value harmony and solidarity.

Low-context communication—communication where information is present in the messages transmitted and presented directly.

High-context communication—communication where people expect others to know how they're thinking and feeling and present messages indirectly.

really don't agree and you should know this, so in the future don't expect me to act as if I have agreed with what you said." So, for example, most people from Asian cultures will talk for hours without clearly expressing an opinion and they are likely to be uncomfortable with direct verbal expressions of love and respect.

The second way that cultures differ is in how comfortable they are with uncertainly. Although we all live in a world of uncertainty, societies respond to this uncertainty differently. Cultures characterized as **low uncertainty avoidance** (United States, Sweden, Denmark) are more comfortable with uncertainty (less effort is put into reducing uncertainty). As a result they more comfortably tolerate differing ideas, behavior, and opinions. A culture with **high uncertainty avoidance** (Greece, Portugal, Japan) is uncomfortable with uncertainty, which creates anxiety among its people, and more effort is put into avoiding it. These societies emphasize providing security and reducing risk. One way they do this is to be less tolerant of deviant ideas and behaviors.

A third way cultures differ is in how strongly traditional sex roles are adhered to. What Hofstede refers to as **masculine cultures** (Japan, Italy, Mexico) are those that expect people to maintain traditional sex roles. In these societies men take more assertive and dominant roles and women take more service-oriented and caring roles (Hofstede, 1983, p. 85). Masculine societies also value masculine roles more highly and as a result emphasize materialism and acquisitiveness. **Feminine cultures** (Sweden, Norway, the Netherlands) are those that expect men and women to take a variety of roles. As a result, these cultures emphasize relationships, concern for others, and overall quality of life.

A fourth way in which cultural groups differ is in how powerful people are viewed and treated. **Power distance** is the extent to which a society accepts the fact that power in institutions and organizations is distributed unequally. In **high power-distance cultures** people show respect for the powerful. As a result, titles, rank, and status determine how a person is talked to. In **low power-distance cultures** inequalities in power are played down. People know that some individuals have more authority, but people don't fear that authority nor are they in awe of it. So their communication is less deferential. Figure 4.1 suggests where the United States falls on each of these dimensions.

This analysis considers national cultures—the differences between and among countries. But we also need to note that different cultures are represented

Low uncertainty avoidance— societies that accept uncertainty and thus are more tolerant of differing behavior and opinions.

High uncertainty avoidance— societies that are uncomfortable with uncertainty, which creates anxiety among its people.

Masculine cultures—cultures that expect people to maintain traditional sex roles.

Feminine cultures—cultures that expect both men and women to take a variety of roles.

Power distance—the extent to which a society accepts the fact that power in institutions and organizations is distributed unequally.

High power-distance societies—societies in which people show respect for authority.

Low power-distance societies—societies in which inequalities are played down.

Figure 4.1

UNITED STATES VS. OTHER NATIONAL CULTURES

Highest of all countries on individualism.

Well below average on uncertainty avoidance.

Well above average on masculinity.

Below average on power distance.

How might culture affect the conversation between the people in this picture?

within nearly every country. Within the United States in particular are a multitude of cultures that differ from one another even when their members speak the same language. People who speak different languages expect to have some problem communicating and thus seem willing to take extra care. Surprisingly, misinterpreting word meaning can be more of a problem for two people from different subcultures who are members of the same speech community because they may assume that they are culturally similar when in fact they are not.

Similarly, we often judge people based on language differences. In the Diverse Voices selection that follows, Castelan Cargile discusses the role that accent plays in our perceptions of others.

Understanding Gender Differences in Language Over the last two decades, stirred by such book titles as *Men Are from Mars, Women Are from Venus*, people have come to believe that gender differences in verbal messages are widespread. Yet the research strongly suggests that differences between men's speech and women's speech is gender based rather than biologically based, and that the differences between men's talk and women's talk are not nearly as large as portrayed (Wood & Dindia, 1998, pp. 34–36). Whereas **sex** refers biological characteristics that differentiate men from women; **gender** means the culturally determined behaviors and personality characteristics that are associated with, but not determined by, biological sex (Howard & Hollander, 1997, p. 11).

There is no evidence to suggest that the differences that have been identified between women's message construction patterns and those of men cause "prob-

Sex—biological characteristics that differentiate men from women.

Gender—the culturally determined behaviors and personality characteristics that are associated with, but not determined by, biological sex.

lems" for either group (Canary & Hause, 1993, p. 141). Nevertheless, a number of specific differences between women's and men's speech patterns have been found.

Edwin and Shirley Ardener argue that the language differences between men and women in the United States are a result of the male-based culture of the United States. Because men have created the meanings for language, the feminine voice has been "muted" (Littlejohn, 2002, p. 224). As a result, women are less expressive in public situations than men are and monitor their own communications more intensely than do men. Anthony Mulac noted two differences in language usage between men and women that seem to have the greatest support as follows (Mulac, 1998, pp. 133–134):

1. Women tend to use both more intensifiers and more hedges than men. Intensifiers are words that modify other words and serve to strengthen the idea represented by the original word. So, according to studies of the actual speech practices of men and women, women are more likely to use words such as *awfully, quite,* and *so* (as in "It was quite lovely" or "This is so important"). Hedges are modifying words that soften or weaken the meaning of the idea represented by the original word. According to the research, women are likely to make greater use of such words as *somewhat, perhaps,* and *maybe* (as in "It was somewhat interesting that . . ." or "It may be significant that . . .").

2. Women ask questions more frequently than men. Women are much more likely to include questions like, "Do you think so?" and "Are you sure?" In general, women tend to use questions to gain more information, get elaboration, and determine how others feel about the information.

But are these two differences really important? Mulac goes on to report that "our research has shown that language used by U.S. women and men is remarkably similar. So similar that in one study native speakers of American English could not correctly identify which language examples were produced by women and which were produced by men" (p. 130). Yet even though the real differences are relatively small, Mulac argues that they have judgmental consequences: People "perceive the female and male speakers differently based on their language use" (p. 147). Mulac's study found that women's speech was perceived as having high social status, being literate, and being pleasant, while male speech was perceived as stronger and more aggressive. And these perceptions remained the same regardless of the sex or age of the observers (p. 148).

Increasing Language Clarity

We speak clearly when our language reduces ambiguity and confusion. Compare these two descriptions of a near miss in a car: "Some nut almost got me a while ago" versus "An hour ago, an older man in a banged-up Honda Civic ran the light at Calhoun and Clifton and almost hit me broadside while I was in the intersection waiting to turn left at the cross street." In the second example, the message used language that was clearer. We are able to clearly express our ideas when we have a

Accents and Language *By Castelan Cargile*

How do we react to the ways others speak? Castelan Cargile, California State University, focuses on what he regards as the most revealing of language behaviors: accents. As you read think of how accents of others (whether they be acquaintances, friends, instructors, or people of different professions) affect your attitude toward them.

One of the many challenges we face as participants in intercultural encounters is coping with language differences. In some cases we may not speak the same language as our conversational partner. When not a single word in an exchange can be understood, the challenge of successful communication is quite obvious. In other cases, however, our partner may be at least competent (if not fluent) in our language or vice versa. And it is these seemingly minor language differences that usually present one of the biggest challenges to successful intercultural communication.

Of the language behaviors that have been investigated, accent is one of the most revealing. Research has shown that listeners have clear attitudes toward those who speak "differently." American listeners who themselves speak with a standard American accent consistently prejudge others with "Appalachian," "Spanish," "German," or "African American" vernacular-accented speech as less intelligent, poorer, less educated, and less status-possessing than standard accented speakers. Surprisingly though, standard accented listeners are not the only ones who look down on many nonstandard accent speakers. Even listeners who themselves speak with a nonstandard accent often judge others who sound like themselves as having low standing.

The complex reality of intercultural communication is not that we think badly of everyone who speaks differently. Indeed, research indicates that some "foreign" accented speakers are not perceived by Americans to be less competent or inferior—for example British-accented English speakers. Similarly, listeners who speak with a standard accent sometimes judge nonstandard-accented speakers to be equal to standard-accented speakers along some dimensions. Yet, the accent attitude research finds that often we prejudge others in unflattering ways based only on their accent. Given this, how should responsible intercultural communicators manage language attitudes?

The first and most important thing to do is to recognize when your responses to others are based on language attitudes alone, and when they are based on more objective, and more reliable information. For example, in universities across the United States, students often respond unfavorably to foreign-born teaching assistants and professors. In fact, on some campuses more than two out of five students withdraw or switch from a class when they find out their teacher is a nonnative speaker of English. In addition, many other students make complaints of the variety that forced Illinois to pass a fluency law for college instructors. Who is responsible for such student dissatisfaction? In some cases, there are real instructors with verifiably poor language skills. In many other cases, though, it may in fact be the stereotypical and prejudicial language attitudes developed by the students themselves that is responsible.

On first hearing an instructor's accent, students often unknowingly make assumptions about the instructor's personality and (language) skills based soley on their own attitudes toward foreign-accented speakers (e.g., this teacher isn't too friendly, too smart, and he doesn't speak good English"). The instructor may, in fact, be or do none of these things that the student assumes. Even so, because language attitudes have the power to initiate selective perceptions, the students may create, in their own minds, evidence to support their views. In particular, they may "hear" the instructor make grammatical mistakes that he has not really made. Students can then, in turn, point to these reasons for responding unfavorably to the instructor. Thus a class may end up with an instructor who speaks grammatically correct and comprehensible English, but because students have unknowingly based their responses on their attitudes toward foreign-accented speech alone, they may feel dissatisfied with their instructor.

The trouble is that we rarely realize this, and as a result we believe the other is entirely responsible for our reactions. Consequently, the first step we should take in dealing with language attitudes is to learn to rec-ognize their role in the evaluation process. Ask yourself, "Am I thinking this about the person only because of the way that he or she speaks?" You may answer "no" to this question; thus indicating that the role that language attitudes are playing is minimal and perhaps justified. You may however answer "yes," suggesting that your attitudes about language use are exerting an undue and likely problematic influence on your behavior.

Once you learn to recognize the role language attitudes play in your responses, a second step should be to seek out and integrate additional information into the evaluation process. For example, in the case of a nonnative English speaking instructor, find out about his or her educational background, prior teaching experiences, and real English competency through patient listening (and perhaps some careful questioning) before passing the easy, ready-made judgment that this person lacks the intelligence and ability to be a successful teacher. Of course, this kind of "fact checking" and follow up is effortful and never easy. It is, however, critical to managing our language attitudes well. Calling on language attitudes in intercultural interaction is nearly unavoidable. Thus, the secret is to tap their potential as a source of information without being poisoned by their power to lead listeners down a road of prejudice and discrimination. ■

Excerpted from Cargile, C. (2000). Language matters. In L. Samovar and R. E. Porter (Eds.), *Intercultural Communication: A Reader* (9th ed., pp. 239–246). Belmont, Calif: Wadsworth.

good vocabulary, use specific language, and date information and index generalizations.

Develop Your Vocabulary

As a speaker, the larger your vocabulary, the more choices you have from which to select the word you want. As a listener, the larger your vocabulary, the more likely you are to understand the words used by others.

Study Vocabulary Books One way to increase your vocabulary is to study one of the numerous vocabulary books available in most bookstores, like *Merriam-Webster's Vocabulary Builder* (Cornog, 1999). You might also study magazine features such as "Word Power," a monthly feature in *Reader's Digest*. By completing this monthly quiz and learning the words with which you are not familiar, you can increase your vocabulary by several words per month.

Find the Definition to New Words You Encounter A second way to increase your vocabulary is to take note of any words that people use in their conversations with you or that you read in a newspaper, magazine, or book that you are not able to define clearly. For instance, suppose you hear, "I was *inundated* with phone calls today!" If you can't define *inundated*, you could ask the speaker to clarify its meaning: "Excuse me, but I'm not sure what you mean by *inundated.*" Or you could write the word down, look up its meaning at the first opportunity, and then go back over what you heard to see whether the dictionary meaning matches what was said. Most dictionaries define *inundated* using synonyms such as *overwhelmed* or *flooded*. So if you then say to yourself, "She was inundated—overwhelmed or flooded—with phone calls today," you are likely to remember that meaning and apply it the next time you hear the word. You can follow the same procedure when you read. As you are reading today's assignments for your courses, circle any words whose meanings you are unsure of. After you have finished the assignment, look them up in the dictionary. Asking speakers to define their words is especially useful when the speaker is using a dialect you are unfamiliar with. If you follow this practice faithfully, you will soon notice an increase in your vocabulary.

Clearly stating verbal messages is hard work, but as you build your vocabulary, you will find that you are better able to express your ideas in everyday conversation. At times you will want to make adjustments in mid-sentence, as in the following examples:

- "To move these things, we'll need a van—I'm sorry, I don't mean a van, I mean one of those extra-large station wagons."
- "I think that many of the boss's statements are very [split-second pause while thinking: I want the word that means `know-it-all'] dogmatic."
- "Mike was just a jerk yesterday—well, I guess I mean he was inconsiderate."
- "I agree Pauline is a tough manager, but I think she's a good one because she is fair—she treats everyone exactly alike."

Even when we are relaxed and confident, our word choices may not best reflect what we're trying to communicate. When we are under pressure, our ability to select the best symbols to convey our thoughts is likely to deteriorate. In fact, people under pressure sometimes think one thing and say something entirely different. For example, a math professor might say, "We all remember that the numerator is on the bottom and the denominator is on the top of the fraction, so when we divide fractions. . . ." "Professor," a voice from the third row interrupts, "you said the numerator is on the bottom and. . . ." "Is that what I said?" the professor replies. "Well, you know what I meant!" Did everyone in the class know? Probably not.

You will really know that you have made strides in improving clarity when you find that you can form specific, precise, concrete messages even under pressure.

Choose Specific Language

Often as we try to express our thoughts, the first words that come to mind are general in nature. **Specific words** clear up ambiguity caused by general words by narrowing what is understood from a general category to a particular group within that category. Specific words are more concrete and precise than are general words. What can we do to speak more specifically?

Specific words—words that clear up ambiguity caused by general words.

Figure 4.2

Level of Specificity

A great number of the words we use really describe a category of similar items. Suppose you told you friend that you were about to buy a new car. "Car" is a category. At this point your friend might say, "What kind of a car are you thinking about?" Now you're being asked to be more specific. What could you say? Let's look at he potential continuum from its most general to most specific. Figure 4.2 provides an illustration of this continuum.

We speak more clearly when we select a word that most accurately or correctly captures the sense of what we are saying. At first I might say "Susan laughed at my story" then I might think "No, it wasn't really a laugh," so I say, "To be more accurate, she chuckled." What is the difference between the two? A laugh is a loud show of mirth; a chuckle is a more gentle sound expressing suppressed mirth. Similar? Yes. But different—showing shades of meaning. Specific language is achieved when words are concrete or precise or when detail or examples are used.

Concrete words—words that appeal to our senses.

Use Concrete Words **Concrete words** are words that appeal to our senses. Consider the word "speak." This is an abstract word—that is, we can "speak" in many different ways. So instead of saying that Jill *speaks in a peculiar way*, we might be more specific by saying that Jill *mumbles, whispers, blusters,* or *drones.* Each of these words creates a clearer sense of the sound of her voice.

Precise words—words that narrow a larger category to a smaller group within that category.

Use Precise Words We speak more specifically when we are **precise,** narrowing a larger category to a smaller group within that category. For instance, if Nevah says that Ruben is a "blue-collar worker," she has named a general category; you might picture an unlimited number of occupations that fall within this broad category. If, instead, she is more precise and says he's a "construction worker," the number of possible images you can picture is reduced; now you can only select your image from the specific subcategory of construction worker. So your meaning is likely to be closer to the one she intended. To be even more precise she may identify Ruben as "a bulldozer operator"; this further limits your choice of images and is likely to align with the one she intended you to have.

Try to construct a description of each of these hands that would help someone know which hand you are referring to. Notice how precise and specific your language must be.

In the examples that follow, notice how the use of concrete and precise language in the right-hand column improves the clarity of the messages in the left-hand column.

The senator brought *several* things with her to the meeting.	The senator brought *recent letters* from *her constituency* to the meeting.
He lives in a *really* big house.	He lives in a *fourteen-room Tudor mansion*.
The backyard has *several different kinds* of trees.	The backyard has *two large maples, an oak, and four small evergreens*.
Morgan is a *fair grader*.	Morgan uses *the same standards for grading all students*.
Many students *aren't honest* in class.	Many students *cheat on tests* in class.
Judy *hits* the podium when she wants to emphasize her point.	Judy *pounds on* the podium when she wants to emphasize her point.

Provide Details and Examples While choosing concrete and precise wordings enables us to improve clarity, there are times when a word may not have a more specific or concrete synonym. So another way to achieve specificity is to use a detail or an example to clarify. Suppose Linda says, "Rashad is very loyal." Since the meaning of loyal (faithful to an idea, person, company, and so on) is abstract, to avoid ambiguity and confusion Linda might add, "I mean he never criticizes a friend behind her back." By following up her use of the abstract concept of loyalty with a concrete example, Linda makes it easier for her listeners to "ground" their idea of this personal quality in a concrete or "real" experience.

Acquire and Use Accurate Information Speaking clearly often goes beyond just simple word choice. It requires you to have the information needed on the subject you're

OBSERVE & ANALYZE

Journal Activity

Synonyms

One good way to increase clarity is to play "synonyms." Think of a word, then list words that mean about the same thing. For example, the word *happy* might inspire you to list *glad, joyful,* and *pleased.* When you have completed your list, refer to a book of synonyms, such as *Roget's Thesaurus,* to find other words. Then write what you think is the meaning of each word, focusing on the shades of difference in meaning among the words. When you are done, look up each word, even those that you are sure of the meaning. You will be surprised to find how many times the subtle meaning of even a familiar word escapes you. The goal of this exercise is to select the most specific, concrete, or precise word to express your idea. ■

discussing. Suppose you were talking with friends about the graduation rate of athletes. You might say, "Here, some athletes are graduating about on time, but a whole lot of them aren't." In this context, "some athletes," "about on time," and "a whole lot" are not specific. The range of what people might understand by "some," "about," and "a whole lot" is too wide. See how much clearer the sentence would be if you said, "Here, roughly 60 percent of athletes on scholarship graduate within five years of the time they started. The problem is that in such 'revenue' sports as football and men's basketball, the number drops to under 30 percent." As this example shows, being able to be clear may involve doing research to nail down exact facts and figures.

Date Information

Dating information means to specify the time or time period that a fact was true or known to be true. Why is this important? We draw conclusions based on information. If the information is inaccurate, the conclusions drawn from that information are likely to be inaccurate as well. A common source of inaccuracy is giving the impression that information is current when

dating information-specifying the time period that a fact was true or known to be true.

TEST YOURSELF

Concrete, Precise

1. For each word listed, find three words or phrases that are more specific, or more concrete.

implements	building	nice	education
clothes	colors	chair	bad
happy	stuff	things	car

2. Make the following statements clearer by editing words that are not precise, specific, or concrete:

   "You know I love basketball. Well, I'm practicing a lot because I want to get better."

   "Paula, I'm really bummed out. Everything is going down the tubes. You know what I mean?"

   "Well, she just does these things to tick me off. Like, just a whole lot of stuff—and she knows it!"

   "I just bought a beautiful outfit—I mean, it is really in style. You'll love it."

   "I've really got to remember to bring my things the next time I visit."

in fact it is not. For instance, Parker says, "I'm going to be transferred to Henderson City. As I remember, you are familiar with it." Laura replies, "Yes I am. Let me just say that they've had some real trouble with their schools." On the basis of Laura's statement, Parker may worry about the effect his move will have on his children. What he doesn't know is that Laura's information about this problem in Henderson City is five years old! Henderson City may still have problems, but then again, it may not. Had Laura replied, "Five years ago, I know they had some real trouble with their schools. I'm not sure what the situation is now, but you may want to check," Parker would look at the information differently.

Nearly everything changes with time. Some changes are imperceptible; others are so extensive as to make old information inaccurate, obsolete, and even dangerous. We can make our messages clearer by using the skill of dating to indicate when the information we are conveying was accurate. To date information (1) consider or find out when the information was true and (2) verbally acknowledge it. This seems like a simple skill to put into practice—and it is. But often, we just don't think about the implication of evaluating a situation using old data.

Consider each of the examples that follow. The statements on the left are undated generalizations; those on the right are carefully dated generalizations.

INTER-ACT WITH Technology

How your ideas are worded can make a great deal of difference in whether people will understand or be influenced by what you say. You can find on nearly any word-processing package a thesaurus (a list of words and their synonyms) to access that will help you identify more specific and precise words. For instance, in the Microsoft® Word package, the user can highlight a specific word, click on "Tools," drag down to "Thesaurus" and be presented with synonyms for that word. For practice, select any word that you would like to improve upon and make note of your choices. Then select the choice that you believe would be most meaningful. For instance if you highlighted "difficult" when you clicked on the thesaurus you would be shown "hard," "laborious," "arduous," and "strenuous." If you wanted more choices you could then highlight one of those words and get additional choices. If you were trying to make the point that studying can be difficult, you might decide to use "arduous" as the better word. ■

Palm Springs is really popular with the college crowd.	When we were in Palm Springs *two years ago*, it was really popular with the college crowd.
Professor Powell brings great enthusiasm to her teaching.	Professor Powell brings great enthusiasm to her teaching—at least she did *last quarter* in communication theory.
The Beast is considered the most exciting roller coaster in the country.	*Years ago*, the Beast was considered the most exciting roller coaster in the country.
You think Mary's depressed? I'm surprised. She seemed her regular high-spirited self when I talked with her.	You think Mary's depressed? I'm surprised. She seemed her regular high-spirited self when I talked with her *the day before yesterday*.

We have no power to prevent change. But we can increase the effectiveness of our messages if we verbally acknowledge the reality of change by dating the statements we make.

OBSERVE & ANALYZE

Journal Activity

Clarity

Revise each of the following sentences in a way that makes the meaning more clear:

The food was great.

Mary's stuff is really nice.

The new building is awful.

She's like, you know, really cool.

Stay away from Don—he's a real jerk.

He was really on me for being late.

Jones assigns a lot of outside reading for the course.

I like sweet potatoes, they're neat.

At the PGA lots of players had trouble with the weather. ■

Indexing generalizations-the mental and verbal practice of acknowledging the presence of individual differences when voicing generalizations.

Index Generalizations

Indexing generalizations is the mental and verbal practice of acknowledging the presence of individual differences when voicing generalizations allow people to use what they have their experiences and apply a stance, when Glenda, a third grade of her students who have at or near the bottom of her class izes that students who fail to likely to be in the bottom of the

Although the capacity to generalize carefully is important to all of us in our decision making, the misuse of generalization contributes to perceptual inaccuracies because it ignores individual differences. Thus, just because Alex and Manuel are better at math than Alicia does not mean that boys (or men) in general are better at math than girls (or women) or are better than Alicia.

To avoid making misleading statements or even stating generalizations that may be true, we need to practice indexing, a skill that is borrowed from mathematics, where it is used to acknowledge individual elements within a group (X1, X2, X3, etc.). We mentally index by acknowledging that whether we have observed one, five, or ten or more, we can't always be sure that a generalization using those examples or cases is valid. Thus just because we learn that Brent has bought a top-of-the-line Mercedes (a very expensive car), it does not mean that Brent is rich. So, if we were

SKILL BUILDERS   SPEAKING MORE CLEARLY

SKILL	USE	PROCEDURE	EXAMPLE
Clarify meaning by selecting a less ambiguous word, by narrowing from a general category to a particular group within that category, by selecting a word that is a more precise choice, or by using concrete details or examples.	To help the listener picture thoughts analogous to the speaker's.	1. Assess whether the word is less specific or precise than it should be. 2. Pause to mentally brainstorm alternatives. 3. Select a more specific, precise word and/or add details or an example.	Instead of saying, "Bring the stuff for the audit," say, "Bring the records and receipts from the last year for the audit." Or, instead of saying, "Paul is very loyal," say "Paul is very loyal. He will back you when you're under fire."

SKILL BUILDERS   DATING INFORMATION

SKILL	USE	PROCEDURE	EXAMPLE
Including a specific time referent that indicates when a fact was true.	To avoid the pitfalls of language that allow you to speak of a dynamic world in static terms.	1. Before you make a statement, consider or find out when the information was true. 2. If not based on present information, verbally acknowledge when it was true.	When Jake says, "How good a hitter is Steve?" Mark replies by dating his evaluation: "When I worked with him two years ago, he couldn't hit the curve."

to say "Brent bought a Mercedes, he must be rich," we should add "of course not all people who buy Mercedes are rich."

To use the skill of indexing, (1) consider whether what you want to say is about a specific object, person, or place, or whether it is a generalization about a class to which the object, person, or place belongs. (2) If what you want to say is based on a generalization about the class, qualify your statement appropriately so that your assertion does not go beyond the evidence that supports it.

In the examples that follow, the statements on the left are overgeneralizations, whereas those on the right have been carefully indexed.

Because men are stronger than women, Max is stronger than Barbara.	*In general*, men are stronger than women, so Max is probably stronger than Barbara.
State's got to have a good economics department; the university is ranked among the top twenty in the nation.	Because State's among the top twenty schools in the nation, the economics department should be a good one, *although it may be an exception.*
Jack is sure to be outgoing; Don is, and they're both Joneses.	Jack is likely to be outgoing because his brother Don is (they're both Joneses), *but Jack could be different.*
Your Chevrolet should go fifty thousand miles before you need a brake job; Jerry's did.	Your Chevrolet may well go fifty thousand miles before you need a brake job; Jerry's did, *but, of course, all Chevrolets aren't the same.*

All people generalize at one time or another, but by using indexing, we can avoid the misunderstandings that generalized statements can create.

Speaking Appropriately

In the United States during the past few years we have had frequent discussions and disagreements about "political correctness." Colleges and universities have been in the forefront of this debate. While several issues germane to the debate on political correctness go beyond the scope of this chapter, at the heart of this controversy is the question of what language behaviors are appropriate—and what language behaviors are inappropriate.

Speaking appropriately means choosing language and symbols that are adapted to the needs, interests, knowledge, and attitudes of listeners in order to avoid language that alienates them. Through appropriate language we communicate our respect and acceptance of those who are different from us. In this section we discuss specific strategies that will help you to craft verbal messages that are more likely to be interpreted correctly because they are appropriate.

> **Speaking appropriately—** choosing language and symbols that are adapted to the needs, interests, knowledge, and attitudes of listeners in order to avoid language that alienates them.

Adapt Formality to the Situation

The language you use should reflect the formality of the situation. In an interpersonal setting, we can use informal language when we are talking with our best friend and should use more formal language when we are talking with strangers. In a group setting, we can use more informal language when we are talking with our peers and more formal language when we are talking with those with greater power or authority. When we adhere to these cultural rules our language is appropriate.

One formality in language that we should observe is how we address others. When we address others by their titles followed by their surnames we are being more formal. So, in an education or business setting or at a formal party it is appropriate to call people "Mr. X," "Ms. B," "Rabbi Z," "Dr. S," or "Professor P" until invited to do otherwise. In addition, we have been taught to refer to those older than we are, those of higher status, or those whom we respect by title and surname unless otherwise directed. Unfortunately this is not always the case.

SKILL BUILDERS   **INDEXING GENERALIZATIONS**

SKILL	USE	PROCEDURE	EXAMPLE
Mentally or verbally accounting for individual differences.	To avoid "allness" in speaking.	1. Before you make a statement, consider whether it pertains to a specific object, person, or place. 2. If you use a generalization, inform the listener that it is not necessarily accurate.	"He's a politician and I don't trust him, although he may be different from most politicians I know."

Be Wary of Jargon and Slang

Appropriate language should be chosen so that **jargon** (technical terminology whose meaning is idiosyncratic to a special activity or interest group) and **slang** (informal nonstandard use of vocabulary) do not interfere with understanding. We form special speech communities as a result of the work we do, our hobbies, and of course the subcultures with which we identify. But we can forget that others who are not in our same line of work or who do not have the same hobbies or are not from our cultural group may not understand language that seems to be such a part of our daily communication. For instance, when an environmentalist gets into a conversation with a friend about the Internet, the environmentalist is likely to lose her friend if she talks to him in the language of "PCBs," "brownfields," and "superfund site." If, however, the environmentalist is sensitive to her friend's level of knowledge, she can work to make her language appropriate by discussing ideas in words that her friend understands. In short, anytime you are talking with people outside your specific speech community, you need to carefully explain, if not abandon, the technical jargon or slang.

Jargon—technical terminology whose meaning is idiosyncratic to a special activity or interest group.

Slang—informal nonstandard use of vocabulary.

Avoid Crude Language

Appropriate language avoids profanity and vulgar expressions. There was a time when saying "hell" or "damn" resulted in severe punishment for children and social isolation for adults. Today, unfortunately, we tolerate vile profanities and vulgarities, and in many subcultures their use is commonplace. In part this is because of film and television, whose aim to titillate and entertain has overexposed us to these words and we have become inured to these expressions. It is now common to hear even elementary school children utter strings of "four-letter words" in school hallways, lunchrooms, and playgrounds.

Why do people swear and use coarse language? DeKlerk (1991, p. 165) suggests that children and low-power people swear as a way of asserting power by breaking taboos. So crude speech can indicate that a person is feeling powerless. Despite the trend for our society to tolerate crude speech, however, in most settings, even in informal conversation, many people find crude speech offensive, although politeness may preclude them from saying so. When speakers use vulgarities, they risk being perceived as crude, uneducated, and menacing. It is important to monitor our messages so that vulgarities don't interfere with our intended meanings.

Demonstrate Sensitivity

Language is appropriate when you avoid usages that others perceive as offensive. Some of the mistakes in language that we make result from using expressions that are perceived by others as sexist, racist, or otherwise biased—that is, any language that is perceived as belittling any person or group of people. Two of the most prevalent linguistic usages that are insensitive are generic and nonparallel language.

Generic Language **Generic language** uses words that may also apply only to one sex, race, or other group as though they represent everyone. This usage is a prob-

Generic language—using words that may apply only to one sex, race, or other group as though they represent everyone.

"S.P. — I suppose you realize that around here you're becoming like a son to me."

lem because it linguistically excludes a portion of the population it ostensibly includes. The following paragraphs contain some examples of generic language.

Traditionally, English grammar called for the use of the masculine pronoun *he* to stand for the entire class of humans regardless of gender. Under this rule, standard English called for such usage as "When a person shops, *he* should have a clear idea of what *he* wants to buy." Even though these statements are grammatically correct, they are sexist because the language (he) inherently excludes females. Despite traditional usage, it is hard to picture people of both sexes when we hear the masculine pronoun *he*.

So sensitive language avoids sentences that use only male pronouns when no specific gender reference is intended. You can avoid this in one of two ways. First, use plurals. For instance, instead of saying "Because a doctor has high status, his views may be believed regardless of topic," you could say "Because doctors have high status, their views may be believed regardless of topic." Alternatively, you can use both male and female pronouns: "Since a doctor has high status, his or her views may be believed regardless of topic" Stewart, Cooper, Stewart, and Friedley (1998, p. 63) cite research to show that using "he and she," and to a lesser extent "they," gives rise to listeners including women in their mental images, thus increasing gender balance in their perceptions. These changes are small, but they are more accurate than the generic option and demonstrate sensitivity.

A second problem results from the traditional use of the generic word, part *man*. Generic man refers to the use of *man* as part of a word when the referent is to all humans. Many words have become a common part of our language that are inherently sexist in that they apply to only one gender. Consider the term *man-made*. What this really means is that a product was produced by human beings, but its underlying connotation is that a male human being made the item. Some people try to argue that just because a word has "man" within it does not really affect people's understanding of meaning. But research has demonstrated that people usually visualize men (not women) when they read or hear these words. Moreover, when job titles end in "man," their occupants are assumed to have stereotypically masculine personality traits (Gmelch, 1998, p. 51).

In past generations this masculine generalization may have been appropriate, but that is no longer the case. Using generic terms when speaking about all human beings is troubling, but using them to describe the behavior or accomplishments of women (as in "Sally creates and arranges man-made flowers") is humorous.

For most sexist expressions, you can use or create suitable alternatives. For instance, use *police officer* instead of *policeman*, substitute *synthetic* for *man-made*. Instead of saying *mankind*, change the construction—for example, from "All of *mankind* benefits" to "All the *people in the world* benefit."

Nonparallel Language Nonparallel language is language in which terms are changed because of the sex, race, or other characteristics of the individual. Because

Nonparallel language—is language in which terms are changed because of the sex, race, or other characteristic of the individual.

it treats groups of people differently, nonparallel language is also belittling. Two common forms of nonparallelism are marking and unnecessary association.

Marking means the unnecessary addition of sex, race, age, or other designations to a general word. For instance, doctor is a word representing a person with a medical degree. To describe Sam Jones as a doctor is to treat Jones linguistically as a member of the class of doctors. For example, you might say "Jones, a doctor, contributed a great deal to the campaign." If, however, you said, "Jones, a woman doctor" (or a black doctor, or an old doctor, or a handicapped doctor), you would be marking. Marking is offensive to some people because you may appear to be trivializing the person's role by laying emphasis on an irrelevant characteristic. For instance, if you say "Jones is a really good female doctor" (or black doctor, or old doctor, or handicapped doctor), you may be intending to praise Jones. But your listeners may interpret the sentence as saying that Jones is a good doctor for a woman (or a black or old or handicapped person) but not necessarily as good as a male doctor (or a white or young or nonhandicapped doctor).

If it is relevant to identify a person by sex, race, age, or other characteristic, do so, but leave markers out of your labeling when they are irrelevant. One test of whether a characteristic is a relevant marker and appropriate is whether you would mention the person's sex, race, or age regardless of what sex, race, or age the person happened to be. It is relevant to specify "woman doctor," for example, only if in that context it would be equally relevant to specify "man doctor."

Unnecessary association is putting emphasis on one person's association with another when you are not talking about the other person. You hear a speaker say something like, "Gladys Thompson, whose husband is CEO of Acme Inc., is the chairperson for this year's United Way campaign." In response to this sentence, you might say that the association of Gladys Thompson with her husband gives further credentials to Gladys Thompson. But using the association may be seen to imply that Gladys Thompson is important not because of her own accomplishment but because of her husband's. The following illustrates a more flagrant example of unnecessary association: "Don Jones, the award-winning principal at Central High School and husband of Brenda Jones, local state senator, is chairperson for this year's minority scholarship campaign." Here Brenda Jones's occupation and relationship to Don Jones is clearly irrelevant. In either case, the pairing takes away from the person who is supposed to be the focus. So, avoid noting the association one person has with others when the association is irrelevant.

Very few people can escape all insensitive language. By monitoring your usage, however, you can guard against saying or doing things that offend others because they perpetuate outdated sex roles, racial stereotypes, and other biases.

Avoid Racist Labels You've heard children shout, "Sticks and stones may break my bones, but words will never hurt me." This rhyme

Marking—the unnecessary addition of sex, race, age, or other designations to a general word.

Unnecessary association—emphasizing one person's association with another when you are not talking about the other person.

TEST YOURSELF

Develop nonsexist alternatives for the following terms:

firemen	foreman	serviceman	brakeman
airman	stewardess	craftsman	repairman
councilman	doorman	night watchman	coed
waitress	bellman	anchorman	freshman

may be popular among children because they know it is untrue but it gives them a defense against cruel name-calling. Whether we admit it or not, words do hurt, sometimes permanently. Racist language is a sign of prejudice.

Where does offensive racist language come from? According to Molefi Asante, an internationally known scholar, racist language has its roots in our personal beliefs and attitudes. To a great extent these have been conditioned by the knowledge system to which we have been exposed. Until recently this knowledge system has had a Eurocentric bias. Thus the contributions to the development of humankind by cultures other than European have been ignored or minimized. To get a more complete understanding of Asante's scholarship, read the following Spotlight on Scholars selection.

Great personal damage has been done to individuals throughout history as a result of racist labeling. Of course, we all know that it is not the words alone that are so powerful; it is the context of the words—the situation, the feelings of the participants, the time, the place, or the tone of voice. You may recall circumstances in which a friend called you a racist name and you did not even flinch; yet you can probably recall other circumstances in which someone made you furious by using the same terms. It may be permissible for members of a subculture to use a racial slur when referring to a friend who is also a member of that subculture. But it is inappropriate for a nonmember to use that racial slur, and some members may be offended even if the speaker is from the same group. So in general you will want to avoid racist terms.

We should always be aware that our language has repercussions. When we do not understand or are not sensitive to our listener's frame of reference, we may state our ideas in language that distorts the intended communication. Many times a single inappropriate sentence may be enough to ruin an entire interaction. How can you speak more appropriately? (1) Consider the situation and use language geared to the formality of the relationship and setting; (2) avoid or define jargon and slang; (3) avoid crude language; (4) demonstrate sensitivity; and (5) avoid racist labels.

SKILL BUILDERS   **APPROPRIATENESS**

SKILL	USE	PROCEDURE	EXAMPLE
Using language that adapts to a specific person or persons and the context of the conversation.	To increase interaction effectiveness.	1. Adapt formality of language to the person and situation. 2. Be wary of jargon and slang. 3. Avoid crude language. 4. Demonstrate sensitivity. 5. Avoid racist labels.	Kevin (who is angry about a grade) approaches his professor: "Dr. Allensmith, I was interested in why you evaluated my essay as you did. I'm not sure that other professors would have viewed my topic as being trivial, so I'd like to hear more about your philosophy."

Molefi Kete Asante, Professor of Africology, Temple University, on

The Language of Prejudice and Racism

Molefi Kete Asante is an activist scholar who believes it is not enough to know, one must act to humanize the world. Throughout his career Asante has sought not only to understand what he studied, but also to use that knowledge to help people learn to exert their power.

In 1968, at the age of twenty-six, Asante completed his Ph.D. in Communication at UCLA. As a graduate student, Asante studied language and the rhetoric of agitation. For his dissertation he analyzed the speeches of one of the most zealous agitators of the American Revolution, Samuel Adams. During the late 1960s, however, Asante focused his attention on another revolution occurring in the United States. While he was working on his dissertation he also wrote *The Rhetoric of Black Revolution,* published in 1969.

Grounded in communication and the rhetoric of agitation, Asante noticed how racism and communication were intertwined, and he began to formulate the theory that racism in our culture is embedded in our language system. According to Asante, racism stems from a thought system that values one particular race over another. As a phenomenon of language,

racism is demonstrated by what people say about others and how they justify their personal attitudes and beliefs. What Asante discovered is that our language reflects the "knowledge system" we are taught. In the United States, this knowledge system has reflected a European rather than a multicultural view of human events and achievements. For instance, in most schools the study of the arts, or philosophy, or science focuses only on the contributions made by Europeans or European Americans. As a result of this focus, we "learn" that nothing really important originated anywhere else. We come to value the music, literature, rituals, and values of Europeans over those of other cultural groups. Since racism comes from valuing one particular race above another, Asante reasons, it was inevitable that monoethnic, Eurocentric approaches to education would result in our developing racist thoughts and a racist language structure that reifies these thoughts. To combat racism and racist language, Asante believes we must first accurately learn the contributions that have been made by other racial and cultural groups. History needs to reflect the sub-

stantial contributions that Africa, China, and other non-European groups have made to the development of humankind; literature and art need to include the work of various racial and ethnic groups. When people learn that all racial and cultural groups have made significant contributions, they will be less prone to view themselves as superior or inferior to others.

Seeking to reorient social science thinking regarding Africans and African Americans, Asante wrote three books that discussed the idea of Africans as agents rather than as victims; these works are *Afrocentricity, The Afrocentric Idea,* and *Kemet, Afrocentricity and Knowledge* (see citations in References at the end of the book). Asante has focused his own learning and his scholarship on discovering, reclaiming, and sharing the contributions of African culture and philosophy.

Asante's influence has been widespread. He served as the first Director of Afro-American Studies at UCLA, Department Head of Speech Communication at SUNY Buffalo, and Chair of the Department of African American Studies at Temple University, where he established the first Ph.D. program in African

American Studies. Asante has directed more than seventy-five doctoral dissertations. He is internationally known for his work on Afrocentricity and African culture. He has published fifty-two books and authored more than three hundred book chapters and journal articles. In the process, he has led an intellectual revolution among scholars working in numerous disciplines. Although he is noted for his scholarship, Asante says, "Working with students is the centerpiece of what I do." He currently teaches undergraduate courses on the African American church and twentieth-century mass media in black communities, and graduate courses in ancient Egyptian language and culture and Egyptian origins of rhetoric.

His personal interest in an African heritage has led Asante to trace his family ancestry back to Ghana. Recently, in Ghana he was "enstooled," a ceremony that formally acknowledges a person as a member of Ghanaian royalty. At that ceremony he was given the name Nana Okru Asante Peasah, Kyidomhene of Tafo. ■

Summary

Language is the body of words and the systems for their use in messages that are common to the people of the same speech community. Through language, we describe, classify, and limit; we evaluate; we discuss things outside our immediate experience; and we talk about language itself.

You will be a more effective communicator if you understand that language is learned, is creative, and that people interpret language differently. Language and meaning are complicated because each generation learns language anew, people invent new words and assign new meanings, language is a creative act, and that language is complicated by denotation and connotation. The denotation of a word is its dictionary meaning, which is complicated by the problem of words having more than one dictionary meaning. The connotation of a word is the emotional and value significance the word has for the listener in a particular situation.

Language meaning varies across different speech communities and among subgroups in a single speech community. Subgroups then develop variations on the core language called dialects, which allow subgroups to share meanings unique to their experience. In addition, cultural differences in language result from similarities and differences in behavior between cultures that are individualistic or collectivistic, have low or high uncertainty avoidance, are masculine or feminine, and are low or high in power distance. Gender differences in language

Why do people use crude language when they're in conflict? What are the most common results of such language usage?

result from the feminine voice being muted. Women tend to use more intensifiers and hedges and to add tag questions to sentences more than men.

You can improve your language skills by developing your vocabulary, choosing specific language, acquiring accurate information, using examples and details, by dating information, and by indexing generalizations.

Speaking appropriately means choosing language and symbols that are adapted to the needs, interests, knowledge, and attitudes of listeners, adapting to the situation, being wary of jargon and slang, avoiding crude language, and demonstrating sensitivity.

OBSERVE & ANALYZE

Journal Activity

Monitoring Your Use of Language

Tape-record at least ten minutes of a conversation that you have with a friend or a family member. Talk about a subject that you hold strong views about: affirmative action, welfare, school levies, candidates for office. Be sure to get the permission of the other person before you tape. At first you may feel self-conscious about having a recorder going. But as you get into discussion it's quite likely that you'll be able to converse normally.

Play back the tape and take notes of sections where your language might have been clearer. Based on these notes, write better expressions of your ideas by using more precise and specific/concrete language and by dating and indexing generalizations.

Replay the tape. This time take notes on any racist, sexist, or biased expression that you used. Based on these notes, write more appropriate expressions for the ones you used.

Write a paragraph or two that describes what you have learned from this experience about your use of language. ■

WHAT WOULD YOU DO?

A Question of Ethics

On the first day of class Heather and Terry, who had known each other since freshman year, asked Paul and Martha, who were sitting next to them, if they wanted to hang out with them at the Student Union Grill since class had let out rather early that first day. When they agreed, the four made their way to the Union.

After they had all ordered drinks and a snack, they began talking about what they thought the class would be like. Soon, the conversation began to include other students who were taking the class.

"By the way," Paul said, "do any of you know Porky?"

"Who?" the group responded in unison.

"The really fat guy who was sitting a couple of seats from me. We've been in a couple of classes together. He's a pretty nice guy."

"What's his name?" Heather asked.

"Carl, but he'll always be Porky to me."

"Do you call him that to his face?" Terry asked.

"Aw, I'd never say anything like that to him—Man, I wouldn't want to hurt his feelings."

"Well," Martha chimed in, "I'd sure hate to think that you'd call me 'skinny' when I wasn't around. Or am I the 'bitch,' or some other unflattering term?"

"Come on—what's with you guys?" Paul retorted. "You're trying to tell me that you never talk about another person that way when they aren't around?"

"Well," said Terry, "maybe a couple of times, but I've never talked like that about someone I really like."

"Someone you like?" queried Heather. "Why does that make a difference? Do you mean it's OK to trash talk someone so long as you don't like him?"

1. Sort out the ethical issues in this case. How ethical is it to call people you supposedly like by an unflattering name that you would never call them if they were in your presence?

2. From an ethical standpoint, is whether you like a person or not what determines when such name calling is OK? ■

Chapter Resources

Communication Improvement Plan: Verbal Communication

How would you like to improve your use of language as discussed in this chapter?

Vocabulary development

Increase language clarity (become better at being specific)

Dating

Indexing

Speaking appropriately (formality, jargon and slang, crude language, demonstrating sensitivity, racist language)

Pick one of the above and write a communication improvement plan.

Skill: _____

Problem: _____

_____

_____

_____

Goal: _____

_____

_____

_____

Procedure:

1. _____

2. _____

3. _____

Test of Achieving Goal: _____

_____

Key Words

Language, p. 93

Speech community, p. 93

Words, p. 93

Denotation, p. 95

Connotation, p. 96

Dialects, p. 96

Individualistic cultures, p. 97

Collectivistic cultures, p. 97

Low-context communication, p. 97

High-context communication, p. 97

Low uncertainty-avoidance societies, p. 98

High uncertainty-avoidance societies, p. 98

Masculine cultures, p. 98

Feminine cultures, p. 98

Power distance, p. 98

High power-distance societies, p. 98

Low power-distance societies, p. 98

Sex, p. 99

Gender, p. 99

Specific words, p. 103

Concrete words, p. 104

Precise words, p. 104

Dating information, p. 106

Indexing generalizations, p. 108

Speaking appropriately, p. 110

Jargon, p. 111

Slang, p. 111

Generic language, p. 111

Nonparallel language, p. 112

Marking, p. 113

Unnecessary association, p. 113

Inter-Act with Media

CINEMA

Randa Haines (Director). (1991). *The Doctor.* William Hurt, Christine Lahti, Elizabeth Perkins, Mandy Patinkin, Adam Arkin.

Brief Summary: This film is based on Dr. Ed Rosenbaum's book *A Taste of My Own Medicine.* William Hurt plays a doctor who believes that he must maintain distance from his patients so that he can remain objective and efficient. When he develops throat cancer, he discovers what it is like to be a patient and deal with the hospital bureaucracy. A young female cancer patient helps him to learn how to empathize with patients and to cope with his own illness. He develops an innovative approach to the training of his interns.

IPC Concepts: Language, relationships, message clarity, jargon, ethics.

James L. Brooks (Director). (1983). *Terms of Endearment.* Shirley MacLaine, Debra Winger, Jack Nicholson, John Lithgow, Jeff Daniels, Danny DeVito.

Brief Summary: The Alm tells the story of Emma (Winger), a young woman who marries a college English teacher and is later diagnosed with cancer. She has a very domineering mother, Aurora (MacLaine), with whom she must continually struggle to keep her own identity secure. Prior to developing cancer, she has an affair, partially in response her husband's infidelity. Aurora takes charge of Emma's health care and must contend with the husband, the children, and her own relationship needs. Two scenes stand out in terms of language and interpersonal language usage. The first involves a confrontation between Emma and her husband's mistress. The second takes place between Aurora and the hospital staff charged with caring for her daughter.

IPC Concepts: Medical jargon and relationship jargon.

THEATER

William Shakespeare. *Romeo and Juliet.*

Brief Summary: Virtually any play by Shakespeare will showcase language in interpersonal communication. Shakespeare understood human emotion, romance, and relationships very well, and used language in a creative and insightful manner. This is clearly demonstrated in *Romeo and Juliet.* The language of their tragic love story is a part of our relational language.

IPC Concepts: Language in relationships.

LITERATURE

Dashiel Hammett. (1935) *The Maltese Falcon.* New York: Knopf.

Brief Summary: Sam Spade, the private detective at the center of the story, loses his partner on a late night assignment. Sam is then given the job of helping a mysterious woman who is caught up in a search for the "stuff that dreams are made of," the Maltese Falcon. Hammett has a wonderful way of creating and conveying colorful, memorable characters, and embellishing their interactions with equally colorful language. In this mystery and in the Nick Charles mystery *The Thin Man,* the argot of the criminal underworld and the police world is cleverly interwoven into the story.

IPC Concepts: Language of the lower class of New York in the 1930s. The film does an excellent job of showcasing the argot of police work, the private eye, and the criminal underworld.

Aldous Huxley. (1932). *Brave New World.* Harper & Row: New York; (1958). Brave New World Revisited. Harper & Row: New York.

Brief Summary: Huxley's brilliant depiction of the world of the future in which social interaction is controlled by test tube births, pills to control emotions, consumerism over religion, sex without relationship, and rigid social class based on scientific or genetic distinctions that are artificially created at birth.

IPC Concepts: The language of social interaction, control by science and advertising as propaganda.

ACADEMIC WORK

William Lutz. (1981). *Double-Speak: From "Revenue Enhancement" to "Terminal Living."* New York: HarperCollins Publishers.

Brief Summary: Lutz has studied language misuse for many years. He tracks the misuse in any area where he can find it. his book is a rich collection of the misuse and overuse of jargon, doublespeak, gobbledygook, and euphemistic language in medicine, law, advertising, government, and everyday life.

IPC Concepts: Language misuse, need for message clarity.

George Lakoff & Mark Johnson. (1980). *Metaphors We Live By.* Chicago: University of Chicago Press.

Brief Summary: Lakoff and Johnson examine the way in which metaphors and all language interact with how we think, feel, and act. This is a very useful book to gain insight into how people feel and what they may really be saying, by listening to their use of language.

IPC Concepts: Metaphor, self, relational language.

WHAT'S ON THE WEB

How to Express Difficult Feelings
http://www.drnadig.com/feelings.htm

Brief Summary: This Web site examines the nature and function of language in expressing emotion. The site includes guidelines on language use when in conflict, the difference between thoughts and feelings, and detailed directions on "I" language. There are links to listening and conflict management with this site.

IPC Concepts: language and conflict.

Human Communication Research Centre
http://www.hcrc.ed.ac.uk/Site/site_home.html

Brief Summary: The home page of the Human Communication Research Centre (HCRC), an interdisciplinary research center at the Universities of Edinburgh and Glasgow, focuses on spoken and written language, as well as communication in other media (visual, graphical, and computer-based).

IPC Concepts: Language in human communication.

Assertiveness Prepared by Organizational Development and Training, Department of Human Resources, Tufts University.
http://www.tufts.edu/hr/tips/assert.html

Brief Summary: This site is a really good introduction to the nature of assertiveness, especially on "I" language, with specific instructions and examples that supplement the discussion on both language and influence very nicely.

IPC Concepts: Language and respect.

CHAPTER 5

Communicating Through Nonverbal

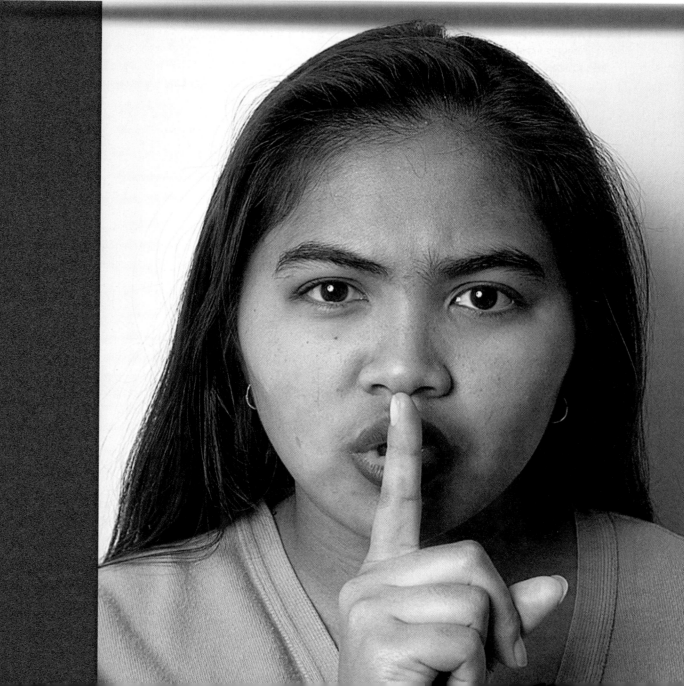

Behaviors

After you have read this chapter, you should be able to answer these questions:

- What are the differences between verbal and nonverbal communication?
- What are the major types and uses of body motions?
- What are the elements of paralanguage, and how does each affect message meaning?
- How do clothing, touching behavior, and use of time affect self-presentation?
- How is communication affected by the use of physical space?
- How do temperature, lighting, and color affect communication?
- What are three ways you can improve the messages you communicate through your nonverbal behavior?
- What are the most significant cultural and gender differences in nonverbal communication?

"You don't want me to buy that denim jacket we looked at this morning, do you?" Clay asked.

"What do you mean 'I don't want you to'?" Maya replied.

"You've got that look on your face."

"What look?"

"You know the look—the one you always get on your face when you don't want me to do something I want to do. But no matter, I'm going to get that jacket."

"I still don't know what look you're talking about, Clay."

"Sure you do. You know how I can tell you do? Because now you're embarrassed that I know and so you're raising your voice."

"I'm not raising my voice, Clay."

"Oh yes you are."

"Clay, you're making me angry."

"You're just saying that because I'm on to you."

"'On to me'? Clay, I don't care whether you get that jacket or not."

"Of course you do. You don't have to tell me in so many words."

"Clay, it's your decision. If you want to get the jacket, get it."

"Well, I don't think I want to—but don't think you talked me out of it."

We've all heard—and said—"actions speak louder than words." Actions are so important to our communication that researchers have estimated that in face-to-face communication as much as 65 percent of the social meaning is a result of nonverbal behavior (Burgoon, Buller, & Woodall, 1989, p. 155). What this means is that the meaning we assign to any communication is based on both the content of the verbal message and our interpretation of the nonverbal behavior that accompanies and surrounds the verbal message. And, as Clay found out, interpreting these nonverbal actions is not always the easiest thing to do.

In the last chapter we discussed language, the verbal elements of interpersonal communication. In this chapter we provide a framework for understanding and improving nonverbal communication behavior. We begin by describing the nature of nonverbal behavior and the way verbal and nonverbal communication messages interrelate. We then look at the major types of nonverbal communication: body motions, paralanguage, self-presentation, and management of the environment. We conclude our discussion by suggesting methods for increasing the accuracy of your nonverbal communication.

The Nature of Nonverbal Communication Behavior

In the broadest sense, the term *nonverbal communication* is commonly used to describe all human communication events that transcend spoken or written words (Knapp & Hall, 2002, p. 5). Specifically, **nonverbal communication behaviors** are those bodily actions and vocal qualities that typically accompany a verbal message. The behaviors are usually interpreted as intentional and have agreed-upon interpretations in a particular speech community (Burgoon, 1994, p. 231).

When we say that nonverbals are interpreted as intentional, we mean that people act as if they are intended even if they are performed unconsciously or unintentionally (Burgoon, 1994, p. 231). So, when Anita says "I've had it" as she slams a book down on the table, we interpret the loudness of her voice and the act of slamming the book down as intentionally emphasizing the meaning of the words.

Likewise, when we refer to agreed-upon interpretations in a culture or speech community, we recognize that although people from around the world use many of the same nonverbal cues, they may interpret them differently. For instance, a smile may convey happiness and pleasure in a situation, or it may be a means of saving face in an uncomfortable situation.

In addition to bodily actions and vocal qualities that accompany verbal messages, nonverbal messages are also conveyed by our use of physical space and our choices of clothing, furniture, lighting, temperature, and color.

We communicate nonverbally even when we aren't speaking. In fact, much of our nonverbal behavior is reactive—we unconsciously respond to what is happening, so others use it as a guide to our true feelings. As we discuss each type of nonverbal behavior, we will describe the behavior that is typical in the United States. Then, because appropriate nonverbal behavior depends on culture, we will describe how some other cultural groups differ in the way that particular type of behavior is used and interpreted.

> **Nonverbal communication behaviors**—bodily actions and vocal qualities that typically accompany a verbal message.

Body Motions

Of all nonverbal behavior, you are probably most familiar with **kinesics,** the technical name for the study of body motions used in communication. In this section we'll consider the types and functions of body motions as well as cultural variations.

> **Kinesics**—the technical name for the study of body motions used in communication.

Types of Body Motions

Body motions include eye contact, facial expression, gesture, and posture.

Eye Contact **Eye contact,** also referred to as **gaze,** is how and how much we look at people with whom we are communicating. Eye contact conveys many meanings. It indicates if we are paying attention. How we look at a person can convey a range of emotions such as anger, fear, or affection. For instance, we describe people in love as looking "doe eyed." Intense eye contact may also be used to exercise dominance (Pearson, West, & Turner, 1995, p. 121). So we comment

> **Eye contact** or **gaze**—how and how much we look at people with whom we are communicating.

What does the absence of eye contact signal in this photo?

on "looks that could kill," and we talk of someone "staring another person down."

Moreover, through our eye contact, we monitor the effect of our communication. By maintaining your eye contact, you can tell when or whether a person is paying attention to you, when a person is involved in what you are saying, and whether what you are saying is causing anxiety.

Although the amount of eye contact differs from person to person and from situation to situation, studies show that talkers hold eye contact about 40 percent of the time and listeners nearly 70 percent of the time (Knapp & Hall, 2002, p. 350). We generally maintain better eye contact when we are discussing topics with which we are comfortable, when we are genuinely interested in a person's comments or reactions, or when we are trying to influence the other person. Conversely, we tend to avoid eye contact when we are discussing topics that make us uncomfortable, when we lack interest in the topic or person, or when we are embarrassed, ashamed, or trying to hide something.

Because people judge others by their nonverbal behavior, you want your eye contact behavior to be perceived as appropriate. You may need to alter your behavior if you find that you maintain a less than normal amount of eye contact even when you are interested in the person or topic of conversation, when you feel confident, or when you have no cause to feel shame or embarrassment.

You can improve your eye contact by becoming conscious of looking at people when you are talking with them. If you find your eyes straying away from that person, work to regain direct contact.

Facial expression—the arrangement of facial muscles to communicate emotional states or reactions to messages.

Facial Expression **Facial expression** is the arrangement of facial muscles to communicate emotional states or reactions to messages. The three sets of muscles that are manipulated to form facial expressions are (1) the brow and forehead; (2) the eyes, eyelids, and root of the nose; and (3) the cheeks, mouth, remainder of the nose, and chin. Our facial expressions are especially important in conveying the six basic emotions of happiness, sadness, surprise, fear, anger, and disgust.

Perhaps the greatest problem with facial expression is the failure of expression to match feelings and meaning. For instance, some people smile or show no expression when they're angry.

You can work to ensure that your facial expression complements your feelings and meaning. Practice being conscious of whether you sense that your face is reflecting your ideas and feelings. If not, try to experience your idea or feeling more strongly.

Gesture Gestures are the movements of our hands, arms, and fingers that we use to describe or to emphasize. Thus, when a person says "about this high" or "nearly this round," we expect to see a gesture accompany the verbal description. Likewise, when a person says "Put that down" or "Listen to me," a pointing finger, pounding fist, or some other gesture often reinforces the point. People do vary, however, in the amount of gesturing that accompanies their speech—some people "talk with their hands" far more than others.

The problem comes when either your gestures are not reinforcing your meaning or they are sending contradictory meanings. You can work to ensure that your gestures complement or emphasize your ideas and feelings. As you talk, think about what you are doing with your hands. Determine what kinds of gestures would further the perception of your meaning. Consciously work to make gestures more meaningful.

Posture Posture is the position and movement of the body. Changes in posture can also communicate. For instance, suddenly sitting upright and leaning forward shows increased attention, standing up may signal "I'm done now," and turning one's back to the other conveys a redirection of attention away from that person.

> **Gestures**—movements of hands, arms, and fingers that we use to describe or to emphasize.

> **Posture**—the position and movement of the body.

How Body Motions Are Used

Body motions in general and gestures in particular help us considerably in conveying meaning (Ekman & Friesen, 1969, pp. 49–98).

1. Body motions may be used to take the place of a word or phrase. We could make a lengthy list of nonverbal symbols that take the place of words or phrases that we use frequently. For instance, pointing thumbs up means "everything is a go"; the extension of the first and second fingers held in a V shape means "peace" or "victory"; shaking the head from side to side means "no" and up and down means "yes"; shrugging the shoulders means "maybe," "I don't care," or "I don't know."

In many contexts nonverbal symbols are used as a complete language. **Sign language** refers to systems of body motions used to communicate, which include sign

> **Sign language**—systems of body motions used to communicate.

languages of the deaf and alternate sign languages used by Trappist monks in Europe and Aborigines in Australia (Leathers, 1997, p. 70). Like verbal languages, sign languages vary by culture and have their own grammar and syntax.

In addition to standing for a word or a phrase, body motions can be used to control. For instance, when a child is doing something wrong, her mother may give her "a look" that the child reads as "Stop what you're doing right now." Whether the nonverbal behavior is a stare, a hand on the arm, a particular tone of voice, or some combination, its purpose is to control. While using nonverbal communication to control may at times be appropriate, unfortunately, these same behaviors become more sinister in abusive relationships. In such relationships the victim may react with fear when the parent or significant other uses a nonverbal threat.

2. Body motions may be used to illustrate what a speaker is saying. We use body motions, especially gestures, to illustrate what we are saying in at least five ways:

- To *emphasize* speech: A man may pound the table in front of him as he says "Don't bug me."
- To show the *path* or *direction* of thought: A professor may move her hands on an imaginary continuum when she says "The papers ranged from very good to very bad."
- To show *position:* A waiter may point when he says "Take that table."
- To *describe:* A speaker may use her hands to indicate size as she says "The ball is about three inches in diameter."
- To *mimic:* A person may nod his head as he says "Did you see the way she nodded?"

Conversely, body motions can detract from a speaker's message if inappropriately used or if their use calls attention to them rather than adding to the speaker's meaning (think of people who wave their hands unnecessarily as they talk).

3. Body motions can display our feelings. Emotional displays take place automatically and are likely to be quite noticeable. For instance, if you stub your toe on a chair as you drag yourself out of bed in the morning, you are likely to grimace in pain. More often than not, these spur-of-the-moment expressions are not intended as conscious communication; nevertheless these reactions will take place automatically, whether or not anyone else is present, and they will probably be quite noticeable.

Occasionally we are fooled by these displays when people purposely deintensify or overreact. For example, a baseball player may remain stone-faced when he is hit by a wild pitch and refuse to rub the spot where the ball struck; at the other extreme, a youngster may howl "in pain" when her older sister lightly bumps her by accident.

4. Body motions may be used to control or regulate the flow of a conversation or other communication transaction. We use shifts in eye contact, slight head movements, shifts in posture, raised eyebrows, and nodding of our head to tell another person when to continue, to repeat, to elaborate, to hurry up, or to finish. Effective communicators learn to adjust what they are saying and how they are saying it on the basis of such nonverbal cues.

5. Body motions may be used to relieve tension. As we listen to people and watch them while they speak, they may scratch their heads, tap their feet, or wring their hands. These unplanned releases of energy serve to reduce the stress a speaker may be feeling.

Cultural Variations

As we have said, the use of body motions and the meanings they convey differ among cultures. Several cultural differences in body motions are well documented.

Eye Contact A majority of people in the United States and other Western cultures expect those with whom they are communicating to "look them in the eye." Samovar and Porter (2001) conclude in their review of research that direct eye contact is not universally considered appropriate (p. 178). For instance, in Japan people direct their gaze to a position around the Adam's apple and avoid direct eye contact. Chinese, Indonesians, and rural Mexicans lower their eyes as a sign of deference—to them too much direct eye contact is a sign of bad manners. Arabs, in contrast, look intently into the eyes of the person with whom they are talking for longer periods—to them direct eye contact demonstrates keen interest. Likewise, there are also differences in use of eye contact among subcultures within the United States. For instance, African Americans use more continuous eye contact than European Americans when they are speaking but less when they are listening (Samovar & Porter, 2001, pp. 178–179).

People who live in the same apartment building are likely to become acquainted. How has where you live influenced whether you talk with your neighbors?

Facial Expression, Gestures, and Movements Studies show that there are many similarities in nonverbal communication across cultures, especially in facial expressions. For instance, several facial expressions seem to be universal, including a slight raising of the eyebrow to communicate recognition, wriggling one's nose, and a disgusted facial look to show social repulsion (Martin & Nakayama 2000, pp. 183–184). In fact, at least six facial expressions (happiness, sadness, fear, anger, disgust, and surprise) carry the same basic meaning throughout the world (Samovar & Porter, 2001, p. 177).

Across cultures, people also show considerable differences in the meaning of gestures. For instance, the forming of a circle with the thumb and forefinger signi-

Journal Activity

Gender Variations in Body Motions

Find a place in the cafeteria or another public spot where you can observe the conversations of others. You are to observe the nonverbal behaviors of three dyads for at least five minutes each. First observe the interaction of two men, then the interaction of two women, and finally the interaction of a man and a woman. Using the following observation tally sheet, record each participant's behavior and any other behavioral cues you note. Using these observation notes, review the material presented earlier on male versus female use of body motions. Did your observations confirm these trends? If they did not, develop an explanation about why they didn't. ■

Nonverbal Behavior Observation Form: Body Motions

Behavior (frequency)	Participant 1 (sex: __)	Participant 2 (sex: __)
Eye contact	High Med Low	High Med Low
Smiling	High Med Low	High Med Low
Forward lean of body	High Med Low	High Med Low
Touches or plays with hair	High Med Low	High Med Low
Touches or plays with clothes	High Med Low	High Med Low
Taps hand or fingers on surface	High Med Low	High Med Low
Arm position relative to body	High Med Low	High Med Low

fies the OK sign in the United States, but means zero or worthless in France, is a symbol for money in Japan, and is a vulgar gesture in Germany and Brazil (Axtell, 1998, pp. 44, 143, 212).

Displays of emotion may also vary. For instance, in some Eastern cultures people have been socialized to deintensify emotional behavior cues, whereas members of other cultures have been socialized to amplify their displays of emotion.

Gender Variations

Men and women also show differences in their use of nonverbal communication behavior (Canary & Hause, 1993, p. 141).

Eye Contact   In the United States women tend to have more frequent eye contact during conversations than men do (Cegala & Sillars, 1989). Moreover, women tend to hold eye contact longer than men regardless of the sex of the person they are interacting with (Wood, 2001, p. 150).

Facial Expression and Gesture   In general, women tend to smile more than men, but their smiles are harder to interpret. Men's smiles generally mean positive feelings, whereas women's smiles tend to be responses to affiliation and friendliness (Hall, 1998, p. 169). Gender differences in the use of gestures are so profound that people have been found to attribute masculinity or femininity on the basis of gesture style alone (Pearson, West, & Turner, 1995, p. 126). For instance, women are more likely to keep their arms close to the body, are less likely to lean forward with the body, play more often with their hair or clothing, and tap their hands more often than men.

Not only do men and women use nonverbal behaviors in different ways, but men and women differ in how they interpret the nonverbal communication behaviors of others. Major difficulties in male–female relationships are often created by inaccurately encoding and decoding nonverbal messages. A number of studies have shown that women are better at decoding nonverbal vocal and facial cues than men (Stewart, Cooper, Stewart, & Friedley, 1998, p. 74).

Paralanguage

Paralanguage, or **vocalics,** is the nonverbal "sound" of what we hear—how something is said. We begin by describing the four vocal characteristics that comprise paralanguage and then discuss how vocal interferences can disrupt message flow.

Vocal Characteristics

By controlling the four major vocal characteristics—pitch, volume, rate, and quality—we can complement, supplement, or contradict the meaning conveyed by the language of our message.

Pitch is the highness or lowness of vocal tone. People raise and lower vocal pitch and change volume to emphasize ideas, indicate questions, and show nervousness. They may also raise the pitch when they are nervous or lower the pitch when they are trying to be forceful.

Volume is the loudness or softness of tone. Whereas some people have booming voices that carry long distances, others are normally soft-spoken. Regardless of their normal volume level, however, people do vary their volume depending on the situation and topic of discussion. For example, people talk loudly when they wish to be heard in noisy settings, they may vary their volume when they are angry, or they may speak more softly when they are being romantic or loving.

Rate is the speed at which a person speaks. People tend to talk more rapidly when they are happy, frightened, nervous, or excited and more slowly when they are problem solving out loud or are trying to emphasize a point.

Quality is the sound of a person's voice. Each human voice has a distinct tone, some voices are raspy, some smoky, some have bell-like qualities, while others are throaty. Moreover, each of us uses a slightly different quality of voice to communicate a particular state of mind. We may associate complaints with a whiny, nasal quality; seductive invitation with a soft, breathy quality; and anger with a strident, harsh quality.

Some of us have developed vocal habits that lead others to consistently misinterpret what we say. For instance, some people have cultivated a tone of voice that causes others to believe they are being sarcastic when they are not. If you have concerns about your vocal characteristics, talk them over with your professor. Your professor can observe you and make recommendations for additional help should you need it.

Vocal Interferences

Although most of us are occasionally guilty of using some **vocal interferences**—extraneous sounds or words

Paralanguage or **vocalics**–the nonverbal "sound" of what we hear–how something is said.

Pitch–the highness or lowness of vocal tone.

Volume–the loudness or softness of tone.

Rate–the speed at which a person speaks.

Quality–the sound of voice.

Vocal interferences–extraneous sounds or words that interrupt fluent speech.

INTER-ACT WITH Technology

As you watch a videotape of a movie or a television program, select a segment where two people are talking with each other for a couple of minutes. The first time you watch, mute the video (turn off the sound). Based on nonverbal behaviors alone, determine the climate of the conversation (whether the people are flirting, in conflict, discussing an issue, kidding around, etc.). What nonverbal behaviors and reactions led you to that conclusion? The second time, watch nonverbals but also listen to vocal variations in volume, pitch, and rate of speed. Do any of these vocal cues add to your assessment? The third time, focus on what the characters are saying. Now analyze the segment. What percentage of meaning came from nonverbal elements? What did you learn from this? ■

that interrupt fluent speech—these interferences become a problem when they are perceived by others as excessive and when they begin to call attention to themselves and so prevent listeners from concentrating on meaning. The most common interferences that creep into our speech include "uh," "er," "well," "OK," and those nearly universal interrupters of American conversations, "you know" and "like."

Vocal interferences may initially be used as "place markers" designed to fill in momentary gaps in speech that would otherwise be silence. In this way they indicate that we are not done speaking and it is still our "turn." So we may use an "um" when we need to pause momentarily to search for the right word or idea. For some speakers the customary filler sounds are "uh" or "er"; for others they are "well" or "um." Although the chance of being interrupted may be real (some people will seek to interrupt at any pause), the intrusion of an excessive number of fillers can lead to the impression that you are unsure of yourself or confused in what you are attempting to say.

Equally prevalent, and perhaps even more disruptive than "uh" and "um" is the overuse of "you know" and "like." The "you know" habit may begin as a genuine way to find out whether what is being said is already known by others. For some, "you know" may be a source of identification—a way to establish common ground with the person being spoken to. Similarly, the use of "like" may start from making comparisons such as "Tom is hot; he looks like Denzel Washington." Soon the comparisons become shortcuts, as in "He's like really hot!" Finally, the use of "like" becomes pure filler: "Like, he's really cool, like I can't really explain it, but I'll tell you he's like wow!" For most people flooding of sentences with "you know" and "like" has become a bad habit that results in disjointed messages and sloppy encoding. Instead of working to clarify their thoughts by choosing precise words, they use "like" and "you know" to abdicate their responsibility to encode their ideas. Soon they are using so many fillers that their messages become unintelligible, shifting most of the responsibility for discerning meaning to the receiver.

Curiously, no matter how irritating the use of "you know" or "like" may be to listeners, they are unlikely to verbalize their irritation. While listeners may not acknowledge irritation and while these interferences may be "accepted" between peers in everyday speech, their habitual use is a handicap in many settings. For example, excessive use of vocal interferences during job interviews, at work, or in class can affect the impression that you make. Since for the most part speech habits persist from one setting to another, if you consistently use these fillers in your everyday speech, you are unlikely to control them easily in more formal settings.

INTER-ACT WITH Technology

Vocal Interferences

Arrange to have a conversation with someone you know quite well. Choose a subject that is of interest to both of you. Tape-record the conversation. Use a stopwatch to time the number of minutes and seconds that you spoke during the conversation. ■

1. Replay the conversation and count the number of times you use each vocal interference described earlier. Which type of vocal interruption do you use most frequently?

2. At what rate did you use vocal interruptions? Compute the rate as follows: rate of vocal interruptions per minute equals number of interruptions divided by number of minutes.

3. Be prepared share the rate you have computed with the class. Compare this rate to that of your classmates. Are you above or below the class average?

By practicing the following steps, you can limit the occurrence of vocal interferences in your speech.

1. Train yourself to hear your interferences. Even people with a major problem seem to be unaware of the interferences they use. You can train your ear in one of two ways:

   a. Tape-record yourself talking for several minutes about any subject—the game you saw yesterday, the course you plan to take next term, or anything else that comes to mind. Before you play the tape, back estimate the number of times you think you peppered your speech with "uh," "you know," and "like." Then compare the actual number with your estimate. As your ear becomes trained, your estimates will be closer to the actual number.

   b. Have a close friend listen to you and raise a hand every time you use a filler such as "uh," "you know," or "like." You may find the experience traumatic or nerve-wracking, but your ear will soon start to pick up the vocal interferences as fast as the listener.

2. Practice to see how long you can go without using a vocal interference. Start out by trying to talk for fifteen seconds. Continue to increase the time until you can talk for two minutes without a single interference. Meaning may suffer; you may spend a disproportionate amount of time avoiding interferences. Still, it is good practice.

3. Mentally note your usage of interferences in conversation. You will be making real headway when you can recognize your own interferences in normal conversation without affecting the flow. When you reach this stage, you will find yourself beginning to avoid or limit the use of interferences.

Self-Presentation

People learn a great deal about us and judge us based on how we present ourselves through our choices of clothing and personal grooming, poise and self-confidence, our use of touching, and the way we treat time.

Clothing and Personal Grooming

Since choice of clothing and personal grooming will communicate a message, you need to determine what message you want to send and then dress and groom accordingly. Lawyers and business managers understand the power of dress and grooming. For instance, an attorney knows that a person charged with drug peddling would be foolish to show up in the courtroom wearing the local gang starter jacket, heavy gold chains, oversized pants, and a backward-facing baseball cap. Similarly, business managers periodically adjust their dress codes to make sure they reflect the images they want their businesses to project. For instance, many companies have been rethinking their decisions about "casual dress days." As Georgie Geyer pointed out in an editorial, "Korn-Ferry International, the nation's largest executive search firm, experimented all summer with 'five-day-a-week' casual. Finally, it declared the experiment a failure, because 'We found that casual dress fostered a casual attitude'" (1999, p. A12).

OBSERVE & ANALYZE

Journal Activity

Clothing Choices

Take an inventory of your wardrobe. Begin by dividing your clothes into three groups: those you wear for "special" dress-up occasions, those you wear for your everyday activities (school and work), and those you wear for leisure or "grubbing around." Count the number of pants, shirts, blouses, skirts, dresses, belts, shoes, and so on that are in each category. Is your wardrobe "balanced" or do you have an overabundance of one type of clothing? Was it easy or difficult for you to categorize your wardrobe in this way? If someone who did not know you were to peruse your closet and drawers, what would be their impression of you? Would it be accurate? ■

Poise–assurance of manner.

Many young people have been consciously choosing clothing styles and other personal grooming behaviors that stretch Western norms of acceptability. From "retro" fashions to hip-hop styles, from blue hair and nail colors to dreadlocks and Mohawks, from tattooing to body piercing, more and more people are choosing to use their physical appearance to differentiate themselves from some groups and to identify closely with others.

Part of being a competent communicator is realizing that your physical appearance sends a message and the meaning of that message depends on the receiver's perceptions as much as it does on your own intentions. While each of us has the right to express our individuality and to communicate our political feelings in our dress and personal grooming, we must realize that when we stretch norms and conventions, we create barriers.

Poise

Poise refers to assurance of manner. As much as 20 percent of the population experiences a high degree of nervousness when encountering strangers, speaking in a group, or making a speech (Richmond & McCroskey, 1995, p. 35). Others may be quite comfortable when encountering strangers one on one, but still get tense in another setting such as speaking in a group or speaking in public. For most people, nervousness decreases as they gain confidence in their ability to function well in a particular setting. Mastery of the skills discussed in this text, for instance, should help you cope with the nervousness you might face in various interpersonal communication situations.

Touch–putting a hand or finger in contact with something.

Touch

Touch, which is, of course, putting a hand or finger in contact with something, is often considered to be the most basic form of communication. Touching behavior is a fundamental aspect of nonverbal communication in general and of self-presentation in particular. We use our hands, our arms, and other body parts to pat, hug, slap, kiss, pinch, stroke, hold, embrace, and tickle. Through touch we communicate a variety of emotions and messages. In Western culture, we shake hands to be sociable and polite, we pat a person on the back for encouragement, we hug a person to show love, we clasp raised hands to demonstrate solidarity. Our touching can be gentle or firm, perfunctory or passionate, brief or lingering. How we touch can communicate our power, our empathy, our understanding.

People differ in their touching behavior and their reactions to unsolicited touch from others. Some people, because of individual preference, family background, or culture, like to touch and be touched; other people do not. Women tend to touch others less than men do, but women value touching more than men do. Women view touch as an expressive behavior that demonstrates warmth and affiliation, whereas men view touch as instrumental behavior, so that touching females is considered as leading to sexual activity (Pearson, West, & Turner, 1995, p. 142).

Although American culture is relatively noncontact oriented, the kinds and amounts of touching behavior within our society vary widely. Touching behavior that seems innocuous to one person may be perceived as overly intimate or threatening by another. Moreover, the perceived appropriateness of touch differs with the context. Touch that is considered appropriate in private may embarrass a person when done in public or with a large group of people.

What you communicate by touching may be perceived positively or negatively. Thus, if you want to be perceived as sensitive and caring, it is a good idea to ask the other person before touching (Burgoon, Walther, & Baesler, 1992, p. 259).

Time

A less obvious aspect of our self-presentation is how we manage and react to others' use and management of what Edward T. Hall (1959) calls "informal time": duration, activity, and punctuality (p. 135).

Duration is the amount of time we regard as appropriate for certain events or activities. For instance, we may expect a sermon to last twenty to thirty minutes, a typical class to run fifty minutes, and a movie to be roughly two hours long. When the length of an event differs significantly from our expectations, we begin to attribute meaning to its duration. For example, if we are told that a job interview will take one hour and it is over in twenty minutes, we may conclude that we didn't get the job. Similarly, if the interview stretches to two hours, we may believe that we are in strong contention for the job. Since our use of time creates its own meanings, we need to learn to attend carefully to polite conventions about the "appropriate duration" of events and activities.

Activity refers to what people perceive should be done in a given period. Many of us work during the day, sleep at night, eat a light meal around midday, and so on. When someone engages in behavior at a time that we deem inappropriate, we are likely to react negatively. For instance, Susan, who prides herself on being available to her employees while at work, may well be put off when Sung Lei calls her at home during the dinner hour to discuss a presentation that is to be delivered at the end of the month. While Sung Lei may think she is presenting herself as organized and interested in her work, Susan may view her call as intrusive.

Punctuality is the extent to which one adheres strictly to the appointed or regular time. In many respects it may be the dimension of time that is most closely related to self-presentation. If you make an appointment to meet your boss in her office at 10 A.M., her opinion of you may differ depending on whether you arrive at 9:50, 10:00, 10:10, or 10:30. Similarly, your opinion of your boss will differ depending on whether she is there or not. In the United States, strict punctuality is the dominant cultural imperative. When a date is made or an appointment set, you are normally expected to be prompt or risk having your early or late arrival be interpreted as meaningful.

Duration–the amount of time that we regard as appropriate for certain events or activities.

Activity–what people perceive should be done in a given period, including the time of day that is considered appropriate for certain activities to take place.

Punctuality–the extent to which one adheres strictly to the appointed or regular time.

Cultural Variations in Self-Presentation

Just as the meanings of body motions and paralanguage are culturally determined, so too do self-presentation behaviors differ in the meanings assigned to them in various cultures.

Touch According to Gudykunst and Kim (1997), differences in touching behavior are highly correlated with culture. In some cultures lots of contact and touching is normal behavior, while in other cultures individual space is respected and frequent touching is not encouraged. "People in high-contact cultures evaluate 'close' as positive and good, and evaluate 'far' as negative and bad. People in low-contact cultures evaluate 'close' as negative and bad, and 'far' as positive and good" (p. 235). According to the research that has been done, Latin America and the Mediterranean countries are high-contact cultures, northern European cultures are medium to low in contact, and Asian cultures are for the most part low-contact cultures. The United States, which is a country of immigrants, is generally perceived to be medium-contact, though there are wide differences between individual Americans due to variations in family heritage.

Time A particularly important area of cultural differences concerns perceptions of time. Some cultures view time monochronically; that is, they see time as compartmental, irreversible, and one-dimensional. It is a scarce resource to be "spent," "saved," and "budgeted." The dominant culture of the United States is monochronically oriented. We compartmentalize our time and schedule one event at a time. In this culture, being even a few minutes late may require you to acknowledge your lateness. Being ten to fifteen minutes late usually requires an apology, and being more than thirty minutes late is likely to be perceived as an insult requiring a great deal of explanation to earn the person's forgiveness (Gudykunst & Kim, 1997, p. 161).

People from other cultural backgrounds, such as those from Latin America, Asia, or the Middle East, tend to view time polychronically, a view that sees time as continuous and involves engaging in several activities at the same time. To those with a polychronic view of time, the concept of "being late" has no meaning. One arrives when one has completed what came before. In Latin American or in Arab cultures, for instance, it is not unusual for either person to be more than thirty minutes late and neither is likely to expect or offer an apology (Gudykunst & Kim, 1997, p. 160). While the dominant culture in the United States is monochronic to the extreme, we again experience wide variations because of our immigrant heritage. In some of our subcultures a polychronic view of time still influences behavior. Those from Latin American or African American backgrounds are likely to use time in a polychronic way.

Cultural differences in perception of time can cause misunderstanding. For instance, a naive U.S. sales representative with a business appointment in Latin America may be very frustrated with what he or she regards as a "cavalier" attitude toward time; likewise, a Latin American with a business appointment in the United States may be frustrated by the perceived "rigidness" of time schedules and the rudeness of the U.S. businessperson who cuts off an important business deal with "I have another appointment."

Communication Through Management of Your Environment

In addition to the way we use body motions, paralanguage, and self-presentation cues, we communicate nonverbally through how we manage the physical environment in which our conversations occur. The principal elements of the environment over which we can exercise control are the space we occupy, the temperature of the surroundings, the lighting levels, and the colors used in the interior decoration.

Space

In any communication episode, the physical environment in which messages are exchanged affects the meanings that are created. This environment includes buildings and other permanent structures, the movable objects within these structures, and the informal space that separates the participants.

Management of Permanent Structures The buildings in which we live and work and the parts of those buildings that cannot be moved fall into the category of permanent structures. Although we may not have much control over the creation of such elements, we do exercise control in our selection of them. For instance, when you rent an apartment or buy a condominium or a house, you consider whether or not the structure is in tune with your lifestyle. People who select a fourth-floor loft may view themselves differently from those who select one-room efficiencies. Businesspeople, doctors, and lawyers usually search with care to find surroundings that fit the image they want to communicate.

In addition, specific features of that choice affect our communication within that environment. For instance, people who live in apartment buildings are likely to become better acquainted with neighbors who live across the hall and next door than with those who live on other floors. Similarly, people who share common space such as laundry facilities or garages are more likely to become acquainted than those who do not.

Management of Movable Objects Within Space We have the opportunity to manage objects in space by arranging and rearranging them to create the desired atmosphere. Whether the space is a dormitory room, a living room, a seminar room, or a classroom, you can move the furnishings around until you achieve the effect you want. In general, the more formal the arrangement, the more formal the communication setting is. Although conclusions about the management of objects within space should not be regarded as absolute, the use of space nevertheless is one index of how people are going to treat you and how they expect you to treat them.

OBSERVE & ANALYZE

Journal Activity

Cultural Differences in Self-Presentation

Interview or converse with two international students from different countries. Try to select students whose cultures differ from one another and from the culture with which you are most familiar. Develop a list of questions related to the self-presentation behaviors discussed earlier. Try to understand how people in the international students' countries differ from you in their use of nonverbal self-presentation behaviors. Prepare to share what you have learned with your classmates. ■

Consider the following arrangements of movable objects and the communication setting created by each.

Living Room

Furniture arranged with chairs facing each other approximating a circle contributes to conversation.

Furniture arranged so that it faces the television emphasizes viewing.

A room with Victorian furniture and hard-backed chairs suggests formal interaction.

A room with a thick carpet, pillows, recliners, and an oversized sectional sofa suggests informal interaction.

Office

A supervisor's office with a chair facing the supervisor across the desk leads to formal conversation. It says, "Let's talk business—I'm the boss and you're the employee."

A supervisor's office with a chair at the side of the desk (absence of a physical barrier) leads to more informal conversation. It says, "Don't be nervous—let's just chat."

Classroom

Several rows of chairs facing the lectern suggests a lecture format.

Chairs grouped in one large circle suggests a give-and-take discussion between students and instructor.

Chairs grouped in four or five smaller circles suggests that the class will work on group projects.

Proxemics—the study of informal space.

Management of Informal Space **Proxemics** is the study of informal space—the space around the place we are occupying at the moment. Managing informal space requires an understanding of attitudes toward the space around us and our sense of personal territory.

Have you ever been speaking with someone and become aware that you were uncomfortable because the other person was standing too close to you? Or maybe you've found yourself starting a conversation and then moving closer to someone as you begin to share an embarrassing story. If you have experienced either of these situations, you are already aware of the way that the space between conversational partners influences their interaction. Edward T. Hall (1969) suggests that in the dominant U.S. culture four distinct distances are comfortable, depending on the nature of the conversation.

Intimate distance, up to eighteen inches, is appropriate for private conversations between close friends.

Personal distance, from eighteen inches to four feet, is the space in which casual conversation occurs.

Social distance, from four to twelve feet, is where impersonal business such as job interviews is conducted.

Public distance is anything more than twelve feet.

These distance categories, based on Hall's research, represent descriptions of what most people consider appropriate or comfortable in various situations.

Judee K. Burgoon, Professor of Communication, University of Arizona on

Nonverbal Expectancy Violation Theory

With seven books and more than 150 articles and book chapters to her credit, Judee K. Burgoon is a leading scholar who has helped to shape how we now think about nonverbal communication. Her fascination with nonverbal behavior dates back to a graduate school seminar assignment at the University of West Virginia, where she was asked to find out what was known about proxemics, the study of space. From that assignment, she says, "I just got hooked. Nonverbal is more elusive and difficult to study and I've always enjoyed a challenge!"

At the time, scholars believed that the road to interpersonal success lay in conforming one's behaviors to social norms about the distances that are appropriate for certain types of interactions and the types of touch that are appropriate for certain people in certain relationships. Thus, people would be successful in their interactions as long as they behaved in accord with these norms. Encouraged by one of her professors to "look for the counterintuitive," Burgoon's research showed that there were situations where violations of these norms resulted in positive, rather than negative consequences. For example, in set-

tings where two people were not well acquainted and one of them began "flirting" by moving closer to the other thus "violating" that person's space, the other person did not always react by moving away from the violator as expected. In fact, at times the person seemed to welcome the violation and at times may even have moved closer. Similarly, she noticed that touching behavior that violated social norms was sometimes rejected and at other times accepted.

To explain what she saw happening, Burgoon developed and began to test what she named "expectancy violation theory," which is based on the premise that we have strong expectations about how people ought to behave when they interact with us. Whether they meet our expectations affects not only how we interact with them, but also affects such outcomes as how competent, credible, and influential we perceive the other to be and what we think of our relationship. She found that how we interpret a violation depends on how we feel about that person. If we like the person we are likely to read the nonverbal violation as positive ("Gee, she put her arm around me—that means

she's really interested in me"), if we don't like the person we are likely to read the same nonverbal violation as negative ("He better take his arm off of me, this is a clear case of harassment"). And, because we have become sensitized to the situation, the violations will be subject to strong evaluations ("Wow, I really like the feel of her arm around my waist" vs. "He's making me feel really uncomfortable"). As Burgoon continued to study violations, she discovered that when a person we really like violates our expectations, we are likely to view the interaction as even more positive than we would have if the person had conformed to our expectations. Over the years, in numerous research studies Burgoon and her students have provided strong support for expectancy violation theory.

Burgoon's scholarship has developed like a river. Her first work was a narrow stream with a focus on proxemics that grew with expectancy violations theory to include all of nonverbal behavior and continues to branch. Presently, in one stream of work, she is studying what determines how people adapt their behavior when they experience any type of communication violation. Why and when do they reciprocate the violation (e.g., if someone shouts, you shout back), or compensate for it (e.g., if someone comes to close to you, you step back)? In a second stream Burgoon is focusing on a specific type of expectancy violation: deception. Here she is trying to sort out the role that nonverbal behavior plays in deceitful interactions. Finally, she has begun a stream of work whose purpose is to identify the essen-

tial properties of interpersonal communication that are different from the properties of media communication. Whatever branch her research takes, Judee Burgoon brings the same readiness to challenge the current thinking that has been the hallmark of her work. For complete citations of many of her recent publications in these areas, see the references for this chapter at the end of the book.

In addition to teaching a number of courses, Burgoon serves as Director of Graduate Studies, where her role of helping students learn how to conduct research and formulate theory gives her great satisfaction. "Mentoring others is among the major gratifications of doing research. The fun is to teach others what I was taught: Always challenge the current assumptions." ■

Of greatest concern to us is the intimate distance—that which we regard as appropriate for intimate conversation with close friends, parents, and younger children. People usually become uncomfortable when "outsiders" violate this intimate distance. For instance, in a movie theater that is less than one-quarter full, people will tend to leave one or more seats empty between themselves and others whom they do not know. If in such a setting a stranger sits right next to you, you are likely to feel uncomfortable or threatened and may even move away.

Intrusions into our intimate space are acceptable only in certain settings and then only when all involved follow the unwritten rules. For instance, people will tolerate being packed into a crowded elevator or subway and even touching others they do not know, provided that the others follow the "rules." The rules may include standing rigidly, looking at the floor or the indicator above the door, but not making eye contact with others. The rules also include ignoring or pretending that they are not touching. Only occasionally will people who are forced to invade each other's intimate space acknowledge the other as a person. Then they are likely to exchange sheepish smiles or otherwise acknowledge the mutual invasion of intimate distance. In the Spotlight on Scholars, we have featured Judee Burgoon, who has focused a great deal of her research on the effects of such intrusions into our intimate space. Her findings develop and test what she calls "expectancy violation theory."

Interpersonal problems occur when one person's use of space violates the behavioral expectations of another. For instance, Lorenzo may come from a family that conducts informal conversations with others at a range closer than the eighteen-inch limit that many European Americans place on intimate space. When he talks to a colleague at work and moves in closer than eighteen inches, the co-worker may back away from him during the conversation. Unfortunately, there are

How do you react when people get closer to you than an arm's length?

times when one person intentionally violates the space expectations of another. When the violation is between members of the opposite sex, it may be considered sexual harassment. Glen may, through violations of informal space, posture, movements, or gestures, "come on" to Donnice. If Donnice does not welcome the attention, she may feel threatened. In this case, Glen's nonverbal behavior may be construed as sexual harassment. In order to avoid perceptions of harassment, people need to be especially sensitive to others' definitions of intimate space.

Whereas our intimate or personal space moves when we move, there is other space that we seek to claim whether or not we are currently occupying it. That is, we are likely to look at certain space as our **territory**—as space over which we may claim ownership. If Marcia decides to eat lunch at the company commissary, the space at the table she occupies becomes her territory. Suppose that during lunch Marcia leaves her territory to get butter for her roll. The chair she left, the food on the table, and the space around that food are "hers," and she will expect others to stay away. If, when she returns, Marcia finds that someone at the table has moved a glass or a dish into the area that she regards as her territory, she is likely to feel resentful.

Territory–space over which we may claim ownership.

OBSERVE & ANALYZE

Journal Activity

Intruding on Personal Space

Find a crowded elevator. Get on it and face the back. Make direct eye contact with the person you are standing in front of. Note their reaction. On the return trip, introduce yourself to the person who is standing next to you and begin an animated conversation. Note the reaction of others around you. Get on an empty elevator and stand in the exact center. Do not move when others board. Note their reactions. Be prepared to share what you have observed with your classmates. ■

Many people stake out their territory with markers. For example, Ramon arrives early for the first day of class, finds an empty desk, and puts his backpack next to it on the floor and his coat on the seat. He then makes a quick trip to the restroom. If someone comes along while Ramon is gone, moves his backpack and coat, and sits down at the desk, that person is violating what Ramon has marked as his territory.

As a student of nonverbal communication, however, you understand that other people may not look at either the space around you or your territory in quite the same way as you do. That the majority of U.S. residents have learned the same basic rules governing the management of space does not mean that everyone shares the same respect for the rules or treats the consequences of breaking the rules in the same way. For example, members of rival street gangs, like competing tribal warlords, may "punish" those who violate their territories with beatings or worse. Thus, it is important to be observant so that you can be sensitive to how others react to your behaviors.

Temperature, Lighting, and Color

Three other elements of the environment that can be controlled and that affect communication are temperature, lighting, and color.

Temperature can stimulate or inhibit effective communication. Temperature can alter people's moods and change their level of attentiveness. Can you recall the difficulty you have had listening to a teacher in a hot, stuffy classroom? Or have you found that you become "edgy" when overheated? If so, you understand how room temperature can affect communication. We know of a common pleas court judge who intentionally keeps his courtroom at sixty-two degrees (Farenheit) year-round because he believes that people listen more attentively if they are moderately cool and he wants the juries in his courtroom to listen carefully and render thoughtful verdicts.

Lighting levels also add meaning to communication messages. In lecture halls and reading rooms, bright light is expected—it encourages good listening and comfortable reading. By contrast, in a chic restaurant, a jazz club music listening room, or a coffee bar, you expect the lighting to be soft and rather dim, which makes for a cozy atmosphere and invites intimate conversation (Knapp & Hall, 2002, p. 126). We often change the lighting level in a room to change the mood and indicate the type of interaction that is expected. Bright lights encourage activity and boisterous conversations, while softer lighting levels calm and soothe, encouraging quiet and more serious conversations.

Color may stimulate both emotional and physical reactions. For instance, red excites and stimulates, blue comforts and soothes, yellow cheers and elevates moods. Knowing this, professional interior designers may choose blues when they are trying to create a peaceful, serene atmosphere for a living room, whereas they may decorate in reds and yellows in a playroom.

In addition, specific colors may convey information about people and events. In European and European American cultures, black is a sign of mourning. Similarly, it is traditional in these cultures for wedding dresses and christening

Latin American and Anglo American Use of Personal Space in Public Places By Elizabeth Lozano

How we use space and how we expect others to treat the space around us are determined by our culture. In this excerpt the author focuses our attention on the ways in which the body is understood and treated by Latin Americans and Anglo Americans, and the cultural differences that become apparent when these two cultural groups find themselves sharing common space.

It is 6:00 P.M. The Bayfront, a shopping mall near a Miami marina, reverberates with the noise and movement of people, coming and going, contemplating the lights of the bay, sampling exotic juice blends, savoring the not-so-exotic foods from Cuba, Nicaragua, or Mexico, and listening to the bands. The Bayfront provides an environment for the exercise of two different rituals: the Anglo American visit to the mall and the Latin American paseo, the visit to the outdoor spaces of the city.

Some of the people sitting in the plaza look insistently at me, making comments, laughing, and whispering. Instead of feeling uneasy or surprised, I find myself looking back at them, entering this inquisitive game and asking myself some of the same questions they might be asking. Who are they, where are they from, what are they up to? I follow their gaze and I see it extend to other groups. The gaze is returned by some in the crowd, so that a play of silent dialogue seems to grow amidst the anonymity of the crowd. The crowd that participates in this complicity of wandering looks is not Anglo American. The play of looks described above has a different "accent," a Hispanic accent, which reveals a different understanding of the plaza and public space.

The Anglo American passersby understand their vital space, their relationship with strangers, and their public interactions in a different manner. If I address them in the street, I better assume that I am confronting them in an alley. But when I am walking by myself along the halls of a Hispanic mall, I am not alone. I do not expect, therefore, to be treated by others as if they were suddenly confronting me in a dark alley. I am in a crowd, with the crowd, and anyone there has access to my attention.

Anglo Americans are alone (even in the middle of the crowd) if they choose to be, for they have a guaranteed cultural right to be "left alone" on their way to and from anywhere. To approach or touch someone without that person's consent is a violation of a fundamental right within Anglo-Saxon, Protestant cultural tradition. This is the right to one's own body as private property. Within this tradition, touching is understood as an excursion into someone else's territory. With this in mind then, it is understandable that Anglo Americans excuse themselves when they accidentally touch someone or come close to doing so. To accidentally penetrate someone else's boundary (especially if that person is a stranger) demands an apology, and a willingness to repair the damage by stepping back from the violated territory.

One can see how rude a Latin American might appear to an Anglo American when the former distractingly touches another person without apologizing or showing concern. But within Latino and Mediterranean traditions, the body is not understood as property. That is, the body is not understood as belonging to its owner. It does not belong to me or to anyone else; it is, in principle, public. It is an expressive and sensual region open to the scrutiny, discipline, and sanction of the community. It is, therefore, quite impossible to be "left alone" on the Latin

American street. For Latin Americans, the access to others in a public space is not restricted by the "privacy" of their bodies. Thus, the Latin American does not find casual contact a form of property trespassing or a violation of rights.

Walking the street in the Anglo United States is very much an anonymous activity to be performed in a field of unobstructive and invisible bodies. Since one is essentially carrying one's own space into the public sphere, no one is actually ever in public. Given that the public is private, no intimacy is granted in the public space. Thus while the Latin American public look or gaze is round, inquisitive, and wandering, the Anglo American is straight, nonobstructive, and neutral.

Civility requires the Anglo American to restrict looks, delimit gestures, and orient movement.

Civility requires the Latin American to acknowledge looks, gestures, and movement and actively engage with them. For the Latin American, the unavoidable nature of shared space is always a demand for attention and a request to participate. An Anglo American considers "mind your own business" to be fair and civil. A Latin American might find this an unreasonable restriction. What takes place in public is everybody's business by the very fact that it is taking place in public.

One can understand the possible cultural misunderstandings between Anglo Americans and Latin Americans. If Anglo Americans protest the "impertinence" of Latin Americans as nosy and curious, Latin Americans would protest the indifference and lack of concern of Anglo Americans.

The scene in the Miami mall could happen just as easily in

Los Angeles, Chicago, Philadelphia, or New York, cities in which Latin Americans comprise an important segment of the population. The influence of this cultural heritage is going to have growing influence in the next few decades on the Anglo American scene, as Hispanics become the largest ethnic and linguistic minority in the United States. The more knowledge we can gain from what makes us culturally diverse, the more we will be able to appreciate what unifies us through the mixing and mutual exchanges of our cultures. ■

Excerpted from Lozano, E. (2000). The cultural experience of space and body: A reading of Latin American and Anglo American comportment in public. In A. Gonzalez, M. Houston, & V. Chen (Eds.), *Our Voices: Essays in Culture, Ethnicity, and Communication: An Intercultural Anthology* (pp. 228–234). Los Angeles: Roxbury Publishing Company.

gowns to be white—the Western European color of purity. Urban gangs use colors to signal membership. So, in some communities gang members wear bandannas or other articles of clothing in a specific color. Unfortunately, people have been killed simply for wearing the wrong color in a particular neighborhood.

Cultural Variations in Management of the Environment

As you would expect, the environments in which people feel comfortable depend on their cultural background. In the United States, where we have ample land, many people live in single-family homes or in large apartments. In other countries, where land is scarce, people live in closer quarters and can feel "lonely" or isolated in larger spaces. In Japan and Europe, most people live in spaces that by our U.S. standards feel cramped. Similarly, people from different cultures have different ideas about what constitutes appropriate distances for various interactions. Recall that in the dominant culture of the United States, the boundary of personal or intimate space is about eighteen inches. In Middle Eastern cultures, however, men move much closer to other men when they are talking (Samovar & Porter, 2001, p. 186). Thus, when an Arab man talks with an American man, one of the two is likely to be uncomfortable. Either the American will feel uncomfortable and invaded or the Arab will feel isolated and too distant for serious conversation.

We also differ in the temperature ranges that we find comfortable. People who originate from warmer climates can tolerate heat more than people who originate from cooler climates. Even the meanings that we assign to colors vary by national culture and religion. In India white, not black, is the color of mourning, and Hindu brides wear red.

But we don't have to go off the North American continent to see variations in the way uses of space may differ. In the Diverse Voices that you have read on pages 141 and 142 notice how Latin American and Anglo American use of space differs.

Increasing the Accuracy of Nonverbal Communication

The question that remains is whether increasing your understanding of body motions and paralanguage can help you use your nonverbal communication more effectively. Although Feldman, Philippot, and Custrini (1991, p. 346) believe that for relatively unskilled communicators, improving their use of nonverbal behavior should improve their social competence, they also recognize that because much of our nonverbal behavior is spontaneous, altering the encoding of our nonverbal behaviors is very difficult. For instance, simply knowing that you are a person who becomes defensive may not enable you to modify your reactions. However, knowing that your typical nonverbal communication behaviors in this situation are grimacing, sighing, and folding your arms will allow you to explain them to people who don't know you well. If you find yourself exhibiting these cues when someone is talking with you, you can say something like, "Please don't think that I don't want to hear what you are saying. The fact is that I automatically grimace in the face of criticism, but really, I need to hear it."

Still, you can improve your nonverbal usage if you are willing to work at it. For example, suppose you have received feedback that you need to look at people more directly when you talk with them. To begin your program of improvement, you might practice by holding "conversations" with objects in your room. For a minute, talk to your book, then shift your gaze to your lamp, and finally, talk to the window. Once you become comfortable maintaining

OBSERVE & ANALYZE

Journal Activity

Managing the Environment

Choose two sites of the same type—for example, two restaurants, two apartments, two dorm rooms, or two doctors' offices. Visit each site, and observe and record the permanent space, the moveable objects, the temperature, lighting, and use of color at each site. Also observe the communication behavior of the people at the site.

If possible, interview the people who "created" these spaces. Ask them to explain why they made the choices that they did when designing the space.

In writing, describe the spaces. Then compare and contrast the decisions that the designers made and speculate on how these decisions influenced the behavior you observed when you visited each site. ■

eye contact with objects, you can continue to practice by having a close friend help you monitor the amount of your eye contact while the two of you converse. Ask your friend to signal you when you lose eye contact. If you need to increase your use of eye contact when you are listening, have your friend tell you about something that happened; then ask how much you maintained eye contact while you were listening. Whether you are practicing improvement in eye contact, facial expression, gesture, or posture, you can follow the same procedure.

You have already studied the skill of perception checking, which allows you to test your interpretation of another's nonverbal behavior. You can use this skill to make your interpretations of other's nonverbal behavior more accurate. For instance, suppose a person smiles and nods her head when you tell her about a mistake she has made. Before you conclude that the person agrees with your observation and accepts your criticism, you might say, "From the smile on your face and your nodding, I get the impression that you had already recognized the mistake you made, or am I off base?" It seems obvious that perception checking may be even

WHAT WOULD YOU DO?

A Question of Ethics

After the intramural mixed-doubles matches on Tuesday evening, most of the players adjourned to the campus grill for a while to have a drink and chat. Although the group was highly competitive on the courts, they enjoyed socializing and talking about the matches for a while before they went home. Marquez and Lisa, who had been paired together at the start of the season, sat down with another pair, Barry and Elana, who had been going out together for several weeks.

Marquez and Lisa had played a particularly grueling match that night against Barry and Elana, a match that they lost largely because of Elana's improved play.

"Elana, your serve today was the best I've seen it this year," Marquez said.

"Yeah, I was really impressed. And as you saw, I had trouble handling it," Lisa added.

"And you're getting to the net a lot better too," Marquez added.

"Thanks, guys," Elana said in a tone of gratitude, "I've really been working on it."

"Well, aren't we getting the compliments today," sneered Barry in a sarcastic tone. Then after a pause, he said, "Oh, Elana, would you get my sweater? I left it on that chair by the other table."

"Come on Barry, you're closer than I am," Elana replied.

Barry got a cold look on his face, moved slightly closer to Elana, and said emphatically, "Get my sweater for me, Elana—now."

Elana quickly backed away from Barry as she said, "OK Barry—it's cool," and she then quickly got the sweater for him.

"Gee, isn't she sweet?" Barry said to Marquez and Lisa as he grabbed the sweater from Elana.

Lisa and Marquez both looked down at the floor. Then Lisa glanced at Marquez and said, "Well, I'm out of here—I've got a lot to do this evening."

"Let me walk you to your car," Marquez said as he stood up.

"See you next week," they said in unison as they hurried out the door, leaving Barry and Elana alone at the table.

1. Analyze Barry's nonverbal behavior. What was he attempting to achieve?

2. How do you interpret Lisa's and Marquez's nonverbal reactions to Barry?

3. Was Barry's behavior ethically acceptable? Explain. ■

more valuable in increasing the accuracy with which we understand the nonverbal behavior of people of the opposite sex or from a different culture or subculture.

Summary

Nonverbal communication refers to how people communicate through the use of body motions, paralanguage, self-presentation cues, and the physical environment. The nature of nonverbal communication is revealed through its contrasts with verbal communication. Nonverbal communication is ambiguous, continuous, multi-channeled, and gives more insight into emotional states than do verbal messages. In addition, the meanings of nonverbal communication behaviors are culturally determined.

Perhaps the most familiar methods of nonverbal communication are what and how a person communicates through body motions and paralanguage. Eye contact, facial expression, gesture, and posture are four major types of body motions. Body motions take the place of words, illustrate what a speaker is saying, display feelings, control or regulate conversations, and relieve tension. Whereas a person's vocal characteristics (volume, rate, pitch, and quality) help us interpret the meaning of the verbal message, a person's vocal interferences ("ah," "um," "you know," and "like") often impede our ability to understand and become annoying.

Although verbal and nonverbal communication work together best when they are complementary, nonverbal cues may replace or even contradict verbal symbols. Generally, nonverbal communication is more to be trusted when verbal and nonverbal cues are in conflict.

Through self-presentation cues, such as clothing, touching behavior, and use of time, people communicate about themselves and their relationship to others. The physical environment is often overlooked, even though we set the tone for conversations and nonverbally communicate through it. The choices people make in their permanent spaces, the way they arrange the objects in those spaces, and the way they control or react to temperature, lighting, and color contribute to the quality and meaning of the communication episodes that occur.

Your understanding of nonverbal communication can contribute to clearer encoding and decoding. Armed with this knowledge, you are equipped to be more effective in all settings. Increasing the accuracy with which we use and understand nonverbal communication behavior is even more critical when we are interacting with people who are different from us.

Chapter Resources

Communication Improvement Plan: Nonverbal Communication

Would you like to improve your use of the following skill or aspects of perception discussed in this chapter?

Eye contact	Poise
Facial expression	Paralanguage
Gesture	Vocal interferences
Posture	Self-presentation

Pick a skill or an area and write a communication improvement plan.

Skill: _____

Problem: _____

_____

_____

_____

Goal: _____

_____

_____

_____

Procedure:

1. _____

2. _____

3. _____

Test of Achieving Goal: _____

_____

Key Words

Nonverbal communication behaviors, *p. 123*
Kinesics, *p. 123*
Eye contact or gaze, *p. 123*
Facial expression, *p. 124*
Gestures, *p. 125*
Posture, *p. 125*
Sign language, *p. 125*
Paralanguage or vocalics, *p. 129*
Pitch, *p. 129*
Volume, *p. 129*
Rate, *p. 129*
Quality, *p. 129*
Vocal interferences, *p. 129*
Poise, *p. 132*

Touch, *p. 132*
Duration, *p. 133*
Activity, *p. 133*
Punctuality, *p. 133*
Proxemics, *p. 136*
Territory, *p. 139*

Inter-Act with Media

CINEMA

Allan Eastman (Director). (1986). *Crazy Moon.* Kiefer Sutherland, Peter Spence, Vanessa Vaughan, Ken Pogue, Eva Napier.

Brief Summary: This is the story of a young, rich teenager who is trying to have a relationship with a deaf girl. Though hearing impaired, she is more fully functional than he is. The film is a good study in how two people can try to communicate when they come from these two cultures—hearing and nonhearing. The girl is also receiving speech therapy to learn how to speak, as well as sign.

IPC Concepts: Nonverbal—gestures, facial, posture, listening, relationship development, deaf culture.

Rob Reiner (Director). (1992). *A Few Good Men.* Jack Nicholson, Demi Moore, Kevin Bacon, Kevin Pollak.

Brief Summary: After a death at the marine base in Cuba, a cocky naval lawyer (Tom Cruise) is assigned to the defense of a pair of marines accused of murder. He arrogantly dismisses the idealism of his superior officer (Demi Moore) and the realism of his partner (Kevin Pollak). The trio meets Colonel Jessup (Jack Nicholson), the colonel in charge of the base. He is even more arrogant than Cruise, besides being openly sexist. The ensuing investigation and trial bring Cruise face to face with himself, his choice to become a lawyer, and respect for his position as a naval attorney. The confrontation between Cruise and Nicholson illustrates a variety of communication concepts in a powerful manner.

IPC Concepts: Nonverbal—posture, facial, gestures, clothing, vocal tone, social standing.

Sydney Pollack (Director). (1982). *Tootsie.* Dustin Hoffman, Jessica Lange, Teri Garr, Dabney Coleman, Charles Durning, Bill Murray, Sydney Pollack, Geena Davis, Estelle Getty.

Brief Summary: The film is about a man who has trouble finding work as an actor due to his dominating and demanding personality. As a solution, he poses as a woman in order to get a job on a television soap opera. His successful portrayal of the woman, both on and off camera, leads him to discover things about himself that he did not know were there. As Michael Dorsey (Hoffman) puts it late in the film, he was "a better man as a woman."

IPC Concepts: Self-presentation, perception, and stereotyping based on nonverbal behavior.

THEATER

William Shakespeare. *The Tempest.*

Brief Summary: This is one of Shakespeare's most memorable and influential plays. Prospero, who has fled from civilization in order to protect himself and his daughter, utilizes the help of a magical character named Ariel. The interaction between Prospero and Ariel depends on the gestures and facial expressions of each character. Further, Ariel only communicates via gestures and facial expressions when around other characters in the story. This is a wonderful dramatization that cleverly draws our attention to nonverbal actions.

IPC Concepts: Gestures.

LITERATURE

Ernest Hemingway. (1952). *The Old Man and the Sea.*

Brief Summary: This is Hemingway's story of Santiago, an old Cuban fisherman who has not caught a fish for over eighty days. His young friend Manolin tries to help him as best as he can, given his own poverty. Santiago goes to fish and catches a large marlin. As the fish tows him further out to sea, Santiago must survive until the fish tires and he can tie it to the small boat. As he returns to his home, he must defend his catch from sharks. Hemingway does a masterful job of describing this man's actions, reactions, and feelings, as this largely nondialogue story unfolds.

IPC Concepts: Nonverbal—gestures, posture, facial expressions, cultural variations.

ACADEMIC WORK

Edward Hall. (1966). *The Hidden Dimension.* Garden City, N.Y.: Doubleday & Company.

Brief Summary: Spatial zones generally are drawn closer for women than for men. Women approach more closely, and seem to prefer side-by-side conversations. The latter may explain differences in use of space—men prefer more face-to-face conversations, and people are generally more aware of space to the front than to the side.

IPC Concepts: Nonverbal communication, especially proxemics.

Dale G. Leathers. (1997). *Successful Nonverbal Communication: Principles and Applications* (3rd ed.). Boston: Allyn & Bacon.

Brief Summary: Leathers does an outstanding job of reporting and discussing research findings on all categories of nonverbal communication. The book is highly readable and very useful. His material on culture, nonverbal behavior, and communication is excellent.

IPC Concepts: Nonverbal communication, intercultural communication.

Dale G. Leathers & Ted H. Emigh. (1980). *Decoding facial expressions: A new test with decoding norms. The Quarterly Journal of Speech, 66*(4), 418-436.

Brief Summary: This is an interesting article for anyone studying nonverbal communication in that it not only presents the statistical results of the study, but it also provides the actual facial photographs used in the Facial Meaning Sensitivity Test. This provides you with an opportunity to look at the actual test being used to collect data, and possibly to replicate the study at a basic level.

IPC Concepts: Nonverbal—facial expression.

WHAT'S ON THE WEB

The Center for Nonverbal Studies (CNS).

http://members.aol.com/nonverbal2/center.htm#Center for Nonverbal Studies

http://members.aol.com/doder1/bodymov1.htm

Brief Summary: These Web sites are of CNS, "a private, non-profit research center located in Spokane, Washington, with a site for conferences and seminars in La Jolla, California. The Center is committed to the idea that, for a deeper understanding of 'who we are' and 'what it means to be human,' more attention should be paid to our nonverbal nature."

IPC Concepts: Areas of special interest include body movement, gesture, facial expression, adornment and fashion, landscape architecture, mass media, and consumer-product design. All the senses—of balance, hearing, smell, sight, space, taste, time, and touch—are channels for nonverbal cues.

Nonverbal Behaviour Nonverbal Communication

http://www3.usa/.es/~nonverbal/index.htm

Brief Summary: This really nice site allows you to look up information on several categories of information on nonverbal behavior and research: people, journals, articles, books, videos, and a miscellaneous category that includes: (1) test your nonverbal communication skills, (2) nonverbal semiotics, (3) special interest groups, (4) in the French/German body, (5) WAIS-Search Engine ANU-Gesture-L, and (6) facial analysis. This site has interesting links. The page is put together by a Spanish psychology student named Jaume Masip.

IPC Concepts: All categories of nonverbal behavior.

CHAPTER 6

Holding Effective

Conversations

After you have read this chapter, you should be able to answer these questions:

- What is a conversation?
- How does a casual social conversation differ from a pragmatic problem-consideration conversation?
- What are conversational rules, and what are their distinguishing features?
- What is the cooperative principle?
- What are the maxims of the cooperative principle, and how does each apply to conversation?
- What are the skills associated with effective conversations?
- What guidelines regulate turn-taking behavior?
- What is conversational coherence, and how can it be achieved?
- Why is politeness important in conversation?
- What are some important considerations for ethical dialogue?
- What are significant cultural variations in conversation?

"Hey Josh, I'm glad you're home. Where have you been?"

"Nowhere."

"What do you mean nowhere? You had to have been somewhere!"

"Well, no Mom, not really. I mean we all went over to Jeff's and just hung out."

"Hung out doing what?"

"You know, just hung out."

"No I don't know. What happened while you were hanging out?"

"We just sat around and talked."

"About what?"

"This and that."

"Josh, you've been gone more than four hours! Tell me something that you talked about."

"I can't remember much. Oh, Jeff told us about a movie he saw and Carrie talked about her cousin's wedding that she went to. And, oh yeah, Becca told us that the Jeffersons are getting a divorce and that Meg, who we thought would be over to hang out with us is going to have to live with her Dad. So we speculated about how well she would deal with that And. . ."

"Whoa! That doesn't sound like 'this and that.' It sounds as if you were talking about some important happenings."

"Yeah, I guess we were."

Conversations are the stuff of which our relationships are made. In fact, as Steve Duck, a leading researcher on relationships, pointed out, "If you were to sit and list the things that you do with friends, one of the top items on the list would surely have to be 'talking'" (1998, p. 7). When conversations go well, they are interesting, informative, stimulating, and just good fun. Yet, many conversations, like Josh and his mom's, are like pulling teeth. By understanding how a conversation works, and how its effectiveness and its value depend on the willingness of participants to be willing to share and to use conversational skills that increase the informative value and the enjoyment of participating.

In this chapter, we begin by describing the characteristics of conversation and identifying two different types. Then we discuss conversational rules, the cooperative principle, and guidelines to help you become a more effective conversationalist.

Characteristics of Conversation

Conversations–locally managed sequential interchange of thoughts and feelings between two or more people.

Conversations are locally managed sequential interchanges of thoughts and feelings between two or more people that are interactive and largely extemporaneous. This definition highlights several key features mentioned by Jan Svennevig (1999) that distinguish conversations from other forms of communication such as speech making and debating (p. 8). First, conversations are *locally managed.* This means that only those involved in the conversation determine the topic, who will speak, the order of speaking, and the length each will speak in a turn. Second, conversations are *sequentially organized*; that is, they have openings, middles, and closings. Third, conversations are *interactive*; that is, they involve at least two people speaking and listening. Fourth, conversations are *largely extemporaneous*, which means the participants have not prepared or memorized what they will be saying.

When people find a conversation satisfying, they tend to seek out each other for additional conversations. For instance, if Dan meets Carl at a party and both find the talk they had about politics stimulating, they are likely to look forward to additional conversations on this topic.

Types and Structures of Conversation

Whether conversations are short or long, most have an identifiable structure or pattern. Let's consider the basic parts of any conversation and then look at two specific types of conversational situations that are structured differently: the casual social conversation and the pragmatic problem-consideration conversation.

Parts of a Conversation

All conversations have identifiable openings, bodies, and conclusions. How obvious or formal each part is will vary depending on how long the conversation is held, how well the participants know each other, and the context of the conversation. Especially when we are in contact with people we don't really know, opening a conversation can be problematic. As Thomas Holtgraves points out, people must indicate their availability and willingness to talk and a topic that is mutually acceptable must be considered (2002, p. 100.) Suppose Marge and Jan (who don't know each other) are waiting for a bus. If neither is busy with another activity, they are of course available. After a few minutes of standing there, Marge says, "Beautiful day, isn't it?" to which Jan replies, "Yeah," and then looks up the street for the bus. Although Jan is available, she shows no willingness to talk—so unless Marge pursues it, there will be no conversation. But if in response to "Beautiful day, isn't it?" Jan says, "Sure is—a great day to be outdoors, isn't it?" she indicates a willingness to continue the conversation. In essence all conversations begin with two utterances, spoken by different people. The first person initiates topic. The second reacts to the first in a way that suggests that the participant is interested or disinterested in continuing the interaction.

Conversations are carried on for an indefinite amount of time on one or more topics. Whereas one conversation could include little more than the opening statement and response another might continue for hours. Most of us have heard of couples who at first meeting "clicked" and spent the next several hours just talking. As we mentioned in Chapter 3 on relationships, conversational topics include idea exchange (information that includes facts, opinions, and beliefs) and gossip (relating information whose accuracy may be questionable about people known to those conversing). In fact, sharing information and gossip makes up a large amount of casual conversation, which appears to be much of what Josh and his friends talked about while "hanging out."

Conversations are usually ended when one person indicates a need or desire to disengage from the interaction. For instance, a person might say, "Oh my, look what time it is . . ." or "This has been great, we'll have to get back together and hash this out some more." Sometimes, the close is not formally discussed but the parties just stop talking. After an unusually long pause indicating closure, a person might say, "Well, it's been great talking with you." At times, one or the other will attempt to extend conversation with a new approach, such as, "Just a second, I wanted to ask you. . ." A statement like this may lead to a lengthy exchange, or may only result in a minimum response before the person who wished to disengage echoes the closure statement and ends the conversation.

Two Common Types of Conversation

Although there may be many ways to categorize conversations, two types of conversations are easy to recognize and commonly occur.

Casual social conversations are interactions between people whose purpose is to enhance or maintain a relationship through spontaneous interactions about nonspecific topics. For instance, when Connie, Jeff, Wanda, and Trevor have dinner together, they might hold conversations on multiple topics, some in which all four participate and others which two sets of two converse on different topics. During dinner they might spend nearly their entire time talking about the upcoming presidential election, or they might talk about a series of topics including a new movie, a television series, last week's football game, politics, or they might gossip about what a friend wore to a party they attended.

You've noticed that gossip is included as a typical casual social conversation topic. And, although at times gossip is malicious and unethical, most of the time it is a harmless form of casual social conversation that has at least some redeeming value. As Eggins and Slade point out, gossip is a powerful socializing force. It reflects a socio-cultural world and at the same time helps to shape that world (1997, p. 279). So, casual conversations are held primarily to meet the participants' interpersonal needs and their sole function is to build or maintain the relationships.

Pragmatic problem-consideration conversations are interactions between people in which the goal of at least one of the participants is to solicit the cooperation of the other in meeting a specific goal. At times this specific goal is known before the conversation begins. For instance, if Glen is concerned about the fair-

Casual social conversations–interactions between people whose purpose is to enhance or maintain a relationship through spontaneous interactions about nonspecific topics.

Pragmatic problem-consideration conversations–interactions between people in which the goal of at least one of the participants is to solicit the cooperation of the other in meeting a specific goal.

ness of workloads, he may ask Susan, his co-worker, to meet with him to generate some ideas about what can be done to better balance the jobs assigned to each person on the team. At other times, the need to consider a particular topic or problem may arise spontaneously during the discussion. For instance, while office mates are talking over lunch, one of them might say, "Garret has really been stressed out lately." This might stimulate the group to consider what they might do to help alleviate Garret's stress.

The Structure of Casual Social Conversation

In a casual social conversation, topics will be introduced by one person and will be accepted or rejected by other participants in no particular order. If others accept it, the topic will be discussed until the participants have expressed all they care to on the topic or until another topic is introduced and captures their attention. A topic is rejected when others choose not to respond and when someone else introduces a different topic that then becomes the focus. This topic change process occurs throughout the conversation.

Figure 6.1 Casual Conversation

CONVERSATION	COMMENTARY
As they look around the theater, Donna says, "They really did an Art Deco thing with this place didn't they?"	Donna introduces a possible topic.
"Yeah . . . Hey," Juanita says as she surveys the audience, "it looks as if this is going to be a sellout."	Juanita acknowledges Donna's statement, chooses not to discuss it, and introduces a different topic.
"Certainly does—I see people in the last row of the balcony."	Donna accepts the topic and extends discussion with a parallel comment.
"I thought this would be a popular show. It was a hit when it toured Louisville . . . and I hear the attendance has been good all week."	Juanita continues the topic by providing new information.
Agreeing with Juanita, Donna adds, "Lots of people I've talked with were trying to get tickets."	Donna and Juanita continue the topic for two more turns.
"Well, it's good for the downtown."	
"Yeah," Donna says as she glances at the notes on the cast. After a few seconds she exclaims, "I didn't know Gloria VanDell was from Cincinnati!"	Donna acknowledges Juanita's reply and then introduces a different topic.

INTER-ACT WITH Technology

Think of times that you've made a call outside your home using a wireless cellular telephone. How do your conversations differ from those you have on wired phones? Are they longer? Shorter? More focused on pragmatic problem considerations than on casual social exchanges? Why do you think this is true? What differences do you see in the way you handle such conversations in comparison to the way you would handle them if you were face to face? ■

Use a search engine (like Google) to locate "The Ten Commandments of cell phone etiquette," an Info World online article published on May 26, 2000. Type in the article title in the "search" space.

For example, Donna and Juanita, who are attending a play together, may engage in a casual conversation before the play begins. Figure 6.1 on the previous page shows the dialogue and a commentary on their conversation.

For the remainder of time before the show starts, Juanita and Donna could converse on one or more topics, sit and read their programs, or follow some combination of conversing and reading.

The Structure of Problem-Consideration Conversations

A pragmatic problem-consideration conversation is structured differently from a casual social conversation because it requires the participants to deliberate and reach a conclusion. As a result, these conversations may appear to be more orderly than casual social conversations and can have as many as five distinguishable parts.

1. Greeting and small talk. Pragmatic problem-consideration conversations may begin with a greeting followed by very brief conversation on social topics in order to develop rapport.

When friends discuss problems that face them, their conversations are likely to become more structured.

2. Topic introduction and statement of need for discussion. In the second stage, one participant introduces the problem or issue that is the real purpose for the conversation. How this topic is presented or framed affects how the discussion will proceed.

3. Information exchange and processing. Once it is established that a problem should be discussed, the the conversation will proceed to a series of speaking turns where participants share information and opinions, generate alternative ideas for solutions, and present the advantages and disadvantages of different options.

Because conversations are spontaneous, they are unlikely to follow a textbook problem-solving format. The conversationalists may begin by generating some alternatives, then while discussing advantages and disadvantages they may share information that might lead to the suggestion of additional alternatives and so on. In the midst of this discussion, they may digress by changing the topic to something unrelated to the problem at hand before circling back to identifying and evaluating alternatives. So while problem-solving conversations will include these messages, the discussion may not be linear.

4. Summarizing decisions and clarifying next steps. As the partners approach the end of their conversation, one person will usually try to obtain closure by summarizing what has been agreed to. The other person will either accept the summary as accurate or will amend it to clarify the areas of agreement as well as any disagreements. At times conversational partners skip this step. Doing so is risky since one partner will act on what he or she perceives to have agreed to, which may not be what the other partner perceives.

5. Formal close. Once the conversationalists have discussed the issue and clarified the next steps that will be taken, they end the discussion of the problem. The ending statements provide a transition that enables conversationalists to move to a social conversation topic, begin a new problem consideration, or simply disengage from one another. The formal closing often includes showing appreciation for the conversation, such "I'm glad we took some time to share ideas. I think we'll be far more effective if the two of us are on the same line." The closing might also leave the door open for later conversation, such as "If you have any second thoughts, give me a call."

The script in the Test Yourself on page 156 exemplifies each of these five parts.

> **OBSERVE & ANALYZE**
>
> ## Journal Activity
>
> ### Problem-Consideration Conversations
>
> Identify two recent problem-consideration conversations that you have had—one that was satisfying and one that was not. Try to recall exactly what was said. Write the scripts for these conversations. Then try to identify each of the five parts of a problem-consideration conversation. Were any parts missing? Retain these scripts for further use later in the chapter. ■

Rules of Conversations

Although conversations may seem to have little form or structure, they are actually conducted based on implicit **rules,** which are "unwritten prescriptions that indicate what behavior is required, preferred, or prohibited in certain contexts" (Shimanoff,

Rules—unwritten prescriptions that indicate what behavior is required, preferred, or prohibited in certain contexts.

TEST YOURSELF

Identifying Parts of Problem-Solving Conversations

For the script below, identify each part of the problem-solving conversation structure:

APRIL: *Hi, Yolanda. How are you doing?*

YOLANDA: *Oh, can't complain too much.*

APRIL: *I'm glad I ran into you—I need to check something out with you.*

YOLANDA: *Can we do this quickly? I've really got to get cracking on the speech I'm doing for class.*

APRIL: *Oh, this will just take a minute. If I remember right, you said that you'd been to the Dells for dinner with Scot. I'd like to take Rob there to celebrate his birthday, but I wanted to know whether we'd really feel comfortable there.*

YOLANDA: *Sure. It's pretty elegant, but the prices aren't bad and the atmosphere is really nice.*

APRIL: *So you think we can really do dinner on fifty or sixty dollars?*

YOLANDA: *Oh, yeah. We had a salad, dinner, and a dessert and our bill was under sixty even with the tip.*

APRIL: *Thanks, Yolanda. I wanted to ask you 'cause I know you like to eat out when you can.*

YOLANDA: *No problem. Gotta run. Talk with you later—and let me know how Rob liked it.*

1980, p. 57). These unwritten rules specify what kinds of messages and behavior will be seen as appropriate in a given physical or social context or with a particular person or group of people. We use these rules to guide our own behavior and as a framework with which to interpret the behavior of others.

When we understand and follow the conversational rules that apply to a particular context, our interactions are more likely to be perceived by others as competent communicators and to build satisfying relationships. When we intentionally or unintentionally violate conversational rules, we risk being perceived as less competent and we undermine the relationship. For example, many people speak much more informally when they interact with same-age friends—in fact at times they may even pepper their speech with obscenities because within the peer group swearing is "OK." So in a peer context, Dan or Marie's crude language may not affect how they are perceived or offend others. Yet if Dan and Marie choose to use crude language in their customer service work settings or when each is talking with elderly relatives, they may be perceived as disrespectful and may unintentionally damage their relationships.

Characteristics of Rules

What makes a rule a rule? As we answer this let's use a common conversational rule as an example: "If one person is talking, then another person should not interrupt."

1. Rules specify appropriate human behavior. This means that rules focus on what to do or not to do.

2. Rules are prescriptive. A rule tells you what to do or say to be successful or effective. If you choose to break the rule you risk being viewed as incompetent or you risk damaging your relationship. For example, if you interrupt, you may be viewed as rude and the speaker may glare at you or verbally upbraid you.

3. Rules are contextual. This means that conversational rules that apply in some situations may not apply under different conditions. So most of the time the rule is, "don't interrupt." But if there is a true emergency—like a fire—this rule doesn't apply. Because rules are contextual some conversational rules differ by culture. So, when we communicate with people of different subcultural backgrounds, we may unintentionally break the conversational rules that guide their behavior and vice versa. For example, cultures differ in how eye contact is used during conversations. In some cultures this rule is to look directly at a speaker while in others the rule is to avoid direct eye contact with a speaker.

4. Rules must allow for choice. This means that a conversational rule by nature allows participants the freedom to comply with or violate the expectation. So, not interrupting is a rule since you can hear the person out or you can choose to interrupt the person. Exhibit 6.1 presents several conversational rules that are common to many cultures.

The Cooperative Principle

Not only are conversations structured by the rules that participants follow or violate, but they also depend on how well conversational partners follow the cooper-

---

E X H I B I T   6 . 1

The following are common conversational rules. Notice that many rules that we use are framed in an "if . . . then" format:

- If your mouth is full of food, then you must not talk.
- If someone is talking, then you must not interrupt.
- If you are spoken to, you must reply.
- If another does not hear a question you ask, then you must repeat it.
- If you are being spoken to, you should direct your gaze to the speaker.
- Or, from a different cultural perspective, if you are being spoken to, you should look at the floor.
- If more than two people are conversing, then each should have equal time.
- If your conversational partners are significantly older than you, then you should refrain from using profanities and obscenities.
- If you can't say something nice, then you don't say anything at all.
- If you are going to say something that you don't want overheard, then drop the volume of your voice.

The cooperative principle–
states that conversations will be satisfying when the contributions made by conversationalists are in line with the purpose of the conversation.

Maxims–rules of conduct that cooperative conversational partners follow.

Quality maxim–requirement to provide information that is truthful.

Quantity maxim–requirement to tailor the amount of information that is sufficient or necessary-not too much and not too little.

Relevancy maxim–requirement to provide information that is related to the topic being discussed.

Manner maxim–requirement to be specific and organized when communicating your thoughts.

ative principle. H. Paul Grice (1975) described the **cooperative principle,** which states that conversations will be satisfying when the contributions made by conversationalists are in line with the purpose of the conversation (pp. 44–46). Based on this principle, Grice identified four conversational **maxims,** or rules of conduct, that cooperative conversational partners follow.

1. The **quality maxim** calls for us to provide information that is truthful. When we purposely lie, distort, or misrepresent, we are not acting cooperatively in the conversation. Being truthful means not only avoiding deliberate lies or distortions but also taking care to avoid misrepresentation. Thus, if a classmate asks you what the prerequisites for Bio 205 are, you should share them if you know them, but you should not guess and offer your opinion as though it were fact. If you don't know or if you have only a vague recollection, you follow the quality maxim by honestly saying, "I'm not sure."

2. The **quantity maxim** calls for us to tailor the amount of information we provide so that we offer the information that is sufficient and necessary to satisfy others' information needs and keep the conversation going. But we are not supposed to become so lengthy and detailed that we undermine the informal give-and-take that is characteristic of good conversations. So, when Sam asks Randy how he liked his visit to St. Louis, Randy's answer, "fine," is uncooperatively brief because it makes it difficult for Sam to continue the conversation. On the opposite extreme, should Randy launch into a twenty-minute monologue that details everything he did including recounting what he ate each day, he would also be violating the maxim.

3. The **relevancy maxim** calls for us to provide information that is related to the topic currently being discussed. Comments that are only tangential to the subject or that seek an abrupt subject change when other conversational partners are still actively engaged with the topic are uncooperative. For example, Hal, Corey, and Li-Sung are in the midst of a lively discussion about the upcoming 5K walk/run for the local homeless shelter when Corey asks whether either Hal or Li-Sung has taken Speech 101. Since Corey's change of subject disrupts an ongoing discussion, he is violating the relevancy maxim.

4. The **manner maxim** calls for us to be specific and organized when communicating our thoughts. We cooperate with our conversational partners when we choose specific language so that it is easy for our partners to understand our meaning. When D'wan asks Remal how to download a computer file, Remal will comply with the manner maxim by explaining the process one step at a time using language that D'wan can understand. Obviously, observing the manner maxim doesn't mean that you have a specific outline for every comment you make.

OBSERVE & ANALYZE

Journal Activity

Conversational Maxims

Refer back to the two conversation scripts you prepared in the exercise on problem-consideration conversations (p. 155). Can you identify specific conversational rules that were used? Which of these were complied with? Which were violated? How does this analysis help you understand your satisfaction with the conversation?

Which of the conversational maxims were followed? If there were violations, what were they and how did they affect the conversation? ■

When Mississippi Chinese Talk *By Gwendolyn Gong, Ph.D.*

In her article from which this excerpt is taken, Dr. Gong, from Texas A&M, explains how Mississippi Chinese use conversational accommodation and topic shifting to politely reduce conversational discomfort for their conversational partners and themselves. As you read this, identify examples of the use of accommodation or deference.

Though my family heritage traces back to an ancestral village in Canton, China, I am a Chinese American, born and reared in the Mississippi Delta. Given that my siblings—in truth, my entire immediate family—served as classic, prolific producers of Southern speech, I find it peculiar that, when I went to graduate school in Indiana, my Hoosier peers and professors saw me as some sort of enigma—an oddity. They would joke, "The picture's fine but adjust the sound." This same type of remark followed me to Texas, where indeed another version of English is spoken. "Adjust the sound." What did that mean? Hadn't these folks ever encountered a Mississippian before? The truth was that they had. But I was different. I was a Mississippi Chinese. Since the late 1800s this lush farming area has served as a homeland for approximately 1200 Cantonese Chinese from Southern China who have gradually assimilated into being Southerners of another ilk: Mississippi Chinese (MC). In my experience, one of the most interesting ways by which I have observed how Southern Genteelism and

Confucianism reveal themselves is in the talk of the MC.

A major feature that typifies MC speech is deference, the courteous submission or acquiescence to the opinions, wishes, or judgment of another speaker, which may manifest itself in two forms: accommodation (i.e., making the non-MC speaker feel comfortable and welcome) and topic shifting (i.e., changing the subject of a conversation). Ironically, accommodation that may provide comfort for the non-MC listener may, on occasion, result in a discomfort for the MC speaker; conversely, topic shifting oftentimes provides relief and control for the MC speaker but frustration for the non-MC listener. For non-MC speakers and listeners, understanding of how deference operates among the MC helps to provide a more effective informed exchange between these two groups.

A number of years ago at the institution where I was teaching, I developed a friendship with a colleague. This woman was a master teacher who spoke with authority and often openly revealed to me her earnest but prejudicial concerns about me as a person. Occasionally, we would

see each other in passing and chat:

"Hi, Gong. I went to a Thai restaurant on Sunday. I asked for some soy sauce, and the waiter looked at me like I was crazy. What was wrong with asking for some soy sauce? The food was so bad—like bad Chinese food—that I covered it with everything. Why was that guy so mad at me?"

"Asking for soy sauce isn't a crime. I don't know why your waiter was upset," I replied sheepishly. I was not certain why she was broaching me on the topic of Thai food: I'm no expert on it, though I do enjoy that particular cuisine.

"We ought to have lunch. What's your schedule?" my colleague inquired.

"I've already eaten. Plus, I've got so much work to finish in my office today. Sorry that I can't join you while you eat." I was uncomfortable, yet truthful.

"What'd ya eat? Betcha had egg rolls, eh? Gong, you're always eating egg rolls—at least you used to. Remember when you first came here years ago? I couldn't believe it—a Chinese, teaching English—with a Southern accent, too. I used to share an office with a fellow named Joe, who'd eat tacos and avocados all the time, and then I'd see you across the hall, eating egg rolls. Right, Gong? Don't ya remember?"

"Well, no I really don't remember, but I suppose it's true," I replied, trying to go along with my colleague. "I do recall Joe and I ate take-out food sometimes. It was a quick way to have lunch." I added, my voice trailing off, diminishing with every syllable. I wished I were anywhere else but here, "talking" with this person. It was embarrassing enough that she made these kinds of remarks to me at all, much less within earshot of

other faculty and students. Where could I hide? I thought to myself: "Hang in there; it'll be over soon."

This is only one conversation among many that this professor and I have shared. Out of my deep belief that she did care about me and out of my respect for her professional accomplishments, I always accommodated this individual's topic selection and conversational moves. I self-consciously defended her, rationalizing that she was just "tone-deaf" and didn't understand her audience very well. She admitted that she'd never known an

American-born Asian like me before. As a result, I reasoned to myself that I should give her a break, help her avoid "losing face," and prevent her from feeling awkward. Yet I always experienced regret that I voluntarily subjected myself to being bullied, demeaned, and belittled by someone espousing true friendship. ■

Excerpted from Gong, G. (2000). When Mississippi Chinese Talk. In A. Gonzalez, M. Houston, & V. Chen (Eds.), *Our Voices: Essays in Culture, Ethnicity, and Communication* (3rd ed., pp. 84–91). Los Angeles: Roxbury Publishing Company.

Conversations, after all, are informal. But following the manner maxim does mean that you organize what you are saying thoughtfully so that others don't have to work too hard to understand you.

While these four maxims are important markers of conversational cooperation, Thomas Holtgraves points out, "conversationalists rarely abide by these maxims. They are often irrelevant, they sometimes say too much or too little, and so on. But it is usually the case that people will mutually assume adherence to the CP (cooperative principle) and maxims, and this assumption serves as a frame for interpreting a speaker's utterances. That is, a speaker's utterances will be interpreted *as if* they were clear, relevant, truthful, and informative" (2002, p. 24).

In addition to the four maxims identified by Grice, Bach and Harnish (1979, p. 64) have proposed two additional maxims that cooperative partners follow.

Morality maxim–the requirement to meet moral/ethical guidelines.

5. The **morality maxim** calls for us to be moral and ethical when we speak. For example, in the United States violations of the morality maxim would include repeating information that had been disclosed confidentially, purposefully deceiving someone as to the truthfulness or accuracy of another's statements, or persuading someone else to do something that the speaker knows is wrong or against the other's personal interests.

6. The **politeness maxim** calls for us to demonstrate respect for other participants by behaving courteously. In our conversations we should attempt to observe the social norms of politeness in the dominant culture and not purposefully embarrass ourselves or others during the interaction. The Diverse Voices feature that you read on pages 159–160 describes how politeness is enacted in Gwendolyn Gong's cultural community. In the next section we will discuss means of practicing politeness.

Politeness maxim–the requirement to be courteous to other participants.

Guidelines for Effective Conversationalists

Regardless of how well we think we converse, almost all of us can learn to be more effective conversationalists. In this section, we discuss several guidelines for helping you become better. These guidelines are listed in Exhibit 6.2.

EXHIBIT 6.2

Guidelines for Effective Conversations
1. Prepare to contribute interesting ideas and information.
2. Ask questions that motivate others to respond.
3. Provide free information.
4. Credit the sources of your ideas.
5. Practice appropriate turn-taking.
6. Maintain conversational coherence.
7. Practice politeness.
8. Engage in ethical dialogues.

Prepare to Contribute Interesting Information

The more you know about a range of subjects, the greater the chances are that you will be able to participate effectively in social conversations. In order to increase what you are able to contribute try to:
1. Keep up to date on current events and issues:
   • Read a newspaper every day.
   • Read one weekly news or special-interest magazine.
   • Follow the news online or through television or radio.

OBSERVE & ANALYZE

Journal Activity

Conversational Variety

During the next three days, intentionally introduce a greater number of unusual or provocative topics in your conversations with others. How well are you able to develop and sustain such conversations? Are these more or less satisfying than conversations on more mundane topics like the weather, sports, and daily happenings? Why? ■

The more you know about a range of subjects, the greater the chance that you will be an interesting conversationalist.

- Watch television documentaries and news specials as well as entertainment and sports programs.

2. Increase your cultural IQ:

- Attend the theater and concerts, as well as going to movies.
- Attend cultural festivals sponsored by different nationalities.
- Study the music, art, or history of another nationality.
- Visit museums and historical sites.
- Read a variety of novels, including the classics.

    Following these suggestions will provide you with a fountain of quality information you can share in social conversations.

Ask Questions that Motivate Others to Respond

What happens in the first few minutes of a conversation can have a profound effect on how well a social conversation develops. Although asking questions comes easy to some, many people seem at a loss for what to do to get a conversation going. While there are countless ways to start a conversation, four common types of questions are commonly used to get a conversation started.

1. Questions about the other's family: How is Susan getting along this year at college? How is your dad feeling? Do you have children? How long have you been married?

2. Questions about a person's work: What do you do for a living? What projects have you been working on lately? What are you majoring in?

3. Questions about sporting or cultural events: How was the fishing trip you went on last week? Did you see how Tiger Woods got out of that impossible situation at last week's tournament? Have you seen the new *Star Wars* movie?

4. Questions about current events: What do you think about the airlines using racial profiling? Can you believe the amount of money CEOs make? Did you see that there was another carload of kids killed on I-75 last Saturday? While these are four types of questions that are commonly used to open conversations with acquaintances, there are obviously many others.

Provide Free Information

Effective conversationalists make it easy for others to continue the conversation by making comments that provide new information to which the partner can respond. **Free information** is extra information offered during a message that can be used by the responder to continue the conversation.

Many people have difficulty sustaining conversations because in replying to questions they give one-word or very brief responses. Suppose Paul asks Jack, "Do you like tennis?" and Jack answers "Yes" and then just looks at Paul, Paul has nowhere to go. To keep the conversation going (or to get it started), Paul has to think of a new line to pursue. If Jack continues supplying only short responses, Paul will eventually become tired and bored and may terminate the conversation.

Suppose, however, that after Jack answers "Yes," he goes on to say "I've only been playing for about a year, but I really enjoy it." Now Paul has a direction to follow. He might turn the conversation to his own experience: "I haven't been playing long myself, but I'm starting to get more confidence, especially with my forehand." Or he might use the information to ask another question: "Have you taken any lessons or clinics?"

As a respondent, it's important to give free information. As the initiator, it's important to listen for the use of free information that is provided. The better the quality of the free information, the more likely it is that the conversation will continue and prove rewarding to both participants.

Free information–extra information offered during a message that can be used by the responder to continue the conversation.

Credit the Sources of Your Ideas

Crediting the source means verbally acknowledging the specific source from which you have drawn your information and ideas. In a term paper you give credit to authors you have quoted or paraphrased by footnoting the sources. Similarly, when you use other people's words or ideas in your oral communication, you should credit the source verbally.

By crediting, you enable the other participants to evaluate the quality of the information you are sharing. Moreover, by crediting ideas from people who are acquaintances, you make them feel better about themselves and avoid hard feelings. For instance, if a friend of yours discusses a creative idea that you dreamed up and verbally acknowledges you as the source, you will appreciate the credit. If, however, the person acts as though the idea were his own, you are likely to be hurt or angry.

Crediting is easy enough. To give credit simply include the name of the person or other source from which you got the idea. For example, in a discussion about course offerings, you might say, "I like the list of courses we have to choose from, but you know, we should really have a course in attitude change—Laura was the one who put me onto the idea, and I can see why it's a good idea." Or in a discussion about the problems in the Mid-East, you might say, "After reading the editorial by Thomas Friedman in Sunday's paper, I changed my mind about the Jewish settlements in the occupied territories."

Crediting the source–verbally acknowledging the specific source from which you have drawn your information and ideas.

CREDITING THE SOURCE

SKILL	USE	PROCEDURE	EXAMPLE
Verbally identifying the source of ideas you are using.	To give credit to sources of information we present in order to clarify the origin of the ideas and to avoid possible hard feelings.	Include the specific source of ideas, whether written or oral.	At a meeting of a group's fund-raising committee, Tina says, "What about buying a television at discount and selling raffle tickets? George was the first one to think of the idea and I think it's a great one. We could probably make a couple of hundred dollars."

Practice Appropriate Turn-Taking

Conversations are most satisfying when all participants feel that they have had their fair share of speaking time. We balance speaking and listening in a conversation by practicing turn-taking techniques.

Although researchers point out that in ordinary conversation people often speak at the same time and that turns are not always easy to identify, as Ford, Fox, and Thompson (2002) point out, the fact is that participants in interaction treat the concept of "turn" as "relevant, real, and consequential in an individual's speaking time/space" (p. 8). Let's consider some of the key aspects of the concept of turn.

1. Effective conversationalists take the appropriate number of turns. In any conversation, the ideal is for all to have approximately the same number of turns. If you discover that you are speaking more than your fair share, try to restrain yourself by mentally checking whether everyone else has had a chance to talk once before you talk a second time. Similarly, if you find yourself being inactive in a conversation, you need to increase your participation level. Remember, if you have information to contribute, you're cheating yourself and the group when you do not share it.

If you find others are wanting to talk, but can't seem to get the floor, you can help those who haven't been able to talk by saying something like, "Donna, I get the sense that you've been wanting to comment on this point."

2. Effective conversationalists speak an appropriate length of time on each turn. People are likely to tune out or become annoyed at conversational partners who make speeches, filibuster, or perform monologues rather than engaging in the ordinary give-and-take of conversation. Similarly, it is difficult to carry on a conversation with someone who gives one- or two-word replies to questions that are designed to elicit meaningful information. Of course, turns do vary in length depending on what is being said. However, if your statements average much longer or much shorter than those of your conversational partners, you need to adjust.

3. Effective conversationalists recognize and heed turn-exchanging cues of others. Patterns of vocal tone, such as changes in volume, pitch, or gestures indicate completion of a point and are the most obvious turn-taking cues (Duncan & Fiske, 1977). When you are trying to get into a conversation, look for those cues.

Does it bother you when one person speaks more often than others?

By the same token, be careful of giving inadvertent turn-exchanging cues. For instance, if you tend to lower your voice when you are not really done speaking or take long pauses for emphasis when you expect to continue, you are likely to be interrupted, because lowering your voice and pausing are turn-taking cues that others are likely to act on. If you find yourself getting interrupted frequently, you might ask people whether you tend to give false cues. Moreover, if you come to recognize that another person has a habit of giving these kinds of cues inadvertently, try not to interrupt when speaking with that person.

4. Effective conversationalists use conversation-directing behavior and comply with the conversation-directing behavior of others. In general, a person who relinquishes his or her turn may define who speaks next. For instance, when Paul concludes his turn by saying "Susan, did you understand what he meant?" Susan has the right to the floor. Skillful turn-takers use conversation-directing behavior to

SKILL BUILDERS   **TURNTAKING**

SKILL	USE	PROCEDURE	EXAMPLE
Engaging in appropriate conversational sequencing.	Determining when a speaker is at a place where another person may talk if he or she wants to.	1. Take your share of turns. 2. Gear turn length to the behavior of partners. 3. Give and watch for turn-taking and turn-exchanging cues. Avoid giving inadvertent turn-taking cues. 4. Observe and use conversation-directing behavior. 5. Limit interruptions.	When John lowers his voice as he says "I really thought they were going to go ahead during those last few seconds," Melissa, noticing he appears to be finished, says, "I did, too. But did you notice. . ."

balance turns between those who speak freely and those who may be more reluctant to speak. Similarly, effective turn-takers remain silent and listen politely when the conversation is directed to someone else.

Of course, if the person who has just finished speaking does not verbally or nonverbally direct the conversation to a preferred next speaker, then the turn is up for grabs and goes to the first person to speak.

5. Effective conversationalists rarely interrupt. Although interruptions are generally considered inappropriate, interrupting for "clarification" and "agreement" (confirming) are interpersonally acceptable (Kennedy & Camden, 1983, p. 55). For instance, interruptions that are likely to be accepted include relevant questions or paraphrases intended to clarify, such as "What do you mean by 'presumptuous'?" or "I get the sense that you think presumptuous behavior is especially bad," and reinforcing statements such as "Good point, Max" or "I see what you mean, Suzie." Interruptions that are likely to be viewed as disruptive or impolite include those that change the subject or that seem to minimize the contribution of the interrupted person.

Maintain Conversational Coherence

Conversational coherence–the extent to which the comments made by one person relate to those made by others previously in the conversation.

Conversational coherence is the extent to which the comments made by one person relate to those made by others previously in the conversation (McLaughlin, 1984, pp. 88–89). Littlejohn (2000) pointed out that conversational coherence is "how communicators create clear meaning" in conversation (p. 83). The more directly messages relate to those that precede them, the more coherent or meaningful is the conversation.

Although many topics of conversation just "come up," we can still work at maintaining conversational coherence while a particular topic is being discussed. In social conversations, where the primary goal is to enjoy each other's company, topics may change and will cover a wide variety of issues. Nevertheless, to maintain coherence, what we say should be related to what was said before. This means that we must listen to what is being said by the person who is speaking. Many of us have developed the bad habit of only half-listening while we rehearse or plan what we want to say next. Most of us have gotten into conversational trouble doing this. To be effective conversationalists, we must give the speaker our full attention and really listen to what is being said. Then we must determine how what we are planning to say relates to the comments just made. If what we want to say is only tangentially related or is unrelated, then we should defer the turn to someone else who may have more relevant comments. If there are only two of us conversing, then we should respond to the speaker's message before introducing a change in topic.

Conservational plan–a consciously constructed conceptualization of one or more sequences of action at achieving a goal.

More of our conversation than we may realize has a definable purpose that is known beforehand. For instance, you may be talking with your family to determine travel plans for the holidays, with your professor about how to study for his tests, or with a friend to get her support for a plan you want to bring to a church committee. In these problem-consideration conversations, coherence can be enhanced by having a conversational plan. A **conversational plan** is a "consciously constructed conceptualization of one or more sequences of action at achieving a goal" (Hobbes & Evans, 1980). Because conversation is a dynamic process in which you cannot plan for every possible response, the plan usually involves an opening approach and some idea of how to proceed given the most likely listener reactions. So, if your goal is to get a friend's support for a proposal you want to bring to a church committee, you should anticipate possible reactions and have clear reasons and supporting data to offer for your plan.

Practice Politeness

Politeness—relating to others in ways that meet their need to be appreciated and protected—is universal to all cultures (Brown and Levinson, 1987). This study of how politeness affects conversation has discovered that although levels of politeness and ways of being polite vary, all people have positive and negative "face needs." **Positive face needs** are the desire to be appreciated and approved, liked and honored. **Negative face needs** are the desire to be free from imposition or intrusion. As Thomas Holtgraves points out, the study of politeness "links the major dimensions of social interaction with the ways in which people talk with one another" (2002, p. 38).

According to politeness theory, to meet people's positive face needs, we make statements that show concern, compliment, or use respectful forms of address. It is

OBSERVE & ANALYZE

Journal Activity

Conversational Coherence

Refer once again to the two scripts that you prepared in the exercise on problem-consideration conversations (p. 155). Analyze each to see how coherent the conversations were. Count the number of times that someone did not directly respond to the statement that immediately preceded it. Was one conversation more coherent than the other? ■

Politeness–relating to others in ways that meet their need to be appreciated and protected.

Positive face needs–the desire to be appreciated and approved, liked and honored.

Negative face needs–the desire to be free from imposition or intrusion.

How might the desire to "win" the Survivor game affect the ethical dialogues between contestants?

polite and to greet your instructor as "Professor Reynolds" (to use a respectful form of address) or to say "Thanks for the tip on how to work out that problem, it really helped" (to compliment).

To meet people's negative face needs, we make statements that acknowledge when we are imposing or intruding upon another. For instance, to recognize that you are imposing you might say to your professor, "I can see you're busy, but I wonder whether you could take a minute to . . ." or "I know that you don't have time to talk with me now, but I wanted to see whether there was a time that we could meet later today or tomorrow."

Sometimes one behavior can meet both positive and negative face needs. For example, knocking on the door and waiting for permission to enter is polite because it both shows respect and recognizes that you are about to impose on someone's solitude or privacy.

Although politeness is always important, it is especially so whenever the central content of a conversation might threaten another person's face. When we say something to a person that might cause the person to "lose face," we commit what Brown and Levinson call **face-threatening acts** (FTAs). We are committing FTAs when our behavior *fails* to meet positive or negative face needs of another. The goal of politeness theory is not to avoid face threatening—it is normal. Rather, the goal is to lessen or eliminate potential conversational or relationship problems that could result from FTAs.

Suppose your professor returned a set of papers and you believe the grade you received did not accurately reflect the quality of the paper. You could say, "I don't think you graded my paper fairly and you need to reconsider the grade you gave me," a statement that is an FTA. Saying something like this, which suggests that the professor was wrong, is likely to threaten the professor with a loss of face and result in the professor becoming defensive. If you need to confront someone with something that might have consequences for their face, you should consider doing so in one of the following ways:

1. **You can make the FTA in a way that includes some form of positive politeness.** "I would appreciate it if you could look at my paper again. I've marked the places that I'd like you to consider. My roommate said that you were fair and usually willing to reconsider if there seemed to be a good reason." Although the request still contains a direct imposition on the professor, "I would appreciate it" is more polite than "You need to." Moreover, the effort to include a positive politeness statement that shows the professor is fair minded and willing to reconsider when there might be a good reason helps to build positive face.

2. **You can make the FTA with negative politeness.** "I'm sure you're very busy and don't have time to reread and remark every paper, but I'm hoping you'll be willing to look at my paper again. To minimize the time it might take, I've marked the places that I'd like you to consider. I've also written comments to show why I phrased those sections as I did." Although the request is still a direct imposition, the statement recognizes that you are

Face-threatening acts (FTAs)—engaging in behavior that fails to meet positive or negative face needs.

imposing. It also suggests that you wouldn't do it if there weren't at least, potentially good reasons. Moreover, you've taken time not only to limit how much the professor needs to look at but also to show why you thought the sections were in keeping with the assignment.

3. **You can make the FTA indirectly or off the record.** "Please don't take this the wrong way, but I was surprised by a few of your comments." By saying this in a casual way, you hope your professor might be curious enough to ask what caused you to be surprised. With this opening you can move to one of the more direct face-saving approaches.

So, the question is, how do we choose whether to be polite and, if so, which of the three strategies do we use? Brown and Levinson (1987) believe this decision is affected by a combination of three factors:

1. **How well people know each other and their relative status.** The less familiar we are with someone and the higher the person's social status, the more effort we will put into being polite.

2. **The power that the hearer has over the speaker.** Most of us will work harder to be polite to those who are powerful than to those who are powerless.

3. **The risk of hurting the other person.** Most of us will work harder to be polite to people we believe to be more vulnerable than to those whom we perceive as less likely to be hurt by our impoliteness.

To show how you might use these three factors in determining how polite you are, let's consider two examples. First, suppose you want to impose on your roommate to take a look at your paper before you turn it in to your professor. Your roommate is your friend, and you get along quite well. The imposition is relatively minor and only mildly threatening—in the past *both* of you have looked at work the other has done. Moreover, your roommate has no special *power* over you. In light of these considerations, you might not put much effort into trying to be polite. You might make this request without much regard to your roommate's negative face needs and say, "Danny, take a look at this paper. I need to hand it in tomorrow."

Second, suppose that you want to ask your professor to preread the same paper before you submit it for a grade. Because your professor is not your friend (you are socially more distant) and because your professor has considerable power over you (he controls your grade), you will probably want to approach your professor more politely than you did your friend. As a result, you are likely to make a statement that includes a form of positive politeness or a statement that includes a form of negative politeness.

OBSERVE & ANALYZE

Journal Activity

Using Politeness

Think about the last time that you committed a face-threatening act (FTA). Try to reconstruct the situation. What did you say? Try to recall as specifically as possible the exact words you used.

Analyze your FTA in terms of familiarity and status, power, and risk. Did you have greater or lesser status? Did you have greater or lesser social power? Was the risk of hurting the person large or small? In light of your analysis, write three different ways that you could have made your request. Try one that uses positive face statements, one that uses negative face statements, and one that combines positive and negative. ■

As you come to better understand face needs, you will become better able to accurately diagnose situations in which you should take particular care to engage in polite behavior. In addition, each of us can make the world a bit more humane by working at being polite regardless of situational imperatives.

Engage in Ethical Dialogue

The final guideline followed by effective conversationalists is to engage in ethical dialogues. According to Johannesen (2000), ethical dialogue or conversation is characterized by authenticity, empathy, confirmation, presentness, a spirit of mutual equality, and a supportive climate.

Authenticity–direct, honest, straightforward communication of all information and feelings that are relevant and legitimate to the subject at hand.

Authenticity is demonstrated by the direct, honest, straightforward communication of all information and feelings that are relevant and legitimate to the subject at hand. To sit in a discussion, disagreeing with what is being said but saying nothing, is inauthentic. It is also inauthentic to agree verbally with something that you really do not believe in.

Empathy–demonstrated by comments that show you understand another's point of view without giving up your own position or sense of self.

Empathy is demonstrated by comments that show you understand another's point of view without giving up your own position or sense of self. Comments such as "I see your point" or "I'm not sure I agree with you, but I'm beginning to understand why you feel that way" demonstrate empathy. Because of the importance of empathy in making effective responses, we will consider it in more detail in Chapter 8.

Confirmation–nonpossessive expressions of warmth for others that affirm them as unique persons without necessarily approving of their behaviors or views.

Confirmation is demonstrated through nonpossessive expressions of warmth for others that affirm them as unique persons without necessarily approving of their behaviors or views. Examples of confirmation might include "Well, Keith, you certainly have an interesting way of looking at things, and I must say, you really make me think through my own views on things" or "Well, I guess I'd still prefer that you didn't get a tattoo, but you really have thought this through."

Presentness–demonstrating a willingness to become fully involved with the other person by taking time, avoiding distraction, being responsive, and risking attachment.

Presentness is demonstrated by becoming fully involved with the other person through taking time, avoiding distractions, being responsive, and risking attachment to them. The most obvious way to exhibit presentness is by listening actively to the person with whom you are conversing. During a conversation you can also demonstrate presentness by asking questions that are directly related to what has been said.

Equality–treating conversational partners on the same level, regardless of the status differences that separate them from other participants.

Equality is demonstrated by treating conversational partners as peers, regardless of the status differences that separate them from other participants. To lord one's accomplishments, one's power roles, or one's social status over another during conversation is unethical because conversations are informal and casual interactions.

Supportiveness–encouraging the other participants to communicate by praising their worthwhile efforts.

Supportiveness is demonstrated by encouraging the other participants to communicate by praising their worthwhile efforts. You will recall from our discussion of relationships in Chapter 3 that positive communication climates are characterized by an exchange of messages that are descriptive, open, and tentative, as well as equality oriented.

When we engage in ethical dialogue, we improve the odds that our conversations will meet our needs and the needs of those with whom we interact.

Cultural Variations in Effective Conversation

Throughout this chapter the guidelines for conversational behavior we have considered assume a Western cultural perspective, specifically the cultural perspective of Anglos whose culture is low context. But just as various verbal and nonverbal rules vary from low-context to high-context cultures, so do the guidelines for effective conversation. Gudykunst and Matsumoto (1996, pp. 30–32) explain four differences in conversational patterns between people of low-context and high-context cultures.

First, while low-context culture conversations are likely to include greater use of such categorical words such as *certainly*, *absolutely*, and *positively*, high-context culture conversations are likely to see greater use of qualifiers such as *maybe*, *perhaps*, and *probably*.

Second, low-context cultures strictly adhere to the relevancy maxim by valuing relevant comments that are perceived by listeners to be directly to the point. In high-context cultures, however, individuals' responses are likely to be more indirect, ambiguous, and apparently less relevant, because listeners rely more on nonverbal cues to help them understand the speaker's intentions and meaning.

Third, in low-context cultures, the quality maxim is operationalized in truth telling. People are expected to verbally communicate their actual feelings about

---

WHAT WOULD YOU DO?

A Question *of* Ethics

Sarah, John, Louisa, Naomi, and Richard all met at a dance party that the university sponsored during First-Year Orientation. During a break, they began sharing where they were from, where they were working, what classes they were taking, and their potential majors. John was having fun talking with Louisa—he thought she was cute and wanted to impress her. When she mentioned that she had been involved in theater during high school and was considering majoring in drama, he began to share his own theater experiences. Everyone was politely listening, and interested at first, but he kept talking and talking. Finally, Naomi interrupted John and changed the subject, for which the rest of the group was quite grateful.

Throughout their twenty-minute conversation, whenever someone would bring up a new subject, John would immediately take center stage and expound on some wild story that only remotely related. Not only was he long-winded, but his stories seemed to be fabricated. He was the hero in every one—either through his intellect or his strength. Besides all this, as John talked he included completely inappropriate side comments that were turn-offs to all of the listeners. One by one, each person found a reason to excuse him- or herself. Soon John was standing alone. Several minutes later, John heard the other four around the corner talking. Before he could round the corner and come into their sight, he heard one of them

say, "Do you guys want to go over to Starbucks so we can talk in peace? That John was really a dork, but I think we can avoid seeing him if we zip out the side door. That way the rest of us can have a chance to talk."

1. Have you ever talked with someone like John? Where did John go wrong in his conversational skills? What should he have done differently?

2. Was it ethical for the group to sneak out? What are the ethical implications of Louisa and the rest of the group sneaking out the back door without saying anything to John? Defend your position. ■

things regardless of how this affects others. Effective conversationalists in high-context cultures, however, operationalize the quality maxim differently. They define quality as maintaining harmony, and so conversationalists will send messages that mask their true feelings.

Finally, in low-context cultures, periods of silence are perceived as uncomfortable since when no one is speaking little information is being shared. In high-context cultures, silences in conversation are often meaningful. When three or four people sit together and no one talks, the silence may indicate truthfulness, disapproval, embarrassment, or disagreement, depending on context.

Summary

Conversations are locally managed sequential interchange of thoughts and feelings between two or more people that are interactive and largely extemporaneous. There are two types of conversations: social conversations between people whose purpose is to enhance or maintain a relationship and problem-consideration conversations between people in which the goal of at least one of the participants is to solicit the cooperation of the other in meeting a goal. Each of these types has a general structure.

Conversations are guided by unwritten prescriptions/rules that indicate what behavior is required, preferred, or prohibited. Four characteristics of conversational rules are that they specify appropriate behavior, they are prescriptive, they are contextual, and that they allow for choice.

Effective conversations are governed by the cooperative principle, which suggests that conversations "work" when participants join together to accomplish conversational goals and make the conversation pleasant for each participant. The cooperative principle gives rise to six axioms: quality, quantity, relevancy, manner, morality, and politeness.

Effective conversationalists follow specific guidelines: They prepare to contribute interesting information by keeping up to date on current events and issues and increasing their cultural IQ. They ask questions that motivate others to respond. They provide free information that can be used by the responder to continue conversation. They credit the sources of the ideas they present. They practice appropriate turn-taking, which includes such behaviors as taking the appropriate number of turns, speaking an appropriate length of time, and rarely interrupting. They maintain conversational coherence by relating their comments to those presented previously. They practice politeness by relating to others in ways that meet their need to be appreciated and protected. And they engage in ethical dialogue.

Inter-Action Dialogue:

Conversations that are likely to be casual social or problem-solving interactions tend to follow unwritten rules. Conversations are most effective when they adhere to quality, quantity, relevancy, manner, morality, and politeness maxims. Skills of effective conversation include asking questions, providing free information, crediting sources, and turn-taking.

Here's a transcript of Susan and Sarah's conversation, with analysis of the conversation in the right-hand column. As you read the dialogue, determine the type of conversation that is taking place. Look for the signs of effective conversation mentioned above. You may want to write down some of your observations before you read the analysis in the right-hand column.

Susan and Sheila are close friends who share the same religious background and the occasional frustrations related to their family beliefs.

CONVERSATION

SUSAN: *So how are you and Bill getting along these days?*

SARAH: *Oh, not too well, Suze. I think we've got to end the relationship. There are so many issues between us that I just don't have the same feelings.*

SUSAN: *Yeah, you know, I could tell. Is there one specific thing that's a problem?*

SARAH: *Yes, and it's ironic because early on I didn't think it would be problem, but it is. You know, he's not Jewish and since we've started talking about marriage, I've realized that it is a problem. While Bill's a great guy, our backgrounds and beliefs just don't mesh. I never realized how important my Jewishness was to me until I was faced with converting. And Bill feels similarly about it.*

SUSAN: *I think I'm kind of lucky, well, in the long run. Remember in high school my parents wouldn't let me go out with anybody who wasn't Jewish? At the time I resented that and we both thought they were reactionary, but now I'm kind of glad. At the time my parents said, "you never know what's going to come out of a high school relationship." Well, they never got that far, but it did force me to think about things.*

SARAH: *Yes, I remember that. you hated it. It's amazing to realize your parents can actually be right about something.*

SUSAN: *Right, it was the pits at the time, but at least it spared me the pain you and Bill are going through. It must be awful to be in love with someone that you realize you don't want as a life partner.*

ANALYSIS

Susan initiates the conversation with a meaningful question.

Sarah answers the question and gives "free information" about her lack of feelings and the presence of multiple problems.

Susan poses a question that suggests the potential for problem consideration.

Sarah accepts Susan's willingness to discuss a problem by sharing specific information that becomes the topical focus of the rest of the conversation—information that meets Grice's conversational maxims.

Susan shifts the topic a bit by speaking about her experiences. This seems to violate the relevancy maxim, but in so doing, she lays the groundwork for later exchanges.

Sarah shows that she recalls what was said. She then adds additional free information to keep the conversation flowing.

Susan confirms that her parents' wisdom spared her pain. She then makes a statement that stimulates further discussion from Sarah.

Conversations

CONVERSATION

SARAH: *Exactly, but I'm glad that my parents didn't restrict my dating to Jewish guys. I've learned a lot by dating a variety of people and I know that I've made this decision independently.*

Bill's a great guy, but for me to be me, I need to partner with a Jewish man—and Bill knows he can't be that. Making this choice has been hard, but it's helped me to grow. I guess I understand myself better.

SUSAN: *So where have you guys left it? Are you going to still see each other? Be friends?*

SARAH: *We hope so. But right now, it's too fresh. It hurts to see him, so we're trying to give each other some space. It will really be tough when I hear he's seeing someone else. But I'll get by.*

SUSAN: *Well, you know I'm here for you. And when you're ready there are some real hotties at Hillel. I'll be glad to introduce you.*

SARAH: *Thanks Suze. So how's your new job?*

SUSAN: *Oh, it's great. I really like my boss and I've gotten a new assignment that fits right in with my major. Plus my boss has been flexible in assigning my hours. I just wish that it wasn't so far away.*

SARAH: *I thought it was downtown.*

SUSAN: *It is, but it takes me over an hour because I have to change buses three times.*

SARAH: *Wow—are you at least able to study while you ride?*

SUSAN: *Not really. I get carsick.*

SARAH: *Oh I forgot. Bummer.*

SUSAN: *Yeah, but I'll survive. Listen, I hate to leave, but I've got a class in ten minutes and if we're late the professor glares when we walk in. I don't need that.*

SARAH: *What a jerk.*

SUSAN: *Yeah, well I've got to run.*

SARAH: *Same time tomorrow?*

SUSAN: *Sure.*

ANALYSIS

Sarah agrees, but then explains her perception of the value of being free to date a variety of people.

Here Sarah confirms that it was her decision to partner with a man of her religion. But she also confirms that the decision was difficult.

Susan pursues the topic by asking questions to probe the consequences of Sarah's decision.

These questions lead Sarah to disclose the difficulties she's experienced as a result of her decision.

Here Sarah opens the door for Susan's support.

Susan picks up on Sarah's need by stating that she stands by her and is even willing to help.

Sarah's thanks serve as a close to the topic. She then asks a question suggesting a change of topic.

Although Susan could probe further, she accepts the change of topic by giving information to support her generalization of "It's great."

Here Sarah could comment on the free information Susan provided. Instead she focuses on location.

Sarah continues the side issue by asking another question.

Susan shows why she can't study.

Sarah tries to save face.

Susan sees no value in continuing this discussion so she cites a reason for ending the conversation.

The girls agree to meet again the next day. As we can see, discussion of this second issue is far less productive than discussion of the first issue.

Chapter Resources

Communication Improvement Plan: Conversation

How would you like to improve your use of language as discussed in this chapter?

    Crediting

    Turn-taking

    Politeness

Pick one of the above topics and write a communication improvement plan.

Skill: _____

Problem: _____

_____

_____

_____

Goal: _____

_____

_____

_____

Procedure:

1. _____

2. _____

3. _____

Test of Achieving Goal: _____

_____

Key Words

Conversations, *p. 150*

Casual social conversations, *p. 152*

Pragmatic problem-consideration conversations, *p. 152*

Rules, *p. 155*

The cooperative principle, *p. 158*

Maxims, *p. 158*

Quality maxim, *p. 158*

Quantity maxim, *p. 158*

Relevancy maxim, *p. 158*

Manner maxim, *p. 158*

Morality maxim, *p. 160*

Politeness maxim, *p. 161*

Free information, *p. 163*

Crediting the source, *p. 163*

Conversational coherence, *p. 166*

Conversational plan, *p. 166*

Politeness, *p. 167*

Positive face needs, *p. 167*

Negative face needs, *p. 167*

Face-threatening acts (FTAs), *p. 168*

Authenticity, *p. 170*

Empathy, *p. 170*

Confirmation, *p. 170*

Presentness, *p. 170*

Equality, *p. 170*

Supportiveness climates, *p. 178*

Inter-Act with Media

CINEMA

Barry Levinson (Director). (1982). *Diner.* Steve Guttenberg, Daniel Stern, Mickey Rourke, Kevin Bacon, Timothy Daly, Ellen Barkin, Paul Reiser.

Brief Summary: A terrific case study for the study of conversation, this film follows a group of friends who meet regularly in a Baltimore diner to discuss their lives, the problems of growing up, and the fun they have had. Students will find this to be a good vehicle for studying techniques of conversation.

IPC Concepts: Conversation—control, turn-taking, conflict, disclosure, relationship development.

Louis Malle (Director). (1981). *My Dinner with Andre.* Andre Gregory, Wallace Shawn.

Brief Summary: Shawn and Gregory discuss their life experiences, especially Gregory's particularly colorful and sometimes strange experiences. The result is a fascinating opportunity to look at the conversation of others. The film portrays characteristics of conversation, rules, cooperation, the need for balance, politeness, and credibility. This may not be the most exciting film ever made, but for the student of conversation, it is not to be missed.

IPC Concepts: Conversation structure, topics, balancing speaking and listening, rules.

THEATER

Noel Coward. (1925). *Easy Virtue.*

Brief Summary: Noel Coward's critique of the hypocrisy of the English upper class is made through a series of conversations between the major characters of this play as they interact with the new wife of the son of a wealthy family. The play is a superb example of ethical concerns in conversation, masks that people wear to hide their true feelings, and games that are played in conversational interactions.

IPC Concepts: Conversational types, purposes, rules, real and false politeness, quality of information, ethical issues.

George Bernard Shaw. (1939). *In Good King Charles' Golden Days.*

Brief Summary: This is the story of Charles II of England and his conversations with an array of fascinating contemporaries, such as Isaac Newton, George Fox, Nell Gwynn, Duchess of Cleveland, James Duke of York, Godfrey Kneller, and Queen Catherine of Braganza.

IPC Concepts: Conversational types, purposes, turn-taking, quality of information.

LITERATURE

Albom, M. (1997). *Tuesdays with Morrie: An Old Man, a Young Man, and Life's Greatest Lesson.* New York: Doubleday.

Brief Summary: This book is the powerful account of the relationship between columnist Mitch Albom and his old college mentor and professor, Morrie Schwartz. Albom recounts the structure and content of many conversations as he re-establishes his relationship with Morrie after many years. Morrie is dying, and Albom takes us through the topics and pathos of each conversation, showing us that there is a lot to learn about conversation and life.

IPC Concepts: Conversation and disclosure, humor, quality information, speaking, and listening.

ACADEMIC WORK

Garner, A. (1980). *Conversationally Speaking: Tested New Ways to Increase Your Personal and Social Effectiveness.* New York: McGraw-Hill.

Brief Summary: This book examines how to listen so others will respond, handle criticism and anxiety in social interactions, and suggests ways of gaining free information and giving compliments.

IPC Concepts: Conversational types, purposes, rules, speaking and listening, quality of information.

Tannen, D. (1990). *You Just Don't Understand: Women and Men in conversation.* New York: William Morrow and Company.

Brief Summary: Tannen discusses patterns of interaction and conversation between men and women, and between women and women. She describes the manner in which each gender structures topics, organizes information, approaches problems, and the purposes for engaging in conversation.

IPC Concepts: Conversational topics and gender-based behavior, quality of information.

Graham, E. E., Papa, M. J. & Brooks, G. P. (1992). *Functions of humor in conversation: Conceptualization and measurement. Western Journal of Communication, 56*(2), 161–183.

Brief Summary: This is an interesting article on conversation and using humor to achieve a variety of communicative functions. The article documents a variety of approaches to the study of humor and uses humor measures to validate the functions that had been identified. The functional approach is helpful when learning how to use humor in interpersonal encounters.

IPC Concepts: Conversation—rules, techniques.

WHAT'S ON THE WEB

VanDruff, D., & VanDruff, M. (1995). *Conversational Terrorism: How Not to Talk.* The Web page is based on this article. The site is currently entitled Conversational Cheap Shots.
http://www.vandruff.com/artu.converse.html

Brief Summary: This Web site describes negative, nonassertive behaviors that can be experienced in conversation. It presents and discusses several categories of behavior that are defensive, aggressive, and monological in nature. The categories are Ad Hominem, Sleight of Mind Fallacies, Delay Tactics, Question as Opportunity ploys, and General Cheap-Shot Tactics and Irritants.

IPC Concepts: Conversation rules, balancing, speaking, and listening.

Love Test
http://www.lovetest.com/

Brief Summary: A fun and somewhat silly exercise that can put students in the mood or mindset to discuss various attraction variables in relationships.

IPC Concepts: Sources of conversation topics based on attraction variables.

The Marriage Toolbox, Paul Michael, Publisher.
http://www.marriagetools.com/betweenus/index.htm

Brief Summary: This site provides an excellent group of topics and questions to initiate conversations regarding intimate relationships.

IPC Concepts: Conversation about relationships.

CHAPTER 7

Listening

Effectively

After you have read this chapter, you should be able to answer these questions:

- What is listening?
- How can you focus your attention?
- What can you do to listen actively?
- What is paraphrasing?
- What are three devices for remembering information?
- How can you evaluate inferences?

"Garret, do you have an extra key to the document cabinet? I misplaced mine, and I have to get into it right away."

"No, I don't have a key, but it doesn't matter because. . ."

"I can't believe it. I was sure that when I left home this morning I had it."

"Bart, it's OK. . ."

"I pulled out my keys—but of course I just had my car key and main door key. I always carry two sets of keys."

"Bart, I've been trying to tell you, just try the . . ."

"It's just like me. I think I've got everything, but just before I check the last time Salina will say something to me and I get sidetracked. Then I just take off . . ."

"Bart, calm down. The door's . . ."

"Calm down?! If I can't get those documents to the meeting, there's going to be hell to pay. We've got six people coming from all over the city just to look at the documents. What am I supposed to say to them?"

"Bart, you don't have to say anything. I've been trying to . . ."

"Oh, sure—I just go in there and say, 'By the way, the documents are locked up in the cabinet and I left my key at home.' Come on, Garret—who's got the other key?"

"Bart, listen!!! I've been trying to tell you—Miller was in the cabinet and, knowing you'd be along in a minute, he left the door open."

"Well, why didn't you tell me?"

Are you a good listener—even when you're under pressure like Bart? Or do you sometimes find that your mind wanders when others are talking to you? How often do you forget something that someone says to you? Do you sometimes feel that other things get in the way of your listening effectiveness? Have any of your close friends or intimates ever complained that you just don't seem to listen to them?

Use the Test Yourself questionnaire below to help assess your basic listening behaviors.

Listening is a fundamental communication skill that affects the quality of our conversations and shapes the course of our relationships. First, listening creates reality. "We listen and create reality based on what we hear in each moment" (Ellinor & Gerard, 1998, p. 99). Second, of the basic communication skills (reading, writing, speaking, and listening) we use listening the most. "From 42 to 60 percent (or more) of our communication time is spent listening, depending on whether we are students, managerial trainees, doctors, counselors, lawyers, or nurses" (Purdy, 1996, p. 4). Unfortunately, after forty-eight hours many listeners can remember only about 25 percent of what they heard (Steil, Barker, & Watson, 1983).

TEST YOURSELF

Listening Behaviors

How frequently do you find yourself engaging in each of the following listening behaviors? On the line, indicate 5 for frequently; 4 for often; 3 for sometimes; 2 for rarely; and 1 for never.

___ 1. I listen differently depending on whether I am listening for enjoyment, understanding, or evaluation.

___ 2. I stop listening when what the person is saying to me isn't interesting to me.

___ 3. I consciously try to recognize the speaker's purpose.

___ 4. I pretend to listen to people when I am really thinking about other things.

___ 5. When people talk, I differentiate between their main points and supporting details.

___ 6. When the person's manner of speaking annoys me (such as muttering, stammering, or talking in a monotone), I stop listening carefully.

___ 7. At various places in a conversation, I paraphrase what the speaker said in order to check my understanding.

___ 8. When I perceive the subject matter as very difficult, I stop listening carefully.

___ 9. When the person is presenting detailed information, I take good notes of major points and supporting details.

___ 10. When people use words that I find offensive, I stop listening and start preparing responses.

In this list, the even-numbered items indicate negative listening behaviors, so you need to reverse the scoring of these items. If you gave yourself 5 count it as 1, 4 count it as 2, 3 count it as 3, 2 count it as 4, 1 count it as 5. The odd-numbered items indicate positive listening behaviors. Count each as given. Sum all your scores. There are 50 points possible. If you score over 40, you are effective in your listening. If you score below 40, identify which questions seemed to cause your lowest scores. You will want to give particular attention to the sections of this chapter that relate to these areas.

Considering its importance and how little attention most of us pay to it, listening may be the most underrated of all communication skills.

What is listening? In her recent book, Judi Brownell pointed out that about ten years ago, members of the International Listening Association sought consensus on a single definition. They produced the following: "**Listening** is the process of receiving, constructing meaning from, and responding to spoken and/or nonverbal messages" (Brownell, 2002, p. 48). Incorporated within this definition are processes of attending, understanding, remembering, evaluating, and responding.

Because each of these listening processes requires distinct, specific skills, we discuss each separately—the first four in this chapter and the fifth, responding, in the next chapter.

Listening–the process of receiving, constructing meaning from, and responding to spoken and/or nonverbal messages.

Attending: Focusing Attention

Listening Problem: Poor listeners may not hear what people say.
Goal: To pay attention.

The first listening process is **attending**–the perceptual process of selecting to concentrate on specific stimuli from the countless stimuli reaching the senses. When attending, we focus our attention in such a way that we are aware of what people are saying and disregard extraneous sounds.

Stop reading for a minute, and try to become conscious of all the sounds around you. Perhaps you notice the humming of an electrical appliance, the rhythm of street traffic, the singing of birds, footsteps in the hall, a cough from an

Attending–the perceptual process of selecting to concentrate on specific stimuli from the countless stimuli reaching the senses.

Which of these people are listening—which are not? How can you tell?

adjoining room. Yet while you were reading, you may have been unaware of these sounds. In fact, our environment is seldom silent. But whereas some sounds intrude on our consciousness, others go unnoticed. Why is it that we "hear" or attend to some sounds and not to others?

Although we physically register any sounds emitted within our hearing range, we exercise psychological control over the sounds we attend to. For instance, as you and a friend are chatting while you walk to class, you both receive and attend to each other's words. At the same time, you may physically "hear" footsteps behind you, the chiming of school bells, and birds singing, but you are able to place them in the background. In fact, you may be so unconscious of background noise that you would deny that certain sounds occurred.

Ineffective listeners exercise insufficient control over which sounds they attend to. Improving your listening skills begins with learning to "pay attention" by bringing some sounds to the foreground while keeping others in the background. People who have developed this skill are able to focus their attention so well that only such really intrusive sounds as a fire alarm, a car crashing into a post, or the cry of their child can intrude on their attention.

Let's consider four techniques for consciously focusing attention.

1. Get physically and mentally ready to listen. Physically, good listeners create an environment conducive to listening and adopt a listening posture. Creating a physical environment conducive to listening means eliminating distractions. For instance, if the radio is playing so loudly that it competes with your roommate who is trying to talk with you, you will turn it down. The physical posture that is most helpful when listening is one that moves the listener toward the speaker, allows direct eye contact, and stimulates the senses. For instance, when the professor tells the class that the next bit of information will be on the test, effective listeners are likely to sit upright in their chairs, lean slightly forward, cease any extraneous physical movement, and look directly at the professor. They are ready to listen.

Likewise, effective listening requires mental preparation. Effective listeners focus their attention by blocking out miscellaneous thoughts that pass through their minds. Recall that when people are talking with you, their ideas and feelings compete with the internal noise created by whatever's on your mind at the moment—a basketball game, a calculus test, a date you're excited about, a movie you've just seen. And what you're thinking about may be more pleasant to attend to than what someone is saying to you. Attending to these competing thoughts and feelings rather than the message is one of the leading causes of poor listening.

2. Make the shift from speaker to listener a complete one. Unlike the classroom, where you are supposed to listen continuously for long stretches, in conversation, you are called on to switch back and forth from speaker to listener so frequently that you may find it difficult at times to make these shifts completely. If, instead of listening, you spend your time rehearsing what you're going to say as soon as you have a chance, your listening effectiveness will take a nosedive. Especially when you are in a heated conversation, take a second to check yourself: Are you preparing speeches instead of listening? Shifting from the role of speaker to that of listener requires constant and continuous effort.

3. Hear a person out before you react. Far too often, we stop listening before the person has finished speaking because we "know what a person is going to say." Yet until the person has finished, we don't have all the data necessary to form an appropriate response—our "knowing" what a person is going to say is really only a guess. Even if we guess right, the person may still feel that we weren't really listening, and the communication will suffer as a result. Accordingly, cultivate the habit of always letting a person complete his or her thought before you stop listening or try to respond. At times your attentive listening may be the best response you can make. Most of us need to learn the value of silence in freeing others to think, feel, and express themselves. As the old Hebrew adage goes, "The beginning of wisdom is silence."

In addition to prematurely ceasing to listen, we often let certain mannerisms and words interfere with hearing a person out, perhaps to the extent of "tuning out." In the Diverse Voices selection on pages 185–186, Dawn and Charles Braithwaite discuss how people often mistreat people who have disabilities. When interacting with people with disabilities the first step is to listen.

Are there any words or ideas that create bursts of semantic noise for you, causing you to stop listening attentively? What is your reaction when people speak of *gay rights, skinheads, conservative Christians, political correctness,* or *rednecks?* Do you tune them in or out? When semantic noise threatens to interfere, counteract this effect and try to let a warning light go on when a speaker trips the switch to your emotional reaction. Instead of tuning out or getting ready to disagree, be aware of this "noise" and work that much harder to listen objectively. If you can do it, you will be more likely to receive the whole message accurately and be able to respond thoughtfully.

4. Adjust the listening behavior to the situation. Listening is similar to reading in that you need to adjust how you listen to the particular goal you wish to achieve and to the degree of difficulty of the material you will be receiving. The intensity with which you attend to a message should depend on whether your purpose or goal consists primarily of enjoyment, learning or understanding, evaluating or critiquing, or responding helpfully to the needs of another.

When your goal is primarily pleasure listening, you can afford to listen without much intensity. People often

---

OBSERVE & ANALYZE

Journal Activity

Adjusting to Listening Goals

Select an information-oriented program on your public television station (such as "NOVA," "News Hour with Jim Lehrer," or "Wall Street Week"). If possible, videotape it before you watch it. Watch at least fifteen minutes of the show while lounging in a comfortable chair or while stretched out on the floor with music playing on a radio in the background. After about fifteen minutes, stop the tape and quickly outline what you have learned. Now, make a conscious decision to use the guidelines for increasing attentiveness during the next fifteen minutes of the show. Turn off the music and sit in a straight-back chair as you watch the program. Your goal is to increase your listening intensity in order to learn, so you need to block out other distractions. After this fifteen-minute segment, you should again outline what you remember. Watch the program a second time and make note of how your attentiveness affected your memory.

Compare your notes. Is there any difference between the amount or quality of the information you retained? Be prepared to discuss your results with your classmates. Are their results similar or different? Why? ■

Communication Between Able-Bodied Persons and Persons with Disabilities

By Dawn O. Braithwaite and Charles A. Braithwaite

Striking up conversations may be most difficult when we encounter people from other cultures, other religions, or different socioeconomic levels, and perhaps especially when we encounter people with disabilities. This excerpt is designed not only to increase our sensitivity, but also to provide some specific guidelines for communication.

Jonathan is an articulate, intelligent, thirty-five-year-old professional man who has used a wheelchair since he became a paraplegic at age twenty. He recalls taking an able-bodied woman out to dinner at a nice restaurant. When the waitress came to take their order, she looked only at his date and asked, in a condescending tone, "And what would *he* like to eat for dinner?" At the end of the meal the waitress presented Jonathan's date with the check and thanked her for her patronage.

[Scenarios like this] represent common experiences for people with physical disabilities and are indicative of what often happens when disabled and able-bodied people communicate.

The passage of the Americans with Disabilities Act (ADA), a "bill of rights" for persons with disabilities, highlighted the fact that they are now a large, vocal, and dynamic group within the United States. Disabled people represent one group within American culture that is growing in numbers. Persons with disabilities

constitute as much as 7 percent of the population.

In the past, most people with disabilities were sheltered, and many were institutionalized; but today they are very much a part of the American mainstream. Each of us will have contact with people who have disabilities within our families, among our friends, or within the workplace.

Persons with disabilities recognize that able-bodied persons often see them as disabled first and as a person second (if at all). The most common theme expressed by people with disabilities in all of the interviews is that they want to be *treated like a person first.*

As for able-bodied persons who communicate with disabled persons, this intercultural perspective leads to the following proscriptions and prescriptions:

Don't:

assume persons with disabilities cannot speak for themselves or do things for themselves

force your help on persons with disabilities

avoid communication with persons who have disabili-

ties simply because you are uncomfortable or unsure

use terms like "handicapped," "physically challenged," "crippled," "victim," and so on, unless requested to do so by persons with disabilities

assume that a disability defines a person

Do:

assume persons with disabilities can do something unless they communicate otherwise

let persons with disabilities tell you if they want something, what they want, and when they want it. If a person with a disability refuses your help, don't go ahead and help anyway. The goal is to give the person with the disability control in the situation

remember that persons with disabilities have experienced others' discomfort before and understand how you might be feeling

use terms like "*people* with disabilities" rather than "*disabled* people." The goal is to stress the person first, before introducing their disability

treat persons with disabilities as *persons first,* recognizing that you are not dealing with a disabled person but with *a person* who *has* a disability. This means actively seeking the humanity of the person you are speaking with, and focusing on the person's characteristics instead of the superficial physical appearance. Without diminishing significance of a physical disability, you can selectively attend to many other aspects of a person during communication. ■

Excerpted from Braithwaite, D. O., & Braithwaite, C. A. (2000). Understanding communication of persons with disabilities as cultural communication. In L. A. Samovar & R. E. Porter (Eds.), *Intercultural Communication: A Reader* (9th ed., pp. 136–145). Belmont, Calif.: Wadsworth.

speak of "vegging out in front of the tube." In most cases, they mean "listening" to comedy or light drama as a means of passing time pleasurably. Unfortunately, many people approach all situations as if they were listening to pass time. Yet how we listen should change qualitatively with the level of difficulty of the information.

In listening situations like attending to directions (how to get to a restaurant), instructions (how to shift into reverse in a foreign car), or explanations (a recounting of the new office procedures), the intensity of your listening is likely to increase, for the goal of understanding requires more careful attending. Moreover, you are likely to engage in a more active listening mode. In the next two sections of this chapter, we consider several skills for adjusting our listening when the goal is understanding and remembering.

At other times you may determine that your goal is to listen critically. Every day we are flooded with countless messages—from friends, family members, co-workers, advertisers, political candidates—designed to influence our behavior. To choose wisely in these situations, we must not only listen more actively, but must also be able to recognize the facts, weigh them, separate emotional appeals, and determine the soundness of the conclusions presented. In the final section of this chapter, we consider several skills for adjusting to critical listening.

In summary, the attending process involves getting ready to listen, making the shift from speaker to listener a complete one, hearing a person out before reacting, and adjusting your attention to the listening goals of the situation.

A special challenge is listening to enable us to give helpful responses. Almost every day people come to us to share their problems and concerns. Sometimes they simply want someone to talk with; other times they come to us for help. Many of the skills we cover in the next chapter are response skills that will work for you in helping situations.

Understanding: Listening Actively

Listening Problem: Poor listeners may hear what is said, but not understand.
Goal: To listen actively.

The second listening process is to use skills to increase understanding. **Understanding** is decoding a message accurately by correctly assigning appropriate meaning to it. Sometimes we do not understand because people use words that are outside our vocabulary. Suppose someone asks "Quelle heure est-il?" and you do not know French. You hear the sounds, but you are unable to understand that the person is asking "What time is it?" A person does not have to be speaking a foreign language, however, for you to have difficulty understanding. In addition to using words that are outside your vocabulary, speakers in any language sometimes talk quickly, shortcut sounds, and mispronounce words so that you may have trouble decoding the message.

Understanding–decoding a message accurately by correctly assigning appropriate meaning to it.

Comprehending what a person means requires **active listening,** a specific technique for improving understanding. Since we can think faster than a speaker can talk, we can learn to process information while it is being given. Active listening involves identifying the organization of the message, paying attention to nonverbal cues, asking questions to get additional information, and paraphrasing the meanings we have understood. Let's consider each of these.

Active listening–a specific technique for improving understanding.

Identifying the Organization

Effective speakers are likely to have an overall organization for the information embedded in the message they present. This organization reflects the purpose or goal, key ideas (or main points), and details of the message to explain or support the main points. Active listeners look for these organizational patterns. Suppose that during an informal parents' discussion group at school Gloria brings up the subject of teenage crime. As Gloria talks, she may focus on the effects of poverty and single-parent homes. She may provide information she has read or heard. When Gloria finishes speaking, the group members will have understood her message if they can identify the causes of teenage crime she presented (her purpose), the two specific factors she cited as causes (her key points), and the evidence she has provided to support each factor (details).

Sometimes people organize their messages in such a way that it is relatively easy to understand the purpose, key points, and details. At other times, however, we must supply the structure for ourselves. You can sort out the purpose, key points, and details of a complex message, and thus increase your understanding of the message, by mentally outlining the message. Asking "What am I supposed to know/do because I listened to this?" will allow you to determine purpose. Asking "What are the categories of information?" and "Why should I do/think this?" will enable you to identify key points. Asking "What's the support?" will enable you to identify the details.

Attend to Nonverbal Cues

Listeners interpret messages more accurately when they observe the nonverbal behaviors accompanying the words, because meaning may be shown as much by the nonverbals as by the spoken words. In Chapter 5 we noted that up to 65 percent of the meaning of a social message may be carried nonverbally. Thus, when Franco says "You really got through to Professor Grant on that one," whether you take his statement as a compliment or a jibe will depend on your perception of the sound of Franco's voice. Likewise, when Deborah says "Go on, I can walk home from here," we have to interpret cues such as tone of voice, body actions, and facial expression to tell whether she is sincerely interested in walking or whether she'd really like a ride.

So, whether you are listening to a co-worker explaining her stance on an issue, a friend explaining the process for hanging wallpaper, or a loved one explaining why he or she is upset with you, you must listen to how something is said as well as to what is said.

Ask Questions

Question–a response designed to get further information, to clarify information already received, or to encourage another to continue speaking.

When we don't have enough information to fully understand a person's message, one effective way to obtain the information is to ask questions. A **question** is, of course, a response designed to get further information, to clarify information already received, or to encourage another to continue speaking. In addition, good questions may also help speakers sharpen their thinking about the points they've

Listening means paying attention to nonverbal as well as verbal cues. What messages are being conveyed by each person's facial expression and gestures?

made. Although you may have asked questions for as long as you can remember, you may notice that at times your questions either don't get the information you want, or they irritate or fluster, or cause defensiveness in the other person. You can increase the chances that your questions will get you the information you want and reduce the likely defensiveness that others might feel if you observe the following guidelines.

1. Note the kind of information you need to increase your understanding. Suppose Maria says to you, "I am totally frustrated. Would you stop at the store on the way home and buy me some more paper?" At this point, you may be a bit confused and need more information to understand what Maria is telling you. Yet if you respond "What do you mean?" you are likely to add to the confusion, because Maria, who is already uptight, won't know precisely what it is you don't understand. To increase your understanding, you might ask Maria one of these three types of questions:

Questions to get more information on important details. "What kind of paper would you like me to get, and how much will you need?"

Questions to clarify the use of a term. "Could you tell me what you mean by 'frustrated'?"

Questions to clarify the cause of the feelings the person is expressing. "What is it that's frustrating you?"

Determine whether the information you need is more detail, clarification of a word or idea, or information on the cause of feelings or events, then phrase your question accordingly.

2. Phrase questions as complete sentences. Under pressure, our tendency is to use one- or two-word questions that may be perceived as curt or abrupt. For instance, suppose Miles says "Molly just told me that I always behave in ways that are totally insensitive to her needs." Instead of asking "How?" you might ask "Did she give you specific behaviors or describe specific incidents when this happened?" Curt, abrupt questions can make speakers defensive instead of helping them focus on the additional information the respondents need.

3. Deliver questions in a sincere tone of voice. Ask questions with a tone of voice that is sincere—not a tone that could be interpreted as bored, sarcastic, cutting, superior, dogmatic, or evaluative. We need to constantly remind ourselves that the way we speak can be even more important than the words we use.

4. Put the "burden of ignorance" on your own shoulders. In order to minimize defensive reactions, especially when people are under stress, phrase your question so as to put the burden of ignorance on your own shoulders. Preface your questions with a short statement that suggests that any problem of misunderstanding may be the result of

INTER-ACT WITH

Technology

Speakerphones, wireless phones, and cellular phones have brought a new level of convenience to communication. These days you can work on your computer, drive, or even cook dinner while you are on the phone. But have these devices affected listening effectiveness? The next time you are using one of these devices, be conscious of how well you are listening. Which of the listening guidelines provided in this chapter should you apply to improve your listening under these conditions? ■

<u>your</u> listening skills. For instance, when Drew says "I've really had it with Malone screwing up all the time," you might say, "Drew, I'm sorry, I'm missing some details that would help me understand your feelings better. What kinds of things has Malone been doing?"

Here are two more examples that contrast inappropriate with more appropriate questioning responses.

> **Tamara:** They turned down my proposal again!
> **Art:** *(inappropriate):* Well, did you explain it the way you should have? (This question is a veiled attack on Tamara in question form.) *(appropriate):* Did they tell you why? (This question is a sincere request for additional information.)
> **Renee:** With all those executives at the party last night, I really felt strange.
> **Javier:** *(inappropriate):* Why? (With this abrupt question, Javier is making no effort to be sensitive to her feelings or to understand them.) *(appropriate):* Gee, what is it about your bosses' presence that makes you feel strange? (Here the question is phrased to elicit information that will help Javier understand, and may help Renee understand as well.)

Note how the appropriate, empathic questions are likely to get the necessary information while minimizing the probability of a defensive reply. The inappropriate questions, on the other hand, may be perceived as an attack by the person being questioned.

In summary, to increase your effectiveness at asking questions: (1) Note the kind of information you need to increase your understanding of the message. (2) Phrase questions as complete sentences. (3) Deliver questions in a sincere tone of voice. (4) Put the burden of ignorance on your own shoulders.

SKILL BUILDERS   **QUESTIONING**

SKILL	**USE**	**PROCEDURE**	**EXAMPLE**
Phrasing a response designed to get further information, to clarify information already received, or to encourage another to continue speaking.	To help get a more complete picture before making other comments; to help a shy person open up; to clarify meaning.	1. Note the kind of information you need to increase your understanding of the message. 2. Phrase questions as specific, complete sentences. 3. Deliver questions in a sincere tone of voice. 4. Put the burden of ignorance on your own shoulders.	When Connie says, "Well, it would be better if she weren't so sedentary," Jeff replies, "I'm not sure I understand what you mean by 'sedentary'—would you explain?"

Paraphrasing

In addition to being skilled questioners, active listeners are also adept at **paraphrasing,** putting their understanding of the message into words. Paraphrasing is not mere repetition of what the speaker has said; rather, it is a message that conveys the images and emotions you have perceived from this message. It states the idea or image that has been sparked in your own mind in your own words. For example, during a meeting with his professor to discuss his performance on the first exam, Charley says, "Well, it looks like I really blew this first test—I had a lot of things on my mind, but I'm really going to study hard next time." If Professor Jensen responds by saying, "If I understand you correctly, there were things happening to you that prevented you from studying, but for the next exam you're going to prepare chapter outlines of the readings and review our class notes each week."

Paraphrasing–putting your understanding of the message into words.

By paraphrasing, you give the speaker a chance to verify your understanding. If Professor Jensen's paraphrase coincides with what Charley meant, Charley might say "Right!" But if her image differs from what Charley intended, Charley has an opportunity to clarify what he meant. For example, he might reply, "Well, I'm going to read and highlight chapters carefully, but I wasn't planning on outlining them." At this point, having clarified the meaning between them, the professor better understands what Charley plans to do.

Types of Paraphrases Paraphrases may focus on content, on feelings underlying the content, or both. In the previous example, the professor's paraphrase, "If I understand you correctly, you're saying that you've learned from your mistakes and you're going outline and review the material periodically," would be a **content paraphrase.** It focuses on the denotative meaning of the message, in this case, what Charley means by "really study."

Content paraphrase–A response that conveys your understanding of the denotative meaning of the verbal message.

As Charley began to speak, if Professor Jensen noticed that he dropped his eyes, sighed, and slowly shook his head, and she said, "So you were really upset with your grade on the last test," her response would be a **feelings paraphrase**—that is, a response that captures the emotions attached to the content of the message.

Feelings paraphrase–A response that conveys your understanding of a speaker's state of mind–the emotions behind the words.

Whether a content or feelings paraphrase is most useful for a particular situation depends on whether you perceive the speaker's emphasis to be on the content of the statement or on his or her feelings about what was said. In real-life settings we often don't distinguish clearly between content and intent paraphrases; and our responses might well be a combination of both. All three types of paraphrases for the same statement are shown in this example.

Statement: "Five weeks ago, I gave the revised manuscript of my independent study to my project advisor. I felt really good about it because I thought the changes I had made really improved my explanations. Well, yesterday I stopped by and got the manuscript back, and my advisor said he couldn't really see that this draft was much different from the first."

Content paraphrase: "Let me see if I'm understanding this right. Your advisor thought that you hadn't really done much to rework your paper, but you put a lot of effort into it and think this draft was a lot different and much improved."

TEST YOURSELF

Writing Questions and Paraphrases

Provide an appropriate question and paraphrase for each of the following statements. To get you started, the first conversation has been completed for you.

1. **Luis:** "It's Dionne's birthday, and I've planned a *big* evening. Sometimes, I think Dionne believes I take her for granted—well, I think after tonight she'll know I think she's something special!"

Question: "What specific things do you have planned?"

Content paraphrase: "If I'm understanding you, you're planning a night that's going to cost a lot more than what Dionne expects on her birthday."

Feelings paraphrase: "From the way you're talking, I get the feeling you're really proud of yourself for making plans like these."

2. **Angie:** "Brother! Another nothing class. I keep thinking one of these days he'll get excited about something. Professor Romero is a real bore!"

Question:

Content paraphrase:

Feelings paraphrase:

3. **Jerry:** "Everyone seems to be talking about that movie on Channel 5 last night, but I didn't see it. You know, I don't watch much that's on the 'idiot box.'"

Question:

Content paraphrase:

Feelings paraphrase:

4. **Kaelin:** "I don't know if it's something to do with me or with Mom, but lately she and I just aren't getting along."

Question:

Content paraphrase:

Feelings paraphrase:

5. **Aileen:** "I've got a report due at work and a paper due in management class. On top of that, it's my sister's birthday, and so far I haven't even had time to get her anything. Tomorrow's going to be a disaster."

Question:

Content paraphrase:

Feelings paraphrase:

Feelings paraphrase: "I sense that you're really frustrated that your advisor didn't recognize the changes you had made."

Combination: "If I have this right, you're saying that your advisor could see no real differences, yet you think your draft was not only different but much improved. I also get the feeling that your advisor's comments really irk you."

In summary, the point of a paraphrase is to make sure that you really understand what the speaker means by what he or she said. If for some reason you misinterpreted the speaker's ideas or feelings, the speaker has the chance to correct your interpretation before the conversation continues. Now the question becomes, when are paraphrases appropriate?

When to Paraphrase Common sense suggests that we need not paraphrase every message we receive; nor would we paraphrase after every few sentences. You will want to paraphrase the ideas and feelings of the other person when

- You need a better understanding of a message—in terms of content, feelings, or both—before you can respond appropriately.
- Misunderstanding the message will have serious consequences.
- The message is long and contains several complex ideas.
- The message seems to have been a reflection of emotional strain.
- You are talking with people for whom English is not their native language.

In summary, to paraphrase effectively, (1) listen carefully to the message, (2) notice what images and feelings you have experienced from the message, (3) determine what the message means to you, and (4) create a message that conveys these images and/or feelings.

SKILL BUILDERS **PARAPHRASING**

SKILL	USE	PROCEDURE	EXAMPLE
A response that conveys your understanding of another person's message.	To increase listening efficiency; to avoid message confusion; to discover the speaker's motivation.	1. Listen carefully to the message. 2. Notice what images and feelings you have experienced from the message. 3. Determine what the message means to you. 4. Create a message that conveys these images and/or feelings.	Grace says, "At two minutes to five, the boss gave me three letters that had to be in the mail that evening!" Bonita replies, "If I understand, you were really resentful that your boss dumped important work on you right before quitting time, when she knows that you have to pick up the baby at daycare."

Remembering: Retaining Information

Listening Problem: Poor listeners may interpret information accurately, but forget it.

Goal: To use memory techniques.

Remembering–using skills to help increase retention of information for recall when it is needed.

The third listening process, **remembering,** involves using skills to help increase retention of information for recall when it is needed. Too often people forget almost immediately what they have heard. For example, you can probably think of many times when you were unable to recall the name of a person to whom you were introduced just moments earlier. How well we remember can be measured by carefully prepared standardized tests. Robert Bostrom is a leader in the field of listening tests. The accompanying Spotlight on Scholars features his work, showing how he became interested in listening and how his effectiveness in testing evolved.

Improving remembering requires conscious application of techniques that imprint ideas on your memory. Here are three techniques that help people remember.

Repeat Information

Repetition–saying something two, three, or even four times.

Repetition—saying something two, three, or even four times—helps listeners store information in long-term memory (Estes, 1989, p. 7). If information is not reinforced, it will be held in short-term memory for as little as twenty seconds and then forgotten. So, when you are introduced to a stranger named Jack McNeil, if you mentally say "Jack McNeil, Jack McNeil, Jack McNeil, Jack McNeil," you increase the chances that you will remember his name. Likewise, when a person gives you the directions "Go two blocks east, turn left, turn right at the next light, and it's in the next block," you should immediately repeat to yourself "two blocks east, turn left, turn right at light, next block—that's two blocks east, turn left, turn right at light, next block."

Construct Mnemonics

Mnemonic device–any artificial technique used as a memory aid.

Constructing mnemonics helps listeners put information in forms that are more easily recalled. A **mnemonic device** is any artificial technique used as a memory aid. One of the most common ways of forming a mnemonic is to take the first letters of a list of items you are trying to remember and forming a word. For example, an easy mnemonic for remembering the five Great Lakes is HOMES (Huron, Ontario, Michigan, Erie, Superior).

When you want to remember items in a sequence, try to form a sentence with the words themselves or assign words using the first letters of the words in sequence and form an easy-to-remember statement. For example, when you studied music the first time, you may have learned the notes on the lines of the treble clef (EGBDF) with the saying "Every good boy does fine." (And for the notes on the treble clef spaces, FACE, you may have remembered the word face.)

Robert Bostrom, Professor of Communication, University of Kentucky, on
Listening

Robert Bostrom's interest in listening began when he was a child, but his career took many turns before he was able to focus his research on listening. As a young man, Bostrom taught high school and coached debate. He returned to do advanced study at the University of Iowa, in part to study with his hero, the foremost authority on listening at the time, Ralph Nichols. Because Bostrom was not assigned to work with Nichols, his early scholarship was focused in a different direction. Still, he continued to read the scholarship on listening and became convinced that the listening tests then in use were not really measuring listening; instead, they seemed to be measuring general intelligence. So Bostrom began to work on a test that would do a better job of measuring how well someone listens.

According to Bostrom, although there are a number of behaviors that might assist listening, it is primarily a mental process. When people listen well, they accurately retain or remember what has been said. So, he reasoned, understanding how memory works is important to understanding listening.

Those who have studied memory differentiate between short-term memory and long-term memory; so too, Bostrom believes, people engage in short-term listening and long-term listening. We engage in long-term listening when we are trying to absorb information that we will need to recall at a later time. This is sometimes called "lecture listening" because one of the dominant contexts for this type of listening is when one person is lecturing information to another. Bostrom believes that when we are participating in interpersonal conversations, we are likely to be engaging in short-term listening. We remember what the other person has said long enough to respond to it, but then we are likely to forget what was said. Perhaps you have experienced this. When asked to recall a recent conversation have you ever had trouble remembering what you discussed? Yet you know that during the conversation you knew what the other person was saying and you responded appropriately. Listening also requires one to interpret what has been said, so Bostrom believes that part of a valid listening test should measure how accurately a person interprets what has been said.

Bostrom's first listening test, called the Kentucky Comprehensive Listening Test (KCLT), has now been given to more than twenty thousand people. While it was originally designed to help scholars conduct research on listening, the test has been found to be a useful diagnostic tool and a motivator for those seeking to improve their listening. Some instructors use this test in classes and find that students enjoy comparing their scores to those of their classmates.

In addition to conducting basic research on listening using the KCLT, Bostrom serves as a consultant to various organizations interested in assessing how well people listen. His work with the Educational Testing Service (ETS) includes designing the listening portion of the Praxis Exam, which is the national certification examination for teachers and a portion of the subject area certification exam for college graduates in communication. He has worked with the National Defense Language Institute to figure out what influences how well people listen to a second or third language.

Bostrom believes that the next step in listening research is to assess our abilities to decode and interpret nonverbal behavior. Now that good research has enabled us to understand how the fundamentals of nonverbal signals operate, it is time to examine the interaction of these signals with memory and retention. Intriguing possibilities stem from the lateral asymmetry of hearing, since left and right sides of the brain engage themselves differently. Another promising area of investigation lies in basic psychobiological differences in persons, such as sensation seeking. Fundamental research in the communicative process is vital to understanding listening. For example, if individuals tend to talk too much, do they then not listen? Or do they listen better? For complete citations of many of Bostrom's publications, see the references for this chapter at the end of the book.

Bostrom is now retired from the University of Kentucky but continues to teach communication theory and research methods at both the graduate and undergraduate levels. He particularly enjoys his work with undergraduates, who he believes seem to get better each year. ■

Take Notes

Do you remember information better and longer if you take notes?

Although note-taking would be inappropriate in most casual interpersonal encounters, it represents a powerful tool for increasing your recall of information when you are involved in telephone conversations, briefing sessions, interviews, and business meetings. Note-taking provides a written record that you can go back to, and it also enables us to take a more active role in the listening process (Wolvin & Coakley, 1996, p. 239). In short, when you are listening to complex information, take notes.

What constitutes good notes will vary depending on the situation. Useful notes may consist of a brief list of main points or key ideas plus a few of the most significant details. Or they may be a short summary of the entire concept (a type of paraphrase) after the message is completed. For lengthy and rather detailed information, however, good notes likely will consist of a brief outline of what the speaker has said, including the overall idea, the main points of the message, and key developmental material (see Figure 7.1 on p. 198). Good notes are not necessarily very long. In fact, many classroom lectures can be reduced to a short outline of notes.

In review, the process of remembering can be facilitated by using various techniques including repeating information several times, creating mnemonics, artificial devices, and when material is complicated, taking notes.

Listening Test

Have a friend assume the role of a fellow worker on your first day in an office job and read the following information to you once, at a normal rate of speech. As the friend reads the instructions, take notes. Then give yourself the test that follows, answering true or false but without referring to your notes. Then repeat the quiz, but use your notes this time. How much does your score improve? Although the temptation is great to read this item to yourself, try not to. You will miss both the enjoyment and the value of the exercise if you do.

"Since you are new to the job, I'd like to fill you in on a few details. The boss probably told you that typing and distribution of mail were your most important duties. Well, they may be, but let me tell you, answering the phone is going to take most of your time. Now about the typing. Goodwin will give the most, but much of what he gives you may have nothing to do with the department—I'd be careful about spending all my time doing his private work. Mason doesn't give much, but you'd better get it right—she's really a stickler. I've always asked to have tests at least two days in advance. Paulson is always dropping stuff on the desk at the last minute.

"The mail situation sounds tricky, but you'll get used to it. Mail comes twice a day—at 10 A.M. and at 2 P.M. You've got to take the mail that's been left on the desk to Charles Hall for pickup. If you really have some rush stuff, take it right to the campus post office in Harper Hall. It's a little longer walk, but for really rush stuff, it's better. When you pick up at McDaniel Hall, sort it. You'll have to make sure that only mail for the people up here gets delivered here. If there is any that doesn't belong here, bundle it back up and mark it for return to the campus post office.

"Now, about your breaks. You get ten minutes in the morning, forty minutes at noon, and fifteen minutes in the afternoon. If you're smart, you'll leave before the 10:30 classes let out. That's usually a pretty crush time. Three of the teachers are supposed to have office hours then, and if they don't keep them, the students will be on your back. If you take your lunch at 11:45, you'll be back before the main crew goes.

"Oh, one more thing. You are supposed to call Jeno at 8:15 every morning to wake him. If you forget, he gets very upset. Well, good luck."

With Notes Without Notes

_____	_____	1. Where are you to take the mail that does not belong here?
_____	_____	2. How often does mail come?
_____	_____	3. When should you be back from lunch?
_____	_____	4. What is Paulson's problem with work?
_____	_____	5. Who gives the most work?
_____	_____	6. What's the problem with Goodwin's request to do work?
_____	_____	7. What are your main jobs, according to the boss?
_____	_____	8. Where are you to take outgoing mail?
_____	_____	9. Where is the post office?
_____	_____	10. How many minutes do you get for your morning break?
_____	_____	11. What is the preferred time to take your lunch?
_____	_____	12. Who are you supposed to give a wake-up call?

1. Harper Hall; 2. Twice a day; 3. 12:30; 4. Last minute; 5. Goodwin; 6. Not work related; 7. Typing/distributing mail; 8. Charles Hall; 9. Harper Hall; 10. ten; 11. 11:45; 12. Jeno.

```
        Duties
                Typing, distribution of mail important
                Answering phone takes most time
        Typing
                Goodwin gives most—question doing private work
                Mason, not much, but get it right—she's a stickler
                Ask for tests 2 days in advance (watch out for Paulson)
        Mail
                10 and 2
                Take to Charles Hall
                Rush stuff goes to campus PO in Harper
                Sort mail from McDaniel—bundle what doesn't belong and mark for
                return to campus PO
        Breaks
                10 min. morning—take before 10:30
                40 min. lunch—take at 11:45
                15 min. afternoon
        Extra
                Call Jeno 8:15
```

Figure 7.1

Sample notes for Listening Test

Evaluating: Listening Critically

Listening Problem: Poor listeners may interpret information accurately and remember it, but not evaluate its merits.

Goal: To listen critically by evaluating inferences.

The fourth listening process is critical analysis. **Critical analysis** is the process of evaluating what you have understood and interpreted in order to determine how truthful, authentic, or believable you judge the meaning to be. For instance, when a person tries to convince you to vote for a particular candidate for office or to support efforts to legalize cloning, you will want to listen critically to these messages so as to determine how much you agree with the speaker and how you wish to respond. If you fail to listen critically to the messages you receive, you risk inadvertently concurring in ideas or plans that may violate your own values, be counterproductive to achieving your goals, or be misleading to others (including the speakers) who value your judgment.

Critical listening requires that you separate facts from inferences and evaluate the quality of inferences.

Critical analysis–the process of evaluating what you have understood and interpreted in order to determine how truthful, authentic, or believable you judge the meaning to be.

Separate Factual Statements from Inferences

Factual statements are those whose accuracy can be verified or proven; **inferences** are claims or assertions based on observation or fact. Separating factual statements from inferences means being able to tell the difference between a verifiable observation and an opinion related to that observation.

Factual statements–statements whose accuracy can be verified or proven.

Inferences–claims or assertions based on observation or fact.

Let's clarify this distinction with an example. If we can document that Cesar received an A in geology, then saying that Cesar received an A in geology is a factual statement. If we go on to say that Cesar studied very hard, the statement is an inference. Cesar may have studied hard to receive his grade, but it is also possible that geology comes easily to Cesar or that Cesar had already learned much of the material in his high school physical science course. If you identify a speaker's statement as an inference, be sure to look for the data on which the inference is based.

The reason for separating factual statements from inferences is that inferences may be false, even if they are based on verifiable facts. Making sound judgments entails basing our opinions and responses to messages on facts or on inferences whose correctness we have evaluated. So, when we encounter such statements as "Better watch it; Carl is really in a bad mood today—did you see the way he was scowling?" or "I know you're hiding something from me; I can tell it in your voice," or "Olga and Kurt are having an affair—I've seen them leave the office together nearly every night," we know that each of them is an inference. Each of them may be true, but none is necessarily true.

An inference is usually presented as part of an argument; that is, a person makes a claim (an inference) and then presents other statements in support of the claim. Here is an example of a simple argument. Joyce says, "Next year is going to be a lot easier than the past year. I got a $200-a-month raise, and my husband's been relieved of some of the extra work he's had to do while they were looking for a replacement for Ed." Her claim "Next year is going to be a lot easier than the past year" is an inference—a statement that requires support to validate it. The statements "I got a $200-a-month raise, and my husband's been relieved of some of the extra work he's had to do while they were looking for a replacement for Ed" are both facts that can be verified. Notice that Joyce's argument suggests that she infers a relationship between her claim and the facts she presents. Her argument is

What questions should listeners be asking themselves as they listen to someone who is trying to influence them?

Separating Fact from Inference

Read the following story only once. Then with out referring back to the story, evaluate each witness's statement as either F (fact) or I (inference).

Two people came hurrying out of a bank with several large bundles, hopped into a long black car, and sped away. Seconds later, a man rushed out of the bank, waving his arms and looking quite upset. You listen to two people discuss what they saw.

___a. "The bank's been robbed!"

___b. "Yes, indeed—I saw the robbers hurry out of the bank, hop into a car, and speed away."

___c. "It was a long black car."

___d. "The men were carrying several large bundles."

___e. "Seconds after they left, a man came out of the bank after them—but he was too late, they'd already escaped."

a. I b. I c. F d. I (men?) e. I

based on the assumption that more money per month and less work for her husband will make the year easier.

Evaluating Inferences

The critical listener asks at least three questions when evaluating any inference:

1. Is there factual information to support the inference? Perhaps there is no supporting information; perhaps there is not enough; or perhaps the supporting information is inaccurate. Joyce does have factual statements for support: She received a raise, and her husband has less work to do.

2. Is the factual support relevant to the inference? Perhaps the actual or implied statement of relevance is logically weak. In the example, increased income is one kind of information that is relevant to "having an easier time." At this stage it would appear that Joyce does have the makings of a sound argument; however, we need to ask a third question.

3. Is there known information that would prevent the inference from logically following the factual statements? Perhaps there is information that is not accounted for that affects the likelihood of the inference. If we learn that the $200-a-month raise involves extra duties for Joyce, then we still might question whether the next year is likely to be "easier" than the last one.

For many of us, the most difficult of the three questions to answer is the second one: "Is the factual support relevant to the inference?" This question is difficult to answer primarily because the listener must be able to verbalize a statement that shows the relevance. The listener must create the statement because in most informal reasoning the link is only implied by the person presenting the argument. Recall that in the first example Joyce never said anything like "A raise and a reduction of work are two criteria for predicting that next year will be a lot easier." Because the relevance is more often implied than stated, we must learn to phrase it.

The key to phrasing the relationship between support and inference in order to judge its relevance is to ask yourself, "What can I say that would make sense for this inference to follow from these facts?" For instance, suppose Hal says "I see frost on the grass—I think our flowers are goners." What can we say that establishes the relevance of the supporting fact "frost on the grass" to the claim "our flowers are goners"? If I were Hal, I would likely be thinking, "The presence of frost means that the temperature is low enough to freeze the moisture on the grass.

If it's cold enough to freeze the moisture on the grass, it's cold enough to kill my flowers." This seems to make sense because we can demonstrate a relationship between frost and the death of unprotected flowers.

Let's try another one. Gina says, "I studied all night and only got a D on the first test—I'm not going to do any better on this one." This statement suggests that Gina sees relevance between the amount of study time before a test and the grade. We could phrase this implied relevance by saying "Since the time of study before the test, which determines the grade, can be no greater, Gina can't improve her grade." In this case, the relevance seems questionable. Her reasoning suggests that the only factor in determining a grade is the amount of study time before the test. Experience would suggest that many other factors, such as previous time spent studying and frame of mind, are of equal if not greater importance.

OBSERVE & ANALYZE

Journal Activity

Effective Listening

Describe five situations during the past day or two in which you were cast as a "listener" (only one of these can be a classroom setting). Was your listening behavior the same or different in each of the instances? What, if anything, determined differences in your approach to your listening in each of these situations? In which of the situations were you the most effective listener? On what basis do you make this evaluation? What behaviors discussed in this chapter seem to best explain how your "effective" listening differed from your "ineffective" listening? ■

TEST YOURSELF

Evaluating Inferences

For each of the following, ask and answer the following three questions: (1) Is the inference supported with meaningful factual statements? (2) Does the stated or implied relevance between the support and the inference makes sense? and (3) Is there any other known information that lessens the quality of the inference? Remember that to do this properly, you must phrase a reasoning link to tie the supporting information to the inference.

a. "The chess club held a raffle, and they made a lot of money. I think we should hold a raffle, too."

b. "Chad is aggressive, personable, and highly motivated—he ought to make a good salesman."

c. "Three of my students last year got As on this test, five the year before, and three the year before that. There certainly will be some As this year."

d. "I saw Kali in a maternity outfit—she must be pregnant."

e. "Listen, I like the way Darren thinks, Solomon is an excellent mathematician, and Marco and Ethan are two of my best students. All four are Alpha Alphas. As far as I'm concerned, the Alphas are the group on campus with academic strength."

f. "If Greg hadn't come barging in, I never would have spilled my iced tea."

g. "Maybe that's the way you see it, but to me when high city officials are caught with their hands in the till and when police close their eyes to the actions of people with money, that's corruption."

h. "Krista wears her hair that way and guys fall all over her—I'm getting myself a hairdo like that."

In short, you are listening critically when you (1)separate facts from inferences, (2) analyze the "facts" to determine their truth, (3) question whether the stated or implied relevance between the facts and the inference makes sense, and (4) question whether there is any other known information that lessens the quality of the inference.

Figure 7.2 summarizes how good listeners and poor listeners deal with the four aspects of listening: attending, understanding, remembering, and evaluating.

	GOOD LISTENERS	**BAD LISTENERS**
ATTENDING	Attend to important information.	May not hear what a person is saying.
	Ready themselves physically and mentally.	Fidget in their chairs, look out the window, and let their minds wander.
	Listen objectively regardless of emotional involvement.	Visibly react to emotional language.
	Listen differently depending on situations.	Listen the same way regardless of type of material.
UNDERSTANDING	Assign appropriate meaning to what is said.	Hear what is said, but either are unable to understand or assign different meaning to the words.
	Seek out apparent purpose, main points, and supporting information.	Ignore the way information is organized.
	Ask mental questions to anticipate information.	Fail to anticipate coming information.
	Silently paraphrase to solidify understanding.	Seldom or never mentally review information.
	Seek out subtle meanings based on nonverbal cues.	Ignore nonverbal cues.
REMEMBERING	Retain information.	Interpret message accurately but forget it.
	Repeat key information.	Assume they will remember.
	Mentally create mnemonics for lists of words and ideas.	Seldom single out any information as especially important.
	Take notes.	Rely on memory alone.
EVALUATING	Listen critically.	Hear and understand but are unable to weigh and consider it.
	Separate facts from inferences.	Don't differentiate between facts and inferences.
	Evaluate inferences.	Accept information at face value.

Figure 7.2

A Summary of the Four Aspects of Listening

WHAT WOULD YOU DO?

A Question *of* Ethics

Janeen always disliked talking on the telephone—she thought that it was an impersonal form of communication. Thus, college was a wonderful respite because when friends would call her, instead of staying on the phone she could quickly run over to their dorm or meet them at a coffeehouse.

One day, during reading period before exams, Janeen received a phone call from Barbara, an out-of-town friend. Before she was able to dismiss the call with her stock excuses Janeen found herself bombarded with information about old high school friends and their whereabouts. Not wanting to disappoint Barbara, who seemed eager to talk, Janeen tucked her phone under her chin and began straightening her room, answering Barbara with the occasional "uh huh,"

"hmm," or "wow, that's cool!" As the "conversation" progressed, Janeen began reading through her mail and then her notes from class. After a few minutes she realized there was silence on the other end of the line. Suddenly very ashamed, she said, "I'm sorry, what did you say? The phone . . . uh there was just a lot of static."

Barbara replied with obvious hurt in her voice, "I'm sorry I bothered you, you must be terribly busy."

Embarrassed, Janeen muttered, "I'm just really stressed, you know, with exams coming up and everything. I guess I wasn't listening very well, you didn't seem to be saying anything really important. I'm sorry. What were you saying?"

"Nothing 'important,'" Barbara answered. "I was just trying to figure out a way to tell you. I know that you were with friends with my brother Billy, and you see, we just found out yesterday that he's terminal with a rare form of leukemia. But you're right, it obviously isn't really important." With that, she hung up.

1. How ethical was Janeen's means of dealing with her dilemma of not wanting to talk on the phone but not wanting to hurt Barbara's feelings?

2. Identify ways in which both Janeen and Barbara could have used better and perhaps more ethical interpersonal communication skills. Rewrite the scenario incorporating these changes.

Summary

Listening is an active process that involves attending, understanding, evaluating, remembering, and responding. Effective listening is essential to competent communication.

Attending is the perceptual process of selecting to concentrate on specific stimuli from the countless stimuli reaching the senses that we consciously process. We can increase the effectiveness of our attention by (1) getting ready to listen, (2) making the shift from speaker to listener a complete one, (3) hearing a person out before we react, and (4) adjusting our attention to the listening goals of the situation.

Understanding is the process of decoding a message accurately by correctly by assigning meaning to it. A key to understanding is to practice active listening: Identify the organization, attend to nonverbal cues, ask questions to get additional information, and paraphrase responses to assure your understanding.

Remembering is the process of storing the meanings that have been received so that they may be recalled later. Remembering is increased by repeating information, constructing mnemonics, and, when feasible, taking notes.

Critical analysis is the process of evaluating what you have understood and interpreted in order to determine how truthful, authentic, or believable you judge the meaning to be. A fact is a verifiable statement; an inference is a conclusion drawn from facts. You are listening critically when (1) you question whether the inference is supported with meaningful factual statements, (2) you question whether the reasoning statement that shows the relationship between the support and the inference make sense, and (3) you question whether there is any other known information that lessens the quality of the inference.

Inter-Action Dialogue:

 Good listening requires attending, understanding (asking questions and paraphrasing), remembering (repeating and forming mnemonics), and analyzing (evaluating inferences). Use your Inter-Act CD-ROM to view the dialogue between Gloria and Jill and analyze the listening behaviors of each.

A transcript of Gloria and Jill's conversation is printed below. You can record your analysis of their behavior in the right-hand column, then complete your analysis online using the Inter-Action Analysis feature on your CD-ROM. From the Dialogue page click "Analysis for Gloria and Jill" to compare your comments to the analysis provided by the authors.

Gloria and Jill meet for lunch on campus.

CONVERSATION

GLORIA: I'm really hungry—I don't know whether I've been working out too hard or what.

JILL: I know. There are some days when I can't figure out what happened, but I just feel starved.

GLORIA: Thanks for meeting me today. I know you're up to here in work, but. . .

JILL: No problem Gloria. I feel bad that we haven't gotten together as much as we used to, so I've been really looking forward to seeing you.

GLORIA: Well, I need to talk with you about something that's been really bothering me. (She notices that Jill is fumbling with something in her purse. Jill—are you listening to me?

JILL: I'm sorry, Gloria. For a minute I couldn't find my cell phone. I wanted to turn it off while we talked, and then I worried that I might have dropped it. but everything's OK. I apologize—that was rude of me. (She then sits up straight and looks directly at Gloria.) I'm ready.

GLORIA: Well, you know I'm working with Professor Bryant on an independent research project this term.

JILL: I recall you mentioning something about it. but remind me of the details.

GLORIA: Last semester when I took her course on family communication I wrote a term paper on how shared dinnertime affected family communication. Well, she really liked it and asked me if I wanted to work with her on a study this term. She said I could get credit.

JILL: How?

GLORIA: I had permission to sign up for four credit hours of independent study.

JILL: That sounds good—so what's the problem?

GLORIA: Well, since she videotapes actual family discussions and then interviews family members, I thought I'd get to help with some of the interviews. But so far all I've been assigned to do is transcribe the tapes and do some library research.

ANALYSIS

Listening Effectively

CONVERSATION

JILL: So you're disappointed because you're not being challenged?

GLORIA: It's more than that. I thought Dr. Bryant would be a mentor: there'd be team meetings, we'd talk over ideas and stuff, but I don't really even get to see her. Her graduate assistant gives me my assignments and he doesn't even stop to explain why I'm being asked to do stuff. I'm not really learning anything.

JILL: So, if I understand, it's not only the type of assignments you're getting but it's also that instead of really being involved, you're being treated like a flunky.

GLORIA: Exactly.

JILL: So when she asked you to work on her study, did she ever sit down and discuss exactly what the independent study would entail?

GLORIA: Not really. I just signed up.

JILL: Well since the term began, have you had any contact with Dr. Bryant?

GLORIA: No. Do you think I should make an appointment to see her?

JILL: I think so, but if you did, what would you say to her?

GLORIA: Well, I'd just tell her how disappointed I am with how things are going. And I'd explain what I hoped to learn this term and ask if she could help me understand how the assignments I'd been given were going to help me learn about family communication research.

JILL: So the purpose of your meeting wouldn't be to get different assignments, but to understand what you are supposed to be learning from the assignments you've done so far?

GLORIA: Right. But I think I'd also like her to know that I really expected to have more contact with her.

JILL: Well, it sounds as if you're clear on what you'd like to ask her.

GLORIA: Yes, but I don't want to get her angry with me. Four credit hours is a lot and it's too late to drop the independent study.

JILL: So you're concerned that she would be offended and take it out on your grade.

GLORIA: A little. But that's probably ridiculous. After all, she's a professional and all the students I know who have gone to see her say that she's really understanding.

JILL: Well, then what do you want to do?

GLORIA: Hm. . . .I'm going to make an appointment to see her. In fact, I'll stop by her office on my way to my next class. Jill, thanks for listening. You've really helped me.

ANALYSIS

Chapter Resources

Communication Improvement Plan: Listening

Would you like to improve your use of the following skills discussed in this chapter?

        Questioning

        Paraphrasing

Pick a skill and write a communication improvement plan

Skill: _____

Problem: _____

_____

_____

_____

Goal: _____

_____

_____

_____

Procedure:

1. _____

2. _____

3. _____

Test of Achieving Goal: _____

_____

Key Words

Listening, *p. 182*

Attending, *p. 182*

Understanding, *p. 187*

Active listening, *p. 187*

Question, *p. 188*

Paraphrasing, *p. 191*

Content paraphrase, *p. 191*

Feelings paraphrase, *p. 191*

Remembering, *p. 194*

Repetition, *p. 194*

Mnemonic device, *p. 194*

Critical analysis, *p. 198*

Factual statements, *p. 198*

Inferences, *p. 198*

Inter-Act with Media

CINEMA

James L. Brooks, (Director). (1997). *As Good as It Gets.* Jack Nicholson, Helen Hunt, Greg Kinnear, Cuba Gooding, Jr., Shirley Knight.

Brief Summary: An obsessive-compulsive writer (Melvin Udall) living in New York City must learn to overcome his illness and his homophobia as he struggles to form single mother relationships with a waitress (Carol Connelly) who serves him breakfast at his favorite restaurant, his gay neighbor (Simon Bishop), with whose care Melvin and Simon's dog, Verdell, is suddenly entrusted.

IPC Concepts: The entire listening process is illustrated.

Randa Haines (Director). (1991). *The Doctor.* William Hurt, Christine Lahti, Elizabeth Perkins, Mandy Patinkin, Adam Arkin.

Brief Summary: This film is based on Dr. Ed Rosenbaum's book *A Taste of My Own Medicine.* William Hurt plays a doctor who believes that he must maintain distance from his patients so that he can remain objective and efficient. When he develops throat cancer, he discovers what it is like to be a patient and deal with hospital bureaucracy. A young female cancer patient helps him to learn how to empathize with patients and to cope with his own illness. He develops an innovative approach to the training of his interns as he learns that really listening to his patients is as important as reading test results, etc. He also learns of the importance of listening to his wife as their relationship is severely tested.

IPC Concepts: Attending to patients, paraphrasing, listening critically, language, relationships, message clarity, jargon, ethics.

Robert Redford (Director). (1980). *Ordinary People.* Donald Sutherland, Mary Tyler Moore, Judd Hirsch, Timothy Hutton, Elizabeth McGovern.

Brief Summary: This story is about a seriously dysfunctional family and its efforts to deal with the death of the eldest son. Both parents lack effective listening skills. The mother refuses to deal with the death and makes the younger son the target of her anger and grief. The father tries to avoid conflict and plays the role of peacemaker. By the end of the film, he learns the value and necessity of active listening to the world around him, and the need to deal with the conflict in a more proactive manner.

IPC Concepts: Attending, listening actively.

Jean Yarbrough (Director). (1945). *Who's on First* in *Naughty Nineties.* Bud Abbott and Lou Costello.

Brief Summary: This is one of the great comedy routines of all time, and it is an effective vehicle for analyzing both the communication and the listening processes. The routine is only one segment in a feature-length film in which Bud and Lou play vaudeville entertainers.

IPC Concepts: Listening—barriers, bad habits, circular communication.

THEATER

Lapine, J., & Sondheim, S. (1985). *Sunday in the Park with George.*

Brief Summary: This is a wonderful musical about artist Georges Seurat (George), and his relationship with his mistress, Dot. In one memorable song from the libretto, she sings out in anguish, "Hello George. Remember me George. I'm here George." George is so consumed by his work that he almost totally fails to attend to her, or to her needs. This failure eventually leads to the end of their relationship.

IPC Concepts: Listening and the need to attend and respond.

LITERATURE

L. Harper. (1960). *To Kill a Mockingbird.*

Brief Summary: Harper Lee's magnificent novel tells the story of three children and the summer during which they come to face their fears about their mysterious neighbor, Boo Radley, and learn about the realities of Southern racism. Scout, Jem, and Dill have a summer of adventures trying to catch a safe glimpse of Boo. However, it is also during this summer that Atticus, Jem and Scout's father, is asked to defend a black man (Tom Robinson) accused of rape and assault. The children learn of the harsh, ugly side of what their father does for a living, and of the racist traditions of their culture. When Scout goes to school in the fall, she must learn how to talk to children who are different from her, and how to control her temper by dealing with her feelings and her self-talk. As the novel moves to its conclusion, Scout finally meets Boo Radley when he comes to Scout and Jem's rescue. Scout realizes that the man's gentle, shy ways should not make him the outcast that he is.

IPC Concepts: This novel illustrates virtually every aspect of the communication process in interpersonal relationships. It deals with trust, perception, empathy, conflict, stereotyping, cultural diversity, and the development of the self. It is especially effective in illustrating the value of listening in the relationship of Scout and Atticus.

ACADEMIC WORK

Wolvin, A., & Coakley, C. G. (1996). *Listening* (5th ed.). Boston: McGraw-Hill.

Brief Summary: This book provides a thorough introduction to the listening process. It goes into depth on the nature of the

process, analysis of barriers to listening, and techniques for improving listening ability.

IPC Concepts: All aspects of the listening process.

Lynch, J. J. (1985). *The Language of the Heart: The Human Body in Dialogue.* New York: Basic Books.

Brief Summary: This is a fascinating discussion of the physiological side of the impact of communication on health. Of particular interest is the relationship between tension, listening, speaking, and blood pressure.

IPC Concepts: Physiological nature and impact of listening.

WHAT'S ON THE WEB

Tips on Effective Listening

http://www.drnadig.com/listening.htm

Brief Summary: This Web site examines the nature and function of listening in effective communication. The site reviews the nature of listening, sources of difficulty for both speaker and listener, listening modes, levels of communication (cliché, facts, etc.), and tips for effective listening. This is an excellent supplement to the discussion in the text. There are links to expressing emotions and conflict management.

IPC Concepts: Attending, understanding, remembering, evaluating.

The Active Listening Exercise prepared by the New England Regional Leadership Program

http://crs.uvm.edu/gopher/nerl/personal/comm/e.html

Brief Summary: This site provides a lengthy explanation of active listening. The document is provided by the Center for Rural Studies, a nonprofit, fee-for-service research organization, based in the College of Agriculture and Life Sciences at the University of Vermont. There is an excellent, extensive discussion of active listening, and a good active listening exercise.

IPC Concepts: Remembering, evaluating.

Harmonious Assertive Communication

http://front.csulb.edu/tstevens/c14-lisn.htm

Brief Summary: Tom G. Stevens's methods to create understanding and intimacy provide a Web-based explanation of empathetic listening. This Web site provides something more than lecture notes or a single chapter, but it is not book-length either. Stevens is a psychologist for the Counseling and Psychological Services at California State University, Long Beach. He is the author of a recent (1998) book, *You Can Choose to Be Happy: "Rise Above" Anxiety, Anger, and Depression* (he has an online version of this book available at his Web site).

IPC Concepts: Listening, understanding.

CHAPTER 8

Responding with
and

Understanding Comforting Others

After you have read this chapter, you should be able to answer these questions:

- How do people respond to the emotional situations of others?

- What is empathy?

- What role does empathy play in building and maintaining relationships?

- What are three approaches to empathizing?

- What cultural considerations affect the ability to empathize well?

- What is the process of providing emotional support to another?

- What are the characteristics of effective and ineffective emotional support messages?

- What are the skills you will want to learn in order to provide comfort to others?

"Kristy, I'm really feeling down and I need to tell you about it. Paul and I went out last night to a movie, and I just felt so good to be with him. After the movie we stopped into The Coffee Bar the way we usually do to talk a bit before we went home. I mean we're only sitting there a few seconds when Paul says, 'Tara, I have to tell you something—I'm seeing another woman.' I thought I was going to die. 'What do you mean you're seeing another woman?' I say. Then he says, 'You know things haven't been going that well between us. There's just no chemistry, so I thought we could just be friends. You know I'll always enjoy talking with you.' Kristy, I was stunned. What was he talking about? 'Things haven't been going well between us!' We've been going out for nearly a year now, my children seem very comfortable with him, and I thought he was getting ready to propose when he hits me with this 'I'm seeing another woman let's be friends' routine!"

"You're kidding!" said Kristy. "Oh, did I tell you that I've got an appointment to get a massage tomorrow? Well, I just can't wait. And I've got a coupon so it's only gonna cost thirty-five dollars for the hour treatment. The masseuse is supposed to be the best. Calla went there last week and just raved about it. Why don't you come too? I think I can get another coupon."

"Kristy, what's with you? Here I am baring my soul to you about how Paul dumped me and all you can talk about is some dumb massage."

"Well, Tara, I was just trying to cheer you up. I thought if we talked about massages it would take your mind off that loser Paul."

"Kristy, just forget it. I've got to go to class."

"All right, so you can't get that excited about my massage, then let's talk about something else."

Can you recall a situation when you went to a friend and shared how hurt you were with an incident that had just happened to you? Did you feel that the person really listened? Did your friend seem to understand and try to help you? Or was your conversation like the one between Tara and Kristy? Notice how Kristy's first response "You're kidding" was followed by changing the topic, what Barbee and Cunningham (1995), refer to as an "escape" strategy, where in effect she was dismissing the importance of Tara's concerns. So how should Kristy have responded in order to be helpful and comforting? In her research, Barbee and Cunningham found that instead of escaping and dismissing, using comforting responses that provide solace and solve problems is perceived by recipients to be supportive—the kind of responses that Tara needed from Kristy (Cunningham & Barbee, 2000).

In our relations we often find ourselves in situations where our partner is emotionally distressed and in need of comfort. How well we respond in these situations not only affects how well our partner copes with the situation but also affects the relationship itself. In this chapter, we will study the concepts and skills of effective supportive communication. We begin by explaining empathy processes and describing how to improve your ability to empathize. Then we discuss the process of providing emotional support to another and the characteristics of effective and ineffective emotional support messages. Finally, we will describe the specific skills you will want to learn in order to provide comfort to others.

Empathy

Appropriate supportive responses depend on our ability to empathize with our communication partner. **Empathy** is the cognitive process of identifying with or vicariously experiencing the feelings, thoughts, or attitudes of another. Scholars recognize that empathy is an important element in understanding and maintaining good interpersonal relationships (Omdahl, 1995, p. 4). When we empathize, we are attempting to understand and/or experience what another understands and/or experiences. It obviously requires more effort to empathize with someone who is very different from us or to empathize with someone who is experiencing something that is out of our realm of experience. But the goal of empathy is to understand the experiences of the other person.

Empathy–the cognitive process of identifying with or vicariously experiencing the feelings, thoughts, or attitudes of another.

Approaches to Empathy

Scholars who study empathy have identified three different approaches that people can use when empathizing: empathic responsiveness, perspective taking, and sympathetic responsiveness (Weaver & Kirtley, 1995, p. 131).

Empathic responsiveness is experiencing an emotional response parallel to another person's actual or anticipated display of emotion (Omdahl, 1995, p. 4; Stiff, Dillard, Somera, Kim, & Sleight, 1988, p. 199). For instance, when Monique tells Heather that she lost her job, Heather will have experienced empathic responsiveness if she senses the sadness that Monique is feeling and feels sad herself.

Empathic responsiveness–experiencing an emotional response parallel to another person's actual or anticipated display of emotion.

The empathic responsiveness approach is most easily used when we have a close or intimate relationship with the other person. Because of the strong relational bond between you, you may identify more easily with the other's emotion and experience it along with the other person. If Heather and Monique have been best friends since third grade, Heather is likely to understand how Monique is feeling. Since she is emotionally attached to Monique, she is more likely to feel with Monique in this situation. If, on the other hand, Heather only met Monique this semester and only sees her in chemistry class, it will be more difficult for Heather to understand what Monique is feeling and she is less likely to be able to feel with Monique. In general, we can use empathic responsiveness most easily with those people who are our intimates.

Perspective taking—imagining yourself in the place of another—is the most common form of empathizing (Zillmann, 1991). While empathic responsiveness stems from feeling what another feels, in perspective taking we imagine ourselves in the situation described, anticipate how we would feel, and then assume that the

Perspective taking–imagining yourself in the place of another.

other person will feel similarly. Although perspective taking is difficult for many of us (Holtgraves, 2002, p. 122), with conscious effort we can learn to imagine ourselves in the place of another. In our example, if Heather personalizes the message by picturing herself being told that she has been fired, anticipates and experiences her own emotions if this were to occur, and then assumes that Monique must be feeling the same way that Heather would feel, then she is empathizing by perspective taking.

Sympathetic responsiveness—a feeling of concern, compassion, or sorrow for another because of the situation.

Sympathetic responsiveness is your feeling of concern, compassion, or sorrow for another because of the situation. Some scholars call this "emotional concern" (Stiff et al., 1988) while others use the more common term "sympathy" (Eisenberg & Fabes, 1990). Sympathetic responsiveness differs from the other two approaches in that you don't attempt to experience the feelings of the other, but rather you focus on intellectually understanding what the speaker has said and experience feelings of concern, compassion, or sorrow for that person. Heather has sympathy for Monique when she understands that Monique is embarrassed and worried, but instead of trying to feel Monique's emotions or experience how she herself would feel in a similar situation, Heather feels concern and compassion for her friend Monique.

Improving Our Ability to Empathize

Although people vary in their ability to empathize, most of us have to learn to increase our empathy and then decide to practice it. Especially for those of us who are overly "I" oriented, we find it difficult to see the world from others' points of view, and as a result, our ability to empathize is often underdeveloped. Under these

Our ability to detect and identify the feelings of others may come from our own experiences in similar situations.

Black and White *By Linda Howard*

Today we tend to label people as Black, White, Asian, Hispanic, etc. But what if you are half one and half another? Linda Howard is a recent high school graduate who has been awarded a four-year scholarship to a prominent university in New England. Listen to a transcript of an interview with her. In what ways can you empathize?

My parents are Black and White American. I come from a long heritage. I am of French, English, Irish, Dutch, Scottish, Canadian, and African descent.

I don't really use race. I always say, "My father's Black, my mother's White, I'm mixed." But I'm American; I'm human. That's my race; I'm part of the human race.

It's hard when you go out in the streets and you've got a bunch of White friends and you're the darkest person there. No matter how light you are to the rest of your family, you're the darkest person there and they say you're Black. Then you go out with a bunch of Black people and you're the lightest there and they say, "Yeah, my best friend's White." But I'm not. I'm both.

I don't always fit in—unless I'm in a mixed group. That's how it's different. Because if I'm in a group of people who are all one race, then they seem to look at me as being the *other* race . . . whereas if I'm in a group full of [racially mixed] people, my race doesn't seem to matter to everybody else. . . . Then I don't feel like I'm standing out. But if I'm in a group of totally one race, then I sort of stand out, and

that's something that's hard to get used to.

It's hard. I look at history and I feel really bad for what some of my ancestors did to some of my other ancestors. Unless you're mixed, you don't know what it's like to be mixed.

I've had people tell me, "Well, you're Black." I'm not Black; I'm Black and White. I'm Black and White American. "Well, you're Black!" No, I'm not! I'm both. It's insulting, when they try and . . . bring it right back to the old standards, that if you have anybody in your family who's Black, you're Black . . . I mean, I'm not ashamed of being Black, but I'm not ashamed of being White either; and if I'm both, I want to be part of both. And I think teachers need to be sensitive to that.

See, the thing is, I mix it at home so much that it's not really a problem for me to mix it outside.

I don't think [interracial identity is] that big of a problem. It's not killing anybody, at least as far as I know, it's not. It's not destroying families and lives and stuff. It's a minor thing. If you learn how to deal with it at a young age, as I did, it really doesn't bother you the rest of your life, like drugs . . .

I think we're all racist in a sense. We all have some type of person that we don't like, whether it's (a person) from a different race, or from a different background, or (a person with) different habits.

But to me a *serious racist* is a person who believes that people of different ethnic backgrounds don't belong or should be in *their* space and shouldn't invade *our* space: "Don't come and invade *my* space, you Chinese person. You belong over in China or you belong over in Chinatown."

Racists come out and tell you that they don't like who you are. Prejudiced people [on the other hand] will say it in like those little hints, you know, like, "Oh, yes, some of my best friends are Black." Or they say little ethnic remarks that they know will insult you but they won't come out and tell you, "You're Black. I don't want anything to do with you." Racists, to me, would come out and do that.

Both racists and prejudiced people make judgments, and most of the time they're wrong judgments, but the racist will carry his one step further . . . A racist is a person that will carry out their prejudices.

I had a fight with a woman at work. She's White, and at the

time I was the only Black person in my department. Or I was the only person who was *at all* Black in my department. And she just kept on laying on the racist jokes. At one point, I said, "You know, Nellie, you're a racist pig!" And she got offended by that. And I was just joking, just like she'd been joking for two days straight—all the racist jokes that she could think of.

I've got a foot on both sides of the fence, and there's only so much I can take. I'm straddling the fence, and it's hard to laugh and joke with you when you're talking about the foot that's on the other side.

She couldn't understand it. We didn't talk for weeks. And then one day, I had to work with her. We didn't say anything for the first like two hours of work. And then I just said, "Smile, Nellie, you're driving me nuts!" and she smiled and laughed. And we've been good friends ever since. She just knows you don't say ethnic things around me; you don't joke around with me like that because I won't stand for it from you anymore. We can be friends; we can talk about anything else—except race. ■

Excerpted from (2000). Case study: Linda Howard, "Unless you're mixed, you don't know what it's like to be mixed. From Nieto, Sonia, *Affirming Diversity: The Sociopolitical Context of Multicultural Education* (3rd ed., pp. 50–60). Boston: Allyn and Bacon. Copyright (c) 2000 by Pearson Education. Adapted by permission of the publisher.

circumstances we may need to exert extra effort to develop our capacity to empathize if we are to increase our interpersonal effectiveness.

Though it may seem trite, the first step is to take the time and make the effort to understand the person who is speaking. This does not mean that we need to have a deep, personal relationship with others in order to empathize with them. It means that we pay serious attention to what others are saying and what they feel about what they are saying. It begins by treating a person as a person with value and not as an object. Understanding others focuses your attention on the other, not on the self. In this chapter's Diverse Voices selection (see page 213), "Black and White," Linda Howard describes what she has experienced as a person who is multiethnic and biracial. As you read this excerpt from an interview with Ms. Howard, see how well you can discern, understand, and feel what she thinks and feels.

How well you empathize also depends on how observant you are of others' behavior and how clearly you "read" the nonverbal messages they are sending. How accurately can you read others' emotions from their nonverbal behavior? Research studies have shown that when people concentrate, they can do quite well. People are especially adept at recognizing such primary emotions as happiness, sadness, surprise, anger, and fear (greater than 90 percent accuracy) and rather good at recognizing contempt, disgust, interest, determination, and bewilderment (80 to 90 percent accuracy) (Leathers, 1997, p. 41). The research also suggests that recognizing facial expressions is the key to perceiving emotion (Leathers, 1997, p. 25).

In order to improve your observations, try the following. When another person begins a conversation with you, develop the habit of silently posing two questions to yourself: "What emotions do I believe the person is experiencing right now?" and "What are the cues the person is giving that I am using to draw this conclusion?" Consciously raising these questions can help you focus your attention on the nonverbal aspects of messages, where most of the information on the person's emotional state is conveyed.

To ensure that you understand another's emotions accurately, use the skill of perception checking. Perception checking is especially useful when the other person's culture is different from our own.

Empathizing also depends on how familiar we are with the situation. It is difficult to use perspective taking in situations that are foreign to our experience or with people who are very different from us. As we increase our experience base, we can increase our ability to use perspective taking. One way to increase our experience base is through the arts, especially by reading and watching live dramatizations, televised portrayals, or films. Through these activities, we can vicariously experience situations that we may not have personally encountered in our own life but which are common to the real lives of others. Then we can draw on these vicarious experiences when we need to visualize another's real situation in order to empathize. For example, you may be an only child. If so, you may have difficulty picturing how you would feel if your sister died. But suppose you have read *Little Women*, by Louisa May Alcott, or watched a film based on this novel. If you cried when Beth died, you can draw on that sadness in order to empathize with a friend whose sister has died.

SKILL BUILDERS   **EMPATHIZING**

SKILL

The cognitive process of identifying with or the vicarious experiencing of the feelings, thoughts, or attitudes of another.

USE

To prepare yourself for making an appropriate comforting response.

PROCEDURE

1. Show respect for the person by actively attending to what the person says.
2. Concentrate on observing and understanding both the verbal and nonverbal messages, using paraphrases and perception checking to aid you.
3. Experience an emotional response parallel to another person's actual or anticipated display of emotion, imagine yourself in the place of the person, feel concern, compassion, or sorrow for the person because of his or her situation or plight.

EXAMPLE

When Jerry says, "I was really hurt when Sarah returned the ring I had given her," Mary experiences an emotional response parallel to Jerry's, imagines herself in Jerry's situation, or feels concern, compassion, or sorrow for Jerry.

In summary, to become more effective at using the cognitive skill of empathizing with others, try the following: (1) Show respect for the person by actively attending to what the person is saying. (2) Concentrate on observing and understanding both the verbal and nonverbal messages, using paraphrases and perception checking to aid you. (3) Experience an emotional response parallel to another person's actual or anticipated display of emotion, imagine yourself in the place of the person, feel concern, compassion, or sorrow for the person because of his or her situation or plight.

Cultural Considerations

As we have seen, empathizing can be difficult even when we are talking with close friends and relatives. Empathizing is even more difficult when communicating with strangers, especially strangers from a different culture. Yet as Samovar and Porter point out in their review of the literature, empathy is a major aspect of effective intercultural communication (2001, p. 286).

Why is empathy so much more difficult across cultures? Primarily because of the increase in the number of communication variables. When we are talking with friends we are likely to share so many communication behaviors that their meanings are easily understood. For instance, if you were born in the United States, when you say something to your friend who shares the same general background and your friend giggles, you can be reasonably sure that your friend was amused by what you said. On the other hand, if you were born and raised in the United States and you are talking with a recently immigrated Japanese acquaintance who giggles at what you have said, it is very likely that the Japanese acquaintance is uncomfortable with what you have said (Martin & Nakayama, 1997, pp. 268–269). Why? Because giggling carries different meanings in different cultures.

When you are communicating with strangers, especially strangers from another culture, you must be very careful about a tendency to stereotype and/or assume that the person thinks the way you do. Moreover, many of us become rather lazy—that is we don't pay as close attention to nonverbal cues as we should. And as Samovar and Porter show, perhaps the greatest problem is lack of motivation. The more distant a person is from us the more indifferent we are likely to become (Samovar & Porter, 2001, p. 288).

So, since we are unlikely to know how people from different cultures think and feel, we need to try harder to make sure that we understand enough about what and how a person is feeling so that we can begin to empathize. First, this calls for us to be even more attentive than usual, which begins by being especially conscious of nonverbal behaviors. Second, if there is any doubt about how the person is feeling, take time to ask. If you suspect that the person is sad, happy, concerned, or embarrassed, take the time to ask. Here is where the skills of paraphrasing and describing behavior are especially useful. By saying, "From the sound of your voice I get the sense that you are really hurt by what Jeff said to you," you get confirmation of your perception—and now you are in a better position to empathize.

Can you learn to empathize with those with whom you have almost nothing in common? Yes. But it takes considerable effort on your part. Especially when you are sincerely interested in the other person and hoping to develop a friendly relationship, taking these steps is vital.

While empathy is the prerequisite for responding appropriately, we now turn our attention to describing specific types of responses that you might use as you demonstrate empathy. These responses can be classified as those that clarify meaning, those that provide comfort to the other, and those that help others to understand their own behavior and its effect on others.

Understanding Emotional Support

Many times in our conversations with others, we may find ourselves in positions where we feel a need to provide emotional support—in effect to comfort the speaker. Comforting means to help people feel better about themselves and their behavior. Comforting occurs when one feels respected, understood, and confirmed.

Research on comforting messages suggests that people who use a relatively high percentage of sophisticated comforting strategies are perceived as more sensitive, concerned, and involved (Burleson & Samter, 1990; Kunkel & Burleson, 1999; Samter, Burleson, & Murphy, 1987).

OBSERVE & ANALYZE

Journal Activity

Empathizing Effectively

1. Describe the last time you effectively empathized with another person. Write a short summary of the episode. Be sure to cover the following: What was the person's emotional state? How did you recognize it? What were the nonverbal cues? Verbal cues? What type of relationship do you have with this person? How long have you known the person? How similar is this person to you? Have you ever had a real or vicarious experience similar to the one the person was reporting? Did you use empathic responsiveness, perspective taking, or sympathetic responsiveness? Why? What was the outcome of this communication episode?

2. During the next two days, make a conscious effort to use empathy guidelines in your daily interactions with others. At the end of each day, assess your progress. How well did you do on each guideline? Where do you need to continue to exert effort? ■

Comforting—to help people feel better about themselves and their behavior.

The new responsibilities of parenthood can seem daunting. How might doctors, family, and friends provide positive support during the first days?

Some comforting responses are statements that show approval of a person's feelings or acknowledge the person's right to have those feelings. Other comforting responses are efforts to commiserate with a person when bad things have happened. Under these circumstances the comforting messages are efforts to reassure, bolster, encourage, soothe, console, and cheer up. In this section we label all these efforts as *supporting*.

Supporting

Supporting response–a statement whose goal is to show approval, bolster, encourage, soothe, console, or cheer up.

Supporting responses are comforting statements whose goal is to reassure, bolster, encourage, soothe, console, or cheer up. They show that we care about people and what happens to them; they demonstrate that the listener empathizes with a person's feelings, whatever their direction or intensity (Burleson, 1994, p. 5). Supporting is not the same as making statements that aren't true or only telling people what they want to hear. Effective supportive statements must be in touch with the facts. Let's look briefly at two supportive approaches, one that supports positive feelings and another that supports negative feelings.

Supporting (Approving) Positive Feelings We all like to treasure our good feelings; when we share them, we don't want them dashed by listeners' inappropriate or insensitive responses. Supporting positive feelings is generally easy, but still requires some care. Consider the following example.

> Kendra *(hangs up the telephone, does a little dance step, and turns to Selena): That was my boss. He said that he'd put my name in for the promotion. I didn't believe he would really choose me!*

Kendra's statement requires an appropriate verbal response. To provide one, Selena must appreciate the feeling people get when they receive good news, or she must envision how she would feel under the same circumstances. Selena responds:

> Selena: *Kendra, way to go, girl! That's terrific! I am so happy for you. You've worked so hard—you deserve this.*

In this case, Selena's response gives her approval for Kendra to be excited. Her response also shows that she is happy because Kendra seems happy.

Supporting responses like Selena's are much needed. Think of the times when you have experienced an event that made you feel happy, proud, pleased, soothed, or amused and you needed to express those feelings. Didn't it further your good feelings when others recognized your feelings and affirmed your right to have them?

Supporting (Giving Comfort) When a Person Experiences Negative Feelings When a person has had an unfortunate experience and is in the midst of or is recalling unpleasant emotional reactions, an effective supporting statement provides much-needed comfort. By acknowledging the person's feelings and supporting the person's right to the feelings, you can help the person further his or her progress at working through the feelings.

Brant Burleson, Professor of Communication, Purdue University on

Comforting

The seeds for Brant Burleson's interest in comforting behavior were sown during his undergraduate days at the University of Colorado at Boulder where he was taught that all communication was persuasion. This proposition did not square with Burleson's own experiences. As a child of the 50s who came of age during the emotion-filled 60s, Burleson had witnessed lots of hurt and conflict. But he had also seen people engaging in altruism and acts of comforting. These comforting acts, he reasoned, were not aimed at changing anyone's opinion or behavior, but were simply done to help the other person. So when he entered graduate school at the University of Illinois, Burleson began to study formally how individuals comfort others. He wanted to establish scientifically whether comforting messages were important and whether they made a difference. Since graduate school Burleson's work has done much to accomplish this goal.

In his research Burleson has carefully defined comforting strategies as messages that have the goal of relieving or lessening the emotional distress of others. He has limited his work to looking at how we comfort others who are experiencing mild or moderate sadness or disappointment that happens as a result of everyday events. He has chosen not to study comforting in situations where there is extreme depression or grief because of extraordinary events. He has also chosen to limit his work to the verbal strategies that we use when we comfort. Burleson's care in defining the "domain" of his work is important. By carefully stating the type of emotional distress he is concerned with, and by clearly identifying the limits of his work, Burleson enables those who read his work to understand the types of comforting to which his findings apply.

Early on, Burleson worked with James L. Applegate, who had developed a way of judging the sophistication of particular comforting messages. Sophisticated messages were seen as those that acknowledged, elaborated, and legitimized the feelings of another person. Sophisticated comforting strategies are also more listener centered (aimed at discovering how the distressed person feels), less evaluative, more feeling centered, more likely to accept the point of view of the other person, and more likely to offer explanations for the feelings being expressed by the other person.

More recently, Burleson and others who study comforting have turned their attention to understanding the results of comforting. Early research judged comforting messages only on the extent to which they reduced the immediate distress that a person is feeling. But more recent research shows that the effects of comforting extend beyond this simple instrumental outcome. Effective comforting also helps the other person cope better in the future, improves the quality of personal relationships, and may even enhance physical health. Moreover, skilled comforting should also benefit the comforter. Burleson believes that when we effectively comfort others, we increase our own self-esteem and we become better liked by the person we comfort and those who see us effectively comfort others. Finally, Burleson believes that those who are effective at comforting others are likely to have better long-term relationships. There is a growing list of research studies, some conducted by

Spotlight on Scholars... Comforting *continued*

Burleson and his colleagues, that provides support for his theory. For complete citations of many

of Burleson's and his colleagues' publications, see the reference

list for this chapter at the end of the book. ∎

For some people, making appropriate responses to painful or angry feelings is very awkward and difficult. But when people are in pain or when they are feeling justifiably angry, they need to be comforted by appropriate supporting statements. Because it can be difficult to provide comfort when we are ill at ease, we need to practice and develop skill in making supporting statements.

An appropriate comforting statement shows empathy and sensitivity, and may show a willingness to be actively involved if need be. Consider the following example.

> Bill: *"My sister called today to tell me that Mom's biopsy came back positive. She's got cancer, and it's untreatable."*
> Dwight: *"Bill, you must be in shock. I'm so sorry that this is happening. Is there anything I can do for you?"*

Notice how Dwight begins by empathizing: "Bill, you must be in shock." He continues with statements that show his sensitivity to the seriousness of the situation: "I'm so sorry that this is happening." Finally, he shows that he really cares: He is willing to take time to talk about it, and he asks whether he can do anything for Bill.

We offer these two examples as an introduction to skill development. Later in the chapter we'll see that these are examples of just two approaches or skills that can be learned and used to provide support.

Currently one of the leading scholars—if not *the* leading scholar—on comforting behavior is Brandt Burleson, who is featured in this chapter's Spotlight on Scholars section (see page 219). Over the years Burleson and his colleagues have provided a great deal of scholarship that informs the development of supportive skills.

To better understand just why some comforting messages help people feel better while others don't do anything—or even make people feel worse—Burleson has recently studied theories and research on emotion and the factors that lead to emotional distress. This study of emotion dynamics led to a new understanding of comforting as a conversational process that, at its best, helps distressed others make sense of what has happened to them, work through their feelings, and reappraise the upsetting situation. This view of the comforting process emphasizes the role of empathic listening and the importance of getting upset people to talk about their feelings and experiences in detail. People seem to make sense of their distressing experiences by expressing their thoughts and feelings in narratives or stories. Burleson and his graduate students are currently conducting several studies on sense-making narratives and how these contribute to the reduction of emotional distress.

Characteristics of Effective and Ineffective Emotional Support Messages

A great deal of research has been directed at understanding what types of messages are perceived by receivers as supportive and what types of messages are perceived as unsupportive. **Supportive messages** are helpful and provide comfort because they create a conversational environment that encourages the person needing support to talk about and make sense of the situation that is causing distress. Nonsupportive messages are those that fail to meet these goals. The follow section lists effective and ineffective supportive message types that Burleson found from his recent studies (Burleson, 2003, pp. 565–568).

Supportive messages–create a conversational environment that encourages the person needing support to talk about and make sense of the situation that is causing distress.

Effective and helpful supportive messages are those that:

1. Clearly state that the speaker's aim is to help the other ("I'd like to help you, what can I do?" or "You know that I'm going to be here for you for as long as it takes").

2. Express acceptance, love, and affection for the other ("I love you and understand how upset this makes you" or "I understand that you just can't seem to accept this").

3. Demonstrate care, concern, and interest in the other's situation ("What are you planning to do now?" or "Gosh, tell me more, what happened then?").

4. Indicate that the speaker is available to listen and support the other ("Say, if you need to talk more, please call" or "Sometimes it helps to have someone to listen, and I'd like to do that for you").

5. State that the speaker is an ally ("I'm with you on this." or "Well, I'm on your side, this isn't right").

6. Acknowledge the other's feelings and situation as well as express sincere sympathy ("I'm so sorry to see you feeling so bad, I can see that you're devastated by what has happened" or "You have my sympathy, I couldn't work for a jerk like that either, no wonder you're frustrated").

THE WIZARD OF ID   Brant parker and Johnny hart

USED BY PERMISSION OF JOHNNY HART AND CREATORS SYNDICATE, INC.

7. Assure the other that what they are feeling is legitimate ("With what has happened to you, you deserve to be angry" or "I'd feel exactly the same way if I were in your shoes").

8. Encourage the other to elaborate on their story ("Uh huh, yeah," or "I see. How did you feel about that?" or "Well, what happened before that? Can you elaborate?").

Ineffective and unhelpful supportive messages are those that:

1. Condemn and criticize the other's feelings and behavior ("I think you're wrong to be angry with Paul" or "That's dumb, why do you feel like that?").

2. Imply that the other's feelings are not warranted ("You have no right to feel that way, after all, you've dumped men before" or "Don't you think you're being a bit over-dramatic?").

3. Tell the other how to feel about the situation or that they should ignore how they feel about the situation ("You should be really happy about this" or "Hey, you should just act as if you don't care").

4. Focus attention on the speaker by a lengthy recount of a similar situation faced by the speaker ("I know exactly how you feel because when I. . .").

5. Intrude because they represent a level of involvement or concern greater than the type of relationship would indicate to be appropriate ("I know we've just met, but I know how to help you here").

Supportive Interaction Phases

Although we can attempt to comfort a person with a single supportive statement, complete comforting is rarely accomplished with one message. Rather, in many situations we provide emotional support and comfort over numerous turns in a conversation. In some situations we will have several conversations spread over days, weeks, or even months in which our role is to give emotional support to someone who is having difficulty achieving a cognitive reappraisal and so continues to need our comfort. If Tara (from the chapter opening conversation) really loves Paul it is likely to take her weeks, if not months, to "talk out" her feelings and develop a reappraisal that allows her to find peace. So too, when someone is grieving the death of someone they loved, they are likely to need ongoing supportive interactions.

Whether a distressed person is comforted in one conversation, or requires many conversations, Barbee and Cunningham (1995) identify four well-ordered phases that supportive interactions seem to progress through.

Phase one: Support Activation. Comforting interactions begin when something happens to trigger a supportive response. Supportive activation can be triggered by the words or behaviors of the person needing support/comforting. So in the chapter opener, Tara overtly seeks support when she self-discloses, "Kristy, I'm really feeling down and I need to tell you about it." Alternatively, support activation can be triggered by a relational partner who perceives a need for comforting. For example, Brianne comes home, walks into the kitchen, and finds her mother slumped over the sink silently sobbing into her arm. Brianne rushes over, puts her arms around her mom and asks, "Mom are you alright, what's happened?" Support, then, can be activated either by the people needing comforting or by the comforters.

Phase two: Support Provision. During the second phase of a supportive interaction, comforters enact messages that are designed to support/give comfort to the partner by focusing on the emotions being displayed or on the problem that has been expressed. Although Kristy avoided dealing with Tara's feelings in the chapter opener, once Brianne's mother has shared that she had lost her job, Brianne may have provided solace by saying, "I'm so sorry, I can understand why you're terrified about how we'll pay this month's rent." In this way Brianne supports her mother's feelings.

Phase Three: Target Reaction. Once a comforter has responded to the person needing support, that person will react to what the helper has said or done. This reaction will indicate how successful the helper's message was at comforting the partner. Rather than being comforted by Tara's offer of escape from the topic, Tara was obviously distressed with Kristy's response. "Kristy, what's with you? Here I am baring my soul to you about how Paul dumped me and all you can talk about is some dumb massage." In contrast, Brianne's mother may be somewhat soothed by the solace Brianne has offered. So she calms down a bit and responds, "I'm not just worried about the rent, but there's the car payment, and I just finished paying off the credit card bill. I don't know if I can face going into debt again."

Phase Four: Helper Responses. The subsequent messages of the comforter respond to what the partner has expressed. If the partner who needs comfort has reached a more stable emotional level, the helper may respond by changing the focus of the conversation. In Kristy's response to Tara, she reinterprets her initial response as "trying to cheer you up" by taking "your mind off that loser Paul." To Kristy's way of thinking her previous response was supportive. In this response to Tara she tries to demonstrate her support and soothe Tara through her explanation of her previous remark. Since Brianne's first message provided support, her mother regained some of her composure and disclosed her fears about going into debt. So now Brianne might refocus the discussion into problem solving the family's finances.

If the partner remains in need of further comforting, the interaction will cycle back to a previous phase and continue until one of the partners changes the subject or ends the conversation. When the two meet again, they may begin another

INTER-ACT WITH

Technology

Much of our emotional tone is shared in conversation through nonverbal behavior. Today many people try to maintain close relationships with friends and family who live in other places through e-mail. If it is difficult to accurately ascertain people's emotional state without seeing or hearing the nonverbal behavior, how can we know if our support or comfort is effective? ■

supportive interaction on the same subject, cycling through the same identifiable phases, but fashioning unique messages that, while related, are different from the ones shared during the previous conversation.

As you have probably experienced during your own supportive interactions, these conversations are not always smooth. There may be false starts, interruptions, topic changes and other disruptions during the course of the discussion. And the messages themselves will vary from very brief nonverbal cues, to short verbal messages, to lengthy narratives complete with subplot digressions. Nonetheless, you will be more effective in providing support/comforting if the messages you use during phases two and four incorporate the supportive message skills presented next.

Supportive Message Skills

According to Burleson (2003), most people could benefit from training in emotional support skills. He cites numerous research studies that have found "support attempts that fail," "miscarried helping," and "unsupportive responses." From this Burleson concludes that we "don't offer each other emotional support as often as (we) might, and when (we) do, much of what (we) offer is of poor quality" (p. 562). Based on his analysis, Burleson has identified six supportive message skills. Four of these skills (clarifying supportive intentions, buffering threats to face—which is two skills—and other-centeredness) help us form messages that are sensitive to the emotional needs of the person. Two of these skills (framing information and giving advice) support the person by helping the person problem solve. Depending on the circumstances and the complexity of the situation, you may find that using a single

Although you may be able to use a single skill to provide the necessary support, you are likely to need a combination of skills over time.

skill will provide the necessary support. More likely, in order to be effective, you will use a combination of the skills as you provide comfort. Let's take a look at each of these individual skills.

Clarifying Supportive Intentions

When people are experiencing emotional turmoil, they can have trouble understanding the motives of those wishing to provide support. We **clarify supportive intentions** (indicate that we are trying to support) when we openly state that our goal in the conversation is to support and help our partner. Messages based on this skill may be a prelude to using other support skills. If our partners interpret our messages in a way that makes them doubt our motives, they may be guarded in what they disclose. When we clarify supportive intentions, our partners interpret our messages and are less likely to search for a hidden agenda. In addition, stating that our objective is to support may help our partners to feel a little better, because they know that someone else is "on their side." Finally, once our partners know our intentions, they have a context for understanding our comments. When we don't overtly make our intentions known, our partners—who are in the midst of emotional turmoil—may misinterpret our attempts to comfort. Thus, when Julie says to Kathie, "I'd really like to help you work through this situation you've described," she begins to clarify her supportive intentions.

To clarify supportive intentions: (1) Directly state your intentions by emphasizing your desire to help. (2) Remind your partner of your commitment to your relationship (if necessary). (3) Indicate that helping is your only motive. (4) Phrase your clarification in a way that reflects helpfulness.

Let's consider a more complete example.

> David (*noticing Paul sitting in his cubicle with head in his lap and his hands over his head*): *Paul is everything OK?*
> Paul (*sitting up with a miserable but defiant look on his face*): *Like you should care. Yeah, everything's fine.*
> David: *Paul, I do care. You've been working for me for five years. You're one of our best analysts, so if something's going on, I'd like to help, even if all I can do is to listen. Now what's up?*

With his second response, David conveys his supportive intentions and desire to help. He then assures Paul that he is interested in his well-being. Then he points out the continuing nature of their relationship and Paul's importance to him. Finally, he directly states his willingness to help. Will this statement be enough to convince Paul to open up? Maybe it will. But if not, Paul can restate supportive intention and hope that a second expression will be effective.

> Paul: *Look, you've got a lot to do without listening to my sad story. I can take care of this myself, so just forget it.*
> David: *Paul, I do have lots to do, but I always have time to listen and to help you. I don't want to pry, I just want to help.*

Clarify supportive intentions—openly state that our goal in the conversation is to support and help our partner.

In his second message, David further emphasizes that Paul is important to him and that his only intention is to help.

People needing comforting can feel vulnerable and may need several reassurances of your supportive intentions before they are comfortable disclosing. So you may use several supportive intention messages as you interact. But you will also need to be sensitive to your partner's right to privacy. Repeated statements of supportive intentions can become counterproductive and coercive if your partner ends up disclosing information that the partner would have just as soon withheld. Supporters need to be sensitive to the fine line that exists between helping someone to "open up" and invading someone's privacy. If your only motive is to help the other, then there will be times when your own curiosity must be unsatisfied. Sometimes we can provide emotional support without knowing the full details of a situation.

Buffering Face Threats

Once you've clarified your intentions to provide support, you may discover that the very act of providing emotional support can be threatening to the positive and negative face needs of your partner (recall of discussion of face needs in Chapter 6). On one hand, providing emotional support can threaten positive face if your partners feel that you will respect, like, or value them less because of their situation. For example, Brianne's mother wants her daughter to respect her. So she is likely to be embarrassed and ashamed telling her daughter that she has lost her job.

On the other hand, providing emotional support can also threaten the negative face needs of our partners if they feel that our intrusion is a threat to their

SKILL BUILDERS   **CLARIFYING SUPPORTIVE INTENTIONS**

SKILL	**USE**	**PROCEDURE**	**EXAMPLE**
Openly stating that your goal in the conversation is to support and help your partner.	To enable your partner to easily interpret messages without searching for a hidden agenda. To communicate that someone is "on their side" and to provide a context for understanding supportive comments.	1. Directly state your intentions, emphasizing your desire to help. 2. Remind your partner about your ongoing relationship. 3. Indicate that helping is your only motive. 4. Phrase your clarification in a way that reflects helpfulness.	After listening to Sonja complain about flunking her geology midterm, her friend Deepak replies: "Sonja, you're a dear friend, and I'd like to help if you want me to. I did well enough on the midterm that I think I could be of help; maybe we could meet once a week to go over the readings and class notes together."

needs to be independent and self-sufficient. Support messages carry a hidden meaning. They say to our partners, "you are needy and require my help." So if Anne tells Cindy that she'd like to help her, Cindy may say, "I can take care of this myself, so just forget it." In this case, she is reacting to the negative face-threatening act (FTA) that Anne's supportive intention message unwittingly committed.

Because supportive messages are also FTAs, comforters need to "buffer" or cushion the effect of their messages by utilizing both positive and negative politeness skills. **Positive facework** messages protect the partner's need to be respected, liked, and valued by verbally affirming the person or the person's actions in the present difficulty. **Negative facework** messages support the partner's need for independence and autonomy by verbally using indirect methods when offering information, opinions, or advice.

To perform positive facework: (1) Describe and convey positive feelings about what the other has said or done in the situation. (2) Express your admiration for the person's courage or effort in the situation. (3) Acknowledge how difficult the situation is. (4) Express your belief that the other has the qualities and skills to endure or succeed.

In the examples we have been looking at, when David says to Paul, "You're one of our best analysts . . ." he is performing positive facework by expressing his admiration for Paul's work. In Brianne's conversation with her mom she could do positive facework in several ways. For instance, she could acknowledge how difficult it must be to be fired. Or she might tell her mother how much she admires her mom's determination to stay out of debt. Or she might indicate her firm belief that her mother is talented and resourceful enough to quickly find a new job. Each of

> **Positive facework**–messages that protect the partner's need to be respected, liked, and valued by verbally affirming the person or the person's actions in the present difficulty.
>
> **Negative facework**–messages that support the partner's need for independence and autonomy by verbally using indirect methods when offering information, opinions, or advice.

SKILL BUILDERS   **POSITIVE FACEWORK**

SKILL	USE	PROCEDURE	EXAMPLE
Messages affirming a person or a person's actions in the face of a difficult situation.	To protect the other's positive face needs (to be respected, liked, and valued) in situations where other messages are perceived to be FTAs.	1. Describe and convey positive feelings about what the other has said or done in the situation. 2. Express your admiration for the person's courage or effort in the situation. 3. Acknowledge how difficult the situation is. 4. Express your belief that the other has the qualities and skills to endure or succeed.	Jan has learned that Ken has suffered his brother's anger when Ken intervened in order to help him. Jan says: "I really respect you for the way you have acted during this. It takes a lot of guts to hang in there like you've been doing, especially when you've been attacked for doing so. I know that you've got the skills to help you get through this."

these statements (and countless others) can help Brianne protect her mom's self-esteem as she provides comfort.

Just as positive facework can mitigate the effects of FTAs to positive face needs, so too messages can be formed that reduce the effects that FTAs have on negative face needs.

To perform negative facework, form messages that (1) Ask for permission before making suggestions or giving advice, (2) Verbally defer to the opinions and preferences of the other person, (3) Use tentative language to hedge and qualify opinions and advice, (4) Offer suggestions indirectly by telling stories or describing hypothetical options.

The simplest, yet often overlooked means for performing negative facework is to ask someone if they want to hear your opinions or advice before you offer it. For example, we might say, "Would you like to hear my ideas on this?" At times, our partners are not interested in having us solve their problems, but instead want someone to commiserate. When we brazenly offer unsolicited opinions or advice, the FTAs to our partner's negative face needs may undermine the very support we are trying to provide.

Even when our partners have indicated that they are receptive to hearing our opinions and advice, we should be careful in how we word our messages. Our opinions and advice should be conveyed in a way that acknowledges that our partner is a competent decision maker who is free to accept or reject the advice. Messages such as "This is just a suggestion, you're the one who has to make this decision," express our deference to our partner's opinions. Our messages should use language that hedges and qualifies our opinions making it easier for our partner to disagree with what we have said. For instance, "I'm not sure this will work or that you would want to proceed this way, but if I were in a situation like this I might think about doing. . ." Finally, our supportive messages will be less threatening when we indirectly hint at advice and opinions by relating what others have done in similar situations or by offering hypothetical suggestions. As in, "You know when my friend Tom lost his job, he. . ." or "Gosh, I suppose one option might be to try. . ." When we use the skills of positive and negative facework in our supportive messages, we create a climate in which our partners can receive our comfort without feeling threats to their self-esteem or autonomy.

Other-Centered Messages

According to their theory of conversationally induced reappraisals (Burleson & Goldsmith, 1998), people experience emotional stress when they believe that their current situation is at odds with their life goals. Burleson and Goldsmith believe that to reduce emotional distress a person must "make sense" of what has happened. People feel better if they can re-evaluate specific aspects of the problem situation or change their opinion about how the situation relates to their goals. An important way that people form a reappraisal is by repeatedly telling and elaborating on the story (what happened to them). In this case the role of the comforter is to create a supportive conversational environment in which the emotionally dis-

SKILL BUILDERS   NEGATIVE FACEWORK

SKILL	USE	PROCEDURE	EXAMPLE
Using verbally indirect methods when offering information, opinions, or advice.	To protect the other's negative face needs (for independence and autonomy) when presenting opinions or advice.	1. Ask for permission before making suggestions or giving advice. 2. After stating the advice verbally defer to the opinions and preferences of the other person. 3. Use tentative language to hedge and qualify opinions and advice. 4. Offer suggestions indirectly by telling stories or describing hypothetical options.	Judy has learned that Gloria has really been hurt by the rejection from a best friend. Judy says: "Would you like any advice on this?" Gloria says yes, Judy then offers suggestion. "These are just a few suggestions, but I think you should go with what you think is best. Now, I'm not sure that these are the only way to go, but I think . . ." After stating her opinions, Judy says "Depending on what you want to accomplish, I can see a couple ways that you might proceed . . .

tressed person can tell and elaborate on the story and discuss feelings about what has happened.

During the comforting process a person may show his or her inability to "make sense." Using the skill of **other-centered messages,** a person utilizes active listening, expresses compassion and understanding, and encourages partners to talk about what has happened, elaborate on it, and explore their feelings about the situation.

For many of us, other-centeredness is difficult to master. We may have been raised in families or come from cultures that taught us not to dwell on problems or taught us that it is rude to pry into other people's business. Consequently, even when a friend or intimate starts the conversation, our gut reaction is to change the topic or make light of the situation. When Kristy switched topics and began discussing massages, she might have thought she was being helpful by "taking Tara's mind" off her troubles, or she might have been trying to relieve her own discomfort. Regardless, her topic change was not supportive. It took the focus off of Tara and didn't allow Tara the "space" to work through this painful situation. In our rush to help another, we may also inadvertently change the focus to ourselves. We can become self-absorbed, sharing our own stories, ideas, feelings, and advice instead of concentrating on providing verbal support to our partners.

Other-centered messages–utilize active listening, express compassion and understanding, encourage partners to talk about what has happened, elaborate on it, and explore their feelings about the situation.

The following guidelines are used in creating other-centered messages: (1) Ask questions that prompt the person to tell and elaborate on what happened ("Really, what happened then?"). (2) Emphasize your willingness to listen to an extended story ("You've simply got to tell me *all* about it, and don't worry about how long it takes. I want to hear the whole thing from start to finish"). (3) Use vocalized encouragement ("Uh huh . . .," "Wow . . .," "I see . . .") and nonverbal behavior (head nods, leaning forward, etc.) to communicate your continued interest without interrupting your partner as the account unfolds. (4) Affirm, legitimize, and encourage exploration of the feelings expressed by your partner ("Yes, I can see that you're disappointed. Most people would be disappointed in this situation. Is this as difficult as when . . .?"). (5) Demonstrate that you understand and connect with what has happen but avoid changing the focus to you ("I know that I felt angry when my sister did that to me. So what happened then?").

In the conversation between Tyrone and James that is on your CD-ROM and at the end of this chapter you will see Tyrone using a series of other-centered messages to help James tell and make sense of what has happened.

During supportive interactions, there are times when our partners lack awareness or may have trouble understanding some aspect of the problem situation. At these times, you can assist by providing information, opinions, or advice that can help them to understand or improve the situation. The supportive message skills of framing and advising assist us in forming messages that convey the information or advice in a supportive manner.

Framing

Framing–the skill of providing comfort by offering information, observations, and opinions that enable the receiver to better understand or reinterpret an event or circumstance.

Framing is the skill of providing comfort by offering information, observations, and opinions that enable the receiver to better understand or to see their situation in a different light. Especially when people's emotions are running high, they are likely to perceive events in very limited ways. Many times by sharing information, observations, and opinions we provide a different "frame" through which someone can "see" an event—thus giving them a different (and perhaps less painful) way of interpreting what took place. Consider the following situation.

Travis returns from his first date with Natasha, a woman he has been interested in for some time, he plops down on the couch, shakes his head, and says to his roommate Pete, "Well, that was certainly a disaster. We had a great time at dinner and saw a really funny movie. But when we got to her place, she gave me a quick kiss on the cheek, said 'Thanks a lot,' and quickly got out of the car, ran up the stairs, opened her door, and disappeared inside. I guess I'll chalk that one up. She's clearly not interested in me."

Travis has not only described the events, but he has interpreted Natasha's behavior as rejecting him. Yet, there could be information that Travis doesn't have or hasn't thought about that would lead to other interpretations. For example, Pete might know that Natasha has had several bad experiences with guys who were more sexually forward on first dates than she is comfortable with. He could help Travis to make a different sense or reinterpretation of what has happened by sharing this information: "I can see why you'd think that, it sounds like it was really abrupt. But

SKILL BUILDERS   **OTHER-CENTERED MESSAGES**

SKILL	USE	PROCEDURE	EXAMPLE
Expressing compassion and understanding and encouraging partners to talk about what has happened and to explore their feelings about the situation.	To help partners in their efforts to cognitively reappraise an emotionally disturbing event.	1. Ask questions that prompt the person to tell and elaborate on what happened. 2. Emphasize your willingness to listen to an extended story. 3. Use vocalized encouragement and nonverbal behavior to communicate your continued interest without interrupting your partner as the account unfolds. 4. Affirm, legitimize, and encourage exploration of the feelings expressed by your partner. 5. Demonstrate that you understand and connect with what has happened but avoid changing the focus to you.	Angie begins to express what has happened to her. Allison says: "Really, what happened then?" As Angie utters one more sentence and then stops, Allison says: "You've simply got to tell me *all* about it, and don't worry about how long it takes. I want to hear the whole thing from start to finish." During Angie's discussion, Allison shows her encouragement: "Go on. . .," "Wow. . .," "Uh huh. . .," and she nods her head, leans forward, etc. To affirm, Allison says: "Yes, I can see that you're disappointed. Most people would be disappointed in this situation. Is this as difficult as when. . .?" Allison then continues: "I know that I felt angry when my sister did that to me. So what happened then?"

I think you should know that Natasha has had some bad experiences on first dates with guys who were all over her. So maybe she wasn't rejecting you. She could have just been trying to protect herself." Suppose that Pete doesn't really know what is going on with Natasha. He might comment that his older sister told him that when she likes a guy, she finds the end of first dates particularly awkward. She doesn't want to embarrass the guy or herself by standing around waiting for a long lingering good-bye kiss that never happens. So, she uses the kiss-on-the-cheek ploy to save face and end things quickly. She figures that if the guy is interested, they'll get together again. In this way too, Pete provides Travis with a way of re-framing what has happened by seeing alternative interpretations that he has overlooked.

Sometimes the best way to provide comfort is to provide a different "frame" through which someone can "see" an event, giving them a different (and perhaps less painful) way of interpreting what took place. What might the coach be saying to reframe the situation for the player?

Our framing statements are supportive when they soothe our partners' feelings by helping them see alternative explanations for what has happened that are less threatening to their self-esteem. To form framing messages: (1) Listen to how your partner is interpreting events. (2) Notice information that your partner may be overlooking or overemphasizing in the interpretation. (3) Clearly present relevant, truthful information, observations, and opinions that enable your partner to reframe what has happened.

Notice how the framing statements in the next two examples provide comfort by suggesting less painful interpretations for events.

Karla: *I'm just furious with Deon. All I said was "We've got to start saving money for a down payment or we'll never get a house," and he doesn't say a word, he just gets angry and stomps out of the room.*

Shelby: *Yes, I can see what you mean, and I'd be frustrated too. It's hard to work through issues when someone up and leaves. But perhaps Deon feels guilty about not being able to save. You know his dad. Deon was raised to believe that the measure of a man is his ability to provide for his family. So, when you said what you did, unintentionally, you may have hurt his male ego.*

Micah: *I just don't believe Bradford anymore. We had my annual evaluation last week and she says my work is top-notch, but I haven't had a pay raise in over two years.*

Khalif: *I can see that you're discouraged. No one in my department has gotten a raise either. But have you forgotten that we're still under that salary freeze? At least Bradford is continuing to do performance* reviews so you know where you stand and what you should be eligible for when the freeze is over.

SKILL BUILDERS   FRAMING

SKILL	USE	PROCEDURE	EXAMPLE
Offering information, observations, and opinions with the goal of helping the receiver to understand or reinterpret an event or circumstance.	To support others when you believe that people have made interpretations based on incomplete information or have not considered other viable explanations that would be less threatening to their self-esteem.	1. Listen to how your partner is interpreting events. 2. Notice information that your partner may be overlooking or over-emphasizing in the interpretation. 3. Clearly present relevant, truthful information, observations, and opinions that enable your partner to develop a less ego-threatening explanation of what has happened.	Pam: "Katie must be really angry with me. Yesterday she walked right by me at the market and didn't even say 'Hi'." Paula: "Are you sure she's angry? She hasn't said anything to me. And you know, when she's mad I usually hear about it. Maybe she just didn't see you."

Giving Advice

Sometimes, we can also support others by giving advice. **Advice giving** messages present relevant suggestions and proposals that a person could use to satisfactorily resolve a situation. Advice can comfort our partners when we offer it after we have already established a supportive climate. Unfortunately, we often rush to provide advice before we really understand the problem or have developed a rapport that allows our partner to see the advice as helpful.

In general, advice messages (and to a lesser extent, framing messages) should not be expressed until our supportive intentions are understood, facework has been performed, and we have sustained an other-centered focus to the interaction. Only when we believe that our partners have had enough time to understand, explore, and make their own sense out of what has happened to them, should we offer advice to help them with unresolved issues.

Suppose Shawn is aware that his boss relies on him to help solve major problems that confront the firm. Yet, twice when positions that pay much more than Shawn's have opened up, his boss has recommended others who have done much less for the firm. When Martino becomes aware that Shawn is very concerned and doesn't know what to do about it, he takes the time to talk with Shawn and says. "Shawn, we've helped each other a lot over the years. May I offer some advice?" When Shawn nods, Martino goes on, "I know you have many choices—one of which is to get a different job. But if I were in your shoes, before I did anything radical I would make a point of seeing your boss and carefully stating what you've told me about his reliance on you and how you appreciate his confidence in you. And then I'd describe my disappointment at not being promoted, and then ask him

Advice giving—messages that present relevant suggestions and proposals that a person could use to satisfactorily resolve a situation.

why he hasn't suggested me for these jobs. Now this could irk him, but it seems to me that you might need to run that risk under the circumstances. Still, it's your decision. But I believe my suggestion is worth thinking about."

As we can see from this example, when giving advice (1) Ask for permission to give advice, (2) Word the message as *one* of many suggestions in a way that the recipient can understand, (3) Present any potential risks or costs associated with the following the advice, and (4) Indicate that you will not be offended should your partner choose to ignore your recommendation or look for another choice.

As you probably noticed, by its very nature, advice is an FTA to your partners' negative face needs. Advice implies that your partners are not competent to solve their own problems and thus need your help. So several of the guidelines help you form advice messages incorporating negative facework. Asking permission, phrasing advice as suggestions, framing the advice as only one alternative, and acknowledging your partner as a capable decision maker act to mitigate the face-threatening nature of advice.

Recall the earlier example of Brianne, who was providing emotional support for her mother in the wake of her job loss. Suppose that as her mother calms down she begins to discuss how she will provide for the family's financial needs. After her mother has considered and rejected several of her own ideas, Brianne might offer her own ideas:

Brianne: *"Mom, I have an idea if you'd like to hear it."*
Mom: *"Well, OK."*

SKILL BUILDERS   **GIVING ADVICE**

SKILL	USE	PROCEDURE	EXAMPLE
Presenting suggestions and proposals a partner could use to satisfactorily resolve an emotionally difficult situation.	To comfort our partners when we have established a supportive climate and they are unable to find their own solutions.	1. Ask for permission to give advice. 2. Word the message as *one* suggestion in a way that the recipient can understand. 3. Present any potential risks or costs associated with the following the advice. 4. Indicate that you will not be offended should your partner choose to ignore your recommendation or look for another choice.	After a friend has explained a difficult situation she faces, Felicia might say: "I have a suggestion if you'd like to hear it. As I see it, one way you could handle this is to . . . "This is just one idea—you may come up with a different solution that's just as good. So think this one over, and do what you believe is best for you."

Brianne: *"Well, this is just one alternative. If you don't like it, I'll understand. It's up to you. But here goes. Both Thomas and I are over sixteen. It's time we start helping with the family expenses. So we could each take a part-time job after school and on weekends. That way, you wouldn't have to take the first job you find. Maybe you could even take a short computer course at City Community College so you'd have more technology skills and wouldn't be intimidated when you were asked to work on the computer. I know that Ms. Hayes is looking for someone to take care of her kids from after school until she gets home from work, so I wouldn't even have to leave the neighborhood. Thomas is eighteen so he can probably get on as a clerk at the grocery store. It's union so the pay should be pretty good. I saw a sign up last time we were there. I haven't talked to Thomas yet, but I know that he loves you and will want to help out. The only downside would be that I wouldn't be able to get my homework done before supper, so I guess that will cut into my TV watching. And Thomas might have to spend less time with his girlfriend. Other than that, I can't see why this wouldn't work. What do you think?"*

TEST YOURSELF

Buffering Face Threats

Choose one of the situations below and write multiturn script in which you use the five skills of supportive messages to comfort the speaker. Identify which message skills are present in each of your turns.

1. Your best friend walks into the restaurant, flops down in the booth and sighs, "My manager is trying to fire me or get me to quit. He told me that my error rate was higher than average so he wants me to drive all the way downtown to headquarters, and take another ten hours of training on my own time."

2. As you turn the corner at work, you spy your co-worker, Janet, leaning against the wall, silently sobbing into her hand.

3. Your sister (or brother) storms in the front door, throws her (or his) backpack on the floor, and stomps upstairs. You slowly follow.

Notice how Brianne "front loads" her advice with negative facework. She presents her ideas and how her advice will solve the problem. Then she mentions the costs of this plan. Finally, she refocuses the discussion by asking her mother to comment on this proposal. Although Brianne's mother may reject this proposal, she is likely to perceive that Brianne was sincerely just trying to be helpful rather than perceiving Brianne to be inappropriately bossy.

People expect their relational partners to provide emotional support to them during times of stress or crisis. The five support skills we have just studied work together during supportive interactions to comfort our partners. If comforting behavior does not seem natural to you, you will want to work hard at adding these skills to your repertoire.

Gender and Cultural Similarity and Differences in Comforting

It is popular to believe men and women differ in the value they have for emotional support, with the common assumption that women expect, need, and provide more comfort. One view holds that men and women differ intrinsically in needing comfort, while another view holds that their differences are due to how they have been socialized. Yet, in a recent article Burleson (2003, p. 572) reports that a growing body of research finds that both men and women of various ages place a high value on emotional support from their partners in a variety of relationships (siblings, same-sex friendships, opposite-sex friendships, and romantic relationships). Studies also find that men and women have similar ideas about what messages do a better and worse job of reducing emotional distress. Both men and women find messages that encourage them to explore and elaborate on their feelings to provide the most comfort.

Unfortunately, while both men and women value other-centered comforting messages, research has also found that men are less likely to use other-centered messages when comforting. According to Kunkel and Burleson (1999), this sug-

WHAT WOULD YOU DO?

A Question *of* Ethics

Danny, who had been living with his parents for the two months following his college graduation, spent much time alone and at home since many of his old friends had left the town and he had not met many new people. One Friday, Sharon, one of his co-workers, invited him to a party she was attending. He told his mom that he would be out, but probably would not be too late because he wasn't feeling that well.

The party turned out to be great. Danny met a lot of new people and really enjoyed their company. It was three in the morning when four of the people he'd met asked him to join them for a while at an all-night coffee shop. Once there, the group got into a heated political discussion. It was about five in the morning when Danny finally headed home.

At about noon he awoke and went downstairs to get something to eat. His mother was working in the kitchen, and he noticed she had dark circles under her eyes. "How you doing today, Mom?"

"If you must know, I barely slept last night. I was worried sick about you. What time did you get in anyway?"

"I don't know, five or so. Look, mom, you can't worry about me all the time. I was having a good time for the first night since I've been home. You know, I've been really lonely around here and would think that you'd be glad that I was out with people my own age."

"Oh, so that's all the appreciation I get. Your father and I aren't any fun, huh?"

"That's not what I said—"

"We don't charge you rent, we feed you, and this is the thanks we get? I'm sorry I'm not as good as some college friends, but the least you could have done was call."

"I thought about calling," he lied, "but it was after one o'clock and I didn't want to wake you. Of course I do appreciate what you've done and are doing for me. Can't you understand, though, how I must feel? I'm a grown man and I need some space."

"Fine, maybe you better start looking for your 'own space,' then. But if you are going

to live here, you have to respect that I worry about you and can't have you out at all hours of the night. You are disrespectful and..."

"Mom, this is ridiculous. We shouldn't be having this conversation now—you're tired, and I just got up. I'm not thinking clearly or expressing myself well. Can we talk about this later?"

"Whatever, Danny. You'll have your own way like always. But if you get into an accident or something next time, don't expect me to be there to pick up the pieces."

With that, his mother stormed out of the room. Danny was left with a cold piece of toast wondering how his mother had misinterpreted everything he had said.

1. What ethical interpersonal guidelines did Danny and his mother violate during their conversation?

2. How was Danny responsible for what happened? His mother? What could either of them have said or done to make the situation easier?

gests that "we need more efforts directed at enhancing men's abilities in the comforting realm—both in school and in the home" (p. 334).

Research has also been directed to understanding cultural differences in comforting. While studies have found some differences, Burleson reports (2003, p. 574) members of all social groups find that solace strategies, especially other-centered messages, are the most sensitive and comforting ways to provide emotional support. According to Burleson, differences that have been found in studies include: (1) European Americans, more than other American ethnic groups, believe that openly discussing feelings will help a person feel better. (2) Americans are more sensitive to other-centered messages than are Chinese. (3) Both Chinese and Americans view avoidance strategies less appropriate than a direct approach, but Chinese saw these as more appropriate than Americans did. (4) Both Chinese and American married people viewed the emotional support provided by their spouse to be the most important type of social support they received. (5) African Americans place lower value on partner emotional support skills than do European or Asian Americans. This was especially true for African American women.

Overall, it appears that we are more than likely different when it comes to our desire to be supported by our partners and what types of messages we find to be emotionally comforting.

Summary

Responding with understanding and comforting others begins with being able to empathize. Empathy is shown through empathic responsiveness, perspective taking, and sympathetic responsiveness. When we have empathized we are in a position to provide emotional support and comfort. Empathizing requires detecting and identifying feelings of others. We can increase our ability to empathize through caring and concentrating. Empathizing is especially difficult with strangers and/or across cultures.

Supportive responses are comforting statements that reassure, bolster, encourage, soothe, console, or cheer up another. We can be supportive of another's positive feelings and experiences as well as comforting others in difficult situations. Supportive messages provide comfort when they provide a conversational environment that encourages the other to talk about and make sense of the situation that is causing them distress.

Effective comforting or supportive messages show a desire to help others, to express acceptance, to demonstrate care, to show availability, to be an ally, and to acknowledge feelings as well as to express sympathy.

Although we can attempt to comfort a person with a single statement, supportive interactions often go through the four phases of support: activation, support provision, target reaction, and helper response.

Research has identified the specific supportive message skills of clarifying supportive intentions, buffering face threats with positive and negative facework, using other-centered messages, framing, and giving advice. The desire to be comforted appears to be universal with little substantial differences reported between men and women.

Inter-Action Dialogue:

Providing emotional support to someone requires empathizing, clarifying your supportive intentions, positive and negative facework, use of other-centered messages, framing, and advice giving. Use your Inter-Action CD-ROM to view the dialogue between James and Rob and analyze the comforting behaviors of each.

A transcript of James and Rob's conversation is printed below. You can record your analysis of their behavior in the right-hand column, then complete your analysis online using the Inter-Action Analysis feature on your CD-ROM. From the Dialogue page, click "Analysis for James and Rob" to compare your comments to the analysis provided by the authors.

Rob and James meet after class.

CONVERSATION

ROB: *Hey man, what's up? You look rough.*

JAMES: *Well, I'm not feeling very good. But I'll get by.*

ROB: *Well, tell me what's bothering you—maybe I can help. I've got the time.*

JAMES: *Come on—you've got better things to do than to listen to my sad story.*

ROB: *(sitting down and leaning toward James): Hey, I know you can take care of it yourself, but I've got the time. So humor me. spill it, what's got you so down?*

JAMES: *It's my old man.*

ROB: *Uh huh.*

JAMES: *You know I hardly ever see him, what with him living out west and all.*

ROB: *That's hard.*

JAMES: *(lowering his voice and dropping his head): And, you know, I thought that now that my mom remarried and has a whole bunch of stepkids and grandkids to take care of that maybe I could go out to California to college and, you know, live with my dad.*

ROB: *Yeah, that's understandable. So, did you call him? What did he say?*

JAMES: *Oh, I called him and he said it was fine. Then he said we "could share expenses." Share expenses? I can't even afford the bus ticket out there. And I was hoping he'd pay for the college.*

ROB: *Ouch.*

ANALYSIS

Responding and Comforting

CONVERSATION

JAMES: *Rob, my dad's always had lots of money. Been living the good life. At least that's what he's been telling me all these years. He never sent the support money, but that's because he said he was "building his business." My mom's always been putting him down, but I believed him. Now I don't know what to think. What a fool I was.*

ROB: *Hey, you're no fool. Why wouldn't you believe him? But it sounds like he's been lying to you and now you're really disillusioned. Is that it?*

JAMES: *Yeah, I guess. You know, I always thought that when I was a man the two of us could, you know, get together. I love my mama. She's my hero. She raised me. but I always was proud of my dad with his business and all, and I just wanted to spend time with him. Get to know him.*

ROB: *I can relate. My dad died when I was young, but I'd sure like to have known him better. So have you told your mom about any of this?*

JAMES: *No.*

ROB: *What do you think she'd say?*

JAMES: *Oh, she'd probably just hug me and tell me to let it be.*

ROB: *Can you do that?*

JAMES: *Maybe.*

ROB: *Do you want my advice?*

JAMES: *Sure, why not.*

ROB: *Well, it's your decision, and I'm sure that there are other ways to handle it, but my advice is, do what your mom says—let it go. If he wants to see you, let him call you. You've got a great family here.*

JAMES: *Maybe you're right. I'm so tired of being let down. And my stepdad is a good guy. He's been taking me to the gym and we play a little ball in the driveway. He's not my dad, but even with all the other kids around, at least he makes time to be with me. I guess getting close to my dad is just not meant to happen. And I guess I don't really need him. If he can't even help with college then why would I want to leave here? I mean, I have great friends. . . right?*

ROB: *Right.*

ANALYSIS

Chapter Resources

Communication Improvement Plan: Responding

Would you like to improve your use of the following skills discussed in this chapter?

Empathizing   Other-centered messages

Clarifying supportive intentions   Framing

Positive facework   Giving advice

Negative facework

Pick a skill and write a communication improvement plan.

Skill: _____

Problem: _____

_____

_____

_____

Goal: _____

_____

_____

_____

Procedure:

1. _____

2. _____

3. _____

Test of Achieving Goal: _____

_____

Key Words

Empathy, *p. 211*

Empathic responsiveness, *p. 211*

Perspective taking, *p. 211*

Sympathetic responsiveness, *p. 212*

Comforting, *p. 217*

Supporting response, *p. 218*

Supportive messages, *p. 221*

Clarify supportive intentions, *p. 225*

Positive facework, *p. 227*

Negative facework, *p. 227*

Other-centered messages, *p. 229*

Framing, *p. 230*

Advice Giving, *p. 233*

Inter-Act with Media

CINEMA

Robert Mulligan (Director). (1962). *To Kill a Mockingbird.* Gregory Peck, Mary Badham, Philip Alford, John Megna, Brock Peters, Robert Duvall, Frank Overton, Rosemary Murphy, Paul Fix, Collin Wilcox, Alice Ghostley, William Windom; narrated by Kim Stanley.

Brief Summary: Based on Harper Lee's magnificent novel, this movie tells the story of three children and the summer during which they come to face their fears about their mysterious neighbor, Boo Radley, and the realities of Southern racism. Scout, Jem, and Dill have a summer of adventures trying to catch a safe glimpse of Boo. However, it is also during this summer that Atticus, Jem and scout's father, is asked to defend a black man (Tom Robinson) accused of rape and assault. The children learn of the harsh, ugly side of what their father does for a living, and of the racist traditions of their culture. When Scout goes to school in the fall, she must learn how to talk to children who are different from her and how to control her temper by dealing with her feelings and her self-talk. As the movie moves to its conclusion, Scout finally meets Boo Radley when he comes to Scout and Jem's rescue. Scout realizes that the man's gentle, shy ways should not make him the outcast that he is.

IPC Concepts: This film illustrates virtually every aspect of the communication process in interpersonal relationships. It deals with trust, perception, empathy, conflict, stereotyping, listening, cultural diversity, and the development of the self.

Sydney Pollack (Director). (1982). *Tootsie.* Dustin Hoffman, Jessica Lange, Teri Garr, Dabney Coleman, Charles Durning, Bill Murray, Sydney Pollack, Geena Davis, Estelle Getty.

Brief Summary: The film is about a man who ahs trouble finding work as an actor due to his dominating and demanding personality. As a solution, he poses as a woman in order to get a job on a television soap opera. His successful portrayal of the woman, both on and off camera, leads him to discover things about himself that he did not know. As Michael Dorsey (Hoffman) puts it late in the film, he was "a better man as a woman."

IPC Concepts: Self-presentation, perception, and stereotyping based on nonverbal behavior.

THEATER

Lane, B., & Harburg, E. Y. (1947). *Finian's Rainbow.*

Brief Summary: The play is a musical fantasy about racial injustice. This story is set in the South in the 1940s. An Irish immigrant and his daughter, their leprechaun, a pot of gold, and two young Southern men run afoul of a wealthy, old white aristocrat. As the story unfolds, one of the wishes granted by the pot of gold turns the old man into a black man. He then experiences what life is like for black people in the South. His newly discovered empathy gives him a unique perspective for the resolution of the play.

IPC Concepts: Empathy and diversity.

LITERATURE

Griffin, J. H. (1960). *Black Like Me.* New York: Signet.

Brief Summary: This is one of the most important books to emerge from the American Civil Rights Movement of the 1950s and 1960s. John Howard Griffin, a white man, had his skin pigmentation darkened so that he could pass as an African American and experience what life was really like for black people as he traveled around the South. His experiences present a fascinating discussion of what empathy can be like.

IPC Concepts: Empathy and diversity.

O'Brien, T. (1990). *The Things They Carried.* Boston: Houghton Mifflin.

Brief Summary: The story follows a small unit of soldiers in Vietnam. It focuses on their inner thoughts as they struggle to play their part in the war. They each manage to carry very few personal items with them into combat—items that remind them of their humanity, individuality, and hope for survival and peace. The items also serve as metaphors for the inner baggage that they carry.

IPC Concepts: Emotion, empathy, and self-talk.

ACADEMIC WORK

Goleman, D. (1995). *Emotional Intelligence: Why It Can Matter More than IQ.* New York: Bantam Books.

Brief Summary: Goleman's work advances the argument that emotion can function similar to intelligence for human development and maturity. He argues that we can have an emotional capacity just like we have a cognitive ability, an EQ like an IQ. Goleman explains that EQ is the inner dynamic that helps the individual develop self-control, confidence, persistence, and motivation. These capabilities can be taught when we are growing up. We can improve our EQ as we grow older as well. The concept of EQ helps us to explain why some people who are very intelligent do not seem to be able to function in life as well as people who are less intelligent. Goleman's work is filled with insight and helps balance our understanding of human development.

IPC Concepts: Self, emotion, self-talk.

LeCompte, A. (1999). *Creating Harmonious Relationships: A Practical Guide to the Power of True Empathy.* London: Atlantic Books.

Brief Summary: This book is a good resource for understanding how cognitive processes affect our behaviors and interactions with others. LeCompte discusses a variety of perspectives on the importance of understanding ourselves before we tackle our understanding of others. He discusses psychological research in the communication process and offers illustrations with teenagers and co-workers.

IPC Concepts: Empathy—approaches, increasing ability, responding with understanding.

Redmond, M. V. (1985). The relationship between perceived communication competence and perceived empathy. *Communication Monographs, 52* (4), 377–382.

Brief Summary: Redmond distinguishes the relationship between empathy and communication competence. He cites four dimensions of competence: behavioral flexibility, interaction management, support, and social relaxation. He offers an interesting definition of empathy and stresses the need to carefully define it for both research and understanding the process.

IPC Concepts: Empathy—nature, relationship to competence.

WHAT'S ON THE WEB

Annenberg CPB Project—Personality, Thoughts, and Feelings: What Makes Us Who We Are?

http://www.learner.org/exhibits/personality/thoughts.html

Brief Summary: This Web site focuses on thoughts and feelings and their relationship to behavioral traits, cognitive and emotional traits, and their role as the basis for many of our actions. The site also discusses the function of masks to hide our real self and the corresponding difficulty in empathizing with others.

IPC Concepts: Approaches to empathy, increasing our ability to empathize, interpreting empathic cues.

Empathy

http://www.utexas.edu/ftp/courses/kincaid/ddye/empath.html

Brief Summary: This site contains a very nice poem on empathy. It illustrates the nature of empathy as one person describes it by using a variety of metaphors for empathy.

IPC Concepts: Nature of empathy.

CHAPTER 9

Sharing Personal

Information:

Self-Disclosure and Feedback

After you have read this chapter, you should be able to answer these questions:

- What do we mean by self-disclosure?
- What are guidelines for disclosing?
- When and how does one describe feelings?
- What are the differences between displaying feelings and describing feelings?
- How does one own feelings?
- What is personal feedback?
- What is effective praise?
- How can we give constructive criticism effectively?
- How can we ensure receiving informative criticism?

"Chuck, when that interviewer at the grocery store asked you whether you'd rather have stuffing than potatoes, you said 'yes'!"

"Uh huh," Chuck responded, nodding his head.

"But you never told me you prefer stuffing."

"Well . . . No, I guess I never did."

"Chuck, we've been married more than twenty years and I'm just now learning that you like stuffing more than potatoes."

"Well, I'm sorry, Susan," Chuck said sheepishly.

"Chuck," Susan asked, "are there other things that you like or don't like that you haven't told me about during these more than twenty years?"

"Well, probably."

"Chuck—why aren't you telling me about these things?"

"Well, I don't know, Susan. I guess I didn't think they were all that important."

"Not important? Chuck, almost every night that I cook we have potatoes. We have mashed potatoes, baked potatoes, scalloped potatoes, potatoes au gratin, french-fried potatoes, home-fried potatoes. Chuck, I hate potatoes. I wouldn't care if I never saw a potato again. Now I find out you like stuffing better!"

"Sue, why didn't you ever tell me that you don't like potatoes?"

"Well I, uh-uh . . ."

Poor Chuck—poor Susan—all those years! But is their experience all that unusual? Do we take the time to tell others what we're really thinking and feeling? For a lot of people the answer is a resounding no.

As you have read in Chapter 3, self-disclosure and feedback are means of deepening relationships because it is through these exchanges that people learn more about themselves and each other. As you disclose you move information from the "secret" area of your Johari window to the "open" pane. Similarly, when your partner gives you feedback, information that is in the "hidden" area moves into the open area. As you both disclose and provide feedback to each other, you increase the intimacy of your relationship. Yet many of us don't really understand when self-disclosure is appropriate and how to share our feelings effectively with others. Similarly, we sometimes refrain from providing others with our observations about their behavior because we don't want to hurt their feelings or don't know how to begin politely.

Because the self-disclosure and feedback processes are fundamental to healthy relationships, in this chapter we explain these concepts and elaborate on the skills associated with each. More specifically, we discuss self-disclosure, disclosing feelings, owning feelings, praise, constructive criticism, and asking for criticism.

Self-Disclosure

Almost all effective interpersonal communication requires some degree of self-disclosure. In the broadest sense, **self-disclosure** means divulging biographical data, personal ideas, and feelings. Statements such as "I was 5′6″ in seventh grade" reveal biographical information—facts about you as an individual. Usually, biographical disclosures are the easiest to make, for they are, in a manner of speaking, a matter of public record. By contrast, statements such as "I don't think prisons ever really rehabilitate criminals" disclose personal ideas and reveal what and how you think. And statements such as "I get scared whenever I have to make a speech" disclose feelings. In terms of accuracy in understanding of self and others, it is this last sense in which most people think of self-disclosure—that is, revealing personal information that the other person does not know.

Self-disclosure is the heart of what is called "social penetration theory." The term *social penetration* was coined by Irwin Altman and Dolman Taylor (1973). Initially, they thought relationships' self-disclosure patterns moved steadily from shallow to deeper, more personal ones. Their research, however, has shown that levels of self-disclosure are cyclical. Relational partners go back and forth between achieving greater intimacy by disclosing more and developing distance by refraining from disclosure. This cycle allows partners to manage the tension between the need for privacy and protection and the need to be known and connected with each other (Altman, 1993, p. 27).

Why is self-disclosure difficult? When we self-disclose we "give" knowledge about us to someone else. Since information is power, the more someone knows about us, the greater is their potential to do us harm. So, for most of us, deeper disclosures occur only when we have developed trust that the other person will not use what we have disclosed to hurt us. This is why we disclose biographic and demographic information early in a relationship and more personal information in a more developed relationship (Dindia, Fitzpatrick, & Kenny, 1997, p. 408).

Although knowing a person better may well result in closer interpersonal relations, learning too much too soon about a person may result in alienation. If what we learn about another person causes us to lose trust in the person, our affection is likely to wane—hence the saying, "Familiarity breeds contempt." Because some people fear that their disclosures could have negative rather than positive consequences for their relationships, they refrain from disclosing.

So, although self-disclosure can help people become more intimate with each other, unlimited self-disclosure may have negative effects. By far the most consistent finding of the research on self-disclosure is that self-disclosure is most positive when it is reciprocated (Berg & Derlega, 1987, p. 4). That means that the amount of self-disclosure engaged in by each partner in a relationship should be approximately equal.

Self disclosure—divulging biographical data, personal ideas, and feelings.

Guidelines for Appropriate Self-Disclosure

The following guidelines will help you engage in self-disclosures that can build and sustain healthy relationships.

Through self-disclosure, people move their relationship from non-intimate levels to deeper more personal ones.

1. Self-disclose the kind of information you want others to disclose to you. When people are getting to know others, they begin by sharing information that they see as normally shared freely among people in that type of relationship in that culture. At early stages in the relationship this might include information about interests such as sports, music, TV shows, movies, schools, and views of current events. One way that people signal that a relationship may be moving to a deeper level is when one partner takes a risk and discloses something that would normally be perceived as more appropriate to a more intimate relationship. This disclosure "tests" a new level. If after some time the other person has not reciprocated, then the disclosing partner should reassess the potential for a deeper relationship.

2. Self-disclose more intimate information only when you believe the disclosure represents an acceptable risk. There is always some risk involved in disclosing, but as trust in the relationship grows, you may perceive that disclosure is more revealing in another person, you perceive that disclosing more revealing information is less threatening and, therefore, the risk becomes acceptable. Incidentally, this guideline explains why people sometimes engage in intimate self-disclosure with bartenders or with people they meet in travel. They perceive the disclosures as safe (representing reasonable risk) because the person either does not know them or is in no position to use the information against them. Unfortunately, some people apparently lack the kinds of relationships with family and friends that would enable them to make these kinds of disclosures to them.

3. Continue intimate self-disclosure only if it is reciprocated. Based on the research, it appears that people expect a kind of equity in self-disclosure (Derlega, Metts, Petronio, & Margulis, 1993, p. 33). When it is apparent that self-disclosure will not be returned, you should limit the disclosures you make. Lack of reciprocity usually means that the other person does not wish for the relationship to become more intimate.

4. Move self-disclosure to deeper levels gradually. Because listening to another's self-disclosure can be as threatening as disclosing, people become uncomfortable when the nature of disclosures continually exceeds their preferences for the relationship. Over time, if a relationship matures, deeper disclosure increases as well.

5. Reserve personal sensitive self-disclosure for ongoing intimate relationships. Disclosures about your fears, loves, and deep or intimate secrets are most appropriate in close, well-established relationships. When people disclose deep secrets to acquaintances, they are engaging in potentially threatening behavior. Making such disclosures before a bond of trust is established risks alienating the other person. Moreover, people are often embarrassed by and hostile toward others who try to saddle them with personal information in an effort to establish a relationship where none exists.

INTER-ACT WITH

Technology

While you are online, do you ever go to a chat room where you are talking with people whom you do not really know? Consider both your own and the contributions of those with whom you are "chatting." How do the levels of self-disclosure differ from conversations that you have with people you are conversing with in person? Under which circumstances do you and/or others seem willing to disclose personal information online? ■

Cultural and Gender Differences

As we might expect, levels of self-disclosure and appropriateness of disclosure differ from culture to culture. The United States is considered an informal culture (Samovar & Stefani, 2001, p. 82). As a result, Americans tend to disclose more about themselves than people from other cultures. The level of formality in a culture can be seen in how people dress, the forms of address they use, and the amount of self-disclosure. Germany, for instance, a country that is like the United States in many ways, has a much higher degree of formality. Germans are likely to dress well even if just visiting friends or going to school. They also use formal titles in their interactions with others. And they have fewer close friends. A German proverb states, "A friend to everyone is a friend to no one." Japan is another country that has a much higher degree of formality than the United States.

Particularly in the beginning stages of a cross-cultural friendship, these differences can easily lead to misperceptions and discomfort. For instance, a person from the United States may perceive an acquaintance from an Eastern culture as reserved or less interested in pursuing a "genuine" friendship because of less disclosing, whereas the acquaintance may see the American as discourteously or embarrassingly expressive about personal feelings and other private matters. When we are aware that cultural differences call for varying levels of disclosure, we can vary our level of disclosure so that it is appropriate for our friend.

Regardless of these cultural differences, however, Gudykunst and Kim have discovered that, across cultures, when relationships become more intimate, self-disclosure increases. In addition, they found that the more partners disclosed to each other, the more they were attracted to each other and the more uncertainty about each other was reduced (Gudykunst & Kim, 1997, p. 325).

Consistent with what you might expect, women tend to disclose more than men, are disclosed to more than men, and are more aware than men of cues that affect their amount of self-disclosure (Reis, 1998, p. 213). In their discussion of differences in disclosure, Pearson, West, & Turner (1995, p. 164) suggest that women may disclose more because they are expected to (a kind of self-fulfilling prophecy), because self-disclosing is more important to women, and because the results are more satisfying to women. Interestingly, both men and women report that they disclose more intimate information to women (Stewart, Cooper, Stewart, & Friedley, 1998, p. 110).

Differences in learned patterns of self-disclosure can create misunderstandings between men and women, especially in intimate relationships. In *You Just Don't Understand*, Deborah Tannen (1990, p. 48) argues that in their disclosure patterns men are more likely to engage in **report-talk** (sharing information, displaying knowledge, negotiating, and preserving independence) while women engage in **rapport-talk** (sharing experiences and stories to establish bonds with others). When men and women fail to recognize these differences in disclosure patterns, the stage is set for misunderstandings about whether or not they are being truly open and intimate with one another. "Learning about style differences won't make them go away," Tannen remarks, "but it can banish mutual mystification and blame."

> **Report-talk**—sharing information, displaying knowledge, negotiating, and preserving independence.
>
> **Rapport-talk**—sharing experiences and stories to establish bonds with others.

Disclosing Feelings

At the heart of intimate self-disclosure is sharing your feelings with someone else. And sharing feelings is a risky business. Yet, all of us experience feelings and have to decide whether and how to deal with them. Obviously, one option is to withhold or mask our feelings. But if we decide to disclose our feelings, we can display them or we can describe them.

Masking Feelings

> **Masking feelings**—concealing verbal or nonverbal cues that would enable others to understand the emotions that a person is actually feeling.

In our culture, **masking feelings**—concealing verbal or nonverbal cues that would enable others to understand the emotions that a person is actually feeling—is considered unhealthy and generally regarded as an inappropriate means of dealing with feelings. Masking feelings behavior is exemplified by the good poker player who develops a "poker face"—a neutral look that is impossible to decipher, always the same whether the player's cards are good or bad. Unfortunately, many people use poker faces in their relationships, so that no one knows whether they are hurt, excited, or saddened. For instance, Jerome feels very nervous when Anita stands over him while he is working on his report. When Anita says "That first paragraph isn't very well written," Jerome begins to seethe, yet his expression remains impassive and he says nothing.

Habitually masking feelings leads to a variety of physical problems, including ulcers and heart disease, as well as psychological problems such as anxiety and depression. Moreover, people who withhold feelings are often perceived as cold, undemonstrative, and not much fun to be around.

Is masking your feelings ever appropriate? Perhaps. When a situation is inconsequential, you may well choose to mask your feelings. For instance, a stranger's inconsiderate behavior at a party may bother you, but there is often little to be gained by disclosing your feelings about it. You don't have an ongoing relationship with the person, and you can deal with the situation simply by moving to another part of the room. In the example of Jerome seething at Anita's behavior, however, masking could be costly to both parties because Jerome's feelings of irritation and tension are likely to affect their working relationship as well as Jerome's well-being.

Displaying Feelings

Displaying feelings is the expression of feelings through facial reactions, body responses, or paralinguistic reactions. Although displays of feelings may be accompanied by verbal messages, the feelings themselves are acted out in the nonverbal behavior. Spontaneous cheering over a great play at a sporting event, howling when you bang your head against the car doorjamb, and patting a co-worker on the back for doing something well are all displays of feelings.

Displays are usually appropriate when the feelings you are experiencing are positive. For instance, if your friend Gloria does something nice for you, and you feel thankful, she is likely to view the big hug you give her as appropriate; when your supervisor gives you an assignment you've wanted, a big smile and a "Thank

Displaying feelings—expressing feelings through facial reactions, body responses, or paralinguistic reactions.

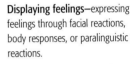

We display feelings through facial reactions, body responses, or paralinguistic reactions. Are the emotions being expressed by each of these women similar? What differences do you detect?

you" is an appropriate display of your feeling of appreciation. In fact, many people need to be more demonstrative of good feelings than they typically are. The bumper sticker "Have you hugged your kid today?" reinforces the point that people we care about need open displays of love and affection.

Displaying feelings becomes detrimental to relationships when the feelings you are experiencing are negative—especially when a display of a negative feelings is perceived to threaten the other. For instance, when Anita says to Jerome "That first paragraph isn't very well written," Jerome might display his feelings of resentment by shouting "Who the hell asked you for your opinion?" This display would probably shock, embarrass, and offend Anita and damage their communication. Although a display of negative feelings may make you feel better temporarily, the frustration or anger that is being experienced is likely to make the other person defensive and damage the conversational climate.

Since displays of feeling often serve as an escape valve for very strong emotions, they can be a more healthy approach to feelings than masking because at least we "get them out of our system." Unfortunately, negative emotional displays can damage our relationships and cause stress in our relational partners. Rather than just display our emotions, we can use the self-disclosure skill of describing feelings to help us share our feelings with others in an appropriate manner.

Describing Feelings

Describing feelings–naming emotions you are feeling without judging them.

Describing feelings is the skill of naming the emotions you are feeling without judging them. Describing feelings increases the likelihood of having a positive interaction and decreases the chances of creating defensiveness. Moreover, when we describe our feelings, we teach others how to treat us because we explain how what has happened affects us. This knowledge gives our relational partners information that they can use to help us deal with our emotions. For example, if you tell Paul that you enjoy it when he visits you, your description of how you feel should encourage him to visit you again. Likewise, when you tell Tony that you are annoyed that he borrows your jacket without asking, he is more likely to ask the next time. Describing your feelings allows you to exercise a measure of control over others' behavior simply by making them aware of the effects their actions have on you.

Many times people think they are describing their feelings when they are displaying feelings or evaluating the other person's behavior. For instance, when questioned, Jerome may believe his outburst,

"Who the hell asked you for your opinion?" is a description of feelings, but it is not. The Test Yourself exercise at the end of this section gives you practice in clarifying the difference between describing feelings, displaying feelings, and expressing evaluations.

If describing feelings is an effective way to communicate, why don't more people do it regularly? There seem to be at least six reasons why people don't describe feelings.

1. Many people mistakenly believe that by saying "I feel" that they are describing their feelings when they are actually evaluating others. Consider the sentence "I feel like you insulted me when you said that I . . ." While the speaker may believe that he has described a feeling, rather than describing a feeling this statement blames. So the use of "I feel" doesn't automatically lead to a description of an emotional state. Stop and think—if a person says something that you perceive as insulting how might you *feel?* Perhaps you feel hurt, rejected, or betrayed. If so, then the descriptive statement might be "I feel hurt (or rejected, or betrayed) when you say that I . . ." Notice how this statement would describe a particular feeling. Let's look at one more example. Suppose that your brother screamed at you for something you did and you said, "I feel that you're angry with me," your statement echoes what the other person said, but does not describe your present feelings. To describe your feelings, you might say "When you talk to me in an angry tone of voice, I feel hurt (or upset, pained, distressed)."

2. Many people do not have an active vocabulary of words for describing the various feelings they experience. They can sense that they are angry; however, they may not be able to distinguish between feeling angry and feeling annoyed, betrayed, cheated, crushed, disturbed, envious, furious, infuriated, outraged, or shocked. Each of these words describes a slightly different aspect of what many people lump together as anger. As shown in Table 9.1, we have a surprising number of words that represent the feelings we experience. If you are to become more effective in describing your feelings, you may first need to work to develop a more complete "vocabulary of emotions."

3. Many people are afraid that describing their true feelings will make them too vulnerable. It is true that if you tell people what hurts you, you risk their using the information against you when they want to hurt you on purpose. So it is safer to act angry than to be honest and describe the hurt you feel; it is safer to appear indifferent than to share your happiness and risk being made fun of. Nevertheless, if you don't take reasonable risks to disclose your feelings in your relationships, you risk having others misunderstand you.

For instance, if Pete calls you by a derogatory nickname that embarrasses you, and you tell Pete that you're embarrassed, Pete has the option of continuing to call you by that name. But if he cares about you, he is likely to stop. On the other hand, if you don't describe your feelings to Pete, he's probably going to continue calling you by that name simply because he doesn't realize that you don't like it. By saying nothing, you reinforce his behavior. While the level of risk varies with each situation, in a healthy relationship, you will more likely improve a relationship by describing your feelings than damage it by doing so.

4. Many people fear that if they describe their real feelings, others will judge them or make them feel guilty about having such feelings. At a tender age, we all learned about "tactful" behavior. Under the premise that "the truth sometimes hurts," we learn to avoid the truth by not saying anything

OBSERVE & ANALYZE

Journal Activity

The Vocabulary of Emotions

Look at each word in Table 9.1, say "I feel. . . ," and try to experience the feeling the word describes. Next make a list of those feelings that you recognize as ones that you experience. Then recall recent situations where you could have used each of these words. Write the message that would have been appropriate for each situation. ■

Table 9.1 A list of more than 200 words that can describe feelings

Words related to *Angry*

agitated	annoyed	bitter	cranky
enraged	exasperated	furious	hostile
incensed	indignant	infuriated	irked
irritated	mad	offended	outraged
peeved	resentful	riled	steamed

Words related to *Helpful*

agreeable	amiable	beneficial	caring
collegial	compassionate	constructive	cooperative
cordial	gentle	kindly	neighborly
obliging	supportive	useful	warm

Words related to *Loving*

adoring	affectionate	amorous	aroused
caring	charming	fervent	gentle
heavenly	passionate	sensitive	tender

Words related to *Embarrassed*

abashed	anxious	chagrined	confused
conspicuous	disconcerted	disgraced	distressed
flustered	humbled	humiliated	jittery
overwhelmed	rattled	ridiculous	shame faced
sheepish	silly	troubled	uncomfortable

Words related to *Surprised*

astonished	astounded	baffled	bewildered
confused	distracted	flustered	jarred
jolted	mystified	perplexed	puzzled
rattled	shocked	startled	stunned

Words related to *Fearful*

afraid	agitated	alarmed	anxious
apprehensive	bullied	cornered	frightened
horrified	jittery	jumpy	nervous
petrified	scared	shaken	terrified
threatened	troubled	uneasy	worried

Words related to *Disgusted*

afflicted	annoyed	nauseated	outraged
repelled	repulsed	revolted	sickened

Table 9.1 A list of more than 200 words that can describe feelings—cont.

Words related to *Hurt*

abused	awful	cheated	deprived
deserted	desperate	dismal	dreadful
forsaken	hassled	ignored	isolated
mistreated	offended	oppressed	pained
piqued	rejected	resentful	rotten
scorned	slighted	snubbed	wounded

Words related to *Belittled*

betrayed	defeated	deflated	demeaned
diminished	disparaged	downgraded	foolish
helpless	inadequate	incapable	inferior
insulted	persecuted	powerless	underestimated
undervalued	unfit	unworthy	useless

Words related to *Happy*

blissful	charmed	cheerful	contented
delighted	ecstatic	elated	exultant
fantastic	giddy	glad	gratified
high	joyous	jubilant	merry
pleased	satisfied	thrilled	tickled

Words related to *Lonely*

abandoned	alone	bored	deserted
desolate	discarded	empty	excluded
forlorn	forsaken	ignored	isolated
jilted	lonesome	lost	rejected
renounced	scorned	slighted	snubbed

Words related to *Sad*

blue	crestfallen	dejected	depressed
dismal	dour	downcast	gloomy
heavyhearted	joyless	low	melancholy
mirthless	miserable	moody	morose
pained	sorrowful	troubled	weary

Words related to *Energetic*

animated	bold	brisk	dynamic
eager	forceful	frisky	hardy
inspired	kinetic	lively	peppy
potent	robust	spirited	sprightly
spry	vibrant	vigorous	vivacious

or by telling "little" lies. Perhaps when you were young, your mother said, "Don't forget to give Grandma a great big kiss." At that time, you may have blurted out, "Ugh—it makes me feel yucky to kiss Grandma. She's got a mustache." If your mother then responded, "That's terrible—your grandma loves you. Now you give her a kiss and never let me hear you talk like that again!," you probably felt guilty for having this "wrong" feeling. Yet the thought of kissing your grandmother did make you feel "yucky," whether it should have or not. In this case, the issue was not your having the feelings but the way you talked about them.

5. Many people fear that describing feelings will cause harm to others or to the relationship. If it really bothers Theo when Lana, his girlfriend, bites her fingernails, Theo may fear that describing his feelings would hurt her and drive a wedge into their relationship. So it's better if Theo says nothing, right? Wrong! If Theo says nothing, he may still be irritated by Lana's behavior. In fact, as time goes on, Theo's irritation may grow and he may eventually distance himself from her because he can't bring himself to talk about the behavior that really bothers him. Lana will be confused and hurt by Theo's coolness, but she won't understand why. If Theo describes his feelings to Lana in a nonjudgmental way, however, they may begin a conversation that allows Lana to understand Theo's feelings and permits them to work on

TEST YOURSELF

Statements that Describe Feelings

In each of the following sets of statements, place a D next to the statement or statements in each set that describe feelings:

1. **a.** That was a great movie!

   b. I was really cheered up by the story.

   c. I feel this is worthy of an Oscar.

   d. Terrific!

2. **a.** I feel you're a good writer.

   b. Your writing brings me to tears.

   c. [You pat the writer on the back] Good job.

   d. Everyone likes your work.

3. **a.** Yuck!

   b. If things don't get better, I'm going to move.

c. Did you ever see such a hole?

d. I feel depressed by the dark halls.

4. **a.** I'm not adequate as a leader of this group.

   b. Damn—I goofed!

   c. I feel inadequate in my efforts to lead the group.

   d. I'm depressed by the effects of my leadership.

5. **a.** I'm a winner.

   b. I feel I won because I'm most qualified.

   c. I did it! I won!

   d. I'm ecstatic about winning that award.

Answers:

1. (b). (a) is an evaluation dressed in descriptive clothing—that the word "feel" is in a statement does not mean the person is truly describing feelings. "this is worthy of an Oscar" is an evaluation, not a feeling; (d) is a display.

2. (b). (a) is evaluative (there's that word "feel" again); (c) is a display; (d) is evaluative.

3. (d). (a) is a display; (b) is the result of feelings but not a description of feelings; (c) is an evaluation in question form.

4. (c) and (d). (b) is evaluative; (c) is similar to (a) except that here the feeling is described, not stated as an evaluation.

5. (d). (a) is evaluative, (b) is evaluative; (c) is a display.

the issue. Perhaps Theo can help Lana break the habit; or Theo might come to realize that Lana's biting her nails is not as big a deal once he has voiced his concerns.

6. Some cultures encourage members to mask their feelings and emotions from others. In cultures where harmony among the group or in the relationship is believed to be more
important than individuals' personal feelings, people choose not to describe their
feelings so that peace is maintained in the relationship.

The skill of describing feelings requires us to: (1) Identify what has triggered the
feeling. The feeling results from some behavior, so identify the behavior. (2)
Mentally distinguish what you are feeling—name the emotion; be specific. This
sounds easier than it sometimes is. When people experience a feeling, they will
sometimes display it without thinking about it. To describe a feeling, you must be
aware of exactly what you are feeling. Table 9.1 provides a vocabulary of emotions
to help develop your ability to select the specific words that describe them. (3)
Verbally state the specific feeling.

Here are two examples of describing feelings:

> *"Thank you for your compliment [trigger]; I [the person having the feeling] feel
> gratified [the specific feeling] that you noticed the effort I made."*
> *"When you criticize my cooking on days that I've worked as many hours as you
> have [trigger], I [the person having the feeling] feel very resentful [the specific
> feeling]."*

To begin with, you may find it easier to describe positive feelings: "You know,
taking me to that movie really cheered me up" or "When you offered to help me
with the housework, I really felt relieved." As you gain success with positive descriptions, you can try describing negative feelings attributable to environmental
factors: "It's so cloudy; I feel gloomy" or "When we have a thunderstorm, I get
really anxious." Finally, you can move to negative descriptions resulting from what

SKILL BUILDERS   **DESCRIBING FEELINGS**

SKILL	USE	PROCEDURE	EXAMPLE
Putting emotional state into words.	For self-disclosure; to teach people how to treat you.	1. Indicate what has triggered the feeling. 2. Mentally identify what you are feeling–think specifically. Am I feeling hate? Anger? Joy? 3. Verbally own the feeling. For example, "I'm (name the emotion)"	"As a result of not getting the job, I feel depressed and discouraged" or "Because of the way you stood up for me when I was being put down by Leah, I'm feeling very warm and loving toward you."

people have said or done: "When you step in front of me like that, I really get annoyed" or "When you use a negative tone of voice while saying that what I did pleased you, I really feel confused."

Owning Feelings and Opinions

Owning feelings or opinions (crediting yourself)—making "I" statements to identify yourself as the source of a particular idea or feeling.

A basic skill of self-disclosure, **owning feelings or opinions** (or crediting yourself), means making "I" statements to identify yourself as the source of a particular idea or feeling. An "I" statement can be any statement that uses a first-person pronoun such as *I, my, me,* or *mine.* "I" statements help the listener understand fully and accurately the nature of the message. Consider the following paired statements:

"Advertising is the weakest department in the corporation."

"I believe advertising is the weakest department in the corporation."

"Everybody thinks Collins is unfair in his criticism."

"It seems to me that Collins is unfair in his criticism."

"It's common knowledge that the boss favors anything that Kelly does."

"In my opinion, the boss favors anything Kelly does."

"Nobody likes to be laughed at."

"Being laughed at embarrasses me."

Instead of owning their feelings and opinions and honestly disclosing them as such, people often express their thoughts and feelings in impersonal or generalized language or attribute them to unknown or universal sources. Why do people use vague referents to others rather than owning their ideas and feelings? There are two basic reasons.

1. To strengthen the power of their statements. Saying "Everybody thinks Collins is unfair in his criticism," means that if listeners doubt the statement, they are bucking the collective evaluation of countless people. Of course, not everybody knows and agrees that Collins is unfair. In this instance, the statement really means that one person holds the belief. Yet because people may think that their feelings or beliefs will not carry much power, they may feel the need to cite unknown or universal sources for those feelings or beliefs.

2. To escape responsibility. Similarly, people use collective statements such as "everybody agrees" and "anyone with any sense" to escape responsibility for their own feelings and thoughts. It seems far more difficult for a person to say "I don't like Herb" than it is to say "No one likes Herb."

The problem with such generalized statements is that at best they are exaggerations and at worst they are deceitful and so unethical. Being both accurate and honest with others requires taking responsibility for our own feelings and opinions. We all have a right to our reactions. If what you are saying is truly your opinion or an expression of how you really feel, let others know and be willing to take responsibility for it. Otherwise, you may alienate people who would have respected your opinions or feelings even if they didn't agree with them.

Giving Personal Feedback

Sometimes in our interactions and relationships with others it is appropriate to comment on the other person's behavior. Messages of this type are referred to as "giving personal feedback." When personal feedback conveys empathy it can help the recipient develop a more accurate self-concept by identifying personal strengths as well as behaviors that may need to be changed. But when we are insensitive in how we phrase feedback, we can damage our relationships and may cause psychological harm to another person.

In some relationships we will need to consider carefully whether it is our place to give feedback; in other relationships we may be expected or required to provide it. For example, you may weigh whether it is your place to tell a friend that she has had too much to drink. But if you are a bartender in a state with dram shop laws, giving patrons this type of feedback will be required of you as part of your job. Similarly, managers, parents, social workers, and others are expected to give personal feedback to employees, children, and clients. So, improving our skills in giving feedback to others about both their positive behaviors and accomplishments and their negative behaviors will have broad use.

There are three skills that we use to give personal feedback. First, effective feedback includes describing behavior. Second, when we highlight positive behavior and accomplishments, we give praise. Third, when we identify negative or harmful behavior, we can provide constructive criticism.

Describing Behavior

When giving feedback many of us have a strong impulse to form our messages around generalized conclusions and evaluations we have reached based on what someone has said or done. So, it is common to overhear feedback like "You're so stupid," "Don't act like a jerk," or "You're really cool." These statements and countless others like them are attempts to provide feedback to the other person, but as stated these messages are evaluative and vague. At times some people may

SKILL BUILDERS   **OWNING FEELINGS OR OPINIONS**

SKILL	USE	PROCEDURE	EXAMPLE
Making an "I" statement to identify yourself as the source of an idea or feeling.	To help others understand that the feeling or opinion is yours.	When an idea, opinion, or feeling is yours, say so.	Instead of saying, "Maury's is the best restaurant in town," say, "I believe Maury's is the best restaurant in town."

not mind having their thoughts or actions judged, but whether the evaluation is positive or negative, feedback stated in this way is rarely helpful and can damage relationships and self-esteem.

Describing behavior—accurately recounting the specific actions of another without commenting on their appropriateness.

Rather than evaluating behavior, effective feedback uses the skill of **describing behavior**—accurately recounting the specific actions of another without commenting on their appropriateness. When we describe behavior we hold ourselves accountable for our observations and any resulting conclusions we have drawn. Consider the following situation. Steve and you are discussing the future of the Republican Party. After you have interrupted Steve for the third time, he could say either: "You're so rude" or "Do you realize that you have interrupted me before I had the chance to finish each of my last three sentences?" Which form of feedback would you feel better about receiving? The first message is a clearly an evaluative generalization and most of us would be embarrassed and might even become defensive were Steve to say this. The second message is an accurate description of our behavior. Since most of us already know that interrupting is not "good form," this feedback, describing the behavior but not voicing an evaluation of it, is more sensitive to our face needs and so provokes less embarrassment and defensiveness.

In other cases, feedback messages that evaluate rather than describe can be frustrating to the receiver. For example, telling someone, "You didn't really do a good job of leading that meeting," is not helpful since the message doesn't inform the recipient about the specific behaviors that led to your impression. As a result, the recipient doesn't know how to change in order to improve. A statement that describes the behavior is more helpful. For example, "Sandy, the meeting lasted an hour longer than was planned and when people brought up and discussed topics that weren't on the agenda, you didn't do anything to steer us back to the business at hand."

Describing behavior seems simple, but can be very difficult to do since it requires us to move backwards in the perceptual process. While we may base our evaluations on a generalized perception, describing behavior requires us to identify the specific stimuli on which our general perception was based. Steve may have concluded that my activity fit the pattern that he associates with the category "rude." But in order to describe my behavior, he must recall and verbalize the exact actions that led him to this conclusion.

The following guidelines will help you describe behavior: (1) Identify the generalized perception you are experiencing. (2) Recall the specific behaviors that have led you to this perception. (3) Form a message in which you report only what you have seen or heard without judging its appropriateness.

The skill of describing behavior is useful in a variety of feedback situations. Once you have described someone's behavior you may want to voice your reaction to the behavior. When your reaction is positive, you can send messages of praise, when your reaction is negative, you can provide constructive criticism. As you will learn in Chapter 11, describing behavior also is used when you wish to work collaboratively to resolve an interpersonal conflict.

SKILL BUILDERS   DESCRIBING BEHAVIOR

SKILL	USE	PROCEDURE	EXAMPLE
Accurately recounting the specific actions of another without commenting on their appropriateness.	Holding ourselves accountable for our observations and any resulting conclusions we have drawn.	1. Identify the generalized perception you are experiencing. 2. Recall the specific behaviors that have led you to this perception. 3. Form a message in which you report only what you have seen or heard without judging its appropriateness.	Instead of saying "She is such a snob," say "She has walked by us three times now without speaking."

Praise

Too often the positive things people say and do or the accomplishments that they achieve are not acknowledged by others. Yet, as you'll recall from our earlier discussion of self-concept, our view of who we are—our identity—as well as our behavior, is shaped by how others respond to us. Praise can reinforce positive behavior and help another to develop a positive self-concept. By praising we can provide feedback to others that what they have said or done is commendable.

Praise is a message describing the specific behaviors or accomplishments of another and the positive effects that this behavior has on others. Praise is not the same as flattery. When we flatter someone, we use insincere compliments to ingratiate ourselves with them. When we praise, our compliments are sincere and reflect our perception of the behavior or accomplishment. When we praise, our sole purpose is to inform others, not to curry favor with them.

For praise to be effective, we focus the praise on specific behaviors and accomplishments and word the message to be in keeping with the significance or value of the accomplishment or behavior. If a child who tends to be forgetful remembers to return the scissors he borrowed, that behavior should be praised so that it is reinforced. Saying "You're so wonderful, you're on top of everything" reinforces nothing, because this is an overly general statement that doesn't identify the particular behavior or accomplishment. Gushing to the child, "Oh, you remembered to return the scissors! I'm so grateful. That was just unbelievably thoughtful of you—I can't wait to tell your mommy about this! She will be so proud of you," is overkill that even a five-year-old will probably perceive as insincere flattery. An effective praise message might simply say something like, "Thanks for

Praise—describing the specific positive behaviors or accomplishments of another and the effects that this behavior has on others.

Praise should focus on a specific action and be in keeping with the value of the accomplishment.

putting the scissors back where they belong—I really appreciate that." This response acknowledges the accomplishment by describing the specific behavior and the positive feeling of gratitude that the behavior has caused. Following are two more examples of appropriate praising.

> Behavior: *Sonya selected and bought a group wedding present for a friend. The gift is a big hit.*
>
> Praise: *"Sonya, the present you chose for Steve was really thoughtful. Not only did it fit our price range, but Steve really liked it."*
>
> Accomplishment: *Cole receives a letter inviting him to a reception at which he is to receive a scholarship award given for academic accomplishments and community service work.*
>
> Praise: *"Congratulations, Cole. I'm so proud of you! It's really great to see that the effort you put into studying, as well as the time and energy you have devoted to the Second Harvest Food Program and Big Brothers, is being recognized and valued."*

While praising doesn't "cost" much, it is valuable and generally appreciated. Not only does praising provide information and acknowledge the worth of another person, but it can also deepen a relationship by increasing its openness. To increase the effectiveness of your praise, use the following guidelines: (1) Make note of the specific behavior or accomplishment that you want to reinforce. (2) Describe the specific behavior and/or accomplishment. (3) Describe the positive feelings or outcomes that you or others experience as a result of the behavior or accomplishment. (4) Phrase your response so that the level of praise appropriately reflects the significance of the behavior or accomplishment.

THE BUCKETS reprinted by permission of United Feature Syndicate, Inc.

If this cartoon is funny, it is primarily because it violates guidelines on effective praise.

Giving Constructive Criticism

Research on reinforcement theory has found that people learn faster and better through positive rewards such as praise, but there are still times when you will want to give personal feedback on behaviors or actions that are negative. While it's best to give this type of feedback when a person specifically asks for it, even when people don't ask, we sometimes need to give constructive criticism. **Constructive criticism** is describing the specific negative behaviors or actions of another and the effects that these behaviors have on others.

Constructive criticism—describing the specific negative behaviors or actions of another and the effects that these behaviors have on others.

SKILL BUILDERS   **PRAISE**

SKILL	USE	PROCEDURE	EXAMPLE
Describing the specific positive behaviors or accomplishments of another and the effects that the behaviors have on others.	To help people see themselves positively.	1. Make note of the specific behavior or accomplishment that you want to reinforce. 2. Describe the specific behavior and/or accomplishment. 3. Describe the positive feelings or outcomes that you or others experience as a result of the behavior or accomplishment. 4. Phrase the response so that the level of praise appropriately reflects the significance of the behavior or accomplishment.	"Marge, that was an excellent writing job on the Miller story. Your descriptions were particularly vivid."

Although the word *criticism* can mean "harsh judgment," the skill of constructive criticism is not based on judgment. Rather it is grounded in empathy and understanding. When we give another constructive criticism, our intention is to help, so we should begin by trying to empathize with the person and by forecasting how he or she will react to the feedback. Then we should work to formulate a message that accurately communicates while attending to the face needs of the message recipient. Unfortunately, most of us are far too free in criticizing others and we are not really all that constructive. At times we overstep our bounds trying to help others "become better persons" even when they aren't interested in hearing from us. Even when the time is right for giving negative feedback, we may not always do a good job of expressing it. While research shows that well-given feedback can actually strengthen relationships and improve interactions, feedback that is not empathically grounded or is poorly understood is likely to hurt relationships and lead to defensive interactions (Tracy, Dusen, & Robinson, 1987).

Before you give constructive criticism, you should make sure that the person is willing to hear it. If you don't know whether a person wants to hear what you have to say, ask. For instance, you might ask a group chairperson, "Are you interested in hearing my comments about the way you handled the meeting?" Remember, however, that even if the answer is yes, you must proceed carefully. You should also limit your comments to recent behavior that a person can do something about.

You'll be more effective in responding with constructive criticism by proceeding with the following guidelines:

1. Begin by describing the behavior. Describing behavior lays an informative base for the criticism and increases the chances that the person will understand what led to your conclusion. Feedback that is preceded with detailed description is less likely to be met defensively. Your description shows that you focus on the behavior rather than attacking the person, and it identifies what needs to change. For example, if DeShawn asks "What did you think of the visuals I used when I delivered my report?" instead of saying "They weren't very effective," a constructive critic might say, "Well, the font size on the first two was kind of small, and from where I was sitting I couldn't read them." This criticism does not attack DeShawn's self-concept, and it tells him what changes could be made to improve the visuals.

2. Whenever possible, preface a negative statement with a positive one. One way to address the face needs of the recipient is to begin your comments by praising some related behavior. Of course, common sense suggests that superficial praise followed by crushing criticism will be seen for what it is. But criticism that is prefaced with valid praise can reduce defensiveness. In the preceding situation, the comment "Well, the charts and graphs helped me understand the rate of change, and the color really helped us to see the differences, but the words on the first two overheads were

OBSERVE & ANALYZE

Journal Activity

Expressing Criticism

Think about the last time you criticized someone's behavior. Which, if any, of the guidelines for constructive feedback did you follow or violate? If you were to do it again, what would you say differently? ■

too small for me to read from where I sat." Here the praise that is provided is relevant and helps DeShawn by providing a complete description.

3. Be as specific as possible. The more specifically you describe the behavior or the actions, the more effectively a person will be able to understand what needs to change and how to change it. In our example, it would not be helpful to say "Some of the slides were kind of hard to read." This comment is so general that DeShawn would have little idea of what to change. Moreover, he might infer that every overhead needs to be redone.

4. When appropriate, suggest how the person can change the behavior. Since the focus of constructive criticism is helping, it is appropriate to provide the person with suggestions that might lead to positive change. So in responding to DeShawn's request for feedback, one might also add, "When I make overheads, I generally try to use 18-point type or larger. You might want to give that a try." By including a positive suggestion, you not only help the person with honest information, you also show that your intentions are positive.

TEST YOURSELF

Providing Feedback

For each of the following situations, write an appropriate feedback message.

1. You have been driving to school with a fellow student whose name you got from the transportation office at school. You have known him for only three weeks. Everything about the situation is great (he's on time, your schedules match, and you enjoy your conversations), except he drives ten to fifteen miles per hour faster than the speed limit and this scares you.

2. A good friend of yours has fallen into the habit of saying "like" and "you know" more than once every sentence. While you know she has a good vocabulary and is a dean's list student, she comes across as uneducated. She is about to graduate and has begun on-campus job interviews. Thus far she has been disappointed because every employer with whom she has spoken has rejected her. She asks why you think she is having such a hard time.

3. After being on your own for five years, for financial reasons you have returned home to live with your parents. While you appreciate your parents' willingness to take you in, you are embarrassed to be living at home. Your mother has begun to treat you the way she did when you were a child. Specifically, she doesn't respect your privacy. She routinely enters your room without knocking, opens your drawers under the guise of putting away your clean clothes, and yesterday you found her looking at your bank statement, which was in an envelope on your desk. You are becoming resentful of these intrusions.

4. Your professor in this class has asked you for feedback on his or her teaching style. Based on your experience in this class, write a message of praise and one of constructive criticism.

Asking for Criticism

At times we seek information from others in order to identify and correct our mistakes. Although asking for constructive criticism is the most direct way of getting feedback, people are often reluctant to do so because they feel threatened by criticism. Instead, people rely entirely on others' nonverbal cues. Yet even when we interpret nonverbal cues accurately, they fail to help us understand why our behavior missed the mark. Nor will such cues help us decide what changes are needed in order for us to improve. By using the verbal skill of asking for criticism, we can accomplish both of these objectives.

So, when do you ask for reactions from others? How do you put yourself in a mental position to listen to negative comments?

1. Think of criticism as being in your best interest. No one likes to be criticized, but through valid criticism we often learn and grow. When you receive a negative appraisal—even when you expected a positive one—try to look at it not as critical of you personally but as a statement that reveals something about your behavior that you did not know. Whether you will do anything about the criticism is up to you, but you cannot make such a decision if you do not know that the behavior exists or how it affects others.

2. Before you ask, make sure that you are ready for an honest response. If you ask a friend "How do you like this coat?" but actually want the friend to agree that the coat is attractive on you, you are not being honest. Once others realize that when you request an appraisal you are actually fishing for a compliment, valuable appraisals will not be forthcoming.

SKILL BUILDERS **GIVING CONSTRUCTIVE CRITICISM**

SKILL	USE	PROCEDURE	EXAMPLE
Describing the specific negative behaviors or actions of another and the effects that the behavior has on others.	To help people see themselves as others see them.	1. Describe the person's behavior accurately. 2. Preface negative statements with positive ones if possible. 3. Be specific. 4. When appropriate, suggest how the person can change the behavior.	Carol says, "Bob, I've noticed something about your behavior with Jenny. Would you like to hear it?" After Bob assures her that he would, Carol continues, "Although you seem really supportive of Jenny, there are times when Jenny starts to relate an experience and you interrupt her and finish telling the story."

3. If you take the initiative to ask for criticism, you will avoid surprises. Taking the initiative in asking for criticism prepares you psychologically to deal with the criticism.

Because many people are reluctant to give feedback that may be perceived as criticism, they're likely to keep their thoughts to themselves. The following guidelines will increase the likelihood that people will give you the kind of feedback that you want and really need to hear.

1. Specify the kind of criticism you are seeking. Rather than asking very general questions about ideas, feelings, or behaviors, ask specific questions. If you say "Colleen, is there anything you don't like about my ideas?" Colleen is likely to consider this a loaded question. But if you say "Colleen, do you think I've given enough emphasis to the marketing possibilities?" you will encourage Colleen to speak openly to the specific issue.

2. Try to avoid negative verbal or nonverbal reactions to the criticism. Suppose you ask a colleague how he likes your ideas for the ad campaign. When he replies "The ideas seem a little understated," you get a sour look on your face or you get so annoyed that you say "Well, if you can do any better, you can take over!" Your colleague will quickly learn not to give you criticism even when you ask for it.

3. Paraphrase what you hear. By paraphrasing the feedback, you ensure that you do not overgeneralize from what has been said.

4. Give reinforcement to those who take your requests for criticism as honest requests. Regardless of whether what you hear makes you feel good or bad, reward people for their constructive criticism. Perhaps you could say, "Thanks for the opinion— I'd like to hear what led you to that conclusion." In this way, you encourage honest appraisal.

SKILL BUILDERS   ASKING FOR CRITICISM

SKILL	**USE**	**PROCEDURE**	**EXAMPLE**
Asking others for their reaction to you or to your behavior.	To get information that will help you understand yourself and your effect on others.	1. Outline the kind of criticism you are seeking. 2. Avoid verbal or nonverbal negative reactions to the criticism. 3. Paraphrase what you hear. 4. Give positive reinforcement to those who take your requests seriously.	Lucy asks, "Tim, when I talk with the boss, do I sound defensive?" Tim replies, "I think so—your voice gets sharp and you lose eye contact, which makes you look nervous." "So you think that the tone of my voice and my eye contact lead the boss to perceive me as defensive." "Yes." "Thanks Tim. I've really got to work on this."

Asking for criticism does not require that you always act on every comment. You may decide against making a change in what you've said or done for other good reasons. But asking for criticism does enable you to make a conscious, rational choice about whether or not you will change your behavior.

WHAT WOULD YOU DO?

A Question *of* Ethics

The Local Employee Fraud Team (LEFT) was a newly formed task force comprising six bright, career-minded employees (four women and two men) whose job it was to design a system to uncover theft on the job for the Comptel Corporation. Their effectiveness hinged on their ability to work closely and secretly. Obviously, each member of the team had to be completely trusted by the others or else the project could fail.

Maria Sanchos, a Mexican American graduate of Yale Law and new member of the company, was excited to be assigned to such an important task force. She put in long hours and found the company of her associates pleasant, except for Theresa Waterson, the leader of the group. Her social skills were as bad as the stereotypical queen bee and Maria could not figure out why she, of all

people, had been appointed to head the project. Occasionally, Theresa would make statements that were colored with stereotypical biases, yet Maria wondered if Theresa really knew how it was affecting her. Increasingly Maria found herself angered by Theresa's views on issues of affirmative action and abortion, even though it had nothing to do with their work. Several times she felt like debating Theresa on these issues, but Maria knew herself well enough to know that when she debated, she could be verbally cruel. The harmonious relationship of the group was at stake and Maria would not risk the group's cohesiveness.

Although Maria was able to control herself in most settings, Maria began to be overly critical of Theresa's views during group meetings and harshly pointed out

what she considered to be illogical thinking and openly upbraided Theresa for her mistakes. When one of the men on the task force privately confronted her, she considered trusting him with her problem, yet she unconsciously feared that self-disclosure would make her seem weak, particularly to a white male. Several days later, when the two other woman in the group confronted her about her behavior toward Theresa, Maria broke down and told them her problem.

1. What are the ethical issues in this case?

2. Did Maria behave ethically in this situation?

3. If you were one of the women advising Maria, what would you recommend that she do?

Summary

In this chapter we have discussed self-disclosure and personal feedback. Self-disclosure statements reveal information about yourself that is unknown to others. There are several guidelines that can help you decide when self-disclosure is appropriate.

Disclosing feelings is especially difficult. We can deal with our feelings in one of three ways: mask them, display them, or skillfully describe them. Instead of owning our feelings and ideas, we often avoid disclosure by making generalized statements. The skill of making "I" statements can help us to more honestly assume ownership of our ideas and feelings.

Personal feedback builds relationships by providing information to others about their behavior and its effects. Positive feedback is accomplished through praising. Negative feedback can be delivered effectively by using the skill of constructive criticism. To learn what others think of your behavior, ask for criticism in a way that will provide you with the most meaningful information.

Inter-Action Dialogue:

Relationships move toward friendship and intimacy through appropriate self-disclosure and feedback. Disclosure includes report-talk and rapport talk. Effective disclosures own opinions and describe feelings. Giving effective feedback requires describing specific behavior and how it affects others. When the effects are positive, praise statements are used; when effects are negative, constructive criticism can be given. Use your Inter-Act CD-ROM to view the dialogue between Maria and Mark and analyze the comforting behaviors of each.

A transcript of Maria and Mark's conversation is printed below. You can record your analysis of their behavior in the right-hand column, then complete your analysis online using the Inter-Action Analysis feature on your CD-ROM. From the Dialogue page, click "Analysis for Maria and Mark," to compare your comments to the analysis provided by the authors.

Maria and Mark have coffee after seeing a movie.

CONVERSATION	ANALYSIS
MARIA: *That was a great movie! The characters were so fascinating and I loved the way we slowly learned about their childhood.*	
MARK: *Yeah, I liked it too, but at times it hit a little too close to home.*	
MARIA: *Really? How do you mean?*	
MARK: *Well, remember how as a little guy he spent so much time alone?*	
MARIA: *Yes, that made me feel kind of sad.*	
MARK: *Oh? Well, my mom and dad both had full-time jobs and my dad often worked a second one as well. So since I was an only child, and we didn't have any other family here, I spent a lot of time alone.*	
MARIA: *That must have been hard on you.*	
MARK: *In a way, yes, but I think it helped me to become independent, resourceful, and very competitive at games and sports.*	
MARIA: *Gee, I guess I understand independent, but why do you say being alone helped you to become resourceful?*	
MARK: *Well, usually no one was home when I came home from school and sometimes my mom had to work late, so I had to get my own supper.*	
MARIA: *So how did that make you resourceful?*	
MARK: *When there were leftovers it wasn't too hard to reheat them, but when there weren't any, I'd have to scrounge around in the cupboards and fridge. I wasn't allowed to use the stove or oven—just the microwave—so I sometimes had to be really creative.*	

Self-Disclosure

CONVERSATION

MARIA: *Really? What did you make?*

MARK: *I was a master of microwave black beans and rice. If you're lucky I'll make them for you someday.*

MARIA: *I think I'll pass. I ate enough beans and rice when I was growing up. My mom wanted us to identify with our "heritage" so she made a big deal of cooking recipes from her childhood a couple of times a week. Unfortunately, she's not a good cook, so we got pretty sick of it. Today, my favorite take-out is Thai—now that's cuisine!*

MARK: *I've never had Thai food. What's so great about it?*

MARIA: *Well it's very spicy-hot, with lots of complex flavoring.*

MARK: *Does it have much MSG? I'm allergic to that.*

MARIA: *I don't know. Hey, back to our previous topic. You said being alone also made you competitive. How?*

MARK: *Well, since I was alone and had no friends to play with, I'd work out ways to compete with myself.*

MARIA: *Really, like what?*

MARK: *I'd play "Horse." You play basketball, don't you?*

MARIA: *Sure. But what's "Horse"?*

MARK: *Well, Horse is usually played with two or more people: One person takes a shot and if he makes it, the other person has to attempt the same shot. If he misses he gets an "h." If he makes it, then he takes a shot and his opponent now has to try to make it. the first one to get all five letters, h,o,r,s,e, loses.*

MARIA: *So how'd that make you competitive?*

MARK: *Well, I used to play against my alter ego. Only he was a lefthander! After awhile I got so I was as good left-handed as I was righthanded. I think that's how I made first string on my high school basketball team. I'm not very fast, but I can shoot with either hand from about anywhere on the court.*

MARIA: *So spending a lot of time alone wasn't all bad.*

MARK: *No. In truth I learned to enjoy my own company and I still like to be alone a lot. In fact, I have trouble enjoying just hanging out or partying with lots of people. It kind of seems like a waste of time. I enjoy smaller groups or one-on-one time, but the party scene leaves me cold.*

MARIA: *Yes, I've noticed that when we're with the group, you don't have much to say. I used to think you thought you were better than us, but I guess I understand why you act that way now. Still, you might want to think about being more vocal. You're really an interesting guy and I think others in the group don't know how to take you.*

ANALYSIS

Chapter Resources

Communication Improvement Plan: Developing Relationships Through Self-Disclosure and Feedback

Would you like to improve your disclosure or feedback skills discussed in this chapter?

> Describing feelings
> Owning feelings and ideas
> Describing behavior
> Praise
> Giving constructive criticism
> Asking for criticism

Choose the skill(s) you want to work on and write a communication improvement plan.

Skill: _____

Problem: _____

_____

_____

_____

Goal: _____

_____

_____

_____

Procedure:

1. _____

2. _____

3. _____

Test of Achieving Goal: _____

_____

Key Words

Self-disclosure, *p. 245*
Report-talk, *p. 248*
Rapport-talk, *p. 248*
Masking feelings, *p. 248*
Displaying feelings, *p. 249*
Describing feelings, *p. 250*
Owning feelings or opinions, *p. 256*
Describing behavior, *p. 258*
Praise, *p. 259*
Constructive criticism, *p. 261*

Inter-Act with Media

CINEMA

John Hughes (Director). (1985) *The Breakfast Club.* Emilio Estevez, Judd Nelson, Molly Ringwald, Anthony Michael Hall, Ally Sheedy, Paul Gleason.

Brief Summary: A group of five high school students spends a Saturday in detention under the supervision of an angry, disrespectful, burned-out teacher. We never come to know their real names. We only know them as the Jock, the Princess, the Delinquent, the Brain, and the Weirdo. While initially presented as a group of stereotyped students, they each disclose enough information to become real flesh-and-blood individuals to each other and to the viewer. This film transcends time and generations in its ability to resonate with a wide range of age groups.

IPC Concepts: Self-disclosure, relationship building, conflict, diversity, expression of emotion.

Barry Levinson (Director). (1982). *Diner.* Steve Guttenberg, Daniel Stern, Mickey Rourke, Kevin Bacon, Timothy Daly, Ellen Barkin, Paul Reiser.

Brief Summary: This film is a terrific case study of conversation. A group of friends meets regularly in a Baltimore diner to discuss their lives, the problems of growing up, and the fun they have had. Students will find the movie to be a good vehicle for studying techniques of conversation.

IPC Concepts: Self-disclosure, relationship development.

Mark Rydell (Director). (1981). *On Golden Pond.* Henry Fonda, Katherine Hepburn, Jane Fonda, Doug McKeon, Dabney Coleman.

Brief Summary: The story is about Norman Thayer (Henry Fonda), a retired schoolteacher who is approaching his eightieth birthday, and his anger and fear of the effect of the aging process on his faculties and ability to function. He and his wife, Ethel Thayer (Katherine Hepburn), are visited at their summer cottage by their daughter, Chelsea (Jane Fonda), her fiancé, Bill (Dabney Coleman), and soon-to-be stepson, Billy (Doug McKeon). The stepson stays with Norman and Ethel for the summer while Chelsea and Bill travel to Europe. Norman and Billy teach each other a lot about fishing, conflict, and each other's perspectives on life.

IPC Concepts: Self-esteem, perception of self and others, self-talk, emotion, and conflict. Note the probable self-talk when Norman is lost in the woods. Also note his disclosure to Ethel about being lost in the woods and his admission to Chelsea about his feelings toward her.

THEATER

Albee, E. (1962). *Who's Afraid of Virginia Woolf?*

Brief Summary: This play, like the movie, is a powerful illustration of the damage that can be done by both not expressing feelings and by expressing them in the wrong way. Both couples are traumatized by the vile disclosure and hurtful barbs exchanged by Martha and George.

IPC Concepts: Disclosure and masking feelings, displaying feelings.

LITERATURE

Styron, W. (1979). *Sophie's Choice.* New York: Random House.

Brief Summary: In this powerful story we follow Sophie move from a fun-loving, carefree woman in playful romantic relationships to a mother who has to make the most difficult choice that a mother can make. The role of disclosure in both relationships, and personal mental health and well-being, is clearly dramatized.

IPC Concepts: Relationships and self-disclosure, masking and displaying feelings.

ACADEMIC WORK

Hugenberg Sr., L. W., & Schaefermeyer, M. J. (1983). Soliloquy as self-disclosure. *The Quarterly Journal of Speech, 69* (2).

Brief Summary: This article examines the nature of disclosure in research and argues that much can be learned about the nature of disclosure by studying its use in dramatic literature. The authors analyze the soliloquy as Shakespeare uses in *Richard III* and 3 *Henry III.* The article offers good examples and an interesting argument.

IPC Concepts: Self-disclosure, nature, qualities, and types.

WHAT'S ON THE WEB

The Six Steps to Self-Disclosure: A Guide for the Sender, by Marty Crouch, Pastoral Counselor.

http://www.martycrouch.com/Disclosure.html

Brief Summary: This Web page offers a good, simple reinforcement for some basics of the process of disclosure framed in terms of assertiveness theory. A helpful chart offers examples of five different types of content for disclosure.

IPC Concepts: Self-disclosure and assertiveness, describing feelings and opinions.

Perry, S. W., Card, C. A. L., et al. (1994). Self-disclosure of HIV infection to sexual partners after repeated counseling. *AIDS Education and Prevention 6*(5), 403–411.

http://hivinsite.ucsf.edu/topics/testing/2098.366e.html

Brief Summary: This site contains an abstract of a journal article on an important aspect of self-disclosure in relationships dealing with a serious illness or a contagious medical condition.

IPC Concepts: Disclosure and ethics.

CHAPTER 10

Using Interpersonal

Influence Ethically

After you have read this chapter, you should be able to answer these questions:

- What is interpersonal power?
- What are the sources of interpersonal power?
- How does interpersonal power affect influence in relationships?
- What does it mean to influence another?
- What ethical considerations affect influence efforts?
- What are the major means of persuasion?
- What are effective means of gaining compliance?
- What is assertiveness?
- How can you be assertive rather than aggressive?

> "As Chet and Marney were sitting at the table eating their breakfast, Chet looked and Marney and said, "Gimme the sports section."
>
> "What was that?" Marney replied.
>
> "I said gimme the sports section."
>
> "Chet, 'Gimme the sports section,' doesn't sound like a very loving husband."
>
> "Come on, you know I love you—but I want the sports section."
>
> "That's the point. You want something, but you're not sounding very considerate in the way you're trying to get it. Why don't you try this, 'Hon, would you please pass me the sports section?'"
>
> Chet paused for a second, and then said, "Hon, would you please pass me the sports section?"
>
> "I'd be delighted to—here," said Marney.
>
> A few minutes later, Chet looked up from his paper and said, "Gimme the sugar."

Stop for a minute and think of a time you tried to get someone to do something for you. Were you successful? Did you pay any attention to thinking about how you should proceed? Did you think about how the person you were talking with might react to the way you went about it? The opening chapter vignette is an example of a lack of real consideration for the other person—and it portrays a style that is all too common, even among people who say they "really care for each other." In this chapter we consider the issue of influence and how it can be achieved effectively and ethically.

Interpersonal influence—symbolic efforts to preserve or change the attitudes or behavior of others.

Interpersonal influence is primarily concerned with symbolic efforts to preserve or change the attitudes or behavior of others (Dillard, Anderson, & Knobloch, 2002, p. 426). It is fundamental to all human relationships and part of most conversations. Therefore, understanding influence processes and learning how to use influence ethically are fundamental to effectiveness in your relationships.

Historically, the formal study of influence was called persuasion. Thinkers and scholars across human history, including the Greek philosophers Socrates, Plato, and Aristotle, and the Roman orator Cicero, studied and wrote about persuasion. Over the years their ideas have been elaborated upon and refined. Today, the study of influence includes not only general strategies for persuasion, but also compliance gaining and assertiveness. In this chapter we will examine each of these areas. To understand influence, we begin by discussing interpersonal power which is the potential a person has in a relationship to influence the other.

Interpersonal Power in Relationships

Interpersonal power—a potential for changing attitudes, beliefs, and behaviors of others.

Interpersonal power is a potential that one person has for changing the attitudes, beliefs, and behaviors of a relational partner. John French and Bertram Raven (1968) proposed that people who have strong power bases will be effective in influencing others. Research has continued to support the claim that people "who are perceived as more expert, attractive, trustworthy, and credible" are likely to be more persuasive (Tedeschi, 2001, p. 116).

French and Raven (1968) identified five major sources of power in relationships: coercive, reward, legitimate, expert, and referent. In 1980, T. R. Hinken and C. A. Schriesheim published a study that sharpened our understanding of these sources.

Perception of Coercive Power

People have **coercive power** if they can harm their partners physically and/or psychologically should the partners resist the influence attempt. As with other types of power, a person can have coercive power and yet never intentionally attempt to use it to influence others. Nonetheless, unintentional influence may occur. This is humorously illustrated in the old vaudeville joke, "Where does a gorilla sit when it enters their room? Anywhere it wants to."

Whether a person actually tries to coerce a partner is not important. What is important is the partner's awareness that the potential is there. Thus, when we recognize that a person can harm us, we may accept their influence.

Coercive power—derives from the perception that people can harm their partners physically and/or psychologically should the partners resist the influence attempt.

Reward Power

People have **reward power** when they are able to provide their partners with monetary, physical, or psychological benefits that the partners desire. So if children perceive that their parents will praise them for cleaning their rooms, they are likely to comply when the parents request them to do so.

Reward power—derives from providing partners with monetary, physical, or psychological benefits that the partners desire.

In the classroom, which sources of power are most commonly available to professors?

Your reward power is based on how much your partner values the rewards you control, how likely you are to bestow the rewards regardless of your partner's compliance with your influence attempt, and how easily your partner can obtain these rewards from someone else. For example, Wendy really wants to attend the 'N Sync concert, but it has sold out (highly valued, not easily obtained elsewhere). Mitchell, her brother, has an extra ticket to this concert (physical benefit that could be provided). Wendy knows that Mitchell has several friends who would also like to go (other competitors for already scarce reward). And she knows of no one else with an extra ticket (no alternative source). Should Mitchell ask Wendy to clean up the dishes after dinner, she may comply, hoping to ingratiate herself so that Mitchell will "reward" her by taking her to the concert.

So, when the rewards you control are of great value to your partner, if your partner believes that you will not bestow the rewards unless he or she complies with your influence attempt, and if your partner does not have other sources for this reward, then there is a high probability that if you try to influence your partner he or she will comply because of the reward power you have. Likewise, if the rewards you control are not valued by your partner, or if your partner believes that you will give the benefits even if he or she does not comply with your influence attempts, or if the benefit can be obtained from some other source, then you will have lower reward power.

Legitimate Power

Legitimate power—derives from using the status that comes from being elected, being selected, or holding a position to influence a partner.

People have **legitimate power** when they use the status that comes from being elected, being selected, or holding a position to influence a partner. The power is called "legitimate" since, in many situations, failure to exercise authority has legal consequences. Teachers have legitimate power with respect to their students, parents with their minor children, older siblings with their younger brothers and sisters, managers with employees, and government officials with specific constituents. So speeders stop by the side of the road when they catch sight of the flashing red light on the top of a police car. Likewise, students may complete lengthy homework because they understand that their teachers have the right to make these assignments.

Expert Power

Expert power—derives from people having knowledge that their relational partners don't have.

People have **expert power** when they have knowledge that their relational partners don't have. Expert power is both subject and relationship specific. Because of her expertise, a friend who is an attorney has the potential to influence decisions about my divorce settlement, but since she is childless, her opinions on how I should raise my kids are not persuasive.

We believe people who appear to know more than we do. In your classes, your instructors can influence your thinking because they usually have more subject-specific knowledge and expertise than you do. Similarly, when our car mechanic, Cubby Saab, tells us that we need new brakes, we are persuaded, because neither of us knows much about auto mechanics.

At times we can be blinded by the perception of expert power. For instance, when buying clothing, a person can be intimidated into buying something by an aggressive sales associate. Salespeople, however, are not always fashion mavens; rather they are hired to sell and their product knowledge may be sketchy. As salespeople gain experience with a line of goods, they may acquire specific product knowledge that is valuable to their clients. We are always grateful to have a knowledgeable sales associate when we have to buy expensive items like a TV or computer.

Referent Power

People have **referent power** when their partners are attracted to them because of their physical appearance, image, charisma, or personality. Let's face it, we want to get along with and impress those we are attracted to and like. So we are likely to allow them to influence our ideas. If your best friend raves about a movie, you are likely to go and see it. The concept of "peer pressure" acknowledges the potency of referent power for adolescents. And corporations hire celebrities to endorse products knowing that they can draw on the referent power of the star in selling their product. Thus Pepsi hired Britney Spears not because she has reward, coercive, legitimate, or expert power, but because of her referent power.

> **Referent power**—derives from people being attracted to others because of their physical appearance, image, charisma, or personality.

Research studies consistently find evidence to support the notion that we can be influenced by those we find physically attractive. Today in the United States, both men and women undergo plastic surgery to increase their attractiveness. Job seekers wear specific clothing to increase the likelihood that they can persuade interviewers to hire them.

We are also attracted to those we find agreeable. Since we tend to like those who pay attention to us and treat us well, improving your interpersonal communication skills, especially your listening, supporting, and conversational skills, is likely to increase your referent power.

Types of Persuasive Messages

Persuasion is the skill of crafting verbal messages to influence the attitudes or behaviors of others using ethical means. It is an ethical means of influence since it relies on verbal arguments rather than force and allows others freedom to resist the influence attempt (Trenholm, 1989, p. 5). Crafting persuasive messages involves giving good reasons, presented by a credible source, in a way that arouses emotions.

> **Persuasion**—the intentional use of verbal messages to influence the attitudes or behaviors of others using ethical means.

Giving Good Reasons

Because people pride themselves on being "rational"—that is, they seldom do anything without some real or imagined reason—you increase the likelihood of persuading them if you can provide them with good reasons. **Reasons** are statements that provide the basis or cause for some behavior or action. They answer the question "Why?" As you think about your efforts to influence, you can probably think

> **Reasons**—statements that provide the basis or cause for some behavior or action.

Claims—statements of belief or requests for action.

of many times that after you made a **claim** (a statement of belief or a request for action) the person you were talking with asked "Why?" In effect, that person is saying, "I can't accept what you've said on face value—give me some reasons!" Suppose I'm talking with a friend about movies, I might ask, "Have you seen *My Big Fat Greek Wedding?*" If my friend says "No," I might then say, "You really need to see it." If my friend says, "Why?" I might then go on to explain, "Well, first, its got a really hilarious plot based on both sets of parents' reaction to their grown child falling in love with a person from a different ethnic background. And the acting is great." My reasoning could be diagrammed as follows:

CLAIM: *You need to see "My Big Fat Greek Wedding." (Why?)*
REASON 1: *Because the story is hilarious.*
REASON 2: *Because the acting is great.*

Ethically, giving reasons is important because when people are provided with a rational basis for why you are making a particular claim, they are able to weigh and evaluate for themselves the substance of the influence attempt. Then they are free to accept or reject the argument. If they deem the reasons to be good enough, they may believe that thinking or behaving a particular way is reasonable. So they may decide to comply with what has been requested. It doesn't matter whether you're trying to persuade someone to take a specific course, select a particular restaurant, go to a particular movie, or vote for a particular candidate, they'll want to know "why?"

Now let's consider the elements of good reasons.

1. Good reasons are relevant to the claim. As you think of the reasons that you might give, you'll find that some reasons are better than others because they relate more

You increase the likelihood of persuading people when you can provide them with good reasons.

directly to the issue at hand. For example, in the reasons offered for seeing "My Big Fat Greek Wedding," "hilarious plot" and "good acting" are relevant reasons. Why? Stop and think for a moment. Ask yourself: "When people go to a movie, what are the criteria that they are likely to use in order to evaluate the quality of that movie?" In answer to that question, you're likely to identify such criteria as *setting, plot, music, directing, length, cinematography, acting,* and *editing.* Why? Because all of these have some relevance to an evaluation.

2. Good reasons can be and are well supported. So we've decided that some reasons are more relevant to making a decision than others. But can we gain belief or action solely by stating good reasons? For instance, if all I say is "You should see *My Big Fat Greek Wedding* because the plot is hilarious and the acting is great" am I likely to convince my friend? Maybe. But it's more likely that my friend will want additional information that justifies these two reasons. So, I'll have to provide some specific support. For instance, in support of the reason "the plot is hilarious" I might say, "Throughout the movie, the bride's father, who is very proud of his Greek heritage, is constantly telling people how specific words, ideas, and objects were originally created by Greeks."

Any time you're trying to persuade using reasons, you need to have some accurate specific information to support the reasons you present. You are likely to be most effective in using good reasons when you have expertise. In fact, the persuasiveness of your reasoning often depends on your listener's acknowledgment of your expert power.

3. Focus on reasons that will have the greatest impact on the person(s) you're trying to influence. We've said that you want to select relevant reasons, that is, reasons that make the most sense in terms of the subject. But there are times when you know something about the person you're talking with that calls for you to give more weight to a particular reason than you ordinarily would. For instance, suppose the friend to whom I recommended seeing *My Big Fat Greek Wedding* is planning a wedding. In this case, I might want to mention that the movie has several scenes that are every bride's nightmare.

In summary, good reasons are relevant to the claim, can be well supported, and are meaningful to the person you're talking with.

Personal Credibility

Good, well-supported reasons alone may be persuasive, but they are even more powerful when presented by a credible source. **Credibility** is the extent to which the target believes in the speaker's expertise, trustworthiness, and likeability. In effect, how persuasive you are may depend on whether the person you are talking with has confidence in you as a person.

You may be able to recall times when no matter how logical the information appeared to be, you didn't believe it because you lacked confidence in the person. The flip side, of course, are situations where people believe or do anything that a highly charismatic person asks even when that person provides no reasons or argues illogically.

Credibility—the extent to which the target believes in the speaker's expertise, trustworthiness, and likeability.

Why do we *ever* allow our opinion of another to be the sole factor in important decisions? In Spotlight on Scholars (see opposite page), Richard Petty, who has studied attitude change, argues that as receivers we follow cognitive and peripheral routes in our consideration of persuasive requests. The cognitive route requires us to weigh and consider the reasons and evidence. We often reserve this route for issues about which we are highly motivated and that are really important to us. We use the peripheral route for issues about which we are not motivated and believe are less important. So, although selecting a movie or a restaurant has some importance to us, it may not be so great that we feel a need to engage in cognitive effort. As a result, we may well rely on the word of a friend even without a great deal of support for the judgment.

Numerous research studies have confirmed that people are more likely to accept messages whose source is perceived to be credible (Chebat, Filiatrault, & Perrien, 1990, p. 165). So when we are considering how to vote on a sales tax proposal, our thinking may go something like this: "I don't want to spend the time to learn about the sales tax proposal. Since Joe is a bright enough guy and has studied the issues, and he and I think a lot alike on many other issues, I'll trust what he recommends." Generally, however, we only allow others to influence us in this way if we believe they are truly credible.

Characteristics of Credibility   Credibility is not the same as blind faith. People will consider your messages to be credible when they believe that you are competent, trustworthy, and likable.

> **Competence**—when people seem to know what they're talking about, have good information, and are perceived as clear thinkers.

> **Trustworthiness**—when people seem to be dependable, honest, and keep the promises they have made, and are perceived to be acting for the good of others more than for self.

1. Competence. When people seem to know what they're talking about, have good information, and are perceived as clear thinkers, we say that they are **competent.** If Alan sees his friend Gloria as unusually well informed on local political issues, Alan may be persuaded to vote for a tax levy simply because Gloria is supporting it. So, the more people perceive you as knowledgeable on a particular subject, the more likely they will pay attention to your views on that subject.

2. Trustworthiness. When people seem to be dependable, honest, and keep the promises they have made, and are perceived to be acting for the good of others more than for self, we say that they are **trustworthy.** People's intentions or motives are particularly important in determining whether another person will view them as trustworthy. For instance, if you are trying on a new pair of slacks and a sales clerk you know is working on commission says to you "Wow, you look terrific in those," you may well question that person's intentions. However, if a bystander who is fashionably dressed looks over at you and comments "I wish I looked as good in those; they really fit you well," you are likely to accept the statement at face value. The bystander has no reason to say anything, so you have no reason to

INTER-ACT WITH

Technology

Watch one of the many "infomercials" on television. Look specifically for efforts to build credibility of the speaker and/or the product, reasons for buying the product, and techniques used to motivate viewers to act. List some of the methods of influence that you find most effective. Which of those methods would you consider for your interpersonal influence efforts? How can you incorporate some of those methods in your interpersonal communication? ■

Richard Petty, Professor of Psychology, the Ohio State University, on
Attitude Change

As an undergraduate political science major, Richard Petty got so interested in how people change their attitudes that he chose to minor in psychology, where he could not only take more courses in attitude change but also learn empirical research methods. He then decided to go on to graduate work in psychology at the Ohio State University, where he could focus on studying attitude change and persuasion. Like many scholars, the subject of his doctoral dissertation—attitude change induced by persuasive communications—laid the foundation for a career of research.

When Petty began his research, the psychological scholarship of the previous forty years had been unable to demonstrate a relationship between people's attitudes and their behavior. Petty believed that the relationship between attitude change and behavior had been obscured by the complexity of the variables involved in assessing attitude change. Now Petty is in the forefront of scholars who have demonstrated that attitude change and behavior are, in fact, related, but in a complex way.

During the last twenty years, Petty has published scores of research articles on his own and with colleagues on various aspects of influence, seeking to discover under what circumstances attitudes affect behavior. His work with various collaborators has been so successful that he has gained international acclaim. Not only have many of his works been published worldwide, but the theory of the Elaboration Likelihood Model of Persuasion (ELM) that he developed in collaboration with John Cacioppo has become the most cited theoretical approach to attitude and persuasion.

According to the ELM theory, attitude change is likely to occur from one of just two relatively distinct "routes to persuasion." The first, central route, is through a person's careful and thoughtful consideration of the true merits of the information presented in support of a claim. The second, peripheral route, is via a simple cue in the persuasion context (such as an attractive source) that induces change without necessitating scrutiny of the central merits of the claim. Following their initial speculation about these two routes to persuasion, Petty and Cacioppo developed, researched and refined their ELM.

The ELM "is a theory about the processes responsible for attitude change and the strength of the attitudes that result from those processes." The ELM hypothesizes that what is persuasive to a person and how lasting any attitude change is likely to be are dependent on how motivated and able people are to assess the merits of a speaker, an issue, or a position. People who are highly motivated are likely to study available information about the claim. As a result, they are more likely to arrive at a reasoned attitude that is well articulated and bolstered by information received via the central route. For people who are less motivated to study information related to the claim, attitude change can result from a number of less resource-demanding processes that do not require the effort of evaluating the relevant information. These people are affected more by information through the peripheral route, but their attitude changes are likely to be weaker in endurance. The ELM explains why some attitude changes are related to behavior but others are not. Specifically, attitude changes that result from considerable thought also result in behavior change, but attitude changes that result from simple peripheral cues (e.g., agreeing simply because the source is an expert), do not.

So what can we learn about influencing others from Petty's research? First, we must recognize that attitude change results from our choices of influence tactics in combination with the choice made by our conversational partners about how deeply they wish to probe into the information. We should strive to present rational influence strategies based on good reasons and supporting evidence when we expect that our conversational partner will think deeply about what we are saying. Likewise, we should draw on our credibility and use emotional influence factors when listener thinking is expected to be superficial. Finally, we must remember that the attitudes changed by considerable mental effort will tend to be stronger than those changed by little thought.

This complexity of attitude change suggests that as communicators we must not only have the necessary information to form well-constructed arguments, but must also have the artistic sense to understand important aspects of those we intend to influence and have the artistic power to use available persuasive means effectively.

Where is Petty going from here? He will certainly continue working on aspects of attitude change for, as he says, "I never finish a project without discovering at least two unanswered questions arising from the research." In addition, he's interested in finding out how people behave when their judgments may have been inappropriate or biased. That is, sometimes it becomes salient to people that they were inappropriately biased by the mere attractiveness of the message source rather than the substance of what they were saying.

Currently Petty teaches both graduate and undergraduate courses in attitudes and persuasion, research methods, and theories of social psychology. Petty has written scores of research articles and several books, all dealing with aspects of attitude, attitude change, and persuasion. For titles of several of his publications, see the references for this chapter at the end of the book. ■

doubt his or her intentions. The more positively you view the intentions of people, the more credible their words will seem to you.

3. Likeability. When people seem to be congenial, attractive, warm, and friendly, we think of them as **likeable.** Until proven wrong, we tend to believe those people that we like. So Ron may let Jose talk him into spending the night camping out in the desert with Jose's Cub Scout troop simply because Ron likes Jose. Scam artists are unethical operators who cultivate the personal characteristics that make them likable in order to use their credibility to persuade others to do things that are not really in their best interest.

Establishing Your Credibility Over time, you can establish your credibility. First, you can *show* that you know what you are doing and why you are doing it—that you are competent. In contrast, if you behave carelessly, take on too many tasks at one time, and do not double-check details, you're likely to be perceived as incompetent.

Second, you can show that you care about the effects on others of what you say and do. Some people develop reputations as manipulators because, though their intentions are good, they fail to state why they behave as they do. Remember, people are not mind readers. When you don't explain your behavior, others may as-

Likeability—when people seem to be congenial, attractive, warm, and friendly.

What qualities would you ascribe to the person talking that would cause others to see him as a credible source?

sume they know your intentions or may misread your behavior. Although you can't change your character or personality on the spur of the moment, you can make your actions reflect your character and personality. For instance, if you perceive yourself as hardworking, you can give yourself totally to the job at hand. Likewise, if you are friendly or likable, you can smile when you meet strangers or offer to help people with their jobs. If people do not see you as a credible person, you may be able to change your image by improving your competence and sharing your intentions.

Third, and perhaps most important, you can establish your credibility by behaving in ways that are ethical—that is, in keeping with the standards of moral conduct that determine behavior. When you believe strongly in the rightness of your cause, you may well be tempted to say or do anything, ethical or not, to achieve your goals. Before you succumb to such temptation, think of all the people in the world who have ridden roughshod over moral or ethical principles to achieve their goals. If your credibility is important to you, then you will not want to adopt the philosophy that the end justifies the means. Even if you achieve your short-term goal, it will be at the cost of satisfying relationships with others.

How you handle ethical questions says a great deal about you as a person. What is your code of ethics? The following behaviors are essentials of ethical persuasion.

1. Tell the truth. Of all the aspects of trustworthiness, this may be the most important. If people believe you are lying to them, they are likely to reject you and your ideas. If they think you are telling the truth but later learn that you have lied, they will look for ways to get back at you. If you are not sure whether information is true, say so. Many times an honest "I really don't know, but I'll find out" is far more positive than trying to deflect a comment or use irrelevant information to try to make points.

2. Resist personal attacks against those who oppose your ideas. There seems to be an almost universal agreement that name-calling is detrimental to your trustworthiness. Even though many people name-call in their interpersonal communication, it is still unethical.

3. Disclose the complete picture. People can make something sound good or bad, better or worse, by the phrasing they select, but if they purposely put a favorable spin on unfavorable information, it is unethical. For instance,

> *Hector's mother asks him, "Why were you out until 3:00 A.M.?" Hector replies indignantly, "It wasn't anywhere near 3:00!" (He got in at 2:20.)*
>
> *Marjorie says to Allison, "I want you to know that I was not the one who told your mother that you were smoking. I'd never do that!" What Majorie fails to say is that she did tell Brenda and suggested to Brenda that perhaps she could tell Allison's mother.*

Such people may tell themselves "I did not tell a lie," but their behavior is still unethical. Messages that are perceived to be ethical are more likely to persuade.

Emotion Appeals

Messages that give good reasons from a credible source are likely to be persuasive. But when you're trying to influence people to act, you can increase the persuasiveness of your message by appealing to their emotions (Jorgensen, 1998, p. 403). Although people can be moved to act on the basis of well-supported reasons from credible sources, others may well *believe* they should do something, but may be reluctant to act on that belief. For instance, Jonas may believe that people should donate money to worthy causes, but he may not do so; Gwen may agree that people should exercise for forty-five minutes, three times a week, but she may not do so. What motivates people to move from simply believing in something to acting on that belief is often the degree of their emotional involvement. Emotions are the driving force behind action, the instrument that prods or nudges us from passive belief to overt action. So, understanding and using emotional appeal can increase effectiveness of our persuasive messages.

The effectiveness of emotional appeals depends on the mood and attitude of the person you are persuading and the language itself. Suppose you are trying to convince your brother to loan you money so that you can buy your textbooks for the semester without waiting for your grant money to be released. In addition to your rational approach, you may want to include several appeals to his emotions. "I'm sure you remember how frustrating it is to go to class unprepared," or "Mom, will be so disappointed if I don't do well in this class," or "I know you love me and want to help me be successful in school."

TEST YOURSELF

Forming Persuasive Messages

Frame a series of messages aimed at persuading a particular person you know to: (1) attend a community college before going to university, (2) stop smoking, (3) get a tattoo, (4) volunteer at a charity event. Begin by identifying three reasons and supporting evidence. Then list ways that you could demonstrate your credibility to speak on each issue. Finally, develop emotional appeals that would impel your partner to act. Check the ethical implications of your plan. Be prepared to share your messages in class.

How can you form messages with strong emotional appeal? Focus on specific examples and experiences. Describe the examples and experiences—often you can develop your descriptions in story form. So, instead of saying "I thought you might be interested in going to the Egyptian exhibit with me—it's supposed to be really good," you might say, "I thought you might be interested in going to the Egyptian exhibit with me. I think it will be like old times when we would spend the whole day getting lost in the museum. Just two brothers, 'bonding.' Remember how exciting it was to be in the midst of a 3-d re-creation of a historical place?"

Compliance-Gaining Strategies

Whereas persuasion is the art getting others to change their beliefs or actions, **compliance gaining** focuses on influencing others to do what you want them to do. In this section we look at specific compliance-gaining strategies that you may consider using in your influence attempts.

In their analysis of the research on compliance-gaining strategies, Kellerman and Cole looked at 74 different lists covering over 840 strategies (1994, p. 6). From these, they identified 64 strategies that overlapped in several studies (pp. 7–10). Dan O'Hair and Michael J. Cody (1987, pp. 286–287) looked at many of these same lists and boiled them down to the seven strategy types that we will present in this section. As you will see, each of these strategy types is based on a unique combination of reasoning, credibility, and emotional appeals.

Compliance-gaining—influencing others to do what you want them to do.

Supporting-Evidence Strategies

In **supporting-evidence strategies,** which draw primarily on reasoning, a person seeks compliance by presenting reasons and/or evidence. To use this strategy, you present the reasons a person should behave as you wish them to. So you might say, "Let me give you what I think are the three best reasons for holding onto the job you have" or "May I borrow your curling iron for a few minutes? When I wear this outfit, I think I look a lot better with just a little curl in my hair."

Supporting-evidence strategies—strategies that draw primarily on reasoning and include all those strategies in which a person seeks compliance by presenting reasons and/or evidence.

Exchange Strategies

Exchange strategies—strategies in which a person seeks compliance by offering trade-offs.

In **exchange strategies** a person seeks compliance by offering trade-offs. Although an exchange strategy does not give reasons directly, it does imply the presence of a reason. To use this strategy, a person might say "I'll help you with calculus if you help me with history" or "I'll agree to the price if you'll throw in free delivery." In short, it uses the negotiated element as a type of a reason: Why will I help you with calculus? Because you'll help me with history. Notice that exchange strategy is also based in credibility. People are likely to comply based on an exchange only if they believe that others will carry out their part of the exchange.

Direct-Request Strategies

Direct-request strategies—all those strategies in which a person seeks compliance by asking another to behave in a particular way.

In **direct-request strategies** a person seeks compliance by asking another to behave in a particular way. A person might say "Can I borrow your pencil?" or "Will you lend me five dollars?" Direct requests generally are not accompanied by reasons. They are based primarily on credibility. In effect, they are saying "You know me. You know I'm trustworthy and cooperative, and I will return what I have asked for." These may also take the form of suggestions, such as "Why don't you think about going out for the golf team?"

Empathy-Based Strategies

Empathy-based strategies—all those strategies in which a person seeks compliance by appealing to another's love, affection, or sympathy.

In **empathy-based strategies** a person seeks compliance by appealing to another's love, affection, or sympathy. Sometimes people word the persuasive statement in a way that tries to show the importance of how others feel about them. So, a person might say "If you really loved me and respected my feelings, you wouldn't try to drive when you had been drinking" or "You know we can't get along without you, and if you don't go in for treatment we're afraid we may lose you." These statements suggest that a person should behave a certain way because of ties based on expertise, trustworthiness, or personality. Other examples are based on showing similarity of values: "Since we're in this together, why don't we join forces?" "You and I have always looked at things the same way, so it's only logical that we do this together." "If you want to get your supervisor to pay attention to you as a person, you're going to have to dress more the way I do." These statements are saying "Because we have so much in common or think so highly of each other, we should behave in similar ways." Empathy-based strategies are primarily grounded in credibility and may use emotional appeal as well.

Face-Maintenance Strategies

Face-maintenance strategies—all those strategies in which a person seeks compliance while using indirect messages and emotion-eliciting statements.

In **face-maintenance strategies** a person seeks compliance while using indirect messages and emotion-eliciting statements. A person might say "Is there something I can get for you now?" Or to make a friend more receptive to suggestions, someone might say "You know I find you really attractive, and I think we share many of the same feelings." Or one might elicit emotions indirectly by saying

"Gee, I really want to look my best tonight, but I just can't seem to get my hair to work right—I wish I had a curling iron." These messages are meant to create emotional bonds between the participants, and these bonds become the basis upon which the request is complied with. So Joan loans Carol her curling iron because of her affection for Joan. Of course, in these strategies one's credibility is also being tapped. Only if Joan finds Carol likable will she have positive feelings that Carol can draw on in this situation.

Other-Benefit Strategies

In **other-benefit strategies** a person seeks compliance by identifying behaviors that benefit the other person. A person might say "I think this car is just right for the kind of driving you do" or "Ken, I believe that going away to college would be in your best interest." In these cases the kindling of emotion is tied to the meeting of interpersonal needs.

> **Other-benefit strategies**—all those strategies in which a person seeks compliance by identifying behaviors that benefit the other person.

Distributive Strategies

In **distributive strategies** a person seeks compliance by threatening or making the person feel guilty. To use this strategy, a person might say "For crying out loud, I'm only asking to borrow your curling iron for a minute, not for the rest of your life" or "You better do this for me, or you've had it." These strategies are based in negative emotional appeals and, though often successful, they are generally regarded as interpersonally unethical.

> **Distributive strategies**—all those strategies in which a person seeks compliance by threatening or making the person feel guilty.

Choosing a Strategy

How should you choose a compliance gaining strategy to use in a particular situation? Miller, Cody, and McLaughlin (1994) point out that situational perceptions are highly important in making these decisions. In short, your choice depends on how effective you believe a particular strategy will be in a given situation. The better you are at assessing the situation, the more likely you are to craft a message that will be effective.

Although there is no one "best" strategy, you may find the following guidelines useful in helping you make your decision.

1. Choose the strategy that you believe is most likely to be effective. Your first consideration is effectiveness. Since people are unique and no strategy will work equally well for everyone, you have to think about the particular person. Will this person respond more favorably to a direct or an indirect method? Will this person appreciate a logical argument or be more likely to comply on the basis of trust in you as a person? Are you in a position to offer some reward?

2. Choose the strategy that will best protect the relationship. Sometimes a strategy that will work will not be good for the relationship. If the relationship is one that you want to preserve, then you will want to select a strategy that will not be perceived as manipulative. Moreover, you are likely to want to select a strategy that will be

OBSERVE & ANALYZE

Journal Activity

Effectiveness of Influence Strategies

Consider the last time someone was effective in influencing you to believe something or to do something. Write down, as nearly as you can remember, the nature of the language that they used to appeal to you. Now, analyze that language. Were they giving you reasons? Appealing to your perception of their credibility? Kindling your emotions?

Next, consider the last time someone failed in influencing you to believe something or to do something. Again, write down, as nearly as you can remember, the nature of the language that they used to appeal to you. Now, analyze that language. Did the person give you reasons? Appeal to your perception of his or her credibility? Kindle your emotions? Why did this attempt fail?

Finally, contrast the two efforts. What conclusions about influencing can you draw from the two experiences? ■

perceived as polite. For instance, if you put pressure on a person by using a threat of punishment, the person is likely to resent the compliance even if given. Distributive strategies are considered to be the least polite of all strategies (Kellermann & Shea, 1996, p. 154). Sometimes failing to win compliance is better than hurting the relationship.

3. Choose the strategy that is most comfortable for you. Sometimes a strategy that will work and will not necessarily hurt the relationship may still be personally uncomfortable for you. There are some persuasive strategies that are a better fit with our personal communication style. Since you are more likely to be effective with a strategy that fits you, all other things being equal, choose the one that best suits you.

Overcoming Resistance

Not all attempts to influence will be successful. Sometimes, even when we have stated well reasoned, credible positions that should have appealed to our partner's emotions, they will resist our influence. As Knowles, Butler, and Linn (2001) point out, "Resistance is the most important component of any social influence attempt that fails to gain compliance" (p. 57). Too often when someone resists, our tendency is to continue to use the techniques we used in the first place. This only adds to a person's resistance. Instead of redoubling our persuasive efforts, one of the easiest ways of dealing with resistance is to ask people to elaborate on their positions. By using effective listening skills you will hear their objections. Then you may be able to answer the objections with additional information or appeals.

Assertiveness

Assertiveness—the art of declaring our personal preferences and defending our personal rights while respecting the preferences and rights of others.

Many people who understand both persuasion and compliance gaining remain ineffective at exerting influence in their relationships because they are not assertive. **Assertiveness** is the art of declaring our personal preferences and defending our personal rights while respecting the preferences and rights of others. It requires us to describe our feelings honestly or verbalize our needs and personal rights. Assertiveness messages may include describing feelings, giving good reasons for a belief, or suggesting behaviors or positions we think are fair. Assertive statements are not exaggerations made for dramatic effect nor do assertive statements attack the other individual. We can understand the specific qualities of assertive behavior best if we contrast it with other ways of interacting when we believe our rights or feelings are in danger of being violated or ignored.

Contrasting Methods of Expressing Our Needs and Rights

When we believe our needs or rights are being ignored or violated by others, we can choose to behave in one of three ways: passively, aggressively, or assertively.

Passive Behavior People behave passively when they do not state their honest opinions, do not describe deeply held feelings, or do not assume responsibility for their actions. So, **passive behavior** is not influential and people who use this method end up submitting to other people's demands, even when doing so is inconvenient, against their best interests, or violates their rights. For example, suppose that when Bill uncrates the new color television set he purchased at a local department store, he notices a deep scratch on the left side. If he is upset about the scratch but keeps the set without trying to get the store to replace it, he is behaving passively.

Passive behavior—when people are reluctant to state their opinions, share feelings, or assume responsibility for their actions.

Aggressive Behavior People exhibit **aggressive behavior** when they belligerently, violently, or confrontationally present their feelings, needs, or rights with little or no consideration for the feelings, needs, or rights of others. Aggressive messages can be judgmental, dogmatic, fault-finding, and depend on coercive power.

Aggressive behavior—when people lash out at the source of their discontent with little regard for the situation or for the feelings, needs, or rights of those they are attacking.

Suppose that after discovering the scratch on his new television set, Bill storms back to the store, confronts the first clerk he finds, and in a loud voice demands his money back while accusing the clerk of being a racist for intentionally selling him damaged merchandise. Such aggressive behavior may or may not be successful in getting the damaged set replaced, but it would certainly damage his relationship with the clerk. Most receivers of aggressive messages, regardless of the relationship, are likely to feel hurt by them (Martin, Anderson, & Horvath, 1996, p. 24). While Bill may not care about his relationship with the store clerk, if he is prone to aggressiveness as a means of influence, he will likely damage other more intimate relationships.

Assertive Behavior People behave assertively when they openly represent their honest opinions, needs, and rights in a manner that persuades others while at the same time respects the feelings, needs, and rights of others. The difference between assertive behavior and passive or aggressive behavior is not in how the individual feels, but rather the way in which they choose to act on that feeling or need. If Bill chooses an assertive response to the damaged TV, he will still feel angry about having received a damaged set. But instead of either doing nothing and living with it or verbally assaulting the clerk, Bill might choose to call the clerk from whom he purchased the set so he can describe the condition of the TV set, his feelings on discovering the scratch, and what he would like to see happen now. For instance he might ask how to return the damaged set and get a new one. He might ask that the store send out a replacement. Bill's assertive messages should accomplish his goals without annoying or hurting the other person.

OBSERVE & ANALYZE

Journal Activity

Passive, Aggressive, and Assertive Behavior

For the next day or two, observe people and their behavior. Make notes of situations where you believe people behaved in passive, aggressive, and assertive ways. Which of the ways seemed to help the people achieve what they wanted? Which of the ways seemed to maintain or even improve their interpersonal relationship with the other person or other people? ■

Distinguishing Among Passive, Aggressive, and Assertive Responses

It is inevitable that in our interpersonal relationships we will need to assert ourselves, so it is important that you learn to distinguish among passive, aggressive, and assertive responses. Let's look at several examples.

At Work Tanisha works in an office that employs both men and women. Whenever the boss has an especially interesting and challenging job to be done, he assigns it to a male co-worker whose desk is next to Tanisha's. The boss has never said anything to Tanisha or to the male employee that would indicate he thinks less of Tanisha or her ability. Nevertheless, Tanisha is frustrated by the boss's behavior.

PASSIVE: *Tanisha says nothing to her boss. She's very frustrated by consistently being overlooked, but says nothing.*

AGGRESSIVE: *Tanisha storms into her boss's office and says, "I'm sick and tired of you giving Tom the plum assignments and leaving me the garbage jobs. I'm every bit as good a worker, and I'm not going to take this anymore."*

ASSERTIVE: *Tanisha arranges a meeting with her boss. At the meeting she says, "I don't know whether you are aware of it, but during the past three weeks, every time you had a really interesting job to be done, you gave it to Tom. To the best of my knowledge, you believe that Tom and I are equally competent—you've never said anything to suggest that you thought less of my work. But when you `reward' Tom with jobs that I perceive as plums and continue to offer me routine jobs, I'm really frustrated. Do you understand my feelings about this?" In this statement, she has both described her perception of the boss's behavior and her feelings about that behavior.*

Would you say that this person is being assertive or aggressive? What leads you to your conclusion?

If you were Tanisha's boss, which of her responses would be most likely to achieve her goal of getting better assignments? Probably the assertive behavior. Which of her responses would be most likely to get her fired? Probably the aggressive behavior. And which of her responses would be least likely to "rock the boat"? Undoubtedly the passive behavior—but then she would continue to get the boring job assignments.

With a Friend Dan is a doctor doing his residency at City Hospital. He lives with two other residents in an apartment they have rented. Carl, one of the other residents, is the social gadfly of the group. It seems whenever he has time off, he has a date. But like the others, he's a bit short of cash. He doesn't feel at all bashful about borrowing clothes or money from his roommates. One evening Carl asks Dan if he can borrow his watch—a new, expensive watch that Dan received as a present from his father only a few days before. Dan is aware that Carl does not always take the best care of what he borrows, and he is very concerned about the possibility of Carl's damaging or losing the watch.

> PASSIVE: *"Sure."*
> AGGRESSIVE: *"Forget it! You've got a lot of nerve asking to borrow a brand-new watch. You know I'd be damned lucky to get it back in one piece."*
> ASSERTIVE: *"Carl, I know I've lent you several items without much ado, but this watch is special. I've had it only a few days, and I just don't feel comfortable lending it. I hope you can understand how I feel."*

What are likely to be the consequences of each of these behaviors? If he behaves passively, Dan is likely to worry the entire evening and harbor some resentment of Carl even if he gets the watch back undamaged. Moreover, Carl will continue to think that his roommates feel comfortable in lending him anything he wants. If Dan behaves aggressively, Carl is likely to be completely taken aback by his explosive behavior. No one has ever said anything to Carl before, so he has no reason for believing that he can't borrow whatever he'd like. Moreover, Dan will damage the relationship. But if Dan behaves assertively, he puts the focus on his own feelings and on this particular object—the watch. His response isn't a denial of Carl's right to borrow items, nor is it an attack on Carl. It is an explanation of why Dan does not want to lend this item at this time.

In a Social Situation Kim has invited two of her girlfriends and their dates to drop by her dormitory room before the dance. Shortly after the group arrives, Nick, who has come with Ramona, Kim's best friend, reaches into his pocket, lights a joint, takes a drag, and passes it to Kim. Kim, who doesn't do drugs, knows that if they are caught she will get kicked out of the dorm and, moreover, she is concerned about anyone in the group getting high and then driving.

> PASSIVE: *Kim takes the joint, holds it for a minute, and then passes it on.*
> AGGRESSIVE: *"Nick, that's really stupid, bringing a joint into my dorm room. Can't anybody here have a good time without getting high, or are you all a bunch of druggies? Now put out that joint and get out of here before somebody notices."*

ASSERTIVE: *"Nick, Ramona probably didn't tell you that I don't get high and you may not know that I can get kicked out of the dorm if you get caught. Besides, I'd feel a lot better if we all stayed clear headed since we have to drive to the dance. So please put the joint away."*

Again, let's contrast the three behaviors. In this case, the passive behavior is not at all in Kim's interest. Kim knows what she believes, she knows the dormitory rules, and even if no one finds out, she'll feel uncomfortable because she did nothing to protect her friends from taking a needless risk with their safety. But the aggressive behavior is hardly better. She knows nothing about Nick, but her outburst assumes bad intentions not only from Nick but also from her friends. If Nick is at all inclined to be belligerent, her method is only going to incite him and damage her relationship with Ramona besides. The assertive behavior accurately and pleasantly presents her position in a way that respects Nick's face need.

Characteristics of Assertive Messages

As these examples demonstrate, assertive messages draw on several of the basic interpersonal communication skills you have learned in this course. These include:

1. Own ideas, thoughts, and feelings. Because the purpose of assertive messages is to represent your position or needs, the message should include "I" statements like, "I think. . .," "I feel. . .," "I would like. . ."

2. Describe behavior and feelings. If we want others to satisfy our needs, then we should provide them with specific descriptive information to justify our requests. We do this by describing the feelings we have and the behavior and outcomes we desire.

3. Maintain eye contact and a self-confident posture. Our nonverbal behaviors should convey our convictions. When we maintain eye contact we are perceived as serious, when we shift our gaze away, it is a sign of submissiveness. Similarly, an erect posture conveys self-confidence.

4. Use a firm but pleasant tone of voice. Aggressiveness is signaled with yelling or harsh vocal tones. Assertive messages should be conveyed at a normal pitch, volume, and rate.

5. Speak fluently. Avoid vocalized pauses and other nonfluences that result in perceptions that you are indecisive.

6. Be sensitive to the face needs of the other. The goal of assertive messages is to influence the other without damaging the relationship. Messages are formed in ways that meet both the positive and negative face needs of the other while still presenting the needs of the speaker.

It's important to recognize that you will not always achieve your goals by being assertive. And just as with self-disclosure and describing feelings, there are risks involved in being assertive. For instance, some people will label any assertive behavior as "aggressive." But people who have

OBSERVE & ANALYZE

Journal Activity

Learning to Respond Assertively

Identify five situations in the past where you were passive or aggressive. Try to write the dialogue for each situation. Then substitute an assertive response for the nonassertive or aggressive reactions you expressed in each case. ■

difficulty asserting themselves often do not appreciate the fact that the potential benefits far outweigh the risks. Remember, our behavior teaches people how to treat us. When we are passive—when we have taught people that they can ignore our feelings—they will. When we are aggressive, we teach people to respond in kind. By contrast, when we are assertive, we can influence others to treat us as we would prefer to be treated.

Useful guidelines for practicing assertive behavior are (1) identify what you are thinking or feeling; (2) analyze the cause of these feelings; (3) choose the appropriate skills to communicate these feelings, as well as the outcome you desire, if any; and (4) communicate these feelings to the appropriate person. If you have trouble taking the first step to being more assertive, try beginning with situations in which you are likely to have a high potential for success (Alberti & Emmons, 1995). In addition, try to incorporate the six characteristics of assertive behavior listed on page 292.

Assertiveness in Cross-Cultural Relationships

Assertiveness is valued and practiced in Western cultures. As Samovar and Porter (2001) point out, "communicaton problems arise when cultures that value assertiveness come in contact with cultures that value accord and harmony" (Samovar & Porter, 2001, p. 85).

Whereas North American culture is known for its assertive communication style, Oriental and South American cultures value accord and harmony (p. 85). For instance "to maintain harmony and avoid interpersonal clashes, Japanese business

SKILL BUILDERS   **ASSERTIVENESS**

SKILL	USE	PROCEDURE	EXAMPLE
Standing up for yourself and doing so in interpersonally effective ways that describe your feelings honestly and exercise your personal rights while respecting the rights of others.	To show clearly what you think or feel.	1. Identify what you are thinking or feeling. 2. Analyze the cause of these feelings. 3. Choose the appropriate skills necessary to communicate these feelings, as well as any outcome you desire. 4. Communicate these feelings to the appropriate person. Remember to own your feelings.	When Gavin believes that he is being unjustly charged, he says, "I have never been charged for a refill on iced tea before–has there been a change in policy?"

TEST YOURSELF

Developing Assertive Responses

For each of the following situations write a passive or aggressive response and then contrast it with a more appropriate assertive response.

1. You come back to your dorm, apartment, or house to type a paper that is due tomorrow, only to find that someone else is using your typewriter.
   Passive or aggressive response:
   Assertive response:

2. You're working at a store part time. Just as your hours are up and you are ready to leave (you want to rush home because you have a nice dinner planned with someone special), your boss says to you, "I'd like you to work overtime if you would–Martin's supposed to replace you, but he just called and can't get here for at least an hour."
   Passive or aggressive response:
   Assertive response:

3. During a phone call to your parents, who live in another state, your mother says, "We're expecting you to go with us when we visit your uncle on Saturday." You were planning to spend Saturday working on your resume for an interview next week.
   Passive or aggressive response:
   Assertive response:

4. You and your friend made a date to go dancing, an activity you really enjoy. When you meet, your friend says, "If it's all the same to you, I thought we'd go to a movie instead."
   Passive or aggressive response:
   Assertive response:

has evolved an elaborate process called nemawashii," a term that means binding the roots of a plant before pulling it out. "In this process, any subject that might cause disorder at a meeting is discussed in advance. Anticipating and obviating interpersonal antagonism allow the Japanese to avoid impudent and discourteous behavior" (Samovar & Porter, 2001, p. 85).

In fact, in collectivist societies, "a style of communication in which respecting the relationship through communication is more important than the information exchanged" (Jandt, 2001, p. 37). Jandt goes on to explain that these societies use group harmony, avoidance of loss of face to others and oneself, and a modest presentation of oneself as means of respecting the relationship. "One does not say what one actually thinks when it might hurt others in the group" (p. 37).

On the other hand, in Latin and Hispanic societies, men, especially, are frequently taught to exercise a form of self-expression that goes far beyond the guidelines presented here for assertive behavior. In these societies, the concept of "machismo" guides male behavior. Thus, the standard of assertiveness considered appropriate in the dominant American culture can seem inappropriate to people whose cultural frame of reference leads them to perceive it as either aggressive or weak.

Thus when we use assertiveness—as with any other skill—we need to be aware that no single standard of behavior ensures we will achieve our goals.

Although what is labeled appropriate behavior varies across cultures, the results of passive and aggressive behavior seem universal. Passive behavior can cause resentment and aggressive behavior leads to fear and misunderstanding. When talking with people whose culture, background, or lifestyle differs from your own, you may need to observe their behavior and their responses to your statements before you can be sure of the kinds of behavior that are likely to communicate your intentions effectively.

OBSERVE & ANALYZE

Journal Activity

Assertiveness

As you observe people, notice situations in which individuals fail to behave assertively. What kind of power were they granting to other people? What kind of power might they have really had that they didn't seem to recognize? ■

WHAT WOULD YOU DO?

A Question *of* Ethics

Collin had always excelled at math. So, as he entered his first college math course, he was excited by the challenge. Since he had placed out of several basic courses, he enrolled in 300-level course titled "Abstract Algebra," to be taught by Greg Morton, a third-year graduate student.

About two weeks into the course, as Collin copied an important theorem from the board, he spotted what seemed to be an inconsistency in the proof. Since no one else in the class seemed bothered, Collin didn't say anything, but resolved that later that evening he would try to figure out what was wrong with his reasoning. That evening, after about a half an hour of work, Collin found that the mistake was Morton's, not his. But he decided not to say anything to Morton about it. A few days later when Morton made another mistake in a proof that Collin verified as he reworked the problem that evening, Collin

became concerned. Not only was Morton teaching the rest of the class incorrect reasoning skills, Collin thought there might come a time when he wouldn't notice a mistake, or might construct a proper proof on an exam and have it graded incorrectly.

Collin didn't know what to do. He was only a freshman and Morton obviously had much more training, but if he let the mistake go again, the rest of the class might be confused. Also, it could affect all of them in later courses when they were required to be able to reproduce what they had learned in Abstract Algebra. He considered writing an anonymous note to his classmates to give them a "heads up." Collin considered talking with Morton directly, but he worried whether he could explain to Morton his concerns without offending him. Collin also considered talking directly to the department chairperson, but he thought Morton was a good

teacher overall, and he didn't want to get him into trouble. Mostly, he was worried that he'd "blow it." He'd never had good interpersonal skills and he wasn't sure he could explain Morton's mistakes to him without offending him. And after all, Morton did control the grading. Finally, Collin wondered if it might just be better to leave well enough alone. After all, he understood the material and he felt he could defend his answers if need be.

1. Identify the ethical issues in this case.

2. What should Collin do?

3. If he chooses to discuss this with Morton, what influence tactics are likely to be most effective?

4. If he chooses to talk with the department chairperson, how should he proceed?

Summary

Influence is the ability to affect people's attitudes and behaviors. Conscious efforts to influence others are accomplished through persuasion, compliance gaining, and assertiveness.

Influence is possible when people believe that they have power over their fate. Social power is the potential ability to influence another person's attitude or behavior. The sources of people's social power may be coercive, reward, legitimate, expert, or referent. People lacking in assertiveness may be overly intimidated by people whom they grant various kinds of social power. Passive people are often unhappy as a result of not stating what they think and feel; aggressive people get their ideas and feelings heard but may create more problems for themselves because of their aggressiveness.

Persuasion is the verbal effort to influence. Persuasion is the product of several elements that may be used alone or in concert. Persuasion can be a product of logical reasoning, of motivation through emotional language, and/or of speaker credibility. Effective interpersonal persuasion is always ethical persuasion; it does not depend on lying, distortion of fact, or acting in the interests of the persuader at the expense of the one being persuaded.

Compliance-gaining messages are classified according to the kinds of power employed by communicators in efforts to gain compliance. The choice of strategy may depend on a communicator's perception of the situation in which compliance is being sought. Many of the strategies used can be grouped under the broad heading of persuasion.

Assertiveness is the skill of stating our ideas and feelings openly in interpersonally effective ways. Some of the characteristics of behaving assertively are owning ideas, thoughts, and feelings; describing behavior and feelings; maintaining eye contact and a self confident posture; using a firm but pleasant tone of voice; speaking fluently; and being sensitive to the face needs of others.

Inter-Action Dialogue:

Influence occurs when one person attempts to change another person's attitudes or actions. Consider type(s) of power exerted in influence efforts, presence of persuasion (reasons and evidence, credibility, emotional appeal), compliance-gaining strategies, and assertiveness. Use your Inter-Act CD-ROM to view the dialogue between Hannah and Paul and notice the influence behaviors of each.

A transcript of Hannah and Paul's conversation is printed below. You can record your analysis of their behavior in the right-hand column or you can complete your analysis online using the Inter-Action Influence Analysis feature on your CD-ROM. On the Dialogue page, click "analysis for Hannah and Paul" then compare your comments to the analysis provided by the authors.

Paul's friend Hannah stops by his dorm to show him what she has done.

CONVERSATION

HANNAH: *Hey Paul, take a look at my term paper.*

PAUL *(quickly reading the first page): Wow, so far this looks great. You must have put a lot of time into it.*

HANNAH: *No, but it should be good, I paid enough for it.*

PAUL: *What?*

HANNAH: *I got it off the Internet.*

PAUL: *You mean you bought it from one of those term paper sites? Hannah, what's up? That's not like you–you're not a cheater.*

HANNAH: *Listen–my life's crazy. I don't have time to write a stupid paper.*

PAUL: *What's stupid about the assignment?*

HANNAH: *I think the workload in this class is ridiculous. The professor acts as if this is the only class we've got. There are three exams, a team project, and this paper. What's the point?*

PAUL: *Well I think the professor assigned this paper for several reasons, to see whether students really know how to think about the material they have studied and to help us improve our writing.*

HANNAH: *Come on, we learned how to write when we were in elementary school.*

PAUL: *That's not what I said. Sure you can write a sentence or a paragraph, but can you really express your own ideas about this subject? What the professor is doing is putting us in a position not only where we show our understanding of the material, but also where we have to show our ability to phrase our thoughts in a sophisticated manner. By writing a term paper we have the chance to*

ANALYSIS

Influence

CONVERSATION

develop our own thinking about a topic. We can read a wide variety of sources and then make up our own minds and in our writing explain our thoughts. And the neat thing is, we'll get feedback about how we did.

HANNAH: *Yes, but you're not listening—I just don't have time.*

PAUL: *So you believe the best way to deal with the situation is to cheat?*

HANNAH: *Man, that's cold. But I'm not the only one doing this.*

PAUL: *Are you saying that since some people cheat it's OK for you to cheat? Like people take drugs or sleep around so it's OK for you?*

HANNAH: *No, don't be silly, but I told you I'm up to here in work. I've got no time.*

PAUL: *Right. So remind me what you did last night.*

HANNAH: *You know. I went to Sean's party. I deserve to have a little social life. I'm only twenty after all.*

PAUL: *Sure, point well taken. So what did you do the night before?*

HANNAH: *Well, I worked until 8:00, then Mary and I grabbed a bite to eat and then went clubbing.*

PAUL: *So, for two nights you chose to do no school work, but you had time to socialize? And you're saying "you're up to here in work." Hannah, I'm just not buying it. your workload is no different from mine. And I manage to get my work done. It's not perfect—like your Internet paper. But it's mine. So who do you hurt when you cheat? Besides your own character you hurt me. Thanks friend.*

HANNAH: *Hey, chill. You've made your point. But what can I do now? The paper's due in two days and I haven't even begun.*

PAUL: *Do you have to work tonight?*

HANNAH: *No.*

PAUL: *Well, then you still have time. It will be a couple of long, hard days, but I'll bring you coffee and food.*

HANNAH: *What a friend. Well, OK, I guess you win.*

PAUL: *Hey wait. Let's seal it by tearing up that bought paper.*

HANNAH: *What! You mean I can't even borrow a few ideas from it?*

PAUL: *Hannah!*

HANNAH: *OK. OK. Just kidding.*

ANALYSIS

Chapter Resources

Communication Improvement Plan: Influencing Ethically

Would you like to improve your use of the following skills discussed in this chapter?

> Persuading
> Gaining compliance
> Assertiveness

Pick a skill and write a communication improvement plan

Skill: _____

Problem: _____

_____

_____

_____

Goal: _____

_____

_____

_____

Procedure:

1. _____

2. _____

3. _____

Test of Achieving Goal: _____

_____

Key Words

Influence, *p. 274*

Interpersonal power, *p. 274*

Coercive power, *p. 275*

Reward power, *p. 275*

Legitimate power, *p. 276*

Expert power, *p. 276*

Referent power, *p. 277*

Persuasion, *p. 277*

Reasons, *p. 277*

Claims, *p. 278*

Credibility, *p. 279*

Competence, *p. 280*

Trustworthiness, *p. 280*

Likeability, *p. 282*

Compliance-gaining strategies, *p. 285*

Supporting-evidence strategies, *p. 285*

Exchange strategies, *p. 286*

Direct-request strategies, *p. 286*

Empathy-based strategies, *p. 286*

Face-maintenance strategies, *p. 286*

Other-benefit strategies, *p. 287*

Distributive strategies, *p. 287*

Assertiveness, *p. 288*

Passive behavior, *p. 289*

Aggressive behavior, *p. 289*

Inter-Act with Media

CINEMA

Roger Mitchell (Director). (2002). *Changing Lanes.* Ben Affleck, Samuel L. Jackson.

Brief Summary: This is the story of two men (a lawyer and a struggling small-businessman) who have an accident on a New York expressway on their way to important appointments. As a result of the accident and a degree of road rage, the men try get even with each other. Both men fail to perceive the other man accurately and, consequently, they make false assumptions about each other. Both men subsequently try to force compliance from the other as their war continues to escalate out of control to the potential ruin of both lives.

IPC Concepts: Dysfunctional approaches to influence. Both characters resort to coercion, force, violence, and every form of power to try to force compliance.

Bruce Beresford (Director). (1989). *Driving Miss Daisy.* Morgan Freeman, Jessica Tandy, Dan Ackroyd, Patti Lupone, Esther Rolle.

Brief Summary: This adaptation of Alfred Uhry's play tells the story of the evolving friendship between an old wealthy woman (Daisy) and her simple, aging chauffeur (Hoke). The film adds the diversity issues of her being Jewish and his being African American. Daisy struggles through most of the story with the changes that she experiences as a result of aging. She slowly learns to accept her chauffeur, and even more slowly, his role as her best friend. Hoke must move very carefully through his interactions with the white community, and must wear a series of carefully constructed masks in order to protect himself and his livelihood, and influence others, like his employer.

IPC Concepts: This film is a powerful dramatization of how influence can take place over the life cycle of a relationship. It demonstrates the gentle manner in which caring for another can overcome barriers to attitudinal change. The film illustrates such concepts as anger and conflict, diversity, masks, power in relationships and how it can change as the basis of the power changes, the life cycles and turning points of relationships, and assertiveness.

THEATER

Tennessee Williams. (1955). *Cat on a Hot Tin Roof.*

Brief Summary: The story revolves around the relationships between Big Daddy, Brick, Maggie, and Big Mama, and the way in which they try to influence each other, especially Big Daddy. Big Daddy lectures Brick on how he has learned to handle all of the lies that he must endure from people who are trying to get their way with him. His expression of "mendacity" is a classic from this powerful play.

IPC Concepts: Influence—direct request strategies; passive, aggressive, and assertive behavior; masks, ethical issues.

LITERATURE

Austen, J. (1818). *Persuasion.* (Or see the film version: Roger Mitchell (Director). (1995). Amanda Root, Ciaran Hinds, Susan Fleetwood, Corin Redgrave, Fiona Shaw, John Woodvine, Phoebe Nicholls, Samuel West, Sophie Thompson, Judy Cornwell, Felicity Dean.)

Brief Summary: A young woman is persuaded by trusted, close friends and family not to marry a young man whom she loves because his social standing and prospects are perceived as not good. The young man goes to sea and rises to captain, securing his social standing and future. Upon returning, the young woman realizes her mistake, and gets a second chance—marrying the young sea captain and going out to sea with her love.

IPC Concepts: Influence as persuasion—good reasons, triggering emotion, reward, power.

ACADEMIC WORK

Drury, S. S. (1984). *Assertive Supervision: Building Involved Teamwork.* Champaign, Ill.: Research Press.

Brief Summary: This is an excellent book on assertiveness in the workplace. It discusses a wide variety of assertive techniques and offers practical examples and ways of applying these techniques in workplace relationships.

IPC Concepts: Nature of assertiveness, methods of expressing rights and needs, characteristics of the assertive style.

Camden, C., Motley, M. T., & Wilson, A. (19840). White lies in interpersonal communication: A taxonomy and preliminary investigation of social motivations. *Western Journal of Speech Communication, 48*(4), 309–325.

Brief Summary: This interesting article looks at eh other side of influence, namely, influence by deception. It offers a brief discussion on types of lies and most of the article is devoted to research on the motivations that people report for lying. These include saving face, avoiding conflict, achieving power, and psychological compensation.

IPC Concepts: Types and frequency of lies, motivations for lying.

WHAT'S ON THE WEB

Harmonious Assertive Communication: Methods to Create Understanding and Intimacy
http://front.csulb.edu/tstevens/c14-lisn.htm

Brief Summary: This Web site focuses on assertive conflict resolution and the requisite skills involved: diplomatically requesting change, emphatic listening, how to escalate and de-escalate conflicts, how to deal with aggression and manipulation.

IPC Concepts: Assertiveness, listening, conflict.

Conflict Resolution Resources at the School of Social and Systemic Studies
http://www.nova.edu/shss/DCAR/

Brief Summary: Maintained by faculty at Nova Southeastern University, the site includes information on the school's academic offerings via distance learning. The school offers graduate degrees in dispute resolution. There is an extensive list of conflict resolution resources: Internet resources and listserves (this is an overwhelming list of resources), newsletters, journals, membership organizations, resource organizations.

IPC Concepts: Conflict management via arbitration.

Assertiveness Prepared by Organizational Development and Training, Department of Human Resources, Tufts University
http://www.tufts.edu/hr/tips/assert.html

Brief Summary: This site offers a really good introduction to the nature of assertiveness and especially on "I" language—with specific instructions and examples that supplement the discussion on both language and influence very nicely.

IPC Concepts: Assertiveness, language.

How to Express Difficult Feelings
http://www.drnadig.com/feelings.htm

Brief Summary: This Web site examines the nature and function of language in expressing emotion. The site includes guidelines on language use when in conflict, the difference between thoughts and feelings, and detailed directions on "I" language. This site has links to listening and conflict management resources.

IPC Concepts: Language and conflict.

CHAPTER 11

Managing Conflict

After you have read this chapter, you should be able to answer these questions:

- What is interpersonal conflict?
- What are some popular views of conflict?
- What are the five types of conflict?
- What are withdrawal, accommodating, forcing, compromising, and collaborating?
- What skills are used in initiating conflict?
- What skills are used in responding to conflict?
- What are the skills involved in mediating a conflict?

> "Oh Hon, I forgot to tell you—Jeff called to remind you that you need to turn in your receipts for that business trip you took last month."
>
> "When did he call?"
>
> "Yesterday."
>
> "Yesterday! And you're just telling me now?"
>
> "I told you I forgot—you'll be able to get them to him in plenty of time."
>
> "That's not the point, Mark. We've gone over this before. Whenever anyone calls with a message that is at all important you're supposed to write a note and leave it where the other person can see it."
>
> "Lisa, this isn't a big deal—I told you in plenty of time."
>
> "But what if you had 'forgotten' for another couple of days? I could be in deep trouble."
>
> "But you're not in trouble."
>
> "Mark, that's not the issue. Remember last week you had a call from Dale about Mary being sick? I wrote you a note and put it on your planner."
>
> "That's right you did."
>
> "See, If you'd just follow my lead—when I get a message for you, I write it down."
>
> "Always?"
>
> "Always."
>
> "So how come this morning when I went over to Jane's for the neighborhood block watch meeting she told me that she called yesterday to tell you it was canceled."
>
> "Uh, well..."
>
> "Don't have much to say, do you?"

Sometimes in our relationships we find ourselves in serious conflict over core issues. But most of the time our conflicts occur over mundane, day-to-day issues. In either case, how we choose to deal with conflict will affect our relationships. For instance, the issue of communicating important telephone messages that Mark and Lisa are discussing may be resolved easily or may escalate into a serious disagreement that may damage their relationship. What happens depends on how each of them chooses to behave.

Most scholars agree that conflict involves some incompatibility between people (Canary, Cupach, & Messman, 1995, p. 4). We define **interpersonal conflict** as a situation occurring when

Interpersonal conflict—a situation in which the needs or ideas of one person are perceived to be at odds with or in opposition to the needs or ideas of another.

the needs or ideas of one person are perceived to be at odds with or in opposition to the needs of ideas or another.

Although many people believe that conflict is a sign of a bad relationship, the reality is that conflicts occur in all relationships. Whether conflict hurts or strengthens a relationship depends primarily on how we deal with it. Since conflict is inevitable, it should be managed in ways that maintain the relationship while satisfying important needs of both parties. As students of interpersonal communication, understanding conflict and developing conflict management skills will make you more effective in dealing with the inevitable conflict episodes you face in your relationships.

How conflict is perceived is culturally based. While you may not like conflict in American culture, conflict is viewed as inevitable. However, in other cultures, especially in Asian cultures, conflict is viewed as dysfunctional to relationships and damaging to social face (Ting-Toomey, 2001, p. 396). In this chapter we present information that is grounded in an American perspective.

We begin by looking at types of conflict. Then we discuss five styles people use to manage conflict, discussing when each approach can be used effectively. Finally, we describe specific communication strategies that can be used to initiate, respond to, or mediate conflict episodes in a collaborative style.

Types of Interpersonal Conflict

Some conflicts are easier to resolve than others. When we can identify the type of conflict that is occurring, we are better equipped to resolve it. Conflicts will generally fall into one of the following five broad categories.

Pseudoconflict

A **pseudoconflict** is a conflict that is apparent, not real. It occurs in a situation where there *appears* to be incompatibility between the needs or ideas of the partners.

A common form of pseudoconflict is **badgering,** light teasing, taunting, and mocking behavior. If badgering is a recognized part of a pair's normal interaction, then it may not signal problems to come. However, badgering becomes destructive when the unspoken goal is to goad a person into a real conflict over some other issue, or when the person being badgered is hurt.

A second common form of pseudoconflict occurs when two people are confronted with goals or needs that they believe cannot be achieved simultaneously when in reality they can. For instance, Carl says, "Hey, the Bengals–49ers game is on television—I've got to see this," to which Cynthia replies, "But you promised that you'd take me to see a movie this afternoon!" Carl and Cynthia both have things they want to do, and it seems as if they are in conflict. However, with some creative adaptation it may be possible to do both. In this case, if Cynthia is willing to delay going to the movie for a few hours, then Carl can watch the game; or if Carl can tape the game to watch later, he and Cynthia can go to the movie now. In this case both parties needs can be accommodated, so there is not a real conflict.

Pseudoconflict—conflict that is apparent, not real.

Badgering—light teasing, taunting, and mocking behavior.

When the conflict is recognized to be pseudoconflict, the parties must deal with the apparent conflict before it becomes real. If they do not or cannot deal with it, the conflict may escalate and become real.

Fact Conflict

Fact conflict, often referred to as simple conflict, occurs when the information one person presents is disputed by the other. These conflicts are "simple" because the accuracy of the information in dispute necessary to resolve the conflict can be verified. For example, Ken says to Marge, "Paul asked if I could go with him to the basketball game next Wednesday," to which Marge replies, "You can't do that; that's Parents' Night at school." "No," says Ken, "Parents' Night is the following Wednesday." At this point Marge and Ken can begin to escalate the argument into a conflict about Ken's insensitivity, or Ken's not paying attention, or Marge's shooting from the hip, or why Ken always puts trivia before the family's welfare, and so on. Or, if they recognize this as a simple conflict over a fact, they can double check the date.

If you find yourself in a conflict over a fact, agree to disengage until a source for verifying the fact can be found or until some guidelines for selecting from among competing sources can be determined.

In short, confine the conflict to the issue at hand and get it resolved before it turns into deeper conflict.

Value Conflict

While pseudoconflicts and fact conflicts can be resolved relatively quickly, when the conflict stems from differences in value systems the conflict management process is more difficult. **Value conflicts** occur when people's deeply held beliefs about what is good or bad, worthwhile or worthless, desirable or undesirable, moral or immoral are incompatible. Value conflict can occur (1) when we differ on what we believe is good or bad or (2) when we differ in the priority we assign to a value we agree on.

Suppose, for example, that Josh and Sarah are going together and would like to get married. In their discussions, they have discovered that they have two serious areas of value conflict. First, Sarah, a conservative Jew, believes that weekly attendance at synagogue is required. Josh, who was also raised in a Jewish environment, doesn't attend temple except on major religious holidays. In this case they hold a similar value, but assign it a different priority. Second, Sarah is a committed vegetarian, while Josh is a diehard meat-and-potatoes kind of guy who never met a steak he didn't like. Here Sarah and Josh are likely to have conflict because they value meat differently. Sarah views eating meat as socially irresponsible, while Josh sees meat as part of a balanced diet.

Many times conflicts over values are unresolvable. At times we must simply be content to respect each other but "agree to disagree." However, if resolution is possible, it will begin with the recognition that the issue is a value conflict. In the

Josh and Sarah scenario, it is important that both of them realize that the other person is not "just being stubborn" or "spoiled" or "just wanting his or her own way."

Instead they must draw on the trust and mutual respect that they have established to recognize that the issue before them is one on which they have incompatible values. Then, recognizing these differences, they may be able to discuss their emotional attachment to the issue. This understanding may enable them to draw upon other values on which they agree to arrive at a mutually satisfying resolution. Once Josh and Sarah acknowledge that each of them is interested in doing what he or she thinks is "right," they can move to a respectful discussion of what to do in any specific case.

As you can see, the less congruence there is between the value hierarchies of two people, the more likely they are to experience value conflicts. Because these conflicts are difficult to resolve, mutually satisfying long-term intimate relationships are likely to be difficult to maintain between individuals whose value hierarchies are dissimilar.

Policy Conflict

Policy conflicts occur when two people in a relationship disagree about what should be the appropriate plan, course of action, or behavior in dealing with a perceived problem. For instance, the chapter opening vignette suggests that Mark and Lisa have resolved their policy conflict over what to do about telephone messages intended for the other person; they appear to have "agreed" that the best policy is to write down the message and give it to the other person. But as that vignette goes on to show, conflict will continue if the parties do not follow through by behaving in accordance with the agreed upon policy.

What is perceived to be an appropriate policy is both situational and culturally based, so this type of conflict is common to most relationships. Many times conflict stems from novel situations (or problems) for which there is no existing relational policy. For instance, Tyrone and Cherise come from families that approach child rearing quite differently. Tyrone comes from a family in which children are given a lot of freedom, while Cherise comes from a family in which children's activities are closely monitored and supervised. So, Tyrone and Cherise may experience a policy conflict over whether to set a curfew for their adolescent children.

At other times policies have been agreed to, but a changing situation causes renewed policy conflict. For instance, Paul and Mary have been going out together for several months. Early on, an informal but never discussed "policy" appeared to be that Paul would pay all the expenses of their dates. Lately, however, Paul has become uncomfortable with this policy. He knows that Mary earns more than he does, and he sees their relationship escalating and expenses mounting. Thus he now sees a problem with the policy—a problem important enough to require discussion and change. Although Mary may understand the problem, her view of how to solve it may or may not agree with Paul's. If they disagree, then they will experience a policy conflict.

Because policy conflicts concern what "should" be done, there is no "right" or "wrong" behavior; the policy that is followed depends on what the parties agree

Policy conflicts—conflicts that occur when two people in a relationship disagree about what should be the appropriate plan, course of action, or behavior in dealing with a perceived problem.

to. These conflicts can be successfully resolved if the parties are willing to consider a plan or course of action that best deals with the perceived problem and with each party's feelings about it. So, Paul and Mary must both recognize that Paul's paying for all dates is creating a problem and then decide the course of action that appears most equitable.

Ego Conflict

Ego conflicts—conflicts that occur when the people involved view "winning" the conflict as central to maintaining their positive self-image.

Ego conflicts occur when the people involved view "winning" the conflict as central to maintaining their positive self-image. When both people see the conflict as a measure of who they are, what they are, how competent they are, whom they have power over, or how much they know, ego conflicts occur. In these situations "winning" the conflict becomes the only means of satisfying needs.

Ego conflicts can develop when discussion of facts or values is undermined by personal or judgmental statements. The more expert you believe yourself to be, the more likely you are to become ego-involved when your word on that issue is questioned. Once your sense of self-worth becomes threatened, your ability to remain rational can be impaired. Before you realize it, emotions come into play, words may be said that cannot be taken back, and a conflict can be blown out of proportion.

When we recognize that we are experiencing ego conflict, we should use face work to de-escalate the conflict to the content level. For instance, suppose Grant says to Darlene, "Where do you get off doubting my word on this? We're talking about *my* family. I know a whole lot more about my brother than you ever could." Darlene might de-escalate the conflict by replying, "Grant, I know that you un-

Conflicts in which values or egos are at issue often escalate. How can peers help to minimize the effects of these conflicts?

TEST YOURSELF

Identifying Types of Conflict

Label the following as S (pseudoconflict), F (fact), V (value conflict), P (policy), or E (ego conflict).

a. Joe wants to live with Mary, but Mary wants the two of them to get married.

b. Stan believes that because he is an insurance salesman, Jerry should not dispute his position on annuities.

c. George defends his failure to present an anniversary gift to Agnes by asserting that their anniversary is not today (May 8) but May 18.

d. Martin calls to announce that he is bringing the boss home for dinner. His wife replies, "That will be impossible. The house is a mess and I need to go shopping."

e. Jane says, "Harry, pick up your clothes—I'm not your maid!" Harry replies, "I thought we agreed that it's your job to take care of the house. I take care of the yard."

a. V b. E c. F d. S e. P

derstand your brother way more than I do. I've only seen him three times and you've lived with him all your life. The point I was trying to make is that your brother hasn't returned the sleeping bag he borrowed over a month ago."

Table 11.1 provides some examples and suggestions for resolving each type of conflict.

Table 11.1 Conflict types and resolution strategies

Type	Dialogue	Resolution Strategy
1. Pseudo conflict	"I've told you those pants have to go. Where's your taste?" "We can't go to the play. I've asked Martha to come over."	Recognize badgering for what it is. Don't let yourself be drawn in. Look for ways of meeting both needs.
2. Fact Conflict	"Parker said that the paper has to be in today."" "No, it can be turned in Tuesday."	Stop and check the facts.
3. Value Conflict	"Tom you've got to tell Jamison what he wants to hear." "But I don't see the world the way he does and I'm not going to say I do."	Look for areas in which both parties agree and work from there. If no agreement, may have to agree to disagree.
4. Policy Conflict	"Myrna, please write down any messages you take." "Why? I remember to tell you without writing it down."	Identify the nature of the problem. Agree on a policy (a plan of action or set of behaviors) that is most likely to provide the best solution.
5. Ego Conflict	"Gloria, I don't think that this design fits the assignment." "Oh, so you think that I'm incapable of doing this job."	Look for ways to move the conflict away from an ego level and back down to a content level.

Styles of Managing Conflict

Think about the last time you experienced a conflict. How did you react? Did you avoid it? Give in? Force the other person to accept your will? Did you compromise? Or did the two of you use a problem-solving approach? Each of these approaches differs in how much you were willing to cooperate in attempting to satisfy the other person's needs or concerns and how assertive you were in trying to satisfy your own needs and concerns. You cooperate more or less depending on how important you believe the relationship to be. You vary your assertiveness depending on how important the issue is to you. When faced with a conflict, you can withdraw, accommodate, force, compromise, or collaborate (Lulofs & Cahn, 2000, pp. 101–102).

Withdrawal

Withdrawal—resolving conflict by physically or psychologically removing oneself from the conflict.

One of the most common, and certainly one of the easiest, ways to deal with conflict is to withdraw or avoid the conflict. When people **withdraw,** they physically or psychologically remove themselves from the conflict. This style is both uncooperative and unassertive because at least one person is refusing to talk about it.

A person may withdraw physically by leaving the site. For instance, as Eduardo and Justina get into an argument about Eduardo's financial support for their son, Eduardo may withdraw physically by saying "I don't want to talk about this" and walk out the door.

What motivates people to withdraw? What is lost as a result?

Conversing about Racism By Bruce A. Jacobs

In the preface to his book Race Manners, *Bruce Jacobs, noted author and poet, provides glimpses of the conversations that Americans need to have with each other if we are to move beyond conflict and effect racial reconciliation. Which do you regard as most valuable?*

Our country is consuming itself in racial rage. Increasingly, talk about race carries either the tone of violence or a sense of sterile, exaggerated civility. The message seems to be, Shut up and behave before somebody gets hurt. Talking about race is, quite literally, dangerous.

How did things become this insane? And why, forty years after White Only and Colored Only signs on water fountains, are we too often willing to accept versions of one another's identities that are as contrived and as facile as car ads?

The reason is that race has become so toxic a topic in America that many of us are afraid to even touch it, as least in public, without some kind of industrial-strength protection. With talk-show vitriol now passing for social discourse, and with racial anger mounting in proportion to the fears and insecurities of a downsized America, the topic of race has acquired the potency of nerve gas. We hold racial opinions clandestinely, muttering them sourly among family and friends. The more desperate among us hurl racial insults (or worse) at perceived enemies from safe hiding places.

It is hard to converse about anything while enraged. And the hold of habitual racism is harder to kick than heroin, particularly when practically everyone you know is a user and every newsstand and television set is a pusher. We have reached the point where our racial hostility and stereotyping regenerate themselves, intensifying as if in an echo chamber, through the inertia of reciprocal resentment. Then periodically, new and outrageous racial incidents provide this juggernaut with fresh momentum. Many African Americans now automatically presume that hostility from any white person, in any situation, is racially based. Many whites leap to the equivalent conclusion about blacks. Sometimes the facts bear out suspicions; sometimes they do not. But we can't see far enough past our own racial panic buttons to discern the difference. Americans have never been very good at this; what few skills we have gained are now rapidly being lost.

Stupid? Self-defeating? Of course. Sometimes, when attacked from just the right angle, racism's very absurdity cries out for laughter. Eddie Murphy does a scathingly hilarious stand-up comedy routine in which he recalls having snapped into the brother-with-an-attitude reflex upon arriving at a Texas airport. A helpful white luggage handler approached, asking, "Is this your bag?" Murphy whirled with centuries' worth of fury. "Yeah, it's my F_ _ _ing bag!" he exploded. "What's wrong? A black man can't have a suitcase?" The audience howls. It's an excruciatingly funny routine for any of us who have learned the habit of anticipating bigotry. White people claim that African Americans can be too touchy. And black people reply that we have good reason for being too touchy.

But maybe Eddie Murphy is showing us precisely the kind of conversation we need to be having. Maybe after the black passenger throws his fit, the white baggage handler grabs his arm and asks him what the hell his problem is. And the black passenger turns and replies that his problem is that a black man was dragged to his death by three white racist psychopaths less than fifty miles from here a month ago, and sometimes it's hard to tell on first sight who wants to carry your bag and who wants to spread your flesh along the pavement. The white baggage handler spits back that he doesn't want to hear it, he's sorry about the hitchhiker but he didn't kill him, and anyway, what good does it do anybody for the black guy to stay so paranoid? The black man replies that maybe being paranoid will, just one time in one town, save his life or spare his pride, and that maybe paranoia is still his one way of feeling in control, of feeling a step ahead of the thousand little ambushes that he knows await him in airports and on country roads. The baggage han-

dler looks at him, thinks for a moment, and then tells him that that's a hell of a way to live. The black man looks right back at him and says, yeah, it sure is.

We have to talk. It is time we stopped allowing our racial conversation to be hijacked by church bombers on the one hand and workshop leaders on the other. Let's dare to push toward some more honest racial

reckoning in our daily lives. Let's break through the private smirks and the public taboos, and begin to get real in talking about race. If not now, when? ∎

Excerpted from Jacobs, B. A. (1999). *Race Manners* (pp. 1–12). New York: Arcade Publishing Inc. Reprinted with permission: © 1999 by Bruce Jacobs.

Psychological withdrawal occurs when one person simply ignores what the other person is saying. Using the same example, when Justina begins to talk about Eduardo's failure to pay child support, Eduardo may ignore her and continue to play with his son as though she has not spoken.

Considered from an individual-satisfaction standpoint, withdrawal creates a lose/lose situation because neither party to the conflict really accomplishes what he or she wants. Although Eduardo temporarily escapes from the conflict, he knows it will come up again. Likewise, Justina experiences frustration at two levels. First, she doesn't get the money, and second, Eduardo's refusal to talk about it further strains the relationship.

When used repeatedly, withdrawal hurts the relationship. Why? Because those who withdraw don't eliminate the source of the conflict, and the withdrawal actually increases the tension. As Roloff and Cloven (1990) say "Relational partners who avoid conflicts have more difficulty resolving their disputes" (p. 49). In ongoing relationships the conflict will undoubtedly resurface. When Eduardo visits again, he and Justina may try to resolve an unrelated issue. In the case of psychological withdrawal, Justina will undoubtedly reintroduce the child support issue.

Another consequence of withdrawal is that it results in what Cloven and Roloff (1991, p. 136) call "mulling behavior." By mulling, they mean thinking about or stewing over an actual or perceived problem until the person perceives the conflict as more severe and begins engaging in blaming behavior. Thus, in many cases, not confronting the problem when it occurs only makes it more difficult to deal with in the long run.

Unhealthy withdrawal can be a primary problem in conflicts among persons of diverse backgrounds. Many people who have harbored stereotypes and prejudices are unwilling to confront them in themselves and have let them get in the way of establishing more meaningful relationships with others. This very issue is considered in the Diverse Voices you read on pages 311–312. Bruce Jacobs, a writer whose works have appeared in a variety of major publications, confronts us with the point that we can't hide deep-seated conflict behind a veil of silence. He discusses how we must be willing to *talk* with each other if we're ever going to be able to resolve our racial conflicts.

Although withdrawal is an ineffective style most of the time, there are at least two sets of circumstances in which withdrawing may be a useful strategy. First, withdrawing permits a temporary disengagement that allows strong emotional reactions to be checked. When it is used for this purpose the withdrawer should so indicate. For example, when Pat and Bill begin to argue heatedly over going to Bill's mother's for Thanksgiving dinner, Pat may stop and say, "Hold it a minute; let me make a pot of coffee and calm down a bit, and then we'll talk about this some more." A few minutes later, having calmed down, Pat may return, ready to approach the conflict in a different way.

The second set of circumstances in which withdrawal is appropriate is when neither the relationship nor the issue is really important. Consider Josh and Mario, who work in different departments of the same company and who have gotten into heated arguments at company gatherings about whether the Giants or the Cardinals is a better ball club. At the next gathering Mario may avoid sitting near Josh or may quickly change the subject when Josh begins the argument anew. In this case, Mario judges that it simply isn't worth trying to resolve the disagreement with Josh—neither the issue nor the relationship is that important. So withdrawal can be effective as a temporary strategy to allow tempers to cool, or when neither an issue nor a relationship is important.

Accommodating

When people **accommodate,** they resolve conflict by satisfying others' needs or accepting others' ideas while neglecting their own. So, This approach is cooperative but unassertive. It preserves friendly relationships, but fails to protect personal rights.

Accommodating—resolving conflict by satisfying others' needs or accepting others' ideas while neglecting our own.

People who are insecure in their relationships accommodate in order to ensure their continuance. For instance, as Juan and Mariana discuss their vacation plans, Mariana says that she'd like to ask two of their friends who will be vacationing the same week to join them. When Juan says that he'd like for the two of them to go alone, Mariana replies, "But I think it would be fun to go with another couple, don't you?" Juan replies, "OK, whatever you want." Even though Juan really wants the two of them to go alone, he sees that Mariana is enthusiastic about all four going together, and so he accommodates.

Considered from an individual-satisfaction standpoint, accommodation is a lose/win situation. The accommodator chooses to lose and the other person gets what he or she wants. From a relational-satisfaction standpoint, habitual accommodation has two problems. First, conflicts resolved through accommodation may lead to poor decision making because important facts, arguments, and positions are not voiced. Second, habitual accommodation results in one person's taking advantage of the other. This can damage one's self-concept and lead to feelings of resentment that undermine relationships.

There are situations, of course, in which it is appropriate and effective to accommodate. When the issue is not important to you, but the relationship is, accommodating is the preferred style. Hal and Yvonne are trying to decide what to have for dinner. Hal says, "I really have a taste for chicken tonight—how about we stir-fry?" Yvonne, who'd prefer a different dish, says, "OK, that will be fine." Yvonne's interest in a different preparation was not very strong, and since Hal really seemed excited about stir-frying, she accommodated. It may also be useful to accommodate in one situation to build "social credits" or goodwill that can be used later. Again, Yvonne goes along with Hal this time so she'll have a little more leverage when a later issue is more important to her.

It should be noted, however, that accommodating is a preferred style of dealing with conflict in some cultures. In Japanese culture, for instance, it is thought to be more humble and face-saving to accommodate than to risk losing respect through conflict (Lulofs & Cahn, 2000, p. 114).

Forcing

Forcing—resolving conflict by attempting to satisfy your own needs or advance your own ideas with no concern for the needs or ideas of others and no concern for the harm done to the relationship.

A third style of dealing with conflict is forcing or competing. When people **force** they attempt to satisfy their own needs or advance their own ideas with no concern for the needs or ideas of the other and no concern for the harm done to the relationship. Forcing can be done through physical threats, verbal attacks, coercion, or manipulation. The expression "my way or the highway" captures the spirit of the forcing style. If the other party accommodates, the conflict subsides. If, however, the other side responds forcibly, the conflict escalates. Forcing is uncooperative but assertive. The forcer wishes to exert his or her will over the other and will argue assertively to do so.

Considered from an individual-satisfaction standpoint, forcing is I win/you lose. The person who is forcing wins—at the expense of the relational partner. From a relational-satisfaction standpoint, forcing usually hurts a relationship, at

CALVIN AND HOBBES © Watterson. Dist. by UNIVERSAL PRESS SYNDICATE. Reprinted with permission. All rights reserved.

least in the short term. But there are times when forcing is an effective means to resolve conflict. In emergencies, when quick and decisive action must be taken to ensure safety or minimize harm, forcing is useful. When an issue is critical to your own or the other's welfare and you know you are right, you may find forcing necessary. Finally, if you are interacting with someone who will take advantage of you if you do not force the issue, this style is appropriate. For example, David knows that, statistically speaking, the likelihood of death or serious injury increases dramatically if one does not wear a helmet when riding a motorcycle. So he insists that his sister wear one when she rides with him, even though she complains bitterly that it messes her hair.

Compromising

When people **compromise** they resolve the conflict by giving up part of what each wants in order to provide at least some satisfaction for both parties. Under this approach both people have to give up part of what they really want or believe, or have to trade one thing they want in order to get something else. Compromising is intermediate between assertiveness and cooperativeness. Each person has to be somewhat assertive and somewhat cooperative to get partial satisfaction. For example, if Heather and Paul are working together on a class project and need to meet outside of class but both have busy schedules, they may compromise on a time to meet.

From an individual-satisfaction standpoint, compromising creates a lose/lose situation, because both people in a sense "lose" even as they "win." From a relational-satisfaction standpoint, compromise may be seen as neutral to positive, because both parties gain some satisfaction.

Although compromising is a popular style, there are significant problems associated with it. One problem of special concern is that the quality of a decision is affected if one of the parties "trades away" a better solution in order to effect the compromise. Compromising is appropriate when the issue is moderately important, when there are time constraints, and when attempts at forcing or collaborating have not been successful.

Compromising—a form of conflict management in which people attempt to resolve their conflict by providing at least some satisfaction for both parties.

Collaborating—resolving conflict by trying to fully address the needs and issues of each party and arrive at a solution that is mutually satisfying.

Collaborating

A fifth style of dealing with conflict is through problem-solving discussion, or collaboration. People **collaborate** when they try to fully address the needs and issues of each party and arrive at a solution that is mutually satisfying. During collaboration people treat their disagreement as a problem to be solved, so they discuss the issues, describe their feelings, and identify the

INTER-ACT WITH

Technology

Suppose you are participating in a newsgroup discussion online in which the topic of conversation is controversial. What kinds of behavior (withdrawal/avoidance, accommodating, forcing/coercing, compromising, or collaborating) do you tend to engage in most? Does your conflict management behavior online differ from your behavior in face-to-face conflicts? If so, what accounts for those differences? ■

What is necessary to stimulate collaboration in resolving an issue of conflict?

characteristics of an effective solution. Collaborating is both assertive and cooperative. It is assertive because both parties voice their concerns; it is cooperative because they work together to gain resolution.

From an individual-satisfaction standpoint, collaborating is win/win, since both people's needs are met. From a relational-satisfaction standpoint, collaboration is positive because both sides feel that they have been heard. They get to share ideas and weigh and consider information. Whatever the solution, it is a truly collaborative effort.

Resolving conflict through collaborative discussion requires many of the communication skills we have discussed previously. Participants must use accurate and precise language to describe their ideas and feelings. They must empathically listen to the ideas and feelings of the other person. Using a problem-solving ap-

---

Table 11.2 Collaborating through problem-solving discussion

1. Define the problem.	What's the issue being considered?
2. Analyze the problem.	What are the causes and symptoms?
3. Develop mutually agreeable criteria for judging alternative solutions.	What goals will a good solution reach?
4. Generate alternative solutions.	What could we do? List before discussing each.
5. Select the solution that best fits the criteria identified.	Select one or a combination from those listed.

proach, they must define and analyze the problem, develop mutually acceptable criteria for judging alternative
solutions, suggest possible solutions, select the solution
that best meets the criteria, and work to implement the
decision (see Table 11.2).

Let's consider a conflict example mentioned earlier: Justina is upset because Eduardo has not paid child
support. To collaborate, both parties must honestly
want to satisfy the other's concerns as well as his or her
own. If they agree to collaborate, each may begin by describing the situation from his or her perspective while
the other listens with empathy and understanding.
Justina may describe for Eduardo the landlord's threats
and her fear of becoming homeless. Eduardo may disclose that he recently took a pay cut in order to take a
new job that has more potential and he has fallen behind on his own bills. From this base they can work together to establish a list of what guidelines or criteria a
solution would have to meet for it to be acceptable to
both of them. Justina might say a good solution would
be one in which she would be sure that she received at least thirty dollars by the
first of each month and thirty dollars by the fifteenth of the month. Eduardo
might say a good solution would be one that allowed him to meet all his financial obligations, including child support, on time.

Together they might brainstorm a list of possible solutions. For example,
Justina might propose that Eduardo bring his laundry to her house and do it while
he visits with his son—this would save him about five dollars a week at the laundry.
Eduardo might suggest that he be allowed to "borrow" the money in their son's
college savings account in order to meet his current child support payments and
pay this money back when he gets a promised raise in six months. Once they have
examined the alternatives, Justina and Eduardo can choose the one or ones that satisfy their criteria.

Does this process sound too idealized? Or impractical? Collaboration is difficult, but when two people commit themselves to trying, chances are they will discover that through discussion they can arrive at solutions that meet both of their
needs and do so in a way that maintains their relationship. Much of the remainder
of this chapter focuses on guidelines for accomplishing good collaborative discussion.

The five different styles of conflict management, with their characteristics,
outcomes, and appropriate usage, are summarized in Table 11.3 (p. 318–319). If we
are to become more effective at interacting in conflict situations, we need to understand each style, we need to know when and at what cost it is likely to be effective, and we need to know when and how to use it.

OBSERVE & ANALYZE

Journal Activity

Conflict Episodes

Describe a conflict episode you have
recently experienced. How did you
and how did the other person behave? What was the outcome of the conflict?
How did you feel about it then? Now? Was
there a different way the conflict might have
been handled that would have resulted in better outcomes? ■

Table 11.3 Styles of conflict management

Approach	Characteristics	Goal	Outlook
Withdrawal	Uncooperative, unassertive	To keep from dealing with conflict	"I don't want to talk about it."
Accommodating	Cooperative, unassertive	To keep from upsetting the other person	"Getting my way isn't as important as keeping the peace."
Forcing	Uncooperative, assertive	To get my way	"I'll get my way regardless of what I have to do."
Compromising	Partially cooperative, partially assertive	To get partial satisfaction	"I'll get partial satisfaction by letting the other person get partial satisfaction as well."
Collaborating	Cooperative, assertive	To solve the problem together	"Let's talk this out and find the best solution possible for both of us."

Communication Skills that Promote Successful Conflict Management

Your primary goal in managing conflict is to be both appropriate and effective. In the Spotlight on Scholars on page 321, we can see how the research of Daniel Canary, Professor of Speech Communication at Arizona State University, has validated the importance of both appropriateness and effectiveness in conflict management. While each of the five conflict styles can be used to manage a conflict, in most interpersonal settings we are concerned about the long-term relationship, so collaboration will be the preferred style.

In the remainder of this chapter we will describe the skills that you can use to resolve a conflict collaboratively. We begin by explaining how to initate a conflict. Then we describe how you can respond to a conflict initiated by your partner. Finally, we present guidelines to help you mediate the conflicts of others.

Communication Skills for Initiating Conflict

Because you have unique needs, feelings, and ideas that will not correspond to your partner's, in any relationship there will be situations where you want to present areas of conflict so that problems can be resolved. If you do this using the communication skills you have previously developed, you are more likely to engage the other

Individual Satisfaction	Relational Satisfaction	Relational Effects	When Appropriate
Lose/lose: neither party gets satisfaction	Negative: no resolution	Drives wedge into relationship: results in muffling and blaming	Either as temporary disengagement or when issue is unimportant
Lose/win: the other party gets satisfaction	Negative: neither party feels good about the process	Hurts relationship because one person takes advantage	To build social credits or when the issue is unimportant
Win/lose: one party, the forcer, gets satisfaction	Negative: physical and psychological pain for the loser	Hurts relationship because one person feels intimidated	In emergencies; when it is critical to one's or others' welfare; if someone is taking advantage of you
Lose/lose or win/win: neither party is fully satisfied	Neutral to positive: at least partial satisfaction for both	May help or hurt because satisfaction is compromised	When issue is moderately important, when time is short, or when other attempts don't work
Win/win: both parties feel satisfied with the process	Positive: relationship strengthened because mutual benefits	Helps the relationship because both sides are heard	Anytime

person in a nondefense-producing collaborative process that resolves the conflict. The following guidelines for initiating conflict (as well as those for responding to conflict in the next section) are based on work from several fields of study (Adler, 1977; Gordon, 1970; Whetten & Cameron, 2002).

1. Recognize and state ownership of the apparent problem. If a conflict is to be resolved, it is important to acknowledge that you are angry, hurt, or frustrated. You may believe that the other person has caused you to feel this way; nonetheless, that person doesn't experience the problem—you do. So it is honest to own what is occurring by owning your own ideas and feelings, making "I" statements (see Chapter 9).

Suppose you are trying to study for a major test in your most difficult course and your neighbor's stereo is so loud that your walls are shaking and you can't concentrate. As this continues, you become agitated because you can't focus on your study. Who has a problem? Your neighbor? No. You have a problem. It's your study that is being disrupted. To resolve your problem, you decide to confront your neighbor.

Remember, your goal is to seek collaboration to resolve the problem. Think of it this way: If two people agree that there is a problem, then they can work to resolve it equitably. In effect, if you can solve your problem without it escalating into a perceived conflict, then your goal will be achieved.

Of course, you could rap on the door and when your neighbor opens her door shout, "Your stereo's too loud, turn it down—I'm trying to study!" Although this bald statement might make you feel better, it is almost guaranteed to arouse defensiveness in your neighbor and lead to an ego conflict. An appropriate way of owning your problem would be to say, "Hi, I'm having a problem that I need your help with. I'm trying to study for a midterm in my most difficult class. . . ."

2. Describe the basis of the potential conflict in terms of behavior, consequences, and feelings. The behavior, consequences, and feelings (b-c-f) sequence is a specific order for communicating your concerns: "When a specific behavior(s) happen(s), the specific consequences result, and I feel (a certain way)" (Gordon, 1971). It's important to include all three of these elements in order for the other person to fully understand what is happening. In each of these instances, you are describing for the other person what you see or hear, what happens to you as a result, and what feelings you experience.

Earlier in this book we discussed the skills of describing behavior and describing feelings. Both of these are designed to lessen defensiveness on the part of the other person. Since people are less inclined to collaborate when they feel threatened, anything we can do to lessen defensiveness should help us achieve our goals. When the b-c-f sequence is used in initiating a conflict, it helps to communicate the problem in nonevaluative terms. Notice, then, that the b-c-f sequence combines the skills of owning feelings, describing behavior, and describing feelings.

In the example of the loud stereo, you begin by owning the problem: "I'm having a problem that I need your help with. I'm trying to study for a midterm in my most difficult class." Now let's see how you might follow up on that opening using the b-c-f sequence. "When I hear your stereo [b], I get distracted and can't concentrate on studying [c], and then I get frustrated and annoyed [f]." The loudness of the stereo is the behavior; the consequences are being distracted and unable to concentrate; and the feelings are being frustrated and annoyed.

Let's try one more example. Suppose a friend has the habit of interrupting you before you finish your ideas. You first own the problem and then describe it by saying, "Glen, I have a problem. When you start talking before I have finished expressing my ideas [b], I'm not able to complete the idea [c], and I get very angry [f]."

3. Avoid evaluating the other person's motives. Since your goal is to resolve your complaint without escalating the conflict, you want to make sure that you do nothing to create defensiveness. So be careful to avoid accusing or distorting what the other person has done. Though a few people may at times be out to get you intentionally, most of the time others' behavior is not an attempt to thwart your needs, but simply an attempt to meet their own. Thus, your neighbor is probably not intentionally undermining your study time, but rather trying to enjoy her leisure time. While using the b-c-f sequence, don't let evaluations and blaming statements creep in. For instance, you wouldn't want to say "When I hear your stereo, which is way too loud for this building. . ." Adding "which is way too loud. . ." is evaluating. You want the focus to be on what is happening to you.

4. Be sure the other person understands your problem. Regardless of our efforts to reduce defensiveness, any time we confront others with a conflict, they are likely to misunderstand what we mean or what we want. Even when we take the greatest care in describing our needs, others may become defensive, try to rationalize, or immediately counterattack. They may get the general drift of the message but misunderstand the seriousness of the problem, or they may completely misunderstand.

Daniel J. Canary, Professor of Communication in the Hugh Downs School of Human Communication, Arizona State University on

Conflict Management

Dan Canary, citing the personal benefit of studying conflict, stated, "I learned how to control my own behavior and become more effective in my personal relationships." Canary's initial curiosity about effective conflict management behaviors was piqued when he was in graduate school at the University of Southern California. At the time he was a classmate of Brian Spitzberg (see Spotlight on Scholars, p. 23–24), who formulated the theory that relational competence is a product of behaviors that are both appropriate and effective, and Bill Cupach, who was studying conflict in relationships. Although Canary saw the connection between their work, it was several years later—after he experienced successful and unsuccessful resolution of significant conflict episodes in his personal life—that he began in earnest to study how the way people behave during conflict episodes affects their relationships.

Scholars can become well known by developing a new theory that more clearly describes what really happens when we interact, by carrying out a series of research studies that test and elaborate on the theories developed by others, or by organizing, integrating, and synthesizing the theories and research work that have been done in an area so that people who are not specialists in the particular area can better understand what is known. Dan Canary's reputation has been made in both of the latter types of scholarship.

Canary's research studies are helping to identify the behaviors that lead to perceiving a person as a competent conflict manager. Canary argues that, although people will view some of the communication behaviors to manage conflict as appropriate and some behaviors as effective, both are necessary to be perceived as competent. Drawing on Sptizberg's competence theory, Canary's research studies are designed to identify conflict behaviors that accomplish both of the goals of appropriateness and effectiveness. The results of his studies consistently show that integrative conflict strategies—problem solving, collaborative, and compromising approaches that display a desire to work with the other person—are perceived to be both appropriate and effective (i.e., competent). Furthermore, his studies have shown that when one partner in

a relationship is thought to be a competent conflict manager, the other one trusts the partner more, is more satisfied with the relationship, and perceives the relationship to be more intimate.

Canary's research studies identify specific conflict management behaviors that are viewed as appropriate and/or effective. Canary has found that when a person acknowledges the arguments of others (e.g., "Uh huh, I can see how you would think that," etc.) and when a person agrees with the arguments that others make to support their points (e.g., "Gee that's a good point that I hadn't really thought about," etc.), the person is viewed as having appropriately handled the conflict. To be viewed as effective, however, requires a different set of behaviors. According to Canary's findings, conflict handling behaviors that are viewed as effective included stating complete arguments, elaborating and justifying one's point of view, and clearly developing one's ideas. Canary noticed that in a conflict situation, what was viewed as appropriate alone had the potential to be ineffective since appropriate behaviors seemed to involve some sort of agreement with the other person.

Canary reasoned that there must be ways to be both appropriate and effective in conflict situations. This led him to consider methods of sequencing or ordering messages in a conflict episode. His preliminary results have revealed that competent communicators (those perceived to be both appropriate and effective) will begin by acknowledging the other's viewpoint, or agreeing with part of the other's argument, *before* explaining, justifying, and arguing for their own viewpoint. Canary believes that

in using this sequence, competent communicators help "frame" the interaction as one of cooperative problem solving rather than framing it as a situation of competing interests where only one party can "win."

Many of Canary's major contributions to the study of conflict in personal relationships are included in two books: *Relationship Conflict* (co-authored with William Cupach and Susan Messman) is a synthesis of the diverse conflict literature that was written for graduate students and other scholars. *Competence in Interpersonal*

Conflict (also co-authored with Cupach) focuses on how readers can increase their competence at managing interpersonal conflict in a variety of settings. For complete citations of these books and additional works by Canary, see the references for this chapter at the end of the book.

Canary teaches courses in interpersonal communication, conflict management, and research methods. His most recent research involves a quickly applied conflict rating system that people can use to observe conflict in an efficient yet valid way.

At times you will need to rephrase or restate what you have said. Remember, effective collaboration depends on understanding the issue, so persevere until you are confident that your partner understands your problem.

Suppose when you approach your neighbor about the stereo, she says, "Oh come on, everyone plays loud music in this neighborhood, and there have been times when I have even heard your stereo." You might reply, "Yes, I understand it's a noisy neighborhood, and loud music normally doesn't bother me. And I'm sorry if I've disturbed you in the past—I didn't mean to. But I'm still having a problem right now, and I was hoping you could help me." Notice that this doesn't say the person wasn't listening or is continuing to be insensitive. It merely attempts to get the focus back on the problem that you are having.

5. Phrase your preferred solution in a way that focuses on common ground. Once you have been understood and you understand the other's position, make your suggestion for resolution. This suggestion is more likely to be accepted if you can tie it to a shared value, common interest, or shared constraint. In our example you might say, "I think we both have had times when even little things got in the way of our being able to study. So even though I realize I'm asking you for a special favor, I hope you can help me out by turning down your stereo while I'm grinding through this material."

6. Mentally rehearse what you will say before you confront the other person, so that your request will be brief and precise. Initiating a collaborative conflict conversation requires us to be in control of our emotions. Yet, by nature and despite our good intentions of keeping on track, our emotions can get the better of us and in the heat of the moment we may say things we shouldn't or we may go on and on and annoy the other person.

Before you go charging over to your neighbor's room, think to yourself, "What am I going to say?" Take a minute to practice. Say to yourself, "I need to own the problem and then follow the b-c-f sequence." Then mentally rehearse a few statements until you think you can do it when your neighbor comes to the door. In your practice keep your comments short. Since problem solving requires interaction, it is important that you draw the other person into the conversation quickly. The longer you talk, the more likely it is that the other person will become defensive. Effective turn-taking during the early stages of a conflict conversation will nurture the problem-solving climate.

Communication Skills for Responding to Conflict

It is more difficult to create a collaborative climate when responding to conflict initiated by another than it is to begin a conflict appropriately. Because most initiators do not use the problem, behavior, consequences, feelings sequence to initiate conflict and instead express their feelings in inappropriate, evaluative terms that threaten you and cause you to become defensive, it can be difficult to overcome your defensiveness and respond appropriately. For instance, suppose your neighbor knocks on your door and says, "Turn down that damn stereo! What kind of inconsiderate idiot are you? Even a moron would realize that playing it at the top of the volume is rude." Face it, even if you were playing the music loudly, the way this person approached you might cause you to want to say, "Well, tough rocks, I'll play my stereo any way I feel like it. If you don't like it, move!" But where does this get you? It may make you feel better for the moment, but it certainly doesn't lay the groundwork for a collaborative discussion.

Your most difficult task as a responder is to take ineffectively initiated conflicts and turn them into productive problem-solving discussions. The following guidelines will help you to respond effectively in these situations.

 **SKILL BUILDERS**

DESCRIBING BEHAVIOR, CONSEQUENCES, AND FEELINGS SEQUENCE

SKILL	USE	PROCEDURE	EXAMPLE
Describing the basis of a conflict in terms of behavior, consequences, and feelings (b-c-f).	To help the other person understand the problem completely.	1. Own the message. 2. Describe the behavior that you see or hear. 3. Describe the consequences that result. 4. Describe your feelings.	Jason says, "I have a problem that I need your help with. When I tell you what I'm thinking and you don't respond (b), I start to think you don't care about me or what I think (c), and this causes me to get very angry with you (f)."

1. Put your "shields up." We *Star Trek* buffs know that when the *Enterprise* is about to be attacked or has just been fired upon, the captain shouts "Shields up!" With its shields in place the ship is somewhat protected from the enemy's fire, and the captain and crew are able to continue to function normally while they consider their strategy. Similarly, when someone becomes overly aggressive in initiating a conflict we need to learn to put our mental "shields" up to enable us to listen and improve our capacity to respond effectively rather than becoming defensive and blindly counterattacking. One method that can help you do this is to remind yourself that the other person obviously has a problem, not you. It also helps to remember that it is unlikely that anything you have said or done has led to this inappropriate over-reaction. In all likelihood the anger being vented toward you is due to an accumulation of frustration, only part of which directly relates to the current issue. So put those shields up, and while you're "counting to ten" think of your options for turning this into a problem-solving opportunity.

2. Respond empathically with genuine interest and concern. When someone initiates a potential conflict, even when it is stated as baldly as "Turn down that damn radio!" the person will be watching you closely to see how you react. If you make light of the other person's concerns, become defensive, or overreact, you will undermine the opportunity to cooperate in problem solving. Even if you disagree with the complaint, effective collaboration means that you show respect to the person by being attentive and empathizing. Sometimes you can do this by allowing others to vent their emotions while you listen. Only when someone has calmed down can you begin to problem solve. In our example, you might well start by saying, "I can see you're angry. Let's talk about this."

3. Paraphrase your understanding of the problem and ask questions to clarify issues. Since most people are unaware of the b-c-f sequence, you may want to form a paraphrase that captures your understanding of b-c-f issues or ask questions to elicit this information. For instance, let's suppose the person says, "What in the world are you thinking?" If information is missing, as with this initiating statement, then you can ask questions that reflect the b-c-f framework. "Can you tell me what it was that I said or did? When that happened, did something else result that I don't realize? How did you feel about that?" It can also be helpful to ask the person if there is anything else that has not been mentioned. Sometimes people will initiate a conflict episode on minor issues when what really needs to be considered has not been mentioned.

4. Seek common ground by finding some aspect of the complaint to agree with. This does not mean giving in to the other person. Nor does it mean that you should feign agreement on a point that you do not agree with. However, using your skills of supportiveness, you can look for points with which you can agree. Adler (1977) says that you can agree with a message without accepting all of its implications. For example, you can agree with part of it, you can agree with it in principle, you can agree with the initiator's perceptions of the situation, and/or you can agree with the person's feelings.

Let's take our ongoing example: "I'm having a problem that I need your help with. I'm trying to study for a midterm in my most difficult class. When I hear your stereo, I get distracted and can't concentrate on studying, and then I get frustrated and annoyed." In your response, you could agree in part: "I agree it's hard to study difficult material." You could agree in principle: "I agree its best to study in a quiet place." You could agree with the initiator's perception: "I can see that you are finding it difficult to study with music in the background." Or you could agree with the person's feelings: "It's obvious that you're frustrated and annoyed."

You do not need to agree with the initiator's conclusions or evaluations. You need not concede. But by agreeing to some aspect of the complaint, you create common ground from which a problem-solving discussion can proceed.

5. Ask the initiator to suggest alternative solutions. As soon as you are sure that you both have agreed on what the problem is, ask the initiator for alternative ways to resolve the conflict. Since the initiator has probably spent time thinking about what needs to be done, your request for alternatives signals a willingness to listen and cooperate. You may find that one of the suggestions seems reasonable to you. If none are, you may be able to craft an alternative that builds on one of the ideas presented. In any case, asking for suggestions communicates your trust in the other person, strengthening the problem-solving climate.

Communication Skills for Mediating Conflict

Sometimes you are called on to mediate or referee a conflict between other people. A **mediator** is an uninvolved third party who serves as a "neutral and impartial guide, structuring an interaction that enables the conflicting parties to find a mutually acceptable solution to their problems" (Cupach & Canary, 1997, p. 205). You can probably think of times when friends have disagreed and have asked for your advice. Mediators can play an important role in resolving conflicts if they observe the following guidelines (Cupach & Canary, 1997; Whetten & Cameron, 2002).

Mediator—an uninvolved third party who serves as a neutral and impartial guide, structuring an interaction that enables the conflicting parties to find a mutually acceptable solution to their problems.

It is often useful to have help in mediating conflict. What is a mediator likely to do to help people resolve conflict?

1. Make sure that the people having the conflict agree to work with you. If one of the parties doesn't really want your help, then you are not likely to be able to do much good. You may be able to clarify this by saying, "I'm willing to help you work on this, but only if both of you want me to." Sometimes people say they want a mediator when in reality they just want to stall discussion or resolution.

2. Help the people identify the real conflict. Many times people seem to be arguing over one thing when the true source of conflict has not been stated. It is important that you help the parties identify the real issue.

3. Maintain neutrality. Even as a mediator who listens empathically, you cannot show favoritism. Any perception of favoritism will destroy the opportunity for successful mediation.

4. Keep the discussion focused on the issues rather than on personalities. Because problem solving is nurtured in a supportive communication climate, the mediator must help participants to make descriptive statements. This can be done through questions that elicit b-c-f statements and by setting ground rules that encourage statements that are problem oriented and not person oriented, descriptive and not evaluative. If, during the discussion, one of the parties begins accusing or insulting, then the mediator can simply remind the violator of the previously agreed to ground rules.

5. Work to ensure equal air time. It's important that mediators control the conversation so that both parties have an equal chance to be heard. The quality of the conversation is increased if each person gives equal input. Mediators can do this by directing questions to a more reticent party and by encouraging turn-taking with statements such as "We've heard your concerns, Erin; now I'd like us to hear how Ed sees this issue."

6. Focus the discussion on helping the parties find a solution. A mediator is not a judge. Mediators should not let themselves be placed in the position of assessing guilt or making decisions. While some interpersonal conflicts involve issues of right and wrong, most arise from differences in perspective. The mediator should avoid making any judgmental statements. If asked for a personal opinion, the mediator might say, "I'm not in a position to judge. What I want to do is help you find a way to resolve this issue that both of you can feel good about." In this way, the mediator focuses the participants on resolving the conflict between them rather than imposing the mediator's solution.

7. Use perception checking and paraphrasing to make sure both parties fully understand and support the agreed upon solution. Sometimes mediators make the mistake of believing that when one party suggests a reasonable solution to which the other party voices no disagreement, the dispute has been resolved. Since silence cannot automatically be interpreted as agreement, a good mediator paraphrases the solution and asks each party whether he or she can support a given alternative. It is also important that mediators check their perceptions of the nonverbal messages that participants send. While a participant may voice agreement, his or her nonverbal behavior may be shouting hesitancy. If the mediator suspects this, it should be explicitly explored through a perception check. For example, the mediator might say, "Marita, you said you agree with the plan, but from the negative headshake you gave, I sense you're really not pleased with it. Is there something specific that is bothering you?" Once you are convinced that both parties are satisfied with the solution, you can move to the final step in the process.

8. Establish an action plan and follow-up procedure. Unfortunately, some mediators stop short, assuming that once a solution has been agreed to in principle, the participants can work out the details unassisted. But making sure that the parties have an action plan with clearly agreed to responsibilities is also part of effective mediating. The action plan should specify what each party is to do and should specify how results will be measured and monitored. Mediators can move participants to this final stage by praising them for reaching agreement on a general solution framework and asking each party to describe what specific behaviors or changes in behavior they will perform to make the solution an actuality.

As you have seen, mediating conflict draws on a variety of basic interpersonal communication skills. Mediators must be assertive, persuasive, and effective at listening, paraphrasing, and questioning. At times they will use interpreting responses to reframe issues in ways that reduce defensiveness. As a mediator you can provide a useful service for friends and family as you help them repair relationships and work to create more positive communication.

Recovering from Conflict-Management Failures

Ideally, conflicts should be resolved as they occur. The biblical admonishment "Never let the sun set on your anger" is sage advice. Nevertheless, there are times when no matter how hard both persons try, they will not be able to resolve the conflict successfully in a way that meets both party's needs. Sillars and Weisberg (1987, p. 143) have pointed out that conflict can be an extremely complex process and that some conflicts may not be resolvable even with improved communication.

Understanding Unresolved Conflicts Especially when the relationship is important to you, it is useful to analyze your inability to resolve the conflict. Ask yourself questions such as the following: Why was this conflict left unresolved? Did one or more of us become competitive? Or defensive? Did I use a style that was inappropriate to the situation? Did we fail to implement the problem-solving method adequately? Were the vested interests in the outcome too great? Did I initiate or respond inappropriately?

By analyzing your behavior, you will become more aware of how you can continue to improve your skills and more aware of how to handle areas of incompatibility in

OBSERVE & ANALYZE

Journal Activity

Conflict Management

Think of a recent conflict you experienced in which the conflict was not successfully resolved. Analyze what happened using the concepts from this chapter. What type of conflict was it? What style did you adopt? What was the other person's style? How did styles contribute to what happened? How well did your behavior match the guidelines recommended for initiating and responding to the conflict? How might you change what you did if you could "redo" this conflict episode?

Write about a recent conflict situation in which you believe you "won" or "lost." What contributed to the outcome? Did you have any control? What skills mentioned in this chapter might have improved the means of resolving the conflict?

Reflect on a time when you won a battle but lost the war; that is, you appeared to come out ahead at the moment but the long-term quality of the relationship was damaged. What behaviors were responsible for the damage? What might you have done to salvage the relationship? ■

your relationships. And, since conflict is inevitable, you can count on using this knowledge again.

Forgiving Whether you ever resolve your conflict, it is important to forgive the party with whom you were in conflict, especially if this is a friend or acquaintance who is or has been a major part of your life. As a cognitive process, forgiveness consists of letting go of feelings of revenge and desires for retaliation. Forgiveness then paves the way for reconciliation, through which you can rebuild trust in a relationship and work toward restoration. As Lulofs and Cahn (2000) have put it, "There is virtual agreement in the literature that forgiveness is a process in which a person lets go of feelings of revenge and his or her right to retaliate against the other person. With few exceptions, forgiveness is not equated with forgetting what has happened. Nor is forgiveness equated with the immediate restoration of trust. Forgiveness is generally conceived of as a process through which people get on with their lives after experiencing some hurt" (p. 329).

WHAT WOULD YOU DO?

A Question of Ethics

Jennie and Sam had been dating for a year when Jennie realized that, although she thought she loved Sam, she wasn't happy with the relationship. When she thought more about it, she noted that Sam had been spending more and more time working at his part-time job, leaving less time for her. One night at dinner Jennie decided to confront the issue.

"Sam, I'm sick and tired of being taken for granted. It seems to me that all you do is work and when you're not working you're so tired that you don't even notice me. But you expect me to be grateful whenever you want to do something. I can't take it anymore—something's got to change!"

Jennie took a deep breath as she waited for Sam to respond. In the past when she'd worked up enough courage to tell Sam "how it is," he'd always responded with guilt and concern—and she fully expected such a response this time. After all, his behavior was way out of line.

"So it's my fault that our relationship isn't going well? Well look at you. When was the last time you paid your share of our expenses? When was the last time you thought about me before you made plans with one of your girlfriends? Maybe if you weren't so selfish and spoiled, you'd notice that I have to work more since you scaled back your work hours so you could be president of

your sorority. And if you ever got home from your precious meetings before midnight, or did the wash, or cleaned the apartment, maybe I wouldn't be too tired to 'notice' you. As it is, I have to do all the chores and 'bring home the bacon.' You're right, something's got to change!"

Jennie was taken aback, hurt, and confused. But most of all, she was very angry. How could Sam yell at her like that? It just wasn't fair.

1. Identify the ethical issues in this case.

2. Construct a dialog, using the guidelines presented throughout the chapter, that would surface the underlying issues in a more ethical manner.

Summary

Interpersonal conflict arises when the needs or ideas of one person are perceived to be at odds with the needs or ideas of another. Even in good relationships conflicts are inevitable.

There are five types of conflict: pseudoconflicts; fact (simple) conflicts over facts, interpretations of facts, definitions, or choices; value conflicts over competing value systems that are brought to bear on the issues; policy conflicts over ways of solving or coping with problems; and ego conflicts that personalize the nature of the conflict. Conflicts become more complicated as they escalate from ones of fact to values to policies to egos.

We manage conflict by withdrawing, accommodating, forcing, compromising, or collaborating. Each of these strategies can be effective under certain circumstances. When we are concerned about the long-term relationship, collaboration will be most appropriate strategy. We can also affect the conflict episode by using specific communication skills and verbal strategies.

To initiate a collaborative conflict resolution conversation use communication skills. Own the problem; describe the potential conflict using the behavior, consequences, feelings sequence; avoid evaluating the other person's motives; be sure that the other person understands your problem; plan what you will say before you confront the other person; and phrase your request so that it focuses on common ground.

When seeking collaboration by responding to another person's initiation, put your shields up, respond empathically, paraphrase your understanding of the problem, seek common ground, and ask the person to suggest alternatives.

When you mediate a conflict, make sure that the people agree to work with you, help them identify the real conflict, maintain neutrality, keep the discussion focused on the issues, work to ensure equal air time, find solutions rather than placing blame, make sure parties understand what they've agreed to, and establish an action plan and follow-up procedure.

Finally, learn from conflict-management failures. Even when you cannot resolve a conflict, you can forgive the other person so that you can get on with your life.

Inter-Action Dialogue:

Conflict occurs when the needs or ideas of one person are perceived to be at odds with or in opposition to the needs or ideas of another. Consider types of conflict, styles of managing conflict, and skills that promote successful conflict management.

   A transcript of Brian and Matt's conversation is printed below, with analysis of the conversation in the right-hand column. You may want to write down some of your observations before you read the analysis.

Brian and Matt share an apartment. Matt is consistently late in paying his share of expenses. Brian has tolerated this for over six months, but has finally had enough and decides to confront Matt.

CONVERSATION	ANALYSIS
BRIAN: *Matt, I need to talk with you.*	
MATT: *What's up?*	
BRIAN: *Well, I have a problem. When I got home from class today, I tried to call my mom, and guess what? The phone's been disconnected.*	*Brian begins by owning the problem and describing what has happened.*
MATT: *You're kidding.*	
BRIAN: *No, I'm not. And when I went next door and called the phone company, you know what they said?*	*This is not really an honest question.*
MATT: *I can guess.*	*Matt acknowledges what has happened.*
BRIAN: *They said the bill hadn't been paid and that this was the fourth month in a row that the bill was over two weeks late.*	*Brian describes what he was told.*
MATT: *Look man, I can explain.*	
BRIAN: *Like you explained not paying the utility bill on time last month? We were just lucky that it was a cool week and that we didn't fry without air conditioning. The candlelit dinner was charming and all that, but I really resented having to go the library to study for my test. Matt, I just can't go on like this. I mean, I gave you my share of the phone bill three weeks ago. I always give you my half of the utility bill the day it arrives. And I'm sick and tired of having to nag you for your share of the rent. For the last four months I've had to cover yours hare by taking money out of what I am saving to buy Angie's engagement ring. I know that you eventually pay me back, but I lose the interest and it's just not fair.*	*Brian interrupts Matt and inappropriately vents his frustration in his comments about the candlelit dinner. Then he displays rather than describes his feelings.*
MATT: *Gosh, I didn't know that you were so upset. I mean it's not like I don't pay. I always make good don't I?*	*Matt begins by acknowledging Brian's feelings which improves the emotional tone of the conversation. Then he defends himself against Brian's attacks.*

Conflict

CONVERSATION

BRIAN: *Yes, so far that's true, but every month it's later and later before you pay me back. And I'm not a lending agency. Why do you expect me to loan you money each month? We work at the same place, make the same money and we've both got the same expenses. If I can come up with the rent and other expenses on time, you can too.*

MATT: *Listen man, I apologize about the phone bill. I thought I'd mailed it. So, I'll check it out with the phone company tomorrow morning. And the utility bill was just a mistake. I lost the bill and didn't realize it hadn't been paid. I know that I've not always had the money for the rent when you asked, but you usually ask me for it a week or more before it's due. You are really good at saving ahead, but I'm not. You say we have the same expenses, but that's not true. I have a car loan and you don't. And since I got that ticket last year, my car insurance has sky-rocketed. Some months I'm living really close to the edge. I know it's no excuse, but I want you to understand that I'm not just some deadbeat who's trying to suck off of you.*

BRIAN: *Matt, I'm sorry I said that we have similar expenses. You're right, yours are higher. And if I understood you correctly, our problems with the utility company and the phone company weren't due to your not having the money, but were because somehow the bills just slipped through the cracks?*

MATT: *Yeah. I'm never very organized but right now things are chaos. Between work, school, and the stuff that's going on with my family I don't know if I'm coming or going.*

BRIAN: *Well, I can understand that you are under a lot of pressure. And I hope you can understand that when you don't pay bills on time, it's not just you that suffers. Angie and I want to buy and house before we get married, so I'm really careful about paying bills on time so that I have a good credit rating. That's why I ask you for the rent so early. When you forget to pay the utility and*

ANALYSIS

Brian conditionally agrees with Matt. But continues to attack Matt and to display but not describe his feelings.

Matt accepts responsibility for the phone problem and apologizes. Then he describes what has happened in the past from his perspective.

Matt compliments Brian on his ability to save. Then he goes on to correct Brian's misperception of similarity of their financial situations.

Matt concludes by acknowledging this information to be an explanation not an excuse.

Brian apologizes. Then he paraphrases Matt's explanation of the late utility payments.

Brian's paraphrase leads Matt to self disclose that is he overwhelmed.

Brian acknowledges Matt's situation. And then describes the consequences that occur to Brian when Matt doesn't pay the bills on time. He also discloses why he is so careful about paying bills.

Here Brian finally uses the b-c-f framework. He describes the consequences of the late payments and his feeling about it.

CONVERSATION

phone bills, not only do we lose service, but since both of our names are on the bill, we both take a hit in our credit ratings. A poor credit rating will make it harder for me to get a loan. And it also will make it harder for you to get credit later. I know that you wouldn't intentionally do anything to hurt me, but the fact is, you have.

MATT: *Whoa, I never really thought about it this way. Man, I'm sorry.*

BRIAN: *Apology accepted. So how can we work this out?*

MATT: *Well, you seem to have thought more about it than I have, do you have any ideas?*

BRIAN: *Yeah, as a matter of fact, a couple of alternatives come to mind. One, we could agree on a date each month to sit down and pay the bills together. That way, I'd know that the bills had been written and sent, and you could control my tendency to bug you for your half of the rent before it really needs to be sent. Or, with each paycheck we could each put a certain amount into a joint account. Then when the bills come in I would just write the checks out of that account, and you wouldn't have to bother with it at all.*

ANALYSIS

Matt acknowledges Brian's comments and apologizes.

Brian, having cooled down now shifts the conversation into a problem solving mode.

As the responder to this conflict Matt wisely defers to Brian and asks him what solutions he has thought about.

In fact, Brian has given this thought.

CONVERSATION

MATT: *Maybe we could do a combination of those things.*

BRIAN: *What do you mean?*

MATT: *Well, I don't want to totally turn control over to you. I mean, I really need to learn how to be responsible for getting stuff done on time. But I'm really jammed for time right now. So how about if we set the date for paying the bills, but also set up the joint account. That way, if something comes up and I don't have the time to sit down with you and pay the bills, you can still get them done on time. But when I do have time, we can do it together. I think I can probably learn some good budgeting habits from you.*

BRIAN: *That's fine as long as you put in your share each pay period. I really get a kick out of managing my personal finances, and I'd be glad to show you what I do. What I do may not work for you, but you might get some ideas that you can adapt to your style. In any case, I'm glad we talked. I was really getting pissed at you and now I'm feeling like things are going to be O.K. So when can we get together to set our bill paying "date" and set up the joint account?*

ANALYSIS

Matt suggests a modification of the proposal.
Brian indicates that he is willing to listen.
Matt suggests a compromise between the two proposals.

Brian agrees but stipulates a condition. Then he goes on to disclose his enjoyment in managing his personal finances.

With the conflict resolved, Brian describes his feelings now versus before they had resolved this issue. The conversation ends with both Matt and Brian believing they have dealt with the issue.

Chapter Resources

Communication Improvement Plan: Conflict Management

Would you like to improve your use of the following aspects of your conflict resolving behavior discussed in this chapter?

        Initiating conflict

        Responding to conflict

        Mediating conflicts of others

Pick an aspect and write a communication improvement plan

Skill: _____

Problem: _____

_____

_____

_____

Goal: _____

_____

_____

_____

Procedure:

1. _____

2. _____

3. _____

Test of Achieving Goal: _____

_____

Key Words

Interpersonal conflict, *p. 304*

Pseudoconflict, *p. 305*

Badgering, *p. 305*

Fact conflict or simple conflict, *p. 306*

Value conflicts, *p. 306*

Policy conflicts, *p. 307*

Ego conflicts, *p. 308*

Withdrawal, *p. 310*

Accommodating, *p. 313*

Forcing, *p. 314*

Compromising, *p. 315*

Collaborating, *p. 315*

Mediator, *p. 325*

Inter-Act with Media

CINEMA

Callie Khouri (Director). (2002). *Divine Secrets of the Ya-Ya Sisterhood.* Sandra Bullock, Ellen Burstyn, James Garner.

Brief Summary: This film tells the story of a dysfunctional mother-daughter relationship. Vivi Walker is the explosive mother and Siddalee Walker is the daughter returning home as a successful playwright. After a confrontation between mother and daughter, friends of Vivi "kidnap" Siddalee for a period of self-confrontation aimed at helping her reach a better understanding of herself and of her mother.

IPC Concepts: Conflict types, styles of managing conflict, the need for better communication skills for more successful conflict management.

Spike Lee (Director). (1989). *Do the Right Thing.* Spike Lee, Danny Aiello, Ossie Davis, Ruby Dee, Richard Edson, Rosie Perez, John Torturro, Bill Nunn (Giancarlo Esposito).

Brief Summary: This is a powerful story of racial diversity, racial animosity, tension, conflict, and the value question of what is meant by doing the right thing. The basic plot involves a successful, white-owned pizza restaurant in an otherwise poor, black neighborhood. The owner, Sal (Danny Aiello), believes that his pizzeria owes nothing to the people of the neighborhood except to serve excellent pizza. Spike Lee plays Mookie, a pizza deliverer, who, on a hot summer day, gets caught up in the middle of tension between Sal and the community. Mookie must determine what the da Mayor (Ossie Davis) means by "do the right thing." The need for this understanding increases as Buggin Out (Esposito) keeps putting pressure on Sal. When Buggin Out recruits Radio Hakeem (Bill Nunn) to join his boycott, the crisis quickly becomes very real. Mookie also faces conflict from Tina (Rosie Perez), the mother of his child.

IPC Concepts: Conflict—pseudo, value, ego, styles, emotion, language.

Stanley Kramer (Director). (1967). *Guess Who's Coming to Dinner.* Spencer Tracy, Katharine Hepburn, Sidney Poitier.

Brief Summary: When a young white girl returns from Europe with her fiancé, her liberal family is thrown into chaos because the fiancé is black. Her father (Spencer Tracy) tries to mask his racial reaction under concern for practical considerations. Her mother (Katharine Hepburn), after an initial negative response, is very supportive. Even the African American maid is opposed. The fiancé (Sidney Poitier) is an internationally recognized doctor who came from very humble surroundings. His parents also join the family for dinner. A series of conversations ensue in which the parents try to discourage the couple from getting married. Each conversation illustrates pseudoconflict, value and ego conflict, styles of managing conflict, as well as approaches to influencing others and the handling of emotion. As the climax of the film approaches, Poitier and Tracy engage in a set of conversations that make this film a classic.

IPC Concepts: Conflict—pseudo, value, ego, styles, emotion, language.

Sidney Lumet (Director). (1957). *Twelve Angry Men.* Henry Fonda, Lee J. Cobb, Ed Begley, E. G. Marshall, Jack Klugman, Jack Warden, Martin Balsam, John Fielder, George Voskovec, Robert Webber, Edward Binns, Joseph Sweeney.

Brief Summary: This film unfolds the powerful story of twelve jurors debating the sentence in a murder trial. We only see the defendant once, at the beginning of the film when the judge is giving instructions to the jury. The balance of the film is about the deliberations and conflicts that eventually result in a unanimous verdict.

IPC Concepts: Every type of conflict is in evidence. Also, stereotyping, emotion, styles of conflict, styles of communication, personality, listening, etc. This is a blockbuster film for communication theory—it's almost as though it was written specifically for communication classes!

THEATER

Edward Albee. (1962). *Who's Afraid of Virginia Woolf?*

Brief Summary: Martha and George are a couple who are unable to have children. Their coping with this fact has led them to create a vicious, desperate, and mean-spirited relationship in which they both engage in games in order to hurt the other person. A young couple is drawn into their games one night after a dinner party.

IPC Concepts: Types of conflict (especially pseudoconflict, fact conflict, and ego conflict), styles of managing conflict, and games and conflict, intimate relationships.

LITERATURE

Alice Walker. (1982). *The Color Purple.* New York: Harcourt.

Brief Summary: This is the story of a poor, used, and abused African American woman, Celie. She is given into an abusive marriage by her abusive father. She suffers in silence until she discovers that her husband, Mister, has been hiding letters from her sister, Nettie, who had moved to Africa with Christian missionaries. Celie finds the letters and secretly reads them whenever she can steal a few minutes between chores, or by hiding them inside her Bible and reading them at church. Her husband has other women but barely knows Celie. His mistress, Shug, befriends Celie and they develop their own intimate relationship. As her love grows with Shug, Celie develops more and more self-esteem and confidence. She is eventually able to stand up to Mister and move out on her own.

IPC Concepts: Self-perception, self-esteem, impact of significant others. Relationships—need for warmth and affection, trust and commitment, conflict, diversity, culture, gender, emotion, gender and intimacy.

ACADEMIC WORK

Ellis, A., & Lange, A. (1995). *How to Keep People from Pushing Your Buttons.* New York: Citidel Press.

Brief Summary: This excellent book explores the theories of Albert Ellis, the famous psychologist. The focus is on how we respond to conflict by allowing our emotions to run wild, rather than remaining in control of our emotions. By focusing on Ellis's ABC process, the book offers practical advice on handling conflict more effectively.

IPC Concepts: Conflict and the management of emotion.

Solomon, M. (1990). *Working with Difficult People.* Englewood Cliffs, N.J.: Prentice Hall.

Brief Summary: Solomon offers excellent resources for examining coping strategies for communicating with specific types of problem people and problems with people.

IPC Concepts: Types and causes of interpersonal conflict, strategies for handling specific types of problems with people.

WHAT'S ON THE WEB

Conflict Resolution Resources at the School of Social and Systemic Studies

http://www.nova.edu/sss/DR/

Brief Summary: Maintained by faculty at Nova Southeastern University, this site includes information on the school's academic offerings via distance learning. The school offers graduate degrees in dispute resolution. There is an extensive list of conflict resolution resources: Internet resources and listserves (this is an overwhelming list of resources), newsletters, journals, membership organizations, and resource organizations.

IPC Concepts: Conflict management via arbitration.

How to Express Difficult Feelings

http://www.drnadig.com/feelings.htm

Brief Summary: This Web site examines the nature and function of language in expressing emotion. The site includes guidelines on language use when in conflict, the difference between thought and feelings, and detailed directions on "I" language. This site has links to listening and conflict management resources.

IPC Concepts: Language and conflict.

CHAPTER 12

Communicating in Intimate

Relationships:
Friends, Spouses, and Family

After you have read this chapter, you should be able to answer these questions:

- What are intimate relationships?
- What are the characteristics of intimate relationships?
- What types of intimate relationships are there?
- What are some problem areas of intimate relationships?
- What are the key characteristics of a family?
- What can we learn from studying the family as a system?
- What is the role of communication in building and maintaining family relationships?
- What are some of the most effective means of overcoming family communication problems?
- What is the relationship between communication patterns and violence in the family?

> As they walked to the door, she turned and said, "Thanks for the ride home."
>
> "Hey, no problem," Luis replied.
>
> "That Footloose is a great place to dance, isn't it? And it's great to dance with someone who moves the way you do—I was impressed!"
>
> "You think I move pretty well, huh? Maybe we could get together again?"
>
> "Sure. I'll probably be there again next Friday."
>
> "OK, I'll look for you . . . Listen, I've got tickets to Phish next week. You want to go with me?"
>
> "You got tickets for Phish? I tried to get tickets, but they sold out the first day they went on sale. Sure, I'll go with you."
>
> "Great! I'll pick you up about 7:30."
>
> "I'll be ready."
>
> "Then it's on," Luis said as he gave her a quick kiss. As she turned and went into the house, Luis danced down the stairs, jumped into the car, and roared up the street. "Look out," he shouted, "I'm in love! . . . Oh, nuts!" he said as he slapped his hands on the steering wheel, "I forgot to ask her name!"

Daniel Perlman and Beverly Fehr (1987) note that the personal relationship literature is "replete with evidence testifying to the importance of relationships in our lives" (p. 19). In fact, every human being has the simultaneous need for community (connection to friends) and attachment (intimacy with a spouse or lover). The absence of either causes loneliness. Luis's experience speaks to the beginning of the most intimate of relationships—romantic love. Yet romantic relationships are not the only kind of intimate relationships that you are likely to have.

In this chapter we will consider characteristics of intimate relationships, types of intimate relationships and relational styles, and problem areas in intimate communication.

Characteristics of Intimate Relationships

Intimate relationships are marked by high degrees of warmth and affection, trust, self-disclosure, and commitment, and are formalized through symbols and rituals (Prisbell & Andersen, 1980). Let's consider each of these characteristics.

Warmth and Affection

Perhaps the first, if not the most important, characteristic of intimacy is warmth and affection. Intimate friends have a great deal of liking for each other. In short, a good intimate relationship is not a trial. If being with the partner seems like work, then something is wrong. One way intimate partners express this liking is through time spent with each other. Intimates always look forward to being with each other because they experience a joy in each other's company, they enjoy talking with each other, and they enjoy sharing experiences.

Trust

Another important characteristic of intimacy is trust. As you'll remember from Chapter 3, **trust** is placing confidence in another in a way that almost always involves some risk. It is a prediction that if you reveal yourself to another, the result will be to your advantage rather than to your disadvantage. We trust those persons who, among other things, will not intentionally harm our interests (LaFollette, 1996, p. 116). And, as Rusbult and colleagues (2001) point out, "As partners develop increased trust in one another, they are likely to become increasingly dependent on one another—that is, they are likely to become increasingly satisfied, increasingly willing to forego alternatives, and increasingly willing to invest in the relationship" (p. 107).

Susan Boon's research (1994, pp. 97–101) articulates four key issues that underlie the development of trust within an intimate relationship. The first of these is dependability. A **dependable partner** is one that can be relied upon at all times under all circumstances. In effect, we must know that the person will be there for us whenever we need him or her. A second issue is responsiveness. A **responsive partner** is one whose actions are geared toward the other person's particular needs. At times this may require that one person sacrifices his or her needs for the good of the other. An **effective conflict resolving partner** is one who can help manage conflicts in a collaborative way. If partners tend to withdraw from potential conflicts, or constantly give in to preserve the peace, or force their goals on the other, trust weakens. When partners can engage in open and constructive conflict, they are exercising their trust in each other- trust that they will be able to work out the conflict in beneficial ways. The fourth issue that undergirds intimacy is faith. A **faithful partner** is one who is secure in the belief that the other person is trustworthy and that the relationship will endure. When you see partners who often question whether the relationship can survive, it seems doomed to failure; when

Intimate relationships—relationships that are marked by high degrees of warmth and affection, trust, self-disclosure, and commitment, and are formalized through symbols and rituals.

Trust—placing confidence in another in a way that almost always involves some risk.

Dependable partner—one that can be relied upon at all times under all circumstances.

Responsive partner—one whose actions are geared toward the other person's particular needs. At times this may require that one person sacrifices his or her needs for the good of the other.

Effective conflict resolving partner—one who can help manage conflicts in a collaborative way.

Faithful partner—one who is secure in the belief that the other person is trustworthy and that the relationship will endure.

you see partners who are jealous of each other's relationships with same-sex and opposite-sex friends, again the partnership seems doomed to failure.

Self-Disclosure

Intimacy demands relatively high levels of self-disclosure. Through the sharing of feelings and the process of self-disclosure people really come to know and to understand each other. Intimate friends often gain knowledge of their partner's innermost being.

As a result of this increasing amount of disclosure they increase their investment in the relationship and develop a sense of "we-ness."

Although it is unrealistic, and perhaps undesirable, to expect to share feelings with a great many others, the achievement of a feelings-sharing level of communication with a few people is a highly beneficial communication goal. When people find that they get satisfaction out of being together and are able to share ideas and feelings, their intimacy grows.

Even with intimate relationships, there may be limits to the amount of self-disclosure that is appropriate. Although communicating private information about self and making personal observations regarding the other are necessary for intimacy to develop, on occasion unconditional openness can short-circuit an otherwise good relationship. Still, as Mills and Clark (2001) point out, "sharing and revealing personal information is so characteristic of strong mutual communal relationships that self-disclosure has been thought of as the essence of close relationships" (p. 20).

INTER-ACT WITH

Technology

Suppose you have important information that you want to communicate to (1) a friend, (2) an acquaintance, and (3) a rival or enemy. In each instance, which means would you be *most likely* to use: face-to-face? telephone? regular mail? e-mail? Would you use the same means in all three situations? If so, why? Would you consider different means for one or two of the situations? If so, why? What is it about each means that makes it more or less desirable for each type of relationship? ■

Commitment

Intimate relationships also require a deep level of commitment. For instance, intimate friendships are characterized by the extent to which a person gives up other relationships in order to devote more time and energy to the primary relationship. Especially when two people are testing the suitability of an enduring relationship—going together, engagement, or marriage—they spend long periods of time together.

Intimate relationships have a great deal of strength. Sometimes when one person moves to another part of town or even to another city, the relationship remains unaffected. Some people see each other only once or twice a year but still consider themselves intimates because they share ideas and feelings freely and rely on each other's counsel when they are together.

In a perfect world, these characteristics would work to ensure that partners were totally content with each other. But in any and all relationships there are times when partners need to recognize that problems are occurring and work to re-establish intimacy. Research by Canary and Stafford (2001) found that five **relational maintenance behaviors,** actions and activities that can be used to sustain desired relational qualities, function to sustain desired relational qualities (2001, p. 134). The five behaviors are positivity (e.g., acting polite and cheerful, being upbeat, and avoiding criticism), openness (discussion about the relationship and sharing thoughts and feelings, etc.), assurances (expressions of love, commitment—implying relationship has a future), use of social networks (spending time with and including mutual friends and family), and sharing tasks.

Relational maintenance behaviors—actions and activities that can be used to sustain desired relational qualities.

Types of Intimate Relationships and Relational Styles

Intimacy is an aspect of different kinds of close relationships it is not synonymous with "love" or exclusivity. **Intimate friends,** then, are people who share a close, caring, and trusting relationship characterized by mutual self-disclosure and commitment. Intimate friends may go out of their way to help each other; they are concerned for each other's welfare.

Intimate friends—people who share a close, caring, and trusting relationship characterized by mutual self-disclosure and commitment.

From early on many of us have developed relationships with people who are likely to be there when we need them. They stand by us regardless of the circumstances, and they listen to our joys and woes nonjudgmentally. People look for same-sex and opposite-sex intimate friends with whom they can share their innermost secrets. Although we have a large number of friends and acquaintances, we are likely to have only a few relationships that we'd define as intimate. Let's consider the nature of platonic male relationships, female relationships, and male-female relationships in order to identify some of the similarities and differences.

Male Relationships

Throughout history, male relationships have been glorified as the epitome of camaraderie. Large numbers of popular books, movies, and television shows have portrayed male comradeship and romanticized the male bonding experience. Yet, using male behavior as a standard for defining intimacy has been questioned. For instance, in 1975 sex-role expert Joseph Pleck wrote that male bonding "may indicate sociability, but does not necessarily indicate intimacy" (p. 441). During the past several years research has shown that male-male intimate behavior is qualitatively different from the standard definition of "high levels of self-disclosure." As Julia Wood and Christopher Inman (1993) have pointed out, men "appear to regard practical help, mutual assistance, and companionship as benchmarks of caring" (p. 291).

A great deal about relationships is revealed by what people talk about. Conversational topics can be classified as topical (politics, work, events), relational (the friendship itself), or personal (one's thoughts and feelings). In general, men's conversations tend to be topical, revolving around sports, sex, work, and vehicles,

Male friendship usually focuses on activities, and men regard practical help, mutual assistance, and companionship as benchmarks of caring.

rather than personal, centered on issues or problems. Research with middle-aged and elderly men shows the same pattern: Men talked to same-sex friends about women, the news, music, art, and sports (Fehr, 1996, p. 119). Thus, of the three categories, men's conversations usually are topical. Likewise, much of men's friendship focuses on activities such as playing video games, attending sporting events, and helping each other with home improvement projects.

Men generally don't spend time with their close friends discussing relationships and personal issues. In a decade-long study of five thousand men and women, Michael McGill (1985) found that only one man in ten has a friend with whom he discusses work, money, and marriage, and only one man in twenty has a friendship in which he discloses his personal or sexual feelings. While data from this study is between eighteen and twenty-five years old, male friendship continues to be heavily based on activities rather than on deep disclosure.

Why is the level of intimacy between men traditionally low? It appears that men are less intimate than women in their same-sex friendships because they choose to be, even though they may not particularly like it. But, as Beverly Fehr (1996) points out, "Even though men may have less intimate friendships than women, intimate friendship is not 'all there is' to friendships" (p. 141). Or, as B. Wellman (1992) said, "To define friendship solely as emotionally supportive companionship is to limit one's world view to a California hot tub" (p. 104).

For many men, the relationships that are most meaningful to them are male-female relationships. Although men don't share much intimate information with each other, they still have a need for relationships with people who will give them help or counsel when they are having difficulty. As one might expect, a large sample of men rated their female friends highest in this nurturing quality but gave their male friends the lowest ratings (Fitzpatrick & Bochner, 1981).

Female Relationships

Whereas men rarely communicate their feelings to their male friends, women's friendships are marked by mutual disclosures. In fact, women's relationships seem to be the total opposite of male friendships. In contrast to male conversation, which we've learned is generally topical, female conversations tend to span the topic categories—topical, relational, and personal—with the focus on relational and personal. Research with middle-aged and elderly adults shows the same pattern: women talk about men, food, relationship problems, family, and fashion (Fehr, 1996, p. 119). Moreover, women's friendships develop more quickly than men's and tend to be more intense.

It would seem that female relationships are rich when measured by many of the criteria of effective interpersonal communication. Nonetheless, women are not always satisfied with their female relationships. Because women care so much about others, they tend to experience the troubles of those close to them as their own. This heavy emotional involvement can take its toll over time, leading to health costs and overdependence on the relationships. Because intimacy is an issue in all relationships, let's look at how men and women differ regarding the issue.

Gender Differences in Intimacy

Recent research continues to support the view that men's friendships are defined in terms of joint activities and women's in terms of shared thoughts and feelings (Reis, 1998, p. 216). Similarly, men's views of intimacy seem related to physical nearness. So, for men, intimacy is based on shared activity in male relationships and sexuality in male-female relationships. In contrast, women's intimacy is based on talking and affection, regardless of whether the friend is female or male (Reis, 1998, p. 218). Yet, despite the apparent differences in behaviors, Reis goes on to say that both men and women define intimacy using the same words: warmth, disclosure of personal feelings, and shared activity (p. 219).

Still, there's no doubt that how men go about showing intimacy differs from women's methods. Reis cites the following conversation he overheard. One man asked another how he was doing. "Terrible," he answered, "I lost my job today, my marriage is falling apart, and the kids are a mess." "That's too bad," the first man replied, with visible sympathy, "But you know, it can be good to talk about your feelings and get them off your chest. So if you've got one or two minutes, come talk to me." And then he ran off to play tennis! (Reis, 1998, p. 225). This is not behavior we'd expect from women in the same situation.

Why do we see such apparent differences in behavior between men and women? To some extent the differences are shown by which of the words defining intimacy are emphasized or enacted. Men tend to emphasize or enact actions, warmth, and shared activities; women emphasize or enact warmth and verbal disclosure of personal feelings. Yet both men and women are sometimes criticized for emphasizing one over the other.

For instance, Duck and Wright (1993) point out that women's emphasis of enacting verbal disclosures legitimizes an unfortunate stereotype of women's friendships as noninstrumental (with less emphasis on action, fun, and companionship) or at least less instrumental than those of men (p. 725).

Men are frequently criticized for failure to express their feelings. Men need to understand that for a woman intimacy is defined as sharing information, feelings, secrets, and insights through such self-disclosing statements as "I really need your presence—I feel so warmly toward you." Women need to understand that for many men intimacy is defined as practical help, mutual assistance, and companionship. Thus, statements about what the man has done for an intimate friend, such as "While you were at the meeting, I washed your car and cleaned up the kitchen," represent a male standard of showing intimacy. So, whereas female intimacy tends to be expressive, male intimacy tends to be instrumental.

In the past, our society has valued a feminine preference for verbal disclosures as the measure of intimacy; recently more emphasis has been placed on the male tendency toward instrumental activity as equally important in determining intimacy (Wood & Inman, 1993, p. 280). Some say that women's expressive style and men's instrumental style are complementary approaches that work well together. Still others maintain that the optimal situation is one in which all people, regardless of gender, embrace both affective and activity-oriented modes of relating to friends (Fehr, 1996, p. 141).

Male-Female Relationships

Male-female relationships may be close, nonsexual friendships or loving sexual relationships that may result in marriage. Intimacy is an important component of both types. Interestingly, older people are less likely to have cross-sex friendships than are younger people; men are more likely to report cross-sex friendships than are women; and unmarried persons are more apt to develop cross-sex friendships than married persons (Werking, 1997, p. 394).

Both cross-sex friendships and loving male-female relationships can be complicated by the fact that men and women seek intimacy in different ways. Male-female relationships are likely to run more smoothly if participants recognize and value the differing approaches. In addition, both men and women can have difficulty distinguishing between satisfying intimate friendship relationships and romantic, sexual relationships. Attempts at male-female relationships, especially when both the man and woman are married to someone else, are frequently misinterpreted.

Some people assume that a close relationship between a man and a woman must become a romantic sexual one. In reality, romance and sex can get in the way of good male-female relationships, for although romance or sex is enhanced by a strong underlying friendship, romance and sex can destroy friendships. While sex can be an expression of intimacy, too frequently sex is performed in the absence of intimacy—or as a substitute for it. Romance and sex may be a kind of adventure pursued not as an expression of a deep level of commitment and for the mutual benefit of both parties, but rather for the selfish pleasure of the individual. As a result, you will want to proceed cautiously before moving a satisfying relationship to a sexual level. Men and women can have long-lasting, satisfying intimate platonic relationships. And much as we may not like to believe it, the continued satisfaction of the partners in such a relationship may depend on them not sexualizing it.

OBSERVE & ANALYZE

Journal Activity

Male-Female Friendships

D o you have nonromantic relationships with members of the opposite sex? List the features that characterize those relationships. Discuss what it is that enables you to keep the relationships on a friendship level. ■

Marriage Relationships

A substantial amount of research has been directed at understanding intimacy in marriage. As we have said earlier, perhaps the ultimate in intimate relationships is a good marriage. When the relationship between life partners is a good one, it meets many tests of the ideal. Perhaps most important, a good marriage is one in which people find greatest satisfaction in being with each other. J. D. Bloch (1980), a psychologist who surveyed more than two thousand Americans, says 40 percent of all married people consider their spouse to be their best friend. In a different sample, 88 percent of married men and 78 percent of married women named their spouse as the person "closest" to them (Fischer & Narus, 1981, p. 449).

Nevertheless, what husbands and wives get from each other is somewhat out of balance. Despite the fact that married women named their spouse as their closest friend, women still need close female friendships to satisfy all their needs. Men, on the other hand, reported that their wives offer them the most satisfaction and emotional support of all the relationships in their lives—more than neighbor, coworker, boss, parent, sibling, or same-sex and opposite-sex friends (Argyle & Furnham, 1983, p. 490).

Despite similarities of apparent needs in marriage partners, there is no one single ideal marriage style. Mary Anne Fitzpatrick, a leading scholar of marriage, has identified characteristics or dimensions that identify different types of couples (Fitzpatrick, 1988, p. 76; Fitzpatrick & Badzinski, 1994, p. 741). Couples can be differentiated on the basis of their "independence," the extent to which they share their feelings with one another. Some couples are highly interdependent, depending on their partners for comfort, expressions of love, and fun. Other couples are more reserved and do not depend on their partners for emotional sharing and support. The second dimension on which couples can be differentiated is their ideology. Ideology is the extent to which the partners adhere to traditional belief systems and values, especially about marriage and sex roles, or hold nontraditional beliefs and values that tolerate change and uncertainty in relationships. The third dimension is one that Fitzpatrick originally called "conflict avoidance" but now calls "communication." Couples types differ in the extent to which they seek to avoid conflict as they interact.

Using these dimensions, Fitzpatrick describes three basic types of enduring couple relationships, which she labels as traditional, independent, and separate.

Traditional couples—those who have a traditional ideology, but maintain some independence in their marriages.

Traditional couples have a traditional ideology, but maintain some independence in their marriages. They follow the values accepted by parents and grandparents. Their values place more emphasis on stability than on spontaneity. They hold to traditional customs: The woman takes her husband's last name in marriage; infidelity is always inexcusable. Traditional relationships show a great deal of interdependence, marked by a high degree of sharing and companionship, and they are apt to engage in rather than avoid conflict.

Independent couples—those who share an ideology that embraces change and uncertainty in the marriage relationship, but like traditional couples, are interdependent and apt to engage in rather than avoid conflict to resolve differences.

Independent couples share an ideology that embraces change and uncertainty in the marriage relationship, but like traditional couples, they are interdependent and apt to engage in rather than avoid conflict to resolve differences. They hold more nonconventional values. Independents believe that relationships should not constrain the partners' freedoms. Independent partners maintain separate physical spaces and sometimes find it difficult to maintain regular daily time schedules.

Separate couples—those who share traditional ideology, but differ from traditional and independent couples in that they engage in less emotional sharing.

Separate couples are characterized by a shared traditional ideology, but differ from the previous two groups in that they engage in less emotional sharing and so are less interdependent. In addition, separate couples tend to avoid conflict. They are conventional in marital and family issues, but like independents, they stress the importance of individual freedom. They have significantly less companionship and sharing in their marriage than partners in either traditional or independent marriages. Separate couples indicate interdependence by keeping a regular daily schedule.

How does a traditional marriage differ from an independent one?

Mary Anne Fitzpatrick, Associate Dean of Social Sciences in the College of Letters and Arts on

Couple Types and Communication

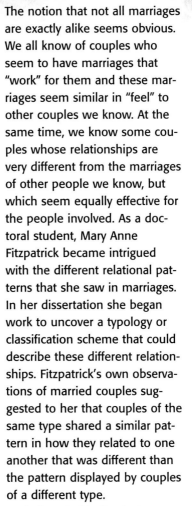

The notion that not all marriages are exactly alike seems obvious. We all know of couples who seem to have marriages that "work" for them and these marriages seem similar in "feel" to other couples we know. At the same time, we know some couples whose relationships are very different from the marriages of other people we know, but which seem equally effective for the people involved. As a doctoral student, Mary Anne Fitzpatrick became intrigued with the different relational patterns that she saw in marriages. In her dissertation she began work to uncover a typology or classification scheme that could describe these different relationships. Fitzpatrick's own observations of married couples suggested to her that couples of the same type shared a similar pattern in how they related to one another that was different than the pattern displayed by couples of a different type.

As is noted in the text, Fitzpatrick has found three distinct types of couples: traditional (both partners have a traditional ideology and are highly interdependent and apt to engage in

rather than avoid conflict), independent (partners share an ideology that embraces change and uncertainty in the marriage relationship, but like the traditional, are interdependent and apt to engage in rather than avoid conflict to resolve differences), and separate (couples are characterized by a shared traditional ideology, but differ from the previous two groups in that they engage in less emotional sharing and so are less interdependent and tend to avoid conflict).

In conducting her research, Fitzpatrick has demonstrated scholarly leadership through her methods. In all of her work, Fitzpatrick has been careful to study a broad range of couples from a wide cross-section of the population. While in some research it may be permissible to study only college students (who are easy to find at a university), Fitzpatrick believes that for theories about communication in marriage and family to be accurate, the people studied must be drawn from the broader base. So she is careful to recruit participants for her studies in a variety of settings and from a variety of backgrounds.

Fitzpatrick believes that her most useful work comes from studies in which she examines the actual conversations of couples and families. Using a research technique called "discourse analysis," Fitzpatrick and other scholars study, categorize, and summarize the flow of actual conversations. By studying the order, topics, and interaction processes through which conversations unfold, Fitzpatrick is able to understand how different types of couples negotiate their relationships. This technique is labor intensive, as each hour of conversation takes about thirty hours of study and coding to turn the conversation into data that can be compared to other conversations.

Finally, Fitzpatrick believes in involving her undergraduate students in her research. Along with her colleagues at the University of Wisconsin and elsewhere, Fitzpatrick is committed to the concept of "scholarship in the service of teaching," meaning that the purpose of scholarship is twofold. First, through scholarship, we create better explanations that more accurately describe the world. These up-to-date explanations should be the substance of what is taught in the modern university. Second, a goal of university teaching is to strengthen the critical thinking and lifelong learning skills of graduates. So involving students in on going research projects equips them to be critical of other studies they read, able to sort out well-done studies from those that are less well executed. Further, it allows students to "get their hands dirty" and in so doing gives them practice in research skills that they can use later to study and find valid answers on their own.

Recently, Fitzpatrick has extended her work on couple types to understanding how the family relationships differ in families headed by different types of couples. She has already completed one project that provided encouraging evidence for her belief that there is a systematic relationship between types of couples and types of families. Currently, Fitzpatrick and her students have begun to code the conversation data from families with adolescent children. Once coded the data will be used to discover how different types of families communicate with one another and handle misunder-

standings. For a list of some of Fitzpatrick's major publications, see the references for this chapter at the end of the book.

Beginning in January 1997, Professor Fitzpatrick took an additional role at the university, becoming Associate Dean of Social Sciences in the College of Letters and Arts. In this capacity, she oversees the operation of thirty-nine departments and programs of the college. At the same time, Fitzpatrick continues to teach and pursue her research program.

While in two-thirds of all the couples she studied, Fitzpatrick found that couples agreed about their marital type, in the remaining third the partners disagreed. When partners disagreed, the wife most frequently classified herself as a "traditional" and the husband more frequently saw himself as a "separate." Fitzpatrick called this pattern "separate-traditionals." In these relationships, the husband and wife agree on the traditional ideology of marriage, but whereas the wife views the marriage as an interdependent relationship where conflict is expressed, the husband views the relationship as one that is more emotionally distant and where conflict should be avoided.

Using these couple types and focusing on actual conversations of couples, Fitzpatrick and her associates, as well as other scholars, have been able to understand how different couple types handle conflict, deal with compliance-gaining messages, display power and control, have casual discussions, and talk about the issues and themes that are important to a marriage.

What Fitzpatrick has concluded is that no couple type is better than the others; rather each type has different kinds of strengths and weaknesses. To provide more insight into Mary Anne Fitzpatrick and her work, we feature her in the above Spotlight on Scholars.

To many of us, an important question is, what is the secret to a long and happy marriage? Researchers have found there are three common characteristics of couples who have stayed together for more than fifty years (Dickson, 1995, pp.

47–48). The first characteristic is **mutual respect**—treating each other with dignity. In short, long-lasting marriages are a product of people's valuing each other for what and who they are.

Mutual respect—treating each other with dignity.

The second characteristic is a **comfortable level of closeness**—spending an appropriate amount of time with each other. This does not mean that longtime partners are with each other all the time. Whereas some long-range partners desire constant companionship, others are happy with relatively low closeness. But the defining point is that both partners continue to know each other. The fact is that many couples grow apart over time—that is, they quit seeking each other's company or come to prefer the company of different people. What we've discovered is that continuing closeness takes effort on the part of the couple. For many couples closeness is developed through such rituals as celebrations, family traditions, and patterned routines (Werner et al., 1993, p. 115). Probably the most important element in maintaining closeness in a relationship is a patterned routine. For instance, some couples make sure that at least one night a week they go out together for dinner and then take in a show or just sit and talk. When people regularly make time to be together, it's easy for them to remember why they were drawn to one another. But if partners let their relationship drift, before long they may lose track of what brought them together in the first place. Yet with families, as with most people, practical matters often get in the way of nurturing the relationship. That is, some families are so busy confronting those things that "must be done" that they forget what it takes to keep a relationship growing. The ritual of patterned routines is designed to foster the relationship and is an essential part of any long-term relationship.

Comfortable level of closeness—spending an appropriate amount of time with each other.

The third characteristic is the **presence of a plan or life vision.** Sometimes this is consciously negotiated. At other times it just seems to happen. But the defining point is that both partners agree on their long-term goals—and, of course, that both partners see each other in those long-term plans. Such partners talk about "we" and "us" rather than "I" or "me."

Presence of a plan or life vision—agreeing on long-term goals.

Family Relationships

A **family** is "a group of intimates who generate a sense of home and group identity, complete with strong ties of loyalty and emotion, and experience a history and a future" (Galvin & Brommel, 1996). Families are structured in different ways. The traditional family consists of two opposite-sex parents living with one or more children from the union of those two parents. Single-parent families have one parent and one or more children. Blended families have two adults and one or more children, some of whom are from the union of those parents to other people. There are other family structures as well, including childless (or empty nest), extended (multiple generations of related people living together), and communal (unmarried people related by nongenetic factors).

Family—a group of intimates who generate a sense of home and group identity, complete with strong ties of loyalty and emotion, and experience a history and a future.

Regardless of type, family relationships develop and change. A person's first intimate friendships are likely to be with family members. For instance, small children first rely on their parents, then perhaps on a brother or sister. Family relationships may remain intimate ones; in many families sisters or brothers continue to see each other as their closest friends throughout their lives. During teen years and beyond, however, many people develop closer friendships with people outside of the family.

Much of the functioning of the family system is a product of the communication within the family. Family communication serves at least three major purposes for individual family members.

Family Communication Contributes to Self-Concept Formation   In Chapter 2 we discussed the role of communication in the formation of one's self-concept. One major responsibility that family members have to one another is to "talk" (family talk includes both verbal and nonverbal communication elements) in ways that will contribute to the development of strong self-concepts in all family members, especially younger children (Yerby et al., 1995). Research by D. H. Demo (1987) emphasized the point that self-concepts are established, maintained, reinforced, and/or modified by communication from family members. Family members' self-concepts are enhanced by:

Recognition and support help family members feel valuable and help them get over difficult times they face. Recall an incident in your own life when a family member gave you support. How did that behavior affect your relationship?

1. Statements of praise ("Jason, you really did a nice job of cleaning your room" and "Mom, that was really nice of you to let Emily stay the night");

2. Statements of acceptance and support ("If you have good reasons to drop out of the band, we accept your decision" and "Andy doesn't see eye to eye with us, but he's welcome in our home because he's your friend, and we respect that"); and

3. Statements of love ("Lee, I know it hurts to play poorly in front of your family, but we love you and we'll be here again next game" and "We both love you very much, Trevor").

Obviously, positive verbal statements can be undermined by nonverbal gestures and tones of voice that cause the receiver to perceive them as sarcasm or put-downs. When people hear "mixed messages," those in which the verbal and the nonverbal messages are in conflict, the nonverbal message is likely to have the greater effect. For example, when a parent says to a child "You know how much I love you," if that statement is not accompanied by nonverbal behavior that is congruent with the verbal message, the child will be confused. If the same parent never has time for the child and rarely praises the child's achievements, the child will not accept the verbal "I love you." If, on the other hand, the verbal "I love you," is accompanied by other posi-

Having a Choice of Who to Be *By Elisa Martinez*

This poem, originally written in Spanish, eloquently reminds us of the importance of celebrating the diversity within each of us. From our families we may inherit strong ethnic identities, and from living in the United States we may develop another one. Rather than being an "either-or," we can choose one "and" the other.

As Mexican Americans, we are often criticized for not flowing in the mainstream of America. Why do "they" insist on speaking "that language" and retaining "that" culture when "they" live in the United States?

I can't answer that question for anyone else. But as for me, I find that it makes life more interesting.

By all appearances, I am one person but in reality I am two.

It is one of me who cries when she hears melancholy memories of mother and father; it is the other who sighs when she hears "Goodnight Sweetheart," with her memories of friends, proms, and malts at the drive-in.

It is one of me who enjoys a slice of medium rare roast beef and the other who wraps it in a tortilla and downs it with hot chili sauce.

It is one of me who jerks in rhythm to "Billy Jean" and the other who swirls gaily to corridos[1] and steps in rhythm to a cumbia.[2] It is one of me who prepares for Santa Claus and the other who breaks the piñata at the Posada.[3] It is one of me who wants to be always on time and the other who gets there just a little bit late.

It is one of me who interprets Serafina in Tennessee Williams' "Rose Tattoo" and the other who becomes "La Siempreviva" in Luis Basurto's "Cada Quién Su Vida."[4]

It is one of me who carves out the face in the pumpkin for Halloween and the other who cleans the sepulcro[5] on Día de Los Muertos.[6]

It is one of me who buys the smoke alarm for the safety of the family and the other who has it disconnected when it drives us mad every time a tortilla burns.

It is one of me who buys medication at the drugstore and the other who washes it down with estafiate.[7]

It is one of me who can appreciate Beverly Sills in concert and the other me who can appreciate "The Poet and Peasant Overture" played beautifully by a group of mariachis.[8]

It is one of me who takes great pains to speak English correctly, giving great care to the rules of grammar, and the other who says Qué cute![9] and Simón que yes![10]

It is one of me who celebrates Mother's Day on the second Sunday in May and other me who celebrates again on May 10.

It is one of me who feels the patriotic emotion when the Stars and Stripes go by and the other who elates at the tri-colored flag with the eagle in the center as she marches by to the rhythm of the bugles.

The other day as I was cleaning house, I was singing that popular Nelson/Iglesias release "To All the Girls I Loved Before." My husband, who incidentally does not appreciate my singing (another Mexican custom), asked, "And who are you, Willie or Julio?"

How neat, I thought, that I DO have a choice. ∎

1 Mexican polka.
2 Salsa-type dance.
3 Twelve-day Christmas celebration.
4 La Siempreviva is the leading lady in "Cada Quién Su Vida" ("To Each His Own").
5 Grave.
6 Day of the Dead.
7 Mexican tea used for health purposes.
8 Group of musicians.
9 How cute!
10 Of course!

From Flores, B. R. (1994). *Chiquita's Cocoon.* (pp. 27–30). New York: Villard Books. Translated by Bettina R. Flores.

tive behaviors that demonstrate commitment and approval, then the child will feel loved.

Among the most important elements of our self-concept that is formed in our families is our ethnic identity: In the Diverse Voices feature (p. 351) we saw how Elisa Martinez tries to balance the ethnic identity she learned from her family and her American (U.S.) identity learned from everyday activities.

Family Communication Supplies Needed Recognition and Support A second responsibility of family members is to interact with each other in ways that recognize and support individual members. Recognition and support help family members feel that they are important and help them get over the difficult times they will face. The importance of this responsibility cannot be overstated. Family members are usually the people with whom we feel safest, and we often turn to them when we need praise, comfort, and reassurance. Yet in many families this important responsibility is forgotten in the rush of day-to-day living. For example, when Judith, the youngest daughter, comes home excited about the gold star she received for her spelling test, her mother and/or father need to take time to recognize the accomplishment regardless of how busy they are or what problems they may have faced that day. Likewise, when parents come home from a rough day at work, their spouse and their children need to behave in ways that show them that home is a safe haven where the difficulties of the workaday world can be set aside. The point is that all family members need to be told when they are doing well and that they can rely on each other. When people can't get recognition and support from within the family, they go outside the family for it.

Family Communication Establishes Models A third responsibility of family members is to communicate in ways that serve as models of good communication for younger family members. Parents serve as role models, whether they want to or not. The saying "Do as I say, not as I do" hardly represents a workable model of behavior because it teaches only hypocrisy. If Julia sees her parents listening, paraphrasing, and comforting each other, Julia will be more likely to paraphrase and comfort her friends and siblings. If, however, Julia sees family members half-listening and being unsympathetic to others, Julia will learn to behave similarly. How many times have we heard a parent say, "I don't understand Tim's or Bea's behavior," when that behavior strongly resembles the parent's?

Modeling behavior is especially important in managing conflict. Children react in vigorous ways when they believe they have been wronged. They will scream, cry, hit, punch, and scratch. As they become more sophisticated, they learn to manipulate, lie, and do whatever is necessary to get their own way. It's the parents' responsibility to socialize children, to teach them how to manage the conflict

OBSERVE & ANALYZE

Journal Activity

Communication in Your Family

For a few days, keep a diary of communication in your family that exemplifies language and nonverbal communication that seem to raise or lower self-concepts, that seem to recognize and support or fail to recognize and support family members, and that seem to provide good or bad models of communication behavior. In general does the family communication appear to be more positive or more negative? What do you see as the effects of family communication styles on individual members of the family and on the family as a unit? ■

in their lives. But telling children how to behave and then engaging in just the opposite behavior will only reinforce aggressive or passive conflict-managing strategies. On the other hand, parents can model collaboration by discussing, weighing and considering, describing their feelings, and being supportive during their disagreements. In so doing they not only protect their own relationship but they also model for their children how loving people work through conflict.

Improving Family Communication

In outlining the importance of effective communication in families, we have alluded to methods for improving family communication. Let's now specifically discuss five guidelines that members (as well as any people in intimate relationships) can use to improve communication in the family.

Opening the Lines of Communication For a number of reasons, lines of communication within a family can become scrambled or broken, causing family members to feel isolated from one another. With the exception of requests and orders from other family members ("Clean up your room," "Don't play the stereo so loudly"), many people actually spend very few minutes each day genuinely communicating with other members of their family. Instead, they spend the bulk of their time interacting with people outside the home.

The first step in opening lines of communication is setting a time specifically for family members to talk. Each member of the family needs the opportunity to recount what happened that day. One good time for families to talk is during the evening meal. Unfortunately, the rush of busy lives and the ever-present television often compete for the attention of family members, even when they are physically together, and thus threaten such conversations. Recent national studies are showing that families are spending much less time together: Family dinners are down by one-third over the past 20 years, and family vacations have decreased by 28 percent (Family Time, 2002) It may be difficult to have significant family time every day of the week, but the consequences of not doing so are becoming increasingly clear.

The next step in opening lines of communication consists of establishing a pattern of communication that family members will follow in interacting with one another. The network of communication in a given family reflects the dominant model or pattern of family communication (see Figure 12.1). Some networks are chains, which means a lower-ranking member of the family (let's say the youngest son) talks to a higher-ranking member (perhaps the oldest daughter), who then relays the messages to the mother or father. Some networks are wheels, with the mother or father at the center and all communication passing through her or him. The most desirable networks have multiple connections, with each member talking with every other member.

Confronting the Effects of Power Imbalances Members of a family are dependent on one another for many things. Children depend on their parents for food, shelter, clothing, and transportation, as well as love. Children depend on one another for friendship and support. Parents need their children's love and companionship, and

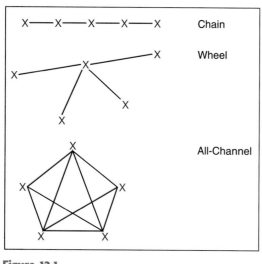

Figure 12.1

Communication Networks

in many cases parents need their children to behave in ways that validate the parents' self-concept. Because of the nature of these dependencies, the distribution of power within the family is unequal. Society gives parents legitimate power over their children, and because parents usually control the family budget and are physically stronger than their children, they wield considerable reward and coercive power. Older children often have great amounts of coercive and referent power over their younger brothers and sisters in addition to the legitimate power given them by the parents. Imbalances in referent power occur between two children when one of the children will go to almost any lengths to please the other (usually older) child. For instance, Todd, a younger child, may endure abusive treatment from his older brother, Mark, because Todd at least has the "privilege" of being with Mark. Within any family with children, then, some of the members will have more power than others. The younger child may be placed in the position of having to please three "parents"—mother, father, and an older brother or sister. If the demands of all three are in accord, few problems should arise. If, however, the older sibling begins to abuse the power relationship, the younger sibling may react by withdrawing or becoming hostile.

Family communication is often strongly influenced by these dependencies and the power distributions that derive from them. In many families children are not treated equally. The parents may realize that one of the children has certain gifts or talents that the others lack, so the parents allow this child privileges that the others do not enjoy. Occasionally, parents simply make a mistake and treat the child unequally because he or she is more demanding or because the parents have forgotten how they treated the other (usually older) children under similar circumstances.

If lines of communication within a family are open, it is possible to identify and confront family power imbalances and the inequities they may be causing within relationships. Each member of the family should feel free to inquire about any family rule or behavior that is a problem for that family member. For instance, suppose the oldest sister in a family is concerned about why she has to be in by 10:30 on weeknights. If lines of communication are open, she will question that rule. If lines of communication are open, parents will explain why they are making and enforcing a 10:30 curfew rather than simply relying on their authority and answering "Because I said so, that's why!" If parents explain to their children and give them reasons for rules, then children are more likely to accept the rules and confide in their parents.

Recognizing and Adapting to Change Members of a family know each other so well that they can often predict how a particular family member will think, feel, or act under many different circumstances. These predictions will not always be accurate, however. All people change with time, though such changes are likely to be gradual, and family members may be the last to recognize them. For example, it isn't

What clues suggest that this family enjoys each other's company?

until Tanya returns from six weeks at summer camp that another member of the family is likely to recognize how she has changed.

Even as children grow and change, their brothers and sisters, and especially their parents, continue to see them as they once were, not as they are or are becoming. Quite often a younger member of the family will hear such statements as "Don't tell me you like asparagus—remember, I'm your brother, I know you" or "You're going to be a doctor? Come on, you faint at the sight of blood." If you are studying away at college, you maybe offended when you return home and your parents continue to treat you as they did when you were in high school.

Recall our discussion in Chapter 2 where we showed that social perceptions are not always accurate. This is true even when those perceptions come from family members who "know each other like the back of their hand." The skill of perception checking is as important for family members as it is for strangers. Moreover, the skill of dating generalizations, discussed in Chapter 4, is another important one for members of a family to master. It may well be true that Maggie didn't like asparagus or that Ginger used to faint at the sight of blood, but as the years go by, Maggie and Ginger change.

How does this representation of a family contrast with the one shown above?

Recognizing and adapting to change appear to be especially difficult as children become teens and strive to achieve independence at the same time that their parents may be experiencing their own midlife transition. Frequently, parents who are occupied with their own adult life transition find it difficult to reexamine and change their relationship with the adolescent child to one that is better suited to the emerging needs of both of them. Thus parents continue to interact with the child in the habitual way and justify the behavior by asserting that the child must earn the right to be treated like an adult. Yet a teenager who is treated like a child will probably rebel or act out, whereas a teenager treated as an adult is likely to reason and discuss.

Recognizing change has another dimension as well. Family members need to be alert to the kinds of changes that may indicate stress or emotional distress in other members. Unfortunately, family members often are unable to notice gradual changes in behavior that serve as signals to problems until the family member is seriously troubled. If family members suspect difficulty, they should be open in confronting family members about their behavior. They should ask such questions as "I've noticed that you don't seem to be yourself. You've withdrawn from most of your activities, you aren't eating well, and you look really sad. Is there something happening that we can help you with?" Family members, like people in all relationships, need to use their supportive communication skills to help other members of the family deal with change.

Respecting Individual Interests Healthy family communication respects individual interests. Chapters 7 and 8 discussed the importance of listening, understanding, and comforting, which certainly applies to family relationships, yet family communication can often be marked by indifference or apathy. Individual family members are sometimes overly concerned with themselves and fail to consider the feelings of others. When something nice happens to one member of the family, the first reaction of other family members should never be "Big deal." If other family members celebrate the accomplishments of a member and show interest in his or her activities, that person is likely to return the favor.

Managing Conflicts Equitably Because interdependent family members have unique needs and power in the family is unevenly distributed, situations that lead to conflict are inevitable. Yet, families differ in their abilities to resolve conflict in effective ways. Families develop rules for how differences between members will be handled. Although these rules are generally determined by the parents' preferred conflict styles, individual children will differ in the extent to which they comply with these rules.

In some families conflict is avoided at all costs. So members learn to avoid conversing about subjects on which there is likely to be disagreement. These families may also withdraw or defer to the position taken by the

OBSERVE & ANALYZE

Journal Activity

Family Power Relationships and Support Systems

Analyze the power relationships between you and (a) your mother or father, (b) your siblings, or (c) your children. How do these dependencies affect your communication? Analyze the support systems in your family. Discuss who listens, who helps, and who can be counted on. ■

most powerful person. So children (and even young adults) obey the will of their parents in order to keep peace.

Other families develop rules that are more democratic. When family members find themselves in conflict, they may hold a family meeting to jointly work out the problem. In these meetings, one or more of the neutral members may serve as a mediator. Conflict mediation and problem solving also may occur in a less formalized process. Nevertheless, the rule in these families is to view conflict as an opportunity to promote win/win outcomes between members.

A third rule of dealing with conflict within the family is characterized by the use of coercive or forcing behaviors. These families often end conflict episodes by acceding to the wishes of the most powerful member. "As long as you're under my roof . . ." and ". . . because I'm the mother, that's why" and "if you don't do . . . , I'll tell mom about when you did . . ." are all examples of forcing.

In some families, forcing behaviors are not met by acquiescence but by resistance. These situations are troublesome since they may escalate into incidents of family violence. Family violence (Yerby et al., 1995, p. 304) is a spiral of family conflict that escalates into attacks upon family members. These attacks take many forms, including wife-battering and spouse abuse, child abuse and neglect, sexual abuse of children, marital rape, sibling abuse, abuse of elderly relatives, psychological abuse of family members, and violence by children.

Unfortunately, in many families almost any conflict can grow to be physical and result in abusive behavior. Because men are generally physically stronger, physical abuse is most often perpetrated by men (Sabourin & Stamp, 1995, p. 213). But verbal aggression can be every bit as harmful to a relationship as physical abuse, and whereas physical abuse is usually a reaction of the man, both men and women engage in verbal abuse.

What causes people to resort to verbal and physical abuse of people they claim to love? While there is strong evidence to suggest that the tendency to use abusive behavior is handed down from generation to generation, those who engage in abuse are likely to lack appropriate communication skills, including those related to constructive conflict management (Sabourin, 1996, p. 213). How can you keep relationships from becoming abusive? The best advice is to reread the material in Chapter 11 and try to apply it in your family relationships.

Problem Areas in Intimate Relationships

In the final section of this chapter we want to consider how jealousy and sex-role stereotyping undermine intimacy.

Jealousy

Jealousy—the suspicion of rivalry or unfaithfulness—is one of the major destructive forces in intimate relationships. According to one study, 57 percent of respondents cited their former friend's jealous feelings or critical attitude toward the

Jealousy—the suspicion of rivalry or unfaithfulness.

respondent's other relationships as a "moderate to very important" reason for the breakup of their relationship (Marsh, 1988, p. 27). The traditional scenario under which the emotion of jealousy occurs is when person A feels that person C is getting affection or favored treatment from person B—favored treatment that A wants (LaFollette, 1996, p. 169).

Jealousy does not seem to be a personality trait, but low self-esteem can make a person susceptible to feeling jealous. When people question their self-worth, they are likely to be insecure in their relationships and perceive "unfaithfulness" in their partners.

There do seem to be some differences in what triggers jealousy in men and women. When women feel ignored or in other ways separated emotionally from their partners, they are likely to feel jealous. On the other hand, men are more likely to feel jealous when their partner gives positive attention to another person. Unfortunately, jealousy poisons intimate relationships by creating self-fulfilling prophesies. For example, as a woman repeatedly expresses her jealousy through accusations and complains about being ignored, isolated, and separated, her partner may seek to protect himself from these unpleasant conversations by withdrawing. As he becomes territorial and angrily accuses her of unfaithfulness for simply speaking with other men, she begins to seek more rational male companionship.

The best way to reduce jealousy in a relationship is to increase the level of trust that exists between partners. Unfortunately, the very nature of jealous behavior makes this difficult to do, especially in situations where one partner suffers from low self-esteem. Only if both partners willingly embrace the situation as a conflict over which to collaborate will they be able to maintain intimacy through supportively discussing and resolving the issues that give rise to the jealousy. Left unresolved, jealousy will eventually choke off relational intimacy.

Sex-Role Stereotyping

Sex-role stereotyping continues to be a problem in many intimate relationships. Because intimate communication entails shared deep personal meaning, both men and women need to be able to step outside the traditional stereotypes, acquire each other's traditional skills, and become well-rounded communicators. Many men need to develop and feel comfortable using the skills that nurture and support others in times of emotional distress; many women need to acquire influence and assertiveness skills so that they present their own point of view clearly and forcefully.

A first step toward improving communication in male-female relationships is for men and women to acknowledge the effects of their early conditioning on their interpersonal communication. For example, Matt has trouble describing his feelings. Yet describing feelings, as you have learned, is one of the most important communication skills. Unless Matt is willing to probe his upbringing to find out why he is having difficulty developing this skill (perhaps he has been conditioned that "big boys don't cry"), he may never integrate this particular skill into his behavior. Similarly, unless Mary understands that the socialization process has encouraged her to be passive (perhaps she has been conditioned that "nice girls don't talk back"), she will find it difficult, if not impossible, to learn to be assertive and stand up for herself.

Unfortunately, sex-role differentiation ensures that women and men have all too few common experiences on which to build empathy. For example, if Marge believes that any form of aggressiveness is unfeminine and therefore undesirable, she will probably have trouble being assertive when returning damaged merchandise to a store. Yet Bob, her husband, may not be able to empathize with Marge's discomfort at all. Likewise, many women complain that their boyfriends, lovers, or husbands don't verbalize affection. A woman frequently feels unloved or unwanted because the man is unwilling to say "I love you" often enough. Although he may in fact not love her, it is more likely that he's simply adhering to the traditional male sex role that discourages men from expressing their feelings. Because the female sex role encourages expressing feelings, women may not be able to empathize with silent men.

Another step toward improving male-female relationships is for men and women to examine the dependency relationships that result from sex-role stereotypes. Because society values traditionally masculine behaviors more highly than it does feminine behaviors, men continue to have a power advantage. Under these circumstances, as you can imagine, a climate of equality in communication between women and men is difficult to establish. A man who adopts a superior attitude toward a woman undermines the effectiveness of their communication.

The fact that society values masculine over feminine behaviors has ramifications for same-sex relationships as well. In our society, for example, Amy may cancel her plans to go shopping with Beth if Joe calls to say he'd like to stop by for lunch. Yet if Joe has plans to go out with his friend Tom, he probably will not cancel them to spend the evening with Amy—even if she really wants to see him. Simply stated, a man's company is more valued than a woman's. Women will sometimes jeopardize their relationships with other women to advance what they believe to be a more socially desirable relationship with a man. Because masculine behavior is more valued, however, men don't often risk same-sex friendships in this way.

A third way to improve male-female relationships is for men and women to monitor sex-role–based tendencies toward communication dominance or passiveness. If, as a normal part of your sex role, you tend to assume either an obviously dominant or an obviously passive communication role, then you are likely to create defensiveness in your communication partners. Remember, a good communication climate results in part from equality, which is impossible to achieve if one person is dominant.

A climate of equality makes people more willing to accept nontraditional sex-role behaviors. Even though more and more women hold nontraditional jobs, many people still have trouble acknowledging their right to do so. And men who pursue nontraditional jobs may have

OBSERVE & ANALYZE

Journal Activity

Sex-Role Stereotypes

Brainstorm a list of "famous old sayings" on sex roles (e.g., "Big boys don't cry"). Take a poll to determine which of the sayings seemed to be the most commonly heard. Discuss your reactions to them when you first heard them and your reactions now. Any differences? ■

even more trouble being accepted. Househusband is all too often a term of ridicule. It does not matter whether you personally wish to lead a nontraditional life. What does matter is this: If you desire successful interpersonal communication, you must be willing to accept behavior that is different from your own.

WHAT WOULD YOU DO?

A Question *of* Ethics

Jackie and Michael had been dating for a year and were talking about marriage when Michael's job transferred him to Columbus for six months. Two months into their separation, Jackie visited Michael's new city and had a chance to meet his co-workers at a party, including Veronica, a beautiful woman a couple of years younger than Jackie. Michael had talked to Jackie about all of his new colleagues, including Veronica, but she had had no idea how attractive Veronica was. In addition, as the evening went on, Jackie could sense that Michael and Veronica were forming a special friendship. She couldn't help but feel a twinge of jealousy for this woman who got to spend time with her boyfriend. Nevertheless, Michael seemed completely attentive to Jackie and they had a wonderful visit.

A couple of weeks later, Gwen, an acquaintance of Jackie's, happened to see Michael and Veronica having dinner together at a restaurant while she was on business in Columbus. The day after her return, Gwen ran into Jackie at the grocery store and casually remarked on seeing Michael with Veronica. When Jackie commented that Michael and Veronica were co-workers, Gwen hesitantly replied, "Well, they certainly seem to have a close working relationship." Jackie blanched. Trying to soothe her, Gwen said, "I'm sure there's an explanation for everything. I mean there could be lots of reasons for him holding her hand. I'm sorry I said anything." But Jackie did not feel better.

Later that evening when Michael called, Jackie immediately confronted him by saying sarcastically, "So, how's Veronica?"

When Michael replied, "What do you mean?" Jackie went on, "Don't give me any of your innocent 'what do I mean' stuff—you were seen and you know it!"

"Oh, Gwen," said Michael, "So you'll take the word of some nosy trouble-making woman and judge me before you find out the real situation. If that's all the more you trust me, then I'm not sure . . ."

"Oh, sure, defend yourself by blaming Gwen. But she did see you. You're right about one thing, this is about trust."

1. What ethical issues are involved in this situation?

2. What could/should Jackie have said to her friend Gwen and to Michael?

3. How could/should Michael have responded?

Summary

Intimate relationships are those in which a high degree of closeness occurs. They are marked by high degrees of warmth and affection, trust, self-disclosure, commitment, and expectation that the relationship will grow and endure.

Four types of intimate relationships are friends (same-sex and opposite-sex friendships), lovers, spouses, and families. Intimate friends are people who like each other; they seek each other out because they enjoy each other's company. Major kinds of intimate relationships are male, female, male-female, spousal, and family.

From an interpersonal communication standpoint, male friendships are far from the ideal when measured by the criterion of intimacy. Their conversation tends to be topical. Whereas male friendships lack intimacy and male conversation is largely topical, women have a greater capacity than men for experiencing the highest levels of intimacy. Moreover, women's talk focuses on relational and personal topics. Although male-female friendship relationships can be tremendously satisfying, they pose a special problem: Many people have difficulty distinguishing between satisfying intimate friendship relationships and romantic, sexual relationships.

Perhaps the ultimate in intimacy is spousal relationships. When the spouse relationship is a good one, it meets many of the tests of the ideal. Marriage relationships generally fit into three types: traditional, independent, and separate.

The family is a basic social unit composed of people who have a past history, a present reality, and a future expectation. Family communication is important because (1) it affects self-concept formation in children, (2) it supplies recognition and support, and (3) it provides models of behavior from members in positions of power for other family members. Family relationships are improved by opening lines of communication, by confronting the effects of power imbalances, by recognizing changes in family members, by respecting individual interests, and by managing conflict.

Problems in relationships often stem from failure to decode verbal and nonverbal communication accurately, from jealousy, and from sex-role stereotyping.

Chapter Resources

Communication Improvement Plan: Intimate Relationships

Would you like to improve your use of the following aspects of your intimate relationship communication discussed in this chapter?

> Male communication
>
> Female communication
>
> Male-female communication
>
> Spousal communication
>
> Family communication

Pick an aspect and write a communication improvement plan

Skill: _____

Problem: _____

_____

_____

_____

Goal: _____

_____

_____

_____

Procedure:

1. _____

2. _____

3. _____

Test of Achieving Goal: _____

_____

Key Words

Intimate relationships, *p. 339*	Traditional couples, *p. 346*
Trust, *p. 339*	Independent couples, *p. 346*
Dependable partner, *p. 339*	Separate couples, *p. 346*
Responsive partner, *p. 339*	Mutual respect, *p. 349*
Effective conflict resolving partner, *p. 339*	Comfortable level of closeness, *p. 349*
Faithful partner, *p. 339*	Presence of a plan or life vision, *p. 349*
Relational maintenance behaviors, *p. 341*	Family, *p. 349*
Intimate friends, *p. 341*	Jealousy, *p. 357*

Inter-Act with Media

CINEMA

Spike Lee (Director). (1994). *Crooklyn.* Alfre Woodard, Delroy Lindo, David Patrick Kelly, Zelda Harris, Carlton Williams, Sharif Rashed, Tse-Mach Washington, Spike Lee.

Brief Summary: This is the story of an African American family in Brooklyn in the 1970s. Their strong-willed mother, Carolyn, holds the family together despite extreme poverty, a free-spirited unemployed father, Woody, and a sometimes dangerous, changing neighborhood. Their neighborhood has undergone tremendous change in terms of its racial and ethnic composition, which has fostered resentment between the groups. The story centers around Troy, the only girl in the family. When family becomes a serious problem, they take Troy to spend the summer with her aunt in the South. Troy strikes up a friendship with her cousin, but longs for her home in Brooklyn. Upon her return, she learns that her mother has become quite ill. Carolyn dies of cancer and the family is filled with insecurity as well as grief.

IPC Concepts: Family, sibling rivalry, conflict, communication between parents, between parents and children, role models, coping with change.

Mira Nair (Director). (1995). *The Perez Family.* Marisa Tomei, Anjelica Huston, Alfred Molina, Chazz Palminteri, Trini Alvarado, Celia Cruz, Diego Wallraff, Trini Alvarado.

Brief Summary: After twenty years of political imprisonment in Cuba, a former Cuban plantation owner, Juan Raul Perez, is released in 1980 as part of the massive prisoner release by Castro. He dreams of being reunited with his wife and family in Miami, but when he arrives in Florida in the company of a young fiery woman, Dorita, who claims to be his wife for immigration purposes, he misses his brother-in-law, who had been looking for a single man. His real wife, Carmela, believes that he has not been released and grieves for him. While Juan tries to find his wife, Dorita tries to create a family so that they can be released to a sponsor in the United States. Dorita's unlikely group slowly becomes a family. Their goal is to survive, learn how to deal with America, and try to find their place in it. They become interdependent and help each other deal with the constant changes in their lives. Eventually Juan is reunited with Carmela, but they realize that they have grown away from each other.

IPC Concepts: Family as a social system, effective communication—illustrates family interdependence, environmental change, goals, and adaptation. Its central question is, what is the real meaning of a family?

John Lee Hancock (Director). (2002). *The Rookie.* Dennis Quaid, Rachel Griffiths, Jay Hernandez, Beth Grant, Angus Jones, Brian Cox.

Brief Summary: Based on a true story, the film is the story of a high school baseball coach (Jim Morris), who is challenged by his team to try out for a place on a professional baseball team. Along the way to achieving his dream of playing professional baseball, Jim must balance his efforts in baseball with his responsibilities to his wife and family. The film reveals Jim's childhood experiences with a remote, absent, unsupportive military father. The struggle to play baseball reveals the flaws and the strengths in Jim's family and shows his special relationship with his son.

IPC Concepts: Trust, disclosure, support, and family relationships.

THEATER

Edward Albee. (1962). *Who's Afraid of Virginia Woolf?*

Brief Summary: Martha and George are a couple who are unable to have children. Their coping with this fact has led them to create a vicious, desperate, and mean-spirited relationship in which they both engage in games in order to hurt the other person. A young couple is drawn into their games one night after a dinner party.

IPC Concepts: Types of conflict, especially pseudoconflict, fact conflict, and ego conflict; games and conflict; intimate relationships, need for honesty, support, warmth; spousal relationships.

LITERATURE

Alice Walker. (1982). *The Color Purple.* New York: Harcourt.

Brief Summary: This is the story of a poor, used, and abused African American woman, Celie. She is given into an abusive marriage by her abusive father. She suffers in silence until she discovers that her husband, Mister, has been hiding letters from her sister, Nettie, who had moved to Africa with Christian missionaries. Celie finds the letters and secretly reads them whenever she can steal a few minutes between chores, or by hiding them whenever she can steal a few minutes between chores, or by hiding them inside her bible and reading them at church. Her husband has relationships with other women but barely knows Celie. Mister's mistress, Shug, befriends Celie, and they develop their own intimate relationship.

IPC Concepts: Self-perception, self-esteem, impact of significant others, relationships—need for warmth and affection, trust and commitment, conflict, diversity, culture, gender, emotion, gender and intimacy.

ACADEMIC WORKS

Covington, S., & Beckett L. (1988). *Leaving the Enchanted Forest: The Path from Relationship Addiction to Intimacy.* New York: Harper & Row Publishers.

Brief Summary: This is a fascinating book on the pattern many people follow when they move from relationship to relationship. The authors offer the explanation that such behavior may be caused by our need for the relationship rush that one experiences when the relationship is new. As the relationship moves on, such a rush is more difficult to experience. Some people may develop a need for, or dependency on, this type of bio-chemical response to a relational partner.

IPC Concepts: Relationship patterns, addiction, gender differences.

Duncan, B. L., & Rock, I. W. (1993, January/February). Saving relationships: The power of the unpredictable. *Psychology Today, 26*(1), 46–51, 86, 90.

Brief Summary: An excellent discussion of problems faced by married couples, this article also explores the role of relational myths in contributing to such problems. The authors suggest communication strategies that couples can employ to improve their relationships. The article stresses the interactive nature of relationships and the power of individual choice in interpreting the actions of the other partner.

IPC Concepts: Relationships—self-disclosure, commitment, trust, spouses.

Dym, B., & Glenn, M. (1993, July/August). Forecast for couples. *Psychology Today, 46*(4), 54–57, 78, 81.

Brief Summary: This article presents a practical discussion of relational stages. The authors posit a three-stage model: expansion and promise, contraction and betrayal, and resolution.

IPC Concepts: Relationships—self-disclosure, commitment, trust, spouses.

WHAT'S ON THE WEB

http://www.stepfamily.org/

Brief Summary: This Web site is devoted to step-relationships and to providing counseling—on the telephone, worldwide, and in person—by Jeannette Lofas and other certified Stepfamily Foundation counselors. Resources include books, audiotapes, and videotapes; training certified Stepfamily Foundation counselors and coaches; free information; research; corporate programs to eliminate the negative spillover effects of divorce and remarriage.

IPC Concepts: Relationships—commitment, warmth, affection, trust.

Love Test

http://www.lovetest.com/

Brief Summary: This fun and somewhat silly exercise can put students in the mood or mindset to discuss various attraction variables in relationships.

IPC Concepts: Intimate relationships—commitment, compatibility, beliefs, and expectations about relationships.

Mapping of Rules (Frederick R. Ford)

http://home.pacbell.net/frccford/index.html

Brief Summary: This site features a list of rules followed by people in several different kinds of families. Features include a Web-based test (with online scoring) which measures five family systems: Two Against the World, Children Come First, Share and Share Alike, Every Man for Himself, and Until Death Do Us Part. Links provide explanations and a bibliography.

IPC Concepts: Relationships and commitments, priorities, support, trust, caring.

CHAPTER 13

Communicating in

the Workplace

After you have read this chapter, you should be able to answer these questions:

- What should you do to prepare for a job interview?
- What are the important elements of a well-written résumé?
- What are the characteristics of open and closed, primary and secondary, and neutral and leading questions?
- How do you conduct a job interview?
- What are some typical questions used by job interviewers?
- How do managers and subordinates develop fair exchanges?
- How can you communicate effectively with co-workers and clients?
- What is leadership? How do you prepare yourself to lead groups?
- How does task leadership differ from person leadership?
- What are the four most important specialized skills necessary for effective leadership?

"At 3:30 sharp Chas arrived at the door of the human resources director of Grover Industries for his interview. The secretary led him into the office and introduced him to Michele Beddington.

"Sit down," Beddington said, "and we'll get started. Well, I've looked over your résumé, and now I have just a few questions. How did you get interested in Grover Industries?"

"Our Student Placement Office said you were hiring."

"And for what kind of a position do you think you would be most suited?"

"One where I could use my skills."

"What skills do you have to offer our company that would make you a good hire for us?"

"Well, I'm a hard worker."

"Are you familiar with our major products?"

"Not really. I haven't had time yet to look you up."

"I see. Well, how do you know that you could be helpful to us?"

"Well, because I work really hard."

"What kinds of experience have you had in business?"

"Um, let's see. Well, I sold magazines for my high school. And my sister-in-law owns her own business and I hear her talking about it a lot."

"OK, what do you see as some of your major skills?"

"I told you, I can work really hard!"

"Well, Chas, companies are impressed by hard workers. We're talking to other applicants, of course. So, I'll be in touch."

When Chas got home Tanya asked, "How did the interview go?"

"Great," Chas replied. "Ms. Beddington was impressed by the fact that I'm a hard worker."

What do you think Chas's chances are for getting the job? Adults spend approximately half their waking hours at work. Thus, many of the relationships that adults maintain are on the job. These relationships differ from friendships and family relationships because, for the most part, they serve different purposes and are not voluntary—you usually don't choose the people you work for or with.

In this chapter we'll explore the interpersonal communication challenges that we face at work. Of course, the first challenge is getting a job. The interpersonal communication process of interviewing is the most frequently used hiring practice and getting an interview often depends on having an effective cover letter and résumé. So, we'll begin by discussing both cover letter and résumé preparation. Then we'll describe effective interviewing both from the perspective of the interviewee and the interviewer. Once hired, we have different types of relationships to manage at work. Our relationships with managers, co-workers, and customers are important to our success. According to business consultant Ralph Weickel, "85 percent of people leave their jobs, voluntarily or through firing, because they did not get along with someone at work" (Kranz, 1999, p. C1). So we will explain the dynamics that lead to satisfying on-the-job relationships. Finally, we'll describe the interpersonal communication skills that enable work group leaders to effectively coach, counsel, and guide work groups.

Presenting Yourself During the Hiring Process

Most organizations use a multistep approach to hiring. Two of the most common elements that companies use to evaluate applicants are résumés and interviews. In this section we will describe how to present yourself in writing and how to effectively present yourself during an interview.

Presenting Yourself in Writing

You may learn of a job through an on-campus placement service, newspaper ad, or tip from a friend. Regardless of how you hear about the job, you usually will write a cover letter introducing yourself to the company and submit a résumé of your qualifications. These two documents are designed to "sell yourself and get an interview" (Schmidt & Conaway, 1999, p. 92).

Writing a Cover Letter The **cover letter** is a short, well-written letter expressing your interest in a particular position and highlighting the qualifications that make you an attractive candidate for the job. It is best to address the letter to a specific person, ideally the person with the authority to hire you (and not, for example, to "The Human Resources Department"). If you do not have the appropriate person's name, you can probably get it by telephoning the company and asking for it. Because you are trying to stimulate the reader's interest in you, make sure that your cover letter does not read like a form letter. The cover letter should be one page or less and specifically request an interview. In a couple of well-written paragraphs it also should include: where and how you learned about the position, the reason you are interested in the company, and your relevant skills and accomplishments (summarized in a few key points that demonstrate how your skill set fits the job requirements). You should always include a résumé with the letter.

> **Cover letter**—a short, well-written letter expressing your interest in a particular position.

The Résumé A **résumé** is a summary of your education, training, skills, and accomplishments. Although there is no universal format for writing a résumé, there is some agreement on what should be included and excluded. Try to approach creating your résumé from the employer's point of view. What will the employer want to know about you in order to decide to meet with you? What do you have to offer that can help the employer solve problems? Think in terms of what the com-

> **Résumé**—a summary of your skills and accomplishments.

pany needs, and present only those skills and accomplishments that show you can do the job. Most important, be tactful but truthful in what you present. While you want to emphasize your strengths, you want to avoid exaggerating facts, a practice that is both deceptive and unethical. An effective résumé includes the following information presented in a visually attractive, easy-to-read format:

1. **Contact information:** Your name, address, and telephone number(s) at which you can be reached. If you live at a temporary address during part of the year, you may want to include your permanent address as well.

2. **Career objective:** A one-sentence statement describing your personal vocational goal. (Important for full-time career positions.)

3. **Employment history:** Paid and nonpaid work experience, beginning with the most recent. Include employer contact information, dates of employment, and a brief list important duties and major accomplishments.

4. **Education:** Colleges, trade schools, and certificate programs attended, degrees or certifications earned (or expected), dates of completion (or expected dates), listing of courses completed that directly relate to the job.

5. **Military experience:** Include highest rank earned, branch of service, job description, honors and achievements, schools completed, skills learned, and discharge status.

6. **Relevant professional affiliations:** Memberships, offices held.

7. **Community activities:** Community service organizations, clubs, or other activities, including offices held and dates.

8. **Special skills:** Fluency in foreign languages, computer expertise.

9. **Interests and activities:** Include only those that are related to your objective.

10. **References:** People who know your work, capabilities, and character, and who are willing to talk with or write to a prospective employer on your behalf. You need not identify your references on the résumé but instead can indicate that "references are available on request." Regardless of whether you list your references or not, you should secure the permission of the people you want use as references before mailing your letters and résumés to potential employers.

Notice that the list does not include such personal information as height, weight, age, sex, marital status, health, race, religion, or political affiliation, nor does it include any reference to salary. Although you may not include the names of your references, you will want to experiment with the design and layout of your résumé—how wide your margins will be, the fonts and font sizes you will use, how each element will be highlighted, spaced, indented, and so on. The final résumé must be visually attractive and easy to read, neat, error free (proofread carefully), and reproduced on a good-quality paper. If you have had little work experience, you will be able to format an attractive one-page résumé. If you have a more extensive and substantial work history, your résumé may run several pages. Ideally, the résumé should be no more than three pages. Figure 13.1 shows a sample cover

Figure 13.1

Sample cover letter

2326 Tower Place
Cincinnati, Ohio 45220
April 8, 2003

Mr. Kyle Jones
Acme Marketing Research Associates
P.O. Box 482
Cincinnati, OH 45201

Dear Mr. Jones:

I am applying for the position of research assistant at Acme Marketing Research Associates that I learned about through the Office of Career Counseling at the University of Cincinnati. I am a senior mathematics major at the University of Cincinnati who is interested in pursuing a career in marketing research. I am highly motivated, eager to learn, and I enjoy working with all types of people. I am excited by the prospect of working for a firm like AMRA where I can apply my leadership and problem-solving skills in a professional setting.

As a mathematics major, I have developed the analytical proficiency that is necessary for working through complex problems. My courses in statistics have especially prepared me for data analysis while my more theoretical courses have taught me how to construct an effective argument. Through my leadership training and opportunities, I have learned to work effectively in groups and have seen the benefits of both individual and group problem solving. My work on the Strategic Planning Committee introduced me to the skills associated with strategic planning. Finally, from my theatrical experience, I have gained the poise to make presentations in front of small and large groups alike. I believe that these experiences and others have shaped who I am and have helped me to develop many of the skills necessary to be successful. I am interested in learning more and continuing to grow. I look forward to having the opportunity to interview with you in the future. I have enclosed my résumé with both my school address and phone number. Thank you for your consideration. I hope to hear from you soon.

Sincerely,

Elisa C. Vardin

letter and Figure 13.2 (p. 370) shows a sample résumé of a person who has just graduated from college.

Electronic Cover Letters and Résumés Electronic cover letters and résumés are those that are sent to the employer online. Electronic résumés have become quite popular with employers and job seekers. For example, from 1995 to 1999 the

Figure 13.2

Sample résumé

Elisa C. Vardin
2326 Tower Avenue
Cincinnati, Ohio 45220
Phone: (513) 861-2497
E-mail: ElisVardin@UC.edu

PROFFESSIONAL OBJECTIVE:

To use my intellectual abilities, quantitative capabilities, communication skills, and proven leadership to further the mission of a high-integrity marketing research organization.

EDUCATIONAL BACKGROUND:

UNIVERSITY OF CINCINNATI, Cincinnati, OH, B.A. in Mathematics June 2003. GPA 3.36. Dean's List.

NATIONAL THEATER INSTITUTE at the Eugene O'Neill Theater Center, Waterford, CT. Fall 2001. Acting, Voice, Movement, Directing, and Playwriting.

WORK AND OTHER BUSINESS-RELATED EXPERIENCE:

REYNOLDS & DEWITT, SENA WELLER ROHS WILLIAMS, Cincinnati, OH. Summer 2002.

Intern at Brokerage/Investment Management Firm. Provided administrative support. Created new databases, performance comparisons, and fact sheets in Excel and Word files.

MUMMERS THEATRE GUILD, University of Cincinnati, Spring 2000–Spring 2003. Treasurer. Responsible for all financial/accounting functions for this undergraduate theater community.

SUMMERBRIDGE CINCINNATI, Cincinnati Country Day School, Cincinnati, OH. Summer 2001. Teacher in program for "at risk" junior high students. Taught 7th grade mathematics, 6th and 7th grade speech communication, sign language; Academic advisor; Club leader. Organized five-hour diversity workshop and three-hour tension-reduction workshop for staff.

STRATEGIC PLANNING COMMITTEE, Summit Country Day School, Cincinnati, OH. Fall 1998–1999. One of two student members. Worked with the Board of Directors developing the first Strategic Plan for a 1000-student independent school (Pre-K through 12).

AYF INTERNATIONAL LEADERSHIP CONFERENCE, Miniwanca Conference Center, Shelby, MI. Summer 1998–2000. Participant in international student conference sponsored by American Youth Foundation.

PERSONAL:

Musical Theater: lifetime involvement, including leads and choreography for several shows. A cappella singing group: 1999–2002, Director 2001–2003. Swing Club: 2000–2002, President and Teacher of student dance club. Junior High Youth Group Leader: 2001. Math Tutor: 2001. Aerobics Instructor: 2001–2002. University of Cincinnati Choral Society: 2000–2003. American Sign Language Instructor: Winter 2001, 2002.

TECHNICAL SKILLS AND TRAINING: SAS, SPSS, EXCEL, ACCESS, WORD. Univariate and Multivariate Statistics (2 courses), Regression Analysis (2 courses).

REFERENCES: Available on request.

percentage of résumés that were received electronically by Microsoft increased from 5 percent to 50 percent (Criscito, 2000, p. 2). By now, that percentage is likely to be considerably higher. Employers like electronic résumés because they then can use computer programs to sift through large numbers of applicants to look for particular qualifications or characteristics. Candidates like electronic résumés because they save time and money.

Although electronic cover letters and résumés contain the same content as traditional paper versions, they may differ in several ways (Schmidt & Conaway, 1999, pp. 98–99). Many of the differences take into account the fact that they will be scanned electronically. Thus, it is wise to avoid using boldface, italics, and bullet points because these design elements "only confuse computerized word searches or interfere with the scanning process" (Schmidt & Conaway, 1999, p. 98). The most important thing to remember for a scannable or e-mail résumé is to keep the format simple. For instance, the sample résumé in Figure 13.2 is more likely to work electronically if the contact information at the top (address, phone, e-mail) is positioned flush left instead of centered on the page. Likewise, any indented material should be moved to flush left, perhaps with a space after each title.

There are three kinds of electronic résumés: the paper résumé that becomes an electronic version when it is scanned into a computer; an ASCII text e-mailable version (a generic computer file that you create especially to send through cyberspace); and a multimedia résumé that is given a home page at a fixed location on the Internet for anyone to visit (Criscito, 2000, p. 2).

A scanned résumé can be attached to an e-mail cover letter and sent directly to a company's recruiters over the Internet. If you already have a paper résumé that has been prepared, saved, and sent as a generic ASCII text file, it has the advantage of being able to be read by anyone, regardless of the word processing software he or she is using (Criscito, 2000, p. 3). ASCII text file résumés can be sent as a file to company recruiters or posted to the home page of a company, a job bank, or a newsgroup. Finally, when you post your résumé on a home page, you increase the likelihood that someone who is seeking employees with your qualifications will see your résumé and inquire about your interest in their company.

TEST YOURSELF

Preparing a Cover Letter and a Résumé

Prepare a cover letter and a résumé that reflects your current experience and expertise.

What is missing on your résumé? Are there some experiences, skills, or accomplishments that would make you more competitive? Develop a plan to gain these experiences, skills, or accomplishments.

Interviewing

Recall a recent job interview that you experienced. Describe the ways in which the interview was difficult for you. Suppose you were to engage in that same interview again: Which of the guidelines presented in the text would be most helpful for you? ■

Presenting Yourself During an Interview

Interviews are used by most organizations to decide whom they will hire. During the interview, company representatives may explore the candidate's qualifications, but the primary purpose of interviews is to judge the candidate's personality and motivation to see how well he or she is likely to fit with the organization, potential co-workers, and managers. The following guidelines can help you effectively present yourself during the interview.

1. Do your homework. Learn about the company's services, products, ownership, and financial health and use this information during the interview. Knowing about a company demonstrates your motivation and your interest in that company. Moreover, you'll be in a better position to discuss how you can contribute to the company's mission.

2. Rehearse the interview. For most of us, job interviews are stressful. To help prepare to perform at your best, it is a good idea to practice. Anticipate questions you will be asked and craft thoughtful answers. Try writing out or saying answers aloud. Figure 13.3 (p. 376) lists some common questions that are frequently asked in interviews. Prepare answers for each of these.

3. Dress appropriately and conservatively. If you know the organization, you will want to dress so that you are a little more conservatively attired than the average employee. While many organizations have a casual dress code, you are not yet an employee and you want to make a good impression. So, it is important that you look neat, clean, and appropriate. When interviewing for professional positions men should wear a collared shirt, dress slacks, tie, jacket, and nonathletic shoes. In some situations men will want to wear suits. Women should wear suits or professional looking dresses. Skirt length and necklines should be modest and midrifts should be completely covered. When possible, wear clothing that covers body art and piercings to avoid having such personal fashion statements negatively influence an interviewer's perception of your qualifications.

4. Plan to arrive early. The interview is the company's first exposure to your work behavior. Regardless of the reason, if you are late for such an important event, the interviewer will conclude that

"I'm in my forties, and it's my firm belief that Digetek could use someone in his forties to excellent advantage."

you are likely to be late for work. So give yourself extra travel time to cover any potential problems. Arriving early gives you a chance to catch your breath, freshen up, and get a feel for the organization. A good rule of thumb is to plan to arrive fifteen to twenty minutes before your appointment.

5. Make appropriate eye contact and listen actively. Remember that your nonverbal communication tells a lot about you. Company representatives are likely to consider eye contact and posture as clues to your self-confidence and your interest in the job.

6. Give yourself time to think before answering a question. If the interviewer asks you a question that you had not anticipated, give yourself a moment to compose your answer. It is better to pause and appear thoughtful than to give a hasty rambling answer that does not present the best of your thinking. If you do not understand the question, try to paraphrase it before providing an answer.

7. Demonstrate your interest by asking questions about the organization and the job. The interview is your chance to find out if you would enjoy working for the company. By asking thoughtful questions, you indicate serious interest in the company and the job. For example, you could ask the interviewer to describe a typical workday, projects, and duties for someone in this job. You could ask what the career progression is. If the interview is conducted at the company's offices, you could ask to see where you would be working. The answers to questions like these will help you know if you would be willing to accept the job if it is offered.

What kinds of questions would you ask to determine whether a person is right for a position?

8. Show your enthusiasm. If you act too "cooly" during the interview, the interviewer is likely to reason that you're uninterested or not highly motivated. Naturally, employers want to hire people who seem excited about their company and the job. So you will want to use your nonverbal behavior (smiling, nodding, and posture) to indicate your enthusiasm.

9. Avoid lengthy discussions of salary or benefits. You should not initiate discussions about salary during a first interview. In later interviews, you might quickly inquire about typical salary range for the position. The time to discuss (and negotiate) salary is after the company has committed to you by offering the job. If the company representative tries to pin you down before an offer is made, try to reframe the discussion by asking, "What do you normally pay someone with my experience and education for this type of position?" This question allows you to get an idea of the salary range without committing yourself to a figure first. People who prematurely talk about salary risk short-changing themselves by quoting a salary that is less than what a company might possibly pay or by not receiving an offer for a job they'd like to have because they quoted a salary a bit higher than the organization can pay.

Similarly, detailed discussions about benefits are appropriate after the company has made you an offer. When you use valuable interview time discussing benefits, organizational representatives are likely to perceive that you are more interested in what you can get from the company rather than what you will bring to the job.

Interviewing Others

In your working life, you will experience interviewing from both sides of the desk; that is, you will be interviewed and you will interview others. For example, you may need to interview customers about their complaints, interview co-workers to get information relevant to your work, or interview prospective vendors or other employees. Understanding how interpersonal communication skills are used in interviewing can make you better at doing this part of your job.

An **interview** is a structured conversation with the goal of exchanging information that is needed for decision making. An interview plan is a list of questions that are designed to get the information that is needed for effective decision making. Interviews, like speeches and essays, have an introductory section, a body, and a concluding section.

Interview—a structured conversation with the goal of exchanging information that is needed for decision making.

Beginning the Interview

Interviewers should begin with a statement of the interview's purpose and and introduction if they have not previously met with the interviewee. In order to create rapport, it is a good idea to begin the interview with several "warm-up" or easy questions. A good interviewer selects questions that are likely to encourage the other person to talk and elaborate on answers. Although warm-up questions can be helpful, participants may be ready to get down to business immediately, in which case warm-up questions may be counterproductive (Cogger, 1982).

Questions Used in the Body of the Interview

During the body of interview the primary questions to which you need answers are asked and answered. The quality of information received usually depends on how questions are phrased. Interview questions may be phrased to solicit open or closed answers. The questions may be neutral or leading, implying a specific type of answer. Some questions will be primary while others will be secondary, or follow-up (Stewart & Cash, 2000, p. 80).

Open questions—broad-based questions that ask the interviewee to respond with whatever information he or she wishes.

Open questions are phrased so to elicit broad-reaching answers. Interviewees must respond at some length with whatever information they can provide. Open questions in a job interview might include "What can you tell me about yourself?" and "What is your one accomplishment that has best prepared you for this job?" In a problem-solving interview with a disgruntled customer, open questions might be "What seems to be the problem?" or "Can you tell me the steps you took in using the product?" Interviewers ask open questions to encourage the person to talk, allowing the interviewer an opportunity to listen and to observe. Open questions take time to answer and give respondents more control, which means that interviewers can lose sight of their original purpose if they are not careful (Tengler & Jablin, 1983).

In contrast, **closed questions** are narrow-focus questions that require the respondent to give very brief (one- or two-word) answers. Closed questions range from those that can be answered yes or no, such as "Have you had a course in marketing?" to those that require only a short answer, such as "Where did you buy the product?" By asking closed questions, interviewers can both control the interview and obtain large amounts of information in a short time. Closed questions seldom enable the interviewer to know why a person gave a certain response, nor are they likely to yield much voluntary information, so a combination of open and closed questions is used in most situations, especially in employment interviews (Stewart & Cash, 2000).

Open and closed questions may be either neutral or leading. **Neutral questions** are those that do not direct a person's answer. "What can you tell me about your work with Habitat for Humanity?" or "What symptoms did you experience?" The neutral question gives the respondent free rein to answer the question without any knowledge of what the interviewer thinks or believes. In contrast, **leading questions** guide the respondents toward providing certain types of information. "What do you like about working for Habitat for Humanity?" steers the respondent to describe only the positive aspects of the work. "Was this as painful as a migraine?" directs the answer by providing the standard for comparison. In most employment interviews, neutral questions are preferred.

Primary questions are the preplanned open and closed questions that the interviewer believes will solicit the information that is needed. Most **Secondary** or **follow-up questions** are spontaneous, and are based on the answers given to primary questions. Some follow-up questions encourage the person to continue ("And then?" "Is there more?"); some probe into what the person has said ("What does 'frequently' mean?" "What were you thinking at the time?"); and some probe the feelings of the person ("How did it feel to get the prize?" "Did it last longer than fifteen minutes?"). The major purpose of follow-up questions is to encourage the person to expand on an answer that seems incomplete or vague. Figure 13.3 (p. 376), presents a sample of the kinds of questions that can be used as part of an employment interview.

Closed questions—narrow-focus questions that require very brief answers.

Neutral questions—questions that allow a person to give an answer without direction from the interviewer.

Leading questions—questions that are phrased in a way that suggests the interviewer has a preferred answer.

Primary questions—open or closed questions that the interviewer plans ahead of time.

Secondary or follow-up questions—planned or spontaneous questions that are designed to pursue the answers given to primary questions.

OBSERVE & ANALYZE

Journal Activity

What Interviewers Look For

Make an appointment to interview a person in the human resources department of a large organization whose job it is to interview candidates for employment. Develop a set of interview questions. Focus your interview on obtaining information about the person's experiences that will help you. For example, you might ask, "What are the characteristics you like to see an interviewee demonstrate?" "How do you decide who to interview?" and so on. Prepare to discuss your findings in class. ■

School:

How did you select the school you attended?

How did you determine your major?

What extracurricular activities did you engage in at school?

In what ways does your transcript reflect your ability?

How were you able to help with your college expenses?

Personal:

What are your hobbies? How did you become interested in them?

Give an example of how you work under pressure.

At what age did you begin supporting yourself?

What causes you to lose your temper?

What are your major strengths? Weaknesses?

Give an example of when you were a leader and what happened.

What do you do to stay in good physical condition?

What was the last nonschool-assigned book that you read? Tell me about it.

Who has had the greatest influence on your life?

What have you done that shows your creativity?

Position:

What kind of position are you looking for?

What do you know about the company?

Under what conditions would you be willing to relocate?

Why do you think you would like to work for us?

What do you hope to accomplish?

What qualifications do you have that would make you beneficial to us?

How do you feel about traveling?

What part of the country would you like to settle in?

With what kinds of people do you enjoy interacting?

What do you regard as an equitable salary for a person with your qualifications?

What new skills would you like to learn?

What are your career goals?

How would you proceed if you were in charge of hiring?

What are your most important criteria for determining whether you will accept a position?

Concluding an Interview

Toward the end of the interview you should always explain to the interviewee what will happen next and how the information you gathered will be used. If the interview will lead to specific decisions, explain how the information will be used in the process. Also let the interviewee know whether and how he or she will receive feedback on the decision. Be sure to thank the interviewee for his or her time and interest. Throughout the interview be careful of your own presentation, try not to waste time, and give the applicant time to ask questions.

Managing Relationships at Work

You will use your interpersonal communication skills to develop and maintain healthy relationships with your colleagues at work, including your managers, employees, co-workers, vendors, clients, and customers. Good communication skills are universally recognized as essential for successful interactions with colleagues at work (Whetten & Cameron, 2002, p. 216).

Communicating in Managerial Relationships

Managers are responsible for seeing that their employees perform their job duties. To do this, managers instruct employees, give them feedback on their job performance, and influence them to meet their personal and work goals. Instructing employees requires managers to be adept in describing behavior, using clear and vivid language, and offering constructive criticism. Providing useful feedback to em-

What kinds of communication skills are recognized as essential for successful interactions with colleagues at work?

ployees requires managers to know how to praise and how to criticize in appropriate ways. Influencing employees to accomplish their tasks well requires managers to understand their employees' needs. Thus, managers must be effective listeners who are skilled at paraphrasing and perception checking. With this information they can then use influence skills to help employees better accomplish their tasks.

Employees also have a responsibility to communicate effectively with their managers. You can increase the likelihood that your conversations with your managers will be effective by using the skills of listening, questioning, paraphrasing, asking for feedback, and asserting yourself.

When both persons in a manager-employee relationship recognize the importance of communication and jointly assume responsibility for sharing meaning, then communication breakdowns are less likely to occur and the needs of both relationship members are likely to be met.

As with any other relationship, the one between a manager and an employee develops over a period of time. Yet, not all individuals who have the same manager establish the same type or level of relationship with that person. In fact, differential treatment from managers is the norm. Workers are aware of such treatment and do talk about it (Sias & Jablin, 1995, p. 5).

Managers look for employees who are willing to perform more than is normally expected (Graen, 1976). As these individuals become more valuable to the manager over time, they establish a greater power base from which to negotiate. In order to maintain a "fair exchange" with these individuals, the manager negotiates special "rewards" for employees performing duties beyond those formally expected of them. Although the rewards may be financial (e.g., bonuses) they are more likely to be in the form of choice task assignments, better office space, public praise for special assignments, access to information not usually shared with employees at that level, and a closer interpersonal relationship with the manager. Employees in these relationships often describe the experience as a mentoring relationship, indicating that what they have gained has helped them to develop skills and expertise beyond the learning that would normally take place on the job. These skills make them more valuable to the organization and will help them to advance in their careers.

Individuals who are performing their role assignments well but who are not doing anything extra to help out the manager may receive good work evaluations, adequate raises, and fair treatment, but they will find it difficult to be promoted or to develop a close working relationship with their manager. Thus, effective employees are likely to ask themselves, "How can I establish a more effective working relationship with my manager?"

To establish a high-quality exchange relationship with your manager you must begin by assessing what skills and expertise you possess that may be of value in helping your manager accomplish the work that falls outside of the formal role prescriptions of your job. These skills may be those that are in short supply in your work unit or those that your manager lacks. If a company is considering a new computer application that the manager is unfamiliar with, an employee might do some research, take a course at the local college, or volunteer for the company training program in order to become a valuable asset.

Once you are aware of what skills you can bring to an exchange relationship, you communicate your willingness to perform extra assignments that require these skills. Thus, if your manager, who might not wish to ask directly for help, says

DILBERT reprinted by permission of the United Feature Syndicate, Inc.

something like "I'm just swamped with work, and now Human Resources says they have to have these affirmative action forms filled out and returned by Monday," a savvy employee sees this as a call for help. Rather than responding "Yeah, Personnel is so unreasonable. Well, I've got to get back to my desk," the savvy employee, seeking to establish an exchange relationship with the manager, might respond with a supportive statement like: "Gee, Barb, I get the feeling you don't really think you'll have time to do it. How can I help?"

The essential bond in a close manager-employee relationship is mutual trust. These relationships are marked by direct interaction between manager and close employees, which reinforces the level of trust between them (Lee & Jablin, 1995, p. 248). Being willing to take on additional assignments will further your relationship only if you are willing to perform such assignments well and on time. Although doing this often means working more, you may be able to negotiate with your manager to be removed from other, mundane assignments.

As we have seen, communication competence is critical in work-based relationships. By skillful use of listening, perception checking, describing, questioning, and paraphrasing, you can control the manner in which your relationships with your managers develop. Without careful and attentive use of these skills, you are likely to have a distant and ineffective working relationship with your manager and, in time, with your employees.

Communicating in Co-Worker Relationships

Your co-workers are the other members of your work group, team, or department who are at the same job level as you. It has been shown that co-workers influence both the quality of our performance and our satisfaction with our jobs (Jablin & Krone, 1994, p. 647). Like other relationships, your relationships with your co-workers are developed through your communication experiences with them. But just as you will not choose your manager, you will also not be in charge of selecting those with whom you work. Thus, as in manager-employee relationships, how well you get along with your co-workers depends on your communication competence. For example, if you choose to be insensitive to the needs and feelings of your co-workers by not listening attentively or being unaware of cultural differences, then you are likely to find that these relationships are not satisfying.

Co-worker cooperation does not mean that co-workers must be close friends or always agree. Indeed, as the workforce becomes more diverse, it is likely that disagreements and misunderstandings between co-workers will become more frequent. Most managers recognize this diversity as a potential strength on which they can draw. They reason that, if well managed, the disagreements and cultural differences may lead to more creative and productive solutions to organizational problems. If this is to happen, co-workers must develop and maintain healthy working relationships. Maintaining them depends on effective interpersonal communication. Skills like turn-taking, listening, collaborative problem-solving approaches to conflict resolution, supportiveness, and effective group communication skills will be critical to workers into the twenty-first century. As the workforce becomes global, understanding the cultural norms that affect organizations in other countries will become increasingly important. In the accompanying Diverse Voices selection, Sheryl Lindsley describes how Mexican cultural imperatives compare to U.S. American imperatives in communication practices and meanings in work relationships.

Communication in Self-Managed Work Teams

The use of self-managed teams or self-managing work groups is increasing in organizations today. In these groups it is the responsibility of the co-workers to decide on and institute work assignments, as well as to problem solve and monitor work quality. The trend toward self-managed teams is expected to spread and may become a dominant fact of organizational life. This will result in co-workers' relationships becoming more important and manager-employee relationships less important.

Self-managed teams succeed in part because people support things that they have helped to create. When the team sets high standards for work and these standards are communicated to and accepted by most group members, the team generates the pressure that will keep that work group productive. A second reason that self-managed teams succeed is that individual co-workers can share a wealth of job-related information that will help new members develop the skills they need to be productive in the organization. A third benefit of self-managed teams is that individuals who have good working relationships with co-workers generally like their jobs and thus are less likely to leave the organization. Because it is expensive to train new employees, most organizations prefer to keep turnover rates low.

Those working in self-managed teams will find that the group process will be facilitated by the skills of paraphrasing, describing behavior, and using precise and specific language, as well as by steps for conflict management and effective listening.

Boundary-spanning roles—roles whose central task is to deal with people outside the organization.

INTER-ACT WITH
Technology

Since 9-11 many businesses are increasing their use of mediated business meetings. Teleconferencing and videoconferencing are becoming common practice. Most organizations have specialists whose jobs are to assist in planning, setting up, and running mediated conferences. Yet many organizations do not provide members with training on how to adapt their behavior to the demands of mediated conferences. Based on your study of verbal and nonverbal communication, develop two lists of ten recommendations you would make for people who are to take part in video- and teleconferences. How are your lists similar? How are they different? ■

Communication in Boundary-Spanning Relationships

Vendors are the representatives of other organizations who supply your organization with things you need to do business. Customers and clients are the people who use the results of your work. In every organization some individuals occupy **boundary-spanning roles,** roles whose central task is to deal with people outside the organization. These boundary-spanning roles require their occupants to form work-related relationships with individuals who are not members of the organization. Examples of typical boundary-spanning roles include sales representatives, customer

Understanding Our Mexican Co-Workers By Sheryl Lindsley

What is deemed appropriate communication behavior in an organization depends on the national culture and language community customs from which the majority of employees come. In this excerpt we read about four ways that Mexican communication behavior differs from North American behavior in work organizations.

"When I go to business meetings, I was raised in a culture where you just get out your reports and start talking about them and that's not how it is here (in Mexico). You talk about family and other things first. I often forget this and so one of my Mexican colleagues will remind me that I'm violating this tradition by saying, 'So (name), how is your dog?' When I hear this then I know I'm not supposed to be talking about business."

This account by a U.S. American reflects the importance of adapting cultural behaviors to achieve communication competency in organizational settings. Four of the five cultural concepts derived from research on doing business in Mexico include: confianza, palanca, estabilidad, and mañana.

Confianza. A Mexican production manager (explains) what she does when she thinks someone is wrong.

"Well, it's hard at first if someone is new, but after you establish trust and confidence, then it's easier. . . I just make suggestions about things, but I don't tell people they are wrong. I just give them information to make the decisions and then they are grateful and the relationship

benefits from this . . . When you just make suggestions and don't tell people what to do and let them learn and make decisions for themselves, then more confidence in the relationship develops and then they owe you. You didn't confront them, you treated them well, with respect, and now they owe you."*

According to this account, indirectness is appropriate in a situation in which another's face (or self-presentation) is vulnerable. Because relationships are generally more central to Mexican than U.S. American organizations, it is no surprise that relationships are carefully nurtured and safeguarded. One of the core aspects of a good relationship is the co-creation of *confianza,* or "trust," which is built through communicative behaviors that adhere to cultural norms for face saving.

Palanca. The concept of *palanca* refers to leverage, or power derived from affiliated connections. It affects organizational relationships in terms of one's ability to get things done by virtue of one's official authority as well as through one's contacts with extensive networks of relationships among family members, relatives, former classmates,

friends, and business associates. These connections are often built over many years and enable one to obtain favors that may transcend institutional rules and procedures or overcome scarcity of resources and services. U.S. Americans may tend to evaluate these practices as "corrupt" without reflecting on the similarities with their own organizational behaviors, or without understanding the rationale for why these behaviors are functional in Mexican culture. Although the differentiation is murky, *palanca* embodies a system of mutual obligation and reciprocated favors, not necessarily money or gifts. For example, some individuals perceive that giving a small fee to a government worker for processing paperwork expeditiously is something positive and similar to the U.S. practice of tipping a waiter or waitress for good service.

Estabilidad. A common sentiment among many Mexicans is, "The family is our first priority and must remain so for the future stability of our country." The need for *estabilidad* or "stability" reinforces the value of personal relationships and permeates organizational behaviors. It reflects the tendency for

Mexicans to place relationships before tasks. This is communicated through a wide range of behaviors, including asking questions about colleagues' families, discussing personal matters before business (e.g., at the beginning of a meeting), taking action to promote the employees' personal well-being, including families in organizational activities, taking time off work to assist family members in need, and establishing, developing, and maintaining long-term relationships.

Some of the ways that managers show responsibility for employees' well-being may be through *compradrazgo* systems in which they become godfathers, godmothers, and mentors for their employees' children. These types of relationships exemplify the extent to which Mexican personal and organizational roles overlap in contrast to U.S. roles that are typically more separated. This often blurred distinction between familial and organizational life also means that Mexicans may give preference to hiring relatives over strangers, helping employees get a better education, or giving them small personal loans. These favors are often reciprocated with strong employee support and loyalty to the manager.

Mañana. In intercultural interaction in organizations, Mexicans and U.S. Americans often find themselves at odds over different understandings and attitudes surrounding the concept of time. Misunderstandings may arise in intercultural interpretation of language.

Spanish language dictionaries say that *mañana* means "tomorrow." But "tomorrow" is a literal translation, not the true cultural meaning of the word. In its normal cultural context, mañana means "sometime in the near future, maybe." Behind the term are such unspoken things as "If I feel like it," "If I have the time," or "If nothing unexpected happens."

U.S. Americans have the tendency to think about mañana as referring to some specific time period due to a primarily external orientation toward time (clocks guide activity). Most Mexicans use time clocks but consider time to be more interpersonally negotiable (relationships guide activities) and mediated by unexpected events beyond one's control. For example, events occur, *"Si Dios quiere"* (God willing). One Mexican manager explained to me, "In Mexico we have a saying, *"Salud, dinero, amor y tiempo para disfrutarlos"* (Health, wealth, love, and time for enjoying them)." He contrasted this with such American sayings as "Time is money." These contrasts in cultural orientation toward time can exacerbate problems in intercultural interaction. When U.S. Americans do not take time to develop and maintain good interpersonal relationships in business, Mexicans may think they do not care about people, only money. Likewise, when Mexicans do not complete tasks "on time," U.S. Americans may think they're lazy.

Experience has shown that intercultural communication competency is critical to organizational success. Through understanding the concepts explained above one can better adapt to working with Mexicans.

Excerpted from Lindsley, S. (2000). U.S. Americans and Mexicans working together: Five core Mexican concepts for enhancing effectiveness. In L. A. Samovar & R. G. Porter (Eds.), *Intercultural Communication: A Reader* (9th ed., pp. 335–340). Belmont, Calif.: Wadsworth.

service technicians, delivery persons, social workers, buyers, purchasing agents, dispatchers, real estate agents, public relations personnel, marketing research interviewers, and caregivers such as nurses. By having to relate to individuals who are not members of their organization or their part of the organization about business-related matters, people in customer relationships must use communication skills to overcome potential pitfalls that otherwise might hinder their effectiveness.

Most boundary-spanning roles involve some type of customer-client relationship. In a study of two stores, as cashiers displayed more courtesy, customers provided more positive evaluations of service and were ultimately more likely to recommend the store to friends and shop at the store, even if other stores were closer (Zabava Ford, 1995, p. 81). Most of us can cite at least one example of a salesperson's behavior that is so extraordinary that we prefer to shop with that salesperson whenever we can. For instance, a woman might buy her cosmetics from only one salesclerk at one department store when she finds that this clerk goes out of her way to explain how to use the products, to recommend colors, and to send cards to the customer when special offers are available. This special attention and extra communication effort on the part of the salesclerk are likely to ensure the loyalty of that customer. This translates directly into profits for the company. Courtesy to customers varies somewhat depending on the sex of the salesperson. A study by Zabava Ford (1995) supports previous research findings that females will display more courteous behaviors toward customers than will men (p. 86).

Unfortunately, many of those who are supposed to deal with the public on behalf of the organization have not been trained to use the communication skills that would be most likely to aid them in the effective performance of their jobs.

What are the signs that the boundary spanner is trying to develop, maintain, or improve customer/client relationships?

Customer service providers need to have refined communication skills such as comforting, listening, responding effectively to conflict, and using equality-oriented language.

In today's business environment effective boundary spanners are spending time listening to, sharing information with, and learning from those with whom they do business. Relationships are viewed as primary, and "deals" are often negotiated to be in both companies' best interest. Obviously it is critical that those who work at these boundaries be adept in using problem-oriented communication strategies. They must also be able to negotiate and use collaborative conflict-resolution skills.

Boundary-spanning roles are fraught with tension because individuals occupying these positions may have little control over the company policies that they must follow and communicate to those with whom they deal. Yet if customers are not satisfied, they will hold the boundary spanner responsible.

Boundary spanners can maintain good communication climates with their customers, however, if they explain to the customer not only the policy they are following but the reason for it. Many discount stores have a no-return policy. In addition to in-store signs, this policy can be communicated to each customer by the cashier at the time of purchase with a simple explanation, "We cannot accept returns and keep our prices low, so be sure to check the merchandise before you leave." Such a practice may reduce the number of customer complaints. Similarly, instead of promising delivery in days, a sales representative should explain to the client that the company policy is to ship 90 percent of all orders in three days but that there is no guarantee that this order might not take longer. A representative who explains delivery in these terms should be able to maintain a good working relationship with a client even if the merchandise is late.

A boundary spanner's lack of control should be clearly and specifically communicated to clients. In this way effective relationships can be established even in the face of business uncertainty. These language skills, when used to honestly communicate the nature of a situation, help establish the boundary spanner as ethical.

Leadership—exerting influence to help subordinates, co-workers, and clients reach their goals

OBSERVE & ANALYZE

Journal Activity

Boundary Spanners

Make a list of the individual boundary spanners you encounter in a typical week with whom you have a continuing relationship. (Don't forget your professors!) Select one satisfying and one unsatisfying episode you have had with a boundary spanner. Compare and contrast the communication processes in each encounter. ■

Leadership in Work Relations

At work, **leadership** means exerting influence to help employees, co-workers, and clients reach their goals (Bass, 1990). Influence, of course, is the ability to bring about changes in the attitudes and actions of others. At work there are many opportunities to lead, whether as a formal manager, team leader, committee chairperson, or informal work group leader. In this section, we are concerned with what leaders can do consciously to help guide people and groups in meeting their goals. First we will look at leadership traits and styles and how you can prepare for leadership. Then we'll consider three of the most important leadership skills: coaching, counseling, and leading group meetings.

Leadership Traits

Leadership traits are distinguishing qualities or characteristics. Traits that are associated with effective leadership are those related to ability, sociability, motivation, and communication skills (Bass, 1990; Shaw, 1981). In ability, leaders exceed average group members in intelligence, scholarship, insight, and verbal facility; in sociability, leaders exceed average group members in dependability, activeness, cooperativeness, and popularity; in motivation, leaders exceed group members in initiative, persistence, and enthusiasm; and leaders exceed average group members in the various communication skills discussed in this text. Although having these traits doesn't guarantee selection as leaders, people are unlikely to be selected as leaders if they do not exhibit at least some of these traits to a greater degree than do those they are attempting to lead.

Leadership traits—distinguishing qualities or characteristics.

Leadership Styles

Leadership style refers to the behavioral patterns that a person enacts when that person is trying to lead. Leadership styles tend to be either task oriented (sometimes called authoritarian) or person oriented (sometimes called democratic), or some combination of the two. Most effective leaders have both task-oriented and person-oriented skills.

Leadership style—behavioral patterns that a person enacts when that person is trying to lead.

Task-oriented leaders exercise more direct control over people and groups. Task leaders will determine what needs to be done and how to go about doing it. **Person-oriented leaders** may suggest ways of proceeding, yet encourage group members to determine what will actually be done.

Task-oriented leaders—leaders who exercise more direct control over people and groups.

Pioneer work by White and Lippitt (1968) suggests the following advantages and disadvantages of each style: (1) More work is done under a task-oriented leader than under a person-oriented leader. (2) The least amount of work is done when no leadership exists. (3) Motivation and originality are greater under a person-oriented leader. (4) Task-oriented leadership may create discontent or result in less individual creativity. (5) More friendliness is shown in person-oriented groups.

Person-oriented leaders—leaders who may suggest ways of proceeding, yet encourage group members to determine what will actually be done.

So which style is to be preferred? Research by Fred Fiedler (1967) suggests that whether a particular leadership style is successful depends on the situation: (1) how good the leader's interpersonal relations are with the group, (2) how clearly defined the goals and tasks of the group are, and (3) to what degree the group accepts the leader as having legitimate authority to lead.

OBSERVE & ANALYZE

Journal Activity

Leadership Style

Identify your leadership style. Are you more of a task-oriented or a person-oriented leader? On what basis did you make this determination? List the strengths and weaknesses of your style. Under what circumstances is your natural style most likely to be effective? Under which leadership style do you work best? Explain each. ■

Preparing for Leadership

Suppose you want to have more opportunities to show your leadership abilities. What can you do to encourage people and groups to support your leadership efforts?

1. Be knowledgeable about the particular tasks. People are more willing to follow when the leader appears to be well informed. The more knowledgeable you are, the better you will be able to analyze individual contributions.

2. Develop mental models for managing meaning. Effective leaders make sure that people share meaning. But because their job requires them to behave spontaneously, they need to anticipate what might happen and have mental models available to deal with various contingencies. Gail T. Fairhurst has done research on one such model, called framing. This chapter's Spotlight on Scholars (p. 387) focuses on Gail Fairhurst and her research.

3. Work harder than anyone else. Since leadership is often a question of setting an example, when a group sees a person who is willing to do more than his or her fair share for the good of the group, they are likely to support the person. Of course, such hard work often takes a lot of personal sacrifice, but the person seeking to lead must be willing to pay the price.

4. Be personally committed to group goals and needs. To gain and maintain leadership takes great commitment to the particular task. The greater your commitment, the greater are the chances that group members will support you.

5. Be willing to be decisive. When leaders fail to be decisive, their groups can become frustrated and short-tempered. Sometimes leaders must make decisions that will be resented; sometimes they must decide between competing ideas about courses of action. Any decisions leaders make may cause conflict. Nevertheless, people who are unwilling or unable to be decisive are not going to maintain leadership for long.

6. Develop people skills as well as task skills. Most effective leaders have both person-oriented and task-oriented skills. Effective leaders make others in their groups feel good by supporting valuable statements, seeing to it that everyone has a chance to contribute, and handling conflicts in ways that don't lead to hard feelings.

Coaching Others at Work

Coaching—a day-to-day, hands-on process of helping others improve their work performance.

Coaching is "a day-to-day, hands-on process of helping others improve their work performance" (Robbins & Hunsaker, 1996, p. 151). A good coach observes what people are doing, shows them the problems or inefficiencies with their methods, offers suggestions for improving their methods, and helps them use the methods effectively. Of course, effective coaching requires a supportive climate and using the active listening skills of paraphrasing, questioning, and supporting.

1. An effective coach is a technically adept and keen observer. You cannot coach effectively if you do not understand the correct or more efficient way to perform the particular behavior. In addition, as a coach your technical expertise is of little value unless you carefully watch people perform and note their deficiencies. For example,

Gail T. Fairhurst, Professor of Communication, University of Cincinnati, on
Leadership in Work Organizations

According to Gail T. Fairhurst, who has been studying organizational communication throughout her career, leadership is not a trait possessed by only some people, neither is it a simple set of behaviors that can be learned and then used in any situation. Rather, Fairhurst's research has convinced her that leadership is the process of creating social reality by managing the meanings that are assigned to certain behaviors, activities, programs, and events. Further, she believes that leadership is best understood as a relational process.

One area in which Fairhurst has focused her work is in examining how organizational leaders "frame" issues for their members. Framing is the process of managing meaning by selecting and highlighting some aspects of a subject, while excluding others. When we communicate our frames to others we manage meaning because we are asserting that our interpretation of the subject should be taken as "real" over other possible interpretations. How organizational leaders choose to verbally frame events is one way that they influence

workers' and others' perceptions.

Framing is especially important when the organization experiences change, such as downsizing. To reduce their uncertainty during times of change, members of the organization seek to understand what the change "means" to them personally and to the way they work in the organization. Leaders are expected to help members understand what is happening and what it means. By framing the change, they select and highlight some features of the change while downplaying others, providing a "lens" through which organizational members can understand what the change means. Most recently Fairhurst has been conducting studies that help us understand the unintentional consequences of the frames that organizations have chosen to use in successive downsizing events.

In *The Art of Framing* (with Robert A. Sarr), Fairhurst reports that leaders use five language forms or devices to frame information: metaphors, jargon or catch phrases, contrast, spin, and stories. Metaphors show how the change is similar to some-

thing that is already familiar. For instance, leaders may frame downsizing with weight and prize-fighting metaphors suggesting that the organization is "flabby and needs to get down to a better fighting weight so it can compete effectively." Jargon or catch phrases are similar to metaphors because they help us understand the change in language with which we are already familiar. Leaders may use jargon and catch phrase frames with words such as becoming "lean and mean." Contrast frames help us understand what the change is by first seeing what it is not. Leaders may use contrast frames by suggesting that the downsizing "is not an attempt to undermine the union, it is simply an attempt to remain competitive." Spin frames cast the change in either a positive or negative light. Leaders may use a positive spin frame by pointing out that the company will not use forced layoffs but will instead use early retirements and natural attrition to reduce the size of the workforce. Story frames make the change seem more "real" by serving as an example, that is, the leader may recount the success that another well-known company had using the same downsizing strategy.

Fairhurst has also studied how the meaning of a change is continually re-framed as members of the organization work out the specifics of how to implement the change. She analyzed the transcripts of tape-recorded conversations between managers and their employees during times when the company was undergoing a significant change in the way that it worked. Her analysis has revealed that employees' reactions to change are often framed as "predicaments" or "problems," showing that they are confused or unclear about the change, or they feel that what they are being asked to do is in conflict with the goals of the change. In response, the leader might counter the employee predica-

ment by using one of several re-frames, for example, "personalization." Using personalization, a leader might point out the specific behaviors that the member needs to adopt in order to be in line with change. Fairhurst suggests that such re-framing techniques help members understand what to do next to bring about the change.

Fairhurst's experience in analyzing the real conversations of managers and employees indicates that many of those in organizational leadership roles are not very good at framing. As a result, leaders may need to be trained to develop mental models that they can draw on to be more effective during their day-to-day interactions with workers. For complete citations of many of Fairhurst's publications, see the references

for this chapter at the end of the book.

In addition to teaching courses in organizational communication at both the graduate and undergraduate levels, Fairhurst works with the Center for Environmental Communication Studies, a research and consulting organization, which she helped found. Through her work with the Center, Fairhurst continues to enhance our understanding of the role communication plays in organizational leadership. In addition, she is also able to lend her expertise to managers who work in environmentally sensitive industries so that they are in a better position to communicate effectively with their workforce and with the public to whom they are ultimately accountable.

Sandy's task force on reducing crime on campus is to present its recommendations at a meeting of the President's Cabinet. If Sandy is an accomplished public speaker who has done premier presentations, she is technically competent to coach team members on their presentations. When they rehearse the presentation, Sandy may carefully observe their trial run and take notes on what she sees.

2. An effective coach both analyzes and supplies specific suggestions for improvement. Some people are good observers, but they don't really know what the employee needs to do to improve. For instance, a new sales associate may be weak on closing deals because he or she misses the cues that people give to show that they're receptive to what the sales associate is saying. An effective coach not only spots the negative, the failure to close, but also uses his or her expertise to help the new sales associate identify the cues that indicate the right time for moving into the close. Key skills for effective coaching are listening, observing, and describing behavior.

3. An effective coach creates a supportive problem-solving environment. Some people are excellent observers and know exactly what needs to be done, but end up antagonizing the other person by being "preachy." An effective coach helps people improve their performance by creating a positive problem-solving environment. To do this, a coach will often begin by acknowledging an area of strength that suggests the other person has undeveloped potential. For instance, in our previous example the coach may praise the new sales associate's product knowledge by saying, "Lydell, I've watched you work, and you have developed a lot of product knowledge. I think you're really going to be good at this job. Would you like to know what you might be able to do to increase your percentage of sales?" This approach helps Lydell to see that they have shared goals. When a person makes a mistake, rather than jumping all over the person, the effective coach might say something like, "Lydell, I think you lost a sale you might have gotten. Can you think of what you might have done differently that will help you close sales like this in the future?" Finally, when the person does succeed, effective coaches praise them but also ask them to reflect on why they were successful. "Lydell, wow—a $300 sale! What did you do this time to close such a big sale?"

Counseling Others at Work

Whereas coaching deals primarily with improving work performance, **counseling** involves helping others deal with their personal problems. Specifically, counseling is the discussion of an emotional problem with another in order to resolve the problem or help the other cope better (Robbins & Hunsaker, 1996, p. 153). Under the pressures of work, and in some cases living in general, people experience such problems as coping with the death of a loved one, lingering illness, divorce and its aftermath, financial problems, the effects of chemical dependence, depression, and overwhelming anxiety that affect their lives in general and their performance at work in particular. Effective counselors maintain confidentiality, listen empathically to others' feelings and circumstances, and help others determine what to do, including seeking professional help.

Counseling—helping others deal with their personal problems.

1. Effective counselors assure confidentiality. Personal problems are just that—personal. Colleagues at work often avoid discussing such issues with their managers, but talk freely to co-workers. Under most circumstances effective counselors do not tell anyone else another's personal problems. Just because a co-worker prefaces a remark with "Don't tell anyone," however, we are not relieved from the ethical responsibility to let the person know the limits to which we will go to maintain his or her confidentiality. There are some circumstances under which maintaining confidentiality would be wrong—for example, keeping confidential information that could jeopardize the health or well-being of others. Under these circumstances ethical counselors first advise the person to disclose the information to an appropriate authority and then, inform the other that the leader is ethically bound to disclose it.

2. Effective counselors are good listeners. Good counseling begins with empathic listening that results in appropriate responses. A good counselor will ask questions for clarification, paraphrase to make sure he or she understands, and most of all provide comforting replies. Supportiveness and, at times, interpreting responses are

Good counseling begins with empathic listening that results in appropriate responses.

key to effective counseling. When people are emotionally distraught, they need to talk out their feelings. Only after they have vented these powerful emotions can they begin the logical problem-solving process.

3. Effective counselors help colleagues find help. At times perhaps the best thing a good lay counselor can do next is to suggest that the person could benefit from professional help. When peer counselors see that problems are long term or severe, they are ethically bound to try to use their leadership to help others seek appropriate professional guidance. To be prepared to do this, it is useful to be familiar with the kinds of services available within your business or organization. Some large companies have employee assistance programs. Various services are also available in the community. And some religious organizations also have professional counselors on staff.

Leaders cannot be expected to and should not act as professional counselors. But because some problems are of short duration and not overly intense, leaders can use their influence to help others sort through and triumph over personal problems.

Leading Group Discussion and Decision Making

In today's work organizations, many decisions are being made by groups of people. Because the cost involved in doing so is high, leaders who are adept at managing group problem solving effectively are valued. A few of the important skills necessary for leading work groups are agenda setting, gatekeeping, questioning, and summarizing discussion and crystallizing consensus.

Agenda Setting An **agenda** is an outline of the topics that need to be covered at a meeting. When possible, the agenda should be in the hands of the group several days before the meeting. Unless group members get an agenda ahead of time, they won't be able to prepare for the meeting.

For a problem-solving discussion, the agenda comprises an outline form of the steps in problem solving. Figure 13.4 shows a satisfactory agenda for a group discussing the question "What should be done to integrate the campus commuter into the social, political, and extracurricular aspects of student life?" Although the meeting is unlikely to follow the exact sequence of the agenda, group members understand that the agenda questions will need to be answered before the group has finished its work.

Gatekeeping **Gatekeeping** means ensuring that everyone has an equal opportunity to speak. Without leader direction, some people are likely to talk more than their fair share. Furthermore, one or two members may contribute little or nothing. As leader you must assume that every member of the group has something to contribute. As a result you may have to hold some members in check and draw other, more reluctant members into the discussion.

How to accomplish balance is a real test of leadership. If you want to clear the road for shy speakers who give clues that they want to speak, you might say something like "Just a second, Lonnie, I think Dominique has something she wants to say here." Then instead of "Dominique, do you have anything to say here?" you may be able to phrase a question that requires more than a yes-or-no answer, such

> **Agenda**–an outline of the topics that need to be covered at a meeting.

> **Gatekeeping**–ensuring that everyone has an equal opportunity to speak.

March 1, 2003
To: Campus commuter discussion group
From: Janelle Smith
Re: Agenda for discussion group meeting, March 8, 2003, 3:00 P.M., Student Union, Conference Room A

Agenda for Group Discussion

Please come prepared to discuss questions 1 through 5. We will consider question 6 on the basis of our resolution of the other questions.

Question: What should be done to integrate the campus commuter into the social, political, and extracurricular aspects of student life?
  1. What percentage of the student body commutes?
  2. Why aren't commuters involved in social, political, and extracurricular activities?
  3. What specific factors hinder their involvement?
  4. What criteria should be used to test possible solutions to the problem?
  5. What are some of the possible solutions to the problem?
  6. What one solution or combination of solutions will work best to solve the problem?

Figure 13.4

Agenda for discussion group meeting

as "Dominique, what do you think of the validity of this approach to combating crime?" When people contribute a few times, it builds up their confidence, which in turn makes it easier for them to respond later when they have more to say.

Similar tact is called for in controlling overzealous speakers. For example, Lonnie, the most talkative member, may be vocal because he has done his homework; if you turn him off, the group's work will suffer. After he has finished a turn but seems to want to speak again, you might try statements such as "Lonnie, you've made some excellent contributions; let's see whether we can get some reactions from other members of the group on this issue." Notice that a statement of this kind does not stop him; it suggests that he should hold off for a while.

Look at Figure 13.5. Figure 13.5A shows a leader-dominated group. The lack of interaction often leads to a rigid, formal, and usually poor discussion. Figure 13.5B shows a more spontaneous group. Because three people dominate and two are not heard from, however, conclusions will not represent group thinking. Figure 13.5C shows something close to the ideal pattern. It illustrates a great deal of spontaneity, total group representation, and—theoretically, at least—the greatest possibility for reliable conclusions. You will have achieved your goal of maintaining balance if the pattern of group discussion resembles that in Figure 13.5C.

Questioning Appropriately Perhaps one of the most effective tools of leadership is the ability to question appropriately to stimulate discussion. You will want to ask questions to initiate, focus, probe, and deal with interpersonal problems.

1. To initiate discussion. When discussion of one point is drying up, you'll want to move discussion to a different point. For instance, "OK, we seem to have a pretty good grasp of the nature of the problem, but we haven't looked at any causes yet. What are some of the causes?"

2. To focus discussion. Sometimes people talk around points. At these times you'll want to ask questions to focus discussion. For instance, to relate a statement to the larger topic in a discussion of marijuana use, you might ask, "Are you saying that the instances of marijuana leading to hard-drug use don't indicate a direct causal relationship?" Or, in response to what has just been said, "How does that information relate to the point that Mary just made?" Or, to ask about an issue or an agenda item, "In what way does this information relate to whether or not marijuana is a health hazard?"

Figure 13.5

Three common patterns of group communication

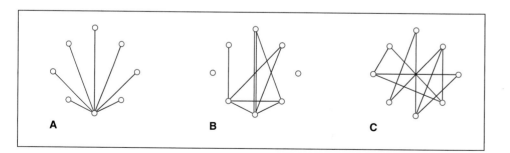

A   B   C

3. To probe for information. When comments are made and apparently accepted without discussion, you'll want to ask questions to probe for additional information. For example, to test the support for an assertion, you can say, "Where did you get that information, Miles?" or "That seems pretty important; what do we have that corroborates the point?" To test the strength of a point, you might ask, "Does that statement represent the thinking of the group?"

4. To deal with interpersonal problems that develop. Sometimes the leader can use questions to help members ventilate personal feelings. For example, "Ted, I've heard you make some strong statements on this point. Would you care to share them with us?" At times a group may attack a person instead of the information that is being presented. Here you can say, "Juan isn't the issue here. Let's look at the merits of the information presented. Do we have any information that runs counter to this point?"

Keep in mind that too frequent use of questions can hurt the discussion that is taking place. The effective leader uses questions sparingly but incisively.

Summarizing and Crystallizing Consensus Often, as a group talks for a considerable time around a topic, the members become uncertain as to what has been said and agreed to. During the discussion individuals might draw six, eight, ten, or even fifteen conclusions that relate to agenda items. Some will be compatible; others will be contradictory.

It is up to the leader to point out intermediate conclusions by summarizing what has been said, pointing out areas of agreement and disagreement before seeking consensus. Following are some phrases that can be used to summarize and assess consensus:

"I think most of us are stating the same points. Are we really in agreement that . . . ?" (State the conclusion.)

"I think we are agreeing on points 1 and 3, but I sense we haven't really discussed recommendation 2. Does that square with your perceptions?" (State the conclusion.)

"Now we're getting into another area. Let's back up and make sure that we are really agreed on the point we've just finished." (State the conclusion.)

"Are we ready to summarize our feelings on this point?" (State the conclusion.)

WHAT WOULD YOU DO?

A Question *of* Ethics

After three years of working at Everyday Products as a clerk, Mark had decided to look for another job. As he thought about preparing a résumé, he was struck by how little experience he had for the kind of job he wanted.

When he talked with Ken about this, Ken said, "Exactly what have you been doing at Everyday?"

"Well, for the most part I've been helping others look for information—I've also done some editing of reports."

"Hm," Ken thought for a while. "Why not retitle your job as editorial assistant? It's more descriptive."

"But my official title is clerk."

"Sure, but it doesn't really describe what you do. This way you show major editorial experience. Don't worry, everybody makes these kinds of changes—you're not really lying."

"Yeah, I see what you mean. Good idea!"

1. Is it interpersonally ethical for Mark to follow Ken's advice? Why?

2. How should we deal with statements like: "Everybody does it"?

Summary

At work we use our interpersonal skills to get a job, to interview others, to relate to colleagues and clients, and to exercise leadership.

Before you interview for a job, you need to take the time to learn about the company and prepare an appropriate cover letter and résumé that are designed to motivate an employer to interview you. If you choose to send your cover letter or résumé electronically, make sure you edit and format it appropriately. For the interview itself, you should be prompt, be alert and look directly at the interviewer, give yourself time to think before answering difficult questions, ask intelligent questions about the company and job, and show enthusiasm for the position.

Once on the job, you may be called on to interview customers about complaints, interview co-workers to get information relevant to your work, or interview prospective employees. To interview well, you need to learn to ask primary and secondary, open and closed, and neutrally worded questions effectively.

The majority of work relationships occur between managers and employees, among co-workers, and between organizational representatives and clients. As a manager you are likely to establish exchange relationships with employees that call for them to do extra work in order to receive intangible rewards for successfully completing additional assignments. In order to engage in exchange relationships employees must communicate their willingness to take on extra work and perform both it and regular assignments well.

Organizational members form relationships with co-workers to satisfy social and informational needs. As organizations move to self-managed work teams, co-worker relationships become even more important. Some workers develop relationships with customers and clients that are important to the effectiveness of the organization.

Most people in an organization seek leadership positions that involve exerting influence to accomplish a goal. How well you lead may depend on your style and how you put it into operation. Some leaders adopt the task-oriented style, focusing on what needs to be done and how to do it; others adopt the person-oriented style, focusing on interpersonal relationships of group members. If you seek a leadership position, you will want to be knowledgeable about the task, work harder than others in the group, be personally committed to group goals and needs, be willing to be decisive, interact freely with others in the group, and develop skills in maintenance and task functions. You may demonstrate your leadership through coaching and counseling others at work, or you may do so by leading team meetings.

Chapter Resources

Communication Improvement Plan: Workplace Communication

Would you like to improve your use of the following skills discussed in this chapter?

      Leading

      Coaching

      Counseling

Pick a skill and write a communication improvement plan.

Skill: _____

Problem: _____

_____

_____

_____

Goal: _____

_____

_____

_____

Procedure:

1. _____

2. _____

3. _____

Test of Achieving Goal: _____

_____

Key Words

Cover letter, *p. 367*

Résumé, *p. 367*

Interview, *p. 374*

Open questions, *p. 374*

Closed questions, *p. 375*

Neutral questions, *p. 375*

Leading questions, *p. 375*

Primary questions, *p. 375*

Secondary or follow-up questions, *p. 375*

Boundary-spanning roles, *p. 380*

Leadership, *p. 384*

Leadership traits, *p. 385*

Leadership style, *p. 385*

Task-oriented leaders, *p. 385*

Person-oriented leaders, *p. 385*

Coaching, *p. 386*

Counseling, *p. 389*

Agenda, *p. 391*

Gatekeeping, *p. 391*

Inter-Act with Media

CINEMA

Steven Soderbergh (Director). (2000). *Erin Brockovich.* Julia Roberts, Albert Finney.

Brief Summary: This film is based on the true story of Erin Brokovich. Erin is a single mother who must find employment after losing a lawsuit over being hit in an auto accident. Her highly unconventional style in the workplace and her direct, assertive style of communication make her both effective in her work, competitive in getting new chances at work, and controversial with co-workers.

IPC Concepts: Interviewing, relationships at work, diversity in the workplace, communicating with managers and co-workers, leadership.

Lasse Hallstrom (Director). (2001). *The Shipping News.* Kevin Spacey, Judi Dench, Julianne Moore, Cate Blanchett, Pete Postlethwaite, Rhys Ifans, Scott Glenn.

Brief Summary: This is a story about a shy man's efforts to achieve a meaningful level of self-respect and respect from others. His relational efforts are a disaster until he returns to his childhood roots in Newfoundland, where he obtains employment at the local newspaper covering the shipping news. His efforts include dealing with an eccentric owner, clashes with the daily manager, forming bonds with his co-workers, and balancing his work with caring for his daughter.

IPC Concepts: Interviews, communicating with supervisors, co-workers, customers, coaching, leadership, and ethical issues.

Barry Levinson (Director). (1987). *Tin Men.* Richard Dreyfuss, Danny DeVito, Barbara Hershey, John Mahoney, Jackie Gayle, Bruno Kirby, J. T. Walsh.

Brief Summary: The story is about a pair of aluminum salesmen in 1963 Baltimore, one who is always on the make and the other is who is something of a loser. The film focuses on their dysfunctional lifestyles, their ethical sales tactics, and their general approach to work. This film offers a somewhat cynical view of one side of the world of sales.

IPC Concepts: Communication between co-workers, with customers, coaching others at work, ethical issues.

THEATER

David Swift. (1967). *How to Succeed in Business Without Really Trying.*

Brief Summary: This play is about J. Pierpont Finch and his speedy rise to the boardroom of the company. He uses humor, a handbook, and charm to get to the top. A musical comedy, it contains some interesting observations on organizational dynamics.

IPC Concepts: Communication, interviewing, leadership, and influence.

LITERATURE

Lewis, M. (1989). *Liar's Poker: Rising Through the Wreckage on Wall Street.* New York: W. W. Norton & Company.

Brief Summary: Though not a novel, this first-hand account of life in a stock brokerage firm during the 1980s is a fascinating look at the daily routines, corporate and communication culture of the brokerage houses, and the rituals, rites of passage, and overall quality of life of these people.

IPC Concepts: Workplace culture, workplace games, manipulation.

ACADEMIC WORKS

Kroeger, O., & Thuesen, J. M. (1988). *Type Talk: The 16 Personality Types that Determine How We Live, Love, and Work.* New York: Tilden Press.

Brief Summary: This book discusses the Myers-Briggs Personality Assessment approach and how to use it in the workplace. There are examples of each personality type, what type of work may suit the type, and how to interact with people of all types. A practical, easy to understand summary and application of this popular approach to personality.

IPC Concepts: Communication, work, and different types of people.

Goleman, D. (1999). *Working with Emotional Intelligence.* New York: Bantam Books.

Brief Summary: This book is an extension of Goleman's original work on the concept of emotional intelligence. The theory explains why people with tremendous talent, IQ, and skill sometimes do not rise above fairly menial jobs, while those with seemingly less talent can go very far in the workplace. Goleman does a good job of showing how and why development and management of our emotions are vitally important to well-balanced people and success at work.

IPC Concepts: Communication, relationships, workplace, emotion, motivation.

WHAT'S ON THE WEB

Interviewing (for jobs, job candidates, by media, exit interviews, etc.). Assembled by Carter McNamara, PhD. This site is sponsored by the Management Assistance Program for Nonprofits.

http://www.managementhelp.org/commskls/intrvews/intrvews.htm

Brief Summary: This site contains a treasure-chest of information on interviewing and many other topics in interpersonal communication, conflict, listening, and so on. There are numerous links to information on these topics, library resources, and exercises. Categories of information include various types of interviews, related library links, online discussion groups, being interviewed by the media, exit interviews, general guidelines for conducting interviews, interviewing for a job, and interviewing job candidates.

IPC Concepts: Employment interviewing, interpersonal skills, conflict management, mediation.

The Interview. A Career Services Web Site Maintained by Virginia Tech.

http://ei.cs.vt.edu/~cs3604/careers/interview.html

Brief Summary: This site includes links to articles on types of interviews, frequently asked interview questions, questions to ask, lawful and unlawful interview questions, the on-campus interviewing program, business etiquette, interview attire, and links other college placement and career sites with information about interviewing.

IPC Concepts: Employment interviewing, getting the interview, preparing and taking part in the interview.

Virtual Résumé Interview Information Resources

http://www.careerspan.com/Jsinterviewing.asp

Brief Summary: The site provides links to practical articles on job interviewing and links to other sites with information about interviewing. It offers articles on interviewing, tips on how to interview in a traditional employment interview and in behavioral interviews. The latter category focuses on the applicant's behavior in order to establish the applicant's competency for the job in question. A sample question is "Give me a specific example of a time when you had to address an angry customer. What was the problem and what was the outcome?" Traditional interview aids include suggestions for résumés, using recruiters, Internet site searches, common mistakes made during interviews, guide to successful interviewing, elements of a successful interview, preparing for interviews, guerilla interviewing, a head-hunter's interview secrets, the telephone interview, and favorite interviewing questions. This is an excellent site for supplementary material on employment interviewing.

IPC Concepts: Employment interviewing, getting the interview, preparing for and taking part in the interview.

CHAPTER 14

Electronically Interpersonal

Mediated Communication

After you have read this chapter, you should be able to answer these questions:

- How is cellular telephone usage changing the nature of telecommunications?
- What is the Internet?
- What is e-mail?
- What are newsgroups?
- What is a chat room?
- How are relationships built online?
- What interpersonal skills are most helpful when online?

> "Hey, Mom, I have a date tonight—can we be done with dinner by seven?"
>
> "Sure, Dawn, who's the lucky guy?"
>
> "Uh, you don't know him."
>
> "So, someone new! What are you two going to do?"
>
> "Oh, we're just going to talk. I can spend hours talking with him. It's like we're real soulmates. He really seems to understand me."
>
> "And what's this fellow's name?"
>
> "Well, I call him J.T."
>
> "What does the 'J' stand for?"
>
> "What difference does it make?"
>
> "None, really. So is he picking you up at seven?"
>
> "No . . ."
>
> "So you're meeting him somewhere?"
>
> "Yes, I guess that's right—we're 'meeting' somewhere."
>
> "And what time do you expect to be back?"
>
> "Back? Well, I won't, because, you see, I'm not really going anywhere."
>
> "Wait a minute—you have a date, your date is not coming to pick you up, and you're not coming back because you aren't really going anywhere! Can you see why I'm a bit lost here?"
>
> "Oh, Mom, get with it. This is the twenty-first century. I have a cyber date with J.T., who lives in Sweden. I met him in a chat room the other day, and we're scheduled to 'meet' at 7:15 tonight. So can you please get dinner ready?"

There are still people, like Dawn's mother, who are bewildered by the concept of "cyber dating"—one type of electronically mediated interpersonal communication. Ten to fifteen years ago, only a few students participated in electronically mediated interpersonal communication, but today most students use the Internet as early as elementary school. And cyber relationships between students from different countries are being encouraged in many schools. So in many homes, children are more familiar than their parents with electronically mediated communication. According to the Pew Network and American

Life Project, three-quarters of all teens between ages twelve and seventeen go on-line regularly (Globus, 2002, p. 13).

Not only has there been a revolution that has led to cyber relationships, but we are also experiencing a telecommunications revolution. The use of digital cellular phones and pagers has become widespread and is changing the way we conduct our relationships. In this chapter, we will examine how telecommunication and electronically mediated communication are affecting interpersonal communication and relationships. We begin by discussing the increasing use of cellular telephones. Then we provide a brief overview of the Internet and how to use it. Next, we discuss several types of electronically mediated interpersonal communication—including e-mail, newsgroups, and chat rooms—and how each type affects how people relate to one another. Then we report what research studies have found to be the effects of electronically mediated interpersonal communication on relationships, including the advent of "cyber stalking." We conclude the chapter by explaining how the interpersonal communication skills you have learned can help you to improve your electronically mediated interpersonal communication.

Cellular and Digital Telephones

Whereas the written communication revolution is taking place online, the oral communication revolution is taking place on cellular and digital telephones. Today, the cellular phone is seen as a convenience that people are entitled to use anywhere, anytime. Many of us feel safer and/or in more control of our lives because of them.

Cellular phones have been a boon to professionals like doctors, police officers, and firefighters—people who are on call in order to react to an emergency. To a much greater extent we feel that we can get in touch with those who may be able to save our or other people's lives.

Many people feel safer and more secure with cellular telephones in their cars. Young people, women, and people with medical conditions are now able to reach those who can help them from within the safety of their car. For instance, many parents equip their automobile with a phone when their children get their driver's licenses. Similarly, many parents carry cell phones so that their children can get in touch with them. This gives parents a sense of comfort to know that they can be reached by their children immediately if any problem occurs.

In our interpersonal relationships many of us "show our importance" or status in a variety of ways. In the past, status symbols have included expensive houses in "the right part of town," expensive clothes in the latest fashions, or driving an expensive car (or even better, having a chauffeur). Today a new sign of status, especially among the young, is carrying a cellular phone. In effect, people are making the statement, "I'm important—people need to talk with me whether I'm walking down the street, sitting on a bus, eating at a restaurant, or sitting in a theater." Whether showing status is really an upside or a downside is probably a matter of perspective. But there is no doubt that many people see their cellular phones as status symbols.

As a result of the tumbling of sales in 2001, phone manufacturers "are busy rolling out new, faster data networks that they hope will spur their slumping industry" (Wildstrom, 2002, p. 24). Companies are producing units that allow for e-mail as well as access to Web sites. In 2002, most of these advances were experimental, but as you are reading this textbook, you are likely to find advertisements for phones that offer a variety of services.

Although access is a great advantage of cellular phones, it can create interpersonal communication problems as well.

Most of us have been conditioned to answer a ringing phone, so instead of viewing an incoming call as an interruption, many people treat an incoming telephone message as a first priority. The phone is answered regardless of what else may be occurring. A dramatic example of this occurred recently in a public speaking class. About a minute and a half into a graded speech that a student was delivering, his cellular phone rang. Instead of ignoring it and continuing his speech, the student stopped his speech, answered the phone, and held a short conversation! After hanging up, the student resumed talking to his audience, but became quite angry when shortly thereafter the professor indicated that he had to stop his speech before he was finished because his time was up!

How do you react to people who talk on their cellular phones in public places?

Telephone conversations, once thought of as private, are now held in public. Many people treat wherever they may be standing or sitting as a telephone booth in which they can carry on their side of the conversation regardless of how inappropriate that conversation might be for others to hear. Terry Golway, writing in *America* magazine, describes the cell phone situation around him as he waits for the 7:58 train out of New York's Penn Station. He writes that on his left a bedraggled Wall Streeter is talking to a client. A fellow in front of him is having trouble with his wife—she's not pleased with his report that he will be coming home late for dinner again. A young man behind him is making plans with a buddy for a night of beers and televised sports. Then on the train itself, several people are engaged in domestic disputes, romantic dreams, dinner plans, or plain old work. He is surprised to see that he is the only one reading a newspaper (Golway, 1998, p. 6).

Golway's experience reinforces the point that through cellular communication we are turning private matters into public knowledge. People are in fact saying, "What's the harm of my sparring with my spouse within earshot of a carload of commuters?" In addition, cellular communication turns people into twenty-four-hour-a-day subjects. Some people boast that they are never really away from their work. Others boast that they are available at any time, at any place, under any circumstances.

Misuse of cellular communication is turning places that used to be completely quiet into places that are quiet no longer. For instance, library officials are reporting more and more stories of times when loud noises ring out as people's pagers summon them to the nearest telephone; or equally as prevalent the ringing of a telephone at the table next to you and a person noisily carrying on a conversation.

Private cell phone calls often disrupt public events. Thus, one person's convenience results in inconvenience to others. You may recall the television commercial depicting a scene in an opera where the singer in a Viking helmet with a spear in her hand becomes so upset with a member of the audience that she hurls her spear at the person's cell phone and pins it to the back of his seat. The audience applauds. To try to stop the interruptions before they occur, most theaters now make a plea for audience members to silence their phones. Unfortunately, these pleas sometimes go unheeded.

The Internet

Written electronic communication is usually transmitted via the **Internet,** an international electronic computer network made up of a collection of thousands of smaller computer networks. It is an information management system made up of information providers and information seekers.

The idea of linking computers to each other began in the mid-1960s. In 1983, this network of computers became known collectively as the Internet. By the last ten years of the twentieth century, being able to use the Internet was an advantage; in these early years of the twenty-first century it is becoming a necessity.

Internet Terminology

With the way that Internet knowledge is expanding, it is likely that you are familiar with most Internet terminology. If not—or if you want to double check your knowledge, we provide the following Internet vocabulary:

The **World Wide Web (WWW)** is a part of the Internet where information is presented in a highly visual, often multi media, format. Information on the Web is presented in **Web pages,** which are somewhat like pages in a book, that may include both text and pictures or graphics. A collection of Web pages belonging to the

Internet—an international electronic computer network made up of a collection of thousands of smaller computer networks.

World Wide Web (WWW)—part of the Internet where information is presented in a highly visual, often multimedia, format.

Web pages—Internet destinations, somewhat like pages in a book, which may include both text and pictures or graphics.

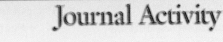

OBSERVE & ANALYZE

Journal Activity

Cellular Telephone Behavior

or the next two days, observe people using cellular phones and record the following information for each observation. ■

Approximate age:
___ under 18   ___ 18–25   ___ 26–35
___ 36–50   ___ over 50

Sex:
___ Male___ Female

Location:
___ on the street   ___ in a restaurant
___ in class   ___ at work
___ in a library   ___ on a bus
___ in a car   ___ in a bar
___ in a store   ___ in an auditorium
___ other (specify)   ___ (movie, concert hall, church, etc.)

Situation:
___ alone   ___ with one other person
___ more than one other

Minutes talking:
___ less than 1   ___ 2–5   ___ 5-10
___ more than 10

Person's demeanor:
___ smiling, happy   ___ tense, hurried
___ obviously upset   ___ businesslike
___ other (specify)

Web site—a collection of Web pages.

Home page—the "first" page at a Web site.

Browser—a device that gives you access to the information across millions of Web sites on the World Wide Web (WWW).

Uniform resource locator or URL—the path name of a document.

Bookmark—a Netscape file used to store Web site addresses for sites that you'd like to visit again.

Search engines—identify Web sites and corresponding URLs.

same organization or person is called a **Web site.** A **home page** is the "first" page at a Web site. It shows you what can be found on the site.

A **browser** is a computer software program that enables you to look over the information on millions of Web sites (called "surfing the Web") on the World Wide Web (WWW). *Netscape Navigator* and Microsoft's *Internet Explorer* are two popular browsers. You need a browser program on your personal computer in order to access the Web.

A **uniform resource locator (URL)** is the path name of a document, or more commonly known as a document's "address." Every site on the Web has a unique URL.

A **bookmark** is a Netscape file used to store Web site addresses for sites that you'd like to visit again. Although this is a feature on all browsers, it may go by a different name, such as "Favorites" on Internet Explorer or "Hotlist" or "Favorite Places List" (names used on other browsers).

Search engines are software programs on the servers that search the Web for you to identify Web pages and sites and their corresponding URLs. Common search engines include Google (http://www.google.com), Yahoo (http://www.yahoo.com), Alta Vista (http://www.altavista.digital.com), Excite (http://www.excite.com), and Lycos (http://www.lycos.com).

To understand how the Internet works, let's look at an example. Suppose that Erin, who is working from her mom's computer at home, wants to do some library research at her school, the University of Cincinnati. Using the Internet, she can access the university's electronic library database. To do so, she opens her mom's browser (in this case, Netscape), and logs on. Then she types in the URL for the Library Research Base, which is http://www.libraries.uc.edu. When Erin types in this URL, she is connected to the university's library Web site. Because she will use this site frequently, she takes advantage of the Netscape "Bookmark" feature. Erin clicks on the "Bookmark" icon on the menu bar and then selects "Add Bookmark" from the pull-down menu. This stores the URL for the library's database (which is on the screen). Then, when Erin wants to go back to that Web site again, she clicks on the Bookmarks icon, scrolls down to the name of the site, and clicks on it (URLs or addresses are normally listed in the Bookmark feature using common words, rather than the actual URL). But suppose that rather than doing research, Erin wants to play games, buy a book, or engage in some other activity. Once on Netscape Navigator she would

"First, they do an on-line search."

use the browser to access sites like Google (http://www.google.com), type in the key words for her search, and the browser would list sites that correspond to the key words that she entered.

Communicating Online

Once online, you usually communicate with others in written form via e-mail, newsgroups, and Internet chat. New types of visually mediated electronic communication are available, but they are not yet in widespread use.

E-Mail

E-mail is the largest application of Internet technology. In the early '90s e-mail was an option available mostly for intraoffice communication; only a small number of people were experimenting with e-mail as a general means of communication. Today, of the 75 percent of teens online, e-mail accounts for most of their one-on-one contact (Globus, 2002, p. 13).

E-mail has two major advantages over regular mail, but it also has at least one major disadvantage. First, e-mail is fast. At times it may be received nearly instantaneously. According to the Inverse Network Technology E-Mail Study, 91 percent of e-mail messages arrive at their destinations within five minutes, and another 5 percent arrive within thirty minutes. (Sherman, 1999, p. 90). Compare this to fastest delivery system for traditional mail: twenty-four-hour overnight delivery. Second, although e-mail is not "free" (we must subscribe to an Internet service), it is not paid for per letter or document. Thus, regardless of the number or of messages length of each, the service cost is the same. Many colleges provide internet e-mail as a service to students, but the cost of this is built into the student fee structure.

Unlike traditional mail, however, e-mail is public, not private. People with the right software can intercept and read nearly any message that is sent. Moreover, e-mail messages can be stored by their recipient and forwarded to others without the original sender's knowledge. As a result, you should think very carefully before sending information that is meant to be private via e-mail.

Using E-Mail to Communicate with Faculty As a student, you should know that a valuable use of e-mail is to communicate with your professors. Why? According to a study by Waldeck, Kearney, and Plax (2001), students find that e-mail is a great way to get clarification. Students are most likely to use e-mail to ask teachers for information about course policies, for guidance on specific tasks such as papers and projects, and for feedback regarding

INTER-ACT WITH
Technology

E-Mail Programs

If you want more information about leading e-mail software programs, visit them from your browser at their Web sites. In the search box, just type in the following:

    Dataviz e-mail

    Eudora Pro 4 mail

    Netscape Navigator Mail

    Outlook Express mail

    Pegasus Mail ■

Have you used E-mail to communicate with your professors in times of need? If you haven't, why not?

performance (p. 65). If visiting your professor during office hours is inconvenient, and you do not wish to bother your faculty member with a phone call, e-mail allows you to get an answer to your question in a manner that is convenient for both of you.

Waldeck, Kearney, and Plax also found that students are reluctant to discuss personal or social issues with teachers in e-mail. They conclude, "students and teachers realize the potential for self-disclosure via e-mail, but simply are not comfortable using the medium frequently for that reason" (p. 66).

Guidelines for Communicating by E-Mail Although e-mail would seem to be more like letter writing than conversation, e-mail messages can be responded to shortly after they are sent so they start to approach a kind of conversation. Let's consider ways that you can improve your e-mail conversations.

1. Take advantage of delayed feedback. One way we can improve the quality of our e-mail messages is to take advantage of its delayed feedback nature. Unfortunately, many people treat e-mail more like a telephone call than like a written letter. As a result we have a tendency to respond with the first thought that comes to mind and pay little attention to how we are phrasing that thought. This can be

Journal Activity

Use of E-Mail

Do you use e-mail? Consider the e-mail you have sent and received over the last week. Try to classify the kinds of messages that you have written (use such headings as social messages to friends, work, or school project-related messages, inquiries to Web sites, messages to faculty, and so on). How many messages a day do you receive? What percentage of those do you reply to? How quickly do you reply? Compare your e-mail use to regular mail. How many letters (not bills, advertisements, or solicitations) do you send or receive each day? ■

a problem, since our receivers don't have the nonverbal behavioral cues that are used in face-to-face interactions to help them interpret what we mean. So, when e-mailing remember that you can and should edit what you write. Before sending a message, don't stop with correcting typos. Rather, analyze the message in terms of *how* you have said something as well as what you have said. Edit the message so that the verbal conveys the appropriate tone that would normally be conveyed by your nonverbal behaviors.

For instance, suppose someone wrote you a short note criticizing something you'd done. A first tendency might be to respond with a counter-attacking comment such as, "If you don't like what I said, tough luck." After writing this, you're likely to feel much better. "I told him what I thought of that, didn't I?" Now pause for a moment. Is what you said really serving any purpose other than venting your emotions? Probably not. In a conversation, when you have "cooled down," you can quickly apologize and perhaps experience little damage to your relationship. But if your partners have several minutes to stew before your apology is received, more damage may result. So when you receive a message to which you have an emotional reaction, carefully consider your response.

2. Include the wording that you are responding to in your e-mail. Even though e-mail exchanges may occur on the same day, the initiator may not remember exactly what he or she wrote to you originally. So, when you respond to specific points that people made in their messages, it is to your advantage to repeat or paraphrase what they said before you respond.

3. Take into account the absence of nonverbal cues to meaning. Whether you're writing a message or responding to a message, keep in mind that the person cannot hear the sound of your voice or see the look on your face or your use of gestures. Since nonverbal communication provides as much 66 percent of the meaning of a message, you should determine what you can do in writing that will "fill in the gaps" of meaning.

Most specialists advise that you choose your words carefully and add more adjectives when appropriate. For instance, instead of writing, "What you said really bugged me," you might write, "What you said had some merit, I was rather curt with my comments, but the way you said it really hurt my feelings." Now the reader will have a much better idea of your feelings about the response.

4. Use common abbreviations sparingly, if at all. Commonly used abbreviations may make your message shorter, but they don't necessarily make it more meaningful. While some frequent e-mail users can easily decode these cryptic notations, many who receive these shorthand citations are at a loss to make sense of them. For instance, abbreviations such as BTW (by the way), FWIW (for what it's worth), IMHO (in my humble opinion) may be common in some chat rooms, but may be uninterpretable by other users. Avoid using all capital letters for emphasis. On the Internet, messages that are in capitals are the equivalent of shouting in face-to-face conversations.

5. Treat e-mail messages as you would other public communications. Because e-mail is so easy to use, there are times when we write e-mail messages that include confidential material—information that we'd ordinarily guard carefully. Keep in mind that a message you write is copied and stored (at least temporarily) on many computers between yours and the recipient's. "In some ways, e-mail messages are like postcards. Anyone 'carrying' the message can read it, even if most would never do so" (Crumlish, 1997, p. 132). So, if you have something to say that is confidential, could be used against you in some way, or could be totally misinterpreted, it is better to convey that message in a letter sent through the post office, UPS, or Federal Express.

Newsgroups

Newsgroup—an electronic gathering place for people with similar interests.

When people exchange personal messages with others on the Internet they use e-mail. One way of communicating with people that we don't know, but who share a common interest, is through newsgroups. A **newsgroup** is "an electronic gathering place for people with similar interests" (Miller, 1999, p. 187). By joining a newsgroup we are able to communicate with people about topics of common interest. Think of a newsgroup as a collecting place for messages on a common topic. To communicate in a newsgroup a user posts a message (called an *article*). These messages may be about a variety of topics that are appropriate for the site. Other users read these articles and, when so disposed, respond. The result is a kind of ongoing discussion in which users (ten, fifty, or maybe even hundreds) may participate. On the Internet there are literally thousands of newsgroup opportunities (Sherman, 1999, p. 137).

Joining a Newsgroup As you surf the Internet you are likely to find Web pages that refer to information located within a newsgroup. If the content interests you, you may want to pursue the opportunity to get involved. To join a newsgroup you need a newsreader program. Your Web browser is likely to have access to a newsreader. Once you have access to a newsreader program, you need the address of you Internet service provider's SMTP (simple mail transfer protocol) server—this is the server that allows you to send e-mail. You also need the NNTP (network news transfer protocol) address—this is the system used to transfer newsgroup articles between your Internet service provider's news service and your newsreader software. For instance, Netscape Navigator has a newsreader named Collabra. After you're connected to your news server, you can choose from any of the thousands of newsgroups to monitor. You can simply go to selected newsgroups, or you can "subscribe" to selected newsgroups. When you subscribe to a newsgroup, there is no formal registration process; this simply means you've added this newsgroup to a list of your favorites that you can access without searching all those available.

Working with Newgroups Once you've subscribed to a newsgroup you can spend your time "listening," posting articles, and/or responding to articles. For example, the Web site iVillage.com has a message board (newsgroup) on the topic African American women at work. Here various people have posted articles on different issues related to this topic. For instance, where one thread might be discussing feelings about working on Martin Luther King Day, another might be discussing how to win over skeptical co-workers.

Listening, called **lurking,** gives you a kind of pseudointeraction with others. For instance, suppose you join a sports newsgroup that is formed to discuss golfing. You'll find that various people will have posted newsgroup articles on issues related to golf. These may range from groups discussing a favorite golfer (like Tiger Woods, Robert Duvall, Julie Inkster, or Sri Pak), to those talking about ways to improve their game (driving, putting, chipping), to those about golf issues (etiquette, rules, etc.). Then you can *lurk* by reading an article and the various responses generated by the article. In this way you get to learn a little about the personalities of posters and repliers.

> **Lurking**—Listening in on newsgroups or chat conversations.

Posting gives you a chance to see whether people want to reply to your particular thoughts. You may post an article and generate little if any response. On the other hand, what you say may touch a nerve and you'll receive many replies, some of which may take the form of **flaming,** a hostile or negative response to what you've written. Some of these are for the specific purpose of getting you engaged in a "flame war." Although you may enjoy such anonymous "face-to-face" verbal combat, more often than not you're wise to avoid taking the bait. In other words, you can just ignore any flaming message that you see.

> **Flaming**—a hostile or negative response to what you've written.

Most importantly, posting leaves the door open for responses that are designed to get you engaged in interaction. That is, if a number of people respond, you may respond to a responder, and thus begin a kind of "relationship."

This leads us to the third way to spend time, and that is to respond. As mentioned, a thoughtful, favorable response may well motivate the poster to respond to your response.

Newsgroup Etiquette Public newsgroup postings may be seen by a wide variety of people, most of whom are sincerely interested in the topic being discussed. Because of the number of people involved, etiquette becomes important and should be observed. "Not observing etiquette in a newsgroup will result in almost instant criticism and reprimand, usually by more than one participant" (Banks, 1997, p. 106). To facilitate discussions, many newsgroups post the Internet etiquette (often labeled **netiquette**) that they expect to be observed in conversations. For instance, items posted in the netiquette for iVillage.com are shown in Figure 14.1.

> **Netiquette**—Internet etiquette.
>
> **FAQs**—frequently asked questions that list the rules followed by participants in a newsgroup.
>
> **Chat**—online interactive message exchange between two or more people.

In addition to etiquette guidelines, many newsgroups post **FAQs** (frequently asked questions) that list the rules followed by participants in that particular newsgroup. In addition to netiquette, newsgroup FAQs may include other information such as the history of the group and the kind of jargon that is acceptable. To find a newsgroup's FAQs, you can look for postings with "FAQ" in the header or post a polite note asking the location of the FAQs.

Internet Chat

Besides joining newsgroups, we can also interact with people that we don't know through online "chat." **Chat** is online interactive message exchange between two or more people. In a chat room as few as two people can hold a conversation; some spaces are licensed for

---

Don't be afraid to post.

Feel free to "lurk" and listen.

Tap into an incredible font of information.

Welcome newcomers.

Agree to disagree, respectfully.

Don't attack each other.

Keep personal information personal.

Keep your posts clean.

Figure 14.1 Netiquette guidelines for iVillage.com

twenty-five, fifty, or hundreds or more participants. Whereas in newsgroups you post articles and people post responses, both parties do not need to be simultaneously online to participate. In a chat room all participants are online and typed responses appear instantly on participant's computer screens. Thus chat rooms approximate face-to-face conversation in that feedback is relatively instantaneous.

Every day millions of people chat online with friends, colleagues, and strangers. Michael Miller, author of numerous computer books, likens online chat to 900-number telephone chat lines—"except you use your keyboard instead of a telephone, and you don't run up bills at $1.99/minute or more" (1999, p. 217). Some people think of chat rooms more like telephone conference calls; instead of conversing orally, they exchange words on computer monitors. Interestingly, S. Globas found that many teens engage in Internet chat because they feel "they can be themselves more when they're online than face to face" (2002, p. 13).

In most chat rooms the conversation is focused on a particular area—music, travel, current events, or almost any topic you can think of. Thus, you want to look for a chat room that is discussing the kinds of things you want to discuss (Snell, 1998, p. 258). On most servers, locating a chat room is relatively easy. If you enter "chat (and) wine," for instance, the search results are likely to provide several sites where you can go to "converse" with others about wine.

Once you've connected to a chat room, you can just "listen" to conversations (called lurking), or you can join in and chat. Although most chats are public—anyone with Internet access can join—you have the option of meeting privately with one or more individuals.

Keeping track of conversation strands in a chat room is difficult. It's like being at a party where numerous groups of people are holding simultaneous conversations, but you are hearing all of them. In a chat room there are usually different "conversations" taking place at once. Since responses appear on the screen in the order in which they are sent, the response that appears last may be unrelated to the comment before it. So, it can be unclear as to who is talking with whom and about what. Often people lurk for a while in order to sort out the various strands and determine if there is one that they want to join.

One unique characteristic of online chat is that in chat rooms the real identity of conversational partners is usually unknown. Most people adopt a cyber identity in the form of a nickname by which they are known. You can be whomever you want—and so can everyone else. You really have no idea whether a person you are talking with is male or female, young or old, rich or poor. There is no way to ensure that conversational partners are really who they are representing themselves to be.

Role of Electronic Communication in Building Relationships

Today communication technologies are changing the way we build and maintain relationships. Prior to 1990, people became acquainted mostly with those with whom they had personal physical contact. At the same time, dating services advertised that they could get people in the same community acquainted with each other within a week. Today, people are able to make acquaintances with people around the world within seconds.

Development of Electronically Mediated (EM) Relationships

Thanks to technological innovation, people are introduced to others they have never seen through newsgroups, Internet chat rooms, and Internet dating services. Moreover, people are likely to try to develop these encounters into personal relationships. A study by Parks and Floyd (1996) found that developing EM personal relationships is quite common (p. 93). For example, Andrea and Matt "meet" each other as they communicate in a newsgroup dedicated to the subject of "environmental concerns." They already believe they have at least one thing in common—an interest in environmental issues. As the postings continue, they notice that they are the only ones who hold a particular view on a certain issue. Moreover, they begin to see that they have other ideas in common as well. At this point, they decide

Increasing numbers of people are likely to try to develop online encounters into personal relationships. Have you developed online relationships? With what result?

to "meet" in a private chat room where they "talk" with each other. Now they are able to begin to explore whether they have other common interests. Before long, they have exchanged e-mail addresses and directly corresponded. If their interest in each other continues to grow, they may arrange to speak on the telephone. If this proves satisfactory, they may arrange to meet in person. At some point during this process, Andrea and Matt have begun to have a personal relationship: maybe a friendship, maybe an intimate relationship.

Of course, many people in EM relationships are perfectly content with just having acquaintances and the opportunity to talk with each other. Parks and Floyd's study shows that nearly a quarter (23.7 percent) of the people in their newsgroup study reported that they communicated with their partners at least three or four times a week, and over half (55.4 percent) communicated with their partners on a weekly basis (p. 85). EM relationships are attractive to some busy people largely because they do not have time to "do the bar scene." Other people who begin relationships in face-to-face settings use EM communication to sustain these relationships when work or school requires them to live at a distance. E-mail, which was developed to be a tool for conducting business, is now widely used by families, friends, and lovers to maintain close connections when living at a distance.

Grandparents, including your authors, keep track of the growth of their new grandchildren through digital photos and videos attached to e-mails.

How likely are we to be able to maintain relationships that begin on the Internet? EM communicators seem to lack many of the things emphasized in traditional discussion of relationship development: physical proximity, information about physical appearance, cues about group membership, and information about the broader social context. However, people in EM settings can overcome these shortcomings by e-mailing, exchanging photographs either electronically or by traditional mail, talking on the telephone, and, ultimately, by arranging face-to-face meetings.

There are important differences between in-person and EM communication that can create difficulties for relationship development. Some critics of EM relationships argue that face-to-face interaction has more social presence than the Internet and the possibility of immediate feedback with face-to-face interaction conveys greater personal closeness (Flaherty, Pearce, & Rubin, 1998, p. 264). In addition, in most EM forms, at least some of the nonverbal message is lost. J. D. Bigelow (1999), of Boise State University, describes three problems (pp. 636–637), which we address next.

EM Communication Is Less Rich than Face-to-Face, Because Text Messages Are Primarily Verbal As a consequence of not being able to see or hear the way people present their messages, we may misinterpret them. Only with videoconferencing is the full range of nonverbal messages available.

Perhaps the most obvious of these limits is absence of nonverbal cues to help us determine meaning. Although we always refer to our EM encounters with others as "talking to people," the words we write seldom carry as much meaning as we think. We may be able to think of ways to sharpen the meanings in EM communication, but we seldom do.

EM Communication, Conducted via Keyboard Entries, Is Slower Paced than Face-to-Face Conversations Although this slower rate may provide a person more time for thought, this slower transmission reduces the spontaneity that is an important characteristic of face-to-face interaction.

EM Communicators Are Perceived to Be Less Supportive Wood and Smith (2001) emphasize that, because of the absence of nonverbal cues, "the relatively 'lean' messages delivered can be perceived as less personal." They go on to say that as a result of this many people "find little warmth in the phosphorescent glow of the computer screen" (p. 73). For instance, suppose you receive a message that says, "I want you to know how much I really care for you." What does this mean? Although it could mean a strong feeling of bonding, it might also be a sarcastic statement that means just the opposite of what the words say. Why the ambiguity? Because there are no nonverbal clues to support or refute the verbal message. In face-to-face communication anywhere from 33 percent to 100 percent of the meaning depends on *how* the message was stated.

Nevertheless, more and more people are turning to EM communication to develop and maintain relationships. EM relationships can be attractive to those who have for one reason or another had difficulty cultivating strong interpersonal relationships in person. Because EM communication is planned, some people are able to show verbal skillfulness and humor in their writing, but are not quick enough to do so in face-to-face settings. And EM relationships can develop without the distraction of physical attraction.

In fact, some individuals report their EM relationships are more satisfying than face-to-face relationships. For instance, a person who had been active in a computer network for church workers said, "I know some of these people better than some of my oldest and best friends" (Parks & Floyd, 1996, pp. 82–83). A variety of studies report instances of EM relationships blossoming into romance and marriage (Markham, 1998). For instance, our son-in-law's brother began cyber dating a woman he met online. Their relationship progressed as we have described. Recently, she quit a job she enjoyed to move to be near him. They are now talking about marriage.

From Online to In-Person Relationships

In face-to-face relationships, trust is built over time. We meet a person and then begin interacting. As a result of the behavior we encounter, we then make decisions about trust. For instance, we loan a book and consider when and if it is returned; we make a date and consider whether and how often the person is on time; we tell the person something that is personal and consider whether that person keeps the information to him/herself or communicates it to others. Through such experiences, we determine whether or not we can trust the person and thus whether or not we want to move toward a more intimate relationship. (Goldberg, 1999, p. 113).

In EM relationships, making a trust evaluation is more difficult. Some of the media through which relationships are developed are very "opaque." That is, we lose most of the spontaneity and most of the information normally available through nonverbal channels. As a result, our capacity to judge the accuracy of the trustworthiness of the behavior of another is limited.

The Dark Side of Electronically Mediated Communication

Despite its appeal, using EM communication to form relationships and acquire information has a number of risks and abuses.

Abuse of Anonymity One type of abuse in Internet-based relationships stems from the common practice of assuming a fictitious online persona. This practice removes both accountability and responsibility. Under the cloak of anonymity people will say things that they do not

OBSERVE & ANALYZE

Journal Activity

Cyber Relationships

Interview someone who has developed a cyber relationship. Ask the person to describe how the relationship developed and what similarities and differences he or she has noticed between this and other more traditionally developed relationships. Find out what the person has done to develop trust in the relationship. If he or she has met the person face-to-face, ask for a description of this meeting. What about the person was surprising to them? What is the status of the relationship now?

To what extent has the fact that the relationship began online influenced how it has developed? Be prepared to share your findings in class. ■

Technological addictions—non-chemical (behavioral) addictions that involve human-machine interaction.

mean and represent themselves as they are not. Kramer and Kramarae (1997) assert that women have the most to lose from this fictitious identity usage (p. 236).

Dishonesty A second risk in cyber relationships lies in the ease with which one can be deceived. In cyberspace, people commonly lie about their sex and physical attributes, and create fictitious careers, homes, and so forth. Unfortunately, some people use cyberspace to prey on others.

When we develop in-person relationships, we usually have independent ways of confirming that the people are what they are representing themselves to be. Because we do not "know" our EM partners in person we are severely limited in our abilities to independently confirm what we are told. It is wise to be skeptical of what people tell you about themselves, especially at the beginning of such a relationship. As Jenny Preece (2000) points out, "Online romances of any sort may fail when real-life meetings result in dashed fantasies. For example, online no one is overweight, but in reality a person's extra twenty-five pounds can make a difference. And dishonesty works only as long as the relationship remains online only" (p. 156).

In the early stages of the relationship, it is wise to limit the personal information you divulge. Remember, in any communication situation, self-disclosure should occur only if it is reciprocated. Even then, begin slowly and with less personal issues before moving to more sensitive information. Recall that what is sent in e-mail is public, not private, communication.

People who are addicted spend inordinate amounts of time online and begin to prefer their cyber relationships to their real ones.

Abuse of anonymity and dishonesty are of special concern for EM relationships formed by children. In 1998, seventeen million children ages two to eighteen were online. That number is expected to grow so that by the time you are reading this text more than forty-two million children are likely to be online (Okrent, 1999, p. 41). It is critically important for parents to monitor their children's EM relationships. Unfortunately, some parents refuse to monitor their kids' online chatting, naively believing it to be violating their privacy and likening it to eavesdropping on their phone calls. But as Okrent warns, "There's a difference: When your child's on the phone, she knows for certain who's on the other end of the line" (p. 41). Parents need to learn how to monitor their children's Internet usage and to use software to block their access to inappropriate and objectionable sites.

Addiction A third potential problem for children and adults alike is **technological addictions,** defined as non-chemical (behavioral) addictions that involve human–machine interaction (Griffiths, 1998, p. 62). People who are addicted spend inordinate amounts of time online and begin to prefer their cyber relationships to their real ones. One example of the ways in which cyber relationships can get in the way of real ones was reported in a *Cincinnati Enquirer* article ("Angry Wife," 1999). It appears that a wife became angry because her husband was on the Internet at 2:05 A.M. He had been online until 4 A.M. the previous day "chatting" with women. In an act of desperation, anger, jealousy, and frustration, this wife tried to cut the power cords on the computer before attacking it with the meat cleaver. She pleaded no contest to domestic violence and resisting arrest and was fined two hundred dollars.

Interpersonal Communication Skills in Cyber Relationships

Several skills that you have learned in this course are especially helpful in cyber relating. We review these skills next and describe how they can help you be more effective when conversing online.

Sender Skills

The following skills can help you as you prepare messages adapted to the more impoverished electronic message environment.

Using Precise, Specific, Concrete Words Since you can't use tone of voice, facial expression, gestures, and other nonverbal means to help clarify your meanings, you must be especially careful that the words you select will really be interpreted correctly. For instance, writing "What do you say we get together sometime?" does little more than express an interest in meeting. In fact, the lack of specifics might make one wonder whether the invitation is real. Writing "What do you say we get together for lunch later this week? I'm available from noon until 2 p.m. Wednesday, Thursday, or Friday. Let me know if any of those times will work for you—and let me know where you'd like to meet" is far more meaningful.

Providing Details and Examples When using such online communication as e-mail, you'll notice the tendency to communicate your ideas in as few words as possible. And although short, concise sentences may at times be a blessing, there are many more times when a statement that is too terse causes problems. For instance, suppose you're sending an e-mail to get information about a project that is in progress. You could just say, "Gwenn, please let me know what's happening with the Morris account." Now this wording may well seem clear enough to you. Gwenn is handling the account, she has accumulated information in relation to that account, and you'd like an update. But Gwenn reads your short note, she may look at it in many ways. First, she may be threatened. She's doing a job, but perhaps you don't trust her, and now you want information to make sure that she's doing her job correctly. Second, she may be bewildered. She's collected a great deal of information. She knows that you don't just want her to forward all that she's amassed, but she has no idea what to include in her "summary." Third, she may be angry. Servicing the account is taking plenty of her time. Now to summarize everything that is happening just isn't worth the time—she figures that when you get it, you'll slip it in a folder and pretty much forget about it. In short, she might have many reactions—many of which might be inaccurate. Just think how much better it would have been for you to say, "Gwenn, please let me know what's happening with the Morris account. I know you're in the midst of a lot of details, so please just let me know whether you've got enough back up to assure you're satisfying their needs, and, if not, what I can do to provide you with what you need."

Or suppose that you said, "Gwenn, please let me know what's happening with the Morris account. You'll recall at the meeting the other day Terry gave us a short list of key dates and a quick summary of needs to assure completion. Something similar to Terry's statement would be fine—recall it really wasn't long, but it did have a few key specifics that help us reply if we're asked by the higher ups."

Describe Your Feelings Clear content (ideas, details, explanations, etc.) helps the receiver understand what you're talking about. Especially when you have an interpersonal relationship, he or she is likely to be as interested in how you feel about what you're saying as in the details of what you're saying. Suppose that Walter says to Julia, "I talked with Bill the other day, but he was trying to make is sound as if we won't get the report for another week." Now if Walter was face-to-face with Julia, his nonverbals might very well give her a sense of how he is feeling about that. But online, Julia has no way of knowing. Thus, Walter would ensure Julia's understanding of his message if he said, "I talked with Bill the other day, but he was trying to make is sound as if we won't get the report for another week. I was really disappointed, because I had told him how important it was for us to have it in our hands by now."

Present Your Ideas Politely For some reason, when we're online there's a tendency to separate ourselves from the person we're talking with. Sometimes this leads to saying things in a way that others will perceive as offensive. So, especially when you're asking another person for something, remember that in some way they're going to have to expend time and energy to comply with your wishes. The more politely you present your wants and needs, the more likely the person will respond to your wants and needs. For instance, suppose you're online with your best friend. Writing "Ken, how about sending me an outline of the ideas you want to cover in the meeting?" may get the results you want if you and Ken are really close and have a good working relationship. But even then Ken may see the request as an intrusion on his time. It would be better to write, "Ken, I want to be well prepared for the meeting you scheduled. I was wondering whether you would have the time to give me the main ideas you want to cover. I'd much appreciate it." At least now you're showing a reason for wanting the outline and you're recognizing that you're intruding on Ken's time.

Receiver Skills

Now that we've considered a few sender skills that are likely to ensure more effective online communication, let's consider receiver skills that you need to apply when you respond.

Listen to What the Person Has Said "Listening" to online material requires you not just to "skim through" it, but to say it out loud. By saying it out loud you come closer to capturing the meaning because you are now adding the nonverbals. For instance if you received the message "I talked with Bill the other day, but he was trying to make is sound as if we won't get the report for another week," you're likely to get more out of the message if you repeat it aloud than if you just skim through it. Especially when you're responding to someone you know well, you may actually be able to capture the sound of their voice as you speak their words.

Be Sensitive to the Person's Feelings Especially if people feel interpersonally involved with you they are going to expect you to empathize with what they've said. Again, even though the printed message may not capture their feelings as well as we'd like, we must still try to be in tune with them. But what if the message is such that you're just not sure about the meaning? Then it's important for you to do what you can to make sure of the accuracy of your understanding. Although you may ask the person for further information, you may well be better off to test your meaning before going on.

Paraphrase Key Ideas Before You Respond As we said, the wording of the messages you receive might not be as precise, specific, or concrete as you'd like in order to ensure your understanding. Instead of assuming that you know exactly what the person meant, paraphrase the meaning that you have gotten from the message. For instance, if you read "I talked with Bill the other day, but he was trying to make it sound as if we won't get the report for another week," when you respond to the comment you might say, "I get the sense that you're not at all happy with Bill's not having the report finished by now—am I right?" Especially if you're conversing in online chat, the person can respond immediately about whether you have really gotten the message.

Be Supportive When a Person Is Sharing Good News Because we do not share the personal space of those with whom we talk online, there's a tendency to be insensitive to the needs of those whose messages you are reading. Regardless of how people might have phrased their messages, they'll still expect that you have fully understood. So, when they share good news with you, they will expect you to react in a positive way. Be supportive. For instance, if Susan writes that she appears to be in line for a promotion that is likely to carry a nice salary increase, you cannot just ignore it—even if such an announcement is tangential to the main aspect of the message. Susan wrote it because she's looking for a reaction. Such good news virtually requires positive response. Thus the least you should write is something like, "Susan, I'll bet you're just glowing over your impending promotion. And with all that you've told me about what you've done, I'll bet that raise is going to be a great one!"

Praise a Person's Accomplishments In the previous paragraph we addressed responding appropriately to good news. But what if the person's achievements alone are the good news? In these cases, whether in online or in face-to-face situations, you should praise them. For instance, if Glen writes, "I don't know whether I mentioned it, but I came in third in the club championship this weekend." No matter what else Glen writes, you need to offer your praise. "Glen, I know that you were hoping to do well, but third place is really something. You've got several golfers there that are really hard to beat. That you came in third must really make you feel quite good. I know I'd be tickled as all get out."

Try to Comfort a Person Who's Hurting Just as close friends share good news, they are likely to share bad news as well. And as we've discussed earlier, people who are close to us seek comforting. Again, because of the lack of sharing the same physical space, we may find ourselves so separated from the person online that we may not feel inclined to get involved. Remember, though, that a person would not say anything unless they were seeking comforting. So, put yourself in their shoes and respond in kind. For instance, if Susan writes, "It's been a pretty bad week—in addition to everything else, Roxy's been acting so poorly that I had to take her to the vet. You know, if it's not one thing, it's another." Online statements like these must not be ignored by a close friend. Put yourself in Susan's shoes. How would you feel if you had a near and dear pet who had to be taken to the vet? Of course, Susan's message gives no real clue of how sick Roxy is or what the outcome might be. If you really value Susan, you'll try to comfort her in some way. "Oh Susan, I know how you feel about Roxy. You didn't really say, but I get the sense that you're worried that this could be really serious. Please let me know if Roxy is all right. I know under these circumstances I'd just be miserable."

WHAT WOULD YOU DO?

A Question *of* Ethics

"I just love the Internet," Ben says.

"How do you spend most of your time? Knowing you, I bet it's playing games," replied Paul.

"Yeah, I do like to play games, but most of all, I like to get into private conversations in chat rooms."

"I didn't know you were into that. Who have you been talking with?"

"Women mostly. You know, women love to talk to other women. You'd be surprised

what they'll share about themselves. I've sure learned a lot."

"About what?"

"Most of all about what they think about men—what they like, don't like. You know what I mean."

"Wait a minute. You say 'women love to talk to other women.' So, how do you get in on those conversations?"

"Easy. Lately, I've used the name 'Kristen.'"

"People do that?"

"Sure."

"So," said Paul, "who do you like to talk with most?"

"Hey, that's easy. Connie."

"And you say she's a woman."

"Well, of course. She's Connie."

"Aren't you Kristen?"

"Oh my gosh. You don't think. . ."

1. What guides whether you use your real name on the Internet?

2. Has Ben lived up to the guidelines?

Summary

In this chapter we focused on using the Internet, electronic communication, the role of electronic communication in building relationships, and the application of interpersonal communication skills to building and maintaining online relationships.

People's use of cellular and digital telephones has changed the nature of telecommunications. Cellular phones are handy for emergencies and ensuring safety and security. They also act as a personal status symbol. Yet the ubiquitous nature of cellular phones and pagers raises expectations about reaching people at any time, turns private conversations into public ones, and disrupts quiet zones and public events.

Most of your electronic communication will be carried out via the Internet, an international electronic computer network made up of a collection of thousands of smaller computer networks. Today, most students can access the Internet through their university library or computer labs or terminals at various locations on campus, through their public library, or on their own home computers. This access connects you to databases of all kinds.

People communicate electronically with others in writing by e-mail, newsgroups, and Internet chat. People communicate with others orally on cellular phones.

E-mail, electronic correspondence conducted between one or more users on a network, is the largest application of Internet technology. An e-mail address comprises a user name, the @ symbol that separates user name from addresses, a service, and a domain. E-mail is different from other mail in that it may be received nearly instantaneously, it is not private, and any number of messages can be sent for the same user fee.

A newsgroup is an electronic gathering place for people with similar interests. People may read articles, post articles, and/or reply to articles.

Internet chat is like a telephone conversation or conference call, but instead of conversing verbally, people exchange words on computer monitors. Unlike e-mail, chat is instantaneous conversation.

New communication technologies are changing the way in which we conduct relationships. Large numbers of people have formed personal relationships with people they met on the Internet, even though the nature of online communication sometimes makes it difficult to build trust.

Although online communication can seem far more impersonal than face-to-face communication, effective communicators still use interpersonal skills appropriately. From a sender perspective, make sure that you write precisely, provide details and examples, describe feelings, and present your ideas politely. From a receiver perspective, make sure that you "listen" carefully, paraphrase when needed, support good news, praise accomplishments, and provide comfort when things are going wrong.

Chapter Resources

Communication Improvement Plan: Communicating Electronically

Would you like to improve an aspect of your electronic communication discussed in this chapter?

        E-mail

        Newsgroups

        Internet chat

        Cellular telephones

        Conducting a relationship online

        Applying interpersonal skills

Pick an aspect of electronically mediated communication and write a communication improvement plan.

Skill: _____

Problem: _____

_____

_____

_____

Goal: _____

_____

_____

_____

Procedure:

1. _____

2. _____

3. _____

Test of Achieving Goal: _____

_____

Key Words

Internet, *p. 403*

World Wide Web (WWW), *p. 403*

Web pages, *p. 403*

Web site, *p. 404*

Home page, *p. 404*

Browser, *p. 404*

Uniform resource locator or URL, *p. 404*

Bookmark, *p. 404*

Search engines, *p. 404*

Newsgroup, *p. 408*

Lurking, *p. 409*

Flaming, *p. 409*

Chat, *p. 409*

FAQs, *p. 409*

Netiquette, *p. 409*

Technological addictions, *p. 414*

Inter-Act with Media

CINEMA

Nora Ephron (Director). (1998). *You've Got Mail.* Tom Hanks, Meg Ryan, Parker Posey, Greg Kinnear, Jean Stapleton.

Brief Summary: This story is about a modern e-mail relationship that is tested due to the real-world pressure of business. The film is a remake of *The Shop Around the Corner,* which used letters instead of e-mail. The two central characters (Hanks and Ryan) must sort out their electronic relationship and their roles as business competitors.

IPC Concepts: E-mail, relational development, strength, and trust of the online relationship.

Barry Levinson (Director). 91994). *Disclosure.* Michael Douglas, Demi Moore, Donald Sutherland, Caroline Goodall, Dylan Baker, Roma Maffia, Dennis Miller.

Brief Summary: Based on the Michael Crichton novel, this film utilizes e-mail in order to show how people can communicate about others in both positive and hurtful ways. The central character (Douglas) is wrongly accused of sexual harassment and his entire career and personal life are thrown into turmoil. E-mail comes into play as his reputation is smeared, and later, as it offers him anonymous help in clearing his name.

IPC Concepts: Electronically mediated communication via e-mail, phone recorder, fax, and television.

Peter Hyams (Director). (1981). *Outland.* Sean Connery, Peter Boyle, Frances Sternhagen, James B. Sikking, Keeka Markham, Clarke Peters, John Ratzenberger.

Brief Summary: While this is essentially a remake of *High Noon* on a small, mining space station, the story is frequently advanced through the use of electronically mediated communication. Cannery, in charge of security for the space station, communicates with his wife via visual phone messages, even recorded messages. He keeps tabs on things and events on the station via visual monitoring screens.

IPC Concepts: Futuristic videophones, relational turning points.

LITERATURE

In an age of electronic communication, it is worthwhile to remember how people initiated and sustained interpersonal relationships via letters. These two books are an excellent way to examine the reality of corresponding with a close friend or family member, and the art of letter writing that could be of use in Internet corresponding.

Sobel, Dava (1999). *Galileo's Daughter: A Historical Memoir of Science, Faith, and Love.* New York: Walker and Company.

Brief Summary: This collection of letters is a fascinating look into a very close relationship. The letters, although written in an archaic form, nonetheless show depth of caring, affection, and concern for both parties. This book is an excellent example of how correspondence via print media can be important and repeated today via electronic media.

IPC Concepts: Interpersonal communication mediated by writing.

Grunwald, L, & Adler, S. J. (Eds.) (1999). *Letters of the Century: America 1900–1999.* New York: Dial.

Brief Summary: Grunwald and Adler have selected 423 letters from the twentieth century to illustrate the power of the written word in social interaction. The collection includes letters from some of the most influential and colorful personalities of the last one hundred years, including Jonas Salk, Mark Twain, and John F. Kennedy. Reading these letters is a wonderful experience, which might be compared to knowing the words to a song and hearing it sung. The letters are organized by decade and include helpful annotations.

IPC Concepts: Interpersonal communication mediated by writing.

ACADEMIC WORKS

Kaye, B. K. & Medoff, N. J. (1999). *The World Wide Web: A Mass Communication Perspective.* London: Mayfield Publishing Company.

Brief Summary: This resource is especially good in Chapter 8 (on the social implications of Web use) and Chapter 12 (on career opportunities via the Web).

IPC Concepts: Introduction to Web technology, terminology, types of e-mail, even legal and ethical concerns.

WHAT'S ON THE WEB

Friendship and Intimacy in the Digital Age, by Timothy Bickmore. http://www.media.mit.edu/~bickmore/Mas714/finalReport.html

Brief Summary: This site contains a final paper presented in the MIT course Systems and Self. This Web article explores the nature of online relationships and examines the acceptance of issues and implications of computer-based intimate friends. The article is based on interviews and a review of the psychological literature on interpersonal relationships. There is also a discussion of the disadvantages of such relationships.

IPC Concepts: Development of relationships, trust and strength of cyber relationships.

Livingood, J. (1995). Revenge of the introverts. *Computer-Mediated Communication Magazine,2*(4), p. 8. Online: http://metalab.unc.edu/cmc/mag/1995/apr/livingood.html

Brief Summary: This short article is based on the thesis that the Internet is an introvert-friendly environment.

IPC Concepts: Personality, relationship development.

Researching Personal Relationships: What's on the Web, by Malcolm Parks (U of Washington) and Joseph Walther (Rensselaer Polytechnic Institute). http://www.rpi.edu/~walthj/inpr96/sld001.htm

Brief Summary: Originally presented at the INPR meeting in Seattle in 1997, this rich seventy-two-slide presentation explores the impact of computer-aided communication (e-mail, moos, etc.) on interpersonal relationships. However, because it is set up in small slide segments, you have to be patient to get through all of them. Joseph Walther has a large bibliography of computer-mediated communication, which supports "researching personal relationships in cyberspace." You will need to go to his personal Web page and click on "CMC Bib." The file is in rtf (rich text format, readable by most word processors). http://www.rpi.edu/~walthj/

IPC Concepts: Nature of online relationships, how they develop, relational issues.

References

Chapter 1

Andersen, P. (2000). Cues of culture: The basis of intercultural differences in nonverbal communication. In L. A. Samovar & R. E. Porter (Eds.), *Intercultural Communication: A Reader* (9th ed., pp. 258–266). Belmont, Calif.: Wadsworth.

Aronson, E. (1999). *The Social Animal.* New York: Worth Publishers.

Carpenter, A. (1996). *Facts about Cities* (2nd ed.). New York: H. W. Wilson.

Edmunds, P. (1998, Oct. 16–18). America's escalating honesty crisis. *USA Weekend,* pp. 14–15.

Horner, E. R. (Ed.). (1998). *Almanac of the 50 States: Data Profiles with Comparative Tables.* Palo Alto, Calif.: Information Publications.

Johannesen, R. L. (2002). *Ethics in Human Communication* (5th ed.). Prospect Heights, Ill.: Waveland Press.

Kellermann, K. (1992). Communication: Inherently strategic and primarily automatic. *Communication Monographs, 59,* 288.

Locke, E. A., Latham, G. P., & Enez, M. (1988, January). The determinants of goal commitment. *Academy of Management Review,* pp. 23–39.

Nieto, S. (2000). *Affirming Diversity: The Sociological Context of Multicultural Education* (3rd ed.). New York: Longman.

Pritchard, M. (1991). *On Becoming Responsible.* Lawrence, KS: University of Kansas Press.

Reardon, K. K. (1987). Interpersonal Communication: Where Minds Meet. Belmont, Calif.: Wadsworth.

Samovar, L. A. & Porter, R. E. (2000). Understanding intercultural communication: An introduction and overview. In L. A. Samovar & R. E. Porter (Eds.), Intercultural Communication: A Reader, (9th ed.), pp. 5–16). Belmont, Calif.: Wadsworth.

Spitzberg, B. H. (2000). A Model of Intercultural Communication Competence. In L. A. Samovar & R. E. Porter (Eds.), *Intercultural Communication: A Reader* (9th ed., pp. 375–387). Belmont, Calif.: Wadsworth.

Spitzberg, B. H., & Cupach, W. R. (1984). *Interpersonal Communication Competence.* Beverly Hills, Calif.: Sage.

Spitzberg, B. H., & Duran, R. L. (1995). Toward the development and validation of a measure of cognitive communication competence. *Communication Quarterly, 43,* 259–274.

Terkel, S. N., & Duval, R. S. (Eds.). (1999). *Encyclopedia of Ethics.* New York: Facts on File.

Watzlawick, P., Beavin, J. H., & Jackson, D. D. (1967). *Pragmatics of Human Communication.* New York: W. W. Norton.

Wellman, C. (1988). Morals and Ethics (2nd ed.). Englewood Cliffs, NJ: Prentice-Hall.

Chapter 2

Aronson, E. (1999). *The Social Animal.* New York: Worth.

Baron, R. A., & Byrne, D. (2000). *Social Psychology* (9th ed.). Boston: Allyn & Bacon.

Berger, C. R., & Bradac, J. J. (1982). *Language and Social Knowledge: Uncertainty in Interpersonal Relations.* London: Arnold.

Campbell, J. D. (1990). Self-esteem and clarity of the self-concept. *Journal of Personality and Social Psychology, 59,* 538.

Centi, P. J. (1981). *Up with the Positive: Out with the Negative.* Englewood Cliffs, N.J.: Prentice Hall.

Demo, D. H. (1987). Family relations and the self-esteem of adolescents and their parents. *Journal of Marriage and the Family, 49,* 705–715.

Forgas, J. P. (1991). Affect and person perception. In J. P. Forgas, (Ed.), *Emotion and Social Judgments* (pp. 263–291). New York: Pergamon Press.

Forgas, J. P. (2000). Feelings and thinking: Summary and integration. In J. P. Forgas (Ed.), Feeling and Thinking: The Role of Affect in Social Cognition (pp. 387–406). New York: Cambridge University Press.

Hattie, J. (1992). *Self-Concept.* Hillsdale, N.J.: Erlbaum.

Hecht M. L., Jackson, R. L., & Ribeau, S. (in press). *African American Communication: Exploring Identity and Culture* (2nd ed.). Mahwah, N.J.: Erlbaum.

Hecht, M. L., & Jones-Corley, J. (2001). A layered perspective on prejudice. *Studies in International Relations, 22,* 93–120.

Hecht, M. L., Marsiglia, F. F., Elek-Fisk, E., Wagstaff, D. A., Kulis, S., Dustman, P., & Miller-Day, M. (in press). Culturally grounded substance use prevention: An evaluation of the keeping it R.E.A.L. curriculum. *Prevention Science.*

Hollman, T. D. (1972). Employment interviewer's errors in processing positive and negative information. *Journal of Psychology, 56,* 130–134.

Jones, M. (2002). *Social Psychology of Prejudice.* Upper Saddle River, N.J.: Prentice Hall.

Jordan, J. V. (1991). The relational self: A new perspective for understanding women's development. In J. Strauss & G. R. Goethals (Eds.), *The Self: Interdisciplinary Approaches* (pp. 136–149). New York: Springer-Verlag.

Jussim, L. J., McCauley, C. R., & Lee, Y-T. (1995). Why study stereotype accuracy and inaccuracy? In Y-T Lee, L. J. Jussim, & C. R. McCauley (Eds.), *Stereotype Accuracy: Toward Appreciating Group Differences* (pp. 3–28). Washington, D.C.: American Psychological Association.

Kenny, D. A. (1994). *Interpersonal Perception: A Social Relations Analysis.* New York: The Guilford Press.

Leary, M. R. (2002). When selves collide: The nature of the self and the dynamics of interpersonal relationships. In A. Tesser, D. A. Stapel, & J. V. Wood (Eds.), *Self and Motivation: Emerging Psychological Perspectives* (pp. 119–145). Washington, D.C.: American Psychological Association.

Littlejohn, S. W. (2002). *Theories of Human Communication* (7th ed.). Belmont, Calif.: Wadsworth.

Michener, H. A., & DeLamater, J. D. (1999). *Social Psychology* (4th ed.). Orlando, Fla.: Harcourt Brace.

Mruk, C. (1999). *Self-Esteem: Research, Theory, and Practice* (2nd ed.). New York: Springer.

Rayner, S. G. (2001). Aspects of the self as learner: Perception, concept, and esteem. In R. J. Riding, & S. G. Rayner, (Eds.), *Self Perception: International Perspectives on Individual Differences* (Vol. 2, p. 42) Westport, Conn.: Ablex Publishing.

Sampson, E. E. (1999). *Dealing with Differences: An Introduction to the Social Psychology of Prejudice*. Fort Worth, TX: Harcourt Brace.

Temple, L. E., & Loewen, K. R. (1993). Perceptions of power: First impressions of a woman wearing a jacket. *Perceptual and Motor Skills, 76,* 345.

Weiten, W. (1998). *Psychology: Themes and Variations* (4th ed.). Pacific Grove, Calif.: Brooks/Cole.

Zebrowitz, L. A. (1990). *Social Perception*. Pacific Grove, Calif.: Brooks/Cole.

Chapter 3

Baxter, L. (1982). Strategies for ending relationships: Two studies. *Western Journal of Speech Communication, 46,* 223–241.

Berger, C. R., & Bradac, J. J. (1982). *Language and Social Knowledge: Uncertainty in Interpersonal Relations*. London: Arnold.

Canary, J. C. & Dainton, M. (2002). Preface. In Canary, J. C. & Dainton, M., Eds. Maintaining Relationships Through Communication: Relational, Contextual and Cultural Variations (pp. xiii–xv.). Mahwah, N.J.: Erlbaum.

Cornog, M. W. (1998). *Merriam Webster's Vocabulary Builder*. Springfield, MA: Merriam Webster.

Cupach, C. R., & Metts, S. (1986). Accounts of relational dissolution: A comparison of marital and nonmarital relationships. *Communication Monographs, 53,* 319–321.

DeKlerk, V. (1991). "Expletives: Men Only?" *Communication Monographs, 589,* 156–169.

Dindia, K. (2000). Relational maintenance. In C. Hendrick & S. S. Hendrick (Eds.), *Close Relationships: A Sourcebook* (pp. 287–300). Thousand Oaks, Calif.: Sage.

Duck, S. (1987). How to lose friends without influencing people. In M. E. Roloff & G. R. Miller (Eds.), *Interpersonal Processes: New Directions in Communication Research* (pp. 278–298). Beverly Hills, Calif.: Sage.

Duck, S. (Ed.). (1997). *Handbook of Personal Relationships* (2nd ed.). New York: John Wiley & Sons.

Duck, S. (1998). *Human Relationships* (3rd ed.). Thousand Oaks, Calif.: Sage.

Duck, S., & Gilmour, R. (Eds.). (1981). *Personal Relationships*. London: Academic Press.

Duck, S., & Pittman, G. (1994). Social and personal relationships. In M. L. Knapp & G. R. Miller (Eds.), *Handbook of Interpersonal Communication* (2nd ed., pp. 677–696). Thousand Oaks, Calif.: Sage.

Fehr, B. (1996). *Friendship Processes*. Thousand Oaks, Calif.: Sage.

Floyd, K., & Morman, M. T. (1998). The measurement of affectionate communication. *Communication Quarterly. 46* (Spring), 144–162.

Gudykunst, W. B., & Kim, Y. Y. (1997). *Communicating with Strangers: An Approach to Intercultural Communication* (3rd ed.). New York: McGraw-Hill.

Guerrero, L. K., & Andersen, P. A. (2000). Cross-cultural variability of communication in personal relationships. In C. Hendrick & S. S. Hendrick (Eds.), *Close Relationships: A Sourcebook* (pp. 171–184). Thousand Oaks, Calif.: Sage.

Kellermann, K., & Reynolds, R. (1990). When ignorance is bliss: The role of motivation to reduce uncertainty in uncertain relations. *Human Communication Research 17,* 67.

Knapp, M. L. & Vangelisti, A. L. (2000). *Interpersonal Communication and Human Relationships*, 4th ed. Boston: Allyn & Bacon.

LaFollette, H. (1996). *Personal Relationships: Love, Identity, and Morality*. Cambridge, Mass.: Blackwell.

Littlejohn, S. W. (2002). *Theories of Human Communication* (7th ed.). Belmont, Calif.: Wadsworth.

Luft, J. (1970). *Group Processes: An Introduction to Group Dynamics*. Palo Alto, Calif.: Mayfield.

Patterson, B. R., Bettini, L., & Nussbaum, J. F. (1993). The meaning of friendship across the life-span: Two studies. *Communication Quarterly 41,* 145.

Schutz, W. (1966). *The Interpersonal Underworld*. Palo Alto, Calif.: Science & Behavior Books.

Shaw, M. (1981). *Group Dynamics: The Psychology of Small Group Behavior* (3rd ed.). New York: McGraw-Hill.

Stafford, L., & Canary, D. J. (1991). Maintenance strategies and romantic relationship type, gender, and relational characteristics. *Journal of Social and Personal Relationships, 8,* 217–242.

Taylor, D. A., & Altman, I. (1987). Communication in interpersonal relationships: Social penetration theory. In M. E. Roloff & G. R. Miller (Eds.), *Interpersonal Processes: New Directions in Communication Research* (pp. 257–277). Beverly Hills, Calif.: Sage.

Thibaut, J. W., & Kelley, H. H. (1986). *The Social Psychology of Groups* (2nd ed.). New Brunswick, N.J.: Transaction Books.

Trenholm, S. (1991). *Human Communication Theory* (2nd ed.). Englewood Cliffs, N.J.: Prentice Hall.

Winstead, B. A., Derlega, V. J., & Rose, S. (1997). *Gender and Close Relationships*. Thousand Oaks, Calif.: Sage.

Chapter 4

Asante, Molefi K. (1998). *The Afrocentric idea*. Philadelphia: Temple University Press.

Asante, Molefi K. (1988). *Afrocentricity*. Trenton, N.J.: Africa World Press.

Asente, Molefi K. (1990). *Afrocentricity and knowledge*. Molefi K. (1988). Afrocentricity.

Canary, D. J., & Hause, K. (1993). Is there any reason to research sex differences in communication? *Communication Quarterly, 41,* 129–144.

Cornog, M. W. (1999). *Merriam-Webster's Vocabulary Builder*,

DeKlerk, V. (1991). "Expletives: Men only?" *Communication Monographs 58,* 156–169.

Dickson, P. (1998). *Slang: The Authoritative Topic-by-Topic Dictionary of American*

Lingoes from All Walks of Life (rev. ed.). New York: Pocket Books.

Encyclopedia.com. (2002). www.encyclopedia.com.

Gmelch, S. B. (1998). *Gender on Campus: Issues for College Women.* New Brunswick, N.J.: Rutgers University Press.

Gudykunst, W. B., & Matsumoto, Y. (1996). Cross-cultural variability of communication in personal relationships. In W. B. Gudykunst, S. Ting-Toomey, & T. Nishida (Eds.), *Communication in Personal Relationships Across Cultures* (pp. 19–56). Thousand Oaks, Calif.: Sage.

Hecht, M. L., Collier, M. J., & Ribeau, S. A. (1993). *African American Communication: Ethnic Identity and Cultural Interpretation.* Newbury Park, Calif.: Sage.

Hofstede, G. (1983). *Culture's Consequences: International Differences in Work-Related Values.* Newbury Park, Calif.: Sage.

Hofstede, G. (1991). *Cultures and Organizations: Software of the Mind.* New York: McGraw-Hill.

Holtgraves, T. (2002). *Language as Social Action: Social Psychology and Language Use.* Mahwah, N.J.: Erlbaum.

Howard, J. A., & Hollander, J. (1997). *Gendered Situations, Gendered Selves: A Gender Lens on Social Psychology.* Thousand Oaks, Calif.: Sage.

Littlejohn, S. (2002). *Theories of Human Communication* (7th ed.). Belmont, Calif.: Wadsworth.

Merriam-Webster's Collegiate Dictionary: Deluxe Edition. (1998). Springfield, Mass.: Merriam-Webster.

Ogden, C. K., & Richards, I. A. (1923). *The Meaning of Meaning.* London: Kegan, Paul, Trench, Trubner.

Richards, I. A. (1965). *The Philosophy of Rhetoric.* New York: Oxford University Press.

Stewart, L. P., Cooper, P. J., Stewart, A. D., & Friedley, S. A. (1998). *Communication and Gender* (3rd ed.). Boston: Allyn & Bacon.

Wood, J. T., & Dindia, K. (1998). What's the difference? A dialogue about differences and similarities between women and men. In D. J. Canary & K. Dindia (Eds.), *Sex Differences and Similarities in Communication: Critical Essays and Empirical Investigations of Sex and Gender in Interaction* (pp. 19–40). Mahwah, N.J.: Erbaum.

Chapter 5

Axtell, R. E. (1998). *Gestures: The Do's and Taboos of Body Language Around the World* (rev. ed.). New York: Wiley.

Burgoon, J. K. (1994). Nonverbal signals. In M. L. Knapp & G. R. Miller (Eds.), *Handbook of Interpersonal Communication* (2nd ed., pp. 229–285). Thousand Oaks, Calif.: Sage.

Burgoon, J. K., Buller, D. B., Dillman, L, & Walther, J. B. (1995). Interpersonal deception: IV. Effects of suspicion on perceived communication and nonverbal behavior dynamics. *Human Communication Research, 22,* 163–196.

Burgoon, J. K., Buller, D. B., & Woodall, W. G. (1989). *Nonverbal Communication: The Unspoken Dialogue.* New York: Harper & Row.

Burgoon, J. K., & Dunbar, N. E. (2000). An interactionist perspective on dominance–submission: Interpersonal dominance as a dynamic, situationally contingent social skill. *Communication Monographs,* Mar., pp. 96–121.

Burgoon, J. K., Walther, J. B., & James Baesler, E. (1992). Interpretations, evaluations, and consequences of interpersonal touch. *Human Communication Research 19,* 259.

Canary, D. J., & Hause, K. (1993). Is there any reason to research sex differences in communication? *Communication Quarterly, 41,* 129–144.

Cegala, D. J., & Sillars, A. L. (1989). Further examination of nonverbal manifestations of interaction involvement. *Communication Reports, 2,* 45.

Ekman, P., & Friesen, W. V. (1969). The repertoire of nonverbal behavior: Categories, origins, usage, and coding. *Semiotica, 1,* 49–98.

Feldman, R. S., Philippot, P., & Custrini, R. J. (1991). Social competence and nonverbal behavior. In R. S.. Feldman & B. Rime (Eds.), *Fundamentals of Nonverbal Behavior* (p. 329–350). New York: Cambridge University Press.

Geyer, G. A. (1999, Sept. 15). Dressing in the name of respect. *Cincinnati Enquirer,* p. A12.

Gudykunst, W. B. (1991). *Bridging Differences: Effective Intergroup Communication.* Newbury Park, Calif.: Sage.

Gudykunst, W. B., & Kim, Y. Y. (1997). *Communicating with Strangers: An Approach to Intercultural Communication* (3rd ed.). Boston: Allyn & Bacon.

Hall, E. T. (1959). *The Silent Language.* Greenwich, Conn.: Fawcett.

Hall, E. T. (1969). *The Hidden Dimension.* Garden City, N.Y.: Doubleday.

Hall, J. A. (1998). How big are nonverbal sex differences? The case of smiling and sensitivity to nonverbal cues. In D. J. Canary & K. Dindia (Eds.), *Sex Differences and Similarities in Communication: Critical Essays and Empirical Investigations of Sex and Gender in Interaction* (pp. 155–178). Mahwah, N.J.: Erlbaum.

Knapp, M. L., & Hall, J. A. (2002). *Nonverbal Communication in Human Interaction* (5th ed.). Belmont, Calif.: Wadsworth/Thomson Learning.

Leathers, D. (1997). *Successful Nonverbal Communication: Principles and Applications* (3rd ed.). Boston-Allyn & Bacon.

Martin, J. N., & Nakayama, T. K. (2000). *Intercultural Communication in Contexts* (2nd ed.). Mountain View, Calif.: Mayfield Publishing.

Pearson, J. C., West, R. L., & Turner, L. H. (1995). *Gender and Communication* (3rd ed.). Dubuque, Iowa: Brown & Benchmark.

Richmond, V. P., & McCroskey, J. C. (1995). *Communication: Apprehension, Avoidance, and Effectiveness* (4th ed.). Scottsdale, Ariz.: Gorsuch Scarisbrick.

Samovar, L. A., & Porter, R. E. (2001). *Communication Between Cultures* (4th ed.). Belmont, Calif.: Wadsworth.

Stewart, L. P., Cooper, P. J., Stewart, A. D., & Friedley, S. A. (1998). *Communication and Gender* (3rd ed.). Boston: Allyn & Bacon.

Wood, J. T. (2001). *Gendered Lives: Communication, Gender, and Culture* (4th ed.). Belmont, Calif.: Wadsworth.

Chapter 6

Bach, K., & Harnish, R. M. (1979). *Linguistic Communication and Speech Acts.* Cambridge, Mass.: The MIT Press.

Brown, P., & Levinson, S. (1987). *Politeness: Some Universals in Language Usage.* Cambridge, U.K.: Cambridge University Press.

Duck, S. (1998). *Human Relationships* (3rd ed.). Thousand Oaks, Calif.: Sage.

Duncan, Jr., S., & Fiske, D. W. (1977). *Face-to-Face Interaction: Research, Methods, and Theory.* Hillsdale, N.J.: Erlbaum.

Eggins, S., & Slade, D. (1997). *Analyzing Casual Conversation*. Washington, D.C.: Cassell.

Ford, C. E., Fox, B. A., & Thompson, S. A. (2002). Introduction. In C. E. Ford, B. A. Fox, & S. A. Thomson (Eds.), *The Language of Turn and Sequence* (pp. 3–13). New York: Oxford University Press.

Grice, H. P. (1975). *Logic and conversation*. In P. Cole & J. L. Morgan (Eds.), *Syntax and Semantics* (Vol. 3, Speech Acts, pp. 41–58). New York: Academic Press.

Gudykunst, W. B., & Matsumoto, Y. (1996). Cross-cultural variability of communication in personal relationships. In W. B. Gudykunst, S. Ting-Toomey, & T. Nishida (Eds.), *Communication in Personal Relationships Across Cultures* (pp. 19–56). Thousand Oaks, Calif.: Sage.

Hobbes, J. R., & Evans, D. A. (1980). Conversation as planned behavior. *Cognitive Science 4*, 349–377.

Holtgraves, T. (2002). *Language as Social Action: Social Psychology and Language Use*. Mahwah, N.J.: Erlbaum.

Johannesen, R. L. (2000). *Ethics in Human Communication* (5th ed.). Prospect Heights, Ill.: Waveland Press.

Kennedy, C. W., & Camden, C. T. (1983). A new look at interruptions. *Western Journal of Speech Communication*, *47*, 55.

Littlejohn, S. W. (2003). *Theories of Human Communication* (7th ed.). Belmont, Calif.: Wadsworth.

McLaughlin, M. L. (1984). *Conversation: How Talk Is Organized*. Newbury Park, Calif.: Sage.

Shimanoff, S. B. (1980). *Communication Rules: Theory and Research*. Beverly Hills, Calif.: Sage.

Svennevig, J. (1999). *Getting Acquainted in Conversation: A Study of Initial Interactions*. Philadelphia: John Benjamins.

Chapter 7

Bostrom, R. N. (1990). *Listening Behavior: Measurement and Applications*. New York: Guilford.

Bostrom, R. N. (1996). Memory, cognitive processing, and the process of "listening,": A reply to Thomas and Levine. *Human Communication Research*, *23*, 298–305.

Bostrom, R. N. (1997). The process of listening. In O. Hargie (Ed.), *Handbook of Communication Skills* (2nd ed., pp. 236–258). New York: Routledge.

Brownell, J. (2002). *Listening: Attitudes, Principles, and Skills* (2nd ed.). Boston, Mass.: Allyn & Bacon.

Ellinor, L., & Gerard, G. (1998). *Dialogue: Rediscover the Transforming Power of Conversation*. New York: Wiley & Sons.

Estes, W. K. (1989). Learning theory. In A. Lesgold & R. Glaser (Eds.), *Foundations for a Psychology of Education* (pp. 1–49). Hillsdale, N.J.: Erlbaum.

Purdy, M. (1996). What is listening? In M. Purdy & D. Borisoff (Eds.), *Listening in Everyday Life: A Personal and Professional Approach* (2nd ed., pp. 1–20). New York: University Press of America.

Steil, L. K., Barker, L. L., & Watson, K. W. (1983). *Effective Listening* Reading, Mass.: Addison-Wesley.

Wolvin, A., & Coakley, C. G. (1996). *Listening* (5th ed.). Dubuque, Iowa: Brown & Benchmark.

Chapter 8

Barbee, A. P., & Cunningham, M. R. (1995). An experimental approach to social support communication: Interactive coping in close relationships. In B. R. Burleson (Ed.), *Communication Yearbook 18* (pp. 381–413). Thousand Oaks, Calif.: Sage.

Burleson, B. R. (1994). Comforting messages: Significance, approaches, and effects. In B. R. Burleson, T. L. Albrecht, & I. G. Sarason (Eds.), *Communication of Social Support: Messages, Interactions, Relationships, and Community* (pp. 3–28). Thousand Oaks, Calif.: Sage.

Burleson, B. R. (2003). Emotional support skills. In J. O. Green & B. R. Burleson (Eds.), *Handbook of Communication and Social Interaction Skills* (pp. 551–594). Mahwah, N.J.: Erlbaum.

Burleson, B. R., & Goldsmith, D. J. (1998). How the comforting process works: Alleviating emotional distress through conversationally induced reappraisals. In P. A. Andersen & L. K. Guerrero (Eds.), *Handbook of Communication and Emotion: Research, Theory, Applications, and Contexts* (pp. 248–280). San Diego: Academic Press.

Burleson, B. R., & MacGeorge, E. L. (2002). Supportive communication. In M. L. Knapp, J. A. Daly, & G. R. Miller (Eds.), *Handbook of Interpersonal Communication* (3rd ed., pp. 374–424). Thousand Oaks, Calif.: Sage.

Burleson, B. R., & Samter, W. (1990). Effects of cognitive complexity on the perceived importance of communication skills in friends. *Communication Research, 17*, 165–182.

Cunningham, M. R., & Barbee, A. P. (2000). Social support. In C. Hendrick & S. S. Hendrick (Eds.), *Close Relationships: A Sourcebook* (pp. 272–285). Thousand Oaks, Calif.: Sage.

Eisenberg, N., & Fabes, R. A. (1990). Empathy: Conceptualization, measurement, and relation to prosocial behavior. *Motivation and Emotion, 14*, 131–149.

Holtgraves, T. (2002). *Language as Social Action: Social Psychology and Language Use*. Mahwah, N.J.: Erlbaum.

Kunkel, A. W., & Burleson, B. R. (1999). Assessing explanations for sex differences in emotional support: A test of the different cultures and skill specialization accounts. *Human Communication Research, 25* (March), 307–340.

Leathers, D. G. (1997). *Successful Nonverbal Communication: Principles and Applications* (3rd ed.). Boston: Allyn & Bacon.

Martin, J. N., & Nakayama, T. K. (1997). *Intercultural Communication in Contexts*. Mountain View, Calif.: Mayfield.

Omdahl, B. L. (1995). *Cognitive Appraisal, Emotion, and Empathy*. Mahwah, N.J.: Erlbaum.

Samovar, L. A., & Porter, R. E. (2001). *Communication Between Cultures* (4th ed.). Belmont, Calif.: Wadsworth.

Samter, W., Burleson, B. R., & Murphy, L. B. (1987). Comforting conversations: The effects of strategy type of evaluations on messages and message producers. *Southern Speech Communication Journal 52*, 263–284.

Stiff, J. B., Dillard, J. P., Somera, L., Kim, H., & Sleight, C. (1988). Empathy, communication, and prosocial behavior. *Communication Monographs, 55*, 198–213.

Weaver III, J. B., & Kirtley, M. B. (1995). Listening styles and empathy. *Southern Communication Journal 60*, 131–140.

Zillman, D., (1991). Empathy: Affect from bearing witness in the emotions of others. In J. Bryant & D. Zillmann (Eds.), *Responding to the Screen: Reception and*

Reaction Processes (pp. 135–167). Hillsdale, N.J.: Erlbaum.

Chapter 9

Altman, I. (1993). Dialectics, physical environments, and personal relationships. *Communication Monographs, 60*, 26–34.

Altman, I., & Taylor, D. (1973). *Social Penetration: The Development of Interpersonal Relationships.* New York: Holt, Rinehart, & Winston.

Berg, J. H., & Derlega, V. J. (1987). Themes in the study of self-disclosure. In J. H. Berg & V. J. Derlega (Eds.), *Self-Disclosure: Theory, Research, and Therapy* (pp. 1–8). New York: Plenum Press.

Derlega, V. J., Metts, S., Petronio, S., & Margulis, S. T. (1993). *Self-Disclosure.* Newbury Park, Calif.: Sage.

Dindia, K., Fitzpatrick, M. A., & Kenny, D. A. (1997). Self-disclosure in spouse and stranger interaction: A social relations analysis. *Human Communication Research, 23* (March), 388–412.

Gudykunst, W. B., & Kim, Y. Y. (1997). *Communicating with Strangers: An Approach to Intercultural Communication* (3rd ed.). Boston: Allyn & Bacon.

Pearson, J. C., West, R. L., & Turner, L. H. (1995). *Gender and Communication* (3rd ed.). Dubuque, Iowa: Wm. C. Brown.

Reis, H. T. (1998). Gender differences in intimacy and related behaviors: Context and process. In D. J. Canary & K. Dindia (Eds.), *Sex Differences and Similarities in Communication: Critical Essays and Empirical Investigations of Sex and Gender in Interaction* (pp. 203–232). Mahwah, N.J.: Erlbaum.

Samovar, L. A., & Porter, R. E. (2001). *Communication Between Cultures* (4th ed.). Belmont, Calif.: Wadsworth.

Stewart, L. P., Cooper, P. J., Stewart, A. D., & Friedley, S. A. (1998). *Communication and Gender* (3rd ed.). Boston, Mass.: Allyn & Bacon.

Tannen, D. (1990). *You Just Don't Understand.* New York: Morrow.

Tracy, K., Dusen, D. V., & Robinson, S. (1987). "Good" and "bad" criticism. *Journal of Communication, 37*, 46–59.

Chapter 10

Alberti, R. E., & Emmons, M. L. (1995). *Your Perfect Right: A Guide to Assertive Living* (7th ed.). San Luis Obispo, Calif.: Impact Publishers.

Chebat, J. C., Filiatrault, P., & Perrien, J. (1990). Limits of credibility: The case of political persuasion. *The Journal of Social Psychology 130*, 157–167.

Dillard, J. P., Anderson, J. W. & Knobloch, L. K. (2002). Interpersonal Influence. In Knapp, M. L. & Daly, J. A. (Eds.) *Handbook of Interpersonal Communication*, 3rd ed., pp. 425–474. Thousand Oaks, Calif.: Sage.

French, Jr., J. R. P., & Raven, B. (1968). The bases of social power. In D. Cartwright & A. Zander (Eds.), *Group Dynamics* (3rd ed., pp. 259–269). New York: Harper & Row.

Hinken, T. R., & Schriesheim, C. A. (1980). Development and application of new scales to measure the French and Raven (1959). Bases of Social Power. *Journal of Applied Psychology 74*, 561–567.

Jandt, F. E. (2001). *Intercultural Communication: An Introduction* (3rd ed.). Thousand Oaks, Calif.: Sage.

Jorgensen, P. E. (1998). Affect, persuasion, and communication process. In P. A. Anderson & L. K. Guerrero (Eds.), *Handbook of Communication and Emotion: Research, Theory, Applications, and Contexts* (pp. 403–422). San Diego: Academic Press.

Kellerman, K., & Cole, T. D. (1994). Classifying compliance gaining messages: Taxonomic disorder in strategic confusion. *Communication Theory, 4*, 3–60.

Kellermann, K., & Shea, B. C. (1996). Threats, suggestions, hints, and promises: Gaining compliance efficiently and politely. *Communication Quarterly, 44*(2), 145–165.

Knowles, E. R., Butler, S., & Linn, J. A. (2001). Increasing compliance by reducing resistance. In J. P. Forgas & K. D. Williams (Eds.), *Social Influence: Direct and Indirect Processes* (pp. 41–60). Philadelphia; Psychology Press.

Martin, M. M., Anderson, C. M., & Horvath, C. L. (1996). Feelings about verbal aggression: Justifications for sending and hurt from receiving verbally aggressive messages. *Communication Research Reports, 13*(1), 19–26.

Miller, L. C., Cody, M. J., & McLaughlin, M. L. (1994). Situations and goals as fundamental constructs in interpersonal communication research. In M. L. Knapp & G. R. Miller (Eds.), *Handbook of Interpersonal Communication* (2nd ed., pp. 263–313). Beverly Hills, Calif.: Sage.

O'Hair, D., & Cody, M. J. (1987). Machiavellian beliefs and social influence. *Western Journal of Speech Communication, 51*, 286–287.

Petty, R. E. DeSteno, D., & Rucker, D. (2001). The role of affect in persuasion and attitude change. In J. Forgas (Ed.), *Handbook of affect and social cognition* (pp. 212–233). Mahwah, N.J.: Erlbaum.

Petty, R. E., Wheeler, S. C., & Bitzer, G. Y. (2000). Attitude functions and persuasion: An elaboration likelihood approach to matched versus mismatched messages. In G. R. Maio & J. M. Olson (Eds.), *Why we evaluate: Functions of attitudes* (pp. 133–162). Mahwah, N.J.: Erlbaum.

Samovar, L. A., & Porter, R. E. (2001). *Communication Between Cultures* (4th ed.). Belmont, Calif.: Wadsworth.

Tedeschi, J. T. (2001). Social power, influence, and aggression. In J. P. Forgas & K. D. Williams (Eds.), *Social Influence: Direct and Indirect Processes* (pp. 109–126). Philadelphia: Psychology Press.

Trenholm, S. (1989). *Persuasion and Social Influence.* Englewood Cliffs, N.J.: Prentice Hall.

Chapter 11

Adler, R. B. (1977). *Confidence in Communication: A Guide to Assertive and Social Skills.* New York: Holt, Rinehart and Winston.

Canary, D. J. (2003). *Maintaining Relationships through Communication: Relational, Contextual, and Cultural Variations.* Mahwah, NJ: Erlbaum.

Canary, D. J., Cupach, W. R., & Messman, S. J. (1995). *Relationship Conflict: Conflict in Parent-Child, Friendship, and Romantic Relationships.* Thousand Oaks, Calif.: Sage.

Canary, D. J., & Hause, K. (1993). Is there any reason to research sex differences in communication? *Communication Quarterly, 41*, 129–144.

Cloven, D. H., & Roloff, M. E. (1991). Sense-making activities and interpersonal conflict: Communicative cures for the mulling blues. *Western Journal of Speech Communication, 55*, 134–158.

Cupach, W. R., & Canary, D. J. (1997). *Competence in Interpersonal Conflict.* New York: McGraw-Hill.

Gayle, B. M., & Preiss, R. W. (2002). An overview of interactional processes in interpersonal communication. In M. Allen, R. W. Preiss, B. M. Gayle, & N. Burrell (Eds.), *Interpersonal Communication Research: Advances Through Meta-Analysis* (pp. 213–226). Mahwah, N.J.: Erlbaum.

Gordon, T. (1970). *Parent Effectiveness Training.* New York: Peter H. Wyden.

Gordon, T. (1971). *The Basic Modules of the Instructor Outline for Effectiveness Training Courses.* Pasadena, Calif.: Effectiveness Training Associates.

Lulofs, R. S., & Cahn, D. D. (2000). *Conflict: From Theory to Action* (2nd ed). Boston: Allyn & Bacon.

Martin, J. N., & Nakayama, T. K. (1997). *Intercultural Communication in Contexts.* Mountain View, Calif.: Mayfield.

Roloff, M. E., & Cloven, D. H. (1990). The chilling effect in interpersonal relationships: The reluctance to speak one's mind. In D. D. Cahn (Ed.), *Intimates in Conflict: A Communication Perspective* (pp. 49–76). Hillsdale, N.J.: Erlbaum.

Sillars, A. L., & Weisberg, J. (1987). Conflict as a social skill. In M. E. Roloff & G. R. Miller (Eds.), *Interpersonal Processes: New Directions in Communication Research* (pp. 140–171). Beverly Hills, Calif.: Sage.

Ting-Toomey, S. (2001). Managing intercultural conflicts effectively. In L. A. Samovar & R. E. Porter (Eds.), *Intercultural Communication: A Reader* (9th ed., pp. 388–399). Belmont, Calif.: Wadsworth.

Whetten, D. A., & Cameron, K. S. (2002). *Developing Management Skills* (5th ed.). Upper Saddle River, N.J.: Prentice Hall.

Chapter 12

Argyle, M., & Furnham, A. (1983). Sources of satisfaction and conflict in long-term relationships. *Journal of Marriage and the Family, 45,* 481–493.

Bloch, J. D. (1980). *Friendship.* New York: Macmillan.

Boon, S. D. (1994). Dispelling doubt and uncertainty: Trust in romantic relationships. In S. Duck (Ed.), *Dynamics of Relationships* (pp. 86–111). Thousand Oaks, Calif.: Sage.

Canary, D. J., & Stafford, L. (2001). Equity in the preservation of personal relationships. In J. Harvey & A. Wenzel (Eds.), *Close Romantic Relationships: Maintenance and Enhancement* (pp. 133–152). Mahwah, N.J.: Erlbaum.

Demo, D. H. (1987). Family relations and the self-esteem of adolescents and their parents. *Journal of Marriage and the Family, 49,* 705–715.

Dickson, F. C. (1995). The best is yet to be: Research on long-lasting marriages. In J. T. Wood & S. Duck (Eds.), *Under-Studied Relationships: Off the Beaten Track* (pp. 22–50). Thousand Oaks, Calif.: Sage.

Duck, S., & Wright, P. H. (1993). Reexamining gender differences in same-gender friendships: A close look at two kinds of data. *Sex Roles, 28,* 709–727.

Family time: An interview with Bill Doherty (2002). The Early Show. CBS Worldwide, Inc.: New York http://www.cbsnews.com/stories/2002/09/20/earlyshow/living/parenting/main522830.shtml.

Fehr, B. (1996). *Friendship Processes.* Thousand Oaks, Calif.: Sage.

Fischer, J. L., & Narus, Jr., L. R., (1981). Sex roles and intimacy in same-sex and other-sex relationships. *Psychology of Women Quarterly,* v. 5, pp. 444–455.

Fitzpatrick, M. A. (1988). *Between Husbands and Wives: Communication in Marriage.* Beverly Hills, Calif.: Sage.

Fitzpatrick, M. A., & Badzinski, D. M. (1994). All in the family: Interpersonal communication in kin relationships. In M. L. Knapp & G. R. Miller (Eds.), *Handbook of Interpersonal Communication* (2nd ed., pp. 726–771). Thousand Oaks, Calif.: Sage.

Fitzpatrick, M. A., & Bochner, A. (1981). Perspectives on self and other: Male-female differences in perceptions of communication behavior. *Sex Roles, 7,* 523–535.

Fitzpatrick, M. A., & Caughlin, J. (2003). Interpersonal communication in family relationships. In M. Knapp & J. Daly (Eds.), *Handbook of Interpersonal Communication* (pp. 726–778). Thousand Oaks, Calif.: Sage.

Fitzpatrick, M. A., & Koerner, A. (2002). A theory of family communication. *Communication Theory, 12*(1), 70–91.

Fitzpatrick, M. A., & Ritchie, L. D. (1994). Communication schemata within the family: Multiple perspectives on family interaction. *Human Communication Research, 20,* 275–301.

Galvin, K. M., & Brommel, B. J. (1996). *Family Communication: Cohesion and Change* (4th ed.). New York: HarperCollins.

LaFollette, H. (1996). *Personal Relationships: Love, Identity, and Morality.* Cambridge, Mass.: Blackwell.

Marsh, P. (Ed.). (1988). *Eye to Eye: How People Interact.* Topsfield, Mass.: Salem House Publishers.

McGill, M. E. (1985). *The McGill Report on Male Intimacy.* New York: Holt, Rinehart, and Winston.

Mills, J., & Clark, M. S. (2001). Viewing close romantic relationships as communal relationships: Implications for maintenance and enhancement. In J. Harvey & A. Wenzel (Eds.), *Close Romantic Relationships: Maintenance and Enhancement* (pp. 13–25). Mahwah, N.J.: Erlbaum.

Perlman, D., & Fehr, B. (1987). The development of intimate relationships. In D. Perlman & S. Duck (Eds.), *Intimate Relationships: Development, Dynamics, and Deterioration* (pp. 13–42). Beverly Hills, Calif.: Sage.

Pleck, J. H. (1975). Man to man: Is brotherhood possible? In N. Glazer-Malbin (Ed.), *Old Family/New Family: Interpersonal Relationships* (pp. 229–244). New York: Van Nostrand.

Prisbell, M., & Andersen, J. F. (1980). The importance of perceived homophily, level of uncertainty, feeling good, safety, and self-disclosure in interpersonal relationships. *Communication Quarterly 28,* 22–33.

Reis, H. T. (1998). Gender differences in intimacy and related behaviors: Context and process. In D. J. Canary & K. Dindia (Eds.), *Sex Differences and Similarities in Communication: Critical Essays and Empirical Investigations of Sex and Gender in Interaction* (pp. 203–231). Mahwah, N.J.: Erlbaum.

Rusbult, C. E., Olsen, N., Davis, J. L., & Hannon, P. A. (2001). Commitment and relationship maintenance mechanisms. In J. Harvey & A. Wenzel (Eds.), *Close Romantic Relationships: Maintenance and Enhancement* (pp. 87–113). Mahwah, N.J.: Erlbaum.

Sabourin, T. C. (1996). The role of communication in verbal abuse between spouses. In D. D. Cahn & S. A. Lloyd (Eds.), *Family Violence from a Communication Perspective* (pp. 199–217). Thousand Oaks, Calif.: Sage.

Sabourin, T. C., & Stamp, G. H. (1995). Communication and the experience of dialectical tensions in family life: An examination of abusive and nonabusive families. *Communication Monographs, 62*(3), 213–242.

Wellman, B. (1992). Men in networks: Private communities, domestic friendships. In P. M. Nardi (Ed.), *Men's Friendships* (pp. 74–114). Newbury Park, Calif.: Sage.

Werking, K. J. (1997). Cross-sex friendship research as ideological practice. In S. Duck (Ed.), *Handbook of Personal Relationships: Theory, Research, and Interventions* (2nd ed., pp. 391–410). New York: Wiley.

Werner, C. M., Altman, I., Brown, B. B., & Ginat, J. (1993). Celebrations in personal relationships: A transactional/dialectical perspective. In S. Duck (Ed.), *Social Context and Relationships* (pp. 109–138). Newbury Park, Calif.: Sage.

Wood, J. T., & Inman, C. C. (1993). In a different mode: Masculine styles of communicating closeness. *Journal of Applied Communication Research, 21,* 279–295.

Yerby, J., Buerkel-Rothfuss, N., & Bochner, A. P. (1995). *Understanding Family Communication* (2nd ed.). Scottsdale, Ariz.: Gorsuch Scarisbrick.

Chapter 13

Bass, B. M. (1990). *Bass and Stogdill's Handbook of Leadership: Theory, Research, and Managerial Applications* (3rd ed.). New York: The Free Press.

Cogger, J. W. (1982). Are you a skilled interviewer? *Personnel Journal 61,* 842–843.

Criscito, P. (2000). *Resumes in Cyberspace* (2nd ed.). Hauppauge, N.Y.: Barron's Educational Series.

Fairhurst, G. T. (2001). Dualism in leadership. In F. M. Jablin & L. Putnam (Eds.), *The New Handbook of Organizational Communication* (pp. 379–439). Thousand Oaks, Calif.: Sage.

Fairhurst, G. T., & Starr, R. A. (1996). *The Art of Framing.* San Francisco: Jossey-Bass.

Fiedler, F. E. (1967). *A Theory of Leadership Effectiveness.* New York: McGraw-Hill.

Graen, G. (1976). Role making processes within complex organizations. In M. D. Dunette (Ed.), *Handbook of Industrial and Organizational Psychology* (pp. 1201–1245). Chicago: Rand McNally.

Jablin, F. M., & Krone, K. J. (1994). Task/work relationships: A life-span perspective. In M. L. Knapp & G. R. Miller (Eds.), *Handbook of Interpersonal Communication* (2nd ed., pp. 621–675). Thousand Oaks, Calif.: Sage.

Kranz, C. (1999, August 9). Employing harmony. *The Cincinnati Enquirer,* pp. C1, C6.

Lee, J., & Jablin, F. M. (1995). Maintenance communication in superior-subordinate work relationships. *Human Communication Research, 22,* 220–257.

Robbins, S. P., & Hunsaker, P. L. (1996). *Training in Inter-Personal Skills: Tips for Managing People at Work.* Upper Saddle River, N.J.: Prentice Hall.

Schmidt, W. V., & Conaway, R. N. (1999). *Results-Oriented Interviewing: Principles, Practices, and Procedures.* Boston: Allyn & Bacon.

Shaw, M. E. (1981). *Group Dynamics: The Psychology of Small Group Behavior* (3rd ed.). New York: McGraw-Hill.

Sias, P. M., & Jablin, F. M. (1995). Differential superior-subordinate relations, perceptions of fairness, and coworker communication. *Human Communication Research, 22,* 5–38.

Stewart, C. J., & Cash, W. B. (2000). *Interviewing: Principles and Practices* (9th ed.). Dubuque, Iowa: William C. Brown.

Tengler, C. D., & Jablin, F. M. (1983). Effects of question type, orientation, and sequencing in the employment screening interview. *Communication Monographs 50,* 253–263.

Whetten, D. A., & Cameron, K. S. (2002). *Developing Management Skills* (5th ed.). Upper Saddle River, N.J.: Prentice Hall.

White, R., & Lippitt, R. (1968). Leader behavior and member reaction in three "social climates." In D. Cartwright & A. Zander (Eds.), *Group Dynamics* (3rd ed., pp. 318–335). New York: Harper & Row.

Zabava Ford, W. S. (1995). Evaluation of the indirect influence of courteous service on customer discretionary behavior. *Human Communication Research, 22,* 65–89.

Chapter 14

Angry wife becomes computer hacker. (1999, June 30). *The Cincinnati Enquirer,* p. B2.

Banks, M. A. (1997). *Web Psychos, Stalkers, and Pranksters.* Scottsdale, Ariz.: The Coriolis Group.

Bigelow, J. D. (1999). The Web as an organizational behavior learning medium. *Journal of Management Education, 23,* 635–650.

Crumlish, C. (1997). *The Internet for Busy People* (2nd ed.). Berkeley, Calif.: Osborne/McGraw-Hill.

Flaherty, L. M., Pearce, K. J., & Rubin, R. B. (1998). Internet and face-to-face communication: Not functional alternatives. *Communication Quarterly, 46,* 250–268.

Globus, S. (2002, February 28). The good and bad and the Internet: Like it or not, life is happening more and more in cyberspace. *Current Health* pp. 13–17.

Goldberg, B. (1999). *Overcoming High-Tech Anxiety: Thriving in a Wired World.* San Francisco: Jossey-Bass.

Golway, T. (1998, November 7). Life in the 90s. *America,* pp. 6–7.

Griffiths, M. (1998). Internet addiction: Does it really exist? In J. Gackenbach (Ed.), *Psychology and the Internet: Intrapersonal, Interpersonal, and Transpersonal Implications* (pp. 61–76). San Diego: Academic Press.

Indicators: Percentage of households with computers. (1999, November 22) *Time,* p. 22.

Kramer, J., & Kramarae, C. (1997). Gendered ethics on the Internet. In J. M. Makau & R. C. Arnett (Eds.), *Communication Ethics in the Age of Diversity* (pp. 226–244). Chicago: University of Illinois Press.

Markham, A. N. (1998). *Life Online: Researching Real Experience in Virtual Space.* Walnut Creek, Calif.: AltaMira.

Miller, M. (1999). *The Lycos Personal Internet Guide.* Indianapolis, Ind.: Que Corporation.

Okrent, D. (1999, May 10). Raising kids online: What can parents do? *Time,* pp. 38–43.

Parks, M. R., & Floyd, K. (1996). Making friends in cyberspace. *Journal of Communication*, 80–97.

Preece, J. (2000). *Online Communities: Designing Usability, Supporting Sociability*. New York: Wiley & Sons.

Sherman, R. A. (1999). *Mr. Modem's Internet Guide for Seniors*. San Francisco: Sybex.

Snell, N. (1998). *Teach Yourself the Internet in 24 Hours* (2nd ed.). Indianapolis: Sams.Net.

Waldeck, J. H., Kearney, P., & Plax, T. G. (2001). Teacher e-mail message strategies and students' willingness to communicate. *Journal of Applied Communication Research, 29*, 54–70.

Wildstrom, S. H. (2002, August 26). Wireless E-mail: A work-in-progress. *Business Week*, p. 24.

Wood, A. F., & Smith, M. J. (2001). *Online Communication: Linking Technology, Identity, and Culture*. Mahwah, N.J.: Erlbaum.

Glossary

Accommodating—*resolving conflict by satisfying others' needs or accepting others' ideas while neglecting our own.*

Acquaintances—*people we know by name and talk with when the opportunity arises, but with whom our interactions are limited.*

Active listening—*a specific technique for improving understanding.*

Active strategy—*getting information about another by asking people who know the person you are interested in.*

Activity—*what people perceive should be done in a given period, including the time of day that is considered appropriate for certain activities to take place.*

Advice giving—*messages that present relevant suggestions and proposals that a person could use to satisfactorily resolve a situation.*

Affection need—*a desire to express and to receive love.*

Agenda—*an outline of the topics that need to be covered at a meeting.*

Aggressive behavior—*when people lash out at the source of their discontent with little regard for the situation or for the feelings, needs, or rights of those they are attacking.*

Assertiveness—*the art of declaring our personal preferences and defending our personal rights while respecting the preferences and rights of others.*

Attending—*the perceptual process of selecting to concentrate on specific stimuli from the countless stimuli reaching the senses.*

Attributions—*reasons we give for others' behaviors.*

Authenticity—*direct, honest, straightforward communication of all information and feelings that are relevant and legitimate to the subject at hand.*

Badgering—*light teasing, taunting, and mocking behavior.*

Bookmark—*a Netscape file used to store Web site addresses for sites that you'd like to visit again.*

Boundary-spanning roles—*roles whose central task is to deal with people outside the organization.*

Browser—*a device that gives you access to the information across millions of Web sites on the World Wide Web (WWW).*

Casual social conversations—*interactions between people whose purpose is to enhance or maintain a relationship through spontaneous interactions about nonspecific topics.*

Channels—*both the route traveled by the message and the means of transportation.*

Chat—*online interactive message exchange between two or more people.*

Claims—*statements of belief or requests for action.*

Clarify supportive intentions—*openly state that our goal in the conversation is to support and help our partner.*

Close friends or **intimates**—*those with whom we share our deepest feelings.*

Closed questions—*narrow-focus questions that require very brief answers.*

Coaching—*a day-to-day, hands-on process of helping others improve their work performance.*

Coercive power—*derives from the perception that people can harm their partners physically and/or psychologically should the partners resist the influence attempt.*

Collaborating—*resolving conflict by trying to fully address the needs and issues of each party and arrive at a solution that is mutually satisfying.*

Collectivistic cultures—*cultures in which group goals are emphasized more than individual goals, because these cultures value harmony and solidarity.*

Comfortable level of closeness—*spending an appropriate amount of time with each other.*

Communication competence—*the impression that communicative behavior is both appropriate and effective in a given relationship.*

Comparison-level of alternatives—*other choices a person perceives as being available that affect the decision of whether to continue in a relationship.*

Competence—*when people seem to know what they're talking about, have good information, and are perceived as clear thinkers.*

Complementary relationships—*relationships in which one person lets the other define who is to have greater power.*

Compliance-gaining—*influencing others to do what you want them to do.*

Compromising—*a form of conflict management in which people attempt to resolve their conflict by providing at least some satisfaction for both parties.*

Concrete words—*words that appeal to our senses.*

Confirmation—*nonpossessive expressions of warmth for others that affirm them as unique persons without necessarily approving of their behaviors or views.*

Connotation—*the feelings or evaluations we personally associate with a word.*

Constructed messages—*those we encode at the moment to respond to a situation for which our known scripts are inadequate.*

Constructive criticism—*describing the specific negative behaviors or actions of another and the effects that these behaviors have on others.*

Content paraphrase—*A response that conveys your understanding of the denotative meaning of the verbal message.*

Context—*the setting in which communication occurs, including what precedes and follows what is said.*

Control need—*a desire to influence the event and people around us.*

Conversational coherence—*the extent to which the comments made by one person relate to those made by others previously in the conversation.*

Conversational plan—*a consciously constructed conceptualization of one or more sequences of action at achieving a goal.*

Conversations—*locally managed sequential interchange of thoughts and feelings between two or more people.*

Content paraphrase—*a response that focuses on the denotative meaning of the message.*

Cooperative principle—*states that conversations will be satisfying when the contributions made by conversationalists are in line with the purpose of the conversation.*

Costs—*outcomes that a person does not wish to incur.*

Counseling—*helping others deal with their personal problems.*

Cover letter—*a short, well-written letter expressing your interest in a particular position.*

Credibility—*the extent to which the target believes in the speaker's expertise, trustworthiness, and likeability.*

Crediting the source—*verbally acknowledging the specific source from which you have drawn your information and ideas.*

Critical analysis—*the process of evaluating what you have understood and interpreted in order to determine how truthful, authentic, or believable you judge the meaning to be.*

Cultural context—*the set of beliefs, values, attitudes, meanings, social hierarchies, religion, notions of time, and roles of the people.*

Culture—*systems of knowledge shared by a relatively large group of people.*

Dating information—*specifying the time period that a fact was true or known to be true.*

Decoding—*the process of transforming messages into the receiver's own ideas and feelings.*

Defensiveness—*a negative feeling or behavior that results when a person feels threatened.*

Denotation—*the direct, explicit meaning a speech community formally gives a word.*

Dependable partner—*one that can be relied upon at all times under all circumstances.*

Describing behavior—*accurately recounting the specific actions of another without commenting on their appropriateness.*

Describing feelings—*naming emotions you are feeling without judging them.*

Dialects—*variations on a core language that allow a subgroup in a speech community to share meanings unique to their experience.*

Direct-request strategies—*all those strategies in which a person seeks compliance by asking another to behave in a particular way.*

Discrimination—*a negative action toward a social group or its members on account of group membership.*

Displaying feelings—*expressing feelings through facial reactions, body responses, or paralinguistic reactions.*

Distributive strategies—*all those strategies in which a person seeks compliance by threatening or making the person feel guilty.*

Diversity—*variations between and among people.*

Duration—*the amount of time that we regard as appropriate for certain events or activities.*

Effective conflict resolving partner—*one who can help manage conflicts in a collaborative way.*

Ego conflicts—*conflicts that occur when the people involved view "winning" the conflict as central to maintaining their positive self-image.*

Empathic responsiveness—*experiencing an emotional response parallel to another person's actual or anticipated display of emotion.*

Empathy—*the cognitive process of identifying with or vicariously experiencing the feelings, thoughts, or attitudes of another.*

Empathy—*demonstrated by comments that show you understand another's point of view without giving up your own position or sense of self.*

Empathy-based strategies—*all those strategies in which a person seeks compliance by appealing to another's love, affection, or sympathy.*

Encoding—*the process of transforming ideas and feelings into symbols and organizing them into a message.*

Equality—*treating conversational partners on the same level, regardless of the status differences that separate them from other participants.*

Ethics—*a set of moral principles that may be held by a society, a group, or an individual.*

Exchange strategies—*strategies in which a person seeks compliance by offering trade-offs.*

Exchange theory—*says that relationships can be understood in terms of the exchange of rewards and costs that takes place during the individuals' interaction.*

Expert power—*derives from people having knowledge that their relational partners don't have.*

External noises—*the sights, sounds, and other stimuli that draw people's attention away from intended meaning.*

Eye contact or **gaze**—*how and how much we look at people with whom we are communicating.*

Face-maintenance strategies—*all those strategies in which a person seeks compliance while using indirect messages and emotion-eliciting statements.*

Face-threatening acts (FTAs)—*engaging in behavior that fails to meet positive or negative face needs.*

Facial expression—*the arrangement of facial muscles to communicate emotional states or reactions to messages.*

Fact conflict or **simple conflict**—*conflict that occurs when the information one person presents is disputed by the other.*

Factual statements—*statements whose accuracy can be verified or proven.*

Fairness—*achieving the right balance of interests without regard to one's own feelings and without showing favor to any side in a conflict.*

Faithful partner—*one who is secure in the belief that the other person is trustworthy and that the relationship will endure.*

Family—*a group of intimates who generate a sense of home and group identity, complete with strong ties of loyalty and emotion, and experience a history and a future.*

FAQs—*frequently asked questions that list the rules followed by participants in a newsgroup.*

Feedback—*verbal and physical responses to people and/or their messages.*

Feelings paraphrase—*a response that captures the emotions attached to the content of the message.*

Feminine cultures—*cultures that expect both men and women to take a variety of roles.*

Flaming—*a hostile or negative response to what you've written.*

Forcing—*resolving conflict by attempting to satisfy your own needs or advance your own ideas with no concern for the needs or ideas of others and no concern for the harm done to the relationship.*

Framing—*the skill of providing comfort by offering information, observations, and opinions that enable the receiver to better understand or reinterpret an event or circumstance.*

Free information—*extra information offered during a message that can be used by the responder to continue the conversation.*

Friends—*people with whom we have negotiated more personal relationships voluntarily.*

Gatekeeping—*ensuring that everyone has an equal opportunity to speak.*

Gender—*the culturally determined behaviors and personality characteristics that are associated with, but not determined by, biological sex.*

Generic language—*using words that may apply only to one sex, race, or other group as though they represent everyone.*

Gestures—*movements of hands, arms, and fingers that we use to describe or to emphasize.*

Good relationship—*one in which the interactions are satisfying to and healthy for those involved.*

Gossip—*talking about people who are not present.*

Halo effect—*perceiving that a person has a whole set of characteristics when you have actually observed only one characteristic, trait, or behavior.*

High-context communication—*communication where people expect others to know how they're thinking and feeling and present messages indirectly.*

High power-distance societies—*societies in which people show respect for authority.*

High uncertainty-avoidance societies—*societies that are uncomfortable with uncertainty which creates anxiety among its people.*

Historical context—*the background provided by the previous communication episodes between the participants that influences understanding in the current encounter.*

Home page—*the "first" page at a Web site.*

Idea exchange messages—*messages that focus on conveying facts, opinions, and beliefs.*

Impersonal relationship—*one in which a person relates to the other merely because the other fills a role or satisfies an immediate need.*

Inclusion need—*a desire to be in the company of other people.*

Incongruence—*the gap between our inaccurate self-perceptions and reality.*

Independent couples—*those who share an ideology that embraces change and uncertainty in the marriage relationship, but like traditional marriage partners, are interdependent and apt to engage in rather than avoid conflict to resolve differences.*

Indexing generalizations—*the mental and verbal practice of acknowledging the presence of individual differences when voicing generalizations.*

Individualistic cultures—*cultures in which individuals' goals are emphasized more than group goals, because these cultures value uniqueness.*

Inferences—*claims or assertions based on observation or fact.*

Influence—*Symbolic efforts to preserve or change the attitudes or behavior of others.*

Integrity—*having a consistency of belief and action (keeping promises).*

Interactive strategy—*getting information about another by conversing with the person in question.*

Internal noises—*the thoughts and feelings that interfere with meaning.*

Internet—*an international electronic computer network made up of a collection of thousands of smaller computer networks.*

Interpersonal communication—*the process through which people create and manage their relationships, exercising mutual responsibility in creating meaning.*

Interpersonal conflict—*a situation in which the needs or ideas of one person are perceived to be at odds with or in opposition to the needs or ideas of another.*

Interpersonal needs theory—*whether or not a relationship is started, built, or maintained depends on how well each person meets the interpersonal needs of the other.*

Interpersonal power—*a potential for changing attitudes, beliefs, and behaviors of others.*

Interpersonal relationship—*a series of interactions between two individuals known to each other.*

Interview—*a structured conversation with the goal of exchanging information that is needed for decision making.*

Intimate friends—*people who like each other and share a close, caring, and trusting relationship characterized by mutual self-disclosure and commitment.*

Intimate relationships—*relationships that are marked by high degrees of warmth and affection, trust, self-disclosure, and commitment, and are formalized through symbols and rituals.*

Jargon—*technical terminology whose meaning is idiosyncratic to a special activity or interest group.*

Jealousy—*the suspicion of rivalry or unfaithfulness.*

Johari window—*a tool for examining the relationship between disclosure and feedback.*

Kinesics—*the technical name for the study of body motions used in communication.*

Language—*the body of words and the systems for their use in messages that are common to the people of the same speech community.*

Leadership—*exerting influence to help subordinates, co-workers, and clients reach their goals.*

Leadership style—*behavioral patterns that a person enacts when that person is trying to lead.*

Leadership traits—*distinguishing qualities or characteristics.*

Leading questions—*questions that are phrased in a way that suggests the interviewer has a preferred answer.*

Legitimate power—*derives from using the status that comes from being elected, being selected, or holding a position to influence a partner.*

Likeability—*when people seem to be congenial, attractive, warm, and friendly.*

Listening—*the process of receiving, constructing meaning from, and responding to spoken and/or nonverbal messages.*

Low-context communication—*communication where information is present in the messages transmitted and presented directly.*

Low power-distance societies—*societies in which inequalities are played down.*

Low uncertainty-avoidance societies—*societies that accept uncertainty and thus are more tolerant of differing behavior and opinions.*

Lurking—*Listening in on newsgroups or chat conversations.*

Manipulation strategies of termination—*intentionally presenting evidence of a serious breach of faith, then leaving it to the other party to take direct action about the situation.*

Manner maxim—*requirement to be specific and organized when communicating your thoughts.*

Marking—*the unnecessary addition of sex, race, age, or other designations to a general word.*

Masculine cultures—*cultures that expect people to maintain traditional sex roles.*

Masking feelings—*concealing verbal or nonverbal cues that would enable others to understand the emotions that a person is actually feeling.*

Maxims—*rules of conduct that cooperative conversational partners follow.*

Meaning—*the substance of messages that you send—the ideas and feelings in your mind.*

Mediator—*an uninvolved third party who serves as a neutral and impartial guide, structuring an interaction that enables the conflicting parties to find a mutually acceptable solution to their problems.*

Messages—*a person's verbal utterances and nonverbal behaviors to which meaning is attributed during communication.*

Mnemonic device—*any artificial technique used as a memory aid.*

Moral dilemma—*a choice involving unsatisfactory alternatives.*

Morality maxim—*the requirement to meet moral/ethical guidelines.*

Mutual respect—*treating each other with dignity.*

Negative face needs—*the desire to be free from imposition or intrusion.*

Negative facework—*messages that support the partner's need for independence and autonomy by verbally using indirect methods when offering information, opinions, or advice.*

Netiquette—*Internet etiquette.*

Neutral questions—*questions that allow a person to give an answer without direction from the interviewer.*

Newsgroup—*an electronic gathering place for people with similar interests.*

Noise—*any stimulus that gets in the way of sharing meaning.*

Nonparallel language—*language in which terms are changed because of the sex, race, or other characteristic of the individual.*

Nonverbal communication behaviors—*bodily actions and vocal qualities that typically accompany a verbal message.*

Open questions—*broad-based questions that ask the interviewee to respond with whatever information he or she wishes.*

Other-benefit strategies—*all those strategies in which a person seeks compliance by identifying behaviors that benefit the other person.*

Other-centered messages—*utilize active listening, express compassion and understanding, encourage partners to talk about what has happened, elaborate on it, and explore their feelings about the situation.*

Owning feelings or opinions (crediting yourself)—*making "I" statements to identify yourself as the source of a particular idea or feeling.*

Paralanguage or **vocalics**—*the nonverbal "sound" of what we hear—how something is said.*

Paraphrasing—*putting your understanding of the message into words.*

Participants—*the people who communicate by assuming the roles of senders and receivers during the communication.*

Passive behavior—*when people are reluctant to state their opinions, share feelings, or assume responsibility for their actions.*

Passive strategy—*getting information about another by observing the person as he or she interacts with others.*

Patterns—*sets of characteristics that differentiate some things from others used to group those items having the same characteristics.*

Perception—*the process of selectively attending to information and assigning meaning to it.*

Perception check—*a message that reflects your understanding of the meaning of another person's nonverbal behavior.*

Personal relationship—*one in which people share large amounts of information with each other and meet each other's interpersonal needs.*

Person-oriented leaders—*leaders who may suggest ways of proceeding, yet encourage group members to determine what will actually be done.*

Perspective taking—*imagining yourself in the place of another.*

Persuasion—*the intentional use of verbal messages to influence the attitudes or behaviors of others using ethical means.*

Physical context—*where communication takes place, the environmental conditions (temperature, lighting, noise level), the distance between communicators, seating arrangements, and time of day.*

Pitch—*the highness or lowness of tone.*

Poise—*assurance of manner.*

Policy conflicts—*conflicts that occur when two people in a relationship disagree about what should be the appropriate plan, course of action, or behavior in dealing with a perceived problem.*

Politeness—*relating to others in ways that meet their need to be appreciated and protected.*

Politeness maxim—*the requirement to be courteous to other participants.*

Positive communication climate—*one that encourages the mutually satisfying discussion of ideas.*

Positive face needs—*the desire to be appreciated and approved, liked and honored.*

Positive facework—*messages that protect the partner's need to be respected, liked, and valued by verbally affirming the person or the person's actions in the present difficulty.*

Positive tone strategies of termination—*use of direct positive communication methods that respect others.*

Posture—*the position and movement of the body.*

Power distance—*the extent to which a society accepts the fact that power in institutions and organizations is distributed unequally.*

Pragmatic problem-consideration conversations—*interactions between people in which the goal of at least one of the participants is to solicit the cooperation of the other in meeting a specific goal.*

Praise—*describing the specific positive behaviors or accomplishments of another and the effects that this behavior has on others.*

Precise words—*words that narrow a larger category to a smaller group within that category.*

Prejudice—*a positive or negative attitude or judgment directed toward people simply because they happen to be members of a specific group.*

Presence of a plan or life vision—*agreeing on long-term goals.*

Presentness—*demonstrating a willingness to become fully involved with the other person by taking time, avoiding distraction, being responsive, and risking attachment.*

Primary questions—*open or closed questions that the interviewer plans ahead of time.*

Proxemics—*the study of informal spaces.*

Pseudoconflict—*conflict that is apparent, not real.*

Psychological context—*the moods and feelings each person brings to an interpersonal encounter.*

Punctuality—*the extent to which one adheres strictly to the appointed or regular time.*

Quality—*the sound of a person's voice.*

Quality maxim—*requirement to provide information that is truthful.*

Quantity maxim—*requirement to tailor the amount of information that is sufficient or necessary to satisfy others' information needs and keep the conversation going.*

Question—*a response designed to get further information, to clarify information already received, or to encourage another to continue speaking.*

Racism, ethnocentrism, sexism, ageism, able-ism—*beliefs that the behaviors or characteristics of one group are inherently superior to those of another group and that this gives the "superior" group the right to dominate or discriminate against the "inferior" group.*

Rapport-talk—*sharing experiences and stories to establish bonds with others.*

Rate—*the speed at which a person speaks.*

Reasons—*statements that provide the basis or cause for some behavior or action.*

Referent power—*derives from people being attracted to others because of their physical appearance, image, charisma, or personality.*

Relational maintenance behaviors—*actions and activities that can be used to sustain desired relational qualities.*

Relationship—*a set of expectations two people have for their behavior based on the pattern of interaction between them.*

Relevancy maxim—*requirement to provide information that is related to the topic being discussed.*

Remembering—*using skills to help increase retention of information for recall when it is needed.*

Repetition—*saying something two, three, or even four times.*

Report-talk—*sharing information, displaying knowledge, negotiating, and preserving independence.*

Respect—*showing regard or consideration for a person and for that person's rights.*

Responsibility—*accountable for one's actions.*

Responsive partner—*one whose actions are geared toward the other person's particular needs. At times this may require that one person sacrifice his or her needs for the good of the other.*

Résumé—*a summary of your skills and accomplishments.*

Reward power—*derives from providing partners with monetary, physical, or psychological benefits that the partners desire.*

Rewards—*outcomes that are valued by a person.*

Role—*a pattern of learned behaviors that people use to meet the perceived demands of a particular context.*

Rules—*unwritten prescriptions that indicate what behavior is required, preferred, or prohibited in certain contexts.*

Scripts—*conversational phrases we have learned from our past encounters.*

Search engines—*identify Web sites and corresponding URLs.*

Secondary or **follow-up questions**—*planned or spontaneous questions that are designed to pursue the answers given to primary questions.*

Self-concept—*self-identity—the idea or mental image that we have about our skills, our abilities, our knowledge, our competencies, and our personality.*

Self-disclosure—*sharing biographical data, personal ideas, and feelings that are unknown to the other person.*

Self-esteem–*our overall evaluation of our competence and personal worthiness.*

Self-fulfilling prophecies–*events that happen as the result of being foretold, expected, or talked about.*

Self-talk–*the internal conversations we have with ourselves.*

Semantic noises–*unintended meanings aroused by a speaker's symbols.*

Separate couples–*those who share traditional ideology, but differ from traditional and independent marriage partners in that they engage in less emotional sharing.*

Sex–*biological characteristics that differentiate men from women.*

Sign language–*systems of body motions used to communicate.*

Skills–*goal-oriented actions or action sequences we can master and repeat in appropriate situations.*

Slang–*informal nonstandard use of vocabulary.*

Small talk–*conversation that meets social needs with relatively low amounts of risk.*

Social context–*the nature of the relationship that exists between the participants.*

Social perception–*a set of processes by which people perceive themselves and others (also known as social cognition).*

Speaking appropriately–*choosing language and symbols that are adapted to the needs, interests, knowledge, and attitudes of listeners in order to avoid language that alienates them.*

Speaking descriptively–*stating what you see or hear in objective language devoid of evaluation and judgment.*

Speaking equally–*phrasing messages that are plain, natural, and down to earth and convey respect for the other person.*

Speaking openly–*honestly sharing thoughts and feelings.*

Speaking tentatively–*phrasing idea and opinions in a way that acknowledges that what you are saying could be inaccurate or there may be other ways to see things.*

Specific words–*words that clear up ambiguity caused by general words.*

Speech community–*a group of people who speak the same language.*

Spontaneous expression–*messages that are encoded without much conscious thought.*

Stabilization–*when each person in a relationship is satisfied with what he or she is receiving from the relationship.*

Stereotypes–*set of beliefs or expectations that we have about people based solely on their group membership.*

Supporting-evidence strategies–*strategies that draw primarily on reasoning and include all those strategies in which a person seeks compliance by presenting reasons and/or evidence.*

Supporting response–*a statement whose goal is to show approval, bolster, encourage, soothe, console, or cheer up.*

Supportive messages–*create a conversational environment that encourages the person needing support to talk about and make sense of the situation that is causing distress.*

Supportiveness–*encouraging the other participants to communicate by praising their worthwhile efforts.*

Symbols–*words, sounds, and actions that are generally understood to represent meaning.*

Symmetrical relationships–*relationships in which people do not agree about who is in control.*

Sympathetic responsiveness–*a feeling of concern, compassion, or sorrow for another because of the situation.*

Task-oriented leaders–*leaders who exercise more direct control over people and groups.*

Technological addictions–*nonchemical (behavioral) addictions that involve human-machine interaction.*

Territory–*space over which we may claim ownership.*

Touch–*putting a hand or finger in contact with something.*

Traditional couples–*those who have a traditional ideology, but maintain some independence in their marriages.*

Trust–*placing confidence in another in a way that almost always involves some risk; putting your well-being in the hands of another.*

Trustworthiness–*when people seem to be dependable, honest, and keep the promises they have made, and are perceived to be acting for the good of others more than for self.*

Truthfulness and **honesty**–*refraining from lying, cheating, stealing, or deception.*

Uncertainty reduction theory–*explains the ways individuals monitor their social environments and come to know more about themselves and others.*

Understanding–*decoding a message accurately by correctly assigning appropriate meaning to it.*

Uniform resource locator or **URL**–*the path name of a document.*

Unnecessary association–*emphasizing one person's association with another when you are not talking about the other person.*

Value conflicts–*conflicts over the deep-seated beliefs people hold about what is good or bad, worthwhile or worthless, desirable or undesirable, moral or immoral.*

Vocal interferences–*extraneous sounds or words that interrupt fluent speech.*

Volume–*the loudness or softness of tone.*

Web pages–*Internet destinations, somewhat like pages in a book, which may include both text and pictures or graphics.*

Web site–*a collection of Web pages.*

Withdrawal–*resolving conflict by physically or psychologically removing oneself from the conflict.*

Withdrawal/avoidance strategies of termination–*use of indirect methods to achieve the goal of termination.*

Words–*arbitrary symbols used by a speech community to represent objects, ideas, and feelings.*

World Wide Web (WWW)–*part of the Internet where information is presented in a highly visual, often multimedia format.*

Index

A

Abbreviations, online, 407
Ableism, 51
Abuse, of anonymity, 413–415
Accommodating style of conflict management, 313–314
Acquaintances, 63
Active listening, 187–193, 417
    defined, 187
Active strategy, 68
Activity, 133
Addiction, 414–415
Adler, R. B., 319, 324
Advice giving, 233–235
Affect, 13. *See also* Affection
Affection, 81–82, 339
Ageism, 51
Agenda setting, 391
Aggressive behavior, 289, 290–292
Alberti, R. E., 293
Allen, Brenda, J., 73–74
AltaVista, 404
Altman, Irwin, 68, 245
Andersen, P. A., 64
Andersen, J. F., 339
Andersen, J. W. 274
Andersen, Peter, 18
Anderson, C. M., 289
Anonymity, 413–414
Appearance. *See* Physical characteristics
Appropriate speaking, 110–114
    adapting to situation, 110
    defined, 110
    sensitivity, 111–114
Aronson, E., 6, 49
Asante, Molefi Kete, 114, 115–116
As Good As It Gets, 206
Assertiveness, 288–295
    characteristics of, 292–293
    cultural differences, 293–295
    defined, 288
    vs. passive and aggressive behavior, 289–292
Assurance, 64
Attending, 33, 182–184, 186
    defined, 182
Attractiveness, 63
Attributions, 53
Authenticity, 170
Axtell, R. E., 128

B

Bach, K., 160
Badgering, 305
Badzinski, D. M., 345
Baesler, J. E., 133
Banks, M. A., 407

Barbee, A. P., 210, 227
Barker, L. L., 181
Baron, R. A., 35
Bass, B. M., 384, 385
Baxter, Leslie, 68, 80
Bearcat online, 401
Beautiful Mind, A, 58
Beavin, J. H., 13
Behavior–consequence–feelings (b–c–f) frame work, 319–320, 323
Berg, D. H., 245
Berger, Charles R., 48, 68
Bettini, L., 63
Bigelow, J. D., 412
Black Like Me, 241
Bloch, J. D., 345
Bochner, Arthur P., 343, 350
Body language. *See* Body motions
Body motions, 123–128
    cultural differences, 127–128
    eye contact, 123–124, 127, 292
    facial expression, 124–125, 127–128, 214
    gender variations, 128
    gestures, 125, 126, 127–128
    posture, 125
    use of, 125–127
Bookmarks, 404
Boon, Susan, 339
Bostrom, Robert, 194, 195–196
Boundary spanners, 380, 383–384
Bradac, James J., 48, 68
Braithwaite, Charles A., 185–186
Braithwaite, Dawn O., 185–186
Brave New World, 119
Breakfast Club, The, 270
Brommel, B. J., 349
Brown, P., 167, 169
Brownel, J., 182
Buerkel-Rothfuss, N., 350
Buffering face threats, 226–228
Buller, D. B., 122
Burgoon, Judee K., 122, 123, 133, 137–138
Burleson, Brant R., 217, 218, 219–220, 221, 224, 228, 236, 237
Butler, S., 288
Byrne, D., 35

C

Cahn, D. D., 310, 314, 328
Camden, C. T., 166
Cameron, K. S., 319, 325, 377
Campbell, J. D., 47
Canary, Daniel J., 62, 64, 100, 128, 304, 319, 321–322, 325, 341

Cargile, Castelan, 101–102
Cash, W. B., 374, 375
Casual social conversation, 152, 153–54
Cat on a Hot Tin Roof, 301
Cegala, D. J., 128
Cellular telephones, 401–403
Centi, P. J., 36
Change, in families, 354–355
Changing Lanes, 300
Channels, 9
Chat, Internet, 409–410
Chebat, J. C., 280
Christmas Story, A, 58
Cincinnati Enquirer, "Angry Wife," 415
Claim, 278
Clarifying supportive intentions, 225–226
Clarity, 100–109
    concrete words, 104
    dating information, 106–107
    indexing generalizations, 108–109
    precise words, 104–105
    specific words, 103–106
    vocabulary building, 102–103
Clark, M. S., 340
Climate. *See* Positive climate
Closed questions, 375
Close friends, 64–65
    See also Intimate relationships
Closeness, 349
Clothing, 131–132, 372
Cloven, D. H., 312
Coaching, 386, 388–389
Coakley, C. G., 196
Cody, Michael J., 285, 287
Coercive power, 275
Cogger, J. W., 374
Coherence, conversational, 166–167
Cole, T. D., 285
Collaborating style of conflict management, 315–318
Collectivist cultures, 97
Collier, M. J., 96
Color, 140–141
Color Purple, The, 335, 363
Confirmation, 170
Comforting, 209–237
    cultural differences, 235–237
    defined, 217
    emotional support, 217–224
    empathy, 211–217
    gender differences, 235–237
    online, 418
    supportive message skills, 224–225
    supporting responses, 218, 220–221
Commitment, 340, 386
Communication competence, 20–26
    defined, 20

Communication process model, 6
   channels, 9
   context, 7–8
   feedback, 9
   messages, 8–9
   noise, 9
   participants, 6
Comparison-level of alternatives, 84–85
Competence, 20–26, 280
   defined, 20
   elements of, 20–21
   improvement plans, 24–26
   skills, 21–22, 24
Complementary relationships, 13
Compliance gaining, 285–288
Compromising style of conflict management, 315
Conaway, R. N. 367, 371
Concrete words, 104, 415
   See also Language
Confidentiality, 389
Confirmation, 170
Conflict, 304–333
   cultural differences, 305
   definition, 304–305
   improvement plan, 334
   skills used in conflict management, 318–328
   styles of management, 310–318
   types of, 305–309
   See also Conflict management
Conflict management, 310–328
   accommodating style, 313–314
   collaborating style, 315–318
   compromising style, 315
   conflict initiation, 318–320, 322–323
   failures in, 327–329
   in families, 356–357, 339
   forcing style, 314–315
   and intimate relationships, 339
   mediation, 325–327, 357
   responding to conflict, 323–325
   withdrawing style, 310, 312–313, 356–357
Connotation, 96
Constructed messages, 12
Constructive criticism, 261–263
Content paraphrasing, 191–193
Context, 7–8, 157
Control, 13, 82
Conversational plan, 166
Conversations, 70–75, 150–175
   characteristics of, 150–151
   coherence, 166–167
   cooperative principle, 157–158, 160–161
   cultural differences, 171
   defined, 150
   and ethics, 160–161, 170
   guidelines, 161–170
   information in, 163
   and politeness, 161, 167–170
   rules of, 155–161
   skills, 22

   structure of, 151–155
   turn taking, 164–166
Cooper, P. J., 112, 128, 248
Cooperative principle, 157–158, 160–161
Cornog, M. W., 102
Cost-reward analysis, 83–84
Counseling, 389–390
Cover letters, 367
   sample, 369
Co-workers, 379–380
Crazy Moon, 146
Creativity, 94
Credibility, 279–280, 282–284
Crediting the source, 163–164
Criscito, P., 371
Critical analysis, 198
Critical listening. *See* Evaluating
Criticism, constructive, 261–263
   asking for, 264–266
Crooklyn, 362
Crude language, 111
Crumlish, C., 408
Cultural context, 7–8
Cultural differences
   assertiveness, 293–298
   comforting, 217–218
   conflict, 305, 314
   conversations, 171
   environment management, 142–143
   and language, 96–100
   nonverbal communication, 127–128, 134
   and perception of others, 48–54
   and reducing uncertainty, 48
   and scripts, 12, 21–22
   self-disclosure, 247–248, 255
   and self-perception, 35–44
   self-presentation, 131–134
   and skills, 21, 22
   and temperature, 143
Culture, 18
Cunningham, M. R., 210, 222
Cupach, William R. 80, 304, 322, 325
Custrini, R. J., 143
Cyber relationships, 415–418

D

Dainton, M., 62
Dating information, 106–107
Davis, J. L., 339
Decisiveness, 386
Decoding, 8
Defensiveness, 75
DeKlerk, V., 111
DeLamater, 49
Demo, D. H., 36, 350
Denotation, 95
Dependable partner, 339
Derlega, V. J., 64, 245, 246
Describing behavior, 257–258, 262
Describing feelings, 250–256
   blocks to, 251, 254
   and conflict management, 319–320, 323
   defined, 250

   online, 416
   vocabulary for, 252, 252–253
Descriptive speaking, 75–76
Dialects, 96
Dickson, F. C., 348
Dickson, P., 95
Differences. *See* Diversity
Differently abled people, 51, 185–186
   See also Diversity
Digital telephones, 401–403
Dillard, J. P., 211, 274
Dindia, K., 64, 99, 245
Diner, 176, 270
Direct-request compliance strategies, 286
Disclosure, 420
Disclosure/feedback ratios, 65–68
Discrimination, 51
Dishonesty, 414
Displaying feelings, 126, 249–250
Dissatisfaction, 79
Distance. *See* Informal space
Distraction. *See* Noise
Distributive compliance strategies, 287
Diverse Voices
   Accents and Language, 101–102
   Black and White, 213–214
   Communication Between Ablebodied Persons and Persons with Disabilities, 185–186
   Conversing About Racism, 311–313
   Friendships that Bridge Differences, 73–74
   Having the Choice of Who to Be, 351
   I Am. . . , 45–46
   Latin American and Anglo American Use of Personal
   Space in Public Places, 141–142
   Social Perception, 19–20
   Understanding Our Mexican Co-Workers, 381–382
   We Wear the Mask, 24
   When Mississippi Chinese Talk, 159–160
Diversity, 16–20
   defined, 16
   See also Cultural differences; Gender
Divine Secrets of the Ya-Ya Sisterhood, The, 334
Doctor, The, 118, 206
Dogmatic statements, 75
Do the Right Thing, 334
Dress, 131–132, 372
Driving Miss Daisy, 300–301
Duck, Steven, 62, 68, 69–70, 150, 344
Duncan, S., Jr., 165
Duration, 133
Dusen, D. V., 262
Duval, R. W., 14, 15

E

Easy Virtue, 177
Edmunds, P., 15
Effective conflict resolving partner, 339
Eggins, S., 152
Ego conflict, 308–309

Eisenberg, N., 212
Ekman, P., 125
Electronically mediated interpersonal communication, 400–419
　application of interpersonal skills, 415–418
　cellular telephones, 401–403
　chat, 409–410
　cover letters, 369, 371
　e-mail, 405–408
　Internet, 403–405
　newsgroups, 408–409
　online relationships, 410–415
　résumés, 369, 371
Ellinor, L., 181
E-mail, 405–408
　faculty, 405–406
　using e-mail more effectively, 406–408
Emmons, M. L., 293
Emotions. *See* Feelings
Empathic responsiveness, 211
Empathy, 22, 170, 211–217
　approaches to, 211–212
　and comforting, 218, 219–220
　and compliance gaining, 286
　and conflict management, 324
　cultural considerations, 216–217
　defined, 211
　emotional support, 217–224
　and gender stereotypes, 358–360
　improving ability, 212, 214–216
　online, 418
　and supporting responses, 218, 220–221
Employment interviews, 372–376
　conducting, 374–376
　defined, 374
Encoding, 8, 12
Encyclopedia.com, 93, 96
Enez, M., 25
Environment management, 135–143
　color cues, 140–141
　cultural differences, 142–143
　lighting levels, 140
　space, 135–140
　temperature, 140
　See also Physical context
Equality, 78, 170, 326, 358–360
　See also Reciprocity
Erin Brockovich, 396
Estes, W. K., 194
Ethics, 14–16, 160–161, 383–384
　defined, 14
　in dialogue, 170
　and gossip, 72
　and influence, 274–296
　online, 414
　questions of, 57, 87 117, 144, 171, 203, 236, 266, 295, 328, 360, 394, 418
Etiquette, 409
Evaluating, 94, 198–202
Evans, D. A., 167
Examples, 105, 415

Exchange compliance strategies, 286
Exchange theory, 83–85, 378–379
Excite, search engine, 404
Expectancy violation theory, 137–138
Expectations, 33
Expert power, 276–277
External noise, 9
Eye contact, 123–125, 127–128

F
Fabes, R. A., 212
Face-maintenance compliance strategies, 286–287
Face needs, 167–170
Face-threatening acts (FTAs), 168–169
Facial expression, 124–125, 127–128, 214–215
Fact conflict, 306
Factual statements, 198–202
Fairhurst, Gail T., 386, 387–388
Fairness, 16
Faithful partner, 339
Family relationships, 349–350, 351–357
　change in, 354–355
　conflict management in, 356–357
　defined, 349
　opening communication lines, 353
　power imbalances in, 353–354
　recognition and support in, 354–355
　respect in, 356
　and self-concept formation, 37, 350, 352
Farewell to Arms, A, 89
Feedback, 65, 257–263
　asking for criticism, 264–266
　constructive criticism, 261–263
　describing behavior, 257–258
　Johari window, 65–68
　praising, 259–260, 417
Feelings
　describing, 250–256, 416
　displaying, 126, 249–250
　masking, 248–249
　and nonverbal communication, 212, 214–216
　owning, 256
　and paraphrasing, 191–193
　and perception of others, 52–53, 212, 214–216
　and persuasion, 284–285
Fehr, Beverly, 63, 338, 342, 343, 344
Feldman, R. S., 143
Female relationships, 343
Feminine cultures, 98
Few Good Men, A, 146
Fiedler, Fred, 385
Filiatrault, P., 280
Filtering, 40
Finding Forrester, 88
Finian's Rainbow, 240
Fischer, J. L., 345
Fiske, D. W., 165
Fitzpatrick, Mary Anne, 245, 343, 345, 346, 347–348
Flaherty, 412

Flaming, 409
Floyd, K., 74, 411, 413
Follow-up questions, 375
Forcing style of conflict management, 314–315
Ford, C. E., 164
Forgas, Joseph P., 52, 53
Form (organization), 9
Formality, 110
Fox, B. A., 164
Framing, 230–232, 233, 386, 387–388
Free information, 163
French, John, 274–275
Frequently asked questions, (FAQs), 409
Fried Green Tomatoes, 88
Friedley, S. A., 112, 128, 248
Friends, 63–65, 341. *See also* Intimate relationships
Friesen, W. V., 125
FTAs. *See* Face-threatening acts
Furnham, A., 345

G
Galileo's Daughter, 421
Galvin, K. M., 349
Gatekeeping, 391–392
Gaze, 123
Gender
　and comforting, 335–337
　and cultural differences, 100
　and empathy, 359
　and intimate relationships, 343–344
　and language, 95
　and nonverbal communication, 128
　and perception of others, 50, 52–53
　and self-disclosure, 247–248
　and self-perception, 47–49
　See also Diversity issues; Sexism
Generalizations, 108
　See also Sterotyping and self-disclosure
Generic language, 111–112
Gerard, G., 181
Gestures, 125, 126, 127–128
Geyer, Georgie, 131
Gilmour, R., 62
Globus, S., 401, 405, 410
Gmelch, S. B., 112
Goldberg, B., 413
Goldsmith, D. J., 225
Golway, Terry, 402
Gong, Gwendolyn, 159–160
Good relationships, 62
Google, 404
Gordon, T., 318, 319
Gossip, 72
Go Tell It on the Mountain, 59
Graen, G., 378
Grice, H. Paul, 158, 160
Griffiths, M., 414
Grooming, 131–132
Group discussion, 390–393
Gudykunst, W. B., 70, 97, 134, 171, 248
Guerrero, L. K., 64
Guess Who's Coming to Dinner, 334–335

H

Hall, Edward T., 128, 133, 136
Hall, J. A., 123, 124, 140
Halo effect, 49–50
Harnish, R. M., 160
Hattie, J., 36, 39
Hause, K., 100, 128
Heart Is a Lonely Hunter, The, 89
Hecht, M. L., 41–42, 43, 96
Hedges, 100
High-context communication, 97, 171–172
High uncertainty avoidance, 98
Hinken, T. R., 275
Historical context, 7
Hobbes, J. R., 167
Hofstede, G., 97, 98
Hollander, J., 99
Hollman, T. D., 49
Holtgraves, T., 92, 151, 160, 167, 212
Homepage, 404
Honesty, 15
Horner, E. R., 18
Horvath, C. L., 289
Howard, J. A., 99
Howard, Linda, 213–214
How to Succeed in Business without Really Trying, 396–397
Hunsaker, P. L., 386, 389

I

Idea exchange, 72
Illustrators, 126
Impersonal relationships, 63
Implicit personality theories, 49
Inclusion, 82
Incongruence, 39
Independent couples, 346
Indexing generalizations, 108–109
Indifference, 80
Individualist cultures, 97
Inferences, 198–202
    defined, 198
Influence, 274–297
    assertiveness, 288–295
    compliance gaining, 285–288
    defined, 274
    as function of interpersonal commu-
      nication, 5–6
    persuasion, 277–285
    power, 274–277
    See also Leadership
Informal space, 136, 138–140
Informal time, 133
Information
    acquisition, 5, 54
    presenting, 161–162
Ingham, Harry, 65
In Good King Charley's Golden Days, 177
Inman, Christopher C., 341, 344
Integrity, 15
Intensifiers, 100
Interaction strategy, 68
Inter-Act with Media, 28–29, 58–59, 88–89, 118–119, 146–147, 176–177,

206–207, 240–241, 270–271, 300–301, 334–335, 362–363, 396–397, 420–421
Inter-Action Dialogues
    comforting, 238–239
    conflict, 330–332
    conversations, 174–175
    influence, 298–299
    listening, 204–205
    self-disclosure, 268–269
Interests, 338
Internal noise, 93
Internet, 403–405
    chat, 409–410
    defined, 403
Internet Explorer, 404
Interpersonal communication
    competence in, 20–26
    defined, 3–4
    diversity, 16–20
    electronically mediated, 400–419
    ethics, 14–16
    functions of, 4–6
    goal statements, 23–26
    importance of, 2–3
    improvement plans, 24–25
    principles of, 11–14
    process of, 6–11
Interpersonal influence, 274
Interpersonal needs theory, 81–83
Interpersonal relationships, 62
    See also Relationships
Interpreting, 34–35
Interviews. *See* Employment interviews
Intimate distance, 136
Intimate friends, 64, 341
Intimate relationships, 64–65, 338–361
    characteristics of, 339–341
    dark side of, 413–415
    defined, 339
    family, 349–350, 351–357
    female, 343
    gender differences, 343–344
    male, 341–343
    male–female, 344–345
    marriage, 345–349
    problem areas, 357–360
    See also Families

J

Jablin, F. M., 375, 378, 379
Jackson, D. D., 13
Jacobs, Bruce, 311–312
Jandt, F. E., 294
Jargon, 111
Jealousy, 357
Johannesen, R. L., 15, 170
Johari window, 65–68
Jones, M., 51
Jordan, J. V., 91
Jorgensen, P. E., 284
Jussim, L. J., 50

K

KCLT (Kentucky Comprehensive Listening Test), 195

Kearney, P., 405–406
Kellerman, Kathy, 11, 70, 285, 288
Kelley, Harold H., 83–85
Kennedy, C. W., 166
Kenny, D. A., 35, 245
Kentucky Comprehensive Listening Test (KCLT), 195
Kim, H., 248
Kim, Y. Y., 70, 134, 211
Kinesics, 139. *See also* Body motions
Kirtley, M. B., 211
Knapp, Mark, 68, 123, 124, 140
Knobloch, L. K., 274
Knowledge, 21, 386
Knowles, E. R., 288
Kramarae, C., 414
Kramer, J., 414
Kranz, C., 367
Krone, K. J., 379
Kunkel, A. W., 217, 237

L

LaFollette, Hugh, 63, 339, 358
Language, 93–117
    appropriateness, 110–114
    clarity, 100–109
    connotation, 96
    and cooperative principle, 157–158
    and creativity, 94
    cultural differences, 96–100
    dating information, 106–107
    defined, 93
    denotation, 95–96
    formality, 110
    gender differences, 100
    indexing generalizations, 108–109
    and meaning, 94–96
    speech community, 93
    uses, 93–94
    vocabulary building, 102–103
Latham, G. P., 25
Leadership, 384–390
    coaching, 386, 388–389
    counseling, 389–390
    framing, 386, 387–388
    meeting management, 390–393
    preparing for, 386
    styles, 385
    traits, 385
Leading questions, 375
Learning, 14
Leathers, D., 126, 214
Leary, M. R., 42
Lee, J. A., 379
Lee, W. T., 50
Legitimate power, 276
Les Miserables, 59
Letters of the Century: America 1900–1999, 421
Levinson, S., 167, 169
Liar's Poker: Rising Through the Wreckage on Wall Street, 397
Life vision, 349
Lighting levels, 140
Likability, 282

Lindsley, Sheryl, 380, 381–382
Linn, J. A., 288
Lippitt, R., 385
Listening, 22, 180–203
    attending, 182–182, 186
    behaviors contrasted, 202
    and conversational coherence, 166–167
    and counseling, 389–390
    defined, 182
    evaluating, 198–202
    online, 417
    and remembering, 194–198
    turn taking, 164–166
    understanding, 187–193
Littlejohn, S. W., 48, 62, 68, 100, 166
Locke, E. A., 25
Loewen, K. R., 49
Low-context communication, 97, 171–172
Low uncertainty avoidance, 98
Lozano, Elizabeth, 141–142
Luft, Joe, 65
Lulofs, R. S., 310, 314, 328
Lurking, 409
Lycos, 404

M
Machismo, 294
Madrid, Arturo, 19–20
Male–female relationships, 344–345
Male relationships, 341–343
Maltese Falcon, The, 119
Manipulation termination strategies, 80
Manner maxim of conversation, 158, 160
Margulis, S. T., 246
Markham, A. N., 413
Marking, 113
Marriage, 345–349
Marsh, P. E., 358
Martin, J. M., 127, 216
Martin, M. M., 289
Martinez, Elisa, 351
Masculine cultures, 98
Masking feelings, 248–249
Matsumoto, Y., 97, 171
Maxims, 158, 160–161
McCauley, C. R., 50
McCroskey, J. C., 132
McGill, Michael, 342
McLaughlin, M. L., 166, 287
Meanings, 8
    connotative, 96
    denotative, 95
    See also Language; Understanding
Mediation, 325–327, 357
Meeting management, 390–393
Memory. *See* Remembering
Merriam-Webster's Collegiate Dictionary: Delux Edition, 95
Messages, 8–9, 22, 40. *See also* Language
Messman, S. J., 304
Metts, S., 80, 246
Michener, H. A., 49
Midsummer Night's Dream, A, 28
Miller, L. C., 287

Miller, Michael, 408, 410
Mills, J., 340
Mixed messages, 350
Mnemonics, 194
Monochronical cultures, 134
Moral dilemmas, 15
Morality maxim of conversation, 160–161
Morals. *See* Ethics
Morman, M. T., 74
Mruk, C., 35, 38, 40
Mulac, A., 100
Mulling behavior, 312
Murphy, L. B., 217
Mutual respect, 349
My Dinner with Andre, 176

N
Nakayama, T. K. 127, 216
Narus, L. R., Jr., 345
Needs, 33, 81–83
Negative face needs, 167
Negative facework, 227–228
Negative politeness, 168–169
Netiquette, 409
Netscape Navigator, 404
Networks of communication, 64, 354
Neutral questions, 375
Newsgroups, 408–409
    defined, 408
    etiquette, 409
New York Times Almanac, 17
Nieto, Sonia, 7
Noise, 9, 184
Nonparallel language, 112–114
Nonverbal communication, 122–145
    and assertiveness, 292–293
    body motions, 123–128
    clothes, 131–132, 372
    and criticism, 265
    cues online, 407
    cultural variations, 127–128, 134, 142–143
    defined, 123
    and differently abled people, 185–186
    and empathy, 212, 214–216
    environment, 135–143
    gender variations, 128
    increasing accuracy, 143–144
    and job seeking, 372
    and listening, 188
    paralanguage, 129–131
    and paraphrasing, 191–193
    and perception checking, 55–56
    and questioning, 188–190
    and self-concept formation, 350–351
    self-presentation, 131–134
Note taking, 196–198
Nussbaum, J. F., 63

O
Ogden, C. K., 96
O'Hair, Dan, 285
Okrent, D., 414
Old Man and the Sea, The, 147

Olsen, N. 339
Omdahl, B. L., 211
On Golden Pond, 270–271
Online relationships, 410–415
    darkside of, 413–415
    development, 411–413
    moving to personal, 413
Openness, 64, 76
Open questions, 374–375
Open speaking, 76
Ordinary People, 206
Organization, 9, 187
Organization stage of perception, 33–34
Other-benefit compliance strategies, 287
Other-centered messages, 228–230, 231
    defined, 229
Outland, 420
Owning feelings/problems, 256–257, 320, 324

P
Paralanguage, 129–131
    vocal characteristics, 129
    vocal interferences, 129–131
Paraphrasing, 191–193
    and conflict management, 324
    and feedback, 265
    and online relationships, 417
Parks, M. R., 411, 413
Participants, 6
Passive behavior, 289, 290–292
Passive strategy, 68
Pattern, 34
Patterson, B. R., 63
Pearce, K. J., 412
Pearson, J. C., 123, 128, 133, 248
Perception checking, 55–56, 215
Perception of others, 48–54
    attributions, 53
    discrimination, 51–52
    diversity issues, 53–54
    and feelings, 52–53, 212, 214–216
    improving, 54–56, 58
    and physical characteristics, 49–50
    prejudice, 51–52
    and self-perception, 44, 46–47
    stereotyping, 50–51, 358–360
    uncertainty reduction theory, 48, 68
Perception process, 32–35
    defined, 32
    stages of, 32–35
    See also Social perception
Perez Family, The, 362
Perlman, Daniel, 338
Perrien, J., 280
Personal distance, 136
Personal grooming, 131–132
Personal relationships, 63
Person-oriented leadership, 385
Perspective taking, 211, 215
Persuasion, 301
Persuasion, 277–285
    credibility, 279–280, 282–284
    defined, 277

and feelings, 284–285
reasoning, 277–279
Petronia, S., 246
Petty, Richard, 280, 281–282
Philippot, P., 143
Physical characteristics, 49–50
Physical context, 7, 183
Pitch, 129
Plax, T. G., 405, 406
Pleck, Joseph, 341
Poise, 132
Policy conflict, 307–308
Politeness, 167–170, 416
    maxim of conversation, 161
Polychronical cultures, 134
Porter, R. E., 7, 127, 143, 216, 247, 293, 294
Positive climate, 75. *See also* Stabilization
Positive face needs, 167
Positive facework, 227
Positive tone termination strategies, 81
Posture, 125
Power, 169, 274–277, 353–354
Power distance, 98
Pragmatic problem-consideration conversation, 152–153, 154–155
Praise, 259–260, 417
Prayer for Owen Meany, A, 28
Precise words, 104–105 415
    See also Language
Preece, Jenny, 414
Prejudice, 51–52
Presentness, 170
Primary questions, 375
Prisbell, M., 74, 339
Pritchard, M., 15
Problem-consideration conversations, 152–153, 154–155
Profanity, 111
Proxemics, 136
    See also Informal space
Pseudoconflict, 305–306
Psychological context, 7
Public distance, 136
Punctuality, 133
Purdy, M., 181
Purposeful communication, 11

Q

Quality maxim of conversation, 158, 171–172
Quality of voice, 129
Quantity maxim of conversation, 158
Questioning
    and active listening, 187–190
    in conversation, 162
    in employment interviews, 374–375, 376
    and meeting management, 392–393
    that motivates response, 162

R

Racism, 51–52, 311–312
    See also Diversity

Racist labels, 113–114
Rapport-talk, 248
Rate, 129
Raven, Bertram, 274, 275
Rayner, S. G., 36, 38
Reardon, K. K., 12
Reasons, 277–279
Receiver role, 6
Reciprocity, 246–247
Referent power, 277
Regulators, 126
Reis, H. T., 248, 343
Relationships, 4, 12–14, 62–87
    beginning, 68, 70–71
    defined, 62
    disclosure/feedback ratios, 65–68
    disintegration, 78–81
    ending, 80–81
    exchange theory, 83–85
    impersonal, 63
    improvement plan, 88
    interpersonal needs theory, 81–83
    and nonverbal communication, 128
    online, 410–415
    social context, 7
    stabilization, 75–78
    theoretical perspectives, 81–85
    types of, 63–65
    See also Conflict; Feedback; Intimate relationships; Online relationships; Self-disclosure
Relevancy maxim of conversation, 158, 171
Remembering, 194–198
    mnemonics, 194
    note taking, 196–198
Repetition, 194
Report-talk, 248
Respect, 16, 214, 356
Responding, 210–237
    and comforting, 217–221
    empathy, 211–217
    paraphrasing, 191–193
Responsibility, 16
Responsiveness, 64
Responsive partner, 339
Résumés, 367–371
    sample, 370
Reward power, 275–276
Rewards, 83–84
Reynolds, R., 70
Ribeau, S. A., 96
Richards, I. A., 94–96
Richmond, V. P., 132
Risk
    and assertiveness, 292–293
    and politeness, 169
    and self-disclosure, 246, 251
    and trust, 64, 339–340
Robbins, S. P., 386, 389
Robinson, S., 262
Roles, 42–43
Roloff, M. E., 312

Romeo and Juliet, 119
Rookie, The, 363
Rose, S., 64
Rubin, R. B., 412
Rules of conversation, 155–161
    in families, 357
Rusbult, C. E., 339

S

Sabourin, Teresa Chandler, 357
Samovar, L. A., 7, 127, 143, 216, 247, 293, 294
Same Time Next Year, 89
Sampson, E. E., 51
Samter, W., 217
Sarr, Robert A., 387
Schmidt, W. V., 367, 371
Scholars, spotlights on
    attitude change, 281–282
    comforting, 219–220
    conflict management, 321–322
    couple types and communication, 347–348
    interethnic communication and ethnic identity, 41–42
    interpersonal competence, 23–24
    language of prejudice and racism, 115–116
    leadership in work organizations, 387–388
    listening, 195–196
    nonverbal expectancy violation theory, 137–138
    personal relationships, 69–70
Schriesheim, C. A., 275
Schutz, William, 81, 82
Scripts, 12, 21–22
Search engines, 404–405
Secondary questions, 375
Security, e-mail, 407–408
Selection, 33
Self-concept, 4, 35–37, 44, 350, 352.
    defined, 35
family influences, 36–37, 350–351
Self-disclosure, 65, 244–267
    cultural differences, 247–248, 255
    defined, 245
    describing feelings, 250–256
    displaying feelings, 126, 249–250
    family, 340
    gender differences, 247–248
    guidelines for, 245–247
    and intimate relationships, 340
    Johari window, 65–68
    masking feelings, 248–249
    owning feelings, 256
    and starting relationships, 74
Self-esteem, 38–40
    See also Self-perception defined
Self-fulfilling prophecies, 39–40
Self-help movement, 40
Self-managed work teams, 380
Self-perception, 35–44

Self-perception (continued)
  accuracy of, 38–40
  and communication style, 47
  defined, 35
  and diversity issues, 47–48
  and perception of others, 44, 46
  and roles, 42–43
  self-concept, 35–37
  self-esteem, 38–40
  self-talk, 44
Self-presentation, 131–134
  clothing, 131–132, 372
  cultural differences, 134
  poise, 132
  time, 133, 134
  touch, 132–133, 134
Self-talk, 44
Semantic noise, 9, 184
Sender role, 6
Sensitivity, 111–114, 417
Separate couples, 346
Sex, 99
Sexism, 51. See also Diversity; Cultural
  Differences; Gender
Sexual harassment, 139
Sexuality, 344–345
Shaw, M. E., 83, 385
Shea, B. C., 288
Sherman, R. A., 405–408
Shimanoff, S. B., 156
Shipping News, The, 396
Sias, P. M., 378
Sign language, 125–126
Sillars, A. L., 128, 327
Similarity, 64
Simon Birch, 32
Simplicity, 33–34
Skills
  and competence, 22
  defined, 21
  and leadership, 386
  See also specific skills
Slade, D., 152
Slang, 111
Sleight, C., 211
Small talk, 72, 154
Smith, M. J., 412
Snell, N., 410
Social context, 7
Social conversations, 152, 153–154
Social distance, 136
Social penetration theory, 245
Social skills, 64
Somera, L., 211
Sophie's Choice, 271
Space management, 135–140
  informal space, 136, 138–140
  moveable objects, 135–136
  permanent structures, 135
Specific words, 103–106, 415
  See also Language
Speech community, 93
Spitzberg, Brian H., 20, 21, 23–24, 321
Spontaneous expression, 12

Spotlight on Scholars. See Scholars, spot-
  lights on
Stabilization, 75–78
  defined, 75
  and speaking descriptively, 75–76
  and speaking openly, 76
  and speaking tentatively, 76–78
  and speaking to others as equals, 78
Stafford, Laura, 64, 341
Stamp, G. H., 357
Steil, L. K., 181
Stereotyping, 50–51, 358–360
  defined, 50
Stewart, A. D., 112, 128, 248
Stewart, C. J., 374, 375
Stewart, L. P., 112, 128, 248
Stiff, J. B., 211, 212
Stimuli, 33–35
Streetcar Named Desire, A, 89
Summarizing, 393
Sunday in the Park with George, 207
Supporting-evidence compliance strate-
  gies, 285
Supporting responses, 218, 220–221, 417
  defined, 221
Supportiveness, 170
Supportive responses
  defined, 221
  interaction phases, 222–224
  message skills, 224–235
Svennevig, J., 151
Symbols, 8,
Symmetrical relationships, 14
Sympathetic responsiveness, 212

T
Tannen, Deborah, 248
Tanno, Delores, V., 45–46
Task-oriented leadership, 385
Task sharing, 64
Taylor, Dolman A., 68, 245
Technological addictions, 414
Tedeschi, J. T., 275
Temperature, 140
Tempest, The, 147
Temple, L. E., 49
Tengler, C. D., 375
Tentative speaking, 76–77
Territory, 139–140
Terkel, S. N., 14, 15
Terms of Endearment, 118
Thibaut, John W., 83–85
Things They Carried, The, 241
Thompson, S. A., 164
Time, 133, 134, 164
Ting-Toomey, S., 190, 309
Tin Men, 396
To Kill a Mockingbird, 28, 207, 240
Tone of voice. See Paralanguage
Tootsie, 146–147, 240
Touch, 132–133, 134
Tracy, K., 262
Traditional couples, 346
Traits, 385

Trenholm, S., 83, 85, 277
Trust, 64, 339–340, 379
Trustworthiness, 280–281
Truthfulness, 15, 158, 283–284
Tuesday's with Morrie, 177
Tuning out, 184
Turner, L. H., 123, 128, 133, 248
Turn taking, 164–166
Twelve Angry Men, 335
Twelve-step groups, 40

U
Uncertainty avoidance, 98
Uncertainty reduction theory, 48, 83
Understanding, 187–193
  and active listening, 187
  and conflict management, 320, 322,
    324
  and paraphrasing, 191–193
  and questioning, 188–190
Uniform Resource Locator (URL), 404
Unnecessary association, 113–114

V
Value conflict, 306–310
Vangelisti, A. L., 68
Victor, Victoria, 58
Violence, 357
Vocabulary, 251, 252–253
  building, 102–103
Vocal characteristics, 129
Vocalics. See Paralanguage
Vocal interferences, 129–131
Voices. See Diverse Voices
Volume, 129
Vulgar expressions, 111

W
Waldeck, J. H., 405, 406
Walther, J. B., 133
Warmth, 339
Watson, K. W., 181
Watzlawick, P., 13
Weaver, J. B., III, 211
Web pages, 403
Web sites, 404
Weisberg, J., 327
Weiten, Wayne, 39
Wellman, B., 342
Wellman, C., 15
Werking, K. J., 344
Werner, C. M., 349
West, R. L., 123, 128, 133, 248
Whetten, D. A., 319, 325, 377
White, R., 385
Who's Afraid of Virginia Woolf?, 271, 335,
  363
Who's on First, 206
Wildstrom, S. H., 402
Winstead, B. A., 64
Withdrawal/avoidance termination strate-
  gies, 80–81
Withdrawing style of conflict manage-
  ment, 310, 312–313, 356–357

Wolvin, A. D., 196
Wonderful Ice Cream Suit, The, 88
Wood, A. F., 412
Wood, Julia T., 99, 128, 341, 344
Woodall, W. G., 122
Words, 93
Workplace communication, 366–395
    conducting interviews, 374–376
    co-workers, 379–380

customers/clients, 380, 383–384
    hiring process, 367–376
    leadership, 384–390
    managerial relationships, 377–379
World Wide Web (WWW), 403
Wright, P. H., 344

Y
Yahoo!, 404

Yerby, J., 350, 357
You've Got Mail, 420

Z
Zabava Ford, W. S., 383
Zebrowitz, Leslie, 50
Zillmann, D., 211

Photo Credits